LINDBERGH

ALSO BY A. SCOTT BERG

Max Perkins: Editor of Genius

Goldwyn: A Biography

LINDBERGH

A. SCOTT BERG

MACMILLAN

First published 1998 by G.P. Putnam's Sons
a member of Penguin Putnam Inc., 375 Hudson Street, New York, New York 10014

This edition published 1998 by Macmillan
an imprint of Macmillan Publishers Ltd
25 Eccleston Place, London SW1W 9NF
and Basingstoke

Associated companies throughout the world

ISBN 0 333 73578 1

1 3 5 7 9 8 6 4 2

A CIP catalogue record for this book is available from
the British Library.

Printed and bound in Great Britain by
Mackays of Chatham plc, Chatham, Kent

CONTENTS

Far or forgot to me is near;
    Shadow and sunlight are the same;
The vanished gods to me appear;
    And one to me are shame and fame.

They reckon ill who leave me out;
    When me they fly, I am the wings;
I am the doubter and the doubt,
    And I the hymn the Brahmin sings.

—EMERSON, "Brahma"

PART ONE

1

KARMA

". . . living in dreams of yesterday, we find ourselves still dreaming

of impossible future conquests . . ."

—C.A.L.

FOR MORE THAN A DAY THE WORLD HELD ITS BREATH . . .
and then the small plane was sighted over Ireland.

Twenty-seven hours after he had left Roosevelt Field in
New York—alone, in the *Spirit of St. Louis*—word quickly
spread from continent to continent that Charles A. Lindbergh
had survived the most perilous leg of his journey—the fifteen-
hour crossing of the Atlantic. He had to endure but a few more
hours before reaching his destination, Paris. Anxiety yielded to
anticipation.

The American Ambassador to France, Myron T. Herrick,
went to St. Cloud after lunch that Saturday to watch the
Franco-American team-tennis matches. When he took his seat
in the front row, five thousand fans cheered. During the course
of the afternoon, people in the stands heard newsboys shouting the headlines of their *éditions spéciales,* announcing Lindbergh's expected arrival that night. In the middle of the match,
Herrick received a telegram—confirmation that Lindbergh had
passed over Valencia in Ireland. All eyes were on the Ambassador as he hastily left courtside, convincing most of the spectators that their prayers were being answered. Before the
match had ended, the stands began to empty.

Herrick rushed back to his residence in Paris, ate a quick
dinner at 6:30, then left for the airfield at Le Bourget, to the
northeast of the city. "It was a good thing we did not delay another quarter of an hour," Herrick recalled, "for crowds were
already collecting along the road and in a short time passage
was almost impossible."

The boulevards were jammed with cars ten abreast. Passengers poked their heads through the sliding roof panels of the Parisian taxis, greeting each other in jubilation. "Everyone had acquired a bottle of something and, inasmuch as the traffic moved very slowly," one reveler recalled of that night in 1927, "bottles were passed from cab to cab celebrating the earthshaking achievement." A mile from the airfield, the flow of traffic came to a stand-still.

Once the radio announced that Lindbergh had flown over southern England, mobs formed in the heart of Paris. Thirty thousand people flocked toward the Place de l'Opéra, where illuminated advertising signs flashed news bulletins. Over the next few hours, the crowds spilled into the Boulevard Poissonière—until it became unpassable—where they expected to find the most reliable accounts of Lindbergh's progress posted in front of the *Paris Matin* offices. "Not since the armistice of 1918," observed one reporter, "has Paris witnessed a downright demonstration of popular enthusiasm and excitement equal to that displayed by the throngs flocking to the boulevards for news of the American flier, whose personality has captured the hearts of the Parisian multitude."

Between updates, people waited in anxious silence. Two French fliers—Nungesser and Coli—had not been heard from in the two weeks since their attempt to fly nonstop from Paris to New York; and their disappearance weighed heavily on the Parisians' minds. Many muttered about the impossibility of accomplishing a nonstop transatlantic crossing, especially alone. Periodically, whispers rustled through the crowd, rumors that Lindbergh had been forced down. After a long silence, a Frenchwoman, dressed in mourning and sitting in a big limousine, wiped away tears of worry. Another woman, selling newspapers, approached her, fighting back her own tears. "You're right to feel so, madame," she said. "In such things there is no nationality—he's some mother's son."

Close to nine o'clock, letters four feet tall flashed onto one of the advertising boards. "The crowds grew still, the waiters frozen in place between the café tables," one witness remembered. "All were watching. Traffic stopped. Then came the cheering message 'Lindbergh sighted over Cherbourg and the coast of Normandy.'" The crowd burst into bravos. Strangers patted each other on the back and shook hands. Moments later, *Paris Matin* posted a bulletin in front of its building, confirming the sighting; and bystanders chanted *"Vive Lindbergh!"* and *"Vive l'Américain!"* The next hour brought more good news from Deauville, and then Louviers. New arrivals onto the scene all asked the same question: *"Est-il arrivé?"*

Fifteen thousand others gravitated toward the Étoile, filling the city block that surrounded a hotel because they assumed Lindbergh would be spending the night there. Many too impatient to stand around in town suddenly decided to witness the arrival. Students from the Sorbonne jammed into buses and subways. Thousands more grabbed whatever conveyance remained available, until more than ten thousand cars filled the roads between the city and Le Bourget. Before long, 150,000 people had gathered at the airfield.

A little before ten o'clock, the excited crowd at Le Bourget heard an approaching engine and fell silent. A plane burst through the clouds and landed; but it turned out to be the London Express. Minutes later, as a cool wind blew the stars into view, another roar ripped the air, this time a plane from Strasbourg. Red and gold and green rockets flared overhead, while acetylene searchlights scanned the dark sky. The crowd became restless standing in the chill. Then, "suddenly unmistakeably the sound of an aeroplane . . . and then to our left a white flash against the black night . . . and another flash (like a shark darting through water)," recalled Harry Crosby—the American expatriate publisher—who was among the enthusiastic onlookers. "Then nothing. No sound. Suspense. And again a sound, this time somewhere off towards the right. And is it some belated plane or is it Lindbergh? Then sharp swift in the gold glare of the searchlights a small white hawk of a plane swoops hawk-like down and across the field—C'est lui Lindbergh. LINDBERGH!"

On May 21, 1927, at 10:24 P.M., the *Spirit of St. Louis* landed—having flown 3,614 miles from New York, nonstop, in thirty-three hours, thirty minutes, and thirty seconds. And in that instant, everything changed—for both the pilot and the planet.

THERE WAS NO HOLDING the one hundred fifty thousand people back. Looking out the side of his plane and into the glare of lights, Lindbergh could see only that the entire field ahead was "covered with running figures!" With decades of hindsight, the woman Lindbergh would marry came to understand what that melee actually signified. "Fame—Opportunity—Wealth—and also tragedy & loneliness & frustration rushed at him in those running figures on the field at Le Bourget," she would later write. "And he is so innocent & unaware."

Lindbergh's arrival in Paris became the defining moment of his life, that event on which all his future actions hinged—as though they were but a predestined series of equal but opposite reactions, fraught with irony. Just as inevitable, every event in Lindbergh's first twenty-five years seemed to have conspired in propelling him to Paris that night. As the only child of woefully ill-matched parents, he had tuned out years of discord by withdrawing. He had emerged from his itinerant and isolated adolescence virtually friendless and self-absorbed. A scion of resourceful immigrants, he had grown up a practical dreamer, believing there was nothing he could not do. A distracted

student, he had dropped out of college to learn to fly airplanes; and after indulging in the footloose life of barnstorming, he had been drawn to the military. The Army had not only improved his aviation skills but also brought
precision to his thinking. He had left the air corps to fly one of the first airmail routes, subjecting himself to some of the roughest weather in the country. Restless, he had lusted for greater challenges, for adventure.

In the spring of 1927, Lindbergh had been too consumed by what he
called "the single objective of landing my plane at Paris" to have considered
its aftermath. "To plan beyond that had seemed an act of arrogance I could
not afford," he would later write. Even if he had thought farther ahead,
however, he could never have predicted the unprecedented global response
to his arrival.

By that year, radio, telephones, radiographs, and the Bartlane Cable
Process could transmit images and voices around the world within seconds.
What was more, motion pictures had just mastered the synchronization of
sound, allowing dramatic moments to be preserved in all their glory and
distributed worldwide. For the first time all of civilization could share as one
the sights and sounds of an event—almost instantaneously and simultaneously. And in this unusually good-looking, young aviator—of apparently
impeccable character—the new technology found its first superstar.

The reception in Paris was only a harbinger of the unprecedented worship people would pay Lindbergh for years. Without either belittling or ag-
grandizing the importance of his flight, he considered it part of the
continuum of human endeavor, and that he was, after all, only a man. The
public saw more than that. Indeed, Harry Crosby felt that the stampede at
Le Bourget that night represented nothing less than the start of a new religious movement—"as if all the hands in the world are . . . trying to touch the
new Christ and that the new Cross is the Plane." Universally admired,
Charles Lindbergh became the most celebrated living person ever to walk the
earth.

For several years Lindbergh had lived according to one of the basic laws
of aerodynamics—the need to maintain balance. And so, in those figures
running toward him, Lindbergh immediately saw inevitable repercussions. At
first he feared for his physical safety; over the next few months he worried
about his soul. He instinctively knew that submitting himself to the idolatry
of the public could strip him of his very identity; and the only preventive he
could see was to maintain his privacy. That reluctance to offer himself to the
public only increased its desire to possess him—the first of many paradoxes
he would encounter in his lifelong effort to restore equilibrium to his world.

"No man before me had commanded such freedom of movement over
earth," Lindbergh would write of his historic flight. Ironically, that freedom

would be denied him thereafter on land. Both whetting and sating the public's appetite for every morsel about him, the press broke every rule of professional ethics in covering Lindbergh. They often ran with unverified stories, sometimes stories they had made up, transforming him into a character worthy of the Arabian Nights. Reporters stalked him constantly—almost fatally on several occasions—making him their first human quarry, stripping him of his rights to privacy as no public figure had ever been before. Over the century, others would reach this new stratum of celebrity.

The unwanted fame all but guaranteed an isolated adulthood. And, indeed, Lindbergh spent the rest of his life in flight, searching for islands of tranquility. Early on, he was was lucky enough to meet Anne Morrow, Ambassador Dwight Morrow's shy daughter, who craved solitude as much as he did. They fell in love and married. Their "storybook romance," as the press always presented it, was, in fact, a complex case history of control and repression, filled with joy and passion and grief and rage. He scourged his wife into becoming an independent woman; and, in so doing, he helped create an important feminist voice—a popular diarist who also wrote one of the most beloved volumes of the century, and another that was one of the most despised.

The Lindberghs' love story had a tragic second act. His fame and wealth cost them their firstborn child. Under melodramatic conditions, Lindbergh authorized payment of a large ransom to a mysterious man in a graveyard; but he did not get his son in return. The subsequent investigation of the kidnapping uncovered only circumstantial evidence; and the man accused of killing "the Lindbergh Baby" never confessed—thus condemning the "Crime of the Century" to eternal debate. Because the victim's father was so celebrated, the case entered the annals of history, and laws were changed in Lindbergh's name. The media circus that accompanied what veteran courtwatchers still refer to as the "Trial of the Century" forever affected trial coverage in the United States. The subsequent flood of sympathy for Lindbergh only enhanced his public profile, making him further prey for the media as well as other criminals and maniacs. In fear and disgust, he moved to Europe, where for a time he became one of America's most effective unofficial ambassadors. Several visits to Germany in the 1930s—during which he inspected the Luftwaffe and also received a medal from Hitler—called his politics into question. He returned to the United States to warn the nation of Germany's insuperable strength in the impending European war, then to spearhead the American isolationist movement. As the leading spokesman for the controversial organization known as America First, he preached his beliefs with messianic fervor, incurring the wrath of many, including President Franklin D. Roosevelt. By December 7, 1941, many Americans considered him nothing short of satanic—not just a defeatist but an anti-Semitic, pro-Nazi traitor.

Lindbergh had spent most of his adult life establishing the role of aviation in war and peace, proving himself one of the prime movers in the aviation industry. But because of his noninterventionist stance, Roosevelt refused to allow Lindbergh to fly after Pearl Harbor with the very air force he had helped modernize. He found other ways to serve. As a test pilot in private industry, he developed techniques that increased both the altitude and range of several planes in America's fleet, saving countless lives. The military looked the other way as Lindbergh insisted on engaging in combat missions in the South Pacific; but his failure to condemn Nazi Germany before World War II haunted his reputation for the rest of his life.

One of his greatest services to his country proved to be in helping launch the space program. As the first American airman to exhibit "the right stuff," Lindbergh inspired his country's first astronauts by sheer example. But more than that, he was—unknown to the public—the man most responsible for securing the funding that underwrote the research of Dr. Robert H. Goddard, the inventor of the modern rocket. A friend of the first man to fly an airplane, Lindbergh lived long enough in a fast-moving world to befriend the first man to walk on the moon.

In time, Lindbergh came to believe the long-range effects of his flight to Paris were more harmful than beneficial. As civilization encroached upon wilderness in the world he helped shrink, he turned his back on aviation and fought to protect the environment. He rededicated his life to rescuing nearly extinct animals and to preserving wilderness areas. For years this college dropout advanced other sciences as well, performing medical research that would help make organ transplants possible. He made extraordinary archaeological and anthropological discoveries as well. A foundation would later be established in Lindbergh's name that offers grants of $10,580—the cost of the *Spirit of St. Louis*—for projects that further his vision of "balance between technological advancement and preservation of our human and natural environment."

Lindbergh believed all the elements of the earth and heavens are connected, through space and time. The configurations of molecules in each moment help create the next. Thus he considered his defining moment just another step in the development of aviation and exploration—a summit built on all those that preceded it and a springboard to all those that would follow. Only by looking back, Lindbergh believed, could mankind move forward. "In some future incarnation from our life stream," he wrote in later years, "we may understand the reason for our existence in forms of earthly life."

In few people were the souls of one's forbears so apparent as they were in Charles Lindbergh. As a result of this transmigration, Lindbergh believed the flight that ended at Le Bourget one night in May 1927 originated much farther back than thirty-three and a half hours prior at Roosevelt Field. It started with some Norsemen—infused with Viking spirit—generations long before that.

2

NORTHERN LIGHTS

"I wonder why my folks ever left that place!"

—C.A.L. (flying over Sweden, 1933)

IN THE LATE SUMMER, THE SKY OVER SWEDEN SOMETIMES casts a striking color, an extremely pale but radiant blue. By fall the currents of the surrounding winds and waters shift, producing a quilt of clouds that can go unturned most of the winter.

In 1859, even with the arrival of spring, dark clouds persisted in hanging over one Swede in particular, a prominent figure in Skåne, the country's southernmost province.

Ola Månsson had been born fifty-one years earlier in the village of Gårdlösa in the parish of Smedstorp. Educated in the local grammar school and raised a Lutheran, he had bought a farm in the village of his birth. The Baltic Sea lay but twelve miles from his two hundred acres of flat prairie land, which boasted numerous lakes and a trickling river. At twenty-five he had married a girl from the neighboring parish of Onslunda, Ingar Jönsdotter, eight years his junior. Over the next twenty-two years, they produced eight children.

Because of the middling quality of the soil, Månsson's "River Farm" subsisted off its dairy products and a few basic crops. But Månsson, a strong, stocky man with an imposing nose and piercing eyes, held the respect of his neighbors. Possessed of a dramatic oratorical style and a firm sense of his own rectitude, in 1847 he persuaded his district to elect him to the Farmer Estate in the Riksdag, the Swedish parliament in Stockholm.

Månsson arrived in the multi-islanded capital, six hundred

miles away, at a trying moment in Swedish politics. Social reform was sweeping across the nation, and Månsson often led the charge, advocating a basic liberalism which he felt was in the best interests of his farm-labor constituency. Even as a freshman "Riksdagsman," he argued for tax relief and a loosening of the Lutheran Church's hold over Swedish society. He later advocated laws protecting children, the elderly, women, and Jews. He urged the abolition of the whipping post. He was soon appointed to the powerful appropriations committee, chosen from the entire Riksdag; and he was the odds-on favorite to become the next speaker for the Farmer Estate. But greater visibility brought greater vulnerability.

The liberal press suggested that Ola Månsson was in the pocket of Crown Prince Carl—who was soon to become King Carl XV. Known as "The Farmer King"—largely for his rural tastes, which included a penchant for carousing with farmers and sleeping with their daughters—Carl was said to have bought Månsson's support on several key votes.

In the last weeks of 1858, Ola Månsson fell from political grace even faster than he had risen. Through his position in the Riksdag, he had been appointed as an officer of the State Bank of Sweden in Malmö. Using information furnished by one of Månsson's enemies, the public prosecutor charged Månsson with embezzlement. The accusation stemmed from his having violated bank regulations—acting as an agent for people applying for loans, a conflict of interest compounded by the further accusation that he had exacted one percent commissions in helping secure loans. At first Månsson denied any wrongdoing; but as a paper trail was produced, he admitted that he had accepted some compensation. The courts ordered Månsson's dismissal from his position as an officer of the bank and that he be stripped of his civil rights.

The case went to Sweden's Supreme Court, which Månsson treated with utter contempt. He insisted that his having served as an agent was his personal business. When he was presented on the stand with an extremely compromising document, he ripped it up, only to wipe his buttocks with one of the pieces of paper. On June 4, 1859, the Supreme Court of Sweden unanimously upheld the lower courts' decision, depriving Månsson of his civil rights.

The defendant was not present for the verdict. In the few weeks between his court apppearance and the final ruling, Ola Månsson disappeared. It would be months before Månsson's even more troubling personal travails were revealed, which further explained his sudden flight. Some of the details would not come to light for another century.

During the long parliamentary sessions, Månsson's wife, Ingar, remained on the farm raising their children while Ola enjoyed the many pleasures of

Stockholm, including its women. There the forty-nine-year-old man from Skåne fell in love with Lovisa Callén, a waitress at Lennström's restaurant. She was a simple country girl, born in 1837 not far from Stockholm. Having lost her father, Lovisa went to the city at fifteen as a "piga," a maidservant. She became a skilled seamstress before taking her restaurant job, by which time she had bloomed into a dark-haired, blue-eyed beauty, with a trim figure. In April 1857, the nineteen-year-old discovered she was pregnant.

Her son with Månsson was born on January 20, 1858, five blocks from Lovisa's Stockholm residence, at the home of her midwife. Månsson was in Gårdlösa at the time. The "piga" there was making his bed when she discovered a letter addressed to him, which she turned over to Ingar; it was from Lovisa, announcing the birth of their baby and asking what to call him. The birth was recorded in the capital city's "oakta dopbok," which registered the births of bastards, stating that the child's parents were "unknown." Two days later, the boy was christened Karl August.

For more than a year, Månsson juggled his two families and his thriving career. Had his illegal banking activities not come to light, he might very well have kept his life and child with Lovisa in the shadows. But once he saw the handwriting on the courthouse wall, he began taking English lessons; and in May 1859, while his case was still pending, he had obtained a passport.

By that time, fewer than twenty thousand Swedes had emigrated to the United States, though, over the next sixty years, stories of America would lure more than one million of their countrymen. Månsson was not as financially desperate as most Swedish refugees; but, more than most, he was by necessity intrigued by this place where he could erase his past—where, in his fifties, he and the young mother of their eighteen-month-old son could start a new life.

Månsson returned to Gårdlösa and announced his intention to flee, offering his wife the opportunity to accompany him. When she and the rest of the family refused, he transferred ownership of the River Farm and all his other property to one of his sons, so that they would all be cared for. A robust forty-three at the time of Ola's departure, Ingar would be dead within five years.

Carrying as few possessions as possible—including a gold medal he had once received from his constituents, and Lovisa's only heirloom, a gold watch—Månsson and his new family embarked on a three-day voyage across the North Sea to Hull, on the eastern coast of England. There they boarded a train across the Midlands for Liverpool—120 miles, some seven hours away. A few weeks later, a steamer took them to Quebec, a crossing that lasted a month. Upon arriving in the New World, Ola Månsson decided to give himself and his second family new names. At a time when Swedes were breaking tradition and assuming permanent patronymics—instead of last names that proclaimed whose son or daughter they were—he adopted the surname his two older sons had acquired at the University in Lund, and he adapted their own Christian names.

And so the newly named August Lindbergh, his wife, Louisa Carline Lindbergh, and their baby, Charles August Lindbergh, boarded a train in Quebec and went all the way to Windsor, Ontario, on the Grank Trunk Railway of Canada. Unable to afford the extravagance of a first-class sleeping car, the Lindberghs spent most of a week sitting on wooden benches as the wood-burning locomotive chugged across southern Quebec and Ontario, occasionally attaining a speed of twenty-five miles per hour.

In Windsor the Lindberghs crossed the Detroit River and entered the United States. They spent the better part of another week riding trains to Chicago, then across Illinois until they reached Dubuque on the Mississippi River. There they boarded a boat that carried them three hundred miles north into the year-old state of Minnesota. They disembarked at the Falls of Saint Anthony, a town of three thousand, which would merge in another thirteen years with the flour-milling town of Minneapolis. From there it was seventy-five miles west—by ox-cart and prairie schooner—through wilderness to the village of Litchfield, where the Lindberghs had friends from Sweden. With its open prairie land dotted by hundreds of surrounding lakes, Litchfield looked remarkably like Gårdlösa; but August Lindbergh chose not to settle there. He opted instead to squat on even more virgin timberland fifty miles north, about a mile and one-half outside a place called Melrose in Stearns County. On August 4, 1859, after ten weeks of arduous travel, the journey officially came to an end, when August Lindbergh appeared at the Minnesota District Court to declare his intention to become a Citizen of the United States.

The immigrants settled into the rigors of pioneer life on the edge of the American wilderness, one of only three families in Melrose. They built a sod hut. Even though the Minnesota summer was hotter than those in Sweden, the winters were known to be colder; so Lindbergh at once got to replacing the crude one-room hovel with a log house, cut from trees on the free land he had staked out. Barely had it been finished when Louisa gave birth to the second of six children she would deliver in America over the next thirteen years—Lovisa, Linda, Victor, Juno, Frank, and Lillian. Lindbergh traded his gold medal for a plow, so that after clearing the land he could break the ground.

As the Lindbergh family expanded, so did their house. It became one of the biggest in the county, with a frame addition to the cabin, upstairs bedrooms, and wood siding. On August 2, 1861, while milling wood for the

house—nine miles away in Sauk Center—Lindbergh got too close to the exposed saw. The machinery caught his clothes and tugged him into the spinning blade. Men at the mill ran for help, summoning the local missionary.
The Reverend C. S. Harrison later reported his findings, that the saw "had
taken a slab off his [left] arm and then struck him in the back and hurled him
half way across the mill," gashing him so deep as to expose his beating heart
and part of a lung. He dispatched a man to fetch the nearest surgeon, sixty
miles away. Meantime, locals wrapped Lindbergh in a quilt, piled him into
a lumber wagon and carted him home. Reverend Harrison noticed a spring
of cold water nearby and prescribed constant bathing of the mangled arm;
he also dressed the wound in the back as best he could, picking out cloth and
sawdust before binding the ripped flesh together. The doctor arrived on the
third day after the accident, by which time there was little to do but ampu-
tate the arm at the shoulder.

When Lindbergh was able to get out of bed, he called for the dead limb
so that he could bury it in his garden. "Bring him to me," Lindbergh cried.
Then, taking the fingers of the lifeless left hand, he said, "Gootbye, mine dear
hand. You have been a goot frent to me for fifty years. You haf always been
goot and true to me, but you can't be viv me anymore."

Combatting adversity with stoicism, August Lindbergh established the
work ethic his descendants would emulate. By the next harvest, he had rigged
up a belt with a metal ring, into which he could insert one of the handles of
his scythe, thus allowing him to continue to work. But feeling he could not
do the job of a whole man, he summoned his son Per from the farm in Sweden; another son, Måns, would follow. Lindbergh grew a long, shaggy beard,
making his now permanent scowl even more intimidating. It also proved
practical in washing and drying his remaining hand.

Thousands of Indians lived in the surrounding areas, mostly Sioux and
the friendlier Chippewa, whose birch-bark teepees reminded the immigrants
from old European communities just how new America was. The settlers
viewed the Native Americans as a nuisance more than a threat, for they generally kept to themselves, only occasionally giving the settlers cause for
alarm. In August 1862, Little Crow rebelled against the government's treatment of his tribe and led the Sioux on the warpath. August Lindbergh un-
penned his animals and herded his then-pregnant wife and two children into
a cart, then headed to the stockade fort at St. Cloud, fifty miles east. There
they waited out what came to be known as the Sioux Uprising, while tales
of massacres, tomahawking, and children being shoved into ovens made
their way into the fort. When the Lindberghs returned to their homestead
many weeks later, newborn in arms, they discovered their farm intact and
most of the animals rounded up. Many of the white men in the Minnesota

Valley were not so lucky; three hundred fifty settlers were killed. The Indians won the battle but lost the war. The Sioux were banished from Minnesota by an act of Congress; and each month brought caravans of prairie schooners carrying new settlers.

In October 1867, August Lindbergh officially acquired 160 acres of land in Stearns County at no cost through the Homestead Act; and the following spring he purchased forty adjacent acres for fifty dollars. Life on the new land was hard. The Lindberghs raised all their own food and made most of their necessities—clothes, soap, even bullets. The elements constantly conspired against them. Over three successive summers in the 1870s, grasshoppers ravaged the farm. One year the insects devoured everything but the garden peas, leaving the family to live off pea soup for months. Whooping cough took the lives of three Lindbergh children. When Louisa's housedresses wore through, she took to wearing the few silk frocks she had carried from Sweden—even for such chores as milking the cow. When the cow died, she sold her gold watch to buy another. Louisa often suffered from crying jags. Through it all, August Lindbergh was thrilled to be in America and proud when he became a citizen on December 23, 1870. Both he and his wife learned English as quickly as possible, insisting that it be spoken at home. They both read their Bible, and August studied history for the rest of his life.

Opinionated as ever, August Lindbergh found himself drawn into political discussions. He wrote letters to the editors of the local newspapers; and after organizing the local school district, he sat on its board and served as town clerk, justice of the peace, and postmaster.

His son Charles August grew into the best-looking young man for miles around—almost six feet tall, lithe, smooth-skinned, with a dimpled chin; but he was moody, often brooding. To him, anything easy was hardly worth doing. From the moment he had been old enough to carry a gun, C.A.'s primary obligation was to provide meat for his family. He had a muzzle-loading double-barreled shotgun, and he became a crack shot. He knew he had to account for each kill against the number of homemade bullets he had been given, so if he ever missed, he would sometimes wait for hours until he could line up two birds that he might shoot with the next. Fishing was often done with spears by birch-bark torchlight. For coming home with a deer, all else was forgiven.

No school for C.A. even existed before he was twelve years old. "I had become so imbued with the grandeur of God's Creation that, when a school was started," he remembered years later, "I could not divert my attention from Nature to books." He considered himself the poorest student in the two-room schoolhouse, which he attended until he was eighteen. But C.A. felt he learned something that could never be taught in a classroom—independence, "not only in thinking," he later wrote, "but in action as well. I love independence, and I like to see others independent. But most of all I like to work and cooperate with independent people."

The circumstances of C.A.'s birth and his father's reasons for coming to America were barely discussed and certainly never publicly disclosed; but with the arrival of his Swedish half-brothers, he pieced together the details. His illegitimacy seemed to fuel his ambition, as though compelling him to make the Lindbergh name honorable, to succeed in the public eye. Like his father, he was driven—stubborn, earnest, and even a little angry.

C.A. pursued his studies at the Grove Lake Academy, where, for six dollars a week, Father Daniel J. Cogan, a Catholic priest, and a few other professors taught six dozen young men—mostly enlightened farmers' sons whose fathers recognized the importance of a formal education enough to release them from farmlife in the winter. As much as possible, the teaching was tutorial, rigorously training each young man to think and speak for himself.

Two years at Father Cogan's academy prepared Lindbergh to pursue the study of law. He matriculated at the University of Michigan in Ann Arbor, the closest law school of any merit, which then awarded a degree after but two six-month terms. That left Lindbergh enough of each year to return home and earn money to pay his tuition, which he did by hunting and trapping for muskrats and minks along the river. At school, he kept his nose in his books—avoiding distractions as much as possible, especially girls. He even moved out of a house in which he lodged because he found himself taking too great an interest in a girl rooming there. He graduated in the class of 1883.

Although rural living would always appeal to him, Lindbergh viewed his sheepskin as insurance against his ever having to rely on a farm for his livelihood. He was admitted to the Minnesota bar that summer; and after two years exploring professional possibilities in St. Cloud and a few towns in South Dakota, he settled in fast-growing Morrison county, in a town called Little Falls, fifty miles northwest of where he had grown up.

Over the next ten years, the population of Little Falls would increase tenfold, to 5,000. This bustling community was no longer concerned with clearing the land so much as what to put on it. New farms, new homes, and new businesses—to say nothing of such booming industries as the Weyerhaeusers' lumber mill—all needed lawyers. So did East Coast investors who were loaning considerable sums on Western farmland.

From the neighboring county, August Lindbergh watched his son's practice flourish—enough to suggest there might be a political career in his future. To prevent his own past indiscretion from ever affecting his son's career, on the afternoon of September 15, 1885, August Lindbergh took his common-law wife to Stearns County Courthouse to be formally married. The judge later said he understood that "August Lindbergh was a very conscientious man and believed in being one hundred percent American and that was probably a reason for an American marriage." Lindberghs unknowingly subscribed to that story for generations. And when August Lindbergh died eight years later at the age of eighty-five, the obituaries described a model American. The papers gilded his reputation as a Swedish legislator, then spoke of his coming to America for religious freedom.

The old Swede had lived to see, in less than a generation, his son become one of the leading citizens of Little Falls, the most dynamic attorney in town. Over the next twenty years, C.A. Lindbergh alternately practiced with a partner or two (including his younger brother Frank) or on his own. He soon counted such companies as Little Falls Lumber, McCormick Harvester Machine, and Singer Manufacturing among his clients. No longer content closing deals for others, owning real estate became his passion, a means by which he could trade up.

He took advantage of the boom years by turning property around and by building in Little Falls. Four second-floor rooms in one of his buildings in town served as his office. Throughout these early years of land transactions, something more than C.A.'s success attracted other clients. "What first drew my attention to the man," said his friend Thomas Pederson, "was the very evident respect with which his name was mentioned and the confidence and trust everyone seemed to have in him."

Morrison County thought so as well, electing him county attorney in 1890. He chose not to run for reelection but did not lose his taste for public service. Even in private practice, which included a great deal of corporation work, "a poor man was never turned down because he had no money," noted his brother Frank. "His sympathies were for the 'under dog.' " Lindbergh lived modestly at first—in the boondocks, in the only Little Falls house on the west side of the Mississippi. Then he moved into the boardinghouse of Harriet and Moses LaFond, original town settlers, and met their daughter.

Mary LaFond was sweet and pretty, uncommonly refined for having been raised on the frontier; and he, with his career underway, paid serious attention to a woman for the first time. They married in April 1887 and moved into a substantial brick house he had built in town, where they settled into a kind of civilized domesticity most people thought impossible in still untamed territory. Mary was often talked about for the "fine home" she kept; and over the next five years she brought three daughters into the world—Lillian, Evangeline, and Edith, the last dying in infancy.

"He was a great home lover," Mary's sister later remarked; but C.A. was equally enamored of his twin careers of real estate and law. Indeed, Frank Lindbergh noted, he "worked hard always beginning early in the morning

and he seldom failed to work after supper and into the night." He began buying farms, which he rented out, offering the tenants the privilege of buying
them on easy terms; he erected the first creamery in Little Falls; he bought the
mortgages of settlers and sold them to Easterners who had money to invest
in the community. He was an original shareholder of the First National
Bank, and after but five years in town was asked to sit on its board of directors. The town's other large financial institution, the German-American
National Bank, offered him a large block of stock for the privilege of using
his name as one of their directors. The transaction fascinated Lindbergh,
leading him to question who had actually paid for his shares and to study
banking practices.

In April 1898, C.A.'s prosperous life all but completely crashed. His wife
began suffering from stomach pains, and a doctor in Minneapolis diagnosed
an abdominal tumor. Not until Mrs. Lindbergh was under chloroform did
the doctor realize that his patient was also several months pregnant. He said
the only way to save the mother was to sacrifice the child; but two hours
later, Mary LaFond Lindbergh—only thirty—died as well.

At first, C.A. found comfort in his family. His mother moved into the big
brick house; and he hired a kindergarten teacher to tend to his children—ten-
year-old Lillian and six-year-old Eva. But after eighteen months of grieving,
he craved solitude. With the start of the school term, in September 1900, he
sent his children to a boarding school in Minneapolis and threw himself into
his work. He moved out of his house and into a room on the second floor of
the large Antlers Hotel.

He had hardly unpacked when he noticed another recent arrival at the
Antlers. She was the new science teacher at Little Falls High School—twenty-
four years old and beautiful. It was not just her enormous blue eyes, fair skin,
and shapely figure that made her so striking; it was the confidence she exuded, a worldly air hardly known in those parts. College-educated, she had
also been born and raised in what many people considered the most sophisticated city west of the Atlantic seaboard. She was, in fact, the daughter of
two of its best-known families—the Lodges and the Lands of Detroit, Michigan.

WITH ITS ADVANTAGEOUS SITUATION for boats and trains, and an
abundance of natural resources, Detroit's flowering had been inevitable. By
the middle of the nineteenth century, some of its roads, notably Woodward
Avenue, could be counted among the most beautiful residential streets in the
country. In the rise of post–Civil War industrialism, the city came of age.

One of its renowned citizens was Edwin Albert Lodge, born in London
in 1822. Traumatized by an alcoholic father, he left home in his teens for

America. After several years of wandering, he found himself in St. Thomas, Ontario—halfway between Buffalo and Detroit—where he married a spirited beauty named Emma Kissane. By then Lodge had developed an interest in medicine, particularly the unconventional practice of homeopathy. Over the next ten years the Lodges traveled through Indiana, Ohio, Pennsylvania, and New York, where he became a graduate of (as he later advertised) "one Allopathic, two Eclectic and four Homeopathic Colleges." In 1859 they moved with their six children to Detroit, which had become a center of homeopathic medicine. There, according to one history of homeopathy, he established "one of the [city's] largest and most lucrative practices ever enjoyed by any physician." A formidable figure—tall, dark, and spare, with a scraggly beard—it was said "half the babies in Detroit were named after him."

Lodge also found religion there. A member of the Church of the Disciples, Dr. Lodge became a fanatic, opposing most earthly pleasures. He forbade anyone in his family from dancing or playing cards; and on the Sabbath he further restricted reading newspapers or eating warm meals, because the cooking of them "prevents those preparing them from going to church." Although he was not an ordained minister, he was frequently asked to preach. In preparing his sermons he would underscore the words of Christ in the New Testament in red ink, those of the Disciples in blue; he practiced writing the Lord's Prayer in a space the size of a dime. Never far from controversy, he incurred the scorn of the orthodox medical community.

In time Edwin A. Lodge, M.D., became a cottage industry—as the subtitle on his stationery indicated: "Homoeopathic Chemist, Importer and Publisher." His practice and Homeopathic Dispensary moved every few years. From one location, on Wayne Street, he published the *American Homoeopathic Observer,* which offered as many as twenty different pamphlets on homeopathic subjects in its advertisements. Thus, he administered doses of homilies and Scripture alongside such remedies as "Lodge's Indian Tonix Elixir" and "Lodge's Chinese Dye-Powder for the Hair." He also delivered public addresses on nutrition, marriage, and midwifery to the good people of Detroit. These speeches pestled some common sense about healthy bodies with some slightly loony "scientific theories," with a pinch of fire and brimstone thrown in. His "Private Lecture to Young Men," for example, prepared "men at eighteen" for puberty—which he claimed was largely induced by "the hot-bed rearing of city life"—

by its unnatural excitements, by reading love romances, and the foul trash which is weekly retailed in sensual papers, by waltzes and other dances, by witnessing theatrical representations of love-plays, by operatic entertainments, by love-songs and lascivious poetry from the pens of Byron and other sensual poets. . . .

A devout anti-abortionist, he urged young men to search for "true wealth" in a partner—"intelligence, affection, and health"—before replenishing the earth.

Had Dr. Lodge spent more time examining the health of his own wife, Emma, he would have observed that she was mentally ill—subject to extreme mood swings that culminated in rages. Within a few years of their marriage, he filed a bill of divorcement, which he withdrew when she promised to put an end to her "bad treatment, violent acts, threats and imprudences." She proved unable to "reform," however, stricken with what the next century would probably recognize as a chemical imbalance. Even after she died a few years later, Lodge wrote his mother, "No mention is ever made of that Xantippe who worried me of old," and that "dead or alive I am not willing to have her spoken of by any member of my family in my house or out of it."

Dr. Lodge lost no time in taking a second wife, one Christiana Hanson, a Norwegian widow of a sea captain. She entered the marriage with a son, who assumed the name Lodge; and they had four more children of their own. Three of the Lodge boys became doctors, and one of the sons from his second marriage, John Christian Lodge, became mayor of Detroit and one of its longest-serving councilmen. But for most of his life, Dr. Lodge criticized his children far more than he ever praised them, engaging in constant arguments, sometimes verbally violent behavior. He seemed to find peace only after he retired from the practice of medicine to run a farm on Pine Lake, about five miles from Pontiac, where he could soak up the beauty of God's country.

The most compliant of the eleven Lodge children was Evangeline, from his first marriage. She learned to deal with her father's tempestuous personality by quietly submitting. She worked long hours in the offices and the pharmacy and never engaged in the family quarrels. At twenty-five she married a man who was in many ways like her father.

Controversial and contumacious, Dr. Charles Henry Land was the most progressive dentist in town, often to the consternation of his colleagues. Like the Lodges, the Lands came to the United States from Great Britain by way of Canada. Some of the family had fought as Loyalist soldiers during the American Revolution, and one member had married into the family of General Winfield Scott, the hero of three wars and Supreme Commander of the Union Army. Abandoned as a teenager by his father, Dr. Land had sold newspapers on the streets of New York and worked as a meat packer in Des Moines before he found himself at age twenty-one in Chicago, apprenticing to a dentist. With all the zeal of an autodidact, Charles Land immersed himself in the science of oral medicine. Just when he had built his own successful practice, the great Chicago fire stormed through the city, taking Land's office and home with it. He fled with little more than the clothes on his back, spending that night in October 1871 under a viaduct, where he covered himself in sand for protection. The next day, he persuaded the captain of a lake boat to take him up Lake Michigan and down Lake Huron to the eastern shore of Michigan—on credit.

Land arrived in Detroit practically penniless. As soon as possible, the twenty-four-year-old dentist hung out his shingle, which he literally painted himself. He met with immediate success; and over the next twenty years he revolutionized his profession. Inventing the porcelain jacket crown, as well as two dozen other patented devices and procedures, earned him his appellation, the "Father of Porcelain Dentistry." In 1875, Charles Henry Land married Dr. Lodge's daughter Evangeline. They moved into a brick house just below Grand Circus Park on Woodward Avenue; and over the next four years they produced a daughter and a son, whom they named after themselves.

Dr. Land proved to be as much of a firebrand in Detroit as Dr. Lodge was. The "gold work" dentists vociferously opposed Land's experiments with porcelain and called him a "quack." And when Land began to advertise his practice, publicly announcing his new techniques, he hit a nerve. The Michigan Dental Association expelled Land from their organization over the issue. "That suits me," he told The Evening News. "I want to be removed from any institution which can be so intolerant and nearsighted as this one is proving."

To make matters worse, he formed a company to sell the Land System of Dental Practice, complete with the rights to practice his methods and a guarantee against patent infringers. Many in the profession objected to such patents and raised money to fight Land in court. At one point, he offered to grant his patents to the dental profession, if it would adopt his methods of dentistry; but he was refused. One against many, he spent most of his resources on lawsuits and went bankrupt.

Young Evangeline and young Charles had to grow up with other embarrassments. Mildly eccentric, Dr. Land busied himself with peculiar activities. An amateur lepidopterist, entomologist, ornithologist, taxidermist, and fungiphile, he surrounded himself with his collections, growing the wild mushrooms in his cellar. In his spare time he made porcelain flowers and pottery, which he threw on a wheel he had fashioned from an old dental foot-engine.

It was difficult for the Land children to keep friends, because they moved almost every other year, the size of their house reflecting the state of their finances. Isolated, the Land children grew up appreciating solitude. Evangeline attended Miss Liggett's private school and practiced piano as much as four hours a day. Furthermore, in an age when most fathers discouraged their daughters from becoming too educated, Dr. Land urged his daughter to pursue an additional year of high school at Detroit Central High School and—

even more unusual—to continue her studies at the University of Michigan. She graduated in 1899 with a Bachelor of Science degree, having majored in Chemistry. She was by her own admission "a practical & matter of fact young woman."

Evangeline was also engaging, lively, and utterly unpredictable. Long after her first cousin Emory Scott Land—a midshipman at the Naval Academy who would rise to the rank of Admiral—had invited Evangeline to be his prom date in Annapolis, he referred to her as "the most beautiful girl at Ann Arbor." One of her Lodge cousins thought he was paying an even higher compliment when he recollected years later that Evangeline was, in fact, "a perfect picture of her grandmother, Emma Kissane." The similarity was more than skin-deep: Evangeline Lodge Land was beginning to exhibit symptoms of her grandmother's mental instability as well.

Because of financial pressures, Evangeline's mother suggested she might teach, thinking her daughter would apply for a position in Detroit. But young Evangeline had other ideas. "How wonderful it would be to go to some mining-town and teach chemistry to the children of miners," she mused. "And if I had to live on the outskirts of town, to have a great St. Bernard dog to carry my lunch." A teachers' agency informed her of an opening in Little Falls, Minnesota.

Evangeline had never heard of the town; but she was able to locate it on a map, little more than one hundred miles downstream from the Mississippi's headwaters. And in Captain Willard Glazier's *Down the Great River,* she found a thrilling account of his travels along the Mississippi. The description of his momentous visit to Little Falls, where he was greeted by a brass band, clinched Evangeline's decision.

She traveled by boat to Duluth, Minnesota, where she caught the only train to Little Falls. It arrived at four o'clock one early-September morning, 1900, offering Miss Land a reception far less festive than Captain Glazier's. From the depot, she went directly to the nearby Antlers Hotel and moved into a room with a bay window in the third-floor tower overlooking a lumber mill. Later that day, the school superintendent, Joseph Seal, introduced her to C.A. Lindbergh, and they soon began to walk together to their respective workplaces.

Within weeks of their meeting, Evangeline was writing home to mother about her new friend, "the brightest lawyer in Minnesota." Before their relationship could get too serious, Mrs. Land wanted details about his reputation and the state of his health; she wondered if so successful an attorney might also be unused to physical labor and effete. "He is about four or five inches taller than I," Evangeline replied. "He has light hair and blue eyes. He has broad shoulders and a chest that would make you laugh at your own question." And though he was forty-two to her twenty-four, "He can swim across the Detroit River all day long back and forth as long as you will be willing to watch him when you ask him. He is strong and awkward and well. He hasn't one unsound tooth. So there." Furthermore: "He has not one single stain on his reputation. He does not drink, chew or smoke. His greatest fault is that he works too hard." Beyond that, Evangeline reported that C.A. had two young daughters who were attending private school in Minneapolis and that her presence was suddenly "causing great commotion because I have interested this man whom everybody caters to . . ."

Love had not completely blinded Evangeline to the rest of Little Falls, which, after Detroit, seemed pretty hick. Evangeline was homesick; and her job—which paid $55 a month—only exacerbated her feelings. She felt underappreciated and overburdened, carrying a teaching load of Botany, Chemistry, Physical Geography, Physiology, and Physics. She and her principal came to loggerheads that December, when she broke school rules by moving equipment from the unheated attic-laboratory to her classroom. "I shall tell you one thing," she wrote her mother, "surely that no matter what becomes of me & my friend the lawyer, Little Falls Minnesota shall not see so very much more of this chicken."

Dr. Land advised his daughter to resign at the end of the year, thinking she might come home. Mr. Lindbergh advised the same, hoping she might stay. He tried to change her mind about Little Falls by showing her the best of its social scene. He courted her in a two-horse carriage he had hired, and he sometimes kept Evangeline out as late as nine o'clock, so they could ride home in the moonlight. Soon she was writing home that "this town is not such a wild and woolly place as I first thought it."

A guilty conscience as much as a hasty heart was driving the stoical lawyer from Little Falls. That autumn he received disturbing reports from the school in Minneapolis to which he had farmed out his children. Miss Olive Adele Evers, headmistress of Stanley Hall, cared for the school's only boarders, the two young Lindberghs, in a red-brick house next door; and she wrote their father that they were both extremely anxious little girls, potential discipline problems who provoked fights with the other children. More disturbing was that Eva was biting her fingernails down to the quick and Lillian was literally tearing at the skin of her fingers until they bled. "Two more forlorn children never existed," Eva recalled sixty years after her stay at Stanley Hall. "We suffered extreme homesickness, made father's visits miserable, and did not really adjust to the abrupt change." They yearned for a home.

Evangeline Land was, in fact, only twelve years older than Lillian, closer in age to C.A. Lindbergh's children than to him; and when he asked her to marry, he never defined how he expected her to play her role of stepmother. Nonetheless, she quit her job and returned to Detroit for Christmas vacation to mull over his proposal. In January their engagement was announced.

Charles August Lindbergh and Evangeline Lodge Land married in Detroit on March 27, 1901, at her parents' home. The small parlor there limited the number of guests to closest relatives and a few friends. Because emotional displays made both the bride and groom uncomfortable, they wanted to steal away without being showered with rice. So when Grandmother Lodge had to leave early, Evangeline and C.A. each took her arm to aid her down the steps and into her carriage. Nobody paid any attention when they got in the carriage as well, driving off to her house, where they had already brought their suitcases earlier in the day.

They journeyed west for a "wedding tour" of ten weeks. They stopped at Pike's Peak and the Garden of Gods in Colorado before pushing on to California, where they traveled the entire length of the state—from Tijuana in Baja to the Oregon border. By Sacramento, Evangeline was giving in to feeling that marriage could be sheer bliss . . . until one night, while taking a long walk, she and C.A. found a deserted garden filled with roses. She picked a bouquet of them and carried them back to their hotel room. Only then did C.A. rebuke her for committing "an offence against the law," insisting that they would have to leave town as soon as possible. Not until the sting of the lecture had worn off did she realize that he had been joking. It was an early glimpse of her new husband's perverse sense of humor.

The "happiest part of our trip," Evangeline Lindbergh would later recall, was spent in The Dalles on the Columbia River in northern Oregon, where they rafted and hiked and camped out, several weeks alone together, at peace with nature. They returned to Minnesota on the Northern Pacific Railroad.

On the way to California, C.A. had asked Evangeline whether she would prefer to live in the town of Little Falls or on the outskirts, in the country. Whichever, he wanted to give her the house of her choice. When she did not hesitate to choose the latter, he told her about a farm two and one-half miles south of Little Falls, on the western bank of the Mississippi. Upon their return, Evangeline saw a most winning aspect of her husband: He had written ahead to a business associate named Carl Bolander, an architect and builder, who had constructed a temporary camp for the newlyweds—a tar-roofed, two-bedroom shack of pine, with a kitchen and screened-in porch that could double as a dining room, right on the banks of the river at the foot of their new land.

Most of the Lindberghs' one hundred twenty acres sat on the bluff, one hundred feet above the riverbank encampment. Pikes Creek and a road running parallel to the river cut through this magnificent woodland, thick with white pines, oak, elm, poplar and linden. They agreed to build Evangeline's dream house at the edge of the cliff, where the land dropped precipitously into the so-called "valley-by-the-river"—affording a spectacular vista of the Mississippi.

The three-story house of pine and cedar had double linings of tar paper for extra warmth. Each of the public rooms on the ground floor was finished in fine wood—the den in California redwood, the dining room in quarter-sawed oak, and the living room in birch. All the floors were varnished maple. The second floor had four bedrooms, with a fireplace in the master bedroom. The third floor had servant's quarters and a billiard room. The house also featured two bathrooms, with water pumped by a gas engine from a well dug seventy feet deep. An oversized furnace that burned either wood or coal heated the hot-water radiators.

Evangeline L. L. Lindbergh, as she now signed her documents, was not the only one to realize her dream that summer. Lillian and Eva were released from Stanley Hall. They returned to Little Falls with open arms, embracing their new mother.

"It was a very happy summer," Evangeline remembered of 1901, when the new family shantied along the river. Lillian and Eva slept in a tent; and a maid cooked and cleaned. One day Evangeline, in a freshly ironed gingham dress and feeling good about her country life, slipped on the grass and fell all the way down into the cold river up to her armpits. C.A. stood on the bank and laughed, which infuriated her. But with each day's progress on the house, Evangeline found ways to overlook her husband's flintiness and his dry humor.

She was even warming to Little Falls, delighting in its reputation "for having two saloons for every church and a church for every creed." C.A.'s office was over one of the saloons. His practice was thriving, and he seemed to derive even more pleasure from his home. That autumn the outside of their house was painted light gray with white trim; and by January the inside was furnished—featuring an upholstered davenport and mahogany bookcase, a piano, Oriental rugs, mahogany-colored drapes, oil lamps, water-color paintings, and a beautiful white and gold china service. "It was wonderfully peaceful and beautiful there," Evangeline recalled, "—not a building in sight across the river—nor thru the trees in any direction. Evenings we had only the sound of the rushing water, and birds' songs."

And soon to come . . . a baby's cry, for Evangeline Lindbergh was entering her ninth month of pregnancy. At the end of January, she went to Detroit, so that her uncle Dr. Edwin Lodge could deliver the baby in her parents' home. C.A. visited the last week of the month and saw Evangeline comfortably settled into the large front bedroom of the house on West Forest, then left to attend business back home. He planned to return in a few weeks as the due-date approached.

On the bitter cold night of February third, Evangeline went into labor. Dr. Land sent a telegram to Little Falls, urging C.A. back to Detroit. Uncle Edwin arrived at seven o'clock and went to bed, to rest until the attending nurse summoned him around midnight. He administered no anesthesia. At 1:30 the next morning, the nine-and-one-half-pound child was born.

For months C.A. had crowed that he knew the "new babe would be a son"; and eager to please, Evangline immediately asked in his absence, "Is it a boy?"

"It is," her uncle replied.

"Are you sure?" she inquired.

"Dead sure," he said. "Just look at the size of those feet. He is fine. You ought to have seventeen like him."

But he would be her only child—named for his father, with the addition of a syllable to the middle name: Charles Augustus Lindbergh. Soon after the birth, he was bundled up and laid on a chair near an open window, where he breathed in the winter air.

"Life's values originate in circumstances over which the individual has no control," Charles Lindbergh would write seventy years later, after an odyssey that took him to places nobody had ever journeyed before. Then, with a peculiar sense of detachment bordering on the divine, he described the beginning of his strange, singular destiny by adding: "I was born a child of man, in the city of Detroit, on February 4, 1902, of Swedish, English, Irish, and Scottish ancestry."

3

NO PLACE
LIKE HOME

"A sound individual is produced by a sound lifestream."

—C.A.L.

RAISED IN VIRTUAL ISOLATION AMONG LINDBERGHS, Lodges, and Lands, it was difficult for Charles Lindbergh ever to recognize that his kin might have differed from other people. He was proud that his family tree abounded with independent thinkers in a broad range of disciplines—most of which he would pursue. But he never perceived that many of his ancestors were prideful to the point of arrogance—rebels so far apart from the rest of society as to be above the law, so evangelical as to appear fanatical, so global in their vision as to be shortsighted. For all his fascination with detail, Lindbergh never examined his family history closely enough to see that it included financial malfeasance, flight from justice, bigamy, illegitimacy, melancholia, manic-depression, alcoholism, grievous generational conflicts, and wanton abandonment of families. But those undercurrents were always there. And so this third-generation Lindbergh was born with a deeply private nature and bred according to the principles of self-reliance—nonconformity and the innate understanding that greatness came at the inevitable price of being misunderstood.

THE BABY WAS FUSSED OVER from birth. With his long black hair, which quickly turned to golden curls, his bright blue eyes, and the already discernible Lindbergh dimpled chin, the child's beauty was not lost on anybody—not even the impassive C.A., who arrived in Detroit two days after the deliv-

ery and stayed through the weekend. Witnessing mother and baby with her
parents prompted emotions he had never felt before. "It is the noblest idea
of God and the most beautiful reality in life that ever came to my knowledge," C.A. wrote his mother-in-law after the experience. He became an attentive husband and even a demonstrative father, for a while.

When the baby was five weeks old, Charles's mother took him on his first
journey—almost eight hundred miles to Little Falls. There they joined C.A.
in their new house on the river—staffed with a cook, a maid, and a coach-
man who oversaw the farm and lived in a tenant's house across the road with
a half-dozen men who fenced the land and built a large stable.

From his first three years, Lindbergh would later recall but a handful of
stray memories, mostly of life along the Mississippi. He remembered the
view of the river from his crib; and the swift-moving current, a quarter mile
across, became an endless source of fascination for him. He also remembered
his mother, with her hair powdered white, coming into a room downstairs,
wringing her hands and crying, "Oh! I'm so nervous, I'm so nervous." She
was, in fact, preparing for a small acting performance which she was presenting that night for some party guests. "I can still see my mother coming
into the room and I can still see her washing the powder off her hair after it
was all over," Lindbergh recalled decades later. "I felt that she would be all
right again as soon as the powder was washed off, but I was worried about
the effect it would have on the fish when it reached the river. I remember
being assured by my mother that it would not make the fish nervous too."

Evangeline L. L. Lindbergh had good reason to feel nervous. She never
fit in with the townsfolk of Little Falls. Unlike most of the other local women,
Evangeline was, after all, a city-bred, college-educated woman who had
worked outside the home and who was living in a style more grand than C.A.
had lived with his first wife. That she was also much younger than he only
isolated her even more. "After the marriage," remembered C.A.'s former
sister-in-law, Mrs. Robert Herron, "she kept aloof and never had many
friends." Lindbergh maids regularly gossiped about their mistress's wild temper and wilder spending habits. Tongues wagged about her fits of rage and
willfulness toward C.A. and her constant nagging. In unkind moments,
C.A.'s two sisters referred to Evangeline as the "Anvil Chorus," "A.C." for
short. (Decades later some believed she was the model for Carol Kennicott,
the stifled heroine in Sinclair Lewis's *Main Street,* a novel based on the author's hometown of Sauk Centre, not fifty miles from Little Falls.)

From the beginning the Lindberghs kept their baby outside as much as
possible, even in winter. His first summers were spent in a baby carriage
which sported a large green parasol. C.A. had purchased a flock of angora
goats to clear the land; and there was a constant battle between whoever was
looking after the baby and the animals, who were always butting the carriage

trying to eat the parasol. Charles was weaned on goat's milk and grew up surrounded by animals—cattle, hogs, sheep, chickens, and horses (including a saddle horse and a "bucking bronco"). There were pigeons in the barn, which Charles called "dubs," and a family of six-toed cats that had to be disposed of because they were excessively fond of the "dubs." With few children nearby, a succession of dogs became Charles's playmates.

The boy's prosperous surroundings reflected C.A.'s booming business in town. The senior Lindbergh's legal reputation grew along with his land holdings—which included large parcels on the west side of the river, where he thought Little Falls residences would mushroom next. His passion for land became famous in the county, as did his reputation for buying at the seller's price and selling at the buyer's. As often as not, he was willing to carry paper, assuming mortgages and promissory notes along with his land parcels; he was even known to throw money back to buyers who needed an advance on their taxes. While serving on the boards of the two Little Falls banks, he was often quoted as saying, "To make money, in my opinion, is not the sole purpose of a bank."

His reputation spread to neighboring counties. "Judges, and other attorneys, told stories about him," wrote the senior Lindbergh's friends Lynn and Dora B. Haines, "—not of sharpness and tricks, but of his straight-forward, uncompromising honesty." Except with his wife, from whom he kept most of his finances as private as his emotions.

Early Sunday morning, August 6, 1905, C.A., Evangeline, and Grandmother Land took Charles in one of their four carriages for a long drive northwest of town. They stopped at a farm in which C.A. had an interest and returned to an early afternoon fried chicken dinner, after which they all went into the living room. Evangeline was playing piano, and C.A. was playing with Charles, carrying him up and down the room, shouting so loudly that Evangeline could hardly hear her music. In the midst of this ruckus, the cook entered the room and said as calmly as if she were announcing dinner, "Mrs. Lindbergh, the house is on fire."

Everybody rushed outside and looked at the roof, which was in flames. While the house burned from the third floor down, the boy's nurse hied him to the back of the barn so that he would not be frightened. But she kept screaming, "Charles, you *mustn't* watch!"—which terrified him, indelibly etching his first vivid memory. Evangeline tried to gather valuables, while C.A. and the workmen tried to extinguish the fire. After twenty minutes, there was nothing to do but watch as the fire consumed the building. Charles pulled away from his nurse to see the black cloud covering the house, as its pine and cedar crackled.

The next day, Evangeline walked Charles through the ruins. Hardly a piece of charred wood remained. "Our entire house has sunk into the stone walls of its basement," he would write fifty years later. "Out of the pit, smoke-smutted but sharp-cut against thick leaves and sky, rises our brick chimney, tall and spindly without a house around it." The only object to remain completely undamaged was a small Mexican idol, a red-clay figurine Evangeline had purchased in Tijuana on her honeymoon. Some clothes and furniture and the upright piano were salvaged, as were all of the maid's possessions. (Evangeline suspected her of accidentally starting the fire by knocking over her kerosene lamp; others believed oily rags had been the cause.) "Father will build us a new house," Evangeline assured her three-and-one-half-year-old. "But my toys, and the big stairs," he later remembered thinking, "and my room above the river, are gone forever—"

More than the Lindbergh house went up in smoke. Evangeline never recovered her pearl-and-diamond engagement ring . . . and, indeed, the Lindbergh marriage seemed to go with it. The solid house could never conceal the fact that the relationship within had been shaky from the start, that while C.A. and Evangeline might have been intellectually compatible, they were two decidedly mismatched personalities—in the words of one of his friends, "an entire contrast in tastes, ideals, and ambitions."

While the first house Charles ever knew was still smoldering, the family moved fifteen miles south, into a hotel in Uppsala. Within two weeks, C.A. and Evangeline had decided to rebuild on their original site; and so they moved back to Little Falls. C.A. camped out on the farm, while Evangeline and the children checked into the Buckman Hotel in town, Charles bunking with his mother in a plain room, with a bed, simple wooden furniture, and a washstand. "For me it was a dreary place," Charles would later write. Without the Mississippi rushing outside his window, he spent much of his time hanging over a windowsill and looking down on the rutted, unpaved road below, with its board sidewalks and hitching posts. Whenever cabin fever set in, Evangeline took Charles for extended visits to Detroit. Meantime Lillian and Eva studied hard in the Little Falls schools in hopes of getting into college, for they realized they would be happier there than in what had become a contentious household.

By the end of the year, C.A. was too far out on a financial limb to allow anyone to proceed with that thought. "We are exceedingly poor in cash and will be for some time to come," C.A. was forced to reveal to Evangeline in December 1905, "and our future expenses will have to be adjusted to our cash and not to what we want." He said they had over two hundred thousand dollars worth of property to which he had become a "slave," because there were debts totaling almost forty thousand dollars against the land with property taxes on top of that. "They both, our little daughters, have got to work," C.A. insisted, "and it will be better for them." C.A. began by selling the horses and cattle and discharging the farmhands. Without sacrifice on everyone's part, he explained, "the future of our dear boy might be less advantageous."

All plans that year were suddenly scaled down—starting with the new house. Gradually, Evangeline realized the reasons for rebuilding a structure half the size of its predecessor were not strictly economic. Months before the fire, Lillian and Eva had observed that C.A. had moved out of his wife's bedroom; now they thought he might be moving out of the house altogether. The new house, built upon the basement of the old one, suggested as much.

"I have heard it called the queerest house in Minnesota," Evangeline herself said of the one-and-a-half-story replacement. Only the first floor ever felt finished. The piano was moved into the living room; but the dining room, two bedrooms, sewing room, kitchen, and bathroom were jumbled in such a way as to produce a dark hallway with seven doors leading into it. "We used to laugh and say we had no fear of burglars at night," Evangeline recalled, "because they would be lost and could not find their way around without making too much noise."

For young Charles, the only part of the house that felt like home was the screened-in sleeping porch in the back, overlooking the Mississippi, partially open to the elements. He chose to spend all but the bitterest nights there. "I was in close contact with sun, wind, rain, and stars," Lindbergh remembered of his "bedroom." "My bed, a wide, folding-cot affair, was in the northwest corner. On stormy nights rain blown in through the screen would mist it. Some of the valley's treetops rose slightly above its level."

The second floor, a few small rooms under the gables and eaves, never became much more than an attic. Its pine floorboards remained unfinished, and no doors were hung. Although C.A. had ordered the foundation of the house to be raised so that he could build a library for himself in the basement, that room was never finished either.

Evangeline did everything to make the place her own. She had it painted gray with white trim; and she replanted the two large oval flower beds in front with irises and nasturtium and tiger lilies. Lilac and honeysuckle bushes lined the road in front of the house. Between Little Falls and whichever house in Detroit her parents were living, C.A. was happy to know there was always a place to "park" Evangeline and their son, for he was developing a new passion outside the home—politics.

THE UNITED STATES experienced an awkward adolescence as it entered the twentieth century. By its thirteenth decade as a nation it found itself caught between its agrarian youth and its industrial manhood. Nowhere were the growing pains felt more than in the Upper Mississippi Valley. The sound of an automobile down one of the roads in those parts was still enough to make a field hand lean against his hoe and marvel; but the nation's breadbasket knew that a new kind of wealth was being created in the cities "out East." A new generation of heartlanders began to fear they might be the next victims of the urban money interests.

Minnesota—a farm state with rapidly growing cities vibrant with factories and mills—was especially mindful. By 1905, more than half its residents lived in urban areas. But in Minnesota's Sixth Congressional District, the state's centermost twelve counties, two-thirds of the population were still rural dwellers and the chief source of their income was agriculture; the largest city in the district, St. Cloud, claimed only ten thousand residents. Such districts began looking for new representatives, men who had grown up on farms, been educated at Midwestern colleges, and were willing to leave their small-town law practices for capital cities.

The incumbent congressman of Minnesota's sixth district—two-term Republican Clarence B. Buckman—had evidently used his office to secure timber tracts for his own lumber interests; and many civic leaders in Little Falls, the district's centermost town, felt C.A. Lindbergh was just the man to replace him. Nobody in the district was more concerned about financial abuses of power; and nobody had been more outspoken, regularly firing off letters to the editors of local newspapers. In fact, Lindbergh had just established an experimental farmers' cooperative and a political quarterly of his own, in which he warned against the "favored class" in America, which he said "grabs the profits and leaves the industrious workers only a bare subsistence." Farmers and small businessmen gathered in support.

Lindbergh asked his most important New York real-estate client, Howard P. Bell—who had just lost shore rights at a dam site because of a Buckman political deal—to help him decide whether or not to run. Bell thought it boiled down to personal considerations—"how much is it worth to . . . have the name and general repute of being a Congressman." He granted that it would certainly enhance a law practice, but at "the cost of the thing in time, money, loss of opportunity at home." Unwittingly, Bell had hit upon the final reason to support C.A.'s running: a scandal-free method of separating from his wife. In September 1906, Lindbergh won the Republican nomination by almost seven percent.

Although never at a loss for opinions, Lindbergh was no silver-tongued orator. Recordings of his voice do not exist, but C.A.'s informal writings suggest a trace of a Scandinavian accent and the fact that he never fully mastered English—"Every think running ok"; "Hinclosed are some notes"; "Spected you down soon." But he was, by most reports, compelling—his passion compensating for his lapses in rhetoric. He repeatedly spoke of labor as the provider of "the main wealth of the world," as "the most important factor in our civilization."

Minnesota's Sixth Congressional District elected C.A. Lindbergh to the United States House of Representatives by a comfortable margin over his Democratic opponent, 16,762 to 13,115. The Sixtieth Congress would not convene until December 1907, but C.A. wasted no time in leaving town. While he familiarized himself with Washington, the rest of his family spent most of that year in Detroit with Dr. and Mrs. Land in a house they rented on Cass Avenue. Lillian graduated from Detroit Central High School and was permitted to start college at Ann Arbor, taking her fourteen-year-old sister along with her and seeing her through her third year of high school. Charles understood that his father's election meant "certain changes in life"—many of them, such as attending church, "disagreeable." Above all, it meant the loss of another home.

This period proved so upsetting that most of Lindbergh's childhood became a blurry memory to him. Over the next sixty-five years he would write six autobiographical volumes, much of which dwell on his youth. One began as a letter and swelled into a fifty-page book solely on the subject, which he titled *Boyhood on the Upper Mississippi*. But the title itself bespeaks a sad irony—for Charles Lindbergh spent only a fraction of his youth on the upper Mississippi. Although the images of his time there would forever be the most colorful in his mind's eye, most of his childhood was spent away from the farm.

From 1906 to 1917, he was there but two, sometimes three, months a year. The farther he traveled from Minnesota, the dimmer his recollections. And the most painful memories of his first eighteen years were subjected to selective amnesia, thus yielding but a few sentences in all his writing. Amazingly, when this stickler for accuracy compiled calendars of events in his childhood, they were riddled with errors, with major events forgotten and entire years mixed up. Later in life, Lindbergh would spend hours scrutinizing these formative years without ever analyzing them, averting his glance from that which was most personal—about his ancestors, his parents, or himself. "I have no recollection whatever of my daily routine during the early years of my life," he would admit in his mid-thirties.

Lindbergh never realized that his many pages of Tom Sawyer–like reminiscences—sunny days along the river, skinny-dipping, tree-climbing, watching "river-pigs" break log jams, running over the log jams himself—were, in fact, the exceptional days of his childhood. He was not consciously trying to varnish his youth. He simply learned at an early age to see and hear only that which he wanted to. By five years old he was already, in the words of his half-sister, "painfully shy"—hardly ever having played with another child and almost never having left his mother's sight.

He learned to make much out of little, indulging in solitary pursuits. He became an ardent collector of stones, arrowheads, cigar bands, coins, stamps, guns, lead soldiers, marbles, cigarette cards—almost anything he could find and stash under one of the attic eaves. And he became an inveterate maker of lists, constantly updating accounts of his possessions, as though taking inventory of himself through his things. He was happiest alone, outside, at one with nature. "That farm was one of the most important things in my life," he would write his mother in his mid-forties. "It taught me the value of water, trees, and sky—and solitude. Anyone who has not known these elements has not really lived." Indeed, he later realized, "I am not happy living away from water or where I cannot see the sky on a clear night."

One day, while playing alone on the upper floor of the house, he heard the distant noise of an engine. As it approached he realized it was louder than that of an automobile. He rushed to the window and climbed onto the roof. About two hundred yards away and barely higher than the treetops, he saw an airplane. It had two sets of wings, one above the other, with a man wearing a visored cap backwards sandwiched between. "Except in photographs, I had never seen an airplane before," Charles later wrote. "The aviator, my mother told me, had come to Little Falls to give exhibitions and carry up into the air anyone who dared to ride with him." She explained that it was both a dangerous and expensive proposition.

In the fall of 1907, C.A. Lindbergh gathered his family in the nation's capital for the inauguration of his career as a Congressman. Lillian left college and took her sister, Eva, to join Evangeline and Charles in C.A.'s furnished apartment in the Romaine, at 1831 V Street N.W., near Rock Creek Park. Although the flat was spacious, the walls closed in on them. By Christmas, Lillian and Eva had been dispatched to relatives in St. Cloud. Charles spent as much time as possible playing alone in vacant lots, having imaginary adventures.

On December 2, 1907, Congressman Lindbergh joined his colleagues for the opening of the Sixtieth Congress. It was largely a day of ceremony, the swearing in of members followed by the re-election of the House Speaker, Joseph Gurney Cannon of Illinois. Republicans had controlled the House in all but sixteen years since the Civil War; and, coercive as he was coarse, cigar-chomping "Uncle Joe" Cannon controlled a powerful legislative machine. As was customary, a photograph of the new Congress was taken, remarkable on this occasion because there, in one of the back rows, among the assembly of hoary heads, sat the vigorous forty-nine-year-old C.A. Lindbergh. Standing out even more glaringly in the photograph, in the aisle to his right, is a towheaded boy in a white sailor suit: his son, Charles.

The first two votes to come before this body were over leadership, in which Speaker Cannon and his rules from the Fifty-ninth Congress both received big majorities—Lindbergh's votes among them. Only years later did Lindbergh impart to close friends that he had often asked himself why he had voted as he did. "I had come to Washington to do something, so I voted with the herd"; but, he just as quickly resolved, "I am going to wipe out that stigma if I can." Over the next ten years in office, he would make good on his vow, hardly considering what new stigma such insurgency might bring upon him.

When Lindbergh took office, the Capitol walls were still shaking from a panic that October on Wall Street, a run on the banks that J. P. Morgan helped control. The solution scared Lindbergh more than the problem. Back home in Minnesota, C.A. had been warning people about the inequities in the American economy for years, how each wreck of the economy and rescue by a few powerful bankers only strengthened the Money Trust—"financial combinations in restraint of trade"—at the nation's expense. He could not have arrived on the House floor at a timelier moment, as the crux of the national debate for the next few years would be the economy and the extension of new powers to the people.

During that decade of progressive reform, Lindbergh would prove no stranger in the House well; and there was never any doubt as to where he stood on any issue. He always sided with the hardworking farmer in his district and opposed the high-rolling "speculative parasites."

The "insurgent" Republicans in the Senate—such men as Robert La Follette of Wisconsin, William Borah of Idaho, Albert Beveridge of Indiana, Albert Cummins of Iowa, and Moses Clapp of Minnesota—were debating many of the same issues with somewhat greater success. And so, when William Howard Taft assumed the Presidency from Roosevelt in 1909, many of the defiant House members challenged Speaker Cannon's leadership of their house. Lindbergh claimed credit for being the first to call for Cannon's ouster; and Rep. John Nelson of Wisconsin helped organize a group of rebel Republicans to fight for their cause. Nelson found that Lindbergh was "perhaps the most radical and independent of the group." A sampling of eighteen roll calls between 1906 and 1912, which "reflect deviation from party leadership on the part of certain intransigent Republicans in the House of Representatives," showed nobody scoring higher than C.A. Lindbergh. His strong support of Bull Moose candidate Theodore Roosevelt in 1912 helped his own re-election to a fourth term; but Democrat Woodrow Wilson, the beneficiary of the schism in the Republican party, got elected President.

By then much of America—not just the progressive representatives—had been awakened to the dangers of the nation's powerful bankers. Wrote muckraker Ida Tarbell in the May 1913 issue of *The American Magazine,* "It was a Swede from Minnesota who first raised in Congress the hue-and-cry of the MONEY TRUST HUNT—'a Swede who dreams,' a fellow member describes him—Charles A. Lindbergh." His colleagues never fully embraced his conspiracy theories nor endorsed his legislative proposals, but in 1912 the

House did approve of a Money Trust investigation to be conducted by its Committee on Banking and Currency under the direction of Congressman Arsene Pujo. As Congressman Ernest Lundeen of Minnesota later said, it was Congressman Lindbergh whose "resolutions and speeches resulted in this monumental work. There had been much talk in the country about interlocking directorates, but the Pujo investigation proved their existence.

> It gave the facts, statistics, and data. It called Morgan, Carnegie, and Rockefeller, and all the rest of the financial powers in America to Washington and placed them on the witness stand.

Control of money, tactics of secrecy, and "other forms of domination" were abuses of which the Pujo committee found such bankers as J. P. Morgan guilty. As early as 1908, the same charges were being leveled against C. A. Lindbergh—by his wife. Antagonism had replaced antipathy in their marriage; and by the end of the year, they decided to take one last stab at keeping the family together by separating. Evangeline would return to Minnesota—not to Little Falls, but to Minneapolis, where she could oversee Lillian as she transferred for her second year of college at the University of Minnesota and Eva as she completed high school.

"The crisp days of autumn were interesting enough," Charles would remember of that year, though, in fact, he never did pinpoint which year of his life it was. He could recollect only that it was dreary without his knowing why. Around this time, Lindbergh developed what became a lifelong practice of internal conversations, a series of questions he would pose to himself. "I spend hours on end in dry heated rooms, with stuffy head and whitening skin," he recalled of the period.

> I grow tired of books and toys, and pressing my face against a frosted window. I move aimlessly about, experiment in strange new fields. Why can't I hold ten marbles between ten toes? How long can a cream-filled chocolate last if I eat it with a pin—

He came down with measles that season, and he remembered being visited in bed by a doctor—the only such visit that would occur for sixty-five years—and taking bitter medicine. "The zero-cold months which followed left colorless space in my mind."

Charles also obliterated from memory the years of tension between his mother and his half-sisters. Ever since their mother's death, Lillian and Eva—four years apart in age—had been living out of a portmanteau, always being shipped off to Lindberghs in Minnesota or Lands in Detroit. While Evangeline had been able to deal with them when they were small, she could not cope with two headstrong teenagers at last rebelling against their years of ne-glect. Once settled at the University of Minnesota, Lillian became fond of pretty dresses and parties and a fellow student, Loren Roberts. One night after he kept her out until three o'clock in the morning, Evangeline scolded them both, insisting that it was "not a decent thing to do." Eva sided with her sister and said she just did not see how they could possibly go on living together any longer.

Increasingly, Evangeline took out her anger toward C.A. on his daugh-ters. She became furious at his indulging them with clothes allowances but crying poverty when she asked for the same thing. She resented having to dis-cipline his daughters, to play the role of the wicked stepmother. One night that spring, Eva returned home late, violating a new curfew, only to be greeted by Evangeline's slapping her in the face. "What was that for?" the sixteen-year-old girl asked, only to be told: "That's what you deserve!"

Like her sister, Eva had the good sense to get out, to disengage from Evangeline and get on with her own life. She would attend Carleton College and intern in her father's Washington office before marrying a journalist, George W. Christie. But for all intents and purposes, from the night of that slap, Evangeline had effectively ended her relationship with her husband's daughters. They never lived together again, an explanation for which was never given to Charles. Through it all, Eva had long resented Charles's being so indulged; but she later realized the price he had had to pay—that his youth must have been deeply "troubled," for "there was no normal family life."

In early summer 1909, Evangeline told C.A. that she wanted a divorce. Knowing it would prove unacceptable to the voters of Minnesota's Sixth District, C.A. appealed to her better judgment, urging her to "let things slide" and continue living as they had been.

Evangeline discussed the matter with her mother in a series of letters written largely in numerical code. Each letter of the alphabet was assigned a number—A=7, B=16, C=21, and so forth; and whenever she had something to say about 21-7, she broke for paragraphs at a time into numbers. "I doubt that he can be held to anything and he will offer as little as possible," Evan-geline "enumerated" that June; "all I can see is that if a definite settlement can be made now it will be better—just because he has not the traits that can allow dependence." She admitted that she no longer was even expecting to find happiness, "but as things are it seems that no one is justified in living as he proposes." C.A. argued that if she tried to shake him down in court she would probably end up getting less money out of him than he was allowing her already. Fearing the loss of his congressional seat, he promised to treat her fairly so long as they remained married.

A few months of truce followed, during which C.A. spent time with "the boy" and treated his wife with the utmost respect in public. Evangeline and Charles often lunched with him in the House dining room and sat in the gallery when the legislature was in session. For Woodrow Wilson's inauguration, C.A. got Senator Nelson of Minnesota to make ten-year-old Charles a Senate page for the day, so that he could observe the entire ceremony from a special seat. C.A. even took his wife to two formal receptions at the White House.

But in private, the Lindberghs reverted to their old quarrels, mostly over finances. Evangeline's trump cards remained C.A.'s fear of public exposure and the happiness of "the boy." Even then, C.A.'s behavior was not always predictable, as the strain of his domestic situation often got the better of him. During one visit to his wife's apartment, Charles began fidgeting, punching C.A., until Evangeline said, "You see, C.A., he's cooped up here and needs an outlet for surplus energy." C.A. said, "Get up on the chair, Charles, and I'll fight you." Charles did and kicked him in the groin. C.A. grabbed him by both arms and called him a "fool." On other occasions C.A. teased Charles until he cried.

C.A. meant no harm. This was just his own frustrated way of trying to make a man out of the boy. Like Evangeline, he never scolded or disciplined Charles; and he never spoke down to him. "Shall we go for a tramp, Boss?" C.A. would ask when he wanted to take a walk in the country.

Both parents believed in giving Charles adult responsibilities, obliging him at an early age to exercise judgment. He was only seven when his father gave him a Savage .22-caliber repeating rifle; and the boy surprised them both when his first shot at a duck, more than fifty feet away, hit it right in the head. He received a Winchester 12-gauge automatic shotgun the year after that, before he was even big enough to steady it against his shoulder. C.A. taught him to fish and to swim naked in the chilly waters near the house in Little Falls. Charles especially remembered one day when he slipped on the slimy stones of the Mississippi's bottom into a hole deeper than he was tall. "When I broke surface and coughed in a breath of air," he later recalled, "I was startled to find that my father wasn't running toward me. He just stood on shore and laughed. And then I realized that I was swimming by myself." Within a few summers, Charles was able to swim across Pike Creek in flood and down the Mississippi's rapids.

Charles grew up fast, becoming a rugged individualist like his father. And for all C.A.'s severity, Charles admired his unexpected wit. "Contrary to the impression of many people who knew him," Charles later explained to his father's biographer, "he had a great deal of humor," which he masked with a serious expression, leaving most people unaware that he was enjoying himself tremendously. "A Swedish sense of humor," Evangeline called it. "He could laugh wonderfully," Charles observed; "but he had an extraordinary ability to control his facial expression when he wanted to." Like his father, young Charles grew to gauge the funniness of a situation by how much laughter he suppressed.

The Lindberghs swallowed most of their emotions—except their increasing anger, which Charles learned to ignore. Although he did not recollect ever having to take sides, one parent or the other occasionally dragged him into the fray. After one testy exchange between them, Evangeline asked Charles if he considered it "quarreling" when she responded to C.A.'s insults as she had. "No," he said, "you answered him just right. I don't see what makes Father act so."

Neither did Evangeline, who endured years of escalating humiliations. On two occasions C.A. called her a "bloodsucker" right in front of Charles. He took to questioning her mental condition . . . and, on at least one occasion, he struck her.

As painful was Evangeline's realization that the persistent rumors about C.A. keeping company with another woman—his stenographer, who had moved from Little Falls to Washington—were true. After yet another overheated argument, she grabbed a gun and held it to C.A.'s head. "O.K., Evangeline," C.A. said, "if you must do it, do it." But she could only bring herself to throw the gun down and run off. In the end, she always caved in for the reason her mother reminded her: "As to divorce—you know that on account of Charles we must be careful . . ."

Through it all, the boy was spared the worst of his parents' behavior. "I cannot recall my father ever saying a word against my mother," Charles would later record. "She encouraged me to be with him as much of the time as possible and I believe that both my mother and my father always continued to care for each other although they were seldom together. One of the reasons my mother went to Washington seven or eight out of the ten winters my father was in Congress, was to give me the opportunity of seeing him frequently." But Charles became chronically restless—finding that his parents' living under one roof only bred greater contempt.

As he never settled in one place, Charles learned to take comfort in his rootlessness. Over a decade, Washington, D.C., became their official residence, with a breather in Minnesota every summer, and long visits in Detroit during their trips each way. While there was a semblance of regularity to Charles's vagabond life, it was nonetheless disconcerting having to move every few months and having to spend most of his year in a place he disliked. "Through long winters," he would later write, "I counted the weeks and days until spring when we would return to our Minnesota farm." With its never finished house, the family always referred to it as "camp."

Where "camp" filled Charles with a love of the outdoors, the Land house at 64 West Elizabeth Street in Detroit opened his eyes to the more interior wonders of science, a world of logic and intellect. "I never had a dull moment at Detroit," Lindbergh would later recall of his visits, adding that there was "even more to do than on the farm in Minnesota." Upon entering the small, gray frame house, a narrow hall lay ahead, a door on the left to the patients' parlor, where there was always an intriguing stack of *National Geographic* magazines. Upstairs was a small parlor. To the rear of the room on one side was a curtain that opened into the master bedroom; on the other side a small hall led into the tiny bedroom of Evangeline's brother, Charles; during Evangeline and young Charles's visits, he turned the room with its narrow double bed over to them.

The boy's interests lay downstairs—in Dr. Land's dental rooms and laboratories. His grandfather's rolltop desk was always cluttered with papers and pamphlets and plaster casts of patients' mouths. A box contained a stuffed tarantula, centipede, scorpion, and horned toad; a safe held platinum foil and dental gold; cabinets were filled with polished stones and fossils—even a mammoth's tooth.

When his grandfather was not practicing, Charles played in the two operating rooms, with their hydraulic foot-pumped dental chairs. There were drills of all sizes and drawers "for hand instruments, bottles of acid, amalgum powder, rubber sheets, little wads of cotton to put under the tongue"; stuffed birds and a Rocky Mountain sheep's head stared from all corners of the rooms. A drawing of prehistoric man hung on one wall. And then there was the laboratory that housed a dental furnace, a blowpipe bench-table, shelves full of chemical bottles, and a blacksmith's anvil.

The basement below was even more fun. Because Charles's grandfather and uncle did all their own home maintenance, pipe cutters, threaders, wrenches, coils of wire, and odd lengths of pipe hung everywhere. During each visit, Charles was taught to master a different tool—learning mechanical, chemical, and electrical laws. "Charles," his grandfather often told him, reiterating the mantra of scientific experimentation, "you must have patience."

The basement's most amusing feature was a shooting gallery. When Charles was six, his grandfather gave him a .22-caliber single-shot Stevens rifle, with which he practiced in a short rifle range he and Charles's uncle built. It featured a mechanical, steel-faced target about ten inches in diameter with a one-inch bull's-eye cut out. When a bullet entered the hole, it tripped a mechanism that made an iron bird pop up.

Every night Grandmother Land prepared a large hot meal, at least one chicken or turkey every visit, served on warmed plates. And the dining room table was always brimming with his grandfather's theories: the importance of mastication; the deleterious effects of automobiles on society; the deadly nature of cigarettes, which he called "coffin nails." Lindbergh came to believe that "Science is the key to all mystery."

In time, he realized another wonderful attraction in Detroit was his uncle. "I have no brother," Charles lamented to his mother one day; and she said she would give him hers. From that day forward Charles Land, Jr., was referred to as such. Twenty-three years Charles's senior, "Brother" had apprenticed to his father in dentistry, graduated from the Michigan School of Mines, and prospected in Canada before drifting into a life of avocations. A social misfit, he considered himself an inventor and had several patents to validate his claim. He was never at a loss for time in teaching Charles how to use his drafting instruments—or any other tools lying around the house. Always busy with some project, Brother's presence helped make "64," as the family referred to their residence, a welcome halfway house for Charles, a stimulating stopover between Little Falls and Washington. In all his analysis of why he found Detroit so special, he never considered the possibility that he found pleasure simply in its being the most traditional home he knew— one in which he was but a periodic visitor.

In the fall of 1909, Evangeline and C.A. established separate residences in Washington; but Charles faced a greater dread that year. At almost eight years of age he found himself, for the first time, having to start school. Until then, Evangeline had tutored her son in the rudiments of reading, writing, and arithmetic. ("I like my mother. My mother likes me" were the first two sentences she instructed him to copy.) Entering the second grade at the Force School, he remembered his first year of school as being "forced to sit still in a strange room, amid strange children, and surrounded by strange and unknown conventions . . . a vague memory of countless hours of sitting at a desk . . . waiting, waiting, waiting for the school to close." He was allowed to change schools—as he did almost every year for the next decade. Because Evangeline insisted on their Detroit stopovers, Charles always started the schoolyear late and left early, and was, as a result, always behind in his studies. One of his teachers was distressed enough by his poor penmanship to threaten him with a bad report to his father. "No use to complain to him," the boy said. "He can't write even as well as I."

After several years of spotty education, Evangeline felt a private school might help Charles buckle down. Although C.A. pled poverty and insisted that boys "must get knocked and knock back in order to stand the world's knocking later," he did concede that "it might be an advantage" for Charles to attend a private school because of his "peculiar situation."

In 1913, he entered The Sidwell Friends School, which assembled in the Friends Meeting House on I Street in Northwest Washington. Although he never liked the name of the place, with what he considered its hollow promise of camaraderie, he remained for two years. It was "an improvement, but did not by any means end my troubles," he later wrote. "I did not find much friendship among the children there. I did not understand them, nor they me." Many of them made fun of his name, nicknaming him "Limburger" or sometimes, more simply, "Cheese."

It was later reported that young Lindbergh palled around with his schoolmates Quentin and Kermit Roosevelt, sons of T.R. "The Roosevelt Gang," was known to gather after school at nearby Henry's drug store, where they would order sodas and charge them to the ringleaders' father. But, future myth to the contrary, Lindbergh was not part of that gang or any other. He briefly became friendly with his deskmate and nobody else. "I took as little part in the games as possible and went home immediately after school was over," he recalled. The day the boys were instructed in Greek folk-dancing, Charles caused a ruckus by flatly refusing to join hands. The "Cheese" stood alone.

"Home" became a series of boardinghouses, as Evangeline was always hunting for the least expensive room she could find for the two of them. One was in a boardinghouse at 1440 Massachusetts Avenue run by a prominent Virginia family on their uppers. The landlords lived in the basement rooms, while the "paying guests" climbed a set of long front steps to the reception room and the dining room, which was available to them only for meals. One flight up was the large front bedroom which Charles and Evangeline shared. Another of their houses offered a curtained alcove for the bed; and still another had a kitchenette, where Evangeline cooked their meals. Surrounded only by strange adults, there was never room for Charles to misbehave, or just be a boy. The boardinghouses constricted his already constrained personality; and at an early age, he became an overly polite silent sufferer.

To compensate for his obvious loneliness, Evangeline took Charles to all the national shrines and exhibitions. They often returned to Mt. Vernon, the Smithsonian Institution, the Navy Yards, and the Corcoran Gallery of Art, where young Charles was especially drawn to Hiram Powers's "The Greek Slave," a white marble statue of a naked girl in shackles.

It did not bother C.A. that his son lived such a friendless existence in Washington. So did C.A. "You and I can take hard knocks," he told his son halfway through grade school. "We'll get along no matter what happens." C.A. showed him that hard work was more valuable than socializing, as he often became absorbed in his job to the point of obsession. He usually lunched on a loaf of bread and bottle of milk in his office, and he often slept on the black leather couch beside his desk. "Congressmen's work seemed awfully boring to me," Charles would later write, but he found the long corridors of Congress entertaining.

He amused himself one afternoon by locking all the doors in the toilet rooms from the inside. Another time he dropped light bulbs from the top floor of the House Office Building onto the street below. And Charles never failed to be impressed whenever his father took him onto the House floor itself. Other Congressmen objected to the boy's presence in the chamber, insisting it was "not in keeping with the dignity of the House"; but the Lindberghs went their own way, trying not to laugh at those same men spitting apple peels on the carpet. Another of Charles's favorite spots was in the House lobby, just outside the main chamber, where a weather map showed the entire country, marked in colored chalk. Remembered Lindbergh years later, "I always looked to see what the day was like at Little Falls and Detroit."

Through it all, Charles developed an appreciation of his country's heritage and an appetite for culture. He considered himself a witness to history in the making, and he took photographs at every opportunity. He watched a "Suffragette parade" on Pennsylvania Avenue, and he met Senate legends Champ Clark, Knute Nelson, and "Fighting Bob" La Follette. He asked "Uncle Joe" Cannon for his autograph—the first such request Lindbergh ever made—and was rebuffed, which so embarrassed him that he vowed to "confine my attention to collections which did not inconvenience other people in obtaining them." He saw Teddy Roosevelt in the backseat of an open car pulling up to Union Station and William Howard Taft exercising by walking behind his horse-drawn carriage. He rolled Easter eggs on the White House lawn; and once, his father got Charles excused from school so that he might accompany him inside the White House, where he was presenting President Wilson some Indian gifts. The President shook hands with the boy and asked how he was. Charles said, "Very well, thank you," and later reported that the audience had not scared him any as "the President was just a man even if he is President."

In June 1912, C.A. arranged for Charles to attend the Aeronautical Trials at Fort Myer. Evangeline and Charles traveled by streetcar to Virginia, where they found a grandstand set up. A half-dozen airplanes, tuning up their engines, stood before them. "Then," Lindbergh recalled of the moment, "one of the planes took off and raced a motor car around the oval track in front of us. You could see its pilot clearly, out in front—pants' legs flapping, and cap visor pointed backward to streamline in the wind." The experience was so "intense and fascinating," Lindbergh would recall toward the end of his life, "that I wanted to fly myself."

Almost every Christmas and Easter, Charles and his mother made other trips to broaden his horizons, visiting Philadelphia, Atlantic City, and New York City twice. Once they went from Detroit to Washington by way of the Erie Canal and the Hudson River. In January 1913, weeks before his eleventh birthday, Charles was excused from school so that he could make a most extraordinary voyage.

C.A. sat on a House Committee visiting Panama while the canal was under construction; and his reports home were so enthusiastic, he and Evangeline decided it would be an invaluable opportunity for their son to see this modern wonder being constructed. On January 3, 1913, she and Charles boarded the *Colón,* a second-class boat, in New York City. They shared a stateroom on the port side, saloon deck, and dined with the captain, who explained at dinner that night that the worsening weather was delaying their departure.

The next morning Charles arose a little after five and went on deck, which he found covered in snow with a hard wind blowing, as they weighed anchor. Leaving the *Lusitania* in the berth beside them, they sailed the better part of a week. At daybreak on January 10, the *Colón* pulled into its eponymous homeport, Charles standing at the bow of the hurricane deck, looking through his binoculars at the lights of the approaching city.

The next week was filled with the stuff of boys' dreams, all of which Charles detailed in a diary. He saw the forests and jungles just outside the city, heard the tales of outlaws still terrorizing the towns, gazed on Morgan the Pirate's castle, underground "torcher chambers," alligators, monkeys, green lizards, tarantulas, coral snakes, deer, wild hogs, armadillos, wild turkeys, sloths, sharks, and butterflies galore. He watched great steam shovels gnawing away at mountains, creating the awesome canal. Sailing on the *Ancon,* Evangeline and Charles returned to a pier near Asbury Park, New Jersey, on January twenty-seventh.

Y OU ARE LIVING in an extraordinary time," C.A., then approaching sixty, told Charles back in Washington. "Great changes are coming. Great things are going to happen. I may not live to see them, but you will." Between 1914 and 1916, when the Panama Canal opened for traffic, the world caught glimpses of this new age, evidence of a shrinking world. R. F. Scott had reached the South Pole, and Vilhjalmur Stefansson explored Arctic Canada; Alexander Graham Bell made the first transcontinental telephone call; and Henry Ford produced his millionth car, paving the way for America's becoming an automobile society.

With advancements in technology bringing people everywhere closer, a royal assassination in remote Serbia in August 1914 impacted not only Europe but even farms in the American Midwest. "It is true that Europe is ablaze and the destruction of life and property is tremendous; but nothing should be destroyed here as a result of the war," said Rep. Lindbergh in response to a war revenue tax proposed by the Wilson administration, "so why should we allow the European war to destroy our reason?"

Over the first two years of the Great War, Lindbergh increasingly spoke out, but his suggestions that the Money Trust and industrialists were fueling the war fell on deaf ears. In search of a bigger power base, he sacrificed a sixth Congressional term in order to run for the United States Senate. In the spring of 1916, when Charles was fourteen, C.A. pulled him from school in Washington to help him in his campaign back home. C.A. was not merely providing Charles with another educational experience; he needed his expertise.

Four years earlier, C.A. had sprung "Maria" (pronounced ma-RYE-a) on his family—a Ford Model T tourabout with Ford's standard foot-pedal gearshift, carbide headlights, hand crank, squeeze rubber-bulb horn, folding waterproof cloth top, and quick fasten-on curtains for rainy days. C.A. had bought Maria for campaigning; but Charles was the only family member who had mastered the machine, having learned to drive at eleven. By the 1916 spring primary in Minnesota, the boy had hundreds of miles of driving experience; and he had shot up to almost six feet in height, so that his feet, at last, could comfortably reach the pedals.

In hopes of better serving the campaign, the two Charles Lindberghs picked up a new Saxon Light Six automobile in Minneapolis for $935. The fourteen-year-old drove the crude back roads of Minnesota, which offered only blaze marks painted onto fenceposts and telegraph poles instead of signposts to mark the way. They stayed in small-town hotels for a dollar a night. In and out of Minneapolis and St. Paul, as far downriver as Winona, as far north as Duluth, Charles logged three thousand miles, averaging seventy-five miles a day. When he was not driving, he distributed pamphlets in the meeting halls and on the farms where C.A. spoke. Charles professed little interest in the content of the speeches himself—"While I wanted very much to have my father win," he later wrote, "my primary interest in his campaign trips lay in the opportunity they gave me to be with him and to drive." Hearing him harp upon the themes of trusts and non-intervention, how wartime waste of resources benefited the few at the expense of the many, could not help leaving an impression.

Besides Lindbergh and the reform-minded incumbent Moses Clapp, running for the Senatorial nomination were former Governor A. O. Eberhart and a trust-busting St. Paul lawyer named Frank B. Kellogg. Senator La Follette considered Lindbergh the most "radical" of the contenders, and he felt the less controversial Clapp could "accomplish more for the general movement than any of the announced candidates." Kellogg, with his theme of preparedness for war, won; and Lindbergh finished a humiliating fourth.

Because C.A. would be retreating to Washington for only a few months in the fall, Evangeline felt no obligation to return with Charles. After ten years, they were still little more than gypsies among the establishment there, having made no friends. No sooner had Charles entered Little Falls High School than his mother developed an urge to visit the opposite coast, for reasons never explained to Charles.

The unspoken truth was that Evangeline had family business. Her stepdaughter Lillian, who had never been a robust child, had recently gone with her husband and daughter to California, hoping its climate might help her fight a case of tuberculosis. The climate provided no cure, and the doctors feared for her life. Evangeline wanted to see her one last time, so that their relationship might not end on a lingering dissonant note. Charles pleaded to make the trip—because it meant he would be able to drive. It was agreed that he could attend school in California for the rest of the year and that it would be yet another "great adventure and experience" for him.

Accompanied by Evangeline's brother and a new fox terrier named Wahgoosh (Chippewa for "fox"), they set off that October, expecting to arrive within two weeks. Despite his experience driving the campaign trails of Minnesota, nothing prepared him for the journey to California. They went West by going south and immediately hit bad weather and poor roads. After one particularly heavy rain in Missouri, they had to remain at a small-town hotel until the clay road had dried. They were slowed farther along by the inadequacy of the Saxon for such a trip. Its springs proved too weak to stand the strain, so that every time Charles approached a bump in the road, he had either to slow to a crawl or strain the springs further. After forty days on the road—highways sometimes narrowing to sandy trails—they arrived in Los Angeles. They checked into the Hotel Armondale, downtown on South Flower Street.

Charles's sketchy accounts of his time in California—little more than a few published sentences—reflect his ignorance of its purpose. He did not know that his mother had written Eva to ask if she could visit her ailing sister. "My feelings were running very high," Eva later recalled, "knowing as I did how shamefully she had treated my sister and how strongly we all felt that that had contributed to undermining the health of a sensitive fragile girl." With Lillian failing fast, Eva wrote to her father for advice. When he instructed her to decide for herself, she denied the visit.

Meantime, C.A. rushed across the country to be at his daughter's bedside. Around eleven o'clock on the night of November third, he leaned over to put his lips to her forehead, and she whispered, "Father, I am dying." And in the next moment, she proved to be right.

Evangeline did all she was allowed, which was to send Eva a letter of condolence. In it she said she was "no longer bitter." The letter incensed Eva even more, for she did not know what Evangeline had to be bitter about. Eva asked her father if she even had to reply. As before, C.A. left the decision to Eva, though he did ask her to consider the feelings of young Charles, to give him "as little trub and as much chance as possible.

> He has reached the age of sensitivity and is developing along lines that give promise. I wish to make it as easy for him as possible, but I could not live with her. I would rather be dead a hundred times. She can't help herself. No grudges toward such a person should be entertained, for she wishes when in the right mood to do right. And she has been punished for her eccentricities and always will be. I am sorry for her but can't allow that to destroy my existence as it would if I tried to live with her. . . .

"I am awfully sorry for the boy," C.A. said in closing the subject. "He feels so hurt. To my judgement you should answer for his sake . . . but you need not do it if it [is] too hard against your wish. Yield a little for the sake of the innocent boy . . ."

She did not. She had caught sight of Charles a few times in the past few years; and, frankly, she could not keep her eyes off him. "He was so good-looking," she recalled of the teenager. "I saw him grow tall and he was always handsome. And very shy." But Eva could never get past her feelings for his mother. "I could and do forgive all she did to me," Eva confessed more than sixty years later, "but not what she did to my father and sister. Only insanity explains it. She made life miserable for all of us." And while she said she did always try to "protect" her half-brother, she noted, "I have always felt that Charles was hurt terribly." Eva destroyed Evangeline's condolence letter, never to respond.

Evangeline remained on the West Coast, where Charles entered the eleventh grade at Redondo Union High School in Redondo Beach. He made no friends there, sticking to himself, his family, and his dog, in the small cottage they rented on the beach. As in Washington, his mother prized any education for Charles found outside the classroom over that within. Taking the wheel, the boy drove her in the Saxon on trips from San Diego to San Francisco, visiting the missions along the way. They made another long visit to Catalina Island, where he gathered moonstones. He and his mother found another beach near Redondo with serpentines, which they set about collecting, and one afternoon they gathered too many of the green rocks to carry home. Charles suggested his picking up their Saxon at the local garage and coming back for his mother and their treasures. By the time he returned, night had fallen, and the Saxon's headlamps would not light; so he had to make his way to the beach by the small light on the windshield. A policeman happened to see him and cited him for driving without a license. The next day in court it was further revealed that Charles was also underage. The Lindberghs thought it outrageous that he was prohibited from driving, especially as he had safely delivered his family halfway across the country.

They might have stayed in California indefinitely were it not for a letter from Detroit late in the winter of 1917. Grandmother Land had developed breast cancer; and by April, Evangeline and her brother decided their California sojourn must end. Brother went ahead by train; and, disobeying the court order, Charles drove his mother and dog the forty days home to Little Falls.

There, Grandmother Land would spend as many of her final hours as possible in a room Evangeline and Charles kept constantly fresh for her with newly cut pine boughs. During the last eighteen months of her life, her only grandchild was forced into early manhood—heading the household, finishing high school, running the farm, keeping the books, caring for his mother and grandmother.

By the time Charles and Evangeline had returned to Little Falls, Woodrow Wilson had been re-inaugurated President largely because he had "kept us out of war." But during the winter of 1916 to 1917, American intervention became inevitable. While his family had been in California, Congressman Lindbergh did not slink away from Capitol Hill. He spent his last months in office taking some of the most dramatic stands of his career.

On February 12, 1917, he delivered a tirade on the floor of the House against the Federal Reserve Board, which he believed was in cahoots with the Money Trust. On the House floor, without warning, he impeached the five members of the Federal Reserve Board of high crimes and misdemeanors—starting with its governor, Warren Harding. He listed fifteen counts, specifically citing such co-conspirators as National City Bank of New York, Kuhn, Loeb, and Company, and J. P. Morgan. "Don't worry if the press slams me," C.A. wrote his daughter Eva. "I hit the board a hard blow, and they are sore."

On March 1, 1917, the United States edged closer to war when the House voted on a bill authorizing the arming of American merchant ships. The tally was 403 to 14, with Lindbergh among that most radical minority, almost all Midwesterners. One month later—a new Congress in place—America entered the war.

C.A. began sniffing out new opportunities. After a hernia operation (which he endured without anesthesia, taking his mind off the pain by discussing international economics for the hour with a friend), he returned to Minnesota. He spent most of his time in the Twin Cities, where he entered third-party politics. Worse than oblivion, he began sliding into political ignominy, becoming a crank. More than ever, Lindbergh took to writing articles and books about his constant bugaboo, the Money Trust. While he was neither a pacifist nor a socialist, he argued that it was not right to send poor farmboys off to war in Europe so that others might profit. "The trouble with war is that it kills off the best men a country has," C.A. used to say.

"It is impossible according to the big press to be a true American unless you are pro-British. If you are really for America first, last, and all the time, and solely for America and for the masses primarily, then you are classed as pro-German by the big press which are supported by the speculators," Lindbergh would write in 1917—words that would resonate in the life of his son twenty years later.

In 1918, C.A. Lindbergh ran in the Republican gubernatorial primary, receiving support from the Nonpartisan League—an agrarian protest party that sought to combat agricultural trusts through state ownership. Socialistic sentiments crept into his speeches. The election will forever stand as one of the most opprobrious in Minnesota's history if not, as it was then considered, "the hottest ever in the U. S." Charles chose never to recall the humiliations of this political fracas in any of his autobiographical writings. But journalist Harrison Salisbury, who was a child in Minneapolis at the time, later searched out the records of the campaign to confirm what he had heard, discovering—

> . . . that mobs trailed Charles Lindbergh, Sr. . . . He was arrested on charges of conspiracy along with the Nonpartisan Leaguers; a rally at Madison, Minnesota, was broken up with fire hoses; he was hanged in effigy in Red Wing, dragged from the speaking platform, threatened with lynching, and he escaped from one town amid a volley of shots.

While there was only talk of tar and feathers, there was an actual record of "the vicious, vituperative, life-threatening mob action against a man who had fought against the war but once we got into it had said: 'A few would destroy democracy to win the war and the rest of us would win the war to establish democracy.' " One day that spring several men presented themselves as government agents at the National Capital Press in Washington, D.C., and announced that the printing plates of Lindbergh's *Why Is Your Country at War* and *Banking and Currency* were to be destroyed because of their "seditious" nature. There was never any official record of the incident or its perpetrators, but the goons did their job. The former title was reprinted a few years later, reset from one of the few hundred copies which had already been published and distributed in Minnesota.

Lindbergh lost the governor's primary by almost fifteen percentage points, but he did not end his political career there. In the summer of 1918 Bernard Baruch invited him to serve on the War Industries Board. Lindbergh was sworn in, but "a storm of protests" from Reserve Banks forced him to resign. He embarked on another venture, in Minneapolis, publishing *Lindbergh's National Farmer,* a large-format magazine that would serve as his mouthpiece while he kept a hand in Minnesota's newest political movement, the coalition between farmers and labor. With Farmer-Labor support, he ran for his old House seat in 1920, only to be trounced by his Republican successor, losing by more than a two-to-one margin.

Swearing off politics, Lindbergh went fishing for new business involvements—a bank, a book, and real estate. His missives to his son were mostly advisory, about finances or farming, occasionally about his professional life. He sent money home in dribs and drabs, only when it was absolutely necessary, and he deeded the Little Falls property over to Charles a few parcels at a time.

With America at war, C.A. felt the farm should step up food production. He stocked it with cattle and sheep, which doubled Charles's duties. "Ours is a grand country and our flag is the Flag," C.A. wrote Charles, inspiriting him for the hard work ahead; "—keep it flying, not as an approval that we like the political machine, but that it represents our country . . ."

On top of basic farm chores, Charles still had his final year of high school to complete. If the road into town was not too snowy, he would bicycle to Little Falls High, often coming home for lunch; if the path was too thick, he would walk—even when temperatures dropped to forty degrees below zero. For the first time, Charles found himself excelling in a few subjects, Physics and Mechanical Drawing; but he found it almost impossible to stay interested in school with all the challenges of the farm. By the second term it seemed unlikely that he would pass the final examinations required for a diploma.

Then one day at a school assembly, the principal announced that "food was so badly needed in connection with the war that any student who wanted to work on a farm could leave school and still receive full academic credit just as though he had attended his classes and taken examinations." Charles would return to Little Falls High only once more, on June 5, 1918, to collect his diploma.

Few of his seventy-five classmates had ever even spoken to him; and years later, when a magazine tried to capture Charles's life in Little Falls, his former classmates could barely sketch a picture of an outsider. "Nobody recalls young Lindbergh's ever having attended a social function or having looked at a girl," read the article. "His favorite pastime was to hang around Martin Engstrom's hardware store, where he could gaze at the latest mechanical gadgets . . ."

Making plans for farm expansion, Charles read up on animal husbandry, and he decided to breed Guernsey cattle, Duroc-Jersey hogs, Shropshire sheep, leghorn chickens, and Toulouse geese. "I concluded that the farm should be mechanized and ordered a La Cross three-wheeled tractor with a two-gang plow," Lindbergh recalled. "Later I ordered and installed an Empire milking machine and took on the Empire agency for the general Little Falls area."

Even with the assistance of a seventy-year-old Norwegian tenant farmer named Daniel Thompson, Charles spent most of his days alone among the heifers and ewes his father had bought. C.A. had got a very good price on the latter because, in fact, they were half-starved. Unfortunately, when lambing time came, most of the mothers died, leaving Charles and Evangeline to nurse the offspring. Every morning he would bring little wet lambs to the kitchen where they warmed them in baskets or tubs and fed them milk from bottles. Some literally died in their laps; but Charles and Evangeline saved sixty of them. The cows were a lot easier to raise but required great amounts of time, as some of them refused to be milked by anyone but Charles.

By the spring of 1918, Charles also had six thousand chicks along with their many other birds. The incubators had to be kept at an even temperature, which meant that during cold nights Charles repeatedly had to awaken himself to regulate them. One morning, however, he found the room black with smoke. The incubator lamp had malfunctioned, roasting all the chicks and burning thousands of eggs.

When he was not tending the animals, trees had to be cut, barked, notched, and fitted to make log houses for the hogs. A suspension bridge needed to be built over Pike Creek, fences had to be built or mended, ice had to be hauled. After experimenting with concrete, he poured a small pond for his ducks, about one yard in diameter and a few inches deep. "I tried to make the sides slope in such a way that the freezing of water in winter would not crack them and so that small ducklings could climb out in summer regardless of the water level." He called his circular creation the "Moo Pond," having been told that "moo" was the Chippewa word for dirty. He signed his name to his handiwork, and added that of his companion Wahgoosh as well. After eighty years of extreme Minnesota weather, the pond remains without a single crack in it.

At a farm auction on November 11, 1918, activity was suspended when the auctioneer stopped gabbling to announce that the armistice in Europe had been signed. "Time was allowed for celebration before the sale continued," Lindbergh later wrote about that moment. Most of the older men who farmed Morrison County knew what they had to return to, but Lindbergh was at a crossroads. He had assumed the war would continue at least until his eighteenth birthday, at which time he would enlist in the armed services. Beyond that he thought he might take a university course in engineering.

Just days before Charles's seventeenth birthday—February 1, 1919—

C.A. wrote a letter appraising his son and praising him as well. It was a rare document not only because it marked one of the few times he remembered his son's birthday but also because its sentiments were as unmasked as any he ever revealed to Charles. He suggested that Charles make a few changes in his life, that he ease up and enjoy himself more. "I am not disappointed with you in any way," C.A. wrote. "I like to see you want to work, but don't want you to overdo the work. I have one thing that I take pride in above all others, and that is that you are able to buck the world alone and independent if it was necessary. I love that quality in a person, and especially in you, because it was hardly forced on you. You gripped it yourself."

Keeping busy kept Charles from feeling lonely. The only times he indulged himself were at night, when he would escape by the golden light of his kerosene lantern. He had discovered the writings of Arctic explorer Vilhjalmur Stefansson, who wrote spellbinding accounts of his life among the Eskimos; and he took a shine to poet Robert W. Service, some of whose ballads he had even committed to memory, such as this stanza from "The Law of the Yukon":

> *This is the Law of the Yukon; that only*
> *the Strong shall thrive;*
> *That surely the Weak shall perish, and*
> *only the Fit survive.*

And beginning with the November 1917 issue of *Everybody's Magazine,* he thrilled at "Tam o' the Scoots," a cliff-hanging serial of a bold, blue-eyed Scottish pilot during the Great War, in nineteen parts.

There was, of course, a bonnie lass at the end of the stories, but the pretty girl was not what intrigued Lindbergh. For this solitary boy up in Minnesota, Tam "represented chivalry and daring in my own day as did King Arthur's knights in childhood stories. If I joined the Army," Lindbergh had decided, "I would apply for the branch of aviation and, if possible, learn to be the pilot of a scout."

For months Charles had even begun to dream of having a plane of his own. During the war he had become addicted to newspaper accounts of aerial combat, anything he could read about Fonck and Richtofen and Rickenbacker and the gallants of the Lafayette Escadrille. And when the war ended, there were still a few more installments of "Tam o' the Scoots" to run in *Everybody's* that he would read—before undressing in the warmth of the sewing room of the Little Falls house, putting on an old fur-lined coat of his father's, and crawling through a window into his bed outside on the sleeping porch. On cold winter nights, Wahgoosh would crawl in beside him. Evangeline would step outside briefly to shake her son's hand goodnight.

In the morning, Wahgoosh would join Charles in a bowl of coffee. Wahgoosh took his with cream and sugar. One morning Evangeline called repeatedly for the dog, but he would not come. Later, Charles found him dead in the well. A deranged neighbor, apparently so enraged at the sheer happiness of Charles's only friend, had beaten the playful fox terrier to death with a crowbar.

Charles kept putting off his decision about the future, opting to keep working the farm. For the first time since infancy, he stayed in one place for more than a year. But after eighteen years of transience, he was ambivalent about staying in Little Falls indefinitely. On one hand, he enjoyed working the Minnesota soil of his forefathers; on the other, he was intrigued with modern machinery and wanted to see more of the world. He bought himself a twin-cylinder Excelsior motorcycle and was exhilarated by "its power and speed"; but he did not know where he wanted to go. His parents told him repeatedly that a college degree "helps you get along in later life."

Thinking he might become a mechanical engineer, he scouted Midwestern colleges and selected the University of Wisconsin in Madison—"probably more because of its nearby lakes than because of its high engineering standards." He began the "difficult and rather heartbreaking procedure" of liquidating the farm's assets, its equipment and animals. And by the end of the summer of 1920, new tenants were working the land.

Then the eighteen-year-old rode his Excelsior 350 miles from Little Falls to Madison. Except for a handful of days here and there over the next few years, Charles would never live on the farm again.

Late that summer, Evangeline Lodge Land Lindbergh also made a big decision about her future. She packed a bag for Madison.

4

UNDER A WING

"Science, freedom, beauty, adventure;
what more could you ask of life?"

—C.A.L.

TRAVELING ALONE BY TRAIN, EVANGELINE ARRIVED BEFORE Charles; and she wasted no time hunting for an apartment for the two of them.

At first blush she did not take to Madison, finding it "a queer place." Situated on an isthmus among a group of lakes, Wisconsin's capital seemed incongruous—with its brand-new, two-million-dollar Capitol dome lording over what might otherwise pass for a small farming village. But she quickly discovered the many charms of this exceptional college community—an intellectual hub of the Midwest.

Just blocks from the campus, at 35 North Mills Street, Evangeline found a third-floor apartment that rented for seventy dollars per month. While the building was closer to the railroad tracks than she would have liked, their flat was more spacious than any of the others she had shared with Charles. It had a living room and front porch, kitchen and dining alcove, a bedroom for each of them, even an extra room in which to study. She had shipped books and furniture from Little Falls to make it feel more like home.

Charles had come to take pride in the fact that he had never been present for the first day of school, and freshman year at the University of Wisconsin proved no exception. His classes in Chemistry, Drawing, English, and a "sub-freshman" course in Mathematics had already begun when he buzzed into town on his Excelsior.

He instantly delighted in the outdoorsy nature of the campus, with its wooded lakeshore trails and the steep walk up to the main building, Bascom Hall, which stood vigil over the campus and town. Once inside the classrooms, however, his mind shut down. After Charles's first mid-semester report in December, his class adviser placed him on probation for poor marks in Chemistry and Math and for failing English. His only creditable work was in Shop and Drawing.

As had been true when he had been a child—a farmboy in Washington, a Congressman's son in Little Falls—Charles felt like a fish out of water. Socializing never came easily to him, and being at a large university only made it more difficult. Since his mid-teens, he had headed a household and run a farm; demoted to freshman, he was suddenly subjected to academic rules, surrounded by academic superiors, and expected to wear a Wisconsin-green beanie.

Lindbergh steered clear of most people, armoring his insecurity in an attitude of aloofness. He become a smart-aleck, less concerned with learning than in outsmarting his teachers. When his English professor told him to write a theme on a close relative, but not a parent or sibling, he said he could not because "it is so many years since I have seen any of them that I am afraid I have forgotten what they look like."

Future English compositions reveal some playfulness about the rigors of academia but an equal lack of respect for them as well. One was a story about a clergyman presenting his passport to St. Peter, only to be turned away because of his failure on earth to use the serial comma; "[a] pity," Peter states, "to permit so many minor mechanical errors to bar good material from eternal commendation." Another essay, "A Day in the University Life of an Engineer," followed a freshman hour by hour, preparing for a Chemistry quiz by attempting "to make up for six weeks' neglected study." More than one paper whose content merited an "A" got downgraded to a "D" because of bad grammar.

Lindbergh abided his time in the classroom only by daydreaming. "Why should one spend the hours of life on formulae, semi-colons, and our crazy English spelling?" he wondered. He did not "believe God made man to fiddle with pencil marks on paper. He gave him earth and air to feel. And now even wings with which to fly. I'd like to stop taking English, and concentrate on engineering. Then, maybe I could take an aeronautical engineering course. I believe I'd be more successful in that. I could work hard to understand the magic in the contours of a wing. But the University of Wisconsin doesn't teach much aeronautics. The Massachusetts Institute of Technology is the best place one could go—but I couldn't pass the entrance requirements there."

The only aspect of university life that held any interest for Lindbergh was in the Reserve Officer Training Corps program. Taking his physical examination—standing six feet and two inches in his bare feet, with long, lanky arms, and weighing in at a lean 148 and a half pounds—he was asked if he bathed regularly. "Sometimes," he kidded, if he "got the chance." When the old local German tailor measured his sleeve-length for his uniform, Charles heard him say "Gott" under his breath.

Field Artillery Cadet Lindbergh immediately took to the values of military life and found his happiest hours in the school armory—the Red Gym, as it was known, a vast Norman-style castle with Romanesque arches and heavy turrets. He looked forward to the discipline of the hour-long drills. He was assigned a Springfield rifle and was taught the manual of arms. He studied the construction and operation of three-inch field guns and the mathematics of fire control. There were also elementary courses in leadership. "On days of ROTC training," Lindbergh recalled, "we wore our uniforms at all classes—proudly." For the first time in his life, the shy loner belonged to a group. Ironically, it was in the military—with its drumming out of any individuation—that Lindbergh discovered his first adult identity.

Lindbergh made a small name for himself as a member of both the University of Wisconsin's rifle and pistol squads. The five men on the rifle team used .22-caliber rifles indoors and .30-caliber Springfields outdoors; the slightly larger pistol team fired Colt .45-caliber automatics. Standing or prone, Lindbergh regularly shot perfect scores, ten consecutive bull's-eyes. For fun, he and a teammate used to shoot twenty-five-cent pieces out of each other's fingers from fifty feet away. The Wisconsin rifle team ended the year number one in the nation; and when it held an outdoor competition to determine its best marksman, Lindbergh took home the prize, a Colt .45.

Whatever time was not accounted for, Charles now spent in the university rifle gallery or at the YMCA, which he joined so that he could "get shower baths and swimming pools at any time." Well into his freshman year, Evangeline noted that he still had not sported his green freshman's cap.

"Scarcely had the staider citizens of the republic caught their breaths," wrote Minnesotan F. Scott Fitzgerald—only six years Lindbergh's senior— "when the wildest of all generations, the generation which had been adolescent during the confusion of the War, brusquely shouldered my contemporaries out of the way and danced into the limelight. This was the generation whose girls dramatized themselves as flappers, the generation that corrupted its elders and eventually overreached itself less through lack of morals than through lack of taste." Charles Lindbergh was not among them. Even at college, he kissed no flappers and went on no dates. Although he had become strikingly handsome—with his smooth chiseled face, dimpled chin, blonde hair, and blue eyes—he went home every night to have dinner with his mother.

Years later there were stories on campus of Lindbergh's taking part in some intramural hijinks, particularly Wisconsin's "bag rush," in which the freshmen and sophomores vied to throw each other into Lake Mendota. But, truer to character, Lindbergh flatly denied any such activity beyond observing. Unlike many a collegian, Lindbergh avoided tobacco and alcohol altogether. His grandfather Land had told him that "cigarettes contained a poison"; and, as he later noted, "I was so revolted by the men I saw in and outside of the saloons I passed in Little Falls that I would have turned away from hard liquor."

He did, however, make two friends freshman year—Richard Plummer and Delos Dudley, son of the university's assistant librarian. Both were engineering students, who also rode motorcycles. Plummer and Dudley would later recall many hours together on motorcycle trips and watching Lindbergh perform dangerous stunts on his Excelsior down the campus hill into town. Lindbergh later denied these stories as well, remembering his rides on Wisconsin's country roads as solitary. In time Lindbergh spent less, not more, time with Plummer and Dudley, as they joined fraternities and began dating girls.

Meantime, Evangeline Lindbergh made the most of her days in Madison. Freed from farm chores, she reveled in the time she found on her hands. She read and substitute-taught Physical Science in one of the local junior high schools. Other residents in their apartment house grew "very curious about our affairs," Evangeline recalled, and pried at every opportunity, trying to figure out the actual relationship between this very good looking young man living with this somewhat matronly woman in her forties who claimed to be married but had no husband.

In fact, C.A. was living most of the year in southern Florida, where he thought he could "make a few thousand by hustling," as he wrote his daughter Eva. He invested what resources he had into real estate in the remote Miami region. He built himself a crude cottage in the wilds and rented lots to campers. He spent most of his nights sleeping in a tent pitched to the trunk of his Buick, eating meals out of tins. The "overhanging dread" of his letters—constantly crying poverty—were the only jarring notes Evangeline recalled of her days in Madison. Convinced of the future in south Florida real estate, C.A. sank deeper into debt. When his mother—the Minnesota pioneer who had once waited tables in Stockholm—died in April 1921, he also sank into melancholia.

Charles made plans to visit his father, whom he had not seen in a year— right after fulfilling his summer ROTC obligation. Upon completing freshman year, he rode his Excelsior to Camp Knox, Kentucky, where he commenced six weeks of field artillery training. He bunked with twenty other cadets, and each regulation and command made him feel he had at last found his niche. He delighted in the detailed ritual, enjoying this perpetual quest for precision.

More than that, after twenty years of living mostly by his own rules under maternal supervision, Charles reveled in martial training—in the comradeship of young men, in the physical challenges, in complying to rules founded on order. At Camp Knox, Lindbergh later recalled with fondness, "I learned to know the imperative note and thrill of the bugle. We rose early, worked hard, slept soundly. The strictness of discipline amazed me, but I enjoyed it, and realized its value in military life."

One weekend Lindbergh joined his fellow cadets on a riverboat trip up the Ohio, where the men fell in with some girls. All Lindbergh recalled of the two-day leave was how tired he was, how he dozed off standing up, his head bobbing against the wall of the boat.

Once Artillery School was completed, Charles left to join his father in Florida. They agreed to meet in Jacksonville. With forty-eight dollars in his pocket, Charles started on this arduous journey—through rural Kentucky, Tennessee, and Georgia—on July 20, 1921. His motorcycle proved barely a match for the primitive roads. There were frequent stops for repairs or buying new parts, but he pressed on, taking almost no time off except to sleep. He picked up quarts of milk along the way for a dime; and it was not until the third day on the road that he stopped for his first real meal, an egg sandwich. Most nights he slept on the ground, between his Excelsior and a tree, using a towel for a pillow and his coat for cover. If the weather was especially bad or if snakes or mosquitoes seemed too prevalent, he pushed on to the nearest farm and asked to use a corncrib, haystack, or sack of peanuts. He awoke more often than not full of bug bites.

A little after noon on the eighth day, he arrived in Jacksonville and stopped at the post office to receive word from his father. Their signals had gotten crossed. C.A. had expected his son to arrive by train; and knowing from Evangeline on which date Charles had started for Florida, C.A. waited around in Jacksonville for most of a week. He left to tend to business up north the day before Charles's arrival.

Charles tooled around Jacksonville for a few hours before deciding to return home. On August sixth he pulled into Madison—with eight dollars. He took a bath and began to overhaul his Excelsior.

Awaiting Charles's return were his second-term grades and a letter from his father. Neither boded well for the young man's future. Failing Mathematics and Chemistry outweighed his good marks in Shop, Military Drill, and English, thus keeping him on probation. C.A.'s letter was even more distressing: "I am at my rope's end," he wrote his son, "for I can sell nothing, am out of funds and the banks are not giving any credit." He was so deep in debt that he said Charles's returning to the University seemed problematic. Fifty dollars a month was all the support he could scare up for his son and his wife, and he suggested that they borrow against the farm.

While C.A. coped with his real estate addiction by heaping new responsibilities onto Charles's shoulders—deeding over more Little Falls land to him and his mother, the taxes and upkeep with it—Evangeline realized she would have to spend the rest of her life supporting herself. She attended summer school to bone up on her Chemistry, then returned to Detroit to find a full-time teaching job. She told C.A. his latest offer of support was outrageous, that she would not consent to borrowing money against the house. As for their son's education, she wrote, "If Charles quits now, he will never try again. . . . It is entirely up to you whether Charles gives up college or continues."

Charles was already thinking about dropping out, contemplating a trip to Alaska before settling back down on the farm. On his way to Little Falls to see how he felt about "camp," he stopped in Minneapolis, where he found his father. C.A. said he would back any decision, though he did warn him against running the farm unless he intended to devote himself to it completely. "That farm," C.A. added, "nearly broke my financial back."

It looked better than he expected, the cattle and crops all healthy. Charles laid a cement floor in the cow barn and visited his Empire milk-machine customers. In his idle moments alone, he hunted crows with his Colt .45 and, inside the house, practiced quick draws with his revolver. "My imagination became a bit too realistic," Lindbergh later admitted, "and I shot a hole through the kitchen-hallway door—well centered, but at too high a level to support my pride of marksmanship." Just the prospect of spending the rest of his life stuck there made him restless.

He returned to Madison—missing the first day of class—with the "desire" to do well in Engineering. But he quickly fell into his old ways. "I have not been a good student," he wrote years later in reconstructing that time. "My mind has been the partner of my body rather than its master. For so long, I can sit and concentrate on work, and then, willy-nilly, my body stands up and walks away—to the shores of Lake Mendota; to the gymnasium swimming pool; to my motorcycle and distant country roads." His imagination took him even farther.

By winter, he was writing to flying schools. Both Nebraska Aircraft Corporation in Lincoln and Ralph C. Diggins School of Aeronautics in Chicago had courses beginning the first week in April. For five hundred dollars the former offered four weeks' work in the various departments of their factory, another week on the flying field, followed by several weeks' training in the air. They urged applying early "in view of the fact that we can only enroll fifty students."

Lindbergh discussed his pie-in-the-sky plans with a few friends, who tried to persuade him not to abandon his studies by citing wartime figures of a pilot's life being but a few hours in the air. Even if Lindbergh wanted to heed their advice about the need for a college education, Wisconsin no longer provided him that option.

In his third semester Lindbergh maintained his high standing in Military Drill and Shop, but he had failed Machine Design, Mathematics, and Physics. On February 2, 1922, two days short of his twentieth birthday, Lindbergh was dropped from the university. His adviser wrote a letter to Mrs. Lindbergh with an unusually personal comment: "It seems to me that Carl [sic] is quite immature, and that a boy of his temperament might do better in some less technical course than engineering." With farming and school behind him, and parental support practically dried up, Lindbergh could see but one course that might elevate his spirits, push him into a profitable career, and allow him to take charge of his future.

Lift, thrust, control . . .

THE CONCEPT OF HUMAN FLIGHT is virtually as old as humankind. Ever since man first walked the earth, he has dreamed of ascending above it. Throughout time and space, across cultures and continents, religions have been founded on man's ascent to heaven above. But it would take millennia before heavenly aspiration and earthly inspiration conspired to create a conveyance for human flight that harnessed its three essential elements—lift, thrust, and control. Charles Lindbergh had been born at the very moment when the final experiments for that first flight were being performed.

As each great world civilization came into its own, so too did its contribution to the metamorphosing sciences of aviation—often unwittingly. Centuries before the birth of Christ, the Chinese toyed with the kite. More than a thousand years later and half a world away, windmills sprouted in Europe, from Iberia to the Low Countries, providing energy from a propeller. Renaissance Italians studied birds, in an attempt to replicate their structure in machines with flapping wings—ornithopters.

During the Age of Reason the French experimented with different gases, inflatable objects, and parachutes. On June 5, 1783, two brothers, Joseph Michel and Jacques Etienne Montgolfier, filled a balloon with hot air and set it soaring six thousand feet. England—birthplace of Newtonian physics and the steam engine—approached aviation during the Industrial Revolution analytically, formulating the science of aerodynamics. Henson and Stringfellow would experiment with flying ships powered by propellers and steam; Sir George Cayley cracked such aeronautical enigmas as camber (the curve in a surface and how it affected lift), empennage (the tail of the flying ship with its pivoting rudder), and dihedrals (the angles formed by two plane surfaces). The Germans, valuing mechanical efficiency, made great strides with their engines through the contributions of Benz and Daimler; they also took the lead in developing dirigibles, powered airships which were designed to be lighter than the air they displaced. In the 1890s another pair of brothers, Gustav and Otto Lilienthal, ushered in a new age in aviation when they abandoned their earlier notions of building an ornithopter for a more efficient display of aviation—fixed-wing gliders.

Entering the twentieth century, American know-how applied all those elements that began with a pair of wax wings in Crete thousands of years earlier. An engineer named Octave Chanute designed ingeniously trussed biplane gliders. Samuel P. Langley, Secretary of the Smithsonian Institution, created a man-carrying "Aerodrome," a gasoline-powered airplane (a term then just coming into use), with a set of wings in the front of the machine and another in the rear. On October 7 and again on December 8, 1903, he catapulted a pilot aloft in the contraption, only to watch it dive into the Potomac River on both occasions.

That very week aviation's third extraordinary set of brothers, two industrious boys with a job-printing office and a bicycle shop in Dayton, Ohio, were testing the winds on the outer banks of North Carolina, among the low hills and sandy dunes of Kill Devil Hill and Kitty Hawk. Orville and Wilbur Wright had been obsessed with flight for five years. And at 10:30 on the cold morning of Thursday, December 17, 1903—against a twenty-seven-mile wind—Orville lay prostrate on the bottom wing of their biplane. He warmed up the motor—a four-cylinder, twelve-horsepower engine of their own design—and pulled a wire, which released it from an iron-covered wooden monorail they had laid. Bicycle chains clanked, two propellers whirled, and the machine started to move. Wilbur ran alongside for about forty feet, but then the machine lifted, thrust forward 120 feet, and was under complete control of its pilot—for twelve seconds. By the end of that day the airplane had made several flights, the longest being Wilbur's, 852 feet in 59 seconds. Within a year the Wright brothers built a new flying machine back in Dayton which flew almost three miles in five minutes. A year after that the Wright Flyer III, which was sophisticated enough to bank and turn and circle, flew more than half an hour, covering almost twenty-five miles.

The world did not rush in to embrace the Wrights. Other airmen were testing other heavier-than-air machines; many still pursued lighter-than-air conveyances; and a few even fooled with jet propulsion and rocketry. In 1908, the Wrights brought their latest Flyer to France, just outside Le Mans; and on the eighth day of the eighth month of the eighth year of the century, Wilbur put their machine through its paces before a group of spectators, stunning them not just with its maneuverability—it could even perform a figure eight—but with the sheer ease of it all. He rang out the year with a seventy-eight-mile flight that lasted two hours and twenty minutes. The Wright brothers were at last hailed as the leaders in aviation.

Louis Blériot of France was one of their first champions. An engineer, inventor, and pilot, on July 25, 1909, he flew a monoplane from Calais to Dover, England—across the Channel in thirty-seven minutes, capturing a thousand-pound prize. The economic, social, and political implications of that flight were boundless.

The next year saw aviation meets from Los Angeles to Cairo; Zeppelin airships launched passenger service in Germany; planes became more enclosed, and many incorporated metal into their construction, though they were mostly made of wood, trussed with wire, and covered in linen. In 1911, C. P. Rodgers flew from Long Island, New York, to Long Beach, California—in seven weeks, making more than eighty stops along the way; in 1913 France's Roland Garros flew nonstop across the Mediterranean . . .

When the world went to war in 1914, a few hundred planes took to the air. Their initial function was reconnaissance, but scout aircraft quickly turned into fighters, which would go one-on-one against each other in scrappy "dogfights." The war forced rapid development of the infant aircraft industry, cramming decades of progress into a few years—all aimed at enhancing speed, strength, and strategy. The most skilful of these knights of the air earned the unofficial rank of "ace"; and many of them became celebrated international heroes—Fonck, Nungesser, and Garros of France, "The Red Baron" von Richtofen of Germany, and the American "Ace of Aces," Edward V. Rickenbacker. British aviation historian Charles H. Gibbs-Smith calculated that in Britain alone the number of people employed in the aircraft industry between 1914 and 1918 grew from a few hundred to 350,000, building more than 50,000 planes.

With the world becoming air-minded, commerce took hold of this tried if not always true invention. Accidents, though not frequent, were usually fatal; but if planes could serve in war, surely there was a place for them in peace. As The Ralph C. Diggins School of Aeronautics blared in its sales brochure:

> Commercial Aviation is but THREE years old and it is growing with tremendous speed. Aviation will grow faster than the automobile industry. The experimental stage is past. . . . every day from stations in many parts of the world planes take off with cargoes of passengers, freight and mail.

> . . . THINK! DECIDE!! ACT!!!

At last, Lindbergh did; but he opted against the Diggins School in Chicago in favor of the Nebraska Aircraft Corporation. In addition to training in every aspect of aircraft building, maintenance, and flying, they also offered every "assistance possible on our part" in job placement. "In the past week," they wrote Lindbergh that winter, "we have furnished $500 per month jobs to three men under our recommendation."

Evangeline Lindbergh had followed her son's interest in aviation as it developed, but C.A. knew nothing of it until Charles had flunked out of college. "My father was greatly concerned about my plans," Lindbergh remembered years later. "He spoke of the danger of aviation, and told me there would always be a place for me in his business if I wanted it; but he did not argue against my decision." To the contrary, he footed the bill—with the understanding that Charles would consider attending the University of Nebraska in Lincoln after completing the flying course. Lindbergh mailed in his $125 deposit.

He and his mother parted company in Madison in March 1922. She would complete that schoolyear teaching, then take graduate courses in Education at Columbia University in New York. He arrived in Lincoln on April 1, 1922, a Saturday, and checked into the Hotel Savoy. "It looked like a fine and respectable place," Lindbergh wrote his friend Plummer back in Madison, "1.25 per, clean room and running water." The bellboy showed him to his room and seemed reluctant to leave until Lindbergh tipped him, fifteen cents. "Five minutes later," Lindbergh wrote, "I was duly rewarded by having him knock on my door and say, 'Say boss! Jes let me know if you need a gal to-night.' " Lindbergh wrote his mother instead, observing, "The morals in Lincoln are Ab. 0."

Monday his new adventure began, but not exactly as he had envisioned. Between the time Lindbergh had signed up with Nebraska Aircraft and his arrival there, management of the company had changed hands. The new owner was the entrepreneurial Ray Page—known as the "Skipper"—who changed the name of the company to Lincoln Standard Aircraft, stepped up the conversion of "veteran" planes into more modern flying machines, and started Page's Aerial Pageant on the side. During this period of corporate turnover, the idea of a flying school had fallen between the cracks, and only one student appeared that April. It was the first time Lindbergh had ever made the first day of class.

He handed over the balance of his tuition and was put right to work dismantling 220 h.p. Hispano-Suiza motors. By the next day he was "doping" wings—applying a varnish to the fabric with which most airplane fuselages and wings were made, thereby waterproofing and strengthening them. He participated in every process of reconditioning the planes, converting the front cockpits to carry two passengers and replacing the engines. "So far I have had work that is not very exciting," Charles wrote his mother after less than a week on the job, "but interesting to *me.*"

By Friday he could barely contain himself, as they hauled out an actual plane, a Lincoln Standard Tourabout. He stood on the airfield all morning—

> watching riggers attach wings and "hook up" ailerons, flippers, and rudder; watching mechanics strain in fuel, drain the sediment bulb, tune up the engine; watching the engineer test cable tautness with his fingers and measure wing droop with his knowing eye.

The next day, Otto Timm, the company's chief engineer and stunt flyer, took Lindbergh for his first flight in that very plane. He shared the front cockpit with a sixteen-year-old Nebraskan named Harlan Gurney—Bud, to the gang at the factory, where he served as odd-jobber and mascot. It was Gurney's first flight as well. When the plane took flight and banked for the first time, Lindbergh felt as though he had lost "all conscious connection with the past," that he lived "only in the moment in this strange, unmortal space, crowded with beauty, pierced with danger." Fifteen minutes in the air, and Lindbergh was forever changed.

Back on the ground he realized he had misunderstood Lincoln. It was not the "jazz town" he had originally suspected but, rather, a sober community, which shuttered up on Sundays. Moving picture theaters closed, a man could not buy a cigar or even ice cream, and just a few miles away two men were arrested for playing quoits. Charles found a boardinghouse at 1429 R Street for twenty dollars a month, only two blocks from the aircraft factory and just as close to the university. He lost interest in his Excelsior, spending all his time at the factory or writing the details of his experience to his mother.

Evangeline could not get over the change in her son, a euphoria she had never seen in him. And though she had not yet got "reconciled to [his] going up in the air," she admitted to feeling more secure knowing "that you really are in Lincoln Nebraska & not in Alaska." She could not help being impressed by the detailed accounts of his finances which he sent to her. His first month in Lincoln—which included such one-time costs as helmet, goggles, a new suit, and three nights at the Savoy—cost a meager $138.50, and that included $5.25 for "Misscelaneous" and $30 for food. Having reached his full height of six feet and two and one-half inches, and weighing little more than 150 pounds with a 30-inch waist, he justly deserved the nickname he picked up at the factory—Slim.

"I know very well that you are careful," Evangeline wrote. "But as far as I can see one dollar a day for eats will not get sufficient food for a person of your size & appetite especially when you are working out of doors." While all the Lindberghs had learned over the years to pinch pennies—Evangeline steamed uncanceled stamps off envelopes for reuse—she made it clear to Charles that money would always be available to him should he need it.

Lindbergh spent most of April learning about airplanes, inside and out. After observing every factoryman at his craft and getting hands-on construction experience, he was assigned to Ira O. Biffle, reputed to have been "the most hard boiled instructor the army had in the war." Lindbergh found him more bark than bite, though embittered since the death of a friend in a plane. Lindbergh's only complaint was that Biff seldom showed up at the field before noon.

Sharp-sighted and coordinated, with quick reflexes, Lindbergh proved to be a natural pilot. "The actual flying of the ship is easy, also the take-off," he wrote his friend Plummer back in Wisconsin. "But the landing is Hell." It was hard at first for Lindbergh to grasp how delicate the controls were, how a half-inch movement of the top of the stick could throw the ship entirely off balance. His only close call came one day in late April when the plane was still on the ground and its old carburetor caught fire. Lindbergh instinctively stuffed his cap into the air intake and extinguished it. By the end of May, he had logged almost eight hours of instruction, and Biff pronounced him ready to solo.

Unfortunately, Ray Page was at that moment in the process of selling the company's training plane to Erold G. Bahl, reputedly the best flyer around Lincoln. While Page felt that Lindbergh was perfectly able to fly, he could not risk turning over the airplane without bond in the event of its sustaining any damage. Lindbergh had neither the money for the bond nor, he realized, enough hours in the air to warrant a pilot's job even if he did solo. Wanting experience, he thought, "Maybe I could get Bahl to take me with him, barnstorming."

"Barnstorming" was a theatrical term—applied to touring actors who often literally performed in barns—which aviation, still its novelty stage, appropriated. It usually involved dropping into towns to give informal exhibitions and sightseeing flights, performing death-defying stunts upon arrival to lure the customers and again upon leaving so they felt they had received their money's worth. Bahl was about to barnstorm through southeastern Nebraska. Lindbergh asked if he could join him as an unpaid assistant. The price was right.

They left in May. Lindbergh's job was to clean the plane and a few farmers' pockets, drumming up business among the small crowds on the prairie. Five dollars bought as many minutes in the air. After a few days Bahl noticed that Lindbergh was luring more money than he expected, so he assumed the young man's expenses. One day Lindbergh suggested that they might draw a bigger crowd if he stood on one of the wings when they flew into town.

Bahl and his new wing-walker returned to Lincoln in June. Hard-up for cash and determined to buy his own plane, Lindbergh picked up fifteen dollars a week back at the factory doing odd jobs. He took a room for $2.25 a week.

Just as he was looking for ways to expand his barnstorming repertoire, one Lt. Charles Hardin blew into town, with his wife Kathryn. They were parachute makers, who gave demonstrations in order to sell their wares. Ray Page put them both to work, in the factory sewing chutes and as part of Page's Aerial Pageant. After watching Hardin fall off a wing two thousand feet in the air, Lindbergh decided that he had to experience that sensation. From the moment of his decision, he later confessed, "life rose to a higher level, to a sort of exhilarated calmness." Years later, Lindbergh tried to analyze why he became possessed by the notion of making a jump. All he concluded was that it was the same impulse that drove him to aviation—"a love of the air and sky and flying, the lure of adventure, the appreciation of beauty."

He asked Hardin for instruction, but not in the basic parachute jump. For his first exit from a plane in flight, Lindbergh wanted to try what was known as a "double jump"—in which one chute opens and is discarded, making way for a second one to deliver the jumper to the ground. One June evening, against a clear sky, Lindbergh made his leap from 1,800 feet, and the first chute opened perfectly. After a few seconds, he cut it loose and waited for the second to open. But several seconds passed and he did not feel the tug that should have followed. Because he had never made such a descent before, Lindbergh had no idea that everything was not right until he began to fall headfirst. Another long moment later, the parachute at last blossomed, carrying him safely to earth. For the rest of his life, Lindbergh remembered feeling no panic over what might have happened to him, only how soundly he slept that night. Easier for him than most, with nobody dependent upon him for anything, Lindbergh decided "that if I could fly for ten years before I was killed in a crash, it would be a worthwhile trade for an ordinary lifetime."

Opportunities suddenly flung themselves at Lindbergh. Bahl offered to take him barnstorming in northwestern Nebraska, for pay; Ray Page offered him a job in the factory; and a pilot named H. J. "Cupid" Lynch, who had recently purchased a Lincoln Standard with a Kansas wheat farmer named "Banty" Rogers, wired Lindbergh that he needed a parachute jumper to barnstorm with him through Kansas and Colorado. Meantime, Charles did not neglect to write his mother late that June that he had not forgotten about college, that whatever his future, he would not return to a straight Engineering course. "I would like, however, to take certain courses," he said, such as calculus, physics, aerodynamics, and structural design.

Ray Page still owed Lindbergh two hours of flight instruction, his solo flight, and some back wages. Striking a deal with him and Charlie Hardin, Lindbergh put all that and twenty-five dollars onto the table and was able to walk away with a brand-new Hardin muslin parachute. He stored his motorcycle in the factory basement and boarded a train for Kansas.

Practically at the end of the line, in Bird City—a few farmhouses in the wheat-filled northwest corner of Kansas—Cupid Lynch and Banty Rogers met Slim Lindbergh at the train that July. The next day Lindbergh put the new parachute through its maiden descent, in order to attract a crowd on the first stop of their summer tour. He and Lynch also took along Rogers's smooth-haired fox terrier, Booster.

"This is sure a great life," Charles wrote his mother, studying in New York that summer. "The states seem small with a plane." Over the next two months, Booster and the barnstormers flew the big skies and small towns of Kansas, Nebraska, Colorado, and Wyoming, with Lindbergh performing as wing-walker, skydiver, and mechanic.

Through the Rocky Mountains they flew as high as ten thousand feet above sea level. And just as exciting, flying from Colorado Springs to Burlington, Colorado, they "hedge-hopped" the last half hour—flying just two feet from the ground at eighty miles per hour, then "zooming" over fences and buildings, sharply ascending a few hundred feet at a forty-five-degree angle. "That is the most fun in this game," Charles carried on. By the end of summer, when they reached Montana, his enthusiasm continued to soar. He advertised himself in the Billings *Gazette Sun* as "Aerial Daredevil Lindbergh"; and he even dragged Booster into the act, putting him in a harness, and letting him fly before the crowds on a rubber mat outside the cockpit, his paws hanging over the cowling. For the first time in his life, the shy farmboy enjoyed being around people.

"It's a sociable place, under a wing," Lindbergh later waxed nostalgic, "and good for business, too.

> People like to come and sit beside you. They start asking questions about flying, and telling about their farms. Pretty soon they begin kidding each other into taking a flight over town. If you help them along a little, they're the best salesmen you could have.

Aviation created a brotherhood of casual acquaintances—people constantly coming and going—in which he felt comfortable. Besides the other pilots and mechanics, he discovered that flying introduced him to "the extremes of human character—from bank presidents to tramps; from sheriffs to outlaws; from professors to idiots; from county preachers to town prostitutes." Indeed, he would write, "Some of the pleasantest hours of my life have been spent in the shade of a wing, waiting for the Nebraska wind to calm when I was learning to fly."

Charles barely had a moment to observe the death of his Grandfather

Land that August. The pioneering dentist worked right up to his final days, when his heart gave out at the age of seventy-five. For the rest of his life Charles would credit him for bequeathing his passion for science, which in large measure led him to aviation and all the marvels "in each curve of an airfoil, in each angle between strut and wire, in the gap of a spark plug or the color of the exhaust flame."

Evangeline returned to Detroit, where she secured a position teaching Chemistry at Cass Technical High School; and at summer's end she could not help reminding Charles, "You say not one word of college." She did not want him to close off options in his life for not having a diploma; but she said she was prepared to support whatever he decided. Charles wrote back about the prospects of buying his own airplane. "You know what you want," Evangeline replied, "—only is a plane a wise investment & has the occupation of pilot any future?"

Lindbergh considered the question when the barnstorming season ended in October, leaving him in Lewistown, Montana. He knew only that it felt wonderfully like "playing hookey from school" that fall not having to show up for class anywhere. He bought a small boat for two dollars, patched the leaks, and planned to ride the rapids of the Yellowstone River as far as he could get on his return to Lincoln—camping and eating canned food along the way. After two days of rain, and spending as much time bailing as he had paddling, he bartered the vessel for a wagon ride to the nearest town. As he remembered, it was Huntley, Montana, where he bought a train ticket and spent the night sleeping at the station, waiting for the next train to Lincoln. There he decided "that the next spring I would be flying my own ship."

Instead of accepting his mother's offer of assistance, Charles felt drawn toward his father, and with good reason. C. A. Lindbergh had fallen on hard times. Living alone in dollar-a-night hotel rooms and picking up his messages care of General Delivery telegraph offices, he kept homing to the Farmer-Labor movement, then enjoying a moment of electability in Minnesota politics. His countenance had turned woeful—with a weary and slightly crazed look in his eyes—but this politician-errant continued to make speeches and to write. At the end of the year he completed his fourth book, *The Economic Pinch,* tilting at the same old windmills—trusts and banks and profiteers who fed off the labor of others.

Because the senior Lindbergh was still an "untamed polar bear," as Farmer-Labor Congressman Knut Wefald once described him, it was difficult for anybody close to him to classify his behavior as "abnormal." But C.A. himself was noticing that his body chemistry seemed out of whack—that he could no longer withstand the cold as he used to and that he periodically suffered moments of melancholia. Trying to jumpstart a law practice in the Twin Cities after sustaining heavy losses in land speculation, he often appeared on the streets of Minneapolis in dirty, ragged clothing. Even more peculiar were a series of bleating letters that year from C.A. to Charles.

"I can't see any reason why you and I should not be in a little closer touch with each other," C.A. wrote. "This life at best is not any too beautiful, so we should be palls [sic] as much as possible. You will soon be going out into the world—and you will find it quite different than you expect in many respects. I may be able to be of some help in advising about conditions. You have been lucky to have your mother with you all these years, but she will not be with you so much in the future."

Neither, C.A. seemed to be suggesting, would he. At sixty-three he was fighting old age, both reveling in Charles's youth and slightly resenting it. "He is in splendid condition," C.A. wrote his estranged wife, "and exercises the most sense of one of his age that I have ever taken notice of." Still, C.A. wrote his daughter Eva, "he has his ways of fun. If nothing happens he may make a mark some time. He will likely freeze to what he earns, except that he wants to go everywhere."

During several visits together that winter, Charles talked to his father about little other than airplanes. By the end of February, C.A. realized that his son's interest in aviation was no mere infatuation; and after belatedly remembering Charles's twenty-first birthday, he agreed to become his business partner and underwrite the purchase of a plane. He had heard that good deals could be made at Souther Field, just outside Americus, Georgia, which warehoused war-surplus aircraft. Because that was not far from C.A.'s real estate investments, Charles offered in return to visit the property outside Miami and work on his house there for a few weeks.

"I leave for Americus to-night," Charles wrote his father on April 20, 1923—after spending days on his belly among thousands of sandburs, digging a sewer ditch by hand—"and will let you know of results there as soon as I can." Even before he had located a plane for sale, he drafted letters to Chambers of Commerce, describing how an "aeronautical exhibition, consisting of parachute drop, wing walking and plane stunting" could be an attraction for their local fairs. He dreamed of new stunts—one in which he would hang by his teeth below a speeding plane—all this and more for $150 a day.

The town of Americus, tucked away in southwestern Georgia, was sleepy country, revived by the World War because of Souther Field and its fourteen active air hangars. After the Armistice, a colorful Georgian named John Wyche bought at government auction 116 planes for sixteen dollars apiece, 525 engines for twenty dollars each, and fourteen thousand propellers for eighty cents a throw. He was selling reconstructed planes for $1,000 each.

The last Army guards had decamped the week Lindbergh arrived, leaving it a "ghost field." After poking around the empty buildings, he made himself at home in one of the barracks. By day, men came out to work on the planes. As the place was hardly crawling with customers, Lindbergh got his pick from most of the stock, and he got John Wyche to halve his price. He selected a Curtiss JN4-D—a Jenny—a two-place, open tandem-cockpit biplane that had been a popular training plane in the war. He also got a brand-new Curtiss OX-5 engine, an extra twenty-gallon tank, and a complete once-over with a fresh coat of olive drab dope in the exchange. The Jenny could fly an hour on ten gallons of gasoline and one quart of oil, reaching a top speed of seventy miles per hour. Lindbergh lived alone on the field for the two weeks that his plane was being assembled, sometimes sleeping by its side in the hangar.

There it dawned on him that he had only flown in a Jenny for a few minutes, that he had but eight hours flying time behind him, and that he still had never soloed. "Everybody at Souther Field took for granted that I was an experienced pilot when I arrived alone to buy a plane," Lindbergh later wrote. "They didn't ask to see my license, because you didn't have to have a license to fly an airplane in 1923."

The day the chief mechanic announced that Lindbergh's plane was ready, he felt he had no choice but to "test her out" in front of everybody present. He taxied the Jenny to the farthest corner of the field, opened the throttle, and took off. When the plane was four feet off the ground, the right wing began to drop. Feeling that the machine was beyond his control, Lindbergh suddenly decided it would be better to land from that height than from any higher. He brought the plane down on one wheel and a wing skid. Out of nowhere, a young aviator named Henderson, dressed in standard pilot's garb of breeches and boots, approached. Overlooking Lindbergh's obvious embarrassment, he offered to fly with him while his own plane was being assembled. A half-dozen takeoffs and landings together, Lindbergh had the hang of it. Henderson suggested Lindbergh wait until the dying winds of day's end before re-attempting to solo.

That afternoon at five he reapproached his Jenny and started the engine. He and his plane were completely alone—except for one old black man who had wandered onto the field, unaware of the significance of the moment. Lindbergh taxied back out and opened the throttle. "No matter how much training you've had," Lindbergh would later state, "your first solo is far different from all other flights. You are completely independent, hopelessly beyond help, entirely responsible, and terribly alone in space." He climbed to 4,500 feet that evening, taking in what seemed like all of Georgia. He felt as though he would have kept going were it not for the sun slipping behind the horizon. When he landed, his sole witness came up to greet him, in awe. There was something about his "praise and courtesy that gave me confidence," Lindbergh would recall more than twenty years later, a feeling of elation surpassed only by the fact that he had landed his plane without "cracking up."

He spent the next week at Souther Field practicing. Another early aviator, Glenn Messer, remembered watching Lindbergh one of those days. He was impressed—not with any particular aviatic prowess, or even an unusual display of physical ability, but with the fact that "for the next few hours all I saw this young skinny feller do was take that plane up and down, over and over, with nothing stopping him. Taking off and landing dozens of times."

While Charles had been in Georgia, Minnesota's senior Senator, Knute Nelson, died, leaving a vacancy to be filled by special election. Like an old fire-horse hearing the bell, C. A. Lindbergh decided to make one last run for office, going after the Farmer-Labor nomination. He thought Charles and his Jenny might be an effective part of the campaign—modernizing the whistle-stop tour and drawing attention to the candidate. At the very least, he thought Charles would be able to barnstorm in Minnesota "and make some spondulix"—the old-fashioned word, even then, for cash. Charles sent his suitcase home by railway express; and he buckled up an extra shirt, pair of breeches, toothbrush, socks, spark plugs, tools, and assorted equipment into the front cockpit of his plane. He left Souther Field on May 17, 1923, and barnstormed his way north.

In the seven months since he had taken up aviation, Lindbergh had parlayed a parachute into a promising flying career, complete with his own Jenny. Every day brought greater mastery of his machine. Nights he slept in a hammock he fashioned from some canvas and slung from his upper wing. Enduring heavy rains and floods, extreme winds, and crude airports as well as surviving several muddy emergency landings, Charles joined his father in the middle of his senatorial campaign in Marshall, Minnesota.

At the first possible moment, he attempted to show C.A. how in a matter of minutes they could saturate an entire town with campaign literature. His father entered the front cockpit carrying hundreds of handbills, which Charles instructed him to throw when he rocked the plane and nodded. "It did not occur to me that he might throw them out all at once," Charles later recalled of the incident; "but he did, and the thick stack of sheets struck the stabilizer with a thud." The circulars did no damage . . . and about as much good—for, as Lindbergh noted, "the distribution of literature in the town wasn't very broad."

A few days later, the candidate and his pilot flew in from Buffalo Lake to Glencoe, landing on a farmer's field southwest of the town. "In an attempt to take the air again," reported the Glencoe *Enterprise,* "one wheel of the plane . . . dropped into a ditch, causing the nose of the machine to plow into the ground with great force. This up-ended the plane, broke one wing, snapped the tail-steering cables, and otherwise damaged it." Nobody was hurt. C.A. left by automobile for Litchfield, where he arrived in time to make a scheduled speech that evening. Charles stayed behind until the plane got repaired, trying to figure out the cause of the accident. C.A. later wrote his daughter Eva that he did not want to believe there was a "plot" to get him, but there was no doubt that the plane had been "munked with."

During their weeks together, C.A. could not help noticing his son's immense charm, his quiet way of drawing people toward him. It was more than his looks, C.A. thought—more that people "seemed to think it strange that he would be so plain and unassuming, and kindly. . . . He does seem like the real stuff," with "the making of a big man, and these are times we need them. In the line of work he is at I do not suppose there is a chance for a big man, and yet there may be."

While Lindbergh wrote up events of this campaign in his autobiographies, he never recorded the results. C.A. ran a distant third, receiving less than twenty percent of the vote and carrying only the eight core counties of his former Congressional district. Afterwards, he returned to his real estate negotiations, constantly robbing Peter to pay Paul, while his son left to barnstorm through Minnesota and northern Iowa.

Most of the time Charles was alone, though his mother did accompany him for a few days, thoroughly enjoying her place in the front cockpit. "Some weeks I barely made expenses," Lindbergh recounted, "and on others I carried passengers all week long at five dollars each. On the whole I was able to make a fair profit in addition to meeting expenses and depreciation."

And then one morning Lindbergh realized a promise he had made to himself years earlier. "I shall never forget flying the first time over the farm in Minnesota where I grew up as a boy," Lindbergh wrote an acquaintance more than forty years later—"the new and seemingly god-like perspective it gave to me."

He landed near the log buildings on the western reaches of the farm. Their hired man, the old Norwegian, Daniel Thompson, was there to greet him, his axe slung familiarly over his shoulder. "Nay doggone," he said, looking over the flying machine, "the man that invented these things vas quite a feller!" When Charles asked about the farm, Thompson replied, "All in veeds." And that was the least of it. A modern dam was about to be built, their valley flooded, trees chopped, and the rapids quelled to a lake. Charles was overcome by nostalgia. "I knew that day," Lindbergh wrote three decades later, "that childhood was gone. My farm on the Mississippi would become a memory, of which, sometime, I'd tell my children . . ."

One evening, while Lindbergh was still barnstorming in southern Minnesota, a car drove up with several young men in it. One of them was a graduate of the Army flying school. After some discussion, he asked Lindbergh why he did not enlist as a flying cadet. "Daredevil Lindbergh"—making a good living off his own plane—was annoyed by the suggestion at first. Then he remembered a group of De Havillands with their 100 h.p. Liberty motors that had landed at Lincoln one day and how he had longed to fly one of them. He realized that flying cadets had access to the most modern and powerful airplanes, not war surplus. Not incidentally, he also "believed every man should be able to take part in defending his country in case of war"; and should there be a war in the future, Lindbergh wanted to be a scout pilot. From his hotel that night he wrote to the Chief of Air Service in Washington. The War Department told him to appear at Chanute Field in Rantoul, Illinois, on January 8, 1924, for his physical and mental examinations. Should he pass, he was told to be prepared to commence his training at Brooks Field, San Antonio, Texas, about March 15, 1924. That left him several months to fly under his own command.

He barnstormed from Minnesota into Wisconsin just ahead of the oncoming cold weather. Heading toward Illinois, he attended the St. Louis Air Meet, held October 4–6, 1923. Combination trade show, swap meet, county fair, and military parade, it became the biggest aeronautical demonstration in the world to date: 125,000 people witnessed the last day's events, which included the Pulitzer Trophy Race. Bud Gurney entered the parachute spot landing contest, and Lindbergh agreed to be his pilot. There at Lambert Field, Lindbergh got to see the latest military aircraft, from Army and Navy racers to big bombers. The winner of the Pulitzer races flew a blue Navy Curtiss biplane with a whining D-12 engine and covered a 125-mile course at an average of 243.7 miles per hour, a 37 mile-per-hour improvement over the 1922 winner. The St. Louis *Globe-Democrat* ran an editorial that said such speed was only possible in a military craft and had "no value for commercial purposes," but few fliers felt the same.

After the meet, Lindbergh picked up a few flying students (including one referred by an acquaintance from Minnesota, a young airplane manufacturer named Marvin Northrop); and he barnstormed a few Illinois towns. But he kept returning to St. Louis, which was becoming a crossroads for the nation's fliers. During this time his side of his regular correspondence with his mother became little more than the posting of a blank card every few days, with only its postmark indicating his whereabouts. He was in the middle of another barnstorming tour of the south, flying a Canuck (a slightly modified Jenny) owned by an automobile dealer named Leon Klink, when he was told to report to Brooks Field, just south of San Antonio, by March nineteenth.

He arrived at Brooks Field on the fifteenth. It was another week before Evangeline Lindbergh learned that her son had enlisted. By then 103 other young men from all corners of the country had joined him.

In no time the young men learned of the "Benzine Boards"—the review board of officers—which would kick half of them out before they could graduate to advanced training at Kelly Field, where another half of them would fail. Fear of flunking a single test haunted every cadet, because two failing marks automatically washed one out. In the past Lindbergh attended school primarily because it was required; at Brooks—for the first time, he would later note—"I had a clear-cut objective that I was overwhelmingly anxious to attain."

Lindbergh scored a 72 on his first exam, in property accounting—barely high enough to pass. With a bad scholastic record behind him and another seventy examinations ahead, he realized he had to change his entire approach to academics. Lindbergh resolved that he "would have to maintain a big margin between my marks and the minimum grade for passing."

He studied harder than he ever had before. Taps blew at ten, but Lindbergh often camped in the latrine, where he read under the all-night lights. "The Army schools taught me what I had never learned before," Lindbergh later noted, "—how to study, even subjects in which I had no interest. For the first time in my experience, school and life became both rationally and emotionally connected."

Lindbergh also liked the "shortness and freshness" of the subjects the Army taught. He learned the essentials of aerodynamics, navigation, and meteorology as well as the "responsibilities and proper conduct of an officer, a smattering of military law, of regulations, of organization, of administration" and the operation of machine guns and methods of bombing. Steadily, Lindbergh's grades ascended into the nineties.

By April, the class got to fly, with seven cadets assigned to each instructor. Lindbergh felt fortunate in falling under the command of Master Sergeant Bill Winston, reputed to hold the record for flying time in the Army, with close to 3,500 hours. Lindbergh, with more than three hundred hours and seven hundred barnstorming flights, came closer to that mark than almost anybody else on the field. The Army still taught flying with Jennies, although the 90 h.p. OX-5 engines had been replaced by 150 h.p. Hispano-Suizas, and the throttles had been moved from the left side to the right. "Barnstorming had made me a skilful pilot," he commented years later, "—far more skilful than my Army instructors in selecting and operating from 'strange fields' for instances. . . . Military training taught me precision and the perfection of flying techniques."

In the midst of the most engrossing experience of his life, a telegram from Minnesota broke Lindbergh's concentration. "FATHER IN HOSPITAL BAD BREAKDOWN," wired Charles's half-sister, Eva Lindbergh Christie, with whom he not had contact in years. In fact, it was worse than that. C. A. Lindbergh had entered the Colonial Hospital in Rochester, Minnesota—where brothers Charles and William Mayo had established a clinic—because of recurring attacks of the grippe. There he demonstrated a rapid loss of much of his short-term memory and the ability to concentrate. "He seems very weak, & quite thin, repeats a great deal, & asks the same question a number of times," Eva reported in a follow-up letter to Charles. His head ached, his voice changed, his hands shook, one foot dragged, and he seemed utterly exhausted. Because he had not lost his ability to reason, Eva thought he had suffered a stroke. But then he lost his sense of taste. Eva was additionally anxious because her father's name was about to be printed on the June primary ballot as a Farmer-Labor candidate for governor.

On Wednesday, April twenty-third, Eva wired Charles again: "COME TO ROCHESTER FATHER VERY LOW." Two hours later, a physician concurred in an even more urgent telegram. The Mayo brothers put Dr. A. W. Adson, whom they considered the best brain surgeon in the country, on the case. After numerous nonsurgical tests, he decided to trephine C.A.'s skull. By the next day, Charles had arranged a furlough and boarded a train that would put him in Rochester by Sunday morning. "I may be 'washed out' . . . for going up home," Charles wrote his friend Leon Klink, who wanted Slim to spend his next furlough barnstorming with him, "but that can't be helped."

Charles arrived to bad news. Dr. Adson had discovered a large, inoperable brain tumor. How much of C.A.'s peculiar behavior in the past year—including his sentimental swings and even a recent premonitory letter to each of his children about his funeral—was the result of the tumor was anybody's guess. Charles sized up the situation and said he would resign from the Army if it would help C.A. in any way. He went to Minneapolis to withdraw his father's name from the gubernatorial election; but nothing could be done because C.A. was unable to sign an affidavit.

Eva graciously informed her stepmother of the graveness of C.A.'s illness, which Evangeline took as her cue to join her son in Rochester. Charles confided to Eva, "I wish she *wouldn't* come." But Evangeline would not be stopped. Dr. Adson told her that C.A.'s case was incurable, that removing the tumor would mean taking one quarter of his brain with it, rendering him completely paralyzed on his right side. Evangeline sat with her husband; and though C.A. could barely speak, it was an emotional encounter for him. Eva fumed that Evangeline must not communicate with C.A. anymore, that he was "upset" over the visit, as evidenced by his crying and a subsequent chill.

And so the wounds Eva and Evangeline had inflicted upon each other for two decades were ripped open all over again. "It was a disastrous episode," Eva later recalled, "which Charles handled with courtesy and determination." Evangeline, for her part, was "glad . . . in a way" that the "bad time with Eva" occurred, "as it opened Charles's eyes a bit." Evangeline kept her distance thereafter.

Charles, on the other hand, was unmistakably a welcome visitor. Barely able to whisper, the felled sixty-five-year-old asked for his boy, and Charles knelt by his side as he tried to speak. After C.A. uttered only part of a sentence, however, his mind wandered off. Charles remained holding his hand, and C.A.'s "eyes brightened," Eva observed, "and for a couple of minutes he was himself."

By Monday, May fifth, there was nothing to do but make C.A. comfortable until he died. Everybody agreed there was no sense in Charles's forfeiting all his work in the Army. He returned to San Antonio; and C.A. was moved to a hospital near Eva, in the northwest corner of Minnesota, where he drifted into a coma. On the Saturday afternoon of May 24, 1924, Charles received a telegram at Brooks Field from Eva, which stated: "FATHER PASSED OUT THIS MORNING. SERVICES AT MINN ACCORDING TO HIS WISHES." Charles immediately wired his mother, as Eva already had.

C.A.'s daughter planned a service in the First Unitarian Church in Minneapolis for Tuesday afternoon, after which she would take the body to St. Paul for cremation. "Later," she wrote Charles, "when you can come, you will comply with Father's wish about throwing his ashes 'to the wind' as he wished, somewhere near the old farmstead he cared so much for." As soon as she could, Eva promised to send Charles their father's watch. "He wanted you to have it," she wrote, "and so do I." Eva would also send the chain that went with it, which she had bought for him. It "represents the 1st money I really earned," she explained, "and I'm glad for you to have that too."

Evangeline wondered whether she ought to attend the funeral. After a sleepless night, she boarded a train that put her in Minneapolis in time for the service. "It is your father," she explained to Charles, "& that's all that counts. I cannot do him any good but my being there again may do some good in the end." She carried a large spray of gladiolus which she placed on the casket in her son's name, and she kissed C.A.'s forehead for Charles as well.

"Boy, just remember your father still lives in you," Evangeline assured him, "and you have done right by us both. You gave him great pleasure in what you have done, perhaps the greatest satisfaction of his life." By day's end Evangeline was glad she had made the trip and that Charles had not—for "it was a day of appeal to the emotions and past affairs and regrets that cannot be made different now." But her own hurt must have deepened upon reading C.A.'s obituaries. Many of them failed to list her as a survivor, noting only that he left Charles and Eva, and that his wife—referring to Eva's mother—had died years earlier.

C.A.'s finances were as messy in death as they had been in life. He left no will and a sheaf of deeds—twenty-three properties, worth a total of $20,000. The rest of his estate—which included stocks, bonds, notes, and personal property—was worth another $5,000. But there were more than $45,000 worth of claims against the estate, mostly in mortgages, which would make any ensuing family feud over administration a pyrrhic victory at best for the winner. And yet Evangeline petitioned through attorneys for appointment as administrator, feeling Eva "has always grabbed all within her reach" and that her "bitterness will make it a hard thing to settle."

Charles wanted only to get back to his books, cramming to catch up on the work he missed while he was away. But in the week following C.A.'s death, Evangeline sent him five letters, each full of estate matters. He took time out from studying for one of his hardest exams to state he would rather have his mother than anybody else serve as administrator, but that whatever was decided, "we can not run the whole thing to suit ourselves. [Eva] must be considered and whatever is done must be straight *all the way around.*" Evangeline agreed, confessing that "in all this I dread nothing so much as that way you have of setting your jaw and gritting your teeth when you are hurt or angry. I can't bear to hurt you."

The probate court appointed the Wells-Dickey Trust Company of Minneapolis administrator of the Lindbergh estate. Most of C.A.'s properties reverted to their mortgagees; and ownership of the farm in Little Falls was divided among the family members—one-third to Evangeline as widow, the remainder divided in thirds, among Charles, Eva, and the late Lillian's daughter. The house remained vacant while the farmland was rented out. As a result of Eva's having vented her anger at her stepmother in court, Charles decided to have nothing more to do with her than he had to, steering clear of her for decades.

C.A.'s legacy to Charles included a lot of stifled anger and sadness. The closest Lindbergh ever got to sorting out those feelings came years later in a recurring dream in which he would see his father with great clarity, and talk with him, and wonder "why we have stayed so long apart when we have had such easy access to each other."

Perhaps inspired by his father's death, Charles became the most forthright personality in his Army class, stalwart and stoical. At the same time, he withdrew even more than he had as a child, when he had found solitude the most effective means of blocking out the marital rancor surrounding him.

He became a chameleon, able to blend into any environment—to be a part of any group but always apart. In flying school, where almost everybody had a nickname, Charles Lindbergh had a dozen of them—including Slim, Charlie, Carl, "Old Swede," even one he would later claim the press made up for its banner headlines, Lindy; but nobody became a close friend. He became the practical joker of "the gang"—dumping a fellow cadet's gear in the middle of the barracks, removing another's to a rooftop, turning a hose on in the bed of a sound sleeper, putting shaving cream into the open mouth of a snorer, dousing a sergeant's pillow with skunk "juice"—though sometimes he did not know when to quit, carrying his pranks to immature if not cruel extremes. While one of his bunkmates who often bragged about his brothel activities lay asleep, naked, one afternoon, Lindbergh painted his erect penis green. He proceeded to tie a long string around the large member, which he had somebody outside the barracks pull. Other cadets often moseyed into town for a night cavorting with women; but Charles cuddled up alone with a stray dog he found, a white mongrel he named Booster.

The military took control of Lindbergh's mind. In aviation, inexactitude could be fatal; and now he applied the same clarity of thought that was required in the air to his precision of expression on the ground. His syntax sharpened; he took to using a dictionary, improving both his spelling and grammar; even his immature handwriting became more legible. As members of his class steadily fell away, Lindbergh's final marks for the year gave him a 93.36 average, the second highest in his class.

At the start of Charles's new school term, he and the thirty-two other survivors of the Benzine Board graduated to Kelly Field, ten miles away, for "advanced training." Life at Kelly was an improvement over Brooks on almost every front. "We get better grub, treatment and work here," he wrote his mother on September 17, 1924. Ground school courses became more advanced as did the planes and maneuvers; the remaining cadets trained in gunnery, photography, and bombing.

Dangers at Kelly Field increased as well. "They wash a man out here even quicker than at Brooks," Charles informed Evangeline, often wondering "how many will be left six months from now." At Kelly, Lindbergh later noted, "we were constantly under observation and our only method of relaxation while flying was when the sky was cloudy and we could get above the clouds."

Lindbergh came close to dismissal once, for flying too well. In early 1925 the cadets were sent on a "cross country" trip—a triangular course from Kelly to Gonzales (sixty miles away) to Cuero (another thirty miles), then back home. The cadets left at five-minute intervals. Lindbergh was the third to take off, but he proved to be the first to land at Gonzales, where he checked in with the instructor and proceeded to Cuero. When he arrived at his second check-point, nobody was there, so he carried on, finishing the race ahead of everybody else. Back at Kelly he was severely lectured "on inattention and inability to locate fields and even towns," for he had obviously landed at the wrong field or was simply lying. To prove his innocence, Lindbergh had to draw a map of the field at which he landed. Upon completing it, word arrived at the operations office that the instructor who was supposed to be checking the pilots in at Cuero had, in fact, got lost that morning and been late in reaching the field himself.

The cadets spent two weeks at Ellington Field, between Houston and

Galveston, where they trained with machine guns. Upon their return to Kelly, the men practiced pursuit, attack observation, bombardment. With the second year of training entering its final months, each cadet specialized in a particular branch. Lindbergh was assigned to pursuit, which required the most versatility. He trained in dog-fighting, ground strafing, and light bombing and spent much of his time flying formations with as many as eight other planes.

On March 6, 1925—only eight days before graduation from the Air Service Advanced Flying School—Lindbergh was part of one such maneuver at five thousand feet. There were three units of three SE-5's each, with Lindbergh on the left of the top unit. Their "enemy" was a DH-4B below. "When we nosed down on the DH," Lindbergh later wrote in his official report, "I attacked from the left and Lieutenant McAllister from the right." The planes collided, locking together. When separating them appeared hopeless, Lindbergh climbed out to the right side of his then vertical cockpit and jumped backward as far from the ship as he could.

Just three weeks earlier two Brooks Field cadets crashed and burned; and eight months earlier two other planes had collided in midair over Kelly Field, killing one pilot. Lindbergh was fortunate to follow the course of the other, his parachute functioning perfectly. While falling he was able to see McAllister descend safely and the two planes, one hundred yards off to the side, twirl earthward, bursting into flames upon hitting the ground. An hour later Lindbergh was in the air again.

Accounts of the crash hit the newspapers from coast to coast. When a man in Detroit commented to Evangeline Lindbergh about her flyboy, "It will not be the last trouble he will have in that game," she replied, "I have more confidence in him than ever and you may be struck dead by an auto before you get home today."

On March 14, 1925, nineteen flying cadets—out of the original group of 104—graduated from the Advanced Flying School at Kelly Field and were commissioned as second lieutenants in the Air Service Reserve Corps. Lindbergh was first in the class. That night the new lieutenants enjoyed a farewell dinner in San Antonio, assembling for the last time. "The gang" decided to remain in contact by circulating a round-robin letter, to which Lindbergh would contribute over the years. Except for rare chance encounters over his lifetime of travels, however, he would only see one or two Army classmates ever again. Lindbergh was already leading a compartmentalized existence, always packing light, carrying few people from one episode of his life to the next.

During the past year, Lindbergh had simply assumed that he would go on active duty upon graduation from Kelly, but few squadrons needed new pilots just then. He had been offered a year's contract cotton dusting in Georgia for $2,400, but the pay seemed too low. He went to Love Field in Dallas to buy a Jenny with most of the year's salary he had squirreled away, but the thousand-dollar price seemed too high.

Evaluating his flying experiences in the past two years, his mind kept turning to Missouri—the Air Races, the job opportunities, the camaraderie at Lambert Field even when the weather had kept him on the ground. In his few months there he had made enough contacts to feel like "an accepted member of the city's little group of pilots." Several of them, in fact, had said a job would always be waiting for him; the young man he considered his closest friend, Bud Gurney, was Missouri-bound; and barnstorming was always good there.

"St. Louis is a city of winds, and the air above Lambert Field is usually rough," Lindbergh would later write. Even so—he thought that third week of March 1925—for him, the winds there had always been favorable.

In Dallas, he boarded the next train north.

5

SPIRIT

"I have felt the godlike power man derives from his
machines . . . the immortal viewpoint of higher air."

—C.A.L.

IN LATE MARCH 1925, LIEUTENANT LINDBERGH'S TRAIN
crossed into Missouri. Surrounded by eight states—whose borders all but connect the Great Lakes to the Gulf of Mexico and
the Alleghenies to the Rockies—Missouri combined qualities
found in the country at large. Not unlike its recent arrival, it
was a mixture of northern industriousness with southern courtesy, eastern diplomacy and western rusticity. Its principal city,
on the western bank of the Mississippi, was in other ways even
more like Lindbergh.

St. Louis was named for Louis IX of France, a king so worshipped he was canonized just twenty-five years after his death.
Louis had been a Crusader—a beacon in the Dark Ages, a
pious traveler renowned for his self-assuredness. Maintaining
his faith and vision, he withstood intense physical discomfort
in order to reach his holy destination. His spirit would take
hold of the Mississippi River's centralmost city that bears his
name, becoming a point of departure for adventurers of unusual zeal. Since 1804, when Jefferson sent Lewis and Clark
from St. Louis to survey the Louisiana territory, the city became more than a gateway to the west. It came to symbolize
the portal to the future.

In 1904, St. Louis became the first American city to host
the modern Olympic Games; and at a World Exhibition that
same year, it enthralled tens of thousands of visitors with a
myriad of electric, incandescent lights. Then it settled into a period of quiet contentment. In the 1920s, St. Louis was coming
alive again. The city passed an $87 million bond issue for local

improvements; business was booming; and Major Albert Bond Lambert, who had commanded a school for balloon pilots during the Great War, bought a former cornfield, which he opened to any aircraft operator free of charge. The one-hundred-seventy-acre clay sod field had no runways, simply a triangular landing space at its center. In winter the cold, the wind, and the frozen grooves in the ground challenged even the best pilots. Since the Air Races in 1923, the field had become the logical intersection for the nation's air traffic. Lambert announced that he would operate the field at his own expense until the city of St. Louis could take it over.

Lindbergh moved into a boardinghouse near Lambert Field in Anglum, farm country ten miles to the northwest of the St. Louis business district. No sooner had he unpacked than Frank and William Robertson, wartime fliers who had started their own company, offered him the best aviation job in town—chief pilot for the airmail. But there was a hitch: The Postmaster General had only recently been authorized to contract with civilian companies for the mail service; and the Robertson Aircraft Corporation's bid for the St. Louis-Chicago route had not yet been accepted. Lindbergh wrote his mother that he would rather fly the mail than try to enlist in the regular army, but he had no idea how long it would take the government to award its routes.

Until then, Lindbergh became a regular at Lambert Field, creating his own opportunities. He obtained a few flying students and carried passengers on short hops. "I found no trouble getting planes 'on shares,' " he later wrote. "New possibilities opened up each day." In an OX-5 Standard, he barnstormed a few weeks in Illinois, Missouri, and Iowa. No matter how silly the work, he took it seriously. There was one flight—recorded in Lindbergh's papers with the exact location discreetly omitted—during which a man wanted to fly over his hometown and urinate on it . . . a wish Lindbergh granted.

In early May 1925, Lindbergh was invited to join Vera May Dunlap's Flying Circus. Their advertisements said Vera May herself would appear in person "and will positively stand erect on top of the upper wing of the airplane without any visible means of support whatsoever while her pilot loops the loop, defying all laws of gravitation." Lindbergh quickly learned that the circus was, in fact, run by an Army "washout" and that Vera May was not especially wild about flying. No matter—"Beans" Lindbergh, as he was billed in Carterville, Illinois, managed to divert the public's attention from Vera May's failure to appear by performing some daredeviltry of his own, stopping his motor three thousand feet in the air and landing with his engine dead. The most dangerous stunt Vera May and her promoter performed was early the morning after the exhibition, when they skipped town, leaving their hotel bill unpaid.

Homing to St. Louis, "Beans" picked up more work around Lambert Field. On June second he tested a new commercial four-passenger plane, an OXX-6 Plywood Special. The ship was handling peculiarly, but he was able to put it successfully into a left spin for two complete turns, holding the stick all the way back and the rudder completely in the direction of the spin. But when he reversed the controls, the ship would not obey. As it kept spinning, it dropped fifteen hundred feet. With less than four hundred feet before crashing, Lindbergh rolled over the right side of the cockpit and pulled his rip cord. Falling faster than his abandoned plane, Lindbergh was in grave danger of their catching each other up; and, in fact, the plane did come within twenty-five feet of him. Of greater concern was a strong wind, which was causing him to drift toward a row of high-tension poles. Forced to hasten his descent by partially collapsing his chute, he landed hard in a potato patch, dislocating his shoulder. Lindbergh became the first man known to have his life saved twice by a parachute, which earned him special status in an unofficial fraternity created by the Irvin Parachute Company called the Caterpillar Club.

Before the end of the day, he was in another plane; and by the end of June he was testing a DH-4 mail plane intended for the airmail run. Of his many barnstorming offers, he chose to fly with a handsome pilot named Orville E. Scott, manager of Lambert Field. Billed now as the "Flying Fool," Lindbergh had—according to the press releases—earned "the reputation of being one of the best all around stunt fliers in the country. Fearing nothing that's possible to be accomplished in the air." In July, he flew in an aerial wedding, carrying a judge into the clouds, alongside another plane with a bride and groom.

Amid all the wonderful nonsense, Lindbergh scheduled an appointment before a board of examining officers as a first step toward obtaining a Regular Army Commission. During his preliminary oral examination, he realized that he was not as prepared as he should be; and midway through the exam, he asked if he could return at a later date. "The board said they thought I might be able to pass the examinations at that time," Lindbergh later recalled, "but that they would accede to my request." Whether it was the increasing interest in his civil flying pursuits or the onerous outline of subjects he would have to pass—including Calculus, a foreign language, English Literature, and Chemistry—Lindbergh never reapplied. After two weeks of Reserve Officer training at Richard Field, Missouri—instructing pilots in Jennies—Lindbergh received an offer from J. Wray Vaughan, president of The Mil-Hi Airways and Flying Circus in Denver—$400 a month.

"I'd always wanted to fly around mountains," Lindbergh would later write, "and Denver was within gliding distance of the Rockies. That would give me a chance to explore the air currents around canyons, slopes, and ridges. I could study the effect of turbulence, about which aviators knew so little and speculated so much." Still waiting on the airmail job, he accepted. Upon arriving at Humphrey's Field, outside the city, he discovered that Mil-Hi Airways and Flying Circus was nothing more than Mr. Vaughan and one old Hisso-Standard with a long green dragon painted on either side of the fuselage. Upon closer examination, Lindbergh realized the green dragons were covering the very plane he and H. J. Lynch had flown in the Kansas wheatfield three years earlier.

Lindbergh hopscotched around eastern Colorado late that summer. "We specialize in Fair and Carnival Exhibition Work, Offering Plane Change in Midair, Wing Walking, Parachute Jumping, Breakaways, Night Fireworks, Smoke Trails, and Deaf Flights," read Lieutenant Lindbergh's new business card. From Sugar Beet Day at Wiley to the Watermelon Celebration at Rocky Ford, he and Vaughan performed. In Lamar he flew his first Deaf Flight, a procedure aviators were promoting as a cure for the hard-of-hearing. "The patient," Lindbergh wrote his mother of the experience, "was a middle-aged man who had been partially deaf for 30 years. I took him up 7,400 ft (he thinks 13,000 ft) and brot him down in a 28 turn spin. He was sure sick and couldn't hear as well as before but the next day his hearing was noticeably improved and the catarrh he had been troubled with had disappeared. He said he had felt better than he had for a long time." Lindbergh received fifty dollars for the treatment.

In October 1925, just as the thrills of barnstorming were becoming routine, the government began awarding the Contract Air Mail routes. Colonial Air Lines received the first, CAM-1, flying between New York and Boston. And Robertson Aircraft Corporation won CAM-2, the Chicago-to-St. Louis run. As promised, Robertson asked Lindbergh to be their chief pilot. Airmail service would not begin until the spring, but he began receiving $200 a month for surveying the route, arranging for landing and emergency fields along the way.

Even with the excitement of the new job, Lindbergh already foresaw its limitations. Although changes in the weather would provide challenges, flying the mail meant following the same route day after day. Before he had even charted its path, he wrote his mother that he was looking forward to the summer, when in order to "break the monotony . . . I expect to take a few weeks off . . . and fly wherever the wind blows again. Hope to make Alaska next year." He intended to take part in the next "On to" competition—a popular long-distance race—whatever the destination.

Lindbergh's restlessness was natural, as it had become the most exciting age of exploration in four hundred years. In 1924, Captain Lowell H. Smith and five American Army lieutenants became the first to circumnavigate the globe in airplanes—27,553 miles in fifteen and one-half days; the Italian

Marchesi de Pinedo flew from Rome to Japan by way of Australia and back, thirty-four thousand miles over six months; and Englishman Alan J. Cobham had just left London on what would prove in four months to be a successful journey to Cape Town. At the end of 1925, Lindbergh heard that United States Navy Commander Richard Evelyn Byrd was preparing to fly over the North Pole and was still in need of two pilots. Lindbergh applied to the Detroit Aviation Society for one of the seats in the cockpit. With over eleven hundred flying hours in thirty different types of planes—and, as he wrote, having "lived in northern Minnesota most of my life"—he thought he was highly qualified. But the personnel for the flight had already been selected.

Lindbergh settled instead into his new routine. "For the first time since I'd entered aviation," he recalled of that fall, "I had a permanent home." Having little social life beyond the airfield, he joined the 110th Observation Squadron of the Thirty-fifth Division Air Service of the Missouri National Guard. Within weeks he was commissioned a First Lieutenant. The squadron, which consisted mostly of pilots from the war who had returned to civilian life, was stationed at Lambert Field. They met two nights a week for ground instruction and drill at a St. Louis armory, and they flew Jennies on Sundays. Lindbergh instructed in the latest techniques of flying and lectured on navigation, parachutes, and aerodynamics. "We'd schedule formation flights over St. Louis, practice acrobatics, and send photographic missions to nearby towns," Lindbergh remembered. "With Army planes and parachutes, I could try maneuvers that were too dangerous for our civil aircraft. One afternoon, I climbed my jenny to 14,000 feet, and brought it down in fifty consecutive turns of a power spin." In early December, he handwrote his first Last Will and Testament, bequeathing his entire estate—which was then a few hundred dollars and the Liberty Standard he had bought from Wray Vaughan—to his mother.

After having shared a room with Bud Gurney in nearby Bridgeton, Lindbergh found more convenient digs at the start of 1926 right on the edge of Lambert Field, just west of the hangars. He rented a room and kitchen—without plumbing or electricity—from Clyde Brayton, an airplane mechanic who lived with his family on the ground floor. Although Charles wrote his mother that he cooked two meals a day there—breakfasts consisting of two eggs on a steak or pork chop, fried potatoes, three slices of buttered toast, two glasses of milk, fruit, and sometimes coffee—she hardly let a week pass without sending him candy, cheese, and nuts along with new handkerchiefs and magazines.

Meantime Robertson Aircraft erected a new hangar as they readied their five mail planes, Army-salvage De Havilland observation planes. The wings of these biplanes were fabric and painted silver, the fuselages were plywood painted maroon, with "U. S. Air Mail" printed boldly in white. Their twelve-cylinder, 400 h.p. Liberty engines enabled them to cruise at ninety miles per hour. The pilot would sit in the rear cockpit, so that he could keep an eye on the mailbags up front. In the Army these planes had been called "flaming coffins," an unfortunately deserved nickname. As chief pilot, Lindbergh insisted that each Robertson pilot be equipped with a new seat-type silk parachute—and "that no penalty would be laid against him if he used it." Lindbergh made the most of his time getting the feel of his DH-4, using it to teach another nine students that January.

The Robertsons gave Lindbergh the task of selecting the two pilots who would be sharing the route. By then, it seemed that Lindbergh had heard from every unemployed flier he had ever known, most of whom had either abandoned the business or were eking out livings barnstorming and crop-dusting. He selected two comrades from the Army Air Service: one was Thomas P. "Nellie" Nelson, who would be based in Chicago; the other was Philip R. "Red" Love, who had just recovered from a cotton-dusting plane crash, which knocked out six teeth, broke his cheekbone, nose, and palate, and injured his back and left ankle, leaving him with an eighteen-stitch scar across his face. Lindbergh offered to share his room and rent at the Brayton house with him.

Although most of his friends were marrying, or at least dating, Slim remained overtly celibate. Off-duty, he seemed most at ease staging dog-fights in old Jennies with Love or loitering with other fliers around a lunch counter in a little shack at Lambert Field run by a local named Louie DeHatre. Many women offered themselves to the daring young men at Lambert, and Lindbergh received an occasional solicitation from a local matchmaker; but he never responded.

Instead, he expended his nervous energy rough-housing with the boys, enjoying practical jokes more than ever. He bragged to his mother in March 1926 that he fed an arrogant loudmouth at the field some laxative tablets, passing them off as candy; and he exploded a stink bomb in the man's glove. Lindbergh also delighted for decades in the time he got Bud Gurney to swallow two big gulps of kerosene, having led him to believe it was water.

On April 15, 1926, Robertson Aircraft inaugurated its domestic airmail route with a formal dedication ceremony before two hundred citizens. Major Lambert's thirteen-year-old daughter, Myrtle, strewed flowers on the wings of Lindbergh's plane and said, "I christen you 'St. Louis.' May your wings never be clipped." The crowd applauded and motion picture cameras clicked. City elders made speeches, including Major Lambert, who predicted that it would only be a few years before airmail service would stretch as far as South America. He added, "The development of the airplane toward safety and reliability is growing far beyond the belief of those who are not acquainted with the aircraft industry."

At 3:50, Lindbergh sat in his plane, Love in another, revving their Liberty engines. At 3:55, a brand-new mail truck drove onto the field, and three pouches carrying 5,600 pieces of mail were loaded into Love's ship. At exactly four o'clock, Lindbergh took off into the northwest to pick up fifteen thousand letters at Springfield.

In St. Louis, Lindbergh became the poster boy for the Air Mail. He appeared in advertisements; and he attended Chamber of Commerce luncheons, describing how even the smallest business could be enhanced by using the airmail. "Our route," Lindbergh explained, ". . . operated on a schedule which saved one business day over train service to New York." A reply could be mailed from New York in the evening and be delivered in St. Louis the following day. In banking, for example, that meant immediate advantages, cutting check-clearance time.

Because airplane crashes were still common occurrences, many questioned the importance of saving a day, especially at the cost of an additional fifteen cents and the risk of the mail's perishing. So, despite first-day indications, popular support for airmail was slow to take off. Robertson Aircraft had bid $2.53 a pound for their airmail contract, which meant that they would have to carry about 125 pounds daily, 2,500 pieces of mail, to break even.

After six weeks, the company was carrying half that amount. "It is difficult for anyone who did not live through that period, to realize the problems which were encountered," Lindbergh recalled years later to William H. Conkling, who had been the Springfield postmaster, "both in persuading people to use the service, and in carrying on an efficient operation with the facilities existing at the time." Only in retrospect was Lindbergh able to laugh at how they used to regard the padlock on a bag of registered mail "as a decided asset to our pay-load," as each extra pound contributed to their very subsistence. For months the St. Louis banks assisted Robertson Aircraft, picking up part of their shortfall. They felt they were investing in the future.

CAM-2 was considered one of the most perilous runs in the country, because of the changeable weather. Navigation was rudimentary at best, with pilots relying on visual contact with the ground—following railroad tracks, rivers, or at night, the glow of a town below. "During the summer months most of our route was covered during daylight," Lindbergh would write, "but as winter approached the hours of night flying increased until darkness set in a few minutes after we left the field at St. Louis." DeHavilland planes had neither landing lights nor navigation lights. "Our total lighting equipment," Lindbergh remembered, "consisted of a pocket flashlight (pilot furnished) and a compass light attached to a button on the end of the stick." Lindbergh later recounted how he "arranged with the mail-truck driver to hang four kerosene lanterns on fence posts on the leeward side of the cow pasture we used as an airmail field at Springfield, as a precaution; and I once had to return and land by the light of the two of them that were still burning." As a rule, Lindbergh recalled, "We went as far as we could, and if the visibility became too bad we landed and entrained the mail."

On September 16, 1926, Lindbergh took off from Lambert Field and made his scheduled stops at Springfield and Peoria, leaving at 5:55 P.M. "There was a light ground haze," Lindbergh later wrote in an official report of the flight, "but the sky was practically clear with but scattered cumulus clouds." Twenty-five miles northeast of Peoria, night fell and a low fog obliterated all view of the ground. He turned back, attempting to drop a flare and land, but it did not ignite. Lindbergh maintained his course until 7:15, at which time he saw several patches of light atop the dark, heavy blanket of fog. He recognized those glows as signs of the towns surrounding Maywood; and he later understood that down on the field the ground crew was directing searchlights skyward. But Lindbergh could not see his way clear to any destination. At 8:20 his engine quit, and he cut into his reserve tank, which held another twenty minutes of fuel. When that was exhausted, Lindbergh headed toward open country, nosing his plane up. "At 5,000 feet," he wrote, "the engine sputtered and died. I stepped up on the cowling and out over the right side of the cockpit, pulling the rip cord after about a 100-foot fall." He did not carry the mail with him, figuring his dry tanks negated the possibility of an explosion. His parachute functioned perfectly . . . but suddenly, in the distance, he heard the sound of his abandoned plane engine. Apparently, when the ship nosed down, residual gasoline drained into the carburetor. Gradually the paths of their descents diverged, and Lindbergh dropped into the fog—one thousand feet into nothingness. He crossed his legs to keep from hooking a branch or wire, and he guarded his face with his hands, and waited.

He landed in a cornfield with stalks taller than he. There was enough ground visibility for him to gather his chute and head down one of the rows to a meadow, in which he saw wagon tracks that led to a farmyard. There some locals asked if he had heard an airplane crash. They found the ship two miles away, crushed into a ball, having caused no damage, then they took the mailbags to the Ottawa, Illinois, post office in time for the 3:30 A.M. train to Chicago. Some farmers let Lindbergh spend the rest of the night with them, for which he later thanked them, enclosing ten dollars for their hospitality.

News of Lindbergh's drop to safety crossed the country, bringing a flurry of personal mail his way. Springfield Postmaster Conkling wired, "We are all greatly rejoiced at the news of your safety which we watched for last night with great anxiety." Even Lindbergh's former Staff Sergeant August W. Thiemann from Kelly Field wrote to congratulate him, pointing out that he was

the only man in the United States known to have saved his life by successfully jumping from a plane three times.

Six weeks later, on November 3, 1926, he became the nation's only four-
time caterpillar. This time he had left Springfield for Peoria, with reports of
satisfactory weather ahead. But only minutes out, both darkness and a four-
hundred-foot ceiling appeared—layered into haze, then rain, and topped by
snow. Again, when he faced no alternative, he directed the plane toward
what he considered the least inhabited country around and dove over the left
side of his ship. Through the clouds he floated, landing on a barbed wire
fence, which broke his fall without ripping his flying suit. The next morning
the plane was recovered. Two of the mail bags were partially full and completely undamaged; the full bag from St. Louis had split open, leaving some
of the mail "oil-soaked" but deliverable. "I don't know whether you possess
any angelistic instinct," Sergeant Thiemann wrote after this emergency jump
hit the newspapers, "but it appears to me as though you are favored by the
angels."

Lindbergh repeatedly displayed grace under pressure. There was, for example, another night when he lost his race against a storm and the dark on
his way to Peoria. Fortunately, he had just persuaded the Robertsons to buy
a used gyroscopic pitch-and-turn indicator, an instrument that indicated
whether an airplane was remaining on its heading. Unfortunately, he had
never tested it. Over the next few minutes, experimenting with stick and
throttle—knowing he had but a fifty-fifty chance of surviving a crash in his
"Flaming Coffin"—Lindbergh taught himself to fly by instruments, and he
made Peoria.

Amid the growing pains of commercial aviation were the most simple
pleasures, including esprit de corps. Another early St. Louis flier recollected
how they all used to delight in "the sweet smell of newly mowed grass
mingling with the tangy, pungent odors of airplane dope, burnt oil and gasoline . . . the appetizing aroma of Louis DeHatre's hamburgers . . . the roar of
a Liberty motor as the C.A.M.2 air mail took off on its flight to Chicago . . ."
And though the Robertston Aircraft pilots often found a telegram informing
them that the mail between New York and Chicago was delayed somewhere
over the Appalachians, Lindbergh and his team completed better than ninety-
eight percent of their scheduled flights.

As he had forecast, Lindbergh's enthusiasm for delivering the mail abated.
He took leave the entire month of August and flew passengers in and out of
Springfield. Upon his return to work, he confessed to his mother, "I am getting tired of the monotony of flying around St. Louis and unless something
new turns up I expect to leave here next May." He wrote the National Geographic Society that October, asking if it was charting any expeditions in

which airplanes would be used but was told there was none. Promoted to Captain in the National Guard, he hoped an opening in the regular Army Air Corps might present some new flying challenges.

Two months shy of his twenty-fifth birthday, Lindbergh took his Army physical. Still a lean 160 pounds with a twenty-nine-inch waist, Slim's hearing was perfect and his vision slightly better than that—20/15 in each eye. In the Psychic Examination portion of the medical report, under the category of Temperamental type, Flight Surgeon Maurice L. Green observed that Lindbergh was "optimum type—slow and purposeful, yet quick of reaction, alert, congenial, intelligent." Under the category of dreams, Dr. Greene noted only that Lindbergh's were "mild" and "vague."

If Dr. Greene was including daydreams, his evaluation was off by miles. Having spent hundreds of hours alone in the clouds, Lindbergh learned to escape the ennui by letting his mind spin, as he had since childhood. He would ask himself a question and roll it over until he could answer no more. During one such moment in the fall of 1926, while jouncing in his salvaged Army DeHavilland, he thought about the new Wright-Bellanca—from everything he had read, the most efficient plane ever built. It could cruise at least fifteen miles an hour faster than his DH, burning half the fuel and carrying twice the payload. "What a future aviation has when such planes can be built," Lindbergh mused; "yet how few people realize it?"

"If only I had the Bellanca," Lindbergh told himself, "I'd show St. Louis businessmen what modern aircraft could do . . ." He would start by taking them to New York in eight or nine hours. Then he wondered just how far a Bellanca could fly if it was carrying nothing but fuel and the engine were throttled down. "It could break the world's endurance record, and the transcontinental," Lindbergh thought, his mind spiraling, "and set a dozen marks for range and speed and weight." And just possibly, he suddenly realized—startling himself with the very notion—"I could fly nonstop between New York and Paris."

LINDBERGH WAS HARDLY the first man to have this lofty thought. In fact, more than seventy people had already crossed the Atlantic by air—most in dirigibles, the rest making the journey in stages, all as members of flying teams. Ten years after Blériot captured the first big purse offered to an aviator, for crossing the English Channel, two Englishmen claimed another prize from the same benefactor—Lord Northcliffe, owner of the *Times* of London and *The Daily Mail*—for crossing the Atlantic from any point in the United States or Canada to any point in Great Britain or Ireland in seventy-two continuous hours. Captain John Alcock and Lieutenant Arthur W. Brown flew almost two thousand miles in sixteen hours, from St. John's to Clifden,

Ireland. While technology advanced, fliers on both sides of the ocean dreamed of a new prize, one which proved for years beyond human attainment.

Raymond Orteig, a French-born American, who owned Manhattan's Lafayette and Brevoort hotels, had come to admire many fliers he had met during the war. Moved by the spirit of cooperation between the United States and France, he wrote the president of the Aero Club of America in a gesture of postwar jubilation. "As a stimulus to the courageous aviators," he stated in May 1919, "I desire to offer . . . a prize of $25,000 to the first aviator of any Allied country crossing the Atlantic in one flight, from Paris to New York or New York to Paris, all other details in your care." The flight could be in a land- or sea-plane, but it had to be a "heavier than air" craft. The offer remained on the table for five years.

In 1924, he revised his proposition. He placed the prize under the auspices of the National Aeronautic Association, removed the time limit, and allowed fliers from any nation to enter. By 1926, there was much discussion in aeronautical circles, even around Louie's lunch shack, about the problems of performance and endurance involved in making such a flight. Years later, Charles Lindbergh would admit that the "offer of the Raymond Orteig prize called my attention to the New York–Paris flight." He said he was "much more interested in the flight than in the prize," but he hastened to add that he did not "mean to imply that the prize was not of definite interest too."

In September 1926, France's most victorious flying ace made a run for the money. René Fonck came to America, where he joined forces with an American syndicate set on winning the prize. After weeks of disputes, Fonck's crew was assembled, including a co-pilot, a navigator-engineer, and a radio operator. Their ship was the S-35, a sesquiplane—a biplane whose lower wing was shorter than its upper—with three engines. It was conceived and constructed by an ingenious Russian émigré named Igor Sikorsky, who was trying to launch his aircraft manufactory. Sikorsky wanted to put the plane through more tests, which would postpone the takeoff until spring; but everybody involved with the flight talked him out of waiting.

On the morning of the fifteenth, Fonck and his crew went to the end of the runway at Roosevelt Field on Long Island to board the S-35. Lindbergh later read newspaper articles detailing the plane's accoutrements—a bed, red-leather upholstery, long-wave and short-wave radio sets, flotation bags in case of an emergency landing, a hot "celebration" dinner to be eaten upon arrival . . . even a last-minute batch of croissants to send them on their way. A large crowd watched as this mighty machine taxied, straining to lift itself off the ground, only to disappear into a gully at the end of the runway. There was a moment of stillness before an explosion rent the air. Fonck and one other were able to flee; the two others perished.

Flying the mail, Lindbergh visualized *his* flight to Paris. "Well, if I can get a Bellanca," he later recalled of that moment of conception, somewhere south of Peoria, "I'll fly alone. That will cut out the need for any selection of crew, or quarreling. If there's upholstery in the cabin, I'll tear it out for the flight. I'll take only the food I need to eat, and a few concentrated rations. I'll carry a rubber boat for emergency, and a little extra water." But first he had to solve the problem of obtaining his new plane: the Wright-Bellanca—with its small body and single high wing—propelled by a Wright Whirlwind engine—air-cooled and radial, reputedly the most reliable source of power in the air. For all the dangers, in Lindbergh's mind "a nonstop flight between New York and Paris would be less hazardous than flying mail for a single winter with our Liberty-powered DHs."

Lindbergh knew that he lacked both the money to buy a new airplane and the credentials that might induce an airplane manufacturer to sponsor his flight. For all his recent experience, he was hardly a Fonck or Byrd or de Pinedo. His reputation hardly extending beyond Lambert Field, he prepared a salespitch to lure people in St. Louis into backing him. "But where shall I start?" he wondered while continuing his airmail rounds. "To whom shall I go with my project? I have friends in the city, but most of them are aviators too, and men in aviation seldom have much money."

He made a date with Earl Thompson, an insurance executive with his own golden-winged Laird, to whom Lindbergh had given flying lessons. At one of the most fashionable addresses in St. Louis, a maid ushered Lindbergh into Thompson's living room. No sooner was he joined by his host than he launched into his appeal, which was ostensibly not for money so much as "advice." Lindbergh had already handwritten a draft of what he called "propaganda" for his trip, a long page which he never showed anybody but which codified for him all the reasons the town burghers should support his venture. "It would show people what airplanes can do," he said. "It would advance aviation, and it would advertise St. Louis." Toward that end, he said he hoped a group of businessmen might back him, not only for the cash but also the cachet he would need in dealing with airplane manufacturers. He figured a Wright-Bellanca—if he could secure one—would cost at least $10,000.

"But the Wright-Bellanca is a land plane—and it has only one engine, hasn't it?" Thompson asked. With that, Lindbergh sensed that he was on his way. Thompson was discussing the possibilities, not dismissing them out of hand. When he suggested a flying boat or a three-motored ship, such as Byrd's Fokker, Lindbergh explained their downsides, that "a flying boat can't take off with enough fuel and a trimotored Fokker would cost a huge amount of money." Moreover, Lindbergh felt that three engines presented three times the chance of engine failure. By the end of the evening, Thompson was interested in the project.

By chance a representative from the Fokker company suddenly appeared one day that fall in St. Louis, where they were thinking of establishing an agency. Fokker had a trimotored plane ready to market, with seats for ten passengers! Out at Louie's lunch stand, he began to talk about the safety of multiengines and "the efficiency of thick airfoils." Before he left, Lindbergh buttonholed the man from Fokker to inquire about the company's ability to produce a plane that could make the New York-to-Paris flight. He said they had already considered that challenge, and if an order were placed right away, Fokker could deliver a ship by spring for $90,000, $100,000 with extras . . . and Fokker would, of course, have to approve of the personnel flying it. When Lindbergh asked about their building a single-engined plane, the man from Fokker dismissed the questioner all together.

More discouraging was the news in late October 1926 that Lieutenant Commander Byrd, the Fokker company's best-known customer, intended to fly from New York to London or Paris the following summer. "He's experienced in organization," Lindbergh had to admit; "and he knows how to get financed." There were also rumors of other fliers going after the Orteig Prize—a pair of Frenchmen, who were planning a flight from Paris to New York, and Americans Noel Davis and Stanton Wooster, who were securing backing from the American Legion.

Lindbergh was not deterred. In fact, he believed more strongly than ever in his ability to make the flight and that its success depended on simplicity—one set of wings, one engine, one pilot. To his mother he revealed on October thirtieth only that "I am working on a new proposition in St. Louis and have been very busy lately." He set an appointment with Major Lambert, who said that if Lindbergh felt it was a practical venture and could "get the right fellows together," he would take part. "He said he already had two thousand dollars raised to help finance the flight," Lambert remembered of the meeting ten years later. "I finally got it out of him that the two thousand dollars represented his savings." Major Lambert pledged $1,000 and indicated that his brother, Wooster, would match it.

His dream officially backed, Lindbergh disclosed his plan to his boss. As much as Major Bill Robertson's endorsement, Lindbergh sought his willingness to adjust the airmail schedule so that he could take time off to arrange for his Paris flight. Robertson was barely making ends meet—facing a weekly deficit from the airmail of almost $400—and was unable to support Lindbergh financially. But if pilots Love and Nelson were willing to cover for him on his route, Robertson said he supported Lindbergh's plan and that Lindbergh could even drop the name of Robertson Aircraft wherever it might prove useful. He suggested that the St. Louis *Post-Dispatch* might finance the whole proposition.

The way Lindbergh's luck had been running, that seemed possible. He feared that might mean turning his airplane into a flying billboard—advertising the newspaper—a repugnant possibility he was willing to consider. Days later he learned that he had nothing to fear. "The *Post-Dispatch* wouldn't think of taking part in such a hazardous flight," one of the editors told him. "To fly across the Atlantic Ocean with one pilot and a single-engine plane! We have our reputation to consider. We couldn't possibly be associated with such a venture!"

Each setback doubled Lindbergh's determination. By late November, it occurred to him that he was asking people to pledge money when he had no guarantee of a plane even being available. He decided to investigate the possibilities in person. He invested one hundred dollars in a new suit, gray felt hat, silk necktie, blue overcoat, and silk scarf. "I haven't the slightest use for them," Lindbergh was thinking as he purchased the fancy togs. "I hate to do things just to make an impression. But right now that may be as essential to my Paris flight as a plane itself will become later."

For the first time since he was ten, Lindbergh arrived at Pennsylvania Station in New York City—on Sunday, November twenty-eighth. The next day, he went to the Wright Aeronautical Corporation factory in Paterson, New Jersey, where he discussed with an executive the possibility of purchasing the Bellanca airplane with its Wright Whirlwind engine. The executive explained that Wright had never intended to manufacture aircraft, that they had built the Bellanca merely to demonstrate their engine, and that they were in the process of selling their rights to that plane to another company. The executive suggested he speak directly to the designer, Giuseppe Bellanca himself, which he did the next evening at the Waldorf-Astoria.

Bellanca was a "serious, slender man—straight black hair, sharp-cut features, medium height," as Lindbergh described him. "One feels, in his presence, genius, capability, confidence." Because Bellanca was then unaffiliated with any company, he was vague in answering questions about production of a plane; but he provided Lindbergh with all the specifications of the vehicle, including his belief that it could stay aloft for fifty hours. After less than an hour, Lindbergh left to catch an 8:20 train for home. He felt so confident of Bellanca's support that he revealed to his mother that the "object of the trip was concerning a contemplated St. Louis NY to Paris flight next spring," adding, "the outcome will be unknown for some time."

Into December most of Lindbergh's plans were put on ice. A volley of telegrams revealed that the plane was still tied up in the negotiations of the Wright Corporation, and the best Bellanca could offer was a new trimotored ship he had designed, which he would sell for $29,000. Lindbergh could not afford it, and he still believed in making the trip on one engine. Meantime he considered a plan of public subscription, inviting the citizens of St. Louis to chip in ten dollars apiece toward a plane with the city's name on it. He remained determined to call on every businessman in St. Louis—and Chicago, if necessary—until he found sufficient backing.

His next call—to the brokerage firm of Knight, Dysart & Gamble—proved shrewd. Lindbergh had selected the devil-may-care son of one of the founding partners, Harry Hall Knight, who worked at the firm and was also president of the St. Louis Flying Club. He told Lindbergh, "Slim, you ought not to be running around worrying about raising money. You've got to put all your attention on that flight if you're going to make it." Within minutes, he had Harold Bixby—a vice president of the State National Bank of St. Louis, a private pilot, and the president of the St. Louis Chamber of Commerce—in his office. Within weeks, Knight and Bixby agreed that they would raise the fifteen thousand dollars Lindbergh said he needed to reach Paris.

The day after Christmas 1926, Lindbergh wrote his mother that "the N.Y. to Paris flight is gradually taking shape and it is now quite probable that we will have a St. Louis expedition ready to hop off from New York next spring." Knowing her obvious concern, he immediately assured her that his "plans will be entirely different from those of Sikorsky and other contemplated expeditions. I may leave the mail service this week to begin organization. If so will be in New York a majority of the time for the next three months."

Lindbergh compiled endless lists: equipment he would need; maps he would have to study; landmarks he would have to learn; and information he would need from the Weather Bureau and the State Department. Unable to count on getting the Wright-Bellanca, Lindbergh also made a list of backup manufacturers. He wired the Travel Air Company in Wichita. When they replied that they would not take the order, he thought of another small outfit, Ryan Aeronautical Company in San Diego, whose high-wing monoplanes were flown on the West Coast mail route. And if they refused him, he would try Curtiss and Boeing and Douglas and Martin. "CAN YOU CONSTRUCT WHIRL-WIND ENGINE PLANE CAPABLE FLYING NONSTOP BETWEEN NEW YORK AND PARIS STOP IF SO PLEASE STATE COST AND DELIVERY DATE," he wired Ryan on February 3, 1927.

The next day—his twenty-fifth birthday—he received the second-best news he had wished for. There was still no word about a Wright-Bellanca, but Ryan replied: "CAN BUILD PLANE SIMILAR M ONE BUT LARGER WINGS CAPABLE OF MAKING FLIGHT COST ABOUT SIX THOUSAND WITHOUT MOTOR AND INSTRUMENTS DELIVERY ABOUT THREE MONTHS." Lindbergh wired back, asking the plane's specifications and if they could produce it any faster. On February sixth, they informed him that the plane would have a gas capacity of 380 gallons and could cruise at one hundred miles per hour—enough to get him to Paris—and they could manufacture it within two months of receiving a fifty-percent deposit.

Then Giuseppe Bellanca sent even better news. "WILLING TO MAKE ATTRACTIVE PROPOSITION ON THE BELLANCA AIRPLANE FOR PARIS FLIGHT," he wired Lindbergh. "SUGGEST YOU COME NEW YORK SOON POSSIBLE SO WE CAN GET TOGETHER IN QUICKEST MANNER." His address had become the Woolworth Building, the offices of Columbia Aircraft, with whom he had gone into business. Days later, Lindbergh sat before the company's pilot, Clarence Chamberlin, and the Columbia board chairman, Charles Levine, a fast-dealing twenty-eight-year-old who had become a millionaire off surplus war materiel and who now owned the one existing Wright-Bellanca.

The meeting seemed promising. Lindbergh impressed Levine with his roster of St. Louis backers; and Levine said while his plane was worth $25,000, he would sell it for $15,000, the difference being his company's contribution to the enterprise. Because the price was higher than any Lindbergh had ever mentioned to his backers, he said he would have to discuss it with them.

"My trip to N.Y. ended very satisfactorily," Charles wrote his mother from the train home. "It will be possible to obtain immediate delivery of the only Bellanca in existence and probably the only plane in the world now flying, which is capable of the Paris flight." He said there would soon be publicity, but it would "not mention a Paris flight before late fall. However we intend to make the attempt sometime around the first of April and hope to misslead any rival attempts by placing the time much later in the year."

The Associated Press was already onto the story. Even before he had secured his plane, headlines announced, "LINDBERGH, MAIL PILOT, MAY FLY FOR SEA AWARD." Upon reading the article in The New York Times, C. F. Schory, Secretary of the contest committee of the National Aeronautic Association, sent Lindbergh a copy of the Orteig regulations and a reminder that the entry must be filed sixty days prior to the start of the flight.

That weekend, Lindbergh learned that Harry Knight, Harry Bixby, and Major Lambert had completed the financing of the plane, having talked Harry Knight's father, the Robertson brothers, and E. Lansing Ray, owner of the St. Louis Globe-Democrat, into investing as well. Bixby sent a memorandum to his fellow board members at the State National Bank, asking them to grant a loan to him and Harry Knight, which they would endorse, for $15,000. The check was cut, and Harry Knight signed it over to Lindbergh. Bixby, wearing his Chamber of Commerce hat, asked Lindbergh, "What would you think of naming [the plane] the 'Spirit of St. Louis'?"

"I am again enroute to New York," Lindbergh wrote his mother hours later, "but this time with a little over $15,000"—every penny of which he would account for. He expected to close the Bellanca deal the following day, then spend the rest of the week in Washington, securing the cooperation of the government agencies on his list. "If neither the French or Byrd are in a position to make the flight sooner," he continued, "we will wait until after Apr. 15th before taking off from N.Y.; otherwise we intend to go without waiting the required 60 days according to the rules of the Raymond Orteig Prize." He sent his mother a six-month subscription to the St. Louis newspaper so that she could clip any articles pertaining to the flight.

According to plan, Lindbergh stood before Charles Levine in his office at the Columbia Aircraft Corporation the next day—February nineteenth— and placed the cashier's check for $15,000 on his polished desktop. "We will sell our plane," Levine said, "but of course we reserve the right to select the crew that flies it." For a moment Lindbergh was dumbstruck. When he finally found the words, he suggested there must have been some misunderstanding, that this point was non-negotiable. Levine countered that his company could not possibly release its plane without selecting its crew but that he was willing to let the St. Louis group paint the name of their city on the fuselage. Angry that he had wasted so much time and money—more than fifty dollars each way—Lindbergh picked up his check and started for the door. "You are making a mistake," Levine argued. "The Bellanca is the only airplane built that is capable of flying between New York and Paris."

"I'm sorry," he replied, "but if you won't sell outright, the sooner I start looking for another plane the better." Before Lindbergh could leave the office, Levine asked him to call the next day. "I had planned on returning to St. Louis that night and replied that I would wait until the next day only if he felt that there was a reasonable possibility of his selling the Bellanca outright," Lindbergh recalled ten years later. "He again asked me to stay over"—another three dollars for a night in a hotel—"and to call him at 11 o'clock in the morning."

In a daze, Lindbergh wandered the streets of Manhattan, even tried to kill time in a motion picture theater. It was a waste of fifty cents, as he could focus on nothing except his eleven-o'clock call. At the appointed hour, Lindbergh telephoned. "Well," Levine said, "have you changed your mind?" Too angered by the question to speak, Lindbergh simply hung up the phone.

On the train home, he assessed the situation. Fokker, Wright, Travel Air, and Columbia had all turned him down; and a number of competitors for the Orteig Prize were cropping up. It appeared that Levine himself intended to make the flight to Paris with Chamberlin; Davis and Wooster were reportedly making progress; a new entrant, Chief of the Army Air Corps, Major General Mason M. Patrick, was reportedly buying a three-engined bomber from the Huff Daland Company; Byrd was officially in the race in his $100,000 Fokker; and word had it that Sikorsky was building another biplane for Fonck. "I'm behind all my competitors," Lindbergh thought,

"—so far behind, in fact, that they don't even consider me in the running. Most of them don't know I exist."

Lindbergh saw only two options. He could go to San Diego and give the Ryan company the chance to make good on their offer; or, whether somebody else beat him to Paris or not, he could surprise the world by crossing the Pacific Ocean instead.

It was sleeting that Monday when Lindbergh got off the train in St. Louis and went to see his backers. Harold Bixby spoke for all of them when he suggested they keep the cashier's check in the bank and their sights on Paris. He urged Lindbergh to return to Union Station and board a train for California. He arrived in San Diego at noon on Thursday, February twenty-fifth—having spent $75 in fare (plus another $22.50 to sleep in a Pullman car, less than $1.50 for each of his meals, and the occasional dime for magazines and candy). Exiting the train, Lindbergh found palm trees gently swaying in the warm air.

San Diego was at once the oldest and newest city in California, a sixteenth-century Spanish settlement whose population had doubled in just the previous decade to 100,000. Where fishing had been the area's first important industry, several small aircraft manufacturers were among the area's newest businesses. Lindbergh took a cab from the downtown Union Depot to Ryan Airlines, at the city's harbor.

Lindbergh's dream factory turned out to be one dilapidated building— with "no flying field, no hangar, no sound of engines warming up; and the unmistakable smell of dead fish from a near-by cannery [mixed] with the banana odor of dope from drying wings." In an instant it all smelled right—an industrious, no-frills operation. Inside a small office he met the company's top brass, chief engineer Donald Hall and Benjamin Franklin Mahoney, a young bond salesman from Pennsylvania who took some flying lessons at the Claude Ryan Flying School, then bought it and began building planes out of war surplus aircraft.

After a Cook's tour of the plant, Lindbergh sat with Mahoney to talk business. Ryan stood by its quoted price of $6,000 without engine; and Mahoney said he would provide the engine and extra equipment at cost, charging no commission for outfitting the plane. As the discussion turned to the machine's performance, Mahoney left Lindbergh alone with Donald Hall. The engineer explained that Lindbergh's needs made the standard Ryan fuselage impossible.

None of the requirements in designing a new plane fazed Hall, but one startled him. He could not believe Lindbergh wanted one cockpit. Once Lindbergh explained that he would "rather have extra gasoline than an extra man," Hall embraced the idea. Conceptually, it made for a more efficient machine—a re-allocation of some 350 pounds, which would mean another fifty gallons of fuel. Already he was sketching, darkening new lines over others as the slightest variation in one aspect of the design affected every other. An increase in the wing span to help the heavy-laden plane take off, for example, meant moving the tail surfaces, which involved replacing the engine.

When Hall asked the exact distance from New York to Paris, and Lindbergh could provide but an approximation, they drove in Hall's old Buick roadster to the public library. Standing before a globe, Lindbergh produced a piece of white string, which he pulled taut from New York up the east coast of North America, then again almost at a right angle across an ocean of blue to Europe. "It isn't a very scientific way of finding the exact distance between two points on the earth's surface," Lindbergh was thinking at the time, but it sufficed for the initial calculation: 3,600 miles. Figuring on the back of an envelope, and adding for a ten percent reserve, Hall recommended four hundred gallons of gasoline.

By the time they returned to the Ryan plant, Mahoney had completed his figures. His company would deliver one Special monoplane with a Wright J-5 motor within sixty days for $10,580. From the office, Lindbergh wired the details to Harry Knight in St. Louis. The next day Knight replied that Lindbergh should close the deal. The order was written up, including the specifics that the plane would have a gasoline capacity of four hundred gallons, a minimum cruising radius of 3,500 miles at 1,550 r.p.m., an oil gauge, temperature gauge, and altimeter. Putting $1,000 down—with a second payment of $6,580 due within the week and $3,000 due upon completion—Lindbergh signed the order on February 25, 1927.

Never had parting with so much money been such a relief for Lindbergh. "I can turn my attention to the flight itself," he thought, "—to the design and construction of the plane, to outfitting it with instruments and emergency equipment, to studying navigation and the weather conditions."

Except for the cost in time, Lindbergh saw only advantages in building a plane from scratch. He could inspect every detail of its structure and become intimate with its workings. The Ryan employees could literally build the plane around him—both his body and his experience—making the plane and its pilot one. And yet it was strange, observed Walter Balderston of the Pacific Scientific Company, who had been asked to install the plane's instruments, that whenever Lindbergh spoke of getting from New York to Paris, he always used the first person plural. "I heard it many times before Lindbergh left San Diego, & particularly noticed his rather peculiar conversational use of it," Balderston would later write in a short memoir. Before there was even a plane built, "He simply would not use the pronoun 'I' when speaking of the flight itself. In the back of his mind somewhere he may have been thinking of his financial backers, but many times he used it when by no stretch of the imagination could it have meant anything or anybody but himself."

Lindbergh moved into room 447 of the U. S. Grant Hotel, downtown San Diego ($2.50 per night); but as he found himself spending most of the next two months camped out at the Ryan factory, he relocated to the YMCA, which was cheaper, and flopped some nights at the San Diego apartment of A. J. Edwards, the Ryan sales manager.

Lindbergh's formula for each element of the plane was: "first consideration to efficiency in flight; second, to protection in a crack-up; third, to pilot comfort." The initial application of that rule came in the placement of the plane's cockpit. Lindbergh wanted it set back in the fuselage, behind the gas tank. When Hall protested because that would preclude any forward vision, Lindbergh replied that there was not much of it in normal flight anyway, what with the nose of the fuselage blocking the view, and that he did not like the idea of being sandwiched between the engine and the gas tank. (When a former submariner at Ryan suggested a periscope—a three-by-five panel in the instrument board through which a frontal view could be obtained—Lindbergh acceded, but only upon Hall's assurance that it was of no "aerodynamical disadvantage.") Night-flying equipment, even parachutes, were sacrificed for the sake of weight, as each saved pound translated into more fuel, which meant greater range. Within days Hall had completed his drawing of the wing and fuselage structure; within the week steel tubes were being cut and welded to form the trusses of the body.

Time and the element of surprise remained of the essence, as the press was both catching and spreading "Atlantic fever." In early March, the news wires reported that Fokker expected to have a new three-engine monoplane for Commander Byrd ready for a May flight; Sikorsky's new plane for Fonck was meant to be built by then as well. Noel Davis's biplane with three Wright Whirlwinds—"The American Legion"—was scheduled for a June crossing. And from Paris came news that two French war aces, Charles Nungesser and the one-eyed François Coli, would have a single-engine plane capable of carrying eight hundred gallons of gasoline ready by summer. The name of Captain Lindbergh, "a St. Louis airmail pilot," was creeping into the press, as San Diego reporters started poking around the Ryan factory. A few short articles drew visitors hoping to catch a glimpse of the young "flying fool" who regarded all this as something other than a "suicidal venture."

"The St. Louis papers will naturally play up this flight for all the spectacular news they can obtain," Lindbergh warned his mother, "so don't pay any attention to their scare headlines. I have planned the flight carefully and with due consideration to single and multimotored ships." He kept trimming his list of emergency landing equipment to the barest essentials—a small,

black-rubber raft (ten pounds), a knife, some flares (stored in a bicycle in-
nertube) and matches, a hacksaw blade, basic fishing equipment, chocolate-
composition rations, and water. Then again, he reconsidered, water weighed
too much; and he had recently heard about a man named Armbrust who had
invented a cup that condensed moisture from one's breath into potable liquid. (If Lindbergh could wait until June, replied C. W. Armbrust to his inquiry, the cup would be in production and available for $7.50; otherwise, he
would have to pay fifty dollars for one of the handmade prototypes. Lindbergh sent a fifty-dollar check.) From A. G. Spalding & Bros. in New York,
he ordered a waterproof cloth suit with sheep wool lining and one long zip-
per after he learned it would weigh but nine pounds. He faced a dilemma
when a stamp collector offered him one thousand dollars to fly one pound
of mail to Paris. Lindbergh knew he had to inform his backers of such an
offer, which equalled any of their shares in the plane; and yet he felt he could
not carry so superfluous a pound. "The plane is nearing completion," he
wrote his mother on March twenty-seventh, "and will be ready for test during the first week in April."

  "I cannot remember one thing that you have ever done that has been to
your discredit," Evangeline wrote her son that March, as though convincing
herself of his safety. "It is a wonderful record you have made, boy." Even so,
she effused, "the happiest day for me will be the day you return." More
than once she stopped herself from overemoting, as on April second, when
she said "the last thing I wish to do is to burden you with sentiment or
bother you in any way." In another letter she did admit, however, "for the
first time in my life I realize that Columbus also had a mother."

  Alas, Columbus also had maritime experience, while Lindbergh had
never flown over great expanses of water nor even for any long distance.
Where Lindbergh had steered his course in the past according to visible landmarks below, he would have to navigate this trip by looking above, charting
a course based on time traveled and the position of the stars. He thought of
consulting with naval officers stationed in San Diego; but, he later admitted
thinking, there was "enough skepticism about my flight now, without adding
to it by showing how inexperienced I am in the technique of long-distance
navigation." Lindbergh decided to plot the course on his own, in private.

  He went to a ship chandler on the San Diego waterfront, but its only
ocean charts were of the Pacific. On March seventh, Lindbergh borrowed a
Ryan monoplane and flew to Los Angeles. In the harbor area of San Pedro
he found a store that sold every chart he could imagine necessary for his Atlantic crossing—Mercator's projections, a gnomonic projection, a time-zone
chart of the world, a chart of magnetic variation, even a few maps showing
prevailing winds over the Atlantic during the spring months. In order to get
the *Spirit of St. Louis* from California to New York, Lindbergh decided to

stand by the trusty guides he had always used, Rand McNally railroad maps available in drugstores for fifty cents per state.

While the Ryan employees created a skeleton for the wings out of spruce and double piano wire, Lindbergh prepared his course. Over a drafting table in Donald Hall's office he spread his charts and applied what he remembered from Army navigation class. He broke the great sweeping curve of his route into three dozen line segments—each representing one hundred miles, approximately one hour of flying time. "At each point," he recalled, "I marked down the distance from New York and the magnetic course to the next change in angle." He proceeded so quickly that he felt he should doublecheck his figures by working the route again, this time using trigonometry. After several days of tedious calculations that led to a virtual duplication of the first half of the course, he quit, extrapolating that the second half was just as correct. When he realized that his markings—"that curving, polygonic line, cutting fearlessly over thousands of miles of continent and ocean"—were enough to direct him to the final dot on the map labeled "Paris," he crossed off his equipment list any radios or even a sextant for further navigation. That savings was worth another twenty-five gallons of gasoline.

Donald Hall kept dashing off new drawings, while factory manager Hawley Bowlus often started work on parts of the plane without the final plans. The thirty-five Ryan employees labored day and night, seven days a week, sometimes round-the-clock, often voluntarily. A young mechanic named Douglas Corrigan, who was pulled from the field and put to work in the factory, remembered working several times past midnight, having to report back at eight the next morning. He said that "everyone was glad to do that as they all seemed to be inspired by the fellow the plane was being built for." Before the final covering was put on the wing, each member of the Ryan crew signed the front spar.

On April eighth, six weeks after Lindbergh had placed his order with Ryan, the motor arrived: Wright Whirlwind J-5C, serial number 7331—a nine-cylinder, air-cooled, radial engine operating on the four-stroke cycle. It weighed five hundred pounds, would normally operate at 1800 r.p.m., and harnessed the power of 223 horses. It was installed in the nose of the fuselage and housed in a cowling of aluminum that had "engine turning"—a circular jewel-like pattern in the burnished metal.

Meantime, the Contest Committee of the National Aeronautic Association accepted the application for the *Spirit of St. Louis*. Because of the many changes made on this "experimental" plane, however, the sixty-day clock for its eligibility would be ticking until the end of May. The license was mailed from Washington—number N-X 211, N being the international designation for the United States, and X signifying that the plane was experimental. For ten dollars, "Gus the Sign Painter" in San Diego went to the factory to bla-

zon in black the top of the right-hand wing and the bottom of the left with
the license number. Fred Ayers, who supervised the covering and finishing of
the plane, painted the number and RYAN NYP (which signified New York
to Paris) on the rudder. In clear block printing, with a few curlicues on the
word "Spirit," he affixed the plane's name on both sides of its "jeweled"
nose.

"FACTORY WORK COMPLETE TODAY," Lindbergh wired Harry Knight on April
twenty-fifth at almost two o'clock in the morning. The next step was to assemble the wing to the fuselage. That first meant getting the two pieces outside the building. Not until the workers removed the landing gear on one side
of the plane could they pass the fuselage through the great door of the Ryan
factory. The wing went less easily. In the constant revising of the plane's design, it had grown ten feet longer than originally planned; and, short of
knocking out part of the factory wall, there appeared no way of freeing it
from the second-story loft where it had been built. Measuring down to a fraction of an inch, they at last realized that by tilting it, they could slide it out
onto the top of an empty boxcar that could be pushed along a railroad siding next to the factory. From there the wing was lowered by contractor's der-
rick onto a waiting truck. The landing gear was re-assembled, and the
fuselage was hoisted up by its tail and attached to the back of Claude Ryan's
1925 Studebaker roadster, then towed tail-first to Dutch Flats, the Ryan test
field on the edge of the city.

Over the course of the next few days and nights, in a hangar at Dutch
Flats, the two great perpendicular pieces were attached. Every detail of the
plane was checked and re-checked until it was unanimously agreed that it
was ready to be pulled onto the dry, grassless field. After two months there
stood this structure of wood and cloth and metal—held together by bolts and
glue—not quite ten feet high. It was considerably shorter than it was wide—
twenty-seven feet, eight inches from spinner to rudder with a wingspan of
forty-six feet. The propeller, purchased from the Standard Steel Propeller
Company and made of duralumin, had two blades, pitched at 16.25 degrees, making a diameter of eight feet, nine inches. The tires of the landing
gear were thirty inches high by five inches. With the exception of the engine
cowling and propeller, practically every bit of the plane's exterior—wing,
fuselage, tail section, external struts (the wings' supports), axles, and tail
skid—was covered with grade A cotton fabric finished with cellulose acetate
dope, in silver-gray. Even the wheels had what appeared to be hubcaps made
of doped fabric laced to the tires, for the sake of streamlining.

Despite the prodigious effort of the Ryan team, Lindbergh had just written his mother that it was "probable that two attempts at the N.Y. Paris
flight will be made before I am ready to go. Either or both may succeed
altho in both cases there are reasons to throw doubt on the successful com-

pletion of the flight." He assured Evangeline that "we are not taking off before everything is ready, and if someone makes the N.Y.–Paris hop we will probably try a Trans-Pacific flight via Honolulu to Australia which would be a still greater accomplishment."

April was a cruel month. On the sixteenth, Commander Byrd's huge Fokker crash-landed on its first trial flight, injuring three crew members and damaging the plane enough to suggest that Byrd might have to forego his spring run for the Orteig Prize. Eight days later, Clarence Chamberlin in the coveted Bellanca, christened *Columbia,* almost met disaster when part of its landing gear tore loose during takeoff. And then on the twenty-sixth, just days before their scheduled departure for Paris, Noel Davis and Stanton Wooster, in the last of their test flights, crashed while taking off in the *American Legion.* They both died. Even before these three accidents, Lloyd's of London was giving odds of ten to one against any successful flight across the Atlantic in 1927.

"I am *glad,* more than glad, that you never get rattled—and always think clearly," Evangeline wrote Charles after reading about the Davis–Wooster crash, putting on her best face; "seems to me some of the N. Y.–Paris people have already been in too much of a hurry." The day after he read of the accident, Lindbergh stepped into the cockpit of his plane to begin its tests.

It felt "strange" settling into the wicker porch chair—with its air cushion—which virtually filled the cabin. The fuel tank before him loomed large, diminishing the instrument panel at eye level—a piece of plywood painted dull black with twenty-one switches, meters, and knobs set therein. Outside the ship, the chief mechanic turned the propeller over several times, contact was made, and the engine kicked in. Lindbergh checked each gauge, opened the throttle, and felt the wheels of the plane pawing at the chocks. He motioned for young Corrigan to duck under the wing and pull them away. The plane began to roll . . . picking up speed as it taxied.

Lindbergh had never felt a plane accelerate so fast, leaving the ground in less than one hundred feet. He spiraled upward to two thousand feet, saw that all his instruments were functioning, then flew over the factory, where its creators ran out to look at the results of their labor. Lindbergh saluted them by rocking the wings and headed out over the bay. Later in the day of that twenty-minute test flight, the three dozen Ryan employees lined up in front of the plane, from one wingtip to the other, for a team photograph, Lindbergh among them.

Over the next ten days, Lindbergh ran the plane through twenty-three test flights, varying in duration from five minutes to a little over an hour. The plane needed only minor adjustments. On May fourth, he performed nine trial runs, testing speed and load, each with a different amount of gasoline, ranging from thirty-eight gallons to three hundred. The day ended before he could attempt the ultimate load; but he knew to quit, if only so that he did not have to put that much stress on his tires, which presumably would never have to endure another landing bearing as much as three hundred gallons remaining in its tanks. "The test flights we have run here have been far above our theoretical performance," Lindbergh wrote his mother reassuringly. "The cruising range will be well over 4,200 miles and it is easily capable of a flight one third again as long as the present world's endurance record."

Stories had already spread that Lindbergh had been training himself to stay awake by taking long walks in San Diego at night. They were completely false. He did, however, fully intend to fly the first leg of his journey by night, to obtain eight hundred miles of practice in the dark. He made final preparations to take off on Friday, May sixth; but storms and fog drifted in, clouding the entire way from San Diego to St. Louis.

Suddenly, not even the weather mattered. Out of the blue, on Sunday the eighth, Nungesser and Coli left Paris's Le Bourget aerodrome in their Levasseur biplane, *L'oiseau blanc,* headed for New York. They were expected to capture the Orteig Prize by Monday. Lindbergh pulled out his charts of the Pacific.

Over the weekend, the ebullience ebbed. Despite the bold headlines, nobody had actually sighted *The White Bird* since it flew over the coast of France. By Sunday Lindbergh realized that the plane must have exhausted its fuel supply, downing Nungesser and Coli somewhere.

Lindbergh's backers and friends in St. Louis prepared for his arrival there. They wanted to throw him a banquet and christen his plane; but Lindbergh knew that the Bellanca stood ready in New York to fly to Paris. Sensing the narrowness of this window of opportunity, Lindbergh thought St. Louis could now be but a pit stop. "[I]f I'm to be successful," he thought, "I can't waste time on ceremonies." On Monday, he learned from the Weather Bureau that the inclement front was, at last, moving on. He went to bed early in preparation for a departure the next day.

On the morning of Tuesday, May tenth, Lindbergh packed a small traveling bag—weight he could afford to carry cross-country—and went to the Ryan factory to say thank-you and good-bye. As he walked out of the factory, one of the Ryan workers shouted, "Send us a wire when you get to Paris."

He drove to Dutch Flats, from which he flew his plane to North Island, home of both Army and Navy installations and Rockwell Field—a fiveminute hop. A gasoline truck waited to fill his plane. Because Lindbergh did not want to leave until day's end, he whiled away most of the afternoon with Donald Hall, lunching with officers, even burning off some nervous energy flying a new Navy Hawk fighter. At 3:15 he returned to his plane, surrounded by reporters and photographers. At 3:40 he climbed into his flying suit, knowing he would not be able to get into it once in the air. At five of four, he decided not to wait any longer. Within seconds he was airborne, escorted by two Army observation planes and a Ryan monoplane.

They went once around North Island, saluted the factory, and headed for St. Louis. The escorts turned back after ninety minutes, leaving Lindbergh to fly into the night that was descending upon the southwestern deserts and Rockies. Except for some engine hacking over Arizona—probably ice forming in the carburetor—the flight proceeded without incident. By sunrise he was entering familiar barnstorming country and was able to deduce that tail winds had pushed him considerably during the night. He landed at Lambert Field at 8:20 Central Standard Time, having flown fifteen hundred miles in fourteen hours and twenty-five minutes, a record for a nonstop flight that distance.

The Robertson brothers and several of his aviation friends greeted him, gathering round Louie's lunch shack while Lindbergh ate ham and eggs. Bill Robertson handed Lindbergh his newly arrived transport-pilot's license, number 69. One of Slim's former flying students, Father Henry Hussman, pastor of St. Henry's Church in St. Louis, presented him a silver medal of Our Lady of Loretto, the patroness of aviators. Representatives of the Vacuum Oil Company, makers of Mobiloil "B," which would be used in the forthcoming flight, assured him that their oil would be ready for him in New York, as would a hotel room and hangar. Knight and Bixby arrived to discuss the options available to him that evening, but Lindbergh first wanted a status report on *The White Bird* and the Bellanca. As there was no news about either flight—Chamberlin still had not left and Nungesser and Coli had not arrived—Lindbergh told his backers, "I'll stay as long as you want me to. But I think I ought to go right on to New York. If I don't, somebody else will beat us to the take-off."

Bixby and Knight agreed. Lindbergh retired early—at his former boardinghouse—and left Lambert Field a little after eight the next morning. Seven hours and twenty-two minutes later, he landed in New York at Curtiss Field, outside Mineola on Long Island. He had crossed the entire country in less than twenty-two hours of flying time, another record. Hundreds waited on the field for him.

Even before the brakeless *Spirit of St. Louis* had rolled to a stop, it was engulfed by newspaper photographers and reporters. "Why can't they wait until I taxi to the line and stop my engine?" Lindbergh wondered. "They'd have better pictures, it would save a lot of time, and I wouldn't have to worry about anyone getting hurt." A wave of mechanics approached, who instinctively cleared a way for the plane.

In a mock ceremony, Casey Jones, the Curtiss company's famous test pilot and airport manager, acted as "mayor" of the field and presented Lindbergh with an old set of office keys. He also provided him a hangar for his plane. Richard Blythe, a partner in the public relations firm of Bruno & Blythe, which had been hired by the Wright Aeronautical Corporation, offered whatever help the flier required. Even before Lindbergh could request a mechanic to examine his engine, Blythe introduced Ken Boedecker and Ed Mulligan, from the Wright organization; the former was one of the company's field service representatives, the latter had been assigned specifically to Lindbergh's plane. After posing Lindbergh for photographs, Blythe ushered him into a press conference, at which the questions quickly descended from aviation to "How do you feel about girls?" After the interview, a tabloid reporter told Lindbergh that his editor wanted to pay several thousand dollars for the exclusive rights to his story.

A small entourage took Lindbergh to the nearby Garden City Hotel, which would become his base until his departure for Paris. Over supper, he learned the status of the contestants vying for the Orteig Prize. Rumors of a rescue of Nungesser and Coli abounded, but there was still not one confirmed report since France of anybody's having seen them. Meantime, Richard Byrd's repaired Fokker—*America*—was resting in a hangar on Roosevelt Field, an adjacent airport, separated from Curtiss by a steep drop. The Bellanca *Columbia* waited in another hangar on Curtiss Field, detained by the weather and personnel problems. The plane's owner, Charles Levine, kept changing his mind as to which two fliers would make the trip.

The men from Wright had engines in all three ships on the airfields of Hempstead Plains. Their task was to service each of them without showing favoritism toward any pilot. After supper Blythe and Boedecker took Lindbergh back to Curtiss Field, where Mulligan was fine-tuning the *Spirit of St. Louis*. He and Boedecker worked past midnight, leaving Lindbergh to retire for the night. By then, Lindbergh's arrival in New York had plainly roused the two other camps into activity.

But there there would be no takeoffs for Paris the next day or for several after that, as bad weather occluded the entire route across the Atlantic. With each passing hour, the number of people from the press grew, as did the number of rubberneckers hoping to get a glimpse of the "dark horse." Fortunately, the rivalry among the pilots remained friendly.

Late that night when Ed Mulligan had inspected Lindbergh's plane, for example, he had noticed a small crack developing in the spinner cap—the propeller's noseguard. By the following morning, the Curtiss Company, one of the Wright Corporation's competitors, was constructing and installing a new one free of charge. Over the next few days, Bellanca and Chamberlin wandered over to see Lindbergh and to wish him luck. Even Commander Byrd paid a call, offering weather information and free use of his runway at Roosevelt Field.

Lindbergh inspected Byrd's runway and found it provided "a longer and better take-off run than I expected to find anywhere around New York." He took the *Spirit of St. Louis* up for six short flights over the next three days. Back on the ground Lindbergh kept revising his lists of every item that would accompany him—from the breeches he would wear to the paper cups into which he would urinate.

The media took a shine to Lindbergh, not only because he was physically the most attractive of all the fliers but also because he was the freshest face in town and the only pilot to make the journey alone. He became the "Human Meteor," the "Flyin' Fool," and the "Kid Flyer." The press did all they could to build him up; and as the wait for Nungesser and Coli dragged on, Lindbergh filled the slot in the front-page headlines. Photographers barged into his Garden City Hotel room trying to snap a picture of him shaving. Reporters in Detroit began to hound his mother. On May thirteenth, she wired her son that she would be arriving in New York the next day.

"Good Lord!" Lindbergh thought. After months of convincing her of the safety of his trip, the press had smoked her out. Although he secretly blamed them for shaking her confidence, he maintained a facade of friendly indifference while they exploited the story of a gray-haired mother bidding farewell to her all-American boy.

Lindbergh met Evangeline at the Garden City train station on Saturday morning, May fourteenth. Borrowing a car, he drove her to Curtiss Field, where she watched him make two test flights. His worst fears about her visit were realized when the press hurled insensitive questions at her, playing up the danger of the flight. Still, mother and son posed dutifully for the photographers, though Mrs. Lindbergh drew the line when one of the cameramen asked Evangeline to kiss her son good-bye. "No," she said with a slightly embarrassed smile. "I wouldn't mind if we were used to that, but we come of an undemonstrative Nordic race."

After a quiet lunch at a restaurant in Hempstead, the Lindberghs returned to the train depot and talked in the car. It had not been much of a visit, just enough to reassure Evangeline that her son "really wanted to go and felt it was the right thing to do." When her train pulled in they got out and she patted his shoulder. "Well, son," she said, "good-bye and good luck." She waved to him from the train window as it pulled away—perhaps, the press suggested, for the last time. Lindbergh was hardly surprised the next day to see one newspaper had a photograph of him kissing his mother, a faked composite picture that substituted their heads onto the bodies of two other people.

Lindbergh now waited only for the weather to change. Fog blanketed the seaboard up to Canada's Maritime Provinces. With time on his hands, he went to Manhattan to tie up loose ends. Carrying photographs he had had taken in St. Louis a few months earlier for just this purpose, he went to the New York Passport Agency and filed an application; the agents issued a passport on the spot. While in the city he called on meteorologist Dr. James H. Kimball at the weather bureau atop the Whitehall Building in the Battery. Kimball spread out his latest weather map and explained how all the isobars were conspiring to make the skies impenetrable. Dr. Kimball wished Lindbergh would take a more southerly route, for the ships in the sea lanes could provide more accurate reports.

With no clearing in sight, Lindbergh became more sociable. He accepted a luncheon invitation to the Oyster Bay home of Colonel Theodore Roosevelt, Jr., who wrote Lindbergh several letters of introduction to friends in Europe, including the American Ambassador. Those, he decided, would be the last ounces of functionless weight he would carry, for he had already agreed to take two other pieces of mail—one for Postmaster Conkling of Springfield, the other for his flying friend Gregory Brandeweide, who had helped him lay out the mail route.

Lindbergh avoided the crowds amassing back at the field as much as possible, but he was happy to make the acquaintance of some of the biggest names in aviation. René Fonck and Tony Fokker stopped by to say hello, as did Charles Lawrance, the president of Wright, and C. M. Keys of Curtiss. Harry Guggenheim, who administered a fund that promoted aviation, made the greatest impression. "I didn't think Lindbergh had much chance to make it," Guggenheim later confessed. In fact, he was "indignant with the authorities for letting him go off on this highly *doubtful* adventure" with so little of "the equipment and aids to navigation available at that time." But Guggenheim masked his concern, extending only encouragement upon saying good-bye. "When you get back," he said, "look me up at the Fund's office."

Charles remained jovial, though in his efforts to lessen the tension, his humor reverted to its most juvenile. Ken Boedecker remembered seeing him pour a whole box of rough bran down the back of Franklin Mahoney, who had come east for the takeoff. One day, Dick Blythe tried to take Lindbergh's mind off the flight for a few hours by taking him to Coney Island. He seemed to lose himself at the amusement park, chuting the chutes, eating hot dogs and popcorn, and listening to the sideshow barkers. "He was happy as a kid turned loose in Coney Island for the first time," wrote Blythe's partner, Harry Bruno, until a woman recognized him and shrieked his name. "Get me out of here," Lindbergh said, and they hightailed it back to Garden City.

The stack of mail in his hotel helped distract him. There were messages from friends, relatives, and complete strangers as well as requests from scores of people for Lindbergh to carry mail for them, which he was meant to post from Paris. Most expected him to perform this service for free, a few enclosed a dollar. Several theatrical agents—including William Morris himself—asked if they could book him upon completion of his flight on a lecture circuit. The president of the Vitamin Food Company wrote Lindbergh that the "crossing will depend on your clear head, steady nerves and endurance," and that without "any thought of advertising" he could not resist sending several jars of his product Vegex—a vegetable extract which "can be taken into the plane in a thermos bottle like coffee or . . . eaten with crackers or bread." As Evangeline wrote her son upon her safe return to Detroit, "You have upset the country's equilibrium."

The other fliers were as excitable as thoroughbreds waiting in the paddock. Byrd's business partner, Rodman Wanamaker, was insisting that Byrd run their Fokker through more tests; a disgruntled former member of the Bellanca team was taking formal action against Levine, legally restraining the plane from taking off. More than ever Lindbergh was grateful that he was flying alone and that he was supported by a team in St. Louis who let him be. That week, he called Harry Knight to say that he would probably be ready to leave before completing the sixty-day waiting period for eligibility for the $25,000 prize. "To hell with the money," Knight told him. "When you're ready to take off, go ahead."

A light rain fell that Thursday, May nineteenth, and all prospects for a departure in the next few days dimmed. With some of his new friends, Lindbergh visited the Wright plant in Paterson, New Jersey. At day's end, they drove into New York City, where Dick Blythe had arranged for Lindbergh to watch one of the season's biggest Broadway hits, "Rio Rita," from backstage. They were driving east on Forty-second Street, when Kenneth Lane, chief airplane engineer for Wright, asked if they should not call Dr. Kimball for the latest weather report.

They pulled over to an office building so that Blythe could telephone. Lindbergh looked up, only to see the tops of the Manhattan skyline enshrouded in fog. Blythe ran back to the car, however, to announce that there had been a sudden change in the atmosphere—a high pressure area was starting to clear patches of weather over the ocean. Putting Broadway behind them, they headed for the East River and grabbed a bite in the Queensboro Plaza. Lindbergh mentally ran through the final checklist. Thinking ahead, Dick Blythe dashed around the corner to a drugstore, where he bought six sandwiches for Slim's trip. The weather was still too nasty to move the plane over to Roosevelt Field, but enough preparations could be made during the night to allow for an early morning departure. They could start by pumping the first hundred gallons of gasoline into the plane while it was still in the hangar. Lane said he would oversee that as well as the final inspection of the plane with his colleagues from Wright. And somebody would have to notify

Carl Schory, the Secretary of the National Aeronautic Association, who would install the recording barograph—which would mark time and altitude on a revolving paper cylinder—the mandatory documentation of the flight.

Strangely, they found few signs of activity in the other camps back at the airfield. Lindbergh had already had a long day; so after a few hours working with his team on his plane, he returned to the Garden City Hotel. Nothing was definite, as Dr. Kimball had hardly promised clear skies—just enough of an opening for a good airmail pilot to get through. "I'll be ready at daybreak," he thought, "and decide then whether or not to start."

6

PERCHANCE
TO DREAM

*"How are we to distinguish the difference between
reality and dream? Dreams result from a relationship
of atoms. So do our bodies."*

—C.A.L.

ALL HE WANTED WAS TO SLEEP, BUT WHEN LINDBERGH RE-
turned to the Garden City Hotel just before midnight, he
found it bustling with activity. An army of reporters clattering
away at typewriters had appropriated the lobby, and they were
all eager to interview him. Lindbergh politely excused himself
from their questions, insisting that he had to go to bed. Even
a long nap, he felt, would sustain him for the thirty-six-hour
ordeal that lay ahead.

The journalists let him retire in peace, as even the hardest-
boiled members of the press no longer attempted to hide their
admiration. Lindbergh's modest manner "won the hearts of
every one who came near him"—as Russell Owens phrased it
in his next front-page piece for the *Times*—partly because he
stood in such sharp contrast to the rest of the current news-
makers—bootleggers, racketeers, and millionaire playboys.
That very day the press carried a story about oilman Harry
Sinclair's jail sentence for his role in the Teapot Dome scandal
and another about an anarchistic maniac who dynamited a
school, killing forty-two children. Charles Augustus Lindbergh
seemed the perfect antidote to toxic times.

It had rained on the opening of the horse-racing season at
nearby Belmont Park that day, but journalists had the derby of
the century to write about. Although Lindbergh did not know
it, Clarence Chamberlin had received the same optimistic

weather report that he had; and Kenneth Boedecker from the Wright Company was preparing the Bellanca *Columbia* for a morning departure as well. Although there seemed to be no sign of activity from the Byrd stable, it struck Lindbergh that the Fokker, *America,* hangared at Roosevelt Field, was in pole position. It could roll right onto the runway, while the *Spirit of St. Louis* would have to be towed there from Curtiss Field.

Lindbergh's backers in St. Louis had thoughtfully sent a member of their Chamber of Commerce, a Missouri National Guardsman named George Stumpf, to Long Island to serve as an aide-de-camp. Lindbergh had no duties for him until that moment, when he asked him to see that he was not disturbed until 2:15, at which time he wished to be awakened.

He was just drifting off when he heard several loud knocks on the door. It was Stumpf. "Slim," the young man asked, "what am I going to do when you're gone?"

"I don't know," Lindbergh managed to say politely. "There are plenty of other problems to solve before we have to think about that one." Now wide awake, he began to consider them all. By 1:40, he realized he would not be getting any sleep that night.

At 2:30, he was back downstairs, dressed in his flying outfit—Army breeches and boots, a light jacket over his shirt, a blue-and-red diagonally striped tie from Vandervoort's in St. Louis. Frank Tichenor and Jessie Horsfall, the publisher and editor of *Aero Digest,* drove him to Curtiss Field. They arrived a little before three in a slow-dripping rain. Through the dark mist Lindbergh saw a crowd of more than five hundred onlookers.

As the steady drizzle kept him inside, there was nothing to do but recheck all the preparations. He and his instrument specialist realized that it would be difficult to read the compass that had been affixed over the pilot's wicker chair and that it should somehow have been incorporated into the instrument panel. A young woman in the waiting crowd came to the rescue with a round compact mirror; a man chewing gum provided the adhesive.

At 4:15, the rain had practically stopped, and weather reports from Massachusetts, Maine, Nova Scotia, and Newfoundland all reported clearings. A few members of the press were allowed to sit inside the hangar while Lindbergh ate a sandwich. When he finished, he ordered his plane wheeled outside. When the soaked crowd of faithfuls discerned the tall, lanky figure, it let out a cheer.

There were no indications of anybody else's taking off that morning as the tailskid of the *Spirit of St. Louis* was lifted and lashed to the back of a motor truck and the engine was shrouded in a tarpaulin. With an escort of six Nassau County motorcycle patrolmen, the plane was hauled to Roosevelt Field. By then word had it that Byrd's backer still believed his plane needed more testing, and the courts were still restraining Chamberlin from taking Levine's Bellanca. The drizzle persisted as the plane was tugged up a gravel road toward the runway. At one point in the muddy journey, they reached ruts deep enough to damage the plane; the caravan waited until some boards were set down to bridge them. Carefully watching his plane, Lindbergh thought, "It's more like a funeral procession than the beginning of a flight to Paris."

The *Spirit of St. Louis* was positioned at the western end of the runway at Roosevelt Field, its nose pointing toward Paris. It would have five thousand feet in which to leave the ground and gain enough altitude to clear telephone wires at the end of the field. Were it a less soggy day, Lindbergh would not have questioned his ability to take off. But with a field turned to mire, no headwinds, and air so heavy that it would lower the engine's r.p.m., the fate of prior overburdened planes raced through his mind.

A truck carrying barrels of the *Spirit of St. Louis*'s fuel supply pulled up, and a small bucket brigade formed. Over the next few hours—just yards from where two members of Fonck's crew had taxied to a fiery death eight months earlier—Ken Lane stood on the engine cowl, slowly pouring gasoline from red five-gallon cans through chamois, filtering the fuel as he filled the plane's five tanks. An ambulance from the Nassau County Hospital rolled onto the field, down to that point at the runway from which the plane was meant to leave the ground.

Hundreds were drawn to Roosevelt Field that morning. People on their way to work joined the all-night revelers on their way home. Besides Lindbergh, they could glimpse some of the most important figures in aviation, including rivals Byrd and Chamberlin along with Bernt Balchen, Bert Acosta, René Fonck, and the attractive "lady flyer" Ruth Nichols. The Dutch manufacturer Anthony Fokker was there, as was a recent Yale graduate named Juan Trippe, the managing director of Colonial Air Transport, which held the airmail contract between New York, Hartford, and Boston. As if to prove that he could have made the journey that day, Byrd asked Lindbergh if he might borrow his own runway to make a trial flight in the *America*. For almost two hours, Byrd put his three-motored Fokker through its paces, cutting in and out of the fog, landing just as Lindbergh's plane was made ready.

By 7:30 on the morning of May 20, 1927, each of the *Spirit*'s tanks was filled to its brim—451 gallons of gasoline, weighing some 2,750 pounds. In addition to the empty plane's basic weight (including equipment and instruments) of 2,150 pounds, there were 140 pounds (twenty gallons) of oil, Lindbergh's 170 pounds (fully clothed), and forty miscellaneous pounds, which included his letters of introduction from Colonel Roosevelt and a bank draft arranged by the St. Louis backers from the Equitable Trust Company of New York for 12,755.10 francs, the equivalent of $500. Frank Tichenor of *Aero Digest* asked if the five sandwiches he was taking were enough. "If I get to Paris," Lindbergh said, "I won't need any more, and if I don't get to Paris, I won't need any more, either." One bystander offered Lindbergh a kitten as a mascot, and several others pressed talismans upon him. Several newspapers would report his taking them, but a pilot who had refused to take navigational equipment, had torn unnecessary pages from his notebook, and had trimmed the margins from his maps to save weight was hardly about to stow a cat—to say nothing of rabbits' feet, wishbones, and horseshoes.

Unwittingly, however, he did pocket a St. Christopher medal. Lindbergh, in his flying suit and leather helmet, had just settled in the cockpit, when he suddenly jumped out. He thought he had forgotten his passport. A member of his crew pointed out the small rack behind him, which held his flashlight and papers. For another moment he paused, looked at the leaden sky, then at the bulging wheels of the *Spirit* sinking into the muddy runway. While he stood there, a woman named Katie Butler, who had come out that morning with a group of Glen Cove schoolteachers, called a policeman over. She removed her St. Christopher from around her neck and whispered some instructions to him. "The officer nodded, took the gift over to the aviator, and put it in his hand," remembered one of the teachers, who then distinctly saw Lindbergh "accept it distractedly and slip it into his pocket without examining it."

At 7:40, Lindbergh reapproached his plane, shook hands with Richard Byrd, and boarded. Ed Mulligan spun the propeller, and Kenneth "Boady" Boedecker twisted the booster magneto, designed to provide a hotter spark. The engine let out a roar, and the chocked airplane tried to buck loose. Lindbergh saw all the gauges before him spin into action, but the tachometer registered only 1,470 r.p.m., thirty revolutions low as a result of the weather.

Ten minutes passed, while the pilot collected himself, pulling together all his flying experience of the past four years: 7,189 flights, 1,790 hours and ten minutes in the air, thirty-two flights in the *Spirit* without incident. He knew conditions were less than favorable. The slight tailwind could be dangerous when taking off from west to east; the humid air had the skin of his plane covered in cold sweat; the horizon was veiled in mist; the engine still had not revved up to 1,500 r.p.m.; and the *Spirit* had never been tested carrying so much weight.

At 7:51 A.M., Lindbergh buckled his safety belt, stuffed each ear with a wad of cotton, strapped on his wool-lined helmet, and pulled his goggles down over his eyes. Turning to Mulligan and Boedecker, he said, "What do you say—let's try it." They went to the blocks, and he nodded. As the wheels were freed, Lindbergh eased his throttle wide open.

In covering the event for the entire world to see, the Fox Film Corporation employed a brand-new technique for their newsreels, a sound-on-film process which they called "Movietone." As the engine spluttered louder and louder, several men under each wing pushed on the struts, finally getting the two-ton, winged gasoline tank to move. It picked up speed, but inside the plane Lindbergh felt the stick wobble, assuming none of the outside pressure required to give the plane lift. At last the vehicle was sloshing forward fast enough to leave the men in its muddy wake, as it fishtailed down the runway.

After more than a thousand feet had passed beneath him, Lindbergh felt play then strength in the stick. At the halfway mark on the runway—the point at which he had to decide whether or not to abort the flight—the *Spirit* still had not reached flying speed, but he felt "the load shifting from wheels to wings." Coordinating his hand-on-throttle and foot-on-rudder movements with the view of the approaching telephone lines, which he could see only by leaning out the side windows, Lindbergh felt the plane leave the ground, only to return again. With less than two thousand feet of runway before him, he picked up speed and, now whooshing through puddles, managed to get the plane to jump off the ground again, only to bounce a second time. With less than a thousand feet, he attempted to lift the plane sharply enough to clear the web of wires in front of it.

At 7:54, the plane was airborne—ten feet above a tractor on the field, over a gully into which he easily could have crashed, and clearing the telephone wires by twenty feet. The cheer of the crowd ripped the air.

The plane headed toward open country, over a golf course and a line of trees. As if catching its breath, it descended slightly, only to regain altitude and slowly climb ever higher. Its wing dipped and caught a glint of the day's first sunlight. "God be with him," said Richard Byrd standing by his plane on the runway. "I think he has a 3-to-1 chance." Clarence Chamberlin said, "My heart was in my throat," as he pulled for the plane to get off the ground. "It was a splendid start," he added, "one of the most thrilling I've ever seen. It took guts." Bert Acosta, who had joined the Byrd team, said he thought Lindbergh was "taking a long chance. You must remember he is alone and has only one motor. If I were inclined to be superstitious, however, I might say that he has a good chance, for he is above all things a lucky flier." Floyd Bennett, who had accompanied Byrd to the North Pole and recently been injured testing the plane for the New York-to-Paris run, also had second thoughts about flying with only one engine; but, he reminded people, the venture depended at least as much on "whether he can keep awake thirty-six hours." Over the AP wire from London came news that Lloyd's was not quoting odds on Lindbergh's chances, because they believed "the risk is too great."

After two minutes in the air the *Spirit of St. Louis* had ascended to two hundred feet, a height safe enough from which to land if necessary; his airspeed was one hundred miles per hour, and the engine was cruising at 1,750

Scandal drove Charles Lindbergh's paternal grandfather—Ola Månsson—to America, where he and his second wife, Louisa, raised their family. They changed their surname to Lindbergh and called their firstborn (standing) Charles August. He became known as C.A.

Charles H. Land—Lindbergh's maternal grandfather—known as the "Father of Porcelain Dentistry"—taught young Charles that "Science is the key to all mystery."

C. A. Lindbergh in 1901—when he was known as "the brightest lawyer in Minnesota" and the handsomest man in Little Falls.

Evangeline Lodge Land left Detroit to teach science in Little Falls, where she fell in love with C.A.

Evangeline Lodge Land Lindbergh and her newborn son, Charles Augustus Lindbergh, in 1902.

Charles had a lonely childhood, with few friends other than his pets. Posed here, in 1913, with Dingo.

The Lindbergh marriage was unhappy, practically from the start. Charles spent most of his time with his doting mother.

C.A. found new passion in politics. Although he and his wife kept separate residences in Washington during his five terms as a Congressman, Evangeline always encouraged Charles to spend time with his father.

C.A. campaigning in northern Minnesota.

Some of Charles's happiest childhood moments were spent on the Upper Mississippi.

In 1920, Charles Lindbergh entered the University of Wisconsin. His mother moved to
Madison to be with him.

After flunking out of college his sophomore year, Lindbergh rode his Excelsior motorcycle to Nebraska, where he learned to fly.

Barnstorming in the 1920s with his friend Harlan "Bud" Gurney.

Second Lieutenant
Charles A. Lindbergh.

Charles A. Lindbergh
(1925)

In 1924, Lindbergh joined the Army Air Corps and was stationed at Brooks Field, Texas.

November 1926. By the time airmail-pilot Lindbergh's plane had gone down for the second time on the St. Louis–Chicago run, he had already been dreaming of the Orteig Prize—$25,000 for the first pilot to fly nonstop between New York and Paris.

The following spring, his plane was built—for $10,580, which he had raised from several businessmen in St. Louis.

May 1927. Lindbergh takes the *Spirit of St. Louis* on a test flight from a Long Island runway. The press was already making the most of the story.

Evangeline L. L. Lindbergh visits her son just before his death-defying flight. "For the first time in my life," she told him, "I realize that Columbus also had a mother."

May 22, 1927. Paris. The "day after." With Ambassador Myron T. Herrick.

June 13, 1927. Lower Broadway. The hero returns.

Triumph. New
York City.

The spirit of St. Louis. Local boy comes home.

Dwight W. Morrow in 1926, just before he ended his career as a partner at J. P. Morgan to become Ambassador to Mexico. Seated with (clockwise) wife, Elizabeth, and children, Elisabeth, Anne, Constance, and Dwight Jr.

In 1930, Anne gave birth to their first child, Charles A. Lindbergh, Jr.

After only a few secret dates, the "Prince of the Air" married the Ambassador's daughter in 1929. Even Anne's old friends congratulated *her*.

Charles and Anne Morrow Lindbergh became international celebrities—the "First Couple of the Skies."

Exploring cliff dwellings in New Mexico in 1929, during one of their whirlwind expeditions.

Anne (photographed
in Nanking) became
Charles's copilot,
navigator, and radio
operator.

Japan, 1931—just before learning of the sudden death of Anne's
father, then a United States Senator from New Jersey.

Anne in the early 1930s
was anxious to develop
her own identity.

Her first book, *North to the Orient*, became the first of many bestsellers.

r.p.m. Past the worry of getting an untested amount of weight off the ground, Lindbergh was able at last to address the next challenge of his journey—navigation. He got his bearings, banking his plane until the needle of his earth-inductor compass reached the center line, 65 degrees, the compass heading for the first segment he had marked on his chart back in San Diego only weeks earlier. He pulled out his map of New York state, to check as often as possible for corresponding landmarks.

Over the grand estates of Long Island he flew low, watching the haze lift over Connecticut. Only then did Lindbergh notice that he was being pursued by Casey Jones, flying a Curtiss Oriole filled with reporters and photographers. He resented their presence. But upon reaching the Sound, the escort plane dipped its wing and turned back, leaving the next thirty-six hundred miles of sky to Lindbergh alone.

Within the hour Richard Blythe sent a wire to Evangeline Lindbergh at Cass Technical High School in Detroit: "CHARLES LEFT AT SEVEN FIFTY ONE THIS MORNING AFTER WONDERFUL TAKE OFF HE WAS FEELING RESTED AND VERY FIT HE WILL BE IN PARIS NEXT." Trying to go about her business as usual, Mrs. Lindbergh asked her principal to make no mention of her son's trip during school hours. She lunched at a small restaurant on Woodward Avenue, as was her custom; but the mob of well-wishing students, strangers on the street, and the press corps made it impossible for her not to issue a statement. Although she knew Charles would want her to say as little as possible, some of her anxiety surfaced. "Tomorrow, Saturday, a holiday for me," she said, "will be either the happiest day in my whole life, or the saddest. Saturday afternoon at 3 o'clock I shall begin looking for word from Paris—not before that." Until then, said Evangeline—hurrying home toward the house at 178 Ashland Avenue that she shared with her brother—"My heart and soul is with my boy on his perilous journey."

New Yorkers instinctively congregated in Times Square, where they hoped to find bulletins about Lindbergh's progress posted on the Broadway side of the Times Square Building. That day alone, the *Times* received more than six hundred telephone inquiries for information.

The American Embassy in Paris had earlier indicated that the French government might frown upon an American attempt at the Orteig Prize while Nungesser and Coli were still missing, but that proved to be misinformation. Their Minister of Marine ordered the big air beacon at Cherbourg lighted to guide Captain Lindbergh inland from the French coast. And the Police Commissioner of Aubervilliers met with aviation authorities at nearby Le Bourget to discuss the possibility of providing extra gendarmes to police the main street leading to the small landing field.

That same day, another attempt at a record-breaking flight commenced. Two members of the Royal Air Force, C. R. Carr and L. S. M. Gillman, took off in a Hawker-Horsley bomber from the Crandley Airdrome outside London bound for Karachi, India, four thousand miles away. The British proudly focused on their own airmen, attempting what was, after all, a longer flight than Lindbergh's; the Associated Press reported that the general English impression of Lindbergh's flight was that it was "foolhardy." But after a few sniffs of disdain, they would be won over by the young American's gallantry, impressed that he was flying alone—over water, which offered little hope of salvation if his plane went down. By day's end, Lindbergh's flight, not Carr and Gillman's, commanded their attention.

Sixty-five vessels traveled the North Atlantic sea lanes that day, but fewer than twenty were believed to be anywhere near Lindbergh's route. Shipping Board statisticians said that "because of uncertainty as to the time of sailing or speed of some of the vessels," none of them could be relied upon for sightings of Lindbergh's plane. Nonetheless, the captain of the S. S. *President Roosevelt,* then sailing from Bremen to New York, altered its course to the north so that it might parallel Lindbergh's; he ordered a searchlight to scan the sky from midnight until dawn.

The flight's first great risk, that of his plane being overloaded with fuel, was behind him. There still remained, however, the possibility of engine failure. Although his Wright Whirlwind had thus far performed precisely, it had never been put to so severe a test—thirty-six nonstop hours of operation, probably through a variety of dangerous weather conditions. "The engine had to make 14,472,000 explosions perfectly and smoothly," noted Lieutenant L. B. Umlauf, aviation engineer for Vacuum Oil. "Even a minor engine problem might bring a sudden and fatal end to a brave and thrilling adventure."

One hour and one hundred miles out of Roosevelt Field, the curtain of mist over Long Island Sound rose. Thirty-five miles obliquely across the Sound to the mouth of the Connecticut River—the most water he had ever flown over—set the stage for what lay ahead—"the trackless wastes, the great solitude, the desertlike beauty of the ocean." Alone in the cockpit, Lindbergh had been at work constantly since his departure. Every fifteen minutes, he had manipulated the system of petcocks regulating gasoline flow, so that a little fuel was used from each tank. He started his second hour by switching to the fuselage fuel tank, off which the plane would feed for an hour. For the duration of the flight he would change tanks every hour, marking a score on his instrument panel at each change-over. He also entered hourly notations in pencil on a white-paper log-sheet he had drawn up in black India ink—a grid in which he would fill in data pulled from each of the dials on the panel before him. At the start of his third hour, he had no more use for his fourth state map—New York, Connecticut, Rhode Island, and Massachusetts lay behind him, unlimited visibility ahead.

Over the Atlantic Ocean, Lindbergh faced his "first real test" of navigation—250 miles without a landmark, just water in every direction. Not until he approached Nova Scotia would he be able to determine how accurate his chart-work back in San Diego had been. He had told himself before commencing the flight that if Nova Scotia were too obscured by fog for him to measure his position, he would turn back to New York. If, on the other hand, he had proceeded accurately enough to compensate for any errors made thus far, he would proceed to the next checkpoint.

With the late-morning sun beating through the *Spirit*'s plastic skylight, Lindbergh felt uncomfortable in his thick flying suit. It occurred to him that it had been more than twenty-four hours since he had actually slept. His helmet and goggles long since removed, he unzipped the suit to cool himself and took a swig of water from his quart canteen. Then he began a discussion with himself insisting that he "must stay alert, and match quality of plane and engine with quality of piloting and navigation. I'd be ashamed to have anyone know I feel tired when I'm just starting."

At noon Nova Scotia appeared. He was slightly dismayed that the large, hilly island had "crept in unobserved" in a quarter of an hour for which he could not account; but he was heartened when he realized that he was only six miles off his mark, a scant two degrees. Over the next four hours he traversed the province. Although he had not eaten in six hours, he forewent lunch, limiting himself to another drink of water. "Mustn't take too much," he told himself, ". . . suppose I'm forced down at sea!" And though the plane was carrying two plastic windows which could be easily inserted, he felt they would adversely curtail the ventilation within the cockpit. He preferred to sacrifice comfort for "the crystal clarity of communion with water, land, and sky."

As the Nova Scotia countryside grew more rugged, the wind kicked up, dark clouds formed, and the air got choppy. Lindbergh made a few short detours but just as happily flew right through some squalls, finding the cold, wet air bracing. By the time he had reached Cape Breton Island, there were clear skies ahead and another two hundred miles of water until Newfoundland.

This was the last jump before making the great leap of faith across the Atlantic. The water was a welcome sight—until he began flying over it again. The virtually constant image of the waves took on a hypnotic monotony. With only eight hours behind him, Lindbergh's eyes were feeling "dry and hard as stones." He was already forcing himself to keep them open, then squeezing them closed as tightly as possible.

The blur below was suddenly sharpened by the appearance of an ice field—huge white cakes reflecting the sun setting behind him. The bright glare against the black sea jolted him to alertness. He realized that he could not rely on natural phenomenon to keep awake; he would have to devise his own means of keeping his senses keen—updating his log, occasionally sipping water. From Placentia Bay to Avalon Peninsula, Newfoundland, he flew toward the approaching night; and at twilight—7:15 by his clock, 8:15 local time—he deviated slightly from his great circle route so that he could fly low over the small city of St. John's, neatly tucked into its deep harbor. It would be his last contact with land until Ireland, and he wanted people to know that he had traveled at least that far. One St. John's merchant was almost close enough to the plane to read its serial number painted underwing; and a member of Newfoundland's cabinet out motoring spotted the plane and followed it along the road as far as he could until . . . the *Spirit of St. Louis* had cleared the wharves below and reached the wide open sea.

In the final moments of dusk, Lindbergh was startled by the sight of an iceberg below. The one soon gave way to many—streaked in gray wisps. And in a moment Lindbergh faced a scrim of fog, followed by the curtain of night.

The second act of Lindbergh's transatlantic journey began in complete darkness—a moonless black night above, a darker ocean below. He would still have a few hours in which to turn back. But while reachable land lay behind him, daylight did not.

For the next fifteen hours, there would be a complete blackout on news from the *Spirit of St. Louis*. Except for the minute chance of a ship at sea spotting him the next day, he was completely detached from the world— bound to the planet only by the gravity which he and his machine would have to resist for another twenty-four hours. While Lindbergh later wrote that no man before him had commanded such freedom of movement over earth, he failed to note that no man before him had ever been so much alone in the cosmos.

In that moment, when Lindbergh lost all contact with earth and climbed above the fog to ten thousand feet, he was also ascending in the public consciousness to Olympian heights. His success would reflect well on the entire human race, placing him in the unique position of overshadowing every other living hero. Indeed, the world had long been host to a succession of athletes, actors, artists, scientists, political and religious leaders, even kings, to whom people looked up; but such admiration was a matter of taste and beliefs. Everybody had a stake in Lindbergh. On May 20, 1927—as night fell— modern man realized nobody had ever subjected himself to so extreme a test of human courage and capability as Lindbergh. Not even Columbus sailed alone.

Practically everybody who lived in America through Lindbergh's flight would remember his or her precise feelings that first night. Forty years later, one housewife recalled how as "a little unattractive fat girl" who had lost most of her family, she had prayed for his safety, thus taking part in his endeavor. Countless millions did the same.

In Indiana, Pennsylvania, the nineteen-year-old son of the local hardware store owner had been laid low with scarlet fever that third week of May. He carved a wooden model of the *Spirit of St. Louis,* then asked his father for a large piece of beaverboard on which he drew a map of the North Atlantic. To the left he crayoned a silhouette of New York's Woolworth Building, and to the right, the Eiffel Tower. Then he warped the board to show the curvature of the earth and tacked on his model of the plane. Young Jimmy displayed the diorama in the front window of J. M. Stewart & Company, inching the plane along with each radio update. "I don't think I got any more sleep than Lindbergh did," James Stewart would recount many years later. "Lindbergh's problem was staying awake; mine was staying asleep that Friday night while he was unreported over the Atlantic between Newfoundland and Ireland."

America's most popular observer of the American scene, humorist Will Rogers, filed his nationally syndicated newspaper column that afternoon from Concord, New Hampshire. "No attempt at jokes today," he wrote uncharacteristically. "A . . . slim, tall bashful, smiling American boy is somewhere over the middle of the Atlantic ocean, where no lone human being has ever ventured before. He is being prayed for to every kind of Supreme Being that had a following. If he is lost it will be the most universally regretted loss we ever had."

That night, forty thousand boxing fans made their way to Yankee Stadium in the Bronx to see a fight between heavyweight favorite Jim Maloney and his rival from Boston, Jack Sharkey. The crowd included such prominent figures as banker Mortimer Schiff, publishing magnates Herbert and Ralph Pulitzer and Condé Nast, Averell Harriman and his tycoon father, industrialist Walter Chrysler, Frank Hague, the powerful Mayor of Jersey City, and John F. "Honey Fitz" Fitzgerald, the former Mayor of Boston. The conversation inside and outside the stadium was all about Lindbergh. Instead of peddling the latest tabloid headlines about the quarter-million-dollar fight about to commence, the newboys sold out their "Extra" editions that night shouting about "Lindy," the sobriquet headline writers used because of its marquee appeal. "Forty thousand persons put Lindbergh first and Sharkey and Maloney second last night," reported the staid *New York Times,* "and forty thousand persons can't be wrong, whether Frenchmen or Americans. The remarkable thing about last night's fight crowd was that they were all wondering how the transatlantic flight would come out and not who would be knocked out."

Sharkey was the upset winner, with a kayo in the fifth round; but the most stirring moment occurred before the fight even began. Announcer Joe

Humphries told the crowd that Lindbergh was at sea and by all reports all was well. His update was based on nothing more than hopeful speculation, but the fans went wild, refusing to be silenced. When his waving motions finally settled them down, a lone, loud voice from the crowd shouted, "He's the greatest fighter of them all." Another round of cheering followed, as Humphries beseeched the spectators for silence. Then he asked the forty thousand to offer a silent prayer that Lindbergh might land safely in France. The entire crowd rose as one, all heads bared.

Similar scenes played out across the country that night. At the Hotel Commodore in Manhattan, twelve hundred industrialists gathered for the American Iron and Steel Institute's annual banquet. Before the chairman of United States Steel delivered the evening's main address, another company head offered an impromptu benediction: "I am proud to live under that flag," he said, pointing to a small star-spangled banner on the table. "I am thinking of a young American boy who left this morning for Paris with a sandwich in his pocket. May God deliver him there safely." And the men in black tie cheered.

Anxiously, the world awakened Saturday to old news. In a three-line banner, *The New York Times* could but report that Lindbergh was speeding across the Atlantic and was last sighted over Newfoundland. A pencil portrait of the delicately featured young man, which made him look even younger than his years, accompanied the lead article. The "skyline" on page one promised a full page of photographs of the aviator, which the paper delivered on page five. Editorial cartoonists across America that day drew variations on the same theme—a picture of a turbulent sea covered by an even more ominous sky, with a tiny plane flying eastward through the clouds. Editorials offered praise and prayers. Thousands of requests streamed in for reprints of the editorial in the New York *Sun,* written by Harold M. Anderson, called "Lindbergh Flies Alone." It became one of the most famous newspaper pieces of its era:

Alone?

Is he alone at whose right side rides Courage, with Skill within the cockpit and Faith upon the left? Does solitude surround the brave when Adventure leads the way and Ambition reads the dials? Is there no company with him for whom the air is cleft by Daring and the darkness is made light by Emprise?

True, the fragile bodies of his fellows do not weigh down his plane; true, the fretful minds of weaker men are lacking from his crowded cabin; but as his airship keeps her course he holds communion with those rarer spirits that inspire to intrepidity and by their sustaining potency give strength to arm, resource to mind, content to soul.

Alone? With what other companions would that man fly to whom the choice were given?

Into the foggy night, Lindbergh sought companionship with the stars. Feeling the tailwinds and deciding that he could afford to expend some gasoline on altitude, he climbed to five thousand feet. "As long as I can hold on to them," he thought, seeing the stars blink through the haze, "I'll be safe." Sleep remained his worst enemy.

Entering the fourteenth hour, cruising at ten thousand feet, the *Spirit of St. Louis* flew through a range of clouds Himalayan in height. With no hope of rising above them, Lindbergh became aware of how cold it was in the cockpit. He removed a leather mitten and put his arm out the window, only to have it stung by cold needles. He aimed his flashlight toward a strut of the plane, on which he saw ice.

He was aware of the danger, as it was already affecting his plane's aerodynamics. "As far north as Newfoundland and in the cold of night," Lindbergh analyzed, "icing conditions probably extend down to the waves themselves"; and if he descended and ice clogged his instruments, he would never be able to climb again. He thought of changing his course and flying south, around the storm; but he had to consider how much gasoline that would cost.

For the next few minutes, as the wind pulled his plane every which way, he followed the clearest path that presented itself, heading south whenever that option existed. At one point he found himself turned completely around, in quest of safe passage. Soon the coating of ice thinned. He observed that both his earth-inductor compass and his liquid compass overhead were malfunctioning. His only hope for getting across the watery abyss lay in the hairline needles of those compasses pointing the way. Lindbergh could only deduce that he was entering a magnetic storm, which he would have to ride out navigating by instinct.

Just then, heavenly assistance arrived. Not only did the expanses between the great thunderheads of the storm widen, but moonlight appeared. Its unexpected illumination disoriented Lindbergh at first, because in shortening the night—racing with the earth's rotation—he had not correctly reckoned when it would show up. Taking off from Roosevelt Field in the early morning had assured Lindbergh the maximum of daylight hours; as it was, he faced but two hours of solid darkness. Entering his thousandth minute in the air, his plane ventured "where man has never been." The last of the ice disappeared from his plane as Lindbergh crossed the halfway mark in his flight. "Now," he thought, "I've burned the last bridge behind me."

After seventeen hours in the air—almost forty since he had last slept—Lindbergh felt disembodied. He seemed able to see without his eyes, and he became numb to both hunger and the cold. He had drunk less than a pint of water. With the first break of light, Lindbergh realized that he had lost control of his eyelids. "My back is stiff; my shoulders ache; my face burns; my eyes smart," he wrote of his physical condition. "It seems impossible to go on longer. All I want in life is to throw myself down flat, stretch out—and sleep."

Lindbergh's body abdicated control to a "separate mind," a kind of automatic pilot that took responsibility for putting his muscles through the motions of flying the plane. The *Spirit of St. Louis* was not a "stable" plane— a machine that might restore its own equilibrium when disturbed by some outside force; and that deficiency proved to be its saving grace. That instability continued to jerk Lindbergh into wakefulness.

During the next three hours of increasing daylight, fog appeared. Into one opening Lindbergh flew within one hundred feet of the ocean. When the ceiling lowered to zero, Lindbergh flew for two hours completely blind at an altitude of fifteen hundred feet. He found it difficult for his mind to function on any level but instinctive survival. He abandoned his log, choosing only to score the switching of gas tanks every hour, and sometimes arriving late to the task.

Into his twenty-second hour, Lindbergh realized that he was drifting into sleep. When the fog periodically dissipated, Lindbergh took his plane close enough to the ocean for the spray off the whitecaps to slap his face. Other times, he let light rain splash into the cockpit. Then, without warning, came another intrusion.

It would be almost three decades before Lindbergh would discuss it publicly, but after almost twenty-four hours of his ordeal—at around five o'clock in the morning by his clock—the fuselage behind him filled with phantoms— "vaguely outlined forms, transparent, moving, riding weightless with me in the plane." He later recorded that these ghosts were benign, vaporous presences. They permeated the fabric walls of the plane, coming and going at will. With human voices they spoke to him above the noise of the engine, advising him on his flight and giving him "messages of importance unattainable in ordinary life." They were human in shape but devoid of real form. With years of hindsight, Lindbergh would grant that these visions would normally have startled him; "but on this fantastic flight," he would recall of the close encounter, "I'm so far separated from the earthly life I know that I accept whatever circumstance may come."

In the next hour, he entertained another vision. Under his left wing, only five miles to the north, Lindbergh saw a coastline, complete with hills and trees and cliffs and islands. The very thought of land that close baffled him, for his calculations put Ireland almost a thousand miles away. Even considering that he had completely lost his bearings, he could not figure out what the land could possibly be—Greenland? Labrador? He shook his head and looked again, assuring himself that he was awake and that he still saw the shore ahead. He finally realized that they were mirages—"fog islands sprung up along my route; here for an hour only to disappear, mushrooms of the sea." He approached one of the islands, only to have it vanish into thick air. Lindbergh wondered how he would ever be able to recognize Europe when he actually reached its shores.

Over the next hour, the fog evanesced. Although there were occasional showers, Lindbergh was able to fly below two hundred feet, often within ten feet of the waves. He felt reconnected to the planet, but he was not sure where he was. He continued to fight sleep and to follow his chart, but mental fatigue made simple computation an exhausting challenge. It was impossible to establish his location because too many variables had entered the equation—his detours over St. John's and around the earlier thunderheads as well as the magnetic storm. He also could not calculate the velocity and direction of the wind for the past twelve hours.

Lindbergh knew only where he was meant to be and that he had been flying for an hour and a day. He reached into his flying-suit pocket for a handkerchief and was surprised to find, among his knife, pencils, and flashlight, the St. Christopher medal. This could not be a hallucination, for he could feel the silver disk showing a saint and child; but he had no idea where it came from. Within minutes, he looked down and saw a dark object swimming through the water. It was a porpoise, the first sign of life he had seen since Newfoundland. The next hour brought a gull.

Drawing on all his reserves to remain awake, Lindbergh remembered he was carrying smelling salts in his first-aid kit. He opened one of the capsules of aromatic ammonia, thinking it would revive him; but he smelled nothing and his eyes would not tear. He floated onward until another vision captured his attention—several small boats looking like dots on a giant canvas. It took another moment before his mind comprehended the significance of the sight. There was no denying that there were fishermen below, who must have shipped out from a nearby harbor. Lindbergh approached one of the boats and saw a man's head poke through a porthole. Within fifty feet of the water and circling the boat, Lindbergh closed the throttle and leaned out his window, shouting, "WHICH WAY IS IRELAND!"

He passed the ship several times but got no response. The men below were no doubt as puzzled by the sight of him as he was of them, for Lindbergh figured he had at least another two and a half hours before reaching land. Flying through a brief rain, he saw another image on the horizon—only this time it seemed more fixed than his other visions. He discerned a jagged coastline, fjords giving way to green fields. He placed a map on his knees; and, looking back and forth between the crude earth outside and the fine lines on his lap, he saw how they corresponded. He had arrived at Dingle Bay on the southwestern coast of Ireland.

Lindbergh was sure this was no mirage. He spiraled down toward a village alive with people running into the streets, looking up, and waving. According to his chart, he was only six segments away from Paris, six hours, six hundred miles. After twenty-eight hours of perilous flight, he was less than three miles off course.

The sun began its descent for the second time since he had left Roosevelt Field. His flight path grazing the southern tip of Ireland, he put the greenery of county Kerry behind him. Revived, only the third act of his flight remained.

Across America, day was breaking, bringing reports from overseas. The steamer *Hilversum* had spotted the *Spirit of St. Louis* hours earlier, five hundred miles from the Irish coast; the steam collier *Nogi* had seen a low-flying gray plane near Valencia. In western Pennsylvania, Jimmy Stewart raced to his father's store at dawn to move his model plane to the southern tip of Ireland, only to have his optimism confirmed by a radio bulletin later in the day.

Almost everybody felt bullish that morning. Wall Street had been prospering for months; and during that half day of business, stocks had their heaviest Saturday trading in a year and a half. Wright Aeronautical was the most impressive gainer, opening at 29 ¾ and closing up 5 ¾ points. Throughout Lindbergh's flight, the exchanges in Amsterdam and Berlin had interrupted their quotations to provide updates. At midnight in Tokyo, thousands of people flocked to the streets. Lloyd's of London at last began issuing odds, 10 to 3 against Lindbergh's making Paris.

The newspapers in France used their boldest typeface for the special editions that afternoon. Although still bemoaning the disappearance of Nungesser and Coli, France set about welcoming Lindbergh as it felt America would have greeted the French pilots. Once it appeared that he would not arrive in daylight, the government ordered the air-route illuminated, lighting the airfields between Cherbourg and Le Bourget.

Since dawn in New York, people descended upon newsstands, turning into mobs as each edition of the city's dozen different newspapers was dropped off. *The New York Times* received over ten thousand calls that day.

"As I write this, you are flying over the wide ocean," wrote Juno Lindbergh Butler—C.A.'s sister—unaware of Charles's progress. "I do not like to think of it but can think of nothing else. When you receive this the 'world will be yours.' It is at your feet now and you cannot imagine how proud we are of you, both for your bravery and because you have kept a level head and a strong heart, with all the adulation that has been heaped upon you." Despite the bad blood that had spilled between the Lindberghs and Charles's mother, Aunt Juno had to grant that part of that day's glory should go to her. "It takes a brave mother to wish her boy goodbye and Godspeed on such a journey with the calm confidence she displayed," she wrote. Meantime, Evangeline sat in her small frame house in Detroit with "Brother," police protection at the front and rear gates, her telephone off the hook.

Under a pleasant sky and over St. George's Channel—one of the lesser gulfs into which the Atlantic dissolves—Lindbergh felt that the "great difficulties of the flight" were behind him. Having burned close to seventeen hundred pounds of fuel, the plane felt unburdened. He had nothing more than the equivalent of a roundtrip between St. Louis and Chicago to complete. Then, without warning, the entire plane shook, as the engine jerked against its mounting.

After twenty-nine hours of the steady rhythm of the Wright Whirlwind, it coughed erratically. As Lindbergh prepared for a forced landing, he considered that it was his hubris that was bringing him down—"Have I grown too confident, too arrogant, before my flight is done?" He realized that the problem was nothing more than his nose tank, the forwardmost of his five, running dry. He had only to turn some valves before gasoline was once again nourishing the thirsty motor.

Counting his pencil marks, Lindbergh reckoned his life was no longer at stake. Even if England or France were fogged in, he had enough gasoline to return to Ireland. Having caught his second wind, he considered flying over Paris, dipping his wings, and continuing on to Rome. Reason prevailed. When he passed over Plymouth, he could not help thinking of the *Mayflower*, which needed two months to reach America; this pilgrim had skirted by Plymouth Rock only thirty hours earlier. Just as the sun was setting, he crossed the English Channel to France, the very coast from where Nungesser and Coli were last sighted.

Looking down on Cherbourg, he took a moment to congratulate himself, realizing that he was at last over "the country of my destination" and that he had made the first nonstop airplane flight between the continents of America and Europe. Crossing the Baie de la Seine to the Normandy coast, with Le Havre off to his left, Lindbergh reached Deauville. He had flown thirty-five hundred miles, breaking the world's distance record for a nonstop airplane flight.

At the mouth of the Seine, Lindbergh celebrated by reaching for food for the first time since he sat in the hangar at Curtiss Field. He vised the stick with his knees and reached under his wicker chair for the paper bag, from which he pulled one of the five wrapped sandwiches. He unscrewed the cap of his canteen and realized that he could at last drink all the water he wanted. The sandwich satisfied his hunger, but it had no taste. Swallowing was an effort, each bite requiring a mouthful of water. That was all he chose to eat. He stuffed the wrapping back into the bag, not wanting "the litter from a sandwich to symbolize my first contact with France."

A few bright lights flashed in the distance, air beacons marking the approach to Paris. To gain greater perspective, Lindbergh climbed to four thousand feet. From that height the ground assumed the appearance of the galaxy above. Lights became more frequent as the country grew less rural; towns appeared as constellations; and bright clusters of cities shone through the clear night air. Ahead in the distance appeared a glow that brightened into something akin to the aurora borealis—"a patch of starlit earth under a starlit-sky—the lamps of Paris—straight lines of lights, curving lines of lights, squares of lights, black spaces in between." He circled once above the Eiffel Tower—which displayed vertical sprays of lights as shooting stars, spelling out "CITROEN"—then headed northeast.

Although he had found Paris, Lindbergh could not locate Le Bourget. At the place he expected the landing field he discovered a black patch that was large enough for that purpose; but its perimetral lighting made no sense. Where an airport should be outlined by regularly spaced lights, this was surrounded by an erratic pattern: one corner of the field appeared to be washed with floodlights; and there seemed to be another string of lights stretching all the way to Paris. He flew another few miles in search of the airport; but after five minutes into rural darkness, he returned to the long strand of lights and spiraled lower. With each glance out the window of his banking plane, more of the airfield revealed itself. Those tens of thousands of surrounding lights, he realized, were the headlamps of automobiles stuck in traffic.

Several times he circled the field, surrendering altitude, surveying the approaching ground. He fastened his safety belt, checked his instrument panel, got a look at the wind sock, and figured where to bring his plane down. He came in close enough to see the texture of the sod, then climbed to a thousand feet for his final approach.

He circled around into the wind, began pulling back on the stick, closing the throttle, cutting his speed, approaching the field until the wheels touched ground, bounced gently and returned to earth, at which time the tail skid touched down. The plane kept rolling into an easy turn, coming to a momentary stop in a dark section right in the middle of Le Bourget. It was 10:24 P.M. Paris time—thirty-three and one-half hours since takeoff. Lindbergh taxied toward the floodlights. Then looking out his window, he was thunderstruck.

The 150,000 people at the airfield stood everywhere—on tops of cars, on tops of the airport buildings, and mostly on the ground behind a fence guarded by the Le Bourget field police, special units of Paris agents, and two companies of soldiers with fixed bayonets. American Ambassador to France Myron T. Herrick was escorted to the overcrowded pavilion at one end of the field for a formal reception of the aviator.

When Lindbergh brought the *Spirit of St. Louis* into the glow of lights on the field, he saw a human tidal wave. "The movement of humanity swept over soldiers and by policemen and there was the wild sight of thousands of men and women rushing madly across half a mile of the not too even ground," reported *The New York Times*'s ace foreign correspondent Edwin L. James. "Soldiers and police tried for one small moment to stem the tide, then they joined it, rushing as madly as anyone else toward the aviator and his plane."

Seventy-three-year-old Ambassador Herrick, who had been around public events most of his life, swore he had never seen anything like it—"not the pandemonium the newspapers always tell about at political conventions, but the real thing. . . . Soldiers and police were swept away, the stout fence was demolished, and the crowd surged toward the airplane." The first to reach Lindbergh were Le Bourget workmen, who cried, *"Cette fois, ça va!"* ("This time, it's done!")

Numerous quotations have been attributed to Lindbergh upon seeing faces pushing their heads inside the *Spirit of St. Louis*—such statements as "I'm Charles Lindbergh" and "Well, I made it"—which he forever denied making. In truth, all he said was, "Are there any mechanics here?"

In the hysterical din, his words meant nothing. Even if somebody had replied in English, Lindbergh probably would not have been able to hear, for the noise of his engine still whirred in his ears, drowning out all sound except the ominous cracking of wood and ripping of fabric. Before he had got the door of his plane open, the first great wave of humanity had crashed over him, keeping him from even putting a foot on the ground. Arms grabbed him, rendering him helpless as he floated over the sea of heads.

After several minutes, he was able to stand on the earth for the first time, and he got caught in the riptide of the masses. A few quick-thinking Frenchmen ran to his rescue. One pulled off Lindbergh's helmet and put it on an American reporter who happened to be standing next to him. In that same instant, a French civil flier named George Delage threw his coat over Lindbergh's shoulders and ran off to get his car while his friend, military pilot Michel Détroyat, pushed Lindbergh to the periphery of the crowd. In the confusion, the mob descended upon the man wearing the helmet, while Détroyat and Lindbergh were able to duck into Delage's Renault.

They drove him to a hangar on the side of the field, where, in its small waiting room, they offered him food and medical attention. They kept most of the lights out, to avoid attracting attention. France was his, they said. Lindbergh's only concern was for his plane, to which he wished to return. Delage and Détroyat made him understand the inadvisability of such a move. He asked about immigration and customs, which got a laugh; and he asked about Nungesser and Coli, which elicited sad expressions.

Détroyat left and returned minutes later with Major Pierre Weiss of the Bombardment Group of the Thirty-fourth A. F. Regiment. Weiss could not believe Delage and Détroyat had been harboring the hero because, he explained, "Lindbergh has just been carried triumphantly to the official reception committee." The four men piled into Delage's Renault and drove across the field, where they waited in Weiss's office; Weiss left to bring Myron Herrick to the actual owner of the hero's helmet.

It was after midnight when Herrick, with his son and daughter-in-law, reached Weiss's darkened office. Lindbergh offered his letters of introduction, which were unnecessary. Herrick said, "Young man, I am going to take you home with me and look after you." Lindbergh drew closer and explained that he still could not hear very well. Herrick repeated his offer, which Lindbergh accepted, though he said he hoped to visit his plane before leaving the field. Again, the obvious arguments against such an attempt were aired. But Lindbergh had been worrying about the cracking and ripping noises he had heard as the crowd had seized him, and he said there were a few items he wished to retrieve.

They drove to the hangar where the *Spirit of St. Louis* had been parked. Lindbergh was shocked to see the crowd had ripped off pieces of the actual plane as souvenirs; a lubrication fitting and the clipboard with his log of the flight were gone. Further inspection revealed, however, that no serious harm had been done. The plane would spend the night under military guard.

Herrick intended to drive Lindbergh into Paris, but through a misunderstanding, Lindbergh, Weiss, Détroyat, and Delage all found themselves packed again into the Renault, detouring several miles over backroads to the west before heading south into the city. They drove through the Saint Ouen gate toward the Place de l'Opéra—where crowds had been dancing in the streets for hours—then straight up the Boulevard Haussmann.

Lindbergh's guides had selected the tomb of the Unknown Soldier as his first stop in Paris. They all got out and stood in silence in the middle of the Étoile, under the Arc de Triomphe. Lindbergh swayed slightly, his legs buckling. They returned to the car and drove to the chancery in the Rue de Chaillot, which they thought was the Ambassador's residence. The police redirected them to No. 2, avenue d'Iéna—one block up a steep hill from the Seine.

Ambassador Herrick had telephoned ahead to his staff to prepare a room and food for their late-night visitor. The French aviators left Lindbergh in the care of Herrick's butler, who served a platter of chicken and side dishes, which Lindbergh declined in favor of an egg and some bouillon. He excused himself to bathe.

Traffic kept the Ambassador from reaching his home until three o'clock that morning. He found his visitor sitting on the edge of a bed in a guest-room, wearing a robe and slippers and a pair of Herrick's pajamas. The street in front of the house had filled with newspapermen, and Herrick suggested that Lindbergh grant them a brief audience. Lindbergh explained that his backers in St. Louis had contracted with *The New York Times* for him to give them an exclusive interview, and that he could not violate those terms. Herrick's son, Parmely, went downstairs to the salon, where some reporters were already waiting, to find the *Times*'s representative, Carlyle MacDonald. As diplomatic as his father, Parmely suggested to MacDonald that "this thing seemed too big an affair to be made the exclusive news of any one paper"; and he asked him to consent to Lindbergh's meeting all the reporters. MacDonald agreed, and the corps of pressmen cheered before being shown upstairs.

Lindbergh's room was blue and gold, with a soft light glowing. He stood to greet his callers, and they insisted he be seated. He grinned and said, "It's almost as easy to stand up as it is to sit down." The journalists peppered him with questions, all of which he answered in few words. After seven or eight minutes, Herrick suggested that any further questions would be an undue strain on Lindbergh—who had by then been awake for sixty-three hours. The newspapermen withdrew. Lindbergh shook Ambassador Herrick's hand and said there was no need to awaken him in the morning, as he was "sure to be up and ready at nine o'clock."

At 4:15 A.M., Lindbergh got into one of the narrow twin beds in his room, a delicate but sturdy Louis XVI replica, with a carved headboard, frame, and footboard in beige and teal. Two meters in length, it was barely long enough for the weary pilot.

As soon as the journalists left, Ambassador Herrick cabled Evangeline Lindbergh in Detroit. "WARMEST CONGRATULATIONS STOP," he said. "YOUR IN-COMPARABLE SON HAS HONORED ME BY BEING MY GUEST STOP HE IS IN FINE CONDITION AND SLEEPING SWEETLY UNDER UNCLE SAMS ROOF."

PART TWO

7

ONLY A MAN

"I was astonished at the effect my successful landing in France had on the nations of the world. To me, it was like a match lighting a bonfire."

—C.A.L.

AROUND ONE O'CLOCK ON SUNDAY AFTERNOON, MAY 22, 1927, Charles Lindbergh awoke in his room at the American Embassy in Paris. Ambassador Herrick had sent in his valet, Walter Blanchard, who drew a bath and raised the curtains at the windows overlooking the Trocadéro Gardens and the Seine. As Lindbergh opened his eyes, he noticed for the first time the splendor of his surroundings. Standing by the bed, Blanchard held open a bathrobe, announced that the bath was ready, and asked how the pilot liked his eggs. Then he left the wide-eyed young man to the tub of warm water and a large cake of yellow soap.

Feeling as though he were awakening into a dream, Lindbergh had no idea that the fantasy was just beginning. Unbeknownst to him, the modern wonders of communication had transformed the twenty-five-year-old "boy" into the most famous man on earth.

While Lindbergh slept, all other news—a massive flood in the Mississippi Valley, rising tensions between Japan and China, Britain's severance of diplomatic relations with Russia, appeal efforts in the Sacco-Vanzetti Case—disappeared from the front pages of most American newspapers and from most people's minds.

After several false alarms, the first authentic report of Lindbergh's landing came through to *The New York Times* at half-past five in the afternoon, six minutes after the *Spirit of St. Louis* had touched down. A bulletin was posted on a window of the *Times* building; and from there, word spread like wildfire—setting off a chain reaction of cheers and horn blasts. "Ferryboats, tugboats, liners, all the little boats and all the big boats that ply the waters of New York Harbor did honor to the man who had flown continuously over the largest stretch of water ever covered by an aviator," reported the *Times*. Every fire company in the city joined in, sounding their sirens and rolling their trucks out on to the streets to spread the word. Several Broadway matinees interrupted their performances to announce that Lindbergh had landed; and later that night, orchestras played "The Star-Spangled Banner" before launching into their overtures. Radio stations played the "Marseillaise." Six thousand patrons at the second show at the Roxy Theatre that night saw—and heard—the Fox Movietone footage of Lindbergh's plane taking off from Roosevelt Field, which brought them to their feet, cheering, stamping, and hugging each other. People shredded telephone books and other papers into confetti and threw it out their windows. Preachers hastily rewrote their Sunday sermons. At the Glen Cove Community Hospital on Long Island, Detective Gordon Hurley announced the birth of his son, Charles Lindbergh Hurley; he would be the first of countless babies to be given the same Christian names. Under a three-line banner headline ("LINDBERGH DOES IT! . . ."), *The New York Times* devoted its entire front page to articles related to Lindbergh and his flight, as it did with every other column inch of text on the following four pages.

Because it was a Saturday afternoon when Lindbergh landed, there was little celebration in St. Louis's downtown business district; but in its suburbs and rural areas, carillons spread the word from steeple to steeple, including the big bells of Christ Church Cathedral, which were rung only on "civic occasions of high importance."

So it was in every city and town in America, each looking for its own special connection to Lindbergh. In Detroit, the hero's mother ended her day of seclusion, coming out to greet the press in a green hat and green dress. Under her cherry tree in the frontyard, she smiled as tears filled her eyes. "I am grateful," she said. "There is no use attempting to find words to express my happiness." She said that she had felt nothing but confidence; but even so, "I am happy that it is over, more happy than I can ever tell. . . . He has accomplished the greatest undertaking of his life, and I am proud to be the mother of such a boy." When word reached San Diego, remembered young Douglas Corrigan, "the whole town went wild, because the people knew that the plane was a local product." In Little Falls, Minnesota, "[P]andemonium broke loose" in front of the newspaper office; a "blaring band," reported the AP wire, "added to the din, whistles shrieked and bells rang." In chronicling the Jazz Age, F. Scott Fitzgerald captured the era's pinnacle by writing:

A young Minnesotan who seemed to have had nothing to do with his generation did a heroic thing, and for a moment people set down their glasses in country clubs and speak-easies and thought of their old best dreams.

A man in Aberdeen, Washington, got so excited by Lindbergh's success that he dropped dead on the street reaching for one of the newspaper extras that afternoon.

Lindbergh captured the attention of people everywhere. Theater audiences and hotel patrons in Berlin burst into applause upon hearing the news; and in Buenos Aires people demanded to know the whereabouts of the kitten alleged to have made the trip. A Hindi periodical outside Bombay observed, "Few things have so deeply stirred the hearts of India and evoked such huge admiration as the marvelous feat of . . . Lindbergh. The triumph he has achieved is a matter of glory, not only for his own countrymen, but the entire human race." The *Times*'s Rome correspondent signaled by wireless that all Italy followed Captain Lindbergh's flight "with breathless interest" because it showed "with what proud contempt man can defy the adverse forces of nature and hurl defiance at destiny." Even the British got caught up in the excitement, shifting their attention from the two Royal Air Force fliers still attempting to reach India. "Well done!" exclaimed the Prince of Wales upon hearing the news. "Lindbergh is no ordinary man," wrote *The Sunday Express*. "He is the stuff heroes are made of. He defied death and snatched his reprieve and pardon. His daring dazzles the world. It is difficult to imagine anything more desperately heroic than his solitary flight across the ocean."

Although feeling a little "stiff," Lindbergh did not soak in the tub for long, as he realized that he had missed his eleven o'clock interview with Edwin L. James and Carlyle MacDonald of *The New York Times*. Ambassador Herrick put his guest at ease, assuring him that all of Paris expected him to sleep for twenty hours and that the *Times* correspondents could easily wait with the two hundred other newspapermen milling on the ground floor of the embassy. Meantime, twenty-five motion-picture camera operators and another fifty photographers set up their equipment outside in the courtyard.

As transatlantic "radio telephone" service did not yet extend to Paris, Lindbergh said he would like to "fly over to London in my machine" so that he could call his mother. "Oh, no more flying for you, my boy, for a little while anyway," Ambassador Herrick replied. But he promised to arrange for a telephone hookup between Paris and Detroit.

Of most immediate concern, Herrick thought, was the matter of clothing, for Lindbergh had packed none and events were already being scheduled that would require more than flying togs. Blanchard came to the rescue with a business suit he had borrowed from a tall friend—who was evidently broader of shoulder and shorter of leg than Lindbergh. The outfit would be temporary as a London tailor with a shop in Paris was summoned to assemble a complete wardrobe—from daywear to tails—as quickly as possible. Nobody around the embassy had feet as large as Lindbergh's, so he padded about in a pair of clean socks, as two servants polished his tan flying boots. While dressing, Lindbergh invited the men from the *Times* into his bedroom.

They talked as he ate his first substantial meal in two and a half days—grapefruit, bacon and eggs, toast, and coffee. While he worked his way through all the plates on the big tray, congratulatory telegrams arrived from several heads of state, including President Calvin Coolidge, who cabled: "The American people rejoice with me at the brilliant termination of your heroic flight. The first non-stop flight of a lone aviator across the Atlantic crowns the record of American aviation . . ."

Outside No. 2, avenue d'Iéna, a huge crowd had been forming under the horse chestnut trees since early morning, its rumblings audible through the thick embassy walls. After Lindbergh sat with the two *Times* reporters and a stenographer in an upstairs salon for the better part of an hour, Ambassador Herrick felt impelled to intrude. Taking the young man by the arm, he ushered him to the front balcony, where masses chanted "Vive Lindbergh! Vive l'Amérique!"

Lindbergh was struck dumb, unsure how to react. "The idea of exhibiting myself embarrassed and disturbed me," Lindbergh would write almost fifty years later. "I had never been asked to do that before."

"Just say you're glad to be in France," somebody suggested; but Lindbergh found the words too trite. Impulsively, he blurted out three of the few words of French he knew—"Vive la France!" The crowd cheered again, which further embarrassed him. Herrick's daughter-in-law, Agnes, approached the balcony with a French flag, which Lindbergh and the ambassador held before them, and the cheering increased. Only then did it dawn on Lindbergh that his flight "had taken on significance extending beyond fields of aviation," and that his notion of spending a few weeks leisurely touring the Old World would have to be changed. "I had entered a new environment of life," he realized, "and found myself surrounded by unforeseen opportunities, responsibilities, and problems."

Shortly after returning inside, Lindbergh was informed that telephone operators were ready to patch him through to Detroit. Although the press would give the impression that mother and son spoke directly to each other, they communicated through an interlocuter in London, who was connected by telephone wire to Paris and radio airwaves to New York, the words finally delivered by telephone wire to Detroit. "Hello, Mother," Charles said. "The trip over was wonderful. I am feeling fine; do not worry about me." Evangeline prescribed "plenty of rest, for you have gone through a tremendous strain." The connection was full of static, but the precise words of their small talk did not much matter—either to the Lindberghs or to the public.

The "conversation" made Lindbergh want to pay his respects to Charles Nungesser's mother. While this outing was being arranged, Lindbergh met with the press and posed for pictures with Myron Herrick. By the end of the day, the photographs and newsreels were flown to all the capitals of Europe. Upon entering one salon of the Ambassador's residence, Lindbergh was shown a huge arrangement of flowers. "Well, that's nice, and I am glad I am able to receive it personally," he said with a laugh. "You know flowers sometimes come in the wrong way and you aren't able to appreciate them." The newspapermen thrilled at the unexpected joke and broke into a cheer.

After a few minutes, Lindbergh left the embassy with Myron Herrick and an entourage for the Boulevard du Temple, across Paris, where Mme. Nungesser lived in one of the city's oldest apartment buildings. Although the visit had not been announced, ten thousand people had gathered outside her residence by the time Lindbergh arrived. Several young women lunged at him in hopes of stealing a kiss; and, Herrick observed, he was "scared to death."

Up six flights of stairs, Mme. Nungesser received Lindbergh's party, kissing the American flier on both cheeks before embracing him. With tears streaming down her cheeks, she said, "You are a very brave young man. I congratulate you from the bottom of my heart. I, too, have a brave son, who I have never ceased to believe is still fighting his way back to civilization." Although it had been more than two weeks since anybody had seen her son, Lindbergh held her hand and told her not to give up hope. Returning to the Embassy by way of the Rue de la Paix, Lindbergh was surprised to see American flags everywhere, even more startled when Herrick explained they were displayed in his honor.

A dinner at the Embassy had long been planned for that night. Because it was "a rather young affair," Ambassador Herrick thought Lindbergh might enjoy himself and chose not to cancel it. Lindbergh's behavior was conspicuous only in its extreme courtesy, which he had acquired during his childhood in Washington. Agnes Herrick had asked some fifty people to arrive after dinner that night to meet the pilot, and every one of them wanted his autograph. The guest of honor smilingly obliged. Lindbergh excused himself early—a little after nine—and retired to his narrow bed, where he was unexpectedly joined by Herrick's wire-haired terrier, Max.

"The next day," Herrick would later write, "serious business began"—

what became the official apotheosis of Charles Lindbergh. Salutations would no longer be extended from individuals, but from institutions and entire nations.

After an early breakfast and a brief meeting with a haberdasher—selecting shirts, shoes, scarves, and spats—Lindbergh asked to see his plane at Le Bourget. He arrived at the field courtesy of the diplomatic cabriolet a little after ten o'clock, unprepared for the ovation he would receive from the airport staff and 34th Aviation Unit. Having braced himself for the sight of holes in the fuselage, his inspection proved more favorable than he had expected. The exhaust pipe had been loosened but not taken, and the motor needed nothing more than some clean oil. A few hours of repair would make the *Spirit of St. Louis* as good as new.

Lindbergh's car returned to Paris for a noon appointment at the Élysée Palace. A military commander greeted him and Ambassador Herrick, ushering them past the cheering crowd. In his borrowed blue suit, Lindbergh was presented to the President of France, Gaston Doumergue, who was in full evening dress. The President pinned the Cross of the Legion of Honor—a gold decoration hanging from a scarlet ribbon—on his lapel. Never in history had the President of the French Republic personally conferred his nation's highest honor, for acts of military bravery or civil achievement, upon an American. Lindbergh bowed politely and returned to his car, which forged through blocks of cheering Parisians.

After Lindbergh and Herrick lunched at the Embassy, the Ambassador urged his guest to nap until their next appointment at the end of the day. But rest was impossible with the steady stream of journalists and emissaries from every country in Europe, each proffering formal invitations to visit their nations. By then several thousand cables and telegrams had arrived. The French Post Office Department announced that it was establishing a special service for his mail alone, which would thenceforth be delivered in sacks. Scores of visiting cards were left at the Embassy, through which Lindbergh would barely have time to run his fingers. One read, "You're a God—Hercules an infant."

At five o'clock Lindbergh appeared before the Aéro-Club of France. Its members presented him their gold medal. Champagne corks rocketed, and Paul Claudel, France's poet-Ambassador to Washington, offered a toast in two languages—"to the happiest woman in America—the mother of this boy." A bewigged waiter bowed low as he offered Lindbergh a slender stemmed glass from his tray. Lindbergh looked for assistance from Herrick, who whispered, "Oh, go ahead and drink it. A toast to your mother is only indirectly to you." And with that, Lindbergh tasted his first sip of champagne. The hall full of Frenchmen cheered and twice brought him to the window, which stoked the hysteria of thousands of Frenchmen waiting outside.

Inside, Lindbergh responded modestly, making his first public address. He said he lacked the words to express his feelings about the wonderful reception in Paris, and he praised Nungesser and Coli "who attempted a greater thing in taking off from Paris for New York than I have done in accomplishing the trip from New York to Paris." Ambassador Herrick pounced on this moment of camaraderie to proclaim, "This young Lochinvar from out of the West brings you better than anything else the spirit of America." Everybody recognized that Lindbergh had become a bridge between the two great nations.

The Aéro-Club offered Lindbergh a gift of 150,000 francs—almost six thousand dollars—which he refused. He asked that the money be used "for the benefit of the families of French aviators who have laid down their lives for the progress of aviation."

Lindbergh was whisked to the Ministry of Finance in the Louvre, where they called on Premier Raymond Poincaré for his congratulations, then back to the embassy for more press conferences with the several hundred journalists who had descended on the avenue d'Iéna from all over the world—twenty-five from Sweden alone, eager to claim him as their own. He sportily answered even the most personal questions—revealing that he liked girls but did not know any and that he thought he would like dancing, though he had never tried it. He was happiest talking about aviation. "Lindbergh never seemed to weary," observed one reporter, "of talking about his earth induction compass . . ." At an appropriate moment, Ambassador Herrick interjected that this "boy is a human being, although we have sort of come to regard him in a much higher light." With that, he led his guest upstairs for a private dinner. They chatted until eleven.

Only when he was alone in his room did Lindbergh sample his first bad taste from any of his recent experiences. Before going to sleep he read that day's *New York Times,* which contained the first of the articles based on material he had been feeding Carlyle MacDonald. In two double columns, covering half the front page, he discovered that MacDonald had transformed his description of the flight into a first-person diary under a Charles Lindbergh byline. "I was shocked and disappointed," Lindbergh remembered more than forty years after reading the account. The long piece was written in a smarmy, aw-shucks style, a poor imitation of Will Rogers. "It was neither accurate nor in accord with my character and viewpoint," Lindbergh recalled. "In other words it made me into quite a different fellow than I was or wanted to be, and it gave quite a distorted picture of the flight itself."

It was an isolating moment for Lindbergh, one in which he realized the press had an agenda all its own. From then on, Lindbergh was suspicious, wary of anybody who would write about him. He saw that the press might forever use him for its own purpose, making him into what it thought the public wanted him to be; he saw that even the one newspaper he held up as the nation's "journal of record" could not be trusted to tell his story accurately. He could only imagine greater distortions that might follow. Lindbergh's parents and grandparents had long saved their important documents; now he resigned himself to save his as well—every shred of evidence that might document all that he did in his life and all that he did not do.

Without realizing that his words would be twisted into the first person, Lindbergh had agreed to an entire series of articles; the second such piece would be appearing stateside in the morning's *Times.* As there was no time for him to write them himself, he could only express his displeasure to MacDonald and hope he would modulate the articles. The journalist complied, not wishing to upset the flow of exclusive interviews Lindbergh would continue to grant. At the soonest possible moment, however, Lindbergh hoped to begin writing the stories himself. He vowed never again to authorize the use of his byline on anything he did not write.

At 12:30 on Tuesday, the American Club in Paris threw a luncheon in Lindbergh's honor. Five thousand members of the American colony vied for the six hundred admission tickets to the dining room at the Hotel Ambassadeurs on the Boulevard Haussmann. Although the event was for Americans, several French luminaries sat at the head table with Lindbergh, including André Citroën, the automobile magnate. Upon Lindbergh's entrance, the luncheon guests exploded into ten solid minutes of applause. A guard stood by his place at the table so that Lindbergh could eat.

Moments later, Ambassador Herrick heard that two hundred French masons and carpenters constructing a building across the street had laid down their tools, striking until they caught sight of Lindbergh. Upon learning this, Lindbergh offered to greet them from the hotel balcony. He left the dining room and stepped onto the balcony, where twenty-five thousand Parisians greeted him. The construction workers threw their caps into the air and tooted their steam whistles. Lindbergh's return to the dining room prompted another ovation. Lindbergh then addressed the crowd, detailing some of the actions that preceded his flight. Summoning Nungesser and Coli once again, he added, "The name of my ship, the *Spirit of St. Louis,* is intended to convey a certain meaning to the people of France, and I sincerely hope it has." The demand to see Lindbergh that day was so ardent that some of the hordes outside smashed the huge plate-glass windows of the hotel in an effort to see their hero. Before he was able to leave the Ambassadeurs, a hundred cooks and scullery boys insisted on greeting him, kissing his hand, while he stood there blushing.

The next day, Lindbergh lunched privately with Louis Blériot at his house, joined only by a few of France's ministers and leaders in French aviation. "I shall always regard you as my master," Lindbergh told the gray-haired man who had flown across the English Channel only eighteen years earlier. "Ah, but you are my son," granted Blériot, "you are the prophet of a new era . . ."

The luncheon party proceeded to the French Chamber of Deputies, where the parliament officially received Lindbergh. The president of the Army Commission of the Chamber praised Lindbergh for accomplishing "the most audacious feat of the century." He added, "It is not only two continents which you have united, but the hearts of all men everywhere in admiration for that simple courage of a man which does great things. . . . Your victory is over nature, over that obstinate trio of time, space and matter, against which man's fight must be incessant if he is to progress."

Between official engagements, Lindbergh continued to meet with members of the world press and diplomatic corps. The deluge of correspondence had been so great that he finally had to appoint the Bankers' Trust company to receive the incoming correspondence. He would actually see but a small fraction of the offerings—the praise from the President of Argentina, Mussolini, and Pope Pius XI . . . and the offer from a Texan to pay the taxes on the Orteig Prize. "There is a hundred and twenty million people in America all ready to tell Lindbergh what to do," wrote Will Rogers in his column four days after the flight. "The first thing we want to get into our heads is that this boy is not our usual type of hero that we are used to dealing with. He is all the others rolled into one and then multiplied by ten, and his case must be treated in a more dignified way." He recommended that the government provide Lindbergh with a pension and a high government position in the American aviation program. "He is our Prince and our President combined," Rogers wrote, "and I will personally pay benefits for him the rest of my life to keep him from having to make exhibitions out of himself. We only get one of these in a lifetime."

America clamored for Lindbergh's return. Major cities spontaneously established welcoming committees, and the whole country was going "aircrazy." James Dole, president of the Hawaiian Pineapple company, offered $25,000 to the first aviator to fly nonstop from the West Coast to Hawaii; Sid Grauman, the Hollywood theater owner, put up $30,000 for a nonstop flight between Los Angeles and Tokyo; the National Aeronautic Association announced $33,000 in prize money for a series of cross-continental flights: the starting dates of all the contests would remain unfixed until Lindbergh's return, as everybody hoped he would enter if not win. At President Coolidge's direction, the Secretary of the Navy offered transportation home for both Captain Lindbergh and his plane.

"From the moment I woke in the morning to that when I fell asleep at night," Lindbergh recounted of his first days in Paris, "every day was scheduled." One day when he thought he had found a few minutes to himself, he was brought one hundred pictures to autograph. Even if he had the time to wander the streets of Paris, he found that he no longer had the "freedom of action" to do so. "I was a prisoner of the ceremonial life that had been arranged for me," he reflected almost fifty years later, "with uniformed officers always outside the door of the building I was in and, always, newspaper reporters and photographers." Ironically, he had felt closer to Paris while flying above it.

Thursday was Ascension Day, a religious holiday for the nation; but Paris continued to celebrate Lindbergh. After meeting informally with the former Commander in Chief of the Allied Armies, Marshal Foch, and lunching with Foreign Minister Briand, Lindbergh rode in an open car down the Champs Élysées, through the Place de la Concorde, and along the Rue de Rivoli to the City Hall. The route was lined with over five hundred thousand—some estimated one million—people. It was the greatest reception Paris had ever accorded a private citizen, rivaling that of President Woodrow Wilson after the war. In the public square at the Hôtel de Ville alone, thirty-five thousand spectators jammed within the police lines.

Lindbergh entered the hall for a brief ceremony, at which he accepted the small gold key to the city. He offered thanks and brief remarks, noting that "I believe my flight is the forerunner of regular commercial air service uniting my country with yours in a manner in which they have never been united before." All through the ceremony the crowd outside could be heard chanting, "Au balcon, au balcon"; and the moment the remarks inside were concluded, Lindbergh rose from the golden chair in which he sat and made his way to the balcony, from which he waved an American flag and smiled his now famous grin. Within the week the City of Paris had designed, struck, and presented a special gold medal to Lindbergh.

He turned in early that night, contemplating offers from around the world—including $300,000 from Adolph Zukor to appear in a motion picture for Paramount Studios which he refused—and invitations from King George of England and King Albert of Belgium—which he accepted. He still mused about touring Europe, especially Sweden, before flying home by way of Greece, Asia, and the Pacific. Those dreams were dashed, however, as his own government pressed for his return.

The next morning, Lindbergh arose at five for a date that he had kept secret from practically everybody. A car drove him to Le Bourget, where the commander of the airport showed him a black Nieuport 300 h.p. fighting plane. After a quick lesson in the controls, Lindbergh took off, heading back toward the city. He flew on his own private tour of Paris, before the city had awakened. After twenty minutes of sightseeing, he returned to the airdrome, where he presented an impromptu half-hour performance of aerial stunts for the French aviators below. Upon landing, he looked in on his own plane and discovered that it had been completely repaired. The French crew had stripped the fuselage of all its fabric and recovered it like new.

After breakfast at the airport restaurant with a few of the fliers, Lindbergh returned to the city and his public duties: lunch at the Ministry of War, where General Pershing joined him; a reception of the French Senators at the Luxembourg Palace; a tour of the Citroën factory; a garden party at the Ministry of Commerce; a reception at the Airmen's Club in the Bois de Boulogne. Ambassador Herrick had invited Raymond Orteig, the hotelier whose prize had inspired Lindbergh's flight, for a private dinner at the embassy. The money would be awarded at a formal occasion in America. For now, Lindbergh wished to discuss his next-day's departure for Belgium and how he could best bid Paris adieu. Lindbergh thought of dropping a message from his plane addressed to the entire city in care of Orteig.

Later that night, Lindbergh got his first taste of Paris after dark, though it too was an institutional affair—a gala performance at the Champs Élysées Theatre for the benefit of the airmen's relief fund. The social elite of Paris turned out en masse. When Lindbergh and Herrick entered the center box, the orchestra struck up "The Star-Spangled Banner," and everybody rose and cheered. "Poor kid was so embarrassed," observed a young woman from Little Falls who happened to be present that night, "he blushed scarlet." American diva Mary Garden appeared onstage dressed as Liberty to sing the national anthem; and when she reached the final phrase—"and the home of the brave"—she thrust her index finger toward Lindbergh, and the theater shook with applause. French actress Cecile Sorel read a poem dedicated to the flier and at the end collapsed to her knees, crying, "Leendbear! Leendbear!" The auctioning of Lindbergh's signature that night fetched $1,600.

Lindbergh was at Le Bourget at 7:30 the next morning, getting grease on his hands for the first time in a week. For three hours he tuned his plane. At eleven, Ambassador Herrick arrived with a cold lunch, which they shared in a hangar. To avoid a recurrence of the hysteria that greeted his arrival, Lindbergh had announced that Paris would be the best place to witness his departure. Most of the city took him at his word.

A few minutes before one o'clock, the *Spirit of St. Louis* took off from exactly the point at which it had landed seven days prior. He headed for Paris, whose streets were lined with hundreds of thousands looking skyward. Lindbergh flew toward the Eiffel Tower, circled it twice, then buzzed low over the Arc de Triomphe; following the Champs Élysées, he looped twice before reaching the Place de la Concorde. "Nothing seemed to be dropped from the airplane," Orteig remembered; "we were rather disappointed, trying to guess what had happened." Then the plane returned, and, as Orteig told it, "my hopes came back and very soon I saw Lindbergh dropping the promised message, tied to a beautiful French flag." Weighted with a little sandbag, the tricolor landed at the foot of the obelisk in front of Orteig's hotel, the Crillon. The crowd rushed to grab the parcel, but it practically fell into the hands of a friend of Orteig, who safely handed it over. "Goodbye! Dear Paris," read the note. "Ten thousand thanks for your kindness to me. Charles A. Lindbergh."

Lindbergh flew toward the center of the city, over which he performed some of his old barnstorming spins and rolls, thrilling the crowd. Then he headed northeast toward Belgium, flying over miles of war-scarred country. "This week will be a kind of a dream to me all my life," read Lindbergh's next *New York Times* piece, written just before his departure in the new style leaning more heavily on his dictation. "I feel I want to go somewhere quiet and think it over."

That was no longer possible. He had less than two hours to himself before reaching the Belgian airdrome at Evere. King Albert had issued orders that the crowd must allow Lindbergh and his plane to land undisturbed. In addition to most of the police force of Brussels, five thousand troops stood guard with fixed bayonets. By three o'clock that afternoon, more than twenty-five thousand people, some said as many as seventy-five thousand, awaited his arrival. Only the Prime Minister stepped forward to welcome the aviator, while everyone behind him cheered. Lindbergh was chauffeured to the American Embassy, where he changed clothes. On his way to the Royal Palace, he was taken to lay a wreath at the Tomb of the Unknown Soldier of Belgium; then King Albert and his family received him. After a few minutes of conversation in English, the King pinned the Badge of a Knight of the Order of Leopold on his lapel. An appearance before the Belgian Aero Club followed, with the awarding of a plaque.

The next morning Lindbergh kept a private engagement with the King and Queen back at Evere, where he showed them his plane and answered questions about his great flight. He returned to the city for a day of receptions. The gilt buildings and even the old gray stone of the magnificent Grande Place in front of the Hôtel de Ville shimmered under a bright sun. The square was packed to capacity with thousands of cheering Belgians, the chimes of St. Gaudule Cathedral filled the air, and American flags waved at every turn. Inside the gothic Guild Hall, before a select group of aldermen, veterans, and the American colony, the highly regarded Burgomaster Max welcomed Lindbergh. "In this City Hall, where I have had the honor to receive so many great and illustrious men," he said, "I am proud to salute a real hero . . . your victory is the victory of humanity. In your glory there is glory for all men." Amid the cheers and handshakes, the Burgomaster handed Lindbergh a leather pouch, which contained a gold medal from the City of Brussels. After the leading baritone of the Brussels Opera sang "The

Star-Spangled Banner," Lindbergh asked that he close the ceremony with the Belgian national anthem. Upon its conclusion, the Burgomaster and Lindbergh stood at the balcony to acknowledge the exultant crowds.

After a week of sixteen-hour diplomatic days, Lindbergh was exhausted. His hours in the air seemed to be the only time he could be by himself. He returned to Evere and pressed on toward England. Over the cemetery at Werington, near Ghent—a final resting place for many American soldiers—Lindbergh flew low. He dropped a wreath of flowers onto the vast sea of white crosses, circled the graveyard twice, and flew under clear skies across the Channel.

From what he knew of British reserve, Lindbergh expected nothing less dignified than the reception he had received in Belgium. In fact, American Ambassador Alanson B. Houghton had arranged a proper ceremony for the flier, in which he would land at Croydon, thirteen miles south of Parliament, taxi around the airdrome in a victory lap for the cordoned-off crowd to see, then leave the plane in a recess close to where he would be presented to British officials. Two and one-half hours after leaving Belgium, the speck of a monoplane was sighted over the towers of London. Despite all the preparation for Lindbergh's reception, nobody had anticipated a crowd of one hundred fifty thousand Englishmen.

That first glint of silver in the sky was enough to throw them into chaos. In an instant, everybody rushed past the ropes onto the field where Lindbergh was meant to land. Above their cheers, the *Spirit of St. Louis* circled, touched the ground, and started to taxi . . . only to take to the air again. Lindbergh had in that instant looked out his window and feared plowing into the masses of people. Those on the ground knew to clear a path for him; and to the sound of a second wave of cheers, he landed just beyond the grasp of the crowd. Not until the police had roped off the plane did Lindbergh exit and make his way to an official car. The Ambassador and Air Minister were lost in the melee, while Lindbergh's driver managed to push through to the control tower. Women fainted, silk hats were crushed, canes and umbrellas went flying, while twelve hundred bobbies helplessly blew their whistles.

The aviator climbed a ladder to the top of the tower and with a megaphone shouted down with glee, "I just want to tell you this is worse than I had in Paris." The thousands of people at his back insisted he address them as well, so Lindbergh crossed to the other side of the tower platform and screamed, "I've just said this is a little worse than Le Bourget, or, I should say, better." After the cheers died down, everybody broke into "For He's a Jolly Good Fellow." Upon its completion, Lindbergh pled with the crowd to allow the Ambassador to pass so that they all might be able to leave. The formal reception was abridged in favor of a retreat to the city. Thousands lining the roads cheered him into London.

Lindbergh's next three days were filled with events to which he had grown accustomed—meals at the embassy with special guests, press conferences, a visit to the tomb of England's "unknown warrior." On his second night in London he was the honored guest at a large banquet of journalists in the Abraham Lincoln Room of the Savoy Hotel. At Lindbergh's place were five sandwiches and a half-gallon jar of water; and when he took his seat, the evening's toastmaster announced, "Captain Lindbergh will now partake of his customary meal."

The next day held more pomp. By then it had been decided that Lindbergh and his plane would return to America by boat. Ambassador Houghton informed him that President Coolidge had "ordered" a warship for his passage. And so, a little before four o'clock on the morning of Tuesday, May thirty-first, Lindbergh was motored to Croydon, where he flew his plane to an airfield in Gosport, near the port of Southampton. There it would be crated for its return home. After explaining how the *Spirit* was to be dismantled and packed, Lindbergh borrowed a plane in which he returned to London, all in time to change into a blue suit for his next round of ceremonies.

After a brief stop at Number 10 Downing Street for Prime Minister Stanley Baldwin's personal congratulations, Lindbergh arrived at Buckingham Palace at 10:45. Presented to King George V, they withdrew to one of the palace salons and sat together, just the two of them. "I was flattered to find his questions showed he had read a great deal about [my flight] and understood it perfectly," Lindbergh "wrote" afterward in the next installment of his travelogue for *The New York Times*. "And interestingly enough, I was able to observe that what interested the King about flying over the Atlantic was just about what interested every one else. The conception of a King as a personage of great aloofness and coldness certainly is belied by King George, who treated me in a straightforward, democratic style." What Lindbergh diplomatically elected not to record was the early fragment of conversation in which His Royal Highness leaned forward and said, "Now tell me, Captain Lindbergh. There is one thing I long to know. How did you pee?"

After fifteen minutes of private conversation, Queen Mary entered with her personal congratulations. She watched while her husband decorated Lindbergh with the Air Force Cross, the highest peacetime honor that may be conferred "upon persons not in the service of the British crown who are credited with great flying achievement." Before leaving the palace, Lindbergh entered a vestibule where he was introduced to the baby Princess Elizabeth, the King's granddaughter. Lindbergh bent down, shook her hand, and patted her cheek. The large crowd that had amassed outside the palace cheered as his car pulled away.

At 11:15 Lindbergh called on the Prince of Wales at York House. He noticed that the charming prince "seemed less interested in my flight itself than the King was, but he displayed great interest in me personally." When the man who would become Edward VIII asked Lindbergh what he was going to do in the future, he replied that he was going to "keep on flying." The press—which would caption the pictures of this meeting "The two most popular young men in the world"—asked Lindbergh what they had talked about. "Oh, about ten minutes," was his reply.

That afternoon Lindbergh visited the House of Commons as the guest of Lord and Lady Astor. The Speaker's welcome inspired a great ovation, and Lindbergh was escorted to the "distinguished strangers gallery." He listened to a few minutes of debate before retiring to the terrace. Upon taking his leave, he received a most unusual display of admiration, some believed the only such demonstration ever extended to an American: the entire House stood as one. On the terrace, Lindbergh had a few minutes with the Chancellor of the Exchequer, Winston Churchill; and the next day in Parliament, Churchill offered a few words about the nation's distinguished visitor. "From the little we have seen of him," Churchill said, "we have derived the impression that he represents all that a man should say, all that a man should do, and all that a man should be."

The British tried to maintain their reserve at all the events Lindbergh attended—the British Air Council luncheon at which he received the *Daily Mail's* gold cup, the Royal Aero Club dinner at the Savoy, the Derby eve ball at Albert Hall, and the Derby itself—but they could not restrain themselves. Wherever he went, bands spontaneously burst into "Yankee Doodle," men on the street cheered and waved handkerchiefs and beseeched him for autographs, and women rushed up to kiss him.

Just as the first boat from Europe containing films and photos of Lindbergh's arrival in Paris reached New York—with special provisions by the Treasury Department that would speed the cargo through customs, so that the images could be transmitted nationwide within hours—there was a change in plans for transporting Lindbergh home. Admiral G. H. Burrage's flagship, the cruiser *Memphis,* which had enough deckspace to carry the *Spirit* as well as room below for the crew of correspondents who wished to make the voyage, was "assigned" to bring him from France.

After two weeks of punctual arrivals at dozens of events, Lindbergh was delayed for the first time, trying to cross the English Channel. While the *Memphis* stopped in Southampton to pick up the two huge crates that held the *Spirit of St. Louis,* fog and rain kept Lindbergh in England one night longer than had been scheduled. He had braved worse weather, but the diplomats refused to let him fly. On the morning of Friday, June second, he left Kenley Airdrome in a borrowed plane and arrived at Le Bourget, where thousands had turned out again to see him. After a few small ceremonies in Paris, Lindbergh quietly left the next morning for Cherbourg to meet the *Memphis*.

Even in the gray cold, ten thousand citizens of Cherbourg stood in the public square, which was dressed with American flags. A plaque was un-veiled, commemorating that spot in France over which Lindbergh first flew. As he shoved off in the launch that delivered him to the U.S.S. *Memphis,* a voice cried from shore, "Come back soon." Lindbergh replied, "You bet I will."

Just as the *Memphis* reached the open sea, another voyage across the At-lantic commenced. After weeks of disputes, the Bellanca *Columbia* finally took off from Roosevelt Field with Clarence Chamberlin as pilot. To every-body's amazement, at the last minute, the unannounced copilot turned out to be none other than Charles Levine, the man who months earlier had re-fused to sell that very plane to Lindbergh. For further dramatic effect, Cham-berlin and Levine were keeping their destination a surprise. Forty-six and one-half hours later, the plane was forced down in Eisleben, Germany, one hundred ten miles short of its intended destination of Berlin.

For days Chamberlin and Levine received boldfaced, front-page coverage, for they had in one swoop smashed two of Lindbergh's records—distance (3,905 miles) and time in the air. Many journalists, especially the corre-spondents in Berlin, tried to outdo the rhetoric about Lindbergh; but neither diction nor distance made any difference. From the outset, the two flights hardly seemed comparable to the public. Lindbergh remained the first to connect the continents by airplane, and he did it alone—arriving exactly where he intended. The articles about Chamberlin and Levine battling the el-ements to reach Europe ended up sharing space with Lindbergh in repose, sailing home. As Lindbergh approached American shores, news of the prepa-ration for his arrival edged Chamberlin and Levine out of the public con-sciousness.

For the next nine days, Lindbergh rewound the fantastic memories of the past two weeks. He caught up on his sleep, and he worked several hours every day with Carlyle MacDonald, dictating the details of his flight and life for a book he had agreed to deliver based on the *Times* articles. "After the receptions at Le Bourget and Croydon," Lindbergh said, ". . . I find myself wondering what sort of reception I will get at New York."

No previous event had ever inspired such a spontaneous outpouring of song, by amateurs and professionals alike—at least two hundred of them, mostly marches and hymns, but also the occasional waltz and fox trot, even a stomp and a mazurka. Most were soubriquets—"Lucky Lindy," "The Lone Eagle," "Eagle of Liberty," "Lindbergh, the Eagle of the U.S.A.," "The Monarch of the Air," "The Flying Idol," "Lindy, the Bird of the Clouds,"

"America's Son," "Columbus of the Air," "Eagle of Liberty," "That Air-plane Man." Even America's songwriter laureate, George M. Cohan, com-posed a tune for publication in all the Hearst newspapers—"When Lindy Comes Home." More serious works came to be composed as well. Kurt Weill and Bertolt Brecht would soon collaborate on a cantata—"Der Lind-berghflug"—fifteen scenes for soloists, chorus, and orchestra in which a tenor portraying Lindbergh sings of his preparations for the flight, and later faces such antagonists as the Fog, the Snowstorm, and Sleep.

The night Lindbergh had landed in Paris, the excitement reached all the way into the Savoy Ballroom in Harlem, where a number of patrons were dancing the latest variations on the Charleston. The whole joint was jump-ing, people elatedly screaming, "Lindy's done it, Lindy's done it." One fel-low on the sidelines, "Shorty George" Snowden, looked over at some young people doing swing-outs, breakaways, and "shine steps," and was alleged to have commented, "Look at them kids hoppin' over there. I guess they're doin' the Lindy Hop." Both the dance and the name caught on.

Thousands expressed themselves in verse. *The New York Times* alone re-ceived more than two thousand poems within a single week. To stanch the flow of unsolicited material, the paper published an editorial stating that "no poem worthy of the event" could be written until at least six months had allowed for "adequate perspective for imaginative treatment." But doggerel continued to arrive, with similes likening him to Gutenberg, Hippocrates, Columbus, and often to Christ.

When publisher Mitchell Kennerley offered cash prizes for the three best poems on the subject of Lindbergh and his flight, he received six thousand entries. Entire books were printed of Lindbergh verses. Effusions in seem-ingly every language were sent to Lindbergh—classroom assignments scrawled in pencil, housewives' musings written in calligraphy, stanzas pri-vately printed, some even decorated in gold leaf. For months it was difficult for any magazine or local newspaper to go without a poetic offering that rhymed "boy" with "joy," "chance" with "France," "night" with "light," "prayer" with "dare," and "youth" with "truth."

The popular French dramatist Sacha Guitry wrote a play called *Lind-bergh,* which would succeed his other theatrical treatments of Pasteur and Mozart. And before Lindbergh had even reached American shores, a dozen biographies of him were in the works, each more hagiographic than the last. No American had been so instantly mythologized, the tales meant to inspire youth and capitalize on patriotism. One successful volume, *The Lone Scout of the Sky,* would be written by James E. West, the Chief Scout Executive of the Boy Scouts of America. The book most eagerly awaited, however, was being written aboard the U.S.S. *Memphis.*

While Lindbergh had as little intention of returning to flying the mail as he had of keeping the Orteig Prize (which he felt belonged to his backers), he had wasted no time considering how he might earn his living. His June second article in the *Times* announced that his criterion in sorting through the many offers coming his way would be simple: "Whatever will aid aviation will interest me. Whatever does not mean help to aviation will not interest me at all." *The Christian Science Monitor* ran a cartoon that showed the aviator holding at bay a group of promotors offering contracts for lectures, theater tours, movies, and books while he cast a pensive eye on the setting sun, which spelled out "achievement." It was the common glorified image of Lindbergh, for newspapers reported that he had already turned down over one million dollars' worth of contracts and product endorsements. But, Lindbergh would later recount, "it was essential that I find ways of earning more money that would leave me as free as possible to pursue the development of aviation."

"The closer we get to the shores of America the more radio messages I receive from cities, towns and persons who want to entertain me," read one of Lindbergh's *Times* columns, radioed from aboard ship. "I suppose I would have to dine out for a year if I were to accept them all, but I am awfully anxious to get back to hard work again just as soon as the receptions are over, and I know the public will help me out on this proposition." In the meantime, he admitted finding it a relief to be able to sleep eight or nine hours and work on his book and "know there are no speeches ahead of me the next day." At the start of his ocean crossing Lindbergh wrote, "I will be ready for anything when I step on dry land again." Six days later that proved to be an idle boast.

At five o'clock in the afternoon of June 10, 1927, the cruiser passed through the Virginia Capes, and Lindbergh got his first taste of the reception that lay ahead. A convoy of four destroyers, two Army blimps, and forty airplanes accompanied the *Memphis* up Chesapeake Bay. Standing on the ship's bridge, as scenes of his lonely childhood approached, the twenty-five-year-old Army captain turned to Admiral Burrage and said, "It is a great and wonderful sight, and I wonder if I really deserve all this."

In Washington, Evangeline Lindbergh arrived as the guest of the President of the United States. Calvin and Grace Coolidge invited her to spend the night on the third floor at 15 Du Pont Circle, their temporary residence while the roof of the White House was being repaired. The only other guest that night was the President's friend Dwight W. Morrow, a partner of J. P. Morgan and Company, who had recently chaired a presidential Aircraft Board. Shortly after dinner, the Coolidges had to excuse themselves for another engagement, leaving Morrow alone to entertain Mrs. Lindbergh. He was grateful for the opportunity, "greatly impressed by her simplicity, dignity, and spirituality." Into the night she regaled Morrow with "countless stories about her son," all "exalting."

It was already hot at dawn that Saturday when the *Memphis* entered its homestretch up the Potomac. The temperature would rise to eighty-eight degrees. A noisy greeting of whistles, horns, bells, and sirens as well as waves and cheers came from most of the citizens of the sleepy town of Alexandria. As the ship passed, heads tilted back to see the aerial escort of eighty-eight planes and the dirigible *Los Angeles* scudding over the *Memphis*.

With the cruiser slowly rounding the bend before the naval yard, Cabinet members and heads of the armed services strained to get their first glimpse of the tall, slim young man in the blue suit on the bridge, holding his hat with one hand and waving with the other. A volley of gun salutes cracked the air, punctuating the roar of the crowd. As the anchor was dropped and the gangway fastened, Admiral Burrage led Lindbergh to the bow for a long welcoming cheer. At a word from Burrage, Lindbergh disappeared inside the ship.

The Admiral ran down the gangway where two White House aides presented a woman dressed in shades of brown and wearing a large, black straw hat. Without saying a word, Burrage offered his arm and escorted the proud Evangeline Lindbergh up the ramp. Once the public realized who it was, every whistle, siren, and cannon in the vicinity sounded. Everyone was overcome with emotion, thinking of that last meeting in Long Island, when nobody knew if mother and son would ever see each other again. Grown men cried.

After a few minutes, the Lindberghs appeared together. To the boom of saluting guns, Lindbergh stepped forward to greet the secretaries of War and the Navy. Then he and his mother stepped into the backseat of the President's touring car, which made its way toward the back of the Capitol. Down the hill to the west, the entourage met up with a cavalry escort on Pennsylvania Avenue, which slowly led them to the Washington Monument. Columns of soldiers and sailors, interspersed with dignitaries, fell in behind. While Lindbergh was abroad, Postmaster General New had touted the use of airmail by encouraging the public to send Captain Lindbergh an airmail letter greeting him home; now three screened mail trucks, carrying over five hundred thousand packages and letters, brought up the rear of the parade. Spectators all along the route waved and cheered and threw their hats into the air. "No returning hero was ever escorted with greater dignity," observed *The New York Times*. Political Washington took no sides that day.

More than two hundred fifty thousand people stood shoulder to shoulder in the hazy heat around the base of the great obelisk and down into Potomac Park, where a grandstand had been erected. Beneath a simple white canopy sat the Coolidges and their guests, including the nation's political, military, and business leaders. The moment the audience spotted Lindbergh, their minute-long demonstration drowned out the huge brass band. Then, most uncharacteristically, the man known as "Silent Cal" orated for several minutes, tracing Lindbergh's personal history right through his royal receptions in Europe. "And now, my fellow citizens," Coolidge said, "this young man has returned. He is here. He has brought his unsullied fame home." With that, the President bestowed upon Lindbergh the first Distinguished Flying Cross—"as a symbol of appreciation for what he is and what he has done"—and announced his promotion to Colonel of the United States Reserve Corps. A demonstration ensued for minutes as Lindbergh stood there—neither bowing nor smiling, just modestly facing the crowd.

Stepping up to the microphones, he spoke plainly in his slightly clipped, boyish voice to the hushed crowd and to another thirty million radio listeners across the country. Some five hundred photographers captured the moment as well, while special trains, planes, and automobiles waited to speed their film to laboratories for worldwide distribution. Lindbergh spoke but one hundred and six unscripted words, the gist of which was that he was a messenger between America and Europe, and that the attention lavished on him was "the affection of the people of France for the people of America." The crowd stood for a moment in absolute silence, stunned by the brevity and the humility of the remarks. The world would little note, nor long remember what he said there, but many people likened his speech to Lincoln's Address at Gettysburg. In lieu of shouts came only sustained, reverential applause. One radio broadcaster sobbed. Under the blazing hot sun, a display of daylight fireworks burst in the sky.

Lindbergh and his party made their way to Du Pont Circle for an early dinner with the Cabinet, followed by a presentation of honors before six thousand at a meeting of the National Press Club in the Washington Auditorium. The Secretary of State handed Lindbergh a bound memorial volume of diplomatic exchanges between the State Department and the Foreign Offices around the world concerning the flight. Dr. Charles G. Abbot, Acting Secretary of the Smithsonian Institution, announced that the Institute was awarding him its distinguished Langley "Medal of Pioneers."

The grandest gesture that night came from the Post Office Department, which announced that it had neither titles nor medals to bestow, and that the department had long labored under the rule that the likeness of a living American could not appear on a postage stamp. But there was nothing to stop them from using his name. And so, Postmaster General New announced that night that his department "has issued a stamp designed for special use with the airmails, which bears your name and a representation of the other member of that very limited partnership in which you made your now famous journey across seas. It is," New declared, just before handing Lindbergh and his mother the first two copies of this issue of five hundred sixty thousand ten-cent stamps depicting the *Spirit of St. Louis,* the "first time a stamp has been issued in honor of a man still living—a distinction which you have worthily won."

Lindbergh began the next day by attending church services with the Coolidges, then laid a wreath at the Tomb of the Unknown Soldier, visited wounded veterans at Walter Reed Hospital, and appeared at a celebration on the Capitol steps of the sesquicentennial of the American Flag. It turned into a celebration of Lindbergh instead, as former Secretary of State and soon-to-be Chief Justice Charles Evans Hughes presented him with the Cross of Honor of the United States Flag Association. Hughes commended Lindbergh as "America's most successful messenger of good-will."

On Monday, June thirteenth, Lindbergh appeared at a 6:45 breakfast reception in the ballroom at the Mayflower Hotel, where the National Aeronautic Association conferred a lifetime membership upon him, an honor held by the Wrights, Chanute, Langley, and Edison. The most magnanimous speech of the morning came from Commander Richard E. Byrd, Lindbergh's former rival on the runway of Roosevelt Field. "When we built the *America* for a transatlantic flight," he said, "it was our object to attempt to help the spirit of good fellowship and the progress of aviation. Colonel Lindbergh has done these two things in a far better way than we ever hoped. We think it very fortunate for the world that Lindbergh got there before we did, and we are glad of it."

Lindbergh went to Bolling Field, where he climbed into the wicker chair of the *Spirit of St. Louis.* The plane had been tuned and given a fresh coat of silver paint; but when Lindbergh heard the engine, it did not sound right. Reluctantly, he borrowed a Curtiss P-1 biplane. He put the crowd at the airfield at ease by offering them a breathtaking display of stunts, showing off with an Immelmann turn, soaring almost straight up and over until he was flying upside down. Flipping into a few barrel rolls, he set off for New York with an escort of the First Pursuit Group of Selfridge Field, Michigan, commanded by Major Thomas G. Lanphier. Commander Byrd rode in one of the planes.

Lindbergh flew at three thousand feet, above his escort, probably too high to see the demonstrations below. In every city along his route—Baltimore, Wilmington, Philadelphia, Trenton—tens of thousands of people filled the streets and the rooftops, waving to him. He landed at Mitchel Field on Long Island, where he was rushed into a waiting car and taken across the field to another plane, the amphibian *San Francisco,* a deep-blue plane with golden wings. The captain volplaned Lindbergh down to the water near Quarantine, the station on Staten Island, where the Atlantic Ocean meets the Narrows.

More than four hundred boats waited in the water, a Marine Parade representing every type of boat in the harbor. One of them, a police launch, pulled over to the *San Francisco* to receive its passenger. Upon the realization that it was Lindbergh, every boat whistled and tooted. The fanfare was loud enough for the twenty thousand people standing along the Palisades of the Hudson River—ten miles away—to hear without straining. Lindbergh was shuttled to the *Macom,* the yacht of the Mayor of the City of New York. A committee welcomed him aboard, but it was too noisy for anybody to hear much, even at the press conference below deck. When one journalist asked if he was wearying of all the receptions, Lindbergh replied, "That's hardly a query I could answer now." For much of the hour it took to reach the Battery, Lindbergh stood on the bridge of the *Macom,* while twenty-two planes flew over in battle formation, dropping fifty thousand blossoms.

When the *Macom* reached Pier A at 12:40 that afternoon, Lindbergh found three hundred thousand people waiting in the Battery. New York City's offices, schools, stock exchanges, and most of the nation's principal financial markets were closed for "Lindbergh Day," as "a mark of respect"; and, at first glance, it seemed that Manhattan's entire population had forced its way to its southern tip. In fact, another four million people were waiting farther uptown, lining the route that lay ahead. Lindbergh's mother met him at the pier, and they entered separate cars. One overpowering roar sustained the entire hour in which Lindbergh rode the mile up Broadway from Battery Park to City Hall, people filling every inch of sidewalk and every window along the way. Through the canyon of buildings, past Wall Street, the ticker tape and other shredded paper was so thick that few could even see Lindbergh or the skyline through the "snowstorm."

More than ten thousand soldiers and sailors led the parade, up to the Mayor's two grandstands, which were filled with three thousand city officials and special guests. Gloria Trumpeters—three women in white robes—sounded the arrival of Lindbergh's car, setting off the vociferation of the one hundred thousand standing outside City Hall. Lindbergh stepped up to the platform, where Grover A. Whalen, Chairman of the Mayor's Committee on Reception, introduced him to Mayor James J. Walker.

"Let me dispense with any unnecessary official side of function, Colonel," said "Gentleman Jimmy" to the young man in the blue suit, "by telling you that if you have prepared yourself with any letters of introduction to New York City they are not necessary." He praised Lindbergh for being a "great grammarian," for introducing to the English language the world's first "flying pronoun"—the "aeronautical 'we.' "

Speaking on behalf of his six million constituents, Mayor Walker said that Lindbergh had "inscribed on the heavens themselves a beautiful rainbow of hope and courage and confidence in mankind." With that, he added,

"Colonel Lindbergh, New York City is yours—I don't give it to you; you won it." He pinned the specially made Medal of New York City on Lindbergh's lapel. It was an elaborate decoration, with Lindbergh's plane and the word "We" struck in platinum and set into the gold medal.

Lindbergh approached the microphones and spoke of his receptions in Europe and the mounting pressure for him to return to America. "The Ambassador in London said that it was not an order to go back home," Lindbergh said, "but there would be a battleship waiting in a few days." He paused for the great wave of laughter to subside, then added that while he had departed with regrets, coming up the Potomac had made him not so sorry that he had taken the Ambassador's advice. "After spending about an hour in New York," Lindbergh added, "I know I am not." His trademark "I thank you" triggered applause that could be stopped only by the singing of "The Star-Spangled Banner."

The parade continued uptown on Fifth Avenue, Lindbergh in the first car with the Mayor and Grover Whalen. They paused at the "Eternal Light" at Twenty-fourth Street so that Lindbergh could place a wreath of roses in memory of New York's fighting men who had made "the supreme sacrifice" in the War. Big American flags billowed along both sides of the avenue, above the steadily thickening crowd. Only children—ten thousand of them, most waving small flags—were given access to the great steps, windows, and front lawn of the Public Library between Fortieth and Forty-second streets. At Fiftieth Street the parade paused again, so that Lindbergh could step out of his automobile to greet Cardinal Hayes of New York, who was seated in a special chair placed in front of the center door of St. Patrick's Cathedral. Upon seeing Lindbergh exit from his car, the Prince of the Church descended the steps to welcome him. "I greet you as the first and finest American boy of the day," said the elderly Cardinal. "God bless you and God bless your mother." Lindbergh bowed slightly and returned to the parade.

At times, Lindbergh and his escorts had to bail confetti out of their car. "I guess when I leave here," Lindbergh yelled to Mayor Walker, "they'll have to print another edition of the telephone book."

"Well, before you leave," the Mayor replied, "you'll have to provide us with another Street Cleaning Department." In fact, two thousand street cleaners were called up to remove what amounted to close to two thousand tons of paper that were tossed that day, the most that had ever rained on the city.

Four hours after arriving in the Battery, Lindbergh faced the three hundred thousand people who had emptied into Central Park's Sheep Meadow for the official honors of New York State. Overhead a skywriter sprayed the words "Hail Lindy." Mayor Walker introduced Lindbergh to Governor Alfred E. Smith, who draped a blue ribbon around Lindbergh's neck, from which hung the Medal of Valor from the State of New York. The medal, created by Tiffany and Company and presented for "intrepidity and courage of the highest order," had never before been awarded to a nonresident of the state. "You are hailed in the Empire State," said Governor Smith, "as an ideal and an example for the youth of America." After a thirty-minute review of the tail end of the parade, Lindbergh and his mother were taken to an apartment at 270 Park Avenue, which had been loaned to them by a friend of the Mayor for the duration of their stay in the city. At the apartment, Lindbergh ate his first food since leaving Washington early that morning. It was also his first quiet moment in ten hours.

Hundreds in New York City had collapsed that day. Many were trampled by the crowd and the mounted police, and one twenty-three-year-old woman suffered a fatal heart attack watching the parade from the roof of the Hotel Seville. By 8:15 that night, a revived Lindbergh was driven to the Long Island estate of Clarence Mackay—head of the Postal Telegraph Company, one of the city's most prominent social leaders, and the disapproving father-in-law of Irving Berlin. At Harbor Hill, his fifty-room mansion in Roslyn, Mackay hosted a dinner for eighty in Lindbergh's honor with several hundred more guests arriving later for dancing. Lindbergh did not return to Park Avenue until after midnight.

By then, Charles Lindbergh had become the most photographed man in the world. Impossibly photogenic, there was not a bad picture to be taken of him. When he smiled, he radiated the endearing innocence of an American farmboy; if caught frowning, his countenance assumed the strength of a Nordic god. Hollywood screenwriter and producer Lamar Trotti said, "Women saw in him the perfection of man, what they conceived their husbands to be and what still constitutes their dream. The men, in turn, experienced quick pulses of the heart and thought wistfully of the things they might have done, things they would like to do, things they wish they had the nerve to do." Although he was barely known but three weeks prior, after the first day of his reception in New York, an estimated 7,430,000 feet of newsreel film had recorded his movements, already two million more feet than existed of the Prince of Wales, previously considered the subject of more frames of documentary film than anybody in history. Where Lindbergh's flight had filled the first five pages of *The New York Times,* his reception accounted for every article for the first sixteen pages. Newspaper stands and tobacconists offered his picture for a quarter. "Welcome Home, Lindy" signs with his picture appeared on the window of practically every taxi. Army recruiting posters had his face pasted on, with the words "Lindbergh the Bold—He was Army trained." Lindbergh kept his head from being turned. As Paul Garber, the Smithsonian's aviation historian noted, "Even more impressive than

Lindbergh's flight across the Atlantic was the way in which he comported himself afterwards."

Over the next four days, the residents of Gotham and the rest of the globe would concur. Speeches dwelled as much on his character as on his achievement. With little more than the most measured thanks, Lindbergh faced screaming fans and laudatory remarks at one reception after another—including the official dinner of the City of New York, which the Hotel Commodore bragged was "the largest ever tendered to an individual in modern history"—thirty-seven hundred guests feasting on six thousand pounds of chicken, two thousand heads of lettuce, one hundred twenty-five gallons of peas, and eight hundred quarts of ice cream. Only the nation's most stately Charles Evans Hughes could do justice to the grandeur of the evening: "We measure heroes as we do ships, by their displacement," he explained. "Colonel Lindbergh has displaced everything."

Wednesday night, after a full day of receptions and a midnight benefit performance of *Rio Rita*—the Ziegfeld musical he had missed weeks earlier, when the weather over the Atlantic had suddenly cleared—Lindbergh took the wheel of a car himself and sped out to Mitchel Field on Long Island. The colonel in charge of the field was apprehensive, but at three o'clock in the morning, he gave Lindbergh an Army pursuit plane with enough gasoline to get him to Bolling Field. He made the trip in a little more than two hours; and within a half hour he was returning to Long Island in his own repaired plane. At 7:40 A.M., Lindbergh flew toward Roosevelt Field, grazing over the runway from which he had made history one month earlier, then landed at Mitchel Field. A car took him to Park Avenue, where he showered and changed from his evening clothes into a blue suit to attend Charles Lindbergh Day in Brooklyn.

The entire borough was closed for the holiday, so that Lindbergh could ride in a parade twenty-two miles long. He was greeted by seven hundred thousand people, one-third of its residents. There were ceremonies at Prospect Park—for two hundred thousand people—and a luncheon, before another ceremony at Roosevelt Field—for twenty-five thousand—where he parked his plane. He was rushed to the Bronx, where the Yankee fans had been promised a visit, but Lindbergh had time only to drive up to the stadium before heading downtown for the six o'clock presentation of the Orteig Prize at the Hotel Brevoort on Fifth Avenue at Eighth Street. There he received a magnificent scroll, a medal, and his check for $25,000. He noted that Orteig's offer had been his impetus to enter the race, for it was "nothing more nor less than a challenge to pilots and engineers in aeronautics to see whether they could build and fly a plane from New York to Paris. I do not believe any such challenge, within reason, will ever go unanswered."

Back at his apartment he changed into evening clothes for a reception of University of Wisconsin alumni and a dinner of the Aeronautical Chamber of Commerce. Later, he dropped in on a party given by William Randolph Hearst, which was also attended by the Mayor and Charlie Chaplin. He returned to the apartment at midnight. At 8:17 the next morning, the wheels of the *Spirit of St. Louis* left the turf of Roosevelt Field for the city that had launched him to fame.

It was a showery nine-hour flight over the Midwest, but that did not dampen the enthusiasm of those below. He circled the cities of Columbus, Dayton, and Indianapolis, where he was joined by aerial escorts, before reaching St. Louis. Five thousand people stood in the drizzle at Lambert Field to welcome him—including his former flying buddies, most of whom could not get past the guards to greet him. He and his mother, who had taken the train to St. Louis, spent the night at the home of backer Harry Knight.

The next day, the sun broke through just as a seven-mile parade through the streets of St. Louis began. Five hundred thousand people lined the way. American flags and pennants with Lindbergh's picture hung everywhere; "Slim did it" was the slogan of the day on lapel pins and hatbands. Although Lindbergh was visibly tired, with dark bags under his eyes, St. Louis kept him awake with the most cacophonous parade he had yet experienced. At the official dinner for thirteen hundred, Lindbergh was presented a scroll and the keys to the city inside a gold jewel box with a raised representation of a map showing the route from St. Louis to Paris. The next day Lindbergh performed aerial acrobatics for one hundred thousand in Forest Park and placed a wreath at the statue of St. Louis.

On Monday, June twentieth, Lindbergh partook in absolutely no public program or ceremony in his honor. For the first time in the month since his departure for France, nothing Lindbergh did that day was especially newsworthy. In fact, when he drove downtown St. Louis in a new car which he had been given, few people even recognized him without all the trappings of ceremony surrounding him. It was only when somebody pointed him out that he found himself running from a crowd intent on grabbing at his clothes and his body.

Evangeline Lindbergh traveled by train to Detroit, so that she could return to her classroom. Her son remained in St. Louis, sifting through some of the congratulations, gifts, and offers among the 3,500,000 letters, one hundred thousand telegrams, and fourteen thousand parcels which had been addressed to him since his return. Western Union had a selection of prepared messages which customers could order—"America's heart goes out to you" or "Time will not dim the splendor of your achievement," for example. Among the thousands of requests for autographs and photographs came scores of marriage proposals and hundreds of thousands of "welcome home" messages from professional organizations, chambers of commerce, and boys' clubs. Cities—such as Boston, Nashville, Sacramento, and Seattle—printed pre-addressed invitations to visit, which required only the sender's signature and a ten-cent airmail stamp.

To honor Lindbergh, thousands rendered his and his plane's likeness in oil paints, watercolors, pencil, charcoal, crayon, and gold as well as tapestries, needlepointed pillows, woven mats, and hooked rugs; one woman crocheted a model of the plane. His bust was sculpted in silver, bronze, ivory, plaster, and soap. He received rolls of Swedish wallpaper with his image repeated, an ivory inlaid billiard cue, a Persian manuscript of the Koran, a Gutenberg Bible, and a stickpin with the *Spirit of St. Louis* cut from a single diamond. Aviation clubs in the Netherlands, Turkey, and Czechoslovakia all conferred lifetime memberships upon him—with a gold medal, a diamond brooch, and a bronze plaque, respectively; and the Masonic Lodge, whose initiation ceremonies Lindbergh had never completed, issued him a Gold Life membership card. The Licensed Newsboys of Springfield, Illinois, chipped in and bought a fountain pen for their hero, a small token for the extra newspapers he helped sell. The Shubert Theatre Corporation issued him a gold and diamond Lifetime Pass to all their theaters throughout Europe and America; the National League of Professional Baseball Clubs sent a gold Lifetime Pass to any of their games.

Then came the wave of requests for his endorsement of products—not just from cigarette and cereal companies but from: Thomas D. Murphy Company of Red Oak, Iowa, which manufactured calendars and offered him two cents on every one of its fifteen-cent items; the Chicago company that was selling $200 busts of the aviator for schools, libraries, and museums; the German firm selling Lindbergh Razor Blades in Turkey; the New York outfit producing bronze *Spirit of St. Louis* letter openers; the Hookless Fastener Company of Meadville, Pennsylvania, which wanted to boast that Lindbergh's new flying suits would use their zippers.

Countless manufacturers did not wait for his approval. Clothiers could outfit men and women from head to toe in Lindbergh fashions: The Bruck-Weiss Company, for example, manufactured the "Lucky Lindy Lid"—a lady's hat of gray felt trimmed with black felt, with flaps on the side simulating plane wings and a gray felt propeller appliquéd in the front; a company in Haverhill produced the "Lucky Lindbergh" shoe for women, which featured the design of the *Spirit of St. Louis* sewn in patent leather with a propeller on the toe and a photograph of Lindy inserted in a leather horseshoe on the side. One of the salesmen of the Thompson Manufacturing Company in Belfast, Maine, realized they could move their boys' breeches faster if they started calling it the "Lindy" pant. A baker in Elkhart, Indiana, renamed his product "Lucky Lindy Bread." Toys and games, watches and clocks, pencils and rulers, and almost any paper product could be adapted to include a Lindbergh theme; anything packaged—from cigars to canned fruit—became fair game for a logo of a single-engined monoplane. Major businesses and institutions advertised in newspapers, welcoming Lindbergh home as a way of drawing attention to themselves. Lucrative proposals came from the deepest pockets in aviation, businessmen who wanted to build an airline around Lindbergh.

As Lindbergh's fame escalated, so did the demand to see him. Alexander Pantages guaranteed Lindbergh $105,000 for fifteen weeks of appearances on his circuit of vaudeville theaters. A French theatrical agent bettered that— $250,000 for five appearances in South America. The Recording Division of Thomas Edison, Inc., wanted Lindbergh to cut a phonograph disk describing his flight, the royalties of which would easily reach six figures. A rival talking-machine company guaranteed a flat $300,000 for such a narration, opening with "The Star-Spangled Banner" and closing with "The Marseillaise." Upon Lindbergh's landing in Paris, Carl Laemmle, founder of Universal Pictures, had offered $50,000 for the flier's appearance in two pictures, one of which he thought could be "The Great Air Robbery." Shortly after seeing the meteoric rise of Lindbergh-mania, he upped his offer to $700,000 for a one-year contract. Yet another company offered $1,000,000 for him to appear in a film in which he would actually marry.

The most extravagant offer came from William Randolph Hearst, whose media empire included Cosmopolitan Pictures. He wanted to star Lindbergh in a motion picture about aviation opposite his mistress, Marion Davies. Hearst had offered Lindbergh $500,000 plus ten percent of the gross receipts. Those extra points in the film would probably have been worth at least as much as his salary—leaving him financially set for life.

Hearst invited Lindbergh to his sumptuous New York house on Riverside Drive, where he handed Lindbergh the motion-picture contract all ready for signing. Lindbergh explained that he never had any intention of going into films, and he felt uncomfortable about signing the document. In order to lure Lindbergh, Hearst assured him that this would not be a moving picture "in the ordinary sense of the word." It would not be a fiction story, but the actual story of Lindbergh's life—"an historical record of a fine life and a great achievement to be preserved in pictures for others to see in years to come." He urged Lindbergh not to consider it merely for himself, "but as an inspiration to others."

"I wish I could do it if it would please you," Lindbergh demurred, "but I cannot, because I said I would not go into pictures." What Lindbergh did not say—until many years later in a book of memoirs—was that he objected to Hearst himself. The mogul, Lindbergh noted, "controlled a chain of news-papers from New York to California that represented values far apart from mine.

> They seemed to be overly sensational, inexcusably inaccurate, and excessively occupied with the troubles and vices of mankind. I disliked most of the men I had met who represented him, and I did not want to become associated with the organization he had built.

"All right," Hearst said at last, "—but you tear up the contract; I have not the heart to do it."

More embarrassed than ever, Lindbergh attempted to hand it back to him. "No," said Hearst quietly, sizing up the young man, "if you don't want to make a picture, tear it up and throw it away." Double-dared, Lindbergh tore the pages in half and tossed them into the fireplace. Hearst watched with what Lindbergh would long remember as "amused astonishment."

As he was leaving, Lindbergh stopped at a table to admire a pair of silver globes, fourteen inches high; one was terrestrial, the other celestial. The silversmith was unknown, but they were thought to be crafted in Hanover around 1700. It was the only known pair in existence, valued then at $50,000. The next day, a messenger arrived at Lindbergh's apartment on Park Avenue, bearing the two silver spheres as a gift.

Within the first month of his return, Lindbergh received more than five million dollars' worth of offers—at a time when income taxes would have taken less than five percent of his earnings and a most lavish rooftop triplex apartment on Park Avenue cost $100,000. The propositions seemed like fool's gold to Lindbergh alongside some vague offers coming from the United States government. Commerce Secretary Herbert Hoover and Aviation Secretaries William P. MacCracken, F. Trubee Davison, and Edward P. Warner, of the Commerce, War, and Navy departments, respectively, hoped Lindbergh might come to Washington to discuss what role he might play in the expansion of commercial aviation. There was talk of creating a new Cabinet post of Secretary of Aviation just for Lindbergh.

After a week of conferences in the capital and New York City, several ideas for promoting aviation emerged, as did a team of advisers who could actualize them. From different backgrounds, these well-educated men of great wealth were all consumed with the notion of public service.

Among them was perhaps the most important but least known figure in the development of American aviation, Harry Guggenheim. His grandfather Meyer Guggenheim was a Jewish peddler who had emigrated from Switzerland to Pennsylvania and parlayed money he had made from a stove-cleaning solvent into a copper mining and smelting empire. Few in America had ever made so much money so quickly, amassing in a few years one of the nation's vastest fortunes.

None of the great Jewish families who had immigrated to America assimilated faster than the Guggenheims, promptly abandoning their orthodoxy, even marrying outside the faith. Meyer's seven sons chose different fields in which to grow the money and different charities in which to re-sow most of it. Daniel Guggenheim became the family's leading industrialist; and among his many philanthropies was a Fund for the Promotion of Aeronautics, which he established in 1926 with $500,000. It could not have come at a more propitious moment, for aviation was then struggling through what Lindbergh would call the "period of transition between invention and commerce." While Guggenheim supplied the money, he left the task of dispensing it to his son, Harry.

A blue-eyed Navy aviator from the War, he and his gentile wife, the former Caroline "Carol" Morton, had recently moved onto an estate adjacent to his father's on the north shore of Long Island. His duties, as described by the Fund, were: "to promote aeronautical education throughout the country; to assist in the extension of aeronautical science; and to further the development of commercial aircraft, particularly in its use as a regular means of transportation of both goods and people." With the rest of his board—which included Air Secretary Trubee Davison and Dwight Morrow—Guggenheim felt "that no man could demonstrate more satisfactorily to the American public the progress of aeronautics than Colonel Lindbergh." In fact, after three weeks of receptions in America, Guggenheim considered him nothing less than a godsend to aviation, a natural generator of only the most positive publicity. The Fund invited Lindbergh to embark on a three-month tour that would take the *Spirit of St. Louis* to all forty-eight states in the Union.

Lindbergh accepted. While planning the trip, he even hired Guggenheim's attorney, Henry Breckinridge—a Princetonian who had served as Woodrow Wilson's Assistant Secretary of War—to act as his personal adviser, to sort through the hundreds of offers coming his way and to challenge the hundreds of illegal abusers of Lindbergh's name in promoting products.

"Col. Lindbergh's airplane tour will be undertaken for the primary purpose of stimulating popular interest in the use of air transport," read the Guggenheim Fund's press release on June 28, 1927. "It will enable millions of people who have had an opportunity only to read and hear about the colonel's remarkable achievement to see him and his plane in action." The fund had two other goals:

> . . . first, to encourage the use of our present air transport facilities for
> mail express and passenger carrying purposes, aerial photography

and other services, and thereby foster the growth of this means of transportation, and second, to promote the development of airports and air communication services.

While Guggenheim, Breckinridge, and the Air Secretaries prepared the itinerary, Dwight Morrow devised a scheme to benefit the flier and his original backers, which would also allow Lindbergh to keep the Orteig Prize. So as not to steal any thunder from the men who had paid for the winning plane, Morrow diplomatically raised $10,000 from his Morgan partners, which he sent to the backers, reimbursing them for their expenses above their initial investments in the plane. He also saw that Lindbergh's own $2,000 share was quietly replaced in his bank account. Finally, Morrow recommended to Harry Guggenheim that the Guggenheim Fund pay Colonel Lindbergh $50,000 for his upcoming tour.

His affairs in the most responsible hands in the nation, Lindbergh could at last devote himself to his most pressing obligation, his book. While Lindbergh had been on public display, Carlyle MacDonald had holed himself up with a staff of secretaries in publisher George Putnam's house in Rye, New York. No sooner were the pages typed than they were rushed to the Knickerbocker Press in New Rochelle, where extra printers had been laid on. "MacDonald did a good job," Putnam later stated, "and a quick one. The crescendo of incoming orders from book-sellers was music to a publisher's ears." The fastest book produced up to that time, a complete set of galley proofs was ready for Lindbergh's approval in less than two weeks of his return to America.

On Saturday, June twenty-fifth, he drove into the city from the Trubee Davison estate on Long Island to read them. He was appalled. MacDonald had not only written the book in the first person, but he had reverted to the bombast Lindbergh thought they had abandoned back in Paris. Lindbergh began blue-penciling the purplest prose, but the task seemed hopeless. More annoying than the factual errors, the entire book struck him as false in tone, "cheaply done." Lindbergh knew he could not renege on his contract, especially as Putnam's had already begun to publicize the book, promising copies by July first. At the same time, the book's editor, Fitzhugh Green, pointed out, "It is your book: we wouldn't want to publish it if it weren't."

Lindbergh saw only one solution—that he would write the book himself. That was more than acceptable to the publishers, until they learned that Lindbergh did not intend to address the job until the autumn, after his cross-country tour. "At that juncture high blood pressure pretty nearly overcame us," George Putnam later recalled. "We were only publishers, to be sure, and he was Lindbergh; but at that a contract was a contract and irate customers were stalking us with knives." At last, Lindbergh figured that if he could hunker down in absolute peace during the month that remained before his tour, he could deliver a complete manuscript. He would use MacDonald's draft as an outline and write ten thousand words a week, a prodigious effort for even a seasoned writer. Lindbergh agreed to start work right after the Fourth of July, which he had promised to spend in Ottawa as part of the diamond jubilee of the Confederation of Canada. There he faced more crowds and received a specially engraved gold medal bearing the profiles of King George V and the Prince of Wales.

Upon his return, Lindbergh settled into Falaise, Harry Guggenheim's twenty-six-room manor house in Sands Point. It had been built in 1923, but upon entering the brick-sheltered courtyard, guests felt transported back to medieval France. The château was complete with high oak-beamed ceilings, detailed work on every door and window, a Norman tower, and an arcaded loggia in the rear practically at the edge of a cliff that dropped to the Long Island Sound. Its topography was reminiscent of Lindbergh's house in Little Falls; but the similarity ended there. Falaise was the epitome of luxurious living, replete with fine antiques and artwork—especially saints and Madonnas.

Lindbergh moved into the northeast bedroom, which had a small balcony and windows looking across the Sound to Connecticut. His suite afforded him complete privacy. The Guggenheims kept visitors at a minimum that July, because whatever time Lindbergh could take from his book went into discussing his forthcoming tour. He worked most of every day—sitting alone at the inlaid wooden desk in his room or at a wooden table outside on the grounds east of the house. He wrote in blue ink with a fountain pen on plain eight-by-ten-inch white bond in his largest, most readable script. Mindful of his contract to deliver at least forty thousand words, he counted his output and ran the total at the top of each page.

As soon as he had a few pages under his belt, Lindbergh read them to Fitzhugh Green over the telephone. "I was much pleased," Green wrote him afterward. "It was clear, precise and well-balanced narrative. My only suggestion is that you might brighten it up a little by a personal touch now and then. But it showed me beyond a doubt that you are quite as competent to write a good book as to fly the Atlantic."

Less than three weeks later, Lindbergh delivered the last of his pages, just under the agreed length. Nobody complained. Lindbergh recorded his life story, from birth to Le Bourget, in serviceable prose, mostly simple sentences; and his calm, objective voice proved especially effective in understating the more melodramatic incidents of his flight. Without Lindbergh's knowledge or approval, Putnam's selected what struck them as an obvious title for the book—"We." Lindbergh would forever complain about it, that his use of "we" meant him and his backers, not him and his plane, as the press had people believing; but his frequent unconscious use of the phrase suggested otherwise.

With a foreword by Myron Herrick—linking him to Joan of Arc, Lafayette, and David, three other exemplars of youthful idealism—a long afterword by Fitzhugh Green—recounting the triumphant marches from Paris to St. Louis—and forty-eight photographs, Putnam's published a highly respectable book of more than three hundred pages. They offered special autographed editions for $25 apiece, all of which were sold before publication. When the typesetters had finished their work, George Putnam had the original manuscript bound in two leather volumes, for which a collector offered $50,000.

Putnam considered accepting the money. He even explained to Colonel Breckinridge that a reading of the contract suggested that he technically owned the pages; and he offered to split the $50,000. Lindbergh considered the suggestion and said, "No. If it's yours, you do as you wish. If it isn't, I want it." Humbled by Lindbergh's rectitude, Putnam backed off. After the author received his pages, he donated them to the Missouri Historical Society in St. Louis.

Lindbergh had not even had the time to reread most of his handwritten manuscript; and the scheduled first flight for the Guggenheim Fund precluded his waiting for galleys. Amazingly, in less than two weeks, books were in the stores. Within a month, "We" had sold close to two hundred thousand copies, and sales showed no signs of letting up before Christmas, for which Putnam's prepared a special boxed edition for boys. It lingered at the top of bestseller lists well into the next year, netting more than six hundred thirty-five thousand copies. It was translated into most major languages in the world and sold in large numbers from Germany to Australia. "We" earned more than a quarter of a million dollars for its author, most of which was paid to him the following year.

Part of the book's success must be credited to the fortunate timing of the Guggenheim Fund tour, which proved to be the most exhaustive author tour ever scheduled. The coinciding of the two events created a publicity storm that resulted in the entire country's becoming obsessed with Lindbergh. Until then, he had been a marvel people outside a few cities could only experience secondhand. The summer of 1927, however, afforded every American the opportunity to become part of the phenomenon, as the frenzy at each stop only fueled the enthusiasm at the next.

The tour began July twentieth at Mitchel Field, Long Island. From there, Lindbergh flew the *Spirit of St. Louis* over Niantic, Connecticut, to Hartford, where he was greeted by one hundred thousand people. The Department of Commerce supplied an advance man named Milburn Kusterer, who had co-

ordinated receptions at each stopping point. Commerce also provided Lindbergh with a personal aide named Donald Keyhoe, who flew in close pursuit
with a mechanic from Wright in a plane piloted, at Lindbergh's request, by
his friend since Kelly Field, Philip Love. The tour continued with hardly a
pause until October twenty-third, zigzagging northward to Portland, Maine,
west across the northern half of the country to Seattle, south to San Diego,
east to Jacksonville then north to New York again. No American was more
than four hundred miles off the Lindbergh route; most lived within fifty
miles.

It was three months of ceaseless adulation, a tour that wavered between
the historical and the hysterical. For most of the places Lindbergh flew over,
touched down, or spent the night, it was the biggest event people had ever
seen. He had already learned not to make eye contact with individuals but
only to see the crowds; and experience quickly taught him to let somebody
else order his breakfast from room service, because his calls were usually met
with long silences and giggles from the telephone operators. He stopped
sending laundry out under his name because it never came back.

Most days on tour began with a short flight to a city for a parade, lunch,
and a meeting with the press. Then he would fly over four or five large
towns—dropping greetings in a muslin sack with an orange streamer—en
route to the next major city for a dinner, reception, and more press. Major
cities staged elaborate welcoming ceremonies. Wherever possible, he inspected sites for airports and talked to engineers and the leading state and
local dignitaries. Spare time was consumed by visits to hospitals and orphanages, then more press.

Lindbergh never failed to put on his best face. He lost his patience only
when the press grilled him about his personal life. Donald Keyhoe remembered Lindbergh's being asked, "Is it true, Colonel, that girls don't interest
you at all?"—to which Lindbergh replied, "If you can show me what that has
to do with aviation, I'll be glad to answer you." He did no stunting on this
tour, and he limited his remarks to one simple message—"that aviation had
a brilliant future, in which America should lead." He insisted to his entourage that no matter how early they had to leave, they must never arrive
late anywhere. Although Lindbergh grew to dread the daily routine, he
thrilled at seeing America as, in his words, "no man had ever known it before."

While Lindbergh found the adoring response "quite similar regardless of
the state," the receptions in some cities could not help standing out because
of their personal significance. In Detroit, he went to the Ford Airport, where
he took Henry Ford, crouched into the cockpit, for his first airplane flight;
Ford's son Edsel got a ten-minute ride as well. After receiving the plaudits of
close to five hundred thousand in the Twin Cities, Lindbergh piloted his

small plane over Melrose, Minnesota—hovering over the very land where Ola Månsson had built a new life for himself in 1859. He flew on to Little Falls, whose streets had been filling since six o'clock that morning. All businesses were closed that Thursday, and there was even restricted postal delivery. Thousands waited at the large pasture three miles north of town where their local hero was meant to arrive. An estimated fifty thousand people from all parts of Minnesota converged upon the small town for the festivities, highlighted by a long parade that featured a dilapidated old heap on which somebody had painted "Lindbergh's First Plane." It was the Saxon Six in which Charles had driven his mother and "Brother" to California and back only ten years prior.

In southern California, the Pacific Electric Railway offered special rates to downtown Los Angeles to watch the parade and hear Lindbergh's speech at the Coliseum; almost one hundred thousand people attended. That night, the city threw a banquet in his honor in the Fiesta Ball Room of the Ambassador Hotel, at which Hollywood royalty paid court. The motion-picture community presented Lindbergh with a gold loving cup, engraved with thirty-six facsimile signatures of the most famous film stars in the world. In less than a month, the first talking picture, *The Jazz Singer,* would put even the biggest names on that loving cup out of business.

Lindbergh's fame kept spreading, etching itself deeper into the public consciousness. He was, parents explained to their children, "living history"; and a worshipful nation paid homage and tribute. Official gifts and citations were presented wherever he stopped—ornate scrolls as well as medals, keys, badges, cups, and plaques, usually in gold. Hartford presented a cane carved of wood from a tree in the Mark Twain Garden, and Nashville presented another made from a tree planted by Andrew Jackson. A Choctaw Indian of Oklahoma conferred upon Lindbergh the name "Tohbionssi Chitokaka," meaning the greatest white eagle.

Lindbergh began to appear in textbooks; schoolchildren wrote essays on him and dedicated their yearbooks to him; and many schools were named for him. The Pennsylvania Railroad rechristened its "St. Louisan" the "The Spirit of St. Louis," and the Milwaukee Railroad named a parlor car "The Lindbergh." Reading, Pennsylvania, named its viaduct after him; Los Angeles named the great light at the apex of City Hall "Lindbergh Beacon." Mountains, lakes, parks, boulevards, islands, bays, and beaches across America and beyond were renamed in his honor.

Lindbergh returned to Mitchel Field on October 23, 1927, his tour having covered 22,350 miles. He had stopped in eighty-two cities, spending the night in sixty-nine of them, where he had been honored at gala dinners and had sat through countless renditions of "Lucky Lindy"—a song he never liked but which bands felt compelled to play whenever he entered the room.

Only once on the entire tour had he arrived late, and that was in Portland, Maine, where the fog was so thick he could not find the airfield. He had flown 260 hours, delivered 147 speeches, and had ridden in 1,285 miles of parade. An estimated thirty million spectators had turned out to see him, one-quarter of the nation.

And Lindbergh's popularity kept growing. When the supervisor of schools at Belleville, New Jersey, asked the local boys what living person they wished to emulate, Lindbergh was the runaway winner, garnering more votes than all the other heroes combined, including Coolidge, Ford, Edison, and General Pershing. "Five centuries have been required to make a saint of Joan of Arc," observed American journalist Marquis Childs, "but in two years Colonel Charles A. Lindbergh has become a demigod."

People behaved as though Lindbergh had walked on water, not flown over it. People sought out patches of cloth from the *Spirit of St. Louis;* old pistons and any other parts from the Wright engine were preserved as relics; the Vacuum Oil Company sent Lindbergh three ounces of the original oil drained from the reservoir of the plane upon its arrival at Le Bourget, which was marked and sealed in a glass ampule for display. One man who had met Lindbergh camping years earlier spent decades searching for the jug from which he had once drunk. And decades later, in 1990, a man in Maine paid $3,000 for the crate in which the *Spirit of St. Louis* had been shipped home, so that it could be enshrined. A Lindbergh Birthplace Association was formed to purchase by public subscription the house at 1120 West Forest Avenue in Detroit. The house in Little Falls was looted of practically anything that was not nailed down. With trophies and gifts for Lindbergh flooding into St. Louis, one man volunteered to guard them for no pay—simply because "Col. Lindbergh is a messenger from God . . . sent here to inspire the people, risking his life every day for the betterment of mankind." Paul Garber asserted, "After the flight, Charles Lindbergh . . . literally became all things to all men."

So long as Lindbergh remained neutral on controversial topics, that remained true. He served as a blank screen onto which each person projected his own best images of man. Nowhere did that become more apparent than in an artifact that dogged Lindbergh for the rest of his life. Of unknown origin, it was a list of "Lindbergh's Character Factors," fifty-nine personality traits in alphabetical order—from Altruism to Unselfishness—which Lindbergh allegedly marked each night with a red cross for those he had fulfilled satisfactorily and a black cross for those he had violated. Constant self-improvement was the obvious purpose, perfection the goal. For fifty years, it circulated around the world reprinted by church groups, boys' clubs, even in dictionaries. It was, as Lindbergh assured the Religion Editor of the Cleveland *Press* in 1973, "pure bunk." While on tour, it was reported that he smoked a cigarette in front of hundreds of people, commenting to Philip Love, "I won't be played for a tin saint." Alas, such behavior only exhibited such checklist virtues as Firmness, Modesty, and Sense of Humor. When it turned out that he did not smoke the cigarette, he won more points for Clean Conduct and Self-Control.

"I feel sure," Harry Guggenheim wrote Lindbergh in late October, "that nothing has so much contributed to the promotion of aviation in America, with the exception of your own historic flight to Paris, as this tour, which you have just completed." Statistics already supported the statement. Within weeks of Lindbergh's flight, Ryan Aircraft had twenty-nine orders for new airplanes—mostly their five-place cabin model—and their workforce had increased from twenty to one hundred twenty. By fall, they were manufacturing three airplanes a week. Airplanes had carried ninety-seven thousand pounds of mail in April and more than one hundred forty-six thousand pounds in September. That year saw a three hundred percent increase in the number of applicants for pilots' licenses in the United States and an increase of more than four hundred percent in the number of licensed aircraft. America's one thousand landing fields and airports would practically double within three years, a third of them with lights.

"It is impossible to predict what the future of aviation will be," Lindbergh had said during his tour, "but I confidently believe that it will become one of the largest industries in the country. Aviation today is in the same position that the automobile was twenty-five or thirty years ago." He believed, as he had since he began flying, that St. Louis was destined to become the nation's "aerial cross-roads"; and within weeks of his tour's conclusion, the City Administration of St. Louis declared its intention to acquire and develop a municipal airport, incorporating General Lambert's field. Cities voting on bonds for airports invited Lindbergh to visit just before elections. Lindbergh Fields began cropping up.

"Lindbergh's significance to business seems greater than that of any mercantile or financial magnate on either side of the Atlantic," wrote *Forbes* that year.

> Progressive bankers, merchants, manufacturers and the public generally, already almost have forgotten that recently it was impossible to get letters of inquiry, money orders, or any other commercial papers across the continent in less time than a business week. . . . After Lindbergh we shall have transocean airmail.

Lindbergh returned from his tour no closer to having decided on his future. While in New York, he became the "catch" of the social season, with invitations every night. John D. Rockefeller, Jr., hoped Lindbergh might "take a family dinner" and meet his five sons—"who, like every other American boy, are very eager to know you." One small stag dinner put him in the same living room with George Gershwin, who mesmerized Lindbergh with a showy rendition of *Rhapsody in Blue,* then stopped playing to ask him about the dangers of his epic flight—specifically, why, at the most dangerous moment, he had not turned back.

During the next month, Lindbergh remained in a tailspin. He put his money in the hands of J. P. Morgan & Co., just as his adviser there, Dwight Morrow, officially terminated his highly lucrative banking career to accept the ambassadorship to Mexico. In thanking Morrow for his past assistance, Lindbergh wrote, "if, by any chance, an opportunity should arise where I might be of any aid to you, please call on me." Almost immediately, Morrow did.

Before assuming his post, Morrow considered ways in which he could lessen the severe tensions between Mexico and the United States. With heavy American investment in Mexican land and petroleum plus a considerable Mexican debt, one newspaper wrote, "After Morrow, come the marines." Instead, Morrow invited Lindbergh to his apartment in New York and asked if he would be willing to fly the *Spirit of St. Louis* south of the border at the end of the year. "I think it would be an excellent thing for Mexico, for aviation, and for the Foundation," Morrow wrote Harry Guggenheim, "and for him."

"I wanted to make another long distance non-stop flight before retiring the plane from use and placing it in [a] museum," Lindbergh recalled. "The plane and engine were practically new and in a number of ways the *Spirit of St. Louis* was better equipped than any other plane for long flights." Such a high-minded mission would also allow him to postpone any of the more mundane possibilities before him. Morrow had expected Lindbergh to tour the Caribbean in stages, making Mexico his "central point," but the thrill for Lindbergh was in attempting another giant leap.

Upon arriving in Mexico, Ambassador Morrow immediately began mending fences between the two countries, proving himself both fair and friendly. His casual air and informal meetings contributed to an unexpected easiness between him and President Plutarco Elías Calles, which the press in both countries happily referred to as "Ham and Eggs Diplomacy." But nothing enhanced America's reputation there more than the announcement that Charles Lindbergh was coming to visit. Lindbergh had grown savvy in diplomatic matters and suggested that his flight would be more symbolic if he flew nonstop between the capitals of the two nations. The cautious Ambassador balked at anything so dangerous until Lindbergh said, "You get me the invitation, and I'll take care of the flying."

He spent the second week of December in Washington, where Chief Justice Taft presented him with the Langley Medal from the Smithsonian Institution and Congress voted to award him the Congressional Medal, previously reserved for military heroes. On December 13, 1927, the *Spirit of St. Louis* was rolled onto Bolling Field, across the Anacostia River from Washington. The flight to Mexico was two-thirds the distance of the New York-to-Paris run, but that still meant twenty-four hours in the air.

Lindbergh lifted the heavily laden plane off a soggy field at 12:25 that Tuesday afternoon, flying down the east coast of Texas then doglegging toward Mexico City. Upon entering the Valley of Mexico, he realized that he had lost his way while flying over a sea of fog. Navigating from a rudimentary map, he could not get his bearings. Hoping to match railroad lines on the ground with those on the map, he roamed the skies for hours. He finally chose to follow some tracks, flying low enough to read the sign at each station. Tired, he could not make sense of town after town being called "Caballeros." He was already late in arriving when he realized that he was reading the signs for the mens' rooms. At last he flew over a city with a wall marked "Hotel Toluca." He located Toluca on his map, thirty miles to the west of his target.

Under a July-like sun, 150,000 people waited at Valbuena Airport that afternoon. Ambassador and Mrs. Morrow had been there since mid-morning; and much of the crowd had slept overnight on the field. Lindbergh had been sighted over Tampico and Toluca, but as the aviator was more than two hours late, Morrow and much of the crowd grew anxious. At 3:16, according to Mrs. Morrow's watch, he arrived, and it was "perfectly thrilling when that plane came to earth." Morrow presented him to President Calles, who handed him the keys of the city. His flight had taken twenty-seven hours and fifteen minutes; and tardy though he was, Lindbergh noted that it had taken the Morrows almost a week to make the same trip.

There was no holding the Mexicans back in their admiration. Guiding Lindbergh from the grandstand to their waiting car, Mrs. Morrow felt the screaming throng was going to rip off his clothes. All the way into the city, the masses threw flowers at him and shouted, "Viva Lindbergh!" Over the next several days—at receptions, dinners, parades, bullfights, folkdancing exhibitions, and rodeos—the Mexicans displayed more exuberance than Lindbergh had seen anywhere. But the Ambassador deliberately blocked out most of the calendar so that Lindbergh could vacation.

He settled into the Embassy for the yuletide. Evangeline Lindbergh accepted the Morrows' invitation to spend the holiday with them and flew down from Detroit. The Morrows, who had been living there with their fourteen-year-old daughter, Constance, and their nineteen-year-old son, Dwight Jr., were joined by their two older daughters, Elisabeth and Anne. For the first time since he had become famous, Lindbergh had a few days at

a time in which to relax; for the first time since he was a small child, he enjoyed an old-fashioned family Christmas, surrounded by a large loving family; and for the first time in his life, he spent hours in the quiet company of
female contemporaries. Although he often lowered his head in their presence,
he could not help noticing how each of the Morrow daughters stood in contrast to the others—Elisabeth, the eldest, beautiful and elegant, socially at
ease; Constance, the youngest, vivacious and witty, not afraid of teasing
their famous guest; and Anne, twenty-one years old and self-conscious.
Sometimes he caught her averting her glance so as not to embarrass him. She
felt more comfortable watching from afar, then running upstairs to confide
in her diary.

"I saw standing against the great stone pillar . . . a tall, slim boy in
evening dress—so much slimmer, so much taller, so much more poised than
I expected," she wrote after laying eyes on him for the first time. "A very refined face, not at all like those grinning 'Lindy' pictures—a firm mouth, clear,
straight blue eyes, fair hair, and nice color." Over the next week, she marveled at his extreme youth and lack of affectation. For Christmas, Mrs. Lindbergh gave Anne and Elisabeth antique Spanish fans, accompanied by cards
with her son's signature.

During the week, Anne seldom came out from behind her present long
enough to learn much about their special visitor. And once Christmas had
passed, Lindbergh became consumed with the next portion of his journey.
During his stay in Mexico, Ambassador Morrow and the State Department
had arranged for Lindbergh to continue touring around Central America
and the Caribbean Sea.

The Morrows saw him off at 5:30 on the morning of December twenty-
eighth, as he left for Guatemela City, seven hours away. By the middle of February, he had flown 9,390 miles in 116 and a half hours in and around Latin
America—traveling from Guatemala to British Honduras, Salvador, Honduras, Nicaragua, Costa Rica, Panama, the Canal Zone, Colombia, Venezuela, St. Thomas, Puerto Rico, the Dominican Republic, Haiti, and Cuba.
The crowds in most places proved too unmanageable for the police; the receptions were usually the greatest those nations had ever seen. The press
consistently applied the term "good will" to these Gulf-and-Caribbean
flights; but Lindbergh would later insist, "good will was a very welcome result, but it was not even a major element" in planning the flights. His interest lay primarily in "the adventure of flying, in demonstrating the airplane's
capabilities, and in the development of aviation in general." He financed the
trip himself.

Lindbergh became the world's first Ambassador of the Air and his nation's youngest emissary. In each of the sixteen countries he visited that winter, he was decorated with their highest honors and presented with

extraordinary gifts—a gold watch from Guatemala, a gold Indian idol from the Canal Zone, a gold brooch from the Dominican Republic, a gold chest of native gold nuggets from Honduras, and a paperweight set with a piece of iron from the anchor of Columbus's flagship *Santa Maria* from Haiti, where they also named a street Lindbergh Avenue. More than anywhere he had ever been, donkey-paced Central America reaffirmed for Lindbergh how indispensable aviation was to the progress of mankind.

Lindbergh himself wrote up his Latin American tour for *The New York Times*. The internationally syndicated pieces, each with a different dateline, had something to interest everybody. As spellbinding as tales of Aladdin on his magic carpet, Lindbergh's dispatches combined adventure with high society, history lessons with visions of the future. One minute he was flying over tropical mountains, the next he was at a Presidential palace—all told with modesty and awe. This real-life action hero had become a regular feature in people's lives.

After two months of being worshiped in "El Dorado," Lindbergh returned to the United States, flying from Havana to St. Louis. The city closed the schools at noon that Tuesday so that every student could gather by the Mississippi and greet him as one. Sixty thousand children, each with an American flag, waited for him—as did almost as many adults—filling the levee for ten city blocks. Lindbergh provided a half-hour stunt show before landing at Lambert Field. With that, he decided that this was to be his plane's last hurrah, and he announced that he was retiring to private life. In the spring, he would fly his plane to Washington—a remarkable flight of 725 miles in less than five hours—where he would donate the plane to the Smithsonian Institution for permanent exhibition.

But the kudos did not stop coming. Just skimming off the cream of the offers, he accepted an Honorary Degree of Doctor of Laws from the University of Wisconsin, out of which he had flunked but six years earlier; he accepted the Congressional Medal of Honor from President Coolidge in a ceremony at the White House; and he accepted a medal and $25,000 from the Woodrow Wilson Foundation "for contributions to international friendship." Lindy Clubs, complete with their own oath, laws, and salute, sprang up. Press coverage did not abate, as each event fostered the next. In an attempt to lure readers, a new magazine called *Time* tried boosting sales at the end of 1927 by naming a "Man of the Year." The first such honoree was Lindbergh.

He tried to concentrate his attention on the development of commercial aviation, entering into conversations with airlines, the Pennsylvania Railroad, even Henry Ford—all of whom were interested in the future of transportation. He also became a paid consultant of the Daniel Guggenheim Fund and the United States government's Bureau of Aeronautics. Still unsettled, he kept himself in constant motion, flying all around the country. "Reporters and photographers had crowded in at every airfield," Lindbergh later recalled of that period. "Automobile-loads of people followed them. The hotels where I stayed at night were watched. I could not walk along a street without being followed, photographed, and shouted at." He had become the first person to be constantly stalked by the media.

And then one day flying westward, Lindbergh crossed the Rocky Mountain ranges of southern Wyoming and eastern Utah and saw desert ahead. The sun was setting in front of him, and he knew a gang of journalists was waiting to ambush him in whichever town he decided to land. Instinctively, he brought his plane down right on the desert floor. "What peace I found there," he later remembered, "on that warm but cooling surface of our planet's sphere!"

Lindbergh spent the night on the dried lake bed and experienced an epiphany. He realized he had been sentenced to a life as a public figure on a scale to which no man before him had ever been subjected. Feeling overexposed, overextended, and overexalted, he wished to "combine two seemingly contrary objectives, to be part of the civilization of my time but not to be bound by its conventional superfluity."

The solution was to simplify. "I would reduce my obligations, give away some of my possessions, concentrate my business and social interests," he later wrote of his new objectives. "I would take advantage of the civilization to which I had been born without losing the basic qualities of life from which all works of men must emanate."

The Missouri Historical Society had asked Lindbergh if they might exhibit his trophies at Forest Park. He agreed to a ten-day display—during which time eighty thousand people visited. He extended his permission to show the prizes indefinitely; and during the next year, one and one-half million people peered into the display cases that took up most of the first floor of the west wing of the Jefferson Memorial Building. Lindbergh never asked for the return of his treasury; in fact, a few years later, he formally deeded the entire lot to the historical society.

While he could share the trophies, he had nobody with whom to enjoy the celebration. Except for the occasional company of his mother, Lindbergh had experienced his entire year of accolades alone. Among the myriads who had glorified "the Lone Eagle," there was only a handful of people he even wanted to see again. Living constantly in the public eye, it was difficult to imagine a personal relationship with anybody ever unfolding naturally. Friendships seemed difficult, a romance out of the question. Solitude seemed the most he could wish for, and that would have to be a hard-fought achievement. The fame he had never sought threatened to turn him into a freak.

In the spring of 1928 Lindbergh grew lonely, longing for intimacy. At the age of twenty-six, he decided "it was time to meet girls." Unconsciously, his mind kept returning to one young woman he had encountered among the millions of his admirers, Ambassador Morrow's daughter—the shy one who always seemed to be looking away. Anne had been taken with him as well, as she revealed only to her diary upon his departure:

The idea of this clear, direct, straight boy—how it has swept out of sight all other men I have known, all the pseudo-intellectuals, the so-phisticates, the posers—all the "arty" people. All my life, in fact, my world—my little embroidery beribboned world is smashed.

8

UNICORNS

"A girl should come from a healthy family, of course.
My experience in breeding animals on our farm had taught me
the importance of good heredity."

—C.A.L.

DWIGHT WHITNEY MORROW WAS THE AMERICAN DREAM incarnate, living proof that hard work could elevate the most humbly born to the nation's power elite. He was often presumed to be descended from one of America's first families, but the life of this influential banker-diplomat-politician—whom Walter Lippmann called the most "trusted" man of his time—actually began in poverty in West Virginia.

In 1873, he was literally born into a world of education—in the building that was Marshall College. His father, James—a teacher's son—had recently been named president of the college, a position whose perquisite of free lodging for him and his growing family was worth more than the meager salary. Shortly thereafter, the James Morrows moved to Allegheny, Pennsylvania, where he assumed a number of teaching jobs over the years, Mathematics and the Bible his favorite subjects. This father of eight never earned more than $1,800 a year.

Although Dwight never grew as tall as five and one-half feet, and was plagued by chronic migraine headaches, poor digestion, and a slightly misshaped arm, no obstacle ever seemed insurmountable to him. He dreamed of following his older brother to West Point and scored highest in his district on the entrance examination. Shortly after being notified that he would receive the appointment, he discovered that he was being passed over in favor of the young man who had placed second—the result of political pull.

Disillusioned but undeterred, Dwight Morrow wrote to

the man who had the final word on appointments to West Point. Just weeks before his eighteenth birthday, he sent a handwritten letter to President Benjamin Harrison himself, reminding him of his special power to appoint ten cadets himself every four years. "A dissapointment [sic] of the kind I received may not seem very much to a man in your position," he wrote the Commander in Chief; "but if you were ever a poor boy, with a poor boy's ambitions you can appreciate my position." Morrow received no satisfaction, not even a personal reply; but the episode proved to be a turning point in his life. Deprived of the opportunities West Point might have afforded him, he grew determined to turn his adversity to greater advantage, to become a man of influence himself. A former teacher in Pittsburgh who knew the Morrows informed Dwight that it was not too late to apply for the next term at his alma mater.

Amherst College became Morrow's lifelong passion. As an undergraduate, he scraped by financially, borrowing money and tutoring; but he was quickly recognized as the most dynamic member of the class of 1895—an A-student, a prizewinner in Mathematics, Writing, and Forensics, as well as the class orator at graduation. He wrote for the campus literary magazines, was elected to Phi Beta Kappa, and made many friends. Upon graduation, Amherst legend has held for more than a century, Dwight Morrow was voted "Most Likely to Succeed" by a unanimous vote save one—his, which he cast for classmate Calvin Coolidge.

Amherst not only opened up the world intellectually for Morrow, but also romantically. In the spring of his sophomore year, the diminutive young man with the Roman nose and determined gaze attended a dance at which he met a freshman from Smith College, across the Connecticut River in Northampton. Elizabeth Reeve Cutter, from Cleveland, was possibly the only coed in Massachusetts whose zeal for college matched his. Outstanding in both scholastics and extracurricular activities, Elizabeth—Betty to most, Bee to a few, and ultimately Betsey to young Mr. Morrow—was racking up as many honors and prizes at Smith as he had at Amherst.

She was no taller than he, with thick eyebrows, high cheekbones, and almost porcelain skin, which made her look like an Eskimo doll. No beauty—which did not matter to Morrow—she was all personality—which did. They quickly realized they were kindred spirits—hardworking, energetic young people at prestigious colleges, with a lot to prove. Although her family's financial circumstances were hardly as dire as that of the Morrows, Elizabeth's drive to succeed was at least as powerful as Dwight's. Since childhood, she had been fueled by a circumstance she seldom mentioned. At the age of nine, her twin sister, Mary, suffered a long illness and died. The result was that Betty charged through life—"determined to accomplish," observed one of her relatives, "enough for two."

Miss Cutter and Mr. Morrow's affections for each other grew slowly, in accordance with the innocence of the times and the seriousness of their natures. Before they spoke of marriage, he had graduated from Columbia Law School and secured a position at the young but illustrious New York law firm of Simpson, Thacher & Bartlett; and she had taught at a private school in Cleveland, studied at the Sorbonne and in Florence, and had several poems published in national magazines. In June 1903—after his salary was raised to $3,000—they wed, honeymooning in the hills of New England, where they visited their respective alma maters.

With abilities equaling their ambitions, the Morrows were always looking ahead. He proved to be an unqualified success at his law firm, putting work before pleasure and often losing himself in thought. Both Morrows preferred the "generous backyard life" of the suburbs to the social pressures of New York City; and directly across the Hudson River from the northernmost tip of Manhattan Island, they discovered the newly incorporated city of Englewood, perched on the Palisades. By commuter train to Jersey City and through the "Hudson Tube," or by ferry down the river, one could commute to lower Manhattan in less than an hour. Already Englewood was becoming known for its fine schools and free library; and the general practitioner made housecalls in his two-seated buggy. The town was attracting a number of bankers, among them Henry P. Davison and Thomas Lamont, power-players at J. P. Morgan & Company.

On their first visit to Englewood, the Morrows learned of a new house for rent on Spring Lane, an easy walk to the town center and the Presbyterian Church. The rent was more than they had budgeted, and the three-story house—with unexpected gables and small windows in odd places—contained more rooms than they needed; but they opted to bank on the future. One night in what they called "the little brown house," Morrow awoke from what he considered "the most horrible" nightmare, in which he had dreamed that they had become *enormously* rich."

Within a few years his income had increased tenfold, and children filled the house. Elisabeth Reeve was born in 1904; Anne Spencer two years later, and Dwight Jr. two years after that. In 1909, the Morrows moved into a larger house of "late gingerbread architecture" on an acre of land on Palisade Avenue, then still a country road. It was a sprawling place, full of trees, with a bedroom for each child. A third daughter, Constance, was born in 1913. "If we keep to our present resolutions and ill fortune does not overtake us," Morrow wrote at the time, "we shall live here for the rest of our lives."

Morrow flourished in corporate law and became a partner at Simpson, Thacher & Bartlett in short order. With his growing list of civic boards and local charities, he found it increasingly difficult to spend time at home. "This,

Betsey, is not the life for you or me," he told his wife. "Once we have made $100,000 we shall retire from the practice of the law. I shall teach history: you will write poetry: the children will earn their own living."

That dream never came true, but his nightmare did. At the end of 1913, Thomas Lamont approached his neighbor to offer him a partnership at J. P. Morgan & Company. Although unexpected, the timing was right for both Morrow and Morgan. He was looking for a new challenge; and the fifty-two-year-old banking empire—at its zenith in power and its nadir in reputation—provided the opportunity. It was, in fact, the very moment when Congressman Charles A. Lindbergh of Minnesota had called for a Congressional probe of Wall Street's concentration of power, the Money Trust. With the sudden death of J. Pierpont Morgan, the firm sought a new senior partner. They selected Morrow—"not merely because of his talent, for talent was plentiful and easy to buy," Calvin Coolidge would later explain, "but . . . for his character, which was priceless."

Morrow wrestled with the fantastic offer for a month. After three weeks of pounding headaches, he saw a political cartoon in a newspaper in which J. P. Morgan was portrayed as a vulture feeding on the entrails of the shareholders of the New York, New Haven and Hartford Railroad. The bank had for the past decade been actively involved in the monopolistic operation of the transportation giant of the northeast; but that involvement had also created a company that greatly improved the public's transportation needs and turned it into a sound investment. The unfairness of the cartoon clinched Morrow's decision. He and his wife stayed up until two o'clock in the morning drafting his resignation letter to his present employers. "We is bankers after we mail this letter," Dwight said to Betsey, filling his pipe. "Well," she replied, "I hope we'll be as happy as we've been as lawyers."

Morrow had suddenly reached the highest echelons of international finance, bringing with him the luster of integrity. Upon entering his new offices at 23 Wall Street, he also became a partner in Drexel & Co. in Philadelphia, Morgan, Grenfell & Co. in London, and Morgan, Harjes & Co. in Paris. Morrow was soon dealing with the heads of General Motors and Du Pont; he helped save the credit of the City of New York; he conferred with the Secretary of the Treasury about financing the War; he worked with Jean Monnet reconstructing postwar Europe.

Domestic changes accompanied the professional challenges. While Dwight and Betty maintained a semblance of modesty in their standard of living in Englewood, his new position forced them to pay more attention to appearances. The Morrows continued to remain active in local affairs, but the demands for their participation on boards of national organizations, chairing school committees, and heading fund drives steadily increased. His work required their taking an apartment in New York City; and though they clung to the image of living in Englewood, the eleventh floor of the new building at 4 East Sixty-sixth Street became the address at which they gradually found themselves residing. Morrow became one of the owners of the fashionable building.

Living in Manhattan, the Morrows began summering on the island of North Haven, in Penobscot Bay, Maine, and winter-vacationing in Nassau. Morrow's new job involved frequent travel to Europe. Whenever possible, he took his children along for the educational benefits, reading appropriate passages from Henry James as they stopped in England and France. Dining with Rockefellers and Vanderbilts, professors and judges, ambassadors and generals, presidents and prime ministers, no doors were closed to the Dwight Morrows.

Everything they touched turned into success. To their children, their marriage seemed ideal while their own lives were enormously privileged. In her early years of motherhood, Betty Morrow dropped everything at five o'clock, so that she could read to her youngsters. In time, they used this children's hour to read by themselves and to write poetry and diaries.

While demands on the Morrow children were few, expectations were infinite. The household was a hotbed of achievement with little room for imperfection. Life proved hardest on Dwight Jr., the only boy, carrying the burden of the great man's name. He was automatically sent to Groton to prepare for Amherst, and before reaching college he began to falter under the pressure, developing a slight stammer. Betty Morrow took greater interest in her daughters.

Elisabeth exceeded her dreams. Blessed with the finest features of her parents, she grew into an exquisite young blonde, delicate in beauty and strong in personality. The apple of her father's eye talked for years of opening her own primary school. She emulated her mother's success at Smith College, adding social sheen that came from prestigious parents. "She was the belle of the ball," noted her youngest sister, Constance, more than sixty years later; "she was sophisticated and graceful and men fell at her feet." Physically, she was fragile, the result of a childhood bout of measles. Her mother, with her lifelong fear of disease, did not cater to her illness. Although Elisabeth had developed a weak heart with a faulty valve, she knew the way to win her mother's approval was to carry on as though she were perfectly fine. That valor made her even more attractive to her many suitors. Most ardent of all of them was one of the sons of Morgan partner Thomas Lamont, Corliss, who also maintained that "Elisabeth was her mother's obvious favorite."

Nine years her junior, Constance would follow her to Milton Academy (and later Smith College) and perform with equal aplomb. Having brains and looks—and young enough not to have to compete with her sisters—she developed the most vibrant personality of all the Morrows.

Anne was caught in the middle of two sisters who seemed to meet their parents' expectations with grace and ease. Not quite as pretty—dark-haired and forever self-conscious about her slightly wide nose—Anne lagged in Elisabeth's shadow. More than anyone in her family, she withdrew, finding comfort in reading and writing. By her mid-teens she had become an inveterate diarist and letter-writer.

She analyzed her every mood with a critical eye. She learned to put herself down before anybody else could, preparing herself and her family for failures then surprising everybody with successes. She became a chronic apologizer, usually unnecessarily. Such self-involvement left her shy but strong. "She was no shrinking violet," remarked one of her oldest friends, "but a real hot-house orchid—one of those rare, complex flowers that look quite fragile but are really quite durable." During her adolescence, Anne developed fortitude from her anger and compassion from her pain.

"Anne was the one student with a soul," recalled one of her friends from Miss Chapin's School in New York City. She was part of a spirited group of teenage girls who came from the best homes and vacationed in the right places. "Anne-Pan" Morrow never lobbied to be their leader; she hung back, quietly attracting them with her selflessness and modesty until they all followed. Far from being antisocial, Anne enjoyed the appreciation from friends that she did not get from her family, especially her mother. She became the best letter-writer of the group, invariably opening with an apology for being so tardy and closing with an apology for being so wordy. It was a subtle trap she set, for most of the replies promptly dismissed the false defects and made way for even greater praise. For the rest of her life, Anne used the same technique, rendering herself incapable of asking directly for what she wanted.

During her five years at Miss Chapin's, Anne attended enough cultural events in New York to realize that her provincialism was threatening to turn her into a snob, as it did her sister Elisabeth. Her poems and stories of the period were full of yearning, for "adventures I have never followed" and "countries I have never seen."

Anne thought she stood a better chance of attaining her goals by breaking ranks with her family. That meant following most of her friends to Vassar College, not Smith. "I want to do something different," she wrote her sister Elisabeth. "I want to start somewhere else. I want to do something entirely independent."

Anne graduated from Miss Chapin's in 1924 the class star. She was captain of the field hockey team, the most accomplished contributor to the literary magazine, and student council president. At the graduation dinner Miss Chapin handed each of the young ladies a questionnaire, which asked:

"What is your life ambition?" Forty years later Mary "Melly" Walker could not remember her own response, but she claimed to remember Anne Morrow's: "I want to marry a hero."

Finding comfort putting others on pedestals, Anne developed crushes—on writers Edna St. Vincent Millay or Michael Strange one week, Corliss Lamont the next. "It's a strange sort of complex," her sister Elisabeth observed in her diary, "and I *wish* she would get over it. I hate to have her working herself up into a nervous state . . ." In the end, Anne enrolled at Smith College. "The chain was just too strong for her to break," her sister Constance explained. "None of us really had a choice."

Difficult though Smith was, Anne Morrow flourished there. Taking courses in creative writing while majoring in English literature, Anne fell under the tutelage of Mina Kirstein Curtiss, who became her newest hero. The daughter of Louis Kirstein, one of the partners in Filene's department store, Mrs. Curtiss was a Smith alumna. Jewish and highly cultured—her brother Lincoln would found the New York City Ballet and her brother George would publish *The Nation*—she received a master's degree in English from Columbia University, before joining the faculty at Smith. Briefly married, she poured her passion into her own writing—books on Proust, Bizet, and Degas—and that of her students. From their first meeting to the end of Mina Curtiss's life, Anne found her "an inspiring teacher, setting standards of scholarship, of creativeness, and of excellence in writing for a generation of students." She guided Anne Morrow toward discovering her own clear and precise literary voice.

Bolstered by Mina Curtiss's approval, Anne tried to break out of her family's restrictive mold. Her classmate Elizabeth Bacon recalled one of those indulgent sophomore-year conversations on the top floor of Emerson House, one in which the girls were talking about poverty, a subject neither of them knew anything about. Suddenly, Anne said, "Bacon, I want to roll in the mud!" Her undergraduate poems, full of allusions to birds and suggestions of budding sexuality, reveal her desire to venture into the real world. She often fixated on another image, the unicorn—a symbol of chastity and purity. Read one of her verses of the period:

> Everything today has been
>   heavy and brown.
> Bring me a Unicorn
>   to ride about the town.

Although Anne persisted in punishing herself with put-downs about her physical and mental shortcomings, she bloomed into an alluring young woman, with radiant blue eyes, a sensitive mouth, and a genuine inner glow—"an aura," people would say about her for the rest of her life. She and Elisabeth attended parties together, and their parents often brought eligible young men home to meet them. The sisters divided the potential beaux into four categories—Sparklers, Twinklers, Worthies, and Lumps. The Morrow girls were most often attracted to the Twinklers—though they were just as happy with Worthies and always felt comfortable around Lumps—"usually other girls' cousins brought in at the last minute." Sparklers, on the other hand, were few and far between; as one of her later fictional characters would note: "Mother said they were unsteady and would never settle down."

Among Anne's first callers was Corliss Lamont. After failing in his pursuit of Elisabeth, he fell deeply in love with Anne's lambent beauty and smoldering nature. She too resisted his amorous intentions, though she was impressed that he had already become a free thinker, departing radically from the conservative politics of his wealthy family.

Within a few years, Corliss would embark upon a career as a writer and philosopher, passionate in his left-wing politics. Shortly before marrying, he could not resist telling Anne about his fiancée, "I do not yet love her as much as I once loved you." He would carry a torch for Anne for the rest of his life, through another three marriages.

The Morrows' world got turned upside down in 1927, once President Coolidge lured his Amherst classmate from the private-business sector into becoming Ambassador to Mexico. The appointment hit Betty Morrow hardest, because giving up his partnership at J. P. Morgan also meant postponing the building of her dream house in Englewood. The architect Chester Aldrich—brother of her dearest friend since college, Amey—had already drawn plans for a Georgian manor. "I wish I thought it was an adventure!" she complained to her diary, but she expressed only enthusiasm about the posting to her husband. Although conflicted, he was ready to make the change. He had long wanted to serve his country; and he had made more than enough money to work for the public good for the rest of his life. In his twelve years at Morgan, he had amassed a fortune in cash, securities, and real estate worth close to ten million dollars. To prove to his wife that he would always consider Englewood their home, he ordered the building of the grand house on a hill in the backwoods of Englewood to proceed.

From his first "ham and eggs" breakfast with President Calles, relations between Mexico and the United States improved, resonating long after his mission had ended. Betty Morrow provided the ballast in his career, as she gamely moved to Mexico and learned Spanish. She and Dwight enrolled Constance in school there. Elisabeth, then teaching in Englewood, took a leave of absence, so that she could partake in the experience. Dwight Jr. remained at Groton, where his moods began to oscillate wildly and he was hearing voices out of nowhere talking about him. Within the year, he would suffer a complete mental breakdown.

Anne remained, in her words, "the youngest, shiest, most self-conscious adolescent that—I believe—ever lived." Still finding herself, she continued to search for heroes. In the spring of 1927, Erasmus caught her fancy; and she was, in fact, writing a paper about him that May twentieth, at the end of her junior year at Smith. The next day, Anne walked by the infirmary, where her friend Elizabeth Bacon was in bed with a case of measles. Anne animatedly shouted into the infirmary window, "Bacon, Bacon, a man has flown the Atlantic. His name is Charles Lindbergh. He flew all alone. He has landed in Paris."

Seven months later, Colonel Lindbergh made his way to the United States Embassy in Mexico City. Dwight and Betty Morrow had entertained him for a week that December before their second daughter arrived by train on her Christmas vacation from Smith. Those seven days, between the twenty-first and twenty-eighth, completely shook her world. "This was to be an objective diary," Anne wrote at the first possible opportunity after reaching her parents' new residence. "It stops here!

> I don't care how much I rave if only I could get down to keep a *little* the feeling of what has happened this last week. I wish to heavens I had written it down as it happened, but I was too moved—and too ashamed of my emotion.

For the first time, Anne surrendered to living in the moment.

Lindbergh's presence threw her into a state of complete distraction, causing her to stammer and stumble at every turn. Her older sister, on the other hand, rose to every occasion, uninhibitedly making delightful conversation. "Why is it that attractive men stimulate Elisabeth to her best and always terrify and put me at my worst!?" Anne wondered.

On Christmas Eve, the Morrows threw a merry staff party, thirty-three for dinner. Entering the dining room, Colonel Lindbergh went looking for his place card next to Anne's. "Well, the older has sat next to me," she imagined his thinking, "I suppose it's the second one's turn. I'll have to sit next to her tonight." But his card was not there, and while looking for hers, she bumped right into him. They exchanged embarrassed apologies.

After dinner there was dancing. "*He* didn't dance but stood apart and watched—not with envy, but with a kind of dazed pleasure," she noted. From afar, she instinctively knew where he was all the time. After dancing a Virginia reel, Anne collapsed on a couch in the hall with a cousin and a few friends of her brother—Worthies verging on being Lumps. They dressed

Anne up with a comb and mantilla and shawl, putting a red carnation in her hair. "I felt glowing and frivolous," Anne confided to her diary that night, "—until suddenly I saw the Colonel behind me and I took them off, feeling silly, and tore the carnation out of my hair."

"She should have been born in Spain, shouldn't she?" one of them said to Lindbergh. Strangely, Lindbergh felt embarrassed too and could barely agree. Anne sat there a little longer, saying nothing until she quietly excused herself and went to bed. When Anne did find herself seated next to Lindbergh at lunch the next day, she became tongue-tied. She did not know that Lindbergh appreciated the silence and that for the first time he felt at home with a girl.

Christmas afternoon, the Morrows spoke of driving to Xochimilco, a town famed for its floating gardens. Lindbergh longed to accompany them but said his presence would spoil their day because of the inevitable crowd. Anne said, "I feel as though the nicest thing we could do for you would be to leave you alone." But Lindbergh chose to tag along. They spent the afternoon in relative peace, punting in a barge down flower-filled lagoons lined with calla lilies and poplars. Most of the people who recognized Lindbergh kept their distance. For a few hours, he had been able to enjoy himself like a normal young man.

The next day, Lindbergh took all the Morrow women for a ride in the five-passenger silver Ford plane that had flown his mother to Mexico. Anne sat right behind Lindbergh and was torn between experiencing the flight and examining the pilot. They flew over the embassy, past a lake, up toward the snowcapped mountain Ixtaccihuatl. "It was a complete and intense experience," Anne wrote afterward. "I will not be happy till it happens again."

Although she never said as much, Anne had fallen in love with Charles Lindbergh that Christmas. It was clear reading between the lines of her diary. She repeatedly told herself how insignificant she must have seemed to him and that she should be grateful just for the privilege of having known him. Returning to Smith College for her last semester, Anne felt as though that one week had changed her more than two decades of education. "Clouds and stars and birds," she wrote, "—I must have been walking with my head down looking at the puddles for twenty years."

Anne became obsessed with Lindbergh. She devoured every book and article she could find about him. Every boy she dated now made her think, "there are *thousands* of him (thank God for one Colonel L.)." One Saturday night that spring she ran alone in the rain to the theater in town where she watched a documentary called "Forty Thousand Miles with Colonel Lindbergh." Then, she returned to her dormitory room to read a story in *The Saturday Evening Post*, which she had stashed away, "Galahad Himself." Its handsome flying hero—Robert Boyd—blushed around women and did not smoke, drink, or dance . . . and was obviously based on Lindbergh. "Boyd" became her code-name for Lindbergh in her letters to her sisters, just as she had named the family station wagon "Memphis" in honor of the ship that brought him home from Europe. Between reading Chaucer and Robert Frost that year, Anne pored over aviation magazines.

"Colonel L. is 'le seul saint devant qui je brûle ma chandelle' ["the only saint before whom I light a candle"]," Anne wrote in her diary, trying to explain to herself why she had become so taken with this new reading matter; "—the last of the gods. He is unbelievable and it is exhilarating to believe in the unbelievable. Then because all that world is so tremendous, new and foreign to me, I could not get further from myself than in it." She found a man with a plane in Northampton who took her flying. Afterward, she gushed in her diary, "He will never know the joy and life it gave me."

CELEBRITY WITHOUT PURPOSE seemed pointless to Lindbergh; and commerical aviation became his crusade. "America has found her wings, but she must yet learn to use them," he wrote of that year. During this "period of adjustment," nobody did more to advance that cause than Charles Lindbergh. In the two years after grounding the *Spirit of St. Louis,* few aspects of American aviation went without the advice or assistance of "The Lone Eagle."

Lindbergh's new goal was to establish transcontinental passenger airline service, connnecting New York with California. Realizing this vision would require speculators with enough foresight to overlook a few years of losses before their million-dollar investments might yield a profit, he returned to his St. Louis backers—Harold Bixby, Harry Knight, and Bill Robertson. Together, they descended upon the one man in the country they thought could satisfy all their business needs.

"The genius of Henry Ford," Lindbergh would later write of the inventor-industrialist, "did not depend much on logic for his business ventures. Intuition played a major part in his phenomenal success." After one of his airplanes crashed, killing its pilot, Ford divined a new plane-building policy. From that day forward, Ford aircraft would be monoplanes (because they were "simpler") made of metal (because "metal's the thing of the future") with more than one engine ("because we aren't going to have any more forced landings"). In one synapse, Ford had leaped to the next generation in aircraft manufacturing. Lindbergh wished to make that leap as well, joining forces as well as resources.

Ford was willing to lend his name and sell his planes but not to invest in the proposed company. He believed in the future of aviation, and even ran the Detroit-Chicago mail route to learn more about such an enterprise. But he also believed in the division of labor and that his personnel were tooled to manufacture not operate. With the most famous pilot and manufacturer of motors on board, the partners next hoped to team with the man who had become the foremost tycoon in aviation.

A Canadian-born wheeler-dealer, Clement M. Keys rose through the penny-ante world of small-time aviation to become chief executive of the Curtiss Airplane Company. A whiz at trades and mergers, he also gained control of a holding company which owned an operation called Transcontinental Air Transport (TAT). Keys was interested in Lindbergh's proposition and suggested that the men from St. Louis approach the railroads, which had an operations system already in place—timetables, ticket-taking, terminals, tracks to follow where navigation was difficult, and trains on which to put passengers in bad weather. He arranged for a meeting with William W. Atterbury, president of the Pennsylvania Railroad.

As this new flying venture would involve rail service until the entire route could be lit at night, and because the "Pennsy" only ran as far west as St. Louis, each side needed the other to realize its belief in Manifest Destiny. For a twenty percent interest in the company, the Pennsy came on board. With paid-in cash capital of $5,000,000, Keys was named president of the company, and Lindbergh chairman of its Technical Committee.

Lindbergh spent most of the next year establishing the TAT route. In a "sister ship" of the *Spirit of St. Louis,* he selected the ten intermediate points between the coasts, then repeatedly checked each stop to ensure that the route was safe and worth the money people would spend to save a few days of travel. Most of his suggestions became the standard for aviation in the United States and, subsequently, around the world. In many cities, he helped create the models for their first modern airports.

Few of the stops had suitable landing fields for the ten trimotored, 1200 h.p. monoplanes Lindbergh ordered from Ford. Columbus, Ohio, for example, had to build and equip an airport of seven hundred acres, to accommodate the new airline. To do so, the city had to pass a bond issue of $850,000 and the Pennsylvania Railroad had to develop a new rail station at that point on their tracks nearest the flying field, with platforms and crossovers so that passengers could easily transfer between planes and trains. Lindbergh believed that passengers would still "prefer the additional comfort of a railroad pullman to the time saved by night flying." But already anticipating the time when the planes could fly through the night, Lindbergh ordered the lighting of three hundred miles of airway between Waynoka, Oklahoma, and Clovis, New Mexico. New airports had to be built and completely outfitted in both those cities as well as Winslow and Kingman, Arizona. While Los Angeles had more than thirty landing fields in its metropolitan area, Lindbergh selected a private airport in Glendale because it was most accessible to the centers of population and least affected by the region's "peculiar fog situation."

Lindbergh insisted upon a national meteorological system, starting with weather stations placed at regular intervals along the TAT route. "On departure from each airport," Lindbergh wrote in one of his first statements for the company, "planes would be given a complete report of weather conditions then existing along their route and also a prediction of conditions which would exist at any time during the flight." In some cities that meant a trainmaster stepping outside and looking up at the sky. Soon every station along the TAT line was equipped with a complete weather station, and they were all linked. The company contracted with the Radio Corporation of America to put ground stations and pilots in direct communication with each other and arranged with the American Telephone and Telegraph Company to install private teletype service between each of the stations along the way.

TAT prepared to offer forty-eight-hour transcontinental trips in the summer of 1929; and Lindbergh was already anticipating that they might shave twelve hours off that by the time they opened for business. While each of those first planes in the TAT fleet would be able to fly twelve passengers at 105 miles per hour, Lindbergh was inspecting designs for other planes with capacities of thirty-two passengers and speeds up to 130 miles per hour and was foreseeing trips across the continent taking less than twenty-four hours!

Handsomely rewarded—$10,000 a year for chairing the Technical Committee plus a signing bonus of $250,000, with which he could purchase forthwith twenty-five thousand shares of company stock at ten dollars per share—Lindbergh worked hard for his piece of this new industry. He suggested Ford might also manufacture aluminum chairs and a toilet in each of the planes TAT was buying from him; he met with the Acme Milling and Refining Company about new ores and alloys that might be used in planes; he talked to General Electric about producing lights for landing fields and magneto compasses; he recommended that Goodyear manufacture tires especially for desert landings, which would be impervious to mesquite, cactus, and sandburs; he designed a special navigational watch with rotating dials, which A. Wittnauer company produced for him and subsequently sold to the trade.

Lindbergh also granted TAT restricted use of his name in its publicity. After public relations representative Harry Bruno parenthetically referred to the company in a publicity story as "The Lindbergh Line," he consented to its further use as the company motto. With the publicity came greater responsibility, for Lindbergh knew that any major accident on "his" line "might well be compared with the sinking of the Titanic."

That spring Lindbergh forged a business relationship with another early mogul of the aviation industry, Juan Terry Trippe. Not of Hispanic origin, as was often assumed—but named for an Aunt Juanita—this enterprising son of a New York banker grew up in Greenwich, Connecticut, graduated from Yale in 1920, and served in the War as a Navy flying instructor. With backing from a few of his wealthy schoolmates, including a Whitney and a Vanderbilt, he formed Eastern Air Transport. Two years later he bought two small competing airlines, Pan American, Inc., and Florida Airways, which he merged into Pan American Airways—all before he was thirty. Alternately described as a pioneer and a pirate, Trippe secured the airmail contract between the United States and Cuba. With its rum and gambling, Havana became a favorite vacation hideaway for Prohibition-parched Americans, which Pan American exploited by establishing daily passenger service from Key West.

While their motives differed, Juan Trippe shared Charles Lindbergh's global visions for aviation. During his five days in Havana on his Caribbean tour, Lindbergh had spent time with Trippe and inspected his base of operation there. He even flew passengers for him, testing one of the new Pan American Fokkers. Both men agreed that after transcontinental routes and before transoceanic routes, it was necessary to span the Americas. More than anybody Lindbergh had met, Trippe had the passion and the power to make that happen. Within months of his TAT deal, Lindbergh also became Technical Adviser to Pan American Airways—again for a salary of $10,000 a year plus the right to purchase about one-tenth of the company's shares at half their present value. Lindbergh would remain active with the company for more than forty years.

Lindbergh was not merely corporate window dressing. As adviser to two airlines, he took to flying where nobody had before him, selecting and surveying routes. He often tested new planes, determining which were best for his companies to purchase. He set down specifications for Pan American planes from the Sikorsky S-40 amphibian in the early days of flying boats all the way through the Boeing 747 of the jet age. In his earliest discussions with Trippe, Lindbergh considered such projects as: dirigibles for transoceanic routes; floating runways, to be anchored at three-hundred-mile intervals across the Atlantic; buoys with rotating beacons for night flying, to be anchored along the Caribbean route; catapult takeoffs for heavily loaded transoceanic planes; refueling in flight to allow for transoceanic range; microfilming airmail letters to reduce their weight. As Pan Am's needs differed from TAT's, there was still a debate between wood or metal construction. In but a matter of years, Lindbergh felt Henry Ford had been right and ordered all-metal monoplanes for the entire Pan Am fleet.

While Lindbergh never cashed in on the $5,000,000 he was offered to endorse products and to appear in movies, within eighteen months of his famous flight, he had earned more than $1,000,000. Lindbergh also received fees up to $10,000 a year for advising the Pennsylvania Railroad and the Daniel Guggenheim Fund; six-figure royalty checks continued to come his way from *"We,"* as did five-figure checks from *The New York Times* for his internationally syndicated articles. J. P. Morgan & Company looked after his investments, two-thirds of which were in stocks, mostly blue chips along with companies with which he felt a personal connection, such as the Guggenheims' Kennecott Copper, Curtiss Flying Service, and a new builder of airplanes, Boeing. Some have suggested that such financial sharpies as Keys and Trippe taught Lindbergh how to avoid income tax; but tax rates were low and Lindbergh's returns were always scrupulously simple. Compiling his own data, which was vetted by officers of Bankers Trust and Morgan, as well as Colonel Breckinridge, he declared all his income and deducted only the most obvious business expenses. Living nowhere on next to nothing, by age twenty-six, Lindbergh had enough of a nest egg never to have to think about earning money again.

He also saw that his mother, then fifty-two, would be financially secure for the rest of her life. Although Charles started sending her $3,000 semiannually, Evangeline L. L. Lindbergh continued to teach in Detroit. She saw no reason to change the way she lived. At the same time, numerous offers came her way, opportunities to write articles and make personal appearances. In the summer of 1928, Constantinople Woman's College offered her an appointment as a visiting professor of Chemistry. Besides the chance to travel through Europe and Asia, Evangeline viewed the job as a way of both teaching and investing in "international good will." She accepted, recruiting as a companion Alice Morrow, whom she had befriended at Christmas in Mexico City. Dwight Morrow's unmarried older sister had been a teacher in Pittsburgh, and the college was pleased to engage her as its official hostess for the winter semester. The two women sailed together in early September, arriving in Turkey fifteen days later.

Not until his mother was seventy-five hundred miles away did Lindbergh approach what he had targeted as his primary obligation that year—marrying and starting a family. By his own admission, America's most eligible bachelor "had never been enough interested in any girl to ask her to go on a date." As a barnstormer, he had resisted the sexual promiscuity that came easily to aviators, finding fly-by-night relationships with women "facile," offering "little chance for selectivity, hardly any desire for permanence and children." In the Army there had been a shanty village near the flying field where prostitutes were available, but Lindbergh never crossed its borders. He later wrote that he thought it "was not an environment conducive to evolutionary progress." His intellectualizing aside, Lindbergh also admitted fifty years later that he had simply been shy and inexperienced and did not want to contend with the problems that attended women—"you had to learn to dance, to talk their language, to escort them properly to restaurants and theaters."

Lindbergh never got over his schoolboy nervousness. Toward the end of his life, he would write at length about the genetic makeup he had sought in a mate, starting with the obvious—"good health, good form, good sight and hearing." The specifics descended from there into a discourse that was more about animal husbandry than human relations. He thought he was displaying a dry wit in emoting less about choosing a wife than a farmer might in selecting a cow. In truth, he never did grow comfortable enough to describe the only courtship in his life. "It's not that he was cold," remarked one of Anne Morrow's friends from her first days visiting Mexico; "he was just immature."

Lindbergh was at a distinct disadvantage in dating. "Girls were everywhere," Lindbergh wrote objectively of his popularity, "but it was hard to get to know them." His singular fame created an unnatural air of "awe, respect, and curiosity." To make matters worse for somebody so inexperienced, the press monitored his every move, ready to turn an innocent glance into an international headline. Reporters trailed him when he began calling on the Morrows that year.

While Anne was still at Smith, he visited Englewood, where her mother and sister Elisabeth were inspecting the construction of their new house. They arranged for Lindbergh to visit the family at the summerhouse they were building at Deacon Brown's Point on North Haven. During a subsequent phone conversation with Lindbergh, Mrs. Morrow referred to her daughter and Lindbergh asked, "Which daughter?" Elisabeth was taken aback that Lindbergh knew—as she wrote Anne—"there was more than me." The press was already conjecturing a summer romance between Elisabeth and Lindbergh.

So was Anne. "I don't think I can bear to face it," she wrote in her diary, imagining Lindbergh's visit: "He will come. He will turn quite naturally to E., whom he likes and feels at ease with. I will back out more and more, feeling in the way, stupid, useless, and (in the bottom of my vain heart) hoping that perhaps there is a mistake and that I will be missed." Her thoughts festered into mild hysteria.

With graduation approaching, Anne became consumed with two dreams, the first largely to keep her mind off the second: she wanted desperately to win the Jordan Prize, awarded for the most original work of prose or verse; and she prayed that Colonel Lindbergh might take some interest in her—that "he liked me." To protect herself from being hurt, she prepared a line of attack against even allowing herself the latter fancy. "Fool, fool, fool," she wrote. "You are completely and irretrievably opposed to him. You have nothing in common. You don't even sincerely care a damn for his world. You are just swept away by the force of his personality."

Her first dream came true, and then some. At graduation, Anne received not only the Jordan Prize but another for the best essay on women of the eighteenth century. What was more, she had a poem published in *Scribner's*. Those triumphs behind her, she could return to fretting about the imminent visit of Lindbergh, as the Morrows set up housekeeping in their new large white summer place, which had cost more than $100,000.

Just as Anne's anxiety over Lindbergh's arrival reached fevered pitch, a rainy front descended upon the coast of Maine, preventing him from getting through. Anne felt relieved, until she learned that Colonel Lindbergh changed his flight plan to go to New York. "Elisabeth of course again," she wrote. "It was like that sudden falling down you have in a dream—kaplunk." Anne and Constance spent summer nights discussing Elisabeth's inevitable wedding to Lindbergh. Newspapers reported that their engagement was imminent.

In the fall of 1928, Lindbergh telephoned the Morrow house in Englewood, the first time he had ever called a girl for a date. But he was calling Anne, not Elisabeth. She was not there, and Mrs. Morrow's secretary, Jo Graeme, told him to telephone the following morning. Refusing to believe that Lindbergh actually wanted her, Anne anxiously grabbed the telephone when he called back. He was just as nervous as she, blurting, "Hello—Miss Anne Morrow—this is Lindbergh himself." Then he charged forward with an obviously prepared statement about a promise he had made to take her flying. After a conversation that threatened to break off with each sentence, they agreed to see each other the following week.

A few days later, Lindbergh arrived for a meeting to "settle a few points" about their date. "Well," he explained, thinking of the press, "we can't go to any of the fields or we'd be engaged the next day. I've been engaged to two girls in one week and I haven't seen either of them." He laughed and blushed, and so did she. Anne later admitted that she had forgotten how tall and good-looking he was.

On October sixteenth, they met in the New York apartment of friends of the Morrows. Anne had thrown together a motley outfit, riding trousers of Constance's, a woolen shirt of her mother's, and thick gray golf stockings of her father's; she wore her own street hat and high-heeled shoes and red leather coat. "Gosh," Anne later wrote, "what a mess I looked." He drove her in his new, black Franklin sedan out to Port Washington, where he had arranged with Harry Guggenheim to use one of his horse pastures as a landing field. On the way out, the awkwardness of their conversation lifted, and she discovered that she could be "*perfectly* natural with him, say anything to him," that she "wasn't *a bit* afraid of him or even worshipful any more."

Upon arriving at Falaise she felt even closer, seeing how "at home" he was in the splendid surroundings and how comfortable he made her feel.

Toward the end of lunch, Lindbergh excused himself to go to Roosevelt Field, where he had rented a De Havilland Moth. Harry and Carol Guggenheim filled Anne with tales of "Slim" and his practical jokes, then took her out to the field, where Lindbergh landed in the small, open-cockpit biplane. He helped her into a parachute and gave her a quick lesson in the controls. Minutes later, they were in the air, high enough to view both coasts of Long Island at once. "I can't describe the flying," Anne later wrote Constance, "—it was too glorious." By the time Anne had returned to New York City she believed "Colonel L. is the kindest man alive *and* approachable." Before they parted, he suggested another flight, perhaps down the New Jersey coast.

Later in the week, Anne and Jo Graeme met him at Teterboro Airport, near Paterson. A reporter was already at Lindbergh's heels asking, "What general direction are you headed?" Lindbergh replied, "Up"; and Anne stifled a giggle. Then he flew his two passengers over the islands of New York City, as far south as Lakehurst, while the setting October sun bathed the entire city in golden light.

By the time Anne and her chaperone had returned to Englewood, reporters were calling and had even staked out the house. A newspaper in Mexico had surmised that the Morrow daughter seen flying with Lindbergh was Elisabeth. Even worse, Ambassador and Mrs. Morrow had clumsily addressed the mistake instead of ignoring it, telling the Embassy staff, "It wasn't Elisabeth, it was Anne—isn't it funny?"

The "joke" even got laughs overseas. Elisabeth Morrow had come down with bronchial pneumonia while traveling abroad and was recuperating in the Mayfair residence of Edward Grenfell, the English partner of the Morgan Bank. "Were you the person I read about in the London paper which said, 'Young, pretty, sparkling, vivacious girl flies with Lone Eagle—resembles Miss Elisabeth Morrow'?" Elisabeth inquired of her younger sister. "Mrs. Grenfell showed it to me and we both roared."

Anne was humiliated, cheered only when Lindbergh visited again that night and got her joking about the press reports. After supper, he took Anne for a drive in his Franklin through a dense fog. For hours they talked, covering a wide range of topics, from politics to his image in the press. He spoke of aviation in a way that made Anne understand that he saw it as but a means to greater ends. "The thing that interests me now," Lindbergh said to her, "is breaking up the prejudices between nations, linking them up through aviation."

When Anne lowered her guard and told him that she hoped to write, he seemed to understand her passion. He even volunteered that he wished he could write. Repeatedly dumbfounded by the sensitivity of his comments,

Anne was finding their silences as comfortable as their conversation. By the time they had returned to Palisade Avenue, she felt completely safe with him. She wrote up the entire evening in her diary and in letters to Constance, all except two salient details: Charles Lindbergh asked her to marry him; and she consented. They agreed not to tell anybody until he had addressed her parents in person.

Lindbergh had fallen in love with Anne Morrow. The evidence of his feelings overwhelmed all the practical considerations he had detailed in his autobiography. The attraction between him and Anne was so strong that he completely overlooked the Morrow family's physical and mental health problems, which he once would have considered obstacles.

Anne was leaving that week for Mexico City, and Charles wondered how he might join her without drawing attention to his trip. By chance, the American military attaché in Mexico invited Lindbergh on a hunting expedition in the northern plains of Coahuila, and Ambassador Morrow asked him to stay at the Embassy afterward. Stopping in St. Louis to vote (for Herbert Hoover), Charles arrived in Mexico City on Friday, November ninth. After dinner that night, Anne and Charles and a young embassy employee went to a dance at the home of Eman Beck, a longtime resident of Mexico City, whose daughter Susanna was becoming one of Anne's closest friends. For once, Anne enjoyed herself, clutching her secret as she watched the adoring women flit around her fiancé.

The next day, Dwight and Betty Morrow took Anne and Lindbergh to the weekend house they had just bought in Cuernavaca, fifty miles south. The Ambassador and Lindbergh talked agriculture all the way down, mostly about cows. The Morrows' sprawling place—which they cleverly named "Casa Mañana"—was enchanting, with red tiled terraces and roofs, tropically planted courtyards, and a swimming pool. Sunday morning, sitting alone with Ambassador and Mrs. Morrow, Charles announced his intentions.

"I think that I can never be surprised again," Betty Morrow would write in her diary later that night. "I am stunned." Upon hearing the news, she rushed to find her daughter and enjoyed a few minutes alone with her in their mirador, a third-floor tower that overlooked all of Cuernavaca. "Anne," she said, mustering all her best wishes, "you'll have the sky!—the sky!" At the same time, she saw that her daughter was "all trembling and upset—& very fearful of herself."

"I think she loves him," Betty Morrow added in her diary. But she had doubts. Anne and Charles had only met four times since Christmas; and they seemed to have come from two different worlds. Before going to sleep that night, Betty checked on her daughter only to find Anne sitting on the side of her bed. "Oh, Mother," she said, "I am so happy."

Lindbergh remained in Mexico with the Morrows for two weeks, as they all tried to get used to the startling news. The Ambassador, who had until that time been nothing less than worshipful, was heard grumbling more than once, "What do we know about this young man?" He urged the young lovers to take some time to get acquainted. Lindbergh had no doubts about the marriage, but he agreed to postpone an announcement as long as possible because he feared the avalanche of publicity.

"He is utterly utterly different from me," Anne kept telling her mother, "but it's all right." By the end of the fortnight, Betty was not completely convinced, though she was sure that Anne was. "I don't believe that she will change," Mrs. Morrow wrote. "I think she is thoroughly in love with Lindbergh. She understands that they are very different—she sees clearly that. There are some things she is going to lose—but he is a romantic figure & a fine virile man who has conquered her imagination. I can't imagine it—but I must." Anne and Charles spoke of a private wedding in North Haven. But until they knew exactly when that would be, they wanted to release no word of the engagement. Lindbergh suggested that the resumption of their separate lives—he returning to his aviation work, she remaining with her family in Mexico—would throw the press completely off their scent.

Until their announcement, Charles insisted that nobody must know, except the few people to whom he and Anne would reveal the news themselves. The Morrows' diplomatic skills were put to the ultimate test that very week when they withheld the news from their daughter Elisabeth, just returning from Europe and being met at the docks by hordes of reporters asking about *her* engagement to Colonel Lindbergh!

Charles informed his mother in Constantinople by mail in two short sentences. "When you are happy," she wrote back, "I am satisfied, for you deserve the greatest happiness life has to offer. You have been too fine always in your attitude toward me for me to be able even to write about it."

Anne and Charles remained apart for most of the next three months, bonded by their great secret and growing affection for each other. Through letters, discreet telephone calls, and coded telegrams, Lindbergh carried on his first romantic relationship. Despite the separation, he felt her love.

The feeling was mutual. "The sheer fact of finding myself loved was unbelievable and changed my world, my feeling about life and myself," Anne would write forty-five years later. "The man I was to marry believed in me and what I could do, and consequently I found I could do more than I realized, even in that mysterious outer world that fascinated me but seemed unattainable. He opened the door to 'real life' and although it frightened me, it also beckoned. I had to go."

While she spent the autumn between Mexico and Englewood, Anne revealed her secret to a few friends. "I don't expect to be happy," she confessed to former beau Corliss Lamont, "but it's gotten beyond that, somehow." Instead, she hoped he would wish her "courage and strength and a sense of humor."

In December 1928, the Morrows' big, new Georgian house was completed, which they called Next Day Hill. Exuding stately grace, the white-painted brick house with stone trim lorded over more than seventy-five acres. In the end, it cost $400,000, complete with morning room, formal library, and a pine living room transported from an old great house in England. Another quarter-million dollars was spent on the furniture and landscaping. The backyard included a dozen vast flower beds, an old apple orchard, and profusions of Betty Morrow's favorite flowers, columbines and larkspur. On New Year's Eve, between four and seven, the Morrows hosted their first party at Next Day Hill, a housewarming attended by nearly one thousand people. The buzz that evening was that Lindbergh might appear and that his engagement to Elisabeth might be announced.

By February, the press was closing in on the truth. Finally, at four o'clock on the twelfth—while Anne was in Mexico City and Charles was in the air between the cities of Belize and Havana, carrying the first airmail between the two American continents—a beaming Ambassador Morrow invited the newspaper correspondents into his Embassy office. When they had all assembled, he leaned over his desk and handed each reporter a small slip of paper on which was typewritten: "Ambassador and Mrs. Morrow announce the engagement of their daughter, Anne Spencer Morrow, to Colonel Charles A. Lindbergh." When pressed for details, Morrow said only, "In matters like this, one guess is as good as another." When reporters caught up with Lindbergh, he evasively added, "Well, then, you know all about it. I have nothing to say."

Within two hours, a friend called the Morrows from Englewood to say the news had been broadcast over the radio. Over the next few weeks, the Embassy received thousands of letters and presents from statesmen and strangers alike. Most of the messages were congratulatory, though millions of hearts around the world were broken. One young girl wrote that she did not really think Anne was pretty enough. Lindbergh's name was everywhere again, in bold type—" 'WE' NOW A TRIO." The entire nation rejoiced anew over this crowning touch to the two-year celebration of the Lone Eagle's triumph. Six Ziegfeld Girls offered to serve as bridesmaids.

Anne Morrow had remained so veiled from the public eye that many newspapers around the world mistakenly published a picture of Lindbergh sitting with the parents of his fiancée and Constance. "Unlike most brides-to-be," Anne later remarked, "it was I who was congratulated, not he." One member of the Embassy merrily sang, "She was only an ambassador's daughter, but he was Prince of the air." Anne thought of him less as a prince than a "knight in shining armor," and she as his attendant. "The role of page came naturally to me," Anne later realized. She did not think that role was a good basis for a marriage, but she thought it was good for her own development— "a role I could play until I grew up." Until then, she could continue to live in somebody else's shadow.

Her sister Elisabeth seemed genuinely happy just being a "bridesmaid." "It is the most perfect and beautiful thing that ever happened," she had written her mother when she learned the news, two weeks before the public announcement. "Of course there will be times when she will have hard and difficult situations to face but they will make her stronger and more capable of living fully. She will *always* be protected and loved by her husband." And at Milton Academy, Constance Morrow had tapped her water glass at dinner the night before the news hit the papers to make the announcement to her schoolmates in Hathaway House. There was tremendous applause and shrieks of surprise. At the next school social, she was stunned to find herself so popular, cut in on every dance. Dwight Jr. had recently entered Amherst, but his mental health once again forced him to drop out of school, this time for treatment with Dr. Austen Fox Riggs in Stockbridge, Massachusetts; but he was excited when told that he would be able to attend the wedding.

While the engagement was a feather in the caps of the Ambassador and his wife, they remained properly concerned about their daughter's welfare. "Poor child!" Betty noted. "With all the world congratulating her, she is having many hard moments." Within days, Charles had joined Anne in Mexico, and she felt suffused with "faith and courage" every time she looked at him. As he gave her nerve, she gave him heart.

Later that week Charles and Anne stole away from the Embassy, flying from Valbuena Field for a private picnic alone on a prairie. Taking off again after their lunch, Lindbergh looked outside the Travel Air cabin monoplane he had borrowed and saw one of its wheels rolling along the ground. To make matters worse, the plane had no safety belts. Charles explained the problem to Anne, but not the possible repercussions. He said that they would fly around for hours, reducing both the load of gasoline and the danger of explosion on impact. He padded Anne with the two seat cushions and instructed her to open the windows so they could crawl out if the plane tipped over. At last, they circled the field, where a frantic crowd had gathered, signaling not to land—as though they had an option. Charles and Anne looked at each other and laughed. Then he began his approach, coming down slowly. With one hand he controlled the plane; with the other he braced himself, grabbing a tube of the fuselage structure. He brought the plane down on one wheel, keeping the opposite axle balanced high for thirty yards before it gouged the ground and the plane turned turtle. Anne suffered but one moment of silent panic, wondering how she would appear in his eyes if she could not face this test. But by the time she realized what had happened, she had crawled out the window and was perfectly fine. He had dislocated his shoulder.

"Anne very cool & composed through it all," her mother observed, "& he is awfully proud of her. I should think he would be!" Although he had a good excuse not to, the next evening Charles insisted on appearing with Anne at a large diplomatic dinner at the Embassy—with his arm in a sling, rigged to a colorful scarf tied around his waist. Terrifying though the plane crash had been, Betty Morrow could not help noticing how the shared experience drew Anne and Charles closer together. "I believe a beautiful thrilling life is ahead of them," she wrote an old friend, "—if only the papers will let them alone after they are married."

Within ten days, Lindbergh left to pilot the inaugural flight between Mexico City and Brownsville, Texas, for Pan American Airways. He spent most of March traveling on airline business, while Anne remained in Mexico, out of sight. By then, there was no doubt in her mind that she was making the right decision, but she found it difficult making one adjustment in particular. Her "intensely private" husband was determined to "keep intact this most private of all relationships"; and toward that end, he had warned his fiancée, "Never say anything you wouldn't want shouted from the housetops, and never write anything you would mind seeing on the front page of a newspaper." Anne believed "an experience was not finished until it was written or shared in conversation"; and, as a result, she kept no thought unexpressed either in diaries or any of a dozen active correspondences all her life. She believed this "lid of caution . . . clapped down on all spontaneous expression" would be the most difficult adjustment she would have to make.

Lindbergh, of course, had grown accustomed to the ubiquity of reporters and false stories. But it hurt him now to see Anne and her family turned into innocent victims of this cat-and-mouse game, having their privacy invaded. Reporters camped outside the gates of Next Day Hill, and photographers hid in the woods around Deacon Brown's Point, North Haven. Morrow servants were regularly offered money for information about the young couple; and the Hearst syndicate even bribed a workman to steal a cache of Anne's letters. Whenever Anne and Charles went driving, they were followed. Charles and Anne instinctively learned to confine themselves to the private estates of family and friends.

Newspapers reported presumptions about the Lindbergh wedding, its guest list growing each week. The media assumed a June wedding in North Haven and a honeymoon by airplane. Because the press had standing cash offers with workers at most airports for any word of Lindbergh's flying activities, Lindbergh secretly placed an order with an officer of the Elco Company for a boat, a thirty-eight-foot motor cruiser. Then, the third week of

May, he ordered his Curtiss Falcon flown to Rochester with instructions to leave it in a hangar fully serviced. As Lindbergh suspected, the press migrated to Roosevelt Field and northern New York, keeping their eyes peeled for a large gathering of Morrows and other dignitaries. They showed no special interest in Dwight Morrow's returning to New Jersey on the last Sunday of the month for a birthday party for his wife.

Although the secret was kept from even the few who had been invited for tea the next day, Monday, May 27, 1929, was chosen for Anne and Charles's wedding. She walked through most of the morning in a daze, picking lilies of the valley and tulips in the backyard to decorate the house. Later, with her mother, sisters, and childhood friend Vernon Munroe, Anne went to the old house on Palisade Avenue, where they cut forget-me-nots and cream columbine and a few sprays of light blue larkspur. Elisabeth arranged the flowers into a bridal bouquet. Charles and his mother arrived from New York together, joining Anne's grandmother and two maternal aunts and the rest of the Morrows for lunch. Anne was too nervous to eat.

Mid-afternoon, Charles excused himself to the library, where he spent a few minutes making a two-and-one-half-page holographic will. In the event of his death he wished to create a trust fund of $200,000 for his mother, and he bequeathed the remainder of his estate to Anne. He also suggested that she select any items she wished from the exhibit of his belongings at the Jefferson Memorial in St. Louis, the rest to be left to the historical society for a permanent exhibit. The will was primarily for Evangeline Lindbergh's protection, as Anne's own trust fund was then worth a half million dollars.

The other guests arrived around four, driving past an indifferent coterie of reporters. A hush hung over the house, creating a funereal mood, or so joked Elisabeth. There was a handful of people from Dwight Morrow's side and another few of Betty Morrow's dearest friends. Dwight Jr. was, in fact, too ill to leave the sanitarium in Massachusetts. Charles had only his mother. Then Reverend Dr. William Adams Brown of the Union Theological Seminary appeared, and it was clear that a wedding ceremony was about to occur. They were twenty-two present in all, the bridal couple included.

Anne readied herself in the ladies' dressing room downstairs. She wore a simple gown of cream-white chiffon—made by the local dressmaker who had sewn clothes for the Morrow daughters since they had been children—and blue heeled slippers. A maid helped Anne with the French lace veil, which fell to her shoulders. Charles, in his blue suit, came into the room, shut the door, and went over to reassure her. At that moment, Anne later recorded, "I knew it would be all right." Then her father, mother, and sisters entered. Each of the women kissed her, before proceeding to the large living room, hidden from the street and overlooking the gardens.

Dwight Morrow smiled at Anne, "very gently & happily," and offered his arm. Together they walked before the hushed group facing the fireplace. In an instant Reverend Brown recited an abbreviated service. Anne and Charles quietly answered his ritual questions, and he slipped the ring on her finger. (It was made from gold nuggets that had been presented to him in Honduras.) Afterward, people approached to kiss her. There were no photographs.

Everybody walked out to the enclosed piazza for refreshments. There was a large fruitcake by Madame Blanche of New York City. It had been made weeks earlier, with a frosting that had become rock-hard. Nobody had read the special instructions from Madame Blanche, saying that a knife had to be dipped in boiling water before attempting each slice. As it was, Charles sawed away at this nearly impenetrable block.

In the middle of everybody's joy, Betty Morrow experienced a moment of terror. As she whispered to Charles that she would get a sharper knife, he grabbed her by the wrist and growled "No! No!" in a tone she had never heard before and would never forget. He managed to hack through the cake, and pieces were passed around.

Anne quietly went upstairs to change into a French blue suit and a blue felt hat. Her mother and sisters followed to say good-bye. At 4:30, everybody waved as the newlyweds slipped out the back of the house and into a car. Charles and Anne drove past the entourage of newsmen waiting at the bottom of the hill, just as they had many times when they went for a drive. The press corps pursued them, but the newlyweds gave them the slip, driving down a blind alley in which Henry Breckinridge was waiting in Lindbergh's Franklin. They exchanged cars. Donning caps and dark glasses, Charles and Anne started their long drive to Long Island. They stopped once to jot and post notes to Betty Morrow. "I do not believe it would be possible to have even wished for a more perfect occasion," Charles wrote his mother-in-law.

The guests lingered at Next Day Hill until 6:45. Not until then had a word about the wedding been released. On his way home, one of the Morrows' friends spoke to the reporters at the bottom of the drive and let the cat out of the bag. By seven o'clock it was on the radio. A few minutes later, Dwight Morrow's secretary, Arthur Springer, distributed to the newsmen the official announcement, one sentence in length; he took no questions. That same afternoon, the *Daily News* carried an article announcing that Lindbergh would be marrying soon, before an assembly of fifteen hundred.

With their two-hour jump on the press, Charles and Anne reached their destination on the Sound at ten o'clock, undetected. According to plan, they found a dinghy tied to a tree, which they hauled by flashlight to the water. As a cold wind blew, Charles rowed his bride out to their cruiser, the *Mouette*, which waited there with lights shining, beckoning them to begin their voyage together.

9

"WE"

"I still expected to devote the greater part of my life that was spent apart from my family in developing fields of aviation."

—C.A.L.

SUMMERY WEATHER WELCOMED THE *MOUETTE* AS IT CRUISED up the Long Island Sound; and the honeymooners enjoyed smooth sailing for most of a week, in complete privacy. Their fourth day at sea, the *Mouette* pulled into the harbor at Block Island for fresh water.

With the world speculating as to where its most famous newlyweds had disappeared, Charles prepared a disguise for coming ashore. A stubbly beard growing in, he pulled a black-checked cap down over his eyes and wore a pair of dark glasses. While his costume seemed to have deflected attention, his boat did not. When some fishermen on the wharf asked about his large cruiser, he kiddingly told them that he was Lindbergh. Eavesdropping from behind the green curtains in the cabin, Anne delighted in the cleverness of his ruse.

Within a few days, they reached Woods Hole, Massachusetts, where the press, at last, discovered them. The Lindberghs spent the next four days pushing their way to the coast of Maine as hard as they could. One morning, a reporter in a launch persisted in circling the *Mouette,* hoping the chop of his boat would make the Lindberghs seasick enough to come topside. They never gave him the satisfaction. After eight hours, Lindbergh decided to get away by gunning the engine, dragging the anchor until they lost the reporter on the open sea.

Each day filled Anne with wonder as she learned the rules of being Mrs. Lindbergh. Four years younger and in the thrall of her new husband, she went along with his every desire, trying to figure out his periodic inconsistencies. She was more than a little surprised, for example, when they pulled into York Harbor, at the southern tip of Maine, where they found a crowd of reporters and towns-people awaiting them. Charles was unusually cheerful, seeming to enjoy showing Anne off to the crowd. Then the chase resumed, as they headed for the cluster of tiny islands that dotted Penobscot Bay.

It was Lindbergh's first visit to the North Haven area, and he adored it on sight—"passing island after island with its deep-green forest and spray-dashed rocks." They both especially liked one of the wildest of the group—Big Garden Island—which Dwight Morrow had just given his daughter as a wedding present. After a few days of complete peace together, they retraced their route, slipping unnoticed into Room 1802 of the Berkshire Hotel on East Fifty-second Street in Manhattan.

While their first three weeks of marriage had been far from the splendor they could afford, it had provided the greatest luxury they could find any-where—time alone. Living on canned goods and ginger ale and a Kellogg's breakfast food called ZO, Anne had surprised herself with her own resiliency. She had found pleasure in the physical labor of their trip and in the rigors of seamanship. "I think it is perfectly thrilling to navigate—use a parallel rule and the compass rose and find magnetic, true, and compass course—and keep the needle on that number—*and actually get there*!" she wrote her brother Dwight, still under doctors' care. "Of course with my usual care-lessness at the end of the trip I discovered that I had been counting the wrong lines in the compass rose. Charles made terrific fun of me and said I did it be-cause those lines were 'prettier.' " Just days short of her twenty-third birth-day, Anne sent her mother a glowing report of her honeymoon—explaining that it was "all so natural & not a bit terrifying—not a terrific change or even strange—and—a great deal of fun!"

No sooner were the Lindberghs back on land than they took to the air. Transcontinental Air Transport had announced the inauguration of its cross-country service; and as Chairman of TAT's Technical Committee, Lindbergh insisted on spending the night at each stop so that he could make a final in-spection of equipment and personnel. His bride accompanied him on this transcontinental dry run; and with each new city, Anne accustomed herself to the rituals of being the hero's wife.

After spending one night in Columbus, the next in Indianapolis, and the next in St. Louis, she realized everywhere they went and probably ever would go, "Charles is Charlemagne"—complete with royal treatment (and giggling telephone operators) to which he no longer even took notice. She could not understand why people now asked for her autograph. To her surprise, she cottoned to all of Charles's friends, down to the grease-monkeys at the air-fields. She was startled to discover Kansas City was in Missouri and that Waynoka, TAT's port city in Oklahoma, was little more than five paved roads and a hotel. Lindbergh, of course, was the guest of honor at the dedication of the town's new airfield—the biggest crowd, said one townsman, "since the dedication of the pavement!" Upon arriving in California, Lindbergh authorized TAT to commence its transcontinental service.

At 6:05 P.M. on July 7, 1929, *The Airway Limited* left Pennsylvania Station in New York for Port Columbus, Ohio. Several of its passengers would continue westward for the forty-eight-hour air-and-rail trip to Los Angeles, mostly journalists given free tickets. The next morning Charles and Anne Lindbergh went to the Grand Central Air Terminal in Glendale, in the San Fernando Valley. The large trimotored *City of Los Angeles*, made of corrugated aluminum alloy that looked like tin, shimmered in the summer sun. Five thousand spectators and a band were on hand for the ceremonies. Several dignitaries spoke, including Governor Frank Merriam of California. Then "America's Sweetheart," Mary Pickford, stood on a ladder and cracked a bottle of grape juice over the nose of the flower-festooned ship. The Lindberghs posed with Miss Pickford for the newsreel and newspaper photographers, then Charles excused himself.

A select group of ten, including Anne, boarded what the newsmen were calling "The Tin Goose." While the copilot revved the engines, Charles Lindbergh came from the cockpit into the cabin and shook hands with each passenger. He would be their pilot that morning. Despite his reassuring grin, some found him looking "tired and tense." The press was already building public suspense, writing at length how Lindbergh had staked "his name and future on the venture," noting that "the slightest mishap would be disastrous."

Anne became TAT's unofficial hostess, showing the other passengers that they too could relax in the air. To her family and friends she raved about every detail of the flight—starting with the cool gray-green of the cabin with its green curtains at each window and blue-shaded lights over each of the adjustable green leather chairs. A white-uniformed attendant provided stationery, maps and postcards, and a small aluminum table for each passenger. After two and one-half hours, the plane touched down in Kingman, Arizona, where everyone disembarked and walked under a long awning on rollers, which connected the plane with the "station." The passengers reboarded after a fifteen-minute stop and, once in the air, partook in a meal which had been specially prepared by the local Harvey House. The attendant set up each passenger's table, covering it with a lavender linen tablecloth. They dined off metal plates on cold meats, salad with sliced pineapple, white and brown bread, sliced grapefruit, cake, and hot coffee poured from a large thermos. Less than two hours later, they had crossed the great Southwestern desert and landed in Winslow.

The *City of Los Angeles* continued east with a fresh crew and without the

Lindberghs. They spent the night in Arizona so that Charles could fly the first passengers on the incoming *City of Washington*. Amelia Earhart—who had become world-famous the year before, as the first woman to fly the Atlantic (Newfoundland to South Wales, along with pilot Wilmer Stultz and a mechanic)—was among them. The success of the new operation quickly found others willing to pay the cross-country fare of $290.

Seeing how wearying it was for Anne to wear a public mask, Charles took her to northern California for a weekend alone in a log-cabin camp in a valley of tall redwoods. They canoed and swam in a mountain stream that ran past their door. Anne's writings from this period were extremely romantic, full of magical images at every turn. "I kicked up golden dust when I opened the gates for C. as we drove through fields and farms today," she wrote her mother from upstate California after a day of simple pleasures. "Maybe it's just the way we feel, C. and I, when we get off together, alone—all gold, that extra golden bloom over everything!"

But Anne was quickly learning that time alone with her husband would always be rare. Aviation, like Wall Street, was booming that year; and Lindbergh's public presence was essential to that industry. Once TAT had completed its foundation line, with hub cities across the country, other airlines in various corners of the nation could connect their routes, creating a web of airlanes that united all the states. The next year, more airlines would span the continent; and Lindbergh would play a part in the growth of all of them, especially as they tried to maintain their footing after that October's stock market crash.

With the addition of new routes, each month saw an increase in passengers taking to the air. But more essential to the survival of a new airline was the presence of a United States mailbag. In fact, most companies fortunate enough to secure a mail contract subsisted on that alone. The most influential man in commercial aviation thus became the man who awarded those contracts—Postmaster General Walter Folger Brown.

A Republican mover and shaker, Brown became an authority on commercial aviation and put that knowledge to both personal and public use. He was blindly ambitious and a visionary who looked out for the public good. With the onset of the Depression, Brown believed the fledgling industry needed a few large, strong companies, not many small, weak ones to see it through hard times and into financial stability. He assumed extraordinary powers, consolidating routes and revoking route certificates at his own discretion.

Lindbergh shared many of the same views about the business of aviation as Brown. Seeing the need to build a broad airline network as quickly as possible, he regarded Brown's energetic reforms as enlightened capitalism. Toward that end, Lindbergh had several meetings in California with Jack

Maddux, a maverick businessman who had started his own bus line and automobile business in the Southwest. His aviation company had been in operation for two years. In 1929 alone, the Maddux Line flew more than a million miles, linking Los Angeles with San Diego and San Francisco as well as the Imperial and San Joaquin Valleys and Baja California. On November sixteenth, the company would merge with TAT.

American Airways received one of the two transcontinental air routes Brown put up for bids in the summer of 1930—the southern route—Atlanta to Dallas to Los Angeles. Then, instead of simply awarding the second contract for a more central route to a bidder, Postmaster General Brown chose to form a new company, all but forcing a merger between TAT-Maddux and Western Air Express. He turned the marriage into a ménage à trois, folding the Mellon-controlled Pittsburgh Aviation Industries Company (PAIC) into the deal not only because of its ability to fly the northeastern leg of the route but also to reward a few friends. The new Transcontinental and Western Air—T&WA—would be run by an executive from PAIC named Richard Robbins. The company would gradually drop its ampersand and make increasing use of its motto, "The Lindbergh Line."

In September 1929, "The Lindbergh Line" suffered its first major catastrophe when one of the TAT trimotor transports disappeared en route from Albuquerque to Los Angeles. The Lindberghs were about to go to Maine; but Charles explained to Anne that it would seem "brutal" to the public—especially to those related to the passengers on the ship—if it appeared that he had gone off on vacation. Charles tried to answer as many questions as he could about the plane's disappearance. Then, despite bad weather, he and Anne took a small fast plane, a Lockheed Vega, out West to join the search party. Even if there was little for Lindbergh to do, the gesture of his flying to the rescue—accompanied by his diminutive wife—was essential to the image of both the company and commercial aviation. After the Lindberghs' arrival in the Southwest, the crashed plane was found on Mount Williams, with no survivors.

Lindbergh visited two other crash-sites during the next eighteen months. Paul Garber, the Smithsonian's first curator of the National Air Museum, said that these public displays were practically as important to commercial aviation as his flight to Paris. "It took Lindy's big smile to get those first passengers into planes, especially after those crashes," he said. "He made it all look so easy . . . and safe enough to take his pretty, young wife along with him."

The Lindbergh name became part of America's daily parlance. Even after the public novelty of their marriage had worn off, Charles and Anne performed a succession of newsworthy deeds which kept them in the headlines. The nation found them more glamorous than movie stars because their romantic adventures together were real. Lindbergh allowed a certain amount of professional exploitation, but he refused to answer questions about his personal life, talking about Anne only insofar as she was becoming an increasingly active partner in aviation.

Over the next year, Charles privately taught Anne to fly, and she studied navigation. "The instructor comes every morning at 10 and we, or I (when C. is at the Lockheed factory) work until lunch," Anne wrote her mother-in-law. "Then he leaves us problems and we work part of the afternoon. Then he comes back right after supper at 7:30 and we work until we drop asleep. . . . It is very interesting work in itself and very wonderful to me that you can get your exact position in a few minutes with a watch, a sextant, a few tables (of spherical geometry) & a little addition and subtraction—that is if you can see two stars or the sun & the moon. . . . Charles makes great fun of me because I can only add and subtract dollars and cents—and get all mixed up with degrees and minutes." During one of their visits to California, she and her husband took up gliding, and Anne became the first licensed female glider in the country. "Women are just as well-fitted to operate a plane as men," Lindbergh told one reporter, "and the physical difference between them that may handicap women in other lines of work need not do so when it comes to flying."

The preceding year, Lindbergh had returned from his Pan American Airways business in Central America via the Yucatán. In the midst of the Mexican jungle he had noticed the ruins of an ancient temple. When he had reached Washington, he telephoned Dr. Charles G. Abbot, Secretary of the Smithsonian, who informed him that he had seen the recent excavation of the Temple of the Warriors at the great Mayan city of Chichén Itzá. His interest in archaeology whetted, Lindbergh read up on the pre-Columbian civilization; and he met Dr. John C. Merriam, president of the Carnegie Institution of Washington, who was supervising other excavations of primitive civilizations. Lindbergh suggested that the airplane could be a valuable tool not only in reaching remote places but in providing "the eyes of birds to the minds of men."

Dr. Merriam told Lindbergh of two archaeological camps near America's Four Corners, not far off TWA's Southwestern route. That summer, Charles and Anne flew from California in an open-cockpit Curtiss Falcon biplane over the Canyon de Chelly, several hundred miles west of the main camp in the area. There they saw a number of small ruins perched so high as to be virtually invisible from the canyon bottom. The Lindberghs made several flights over the long-abandoned community—unmarked on archaeological maps— taking hundreds of photographs of terrain and ruins. They climbed the cliffs and examined the ruins, which, according to the Carnegie Institution's *News Service Bulletin,* had "never before been visited by white people."

The *Bulletin* praised the Lindbergh expedition for several reasons. Above all, the airplane allowed an observer to cover in a few hours territory that might require months on the back of an animal. Their photographs also showed "much better than in any other way, topographical features in proximity to the ruins which must have affected in a vital way the life of the inhabitants." The Lindbergh survey's impact on archaeology was incalculable. Media coverage of this latest adventure spawned a new interest in both the science and the early civilizations.

The Lindberghs explored Central and South America that fall as well. When Charles had flown there just before his marriage, he had been surveying and organizing air routes. In September 1929, Lindbergh returned to those waters with his wife, along with Juan and Betty Trippe. Linking the Gulf and Caribbean countries to the United States was an important step in the development of global transportation in and of itself, as they opened passenger and mail service linking the Americas. In just ten days at the end of September, they stopped in Cuba, Haiti, Puerto Rico, Trinidad, Venezuela, Colombia, Panama, and Nicaragua. "There were mobs of people at every airport," remembered Juan Trippe.

Before each takeoff, Lindbergh walked the dirt airfields, testing its hardness. "One of the fields was a sea of mud," Trippe remembered. "Slim trudged through the mud from one end of the field to another, and after we had taken off, he hung his socks out of the cabin window to dry . . . but one of them blew away. So at the next stop in Curaçao, there was the usual crowd of well-wishers, the band, and the reviewing stand, and there was Slim greeting all the dignitaries wearing only one sock. But that flight marked the first air mail delivered to South America. It opened up a continent."

Lindbergh had been warned that "it would be foolhardy to attempt a flight around the Caribbean, that the weather was too bad and unpredictable, the rain squalls frequent and too heavy to fly through." But the successful 1929 tour by the Lindberghs and the Trippes paved the way for permanent air routes in that territory. More than that, as Trippe would later recount, "The Caribbean was our first laboratory for overwater flying operations. Lindbergh, from his first Caribbean flight on, was in on virtually every decision of a technical nature that Pan American made, and from the very start he showed an understanding also of the economic and political hurdles that had to be surmounted."

Having enjoyed their archaeological sorties in the southwestern United States so much, the Lindberghs concluded their Pan American swing with a visit to the Maya region. With the blessing of Juan Trippe—who encouraged any activity that promoted interest in the skies he serviced—they flew from Nicaragua to Belize. In a Pan American twin-motored amphibian—the S-38—the Lindberghs covered most of the Yucatán peninsula in five days. Accompanied by Dr. A. V. Kidder, they flew from Tikal to Uaxactún in six minutes—what would have been a long day's journey by mule-train. Over Chichén Itzá, Lindbergh himself took what many still consider the finest photograph of the entire city. They explored the southeasternmost state of Quintana Roo. "The greatest thrills of our five days' flying came, of course with the finding of groups of Maya ruins indicating the presence of ancient cities," Dr. Kidder wrote afterward. In less than a week, they discovered as many as six lost sites which might otherwise not have been reached for decades.

Despite the press's embellishing of Lindbergh's archaeological work, he always kept its value in proportion. More than once he was approached by admirers who asked him to tell about the lost Mayan city he had "discovered," to which he would reply, "As a matter of fact I located a small ruined wall almost covered by tropical vegetation."

While spending much of his time exploring the past, Charles Lindbergh's most far-reaching scientific investigations that year were aimed toward the future. Months earlier, on a solo flight in his Ryan monoplane between New York and St. Louis, his mind had begun to wander. Bucking a strong headwind at eighty-five miles per hour, he considered the great human milestones in transportation. "Through the centuries," he realized, "man had developed the wheel to travel over land, the hull to sail across water, and the wing to fly through air." Advancing his thought, he asked himself if man could ever enter space. "If so," he thought, "obviously we would have to overcome the need for wings and the limitations of propellers." Lindbergh wondered from whom he could learn the essentials for sending man into space.

The Lindberghs relaxed for a day in August 1929, at Falaise on Long Island. There occurred one of those serendipitous moments which, in Lindbergh's words, "so often bend the trends of life and history." While Anne had excused herself to write letters upstairs, Charles and the Guggenheims retired to the large living room, where the men invariably discussed aviation. Lindbergh was standing by a window—looking at the Sound and comparing an airplane's speed with a slow string of barges—when Carol suddenly exclaimed, "Listen to this!" She proceeded to read aloud from an article in *Popular Science Monthly* about a recent explosion in Worcester, Massachusetts.

Robert Hutchings Goddard, the forty-seven-year-old Chairman of the Physics Department at Clark University, had spent his sickly childhood reading the works of H. G. Wells and Jules Verne. Finding physics a creative outlet for his own active imagination, he became obsessed with formulating a method of reaching extreme altitudes. He studied at Worcester Polytechnic Institute, earned a doctorate locally at Clark University, and did postgraduate research at Princeton. He kept his thoughts about rockets under his hat as much as possible. But, he quickly learned, experimentation in this nascent field of study cost a lot of money and inevitably attracted a lot of local attention.

The press superficially summarized his work as an attempt to reach the moon. Worse for Goddard than being dismissed as a lunatic was the undue attention being placed on his experimentation, which stripped him of the privacy necessary for trial and error. Cadging grants in a new field of study was difficult enough without having ridicule attached to his work.

Goddard had won a $5,000 grant from the Smithsonian Institution, and a few thousand dollars more from Clark University; but his experiments with gasoline and liquid oxygen quickly burned through his funds. The year Charles Lindbergh first dreamed of flying from New York to Paris, Robert Goddard had launched a ten-foot-tall contraption of steel tubing forty-one feet into the air in 2.5 seconds over a trajectory of 184 feet. Three years later, on his Aunt Effie Ward's farm, in Auburn, he sent another slightly larger model soaring—twenty feet above its sixty-foot launching tower, at which point it veered right and rose another ten feet, landing 171 feet away. This was the projectile—only some 200,000 miles short of the moon, he told journalists in an attempt to lead them from covering his experiments—that Carol Guggenheim had read about.

Upon hearing about the missile, Lindbergh called on the Du Pont Company, among the world's largest manufacturers of chemicals and explosives, and arranged a private audience. On November 1, 1929, he flew to Wilmington, Delaware, where Henry Du Pont had gathered twenty of his organization's leading executives, engineers, and scientists. "Might rockets," Lindbergh asked, "be used to get far out into space or as power-plants for aircraft?" The scientists were skeptical, explaining that the necessary fuel would be too heavy, the temperatures too high, the combustion time too short.

Realizing that his vision was beyond their present horizons, Lindbergh left the group with a simple problem to keep their minds on the subject of rockets. As aviation was just emerging from a period marked by frequent engine failures, he asked if a small rocket could not be devised, one that could be "attached to an airplane for emergency use in case of engine failure on take-off." A single minute of such reserve power, Lindbergh indicated, might be enough to avert a serious crash. Du Pont's chemical director conducted an investigation of the problem which led Henry Du Pont to conclude that it was not worth further consideration. Lindbergh still had not encountered anybody who shared his belief that "rockets would be practical either for aircraft or for flights into space."

In the meantime, he learned that Professor Goddard was a highly regarded physicist, not the mad scientist many had suggested. On a gray afternoon at the end of November, Goddard answered his telephone only to find Charles Lindbergh at the other end. Lindbergh proclaimed interest in Goddard's work in rocketry and asked if they might discuss it in person. Goddard waited until dinner that night before nonchalantly telling his wife, Esther, of his unusual call. "Of course, Bob," she replied. "And I had tea with Marie, the Queen of Rumania."

On Saturday, November 23, 1929, Lindbergh drove to Worcester in his 1927 Franklin sedan. The wary Goddard trusted his visitor on sight, showing him his laboratory and taking him back to his house, where Esther Goddard brought out some milk and a homemade chocolate cake. They sat on the porch for hours, while Goddard did most of the talking—disclosing results of his experiments with paper-thin Duralumin combustion chambers instead of firebrick and liquid fuel instead of explosive powder. "I was tremendously impressed with Goddard," Lindbergh recalled forty years later, "his accomplishments, his knowledge, and his confidence in the future of rocket flight." When Lindbergh asked if he thought it possible to build a rocket that could reach the moon, Goddard said yes, by building a multistage missile, a patent for which he already held. But, Goddard added with a grin suggesting an even wilder concept, "it might cost a million dollars to do so."

Short of that, Lindbergh asked Goddard what he would require to reach more immediate goals. With $25,000 a year for four years, Goddard replied, he could set up a laboratory and launching tower somewhere far from neighbors' complaints, police restrictions, or snooping journalists. He could then accomplish in four years, he said, "what might otherwise take him a lifetime." By the end of the day, and Esther's chocolate cake, Lindbergh was determined to secure that backing.

A few weeks later, Lindbergh met Goddard in Wilmington, where he had arranged another meeting. Lindbergh thought the people at Du Pont would be interested in Goddard's projects; and he knew that the Du Pont Company could easily appropriate $25,000 a year for further research in what he considered "a fascinating and little-known field." The meeting was a dud, as Goddard hesitated to reveal details of his liquid-fueled rocket to people more interested in gun-powder. Lindbergh gave Goddard a lift north, his first plane ride.

After arranging a meeting with the Carnegie Institution, which yielded $5,000, Lindbergh concluded that Goddard would probably find support more readily from a single investor than from an institution, a wealthy benefactor who would not have to answer to a board. In the back of his mind, he kept thinking of Daniel Guggenheim, but he hesitated because Daniel's son, Harry, had become one of his close friends. "Also," Lindbergh later recalled, "I felt that Daniel Guggenheim had done much more than his share in supporting scientific progress when he had contributed five million dollars to set up a philanthropic fund for the promotion of aeronautics."

Revelations of Germany's recent experiments with rockets quickly dispelled Lindbergh's reluctance. Concerned that the United States maintain its postwar position of global supremacy, he went to Hempstead House, a gray stone castle, statelier than Falaise, which sat on a neighboring bluff in Sands Point. Daniel Guggenheim, then in his mid-seventies, met him in the entry hall, where Lindbergh started blurting his interest in rockets and Goddard even before they had sat down. "Then you think that rockets have a future?" Guggenheim asked. "One can't be certain," said Lindbergh; "but if we advance beyond airplanes and propellers, we'll probably have to turn to rockets."

Guggenheim asked Lindbergh to assess Professor Goddard's ability and his financial needs. Lindbergh replied, "I think he knows more about rockets than any other man in the country," and that proper expansion of his knowledge would require $100,000. Guggenheim asked Lindbergh if he thought such research was worth so large an investment. "Well, it's taking a chance," Lindbergh replied, pausing before committing himself, "but—yes, I think it's worth it." Guggenheim said he would back the venture, asking only that an advisory committee be formed and that Lindbergh join it. Lindbergh telephoned Goddard with the news, telling him to start planning the future.

The bulk of Goddard's first two-year budget would pay for machinists and assistants and setting up shop. He allotted himself $5,000 a year in salary. A meteorologist at Clark directed him to a high plateau in the barren southeast corner of New Mexico which promised little fog, few clouds, and mild temperatures. In the summer of 1930, just a year after Lindbergh had first heard Goddard's name in the living room at Falaise, the professor and his wife set up a home and laboratory in the little city of Roswell. Twenty miles away, Goddard and a small team erected a rocket-launching tower made from the galvanized-iron framework of a windmill.

The press release about Daniel Guggenheim's patronage of Goddard's work was couched in the most mundane terms possible, to make the research sound levelheaded. "Perfection of Professor Goddard's rocket," the statement said, "will mean that thermometers, barometers, electrical measuring apparatus, air traps to collect samples of air and other instruments may be sent to extreme altitudes to bring back much-needed information." But Lindbergh already knew that Goddard was laying the foundation for launching a rocket that could reach the moon.

When the Depression began to corrode even the Guggenheim fortune, the Foundation's support for Goddard crumbled, forcing the physics professor back to Clark University. As a result of Lindbergh's importuning, however, Guggenheim restored full funding to Goddard, letting him return to New Mexico. Within a few years he was launching fifteen-foot rockets weighing eighty-five pounds as high as seventy-five hundred feet, gyroscopically controlled, veering off their vertical course by only two degrees.

To keep Guggenheim funds flowing, Lindbergh flew his friend Harry out to Roswell so that they might see an actual launch. But during their visit, two rockets misfired, leaving Goddard "as mortified as a parent whose child misbehaves in front of company." Lindbergh's enthusiasm, however, kept Guggenheim's interest stoked. He even convinced the secretive Goddard to publicize some of his latest results, which not only helped alter public perception toward rockets but also—in the words of G. Edward Pendray, one of the founders of the American Rocket Society—"brought the rocket forcibly to the attention of reputable scientists and engineers as a possible instrument" for reaching high altitudes.

IT WAS DIFFICULT to mark exactly when the Lindberghs' honeymoon ended, as one trip blended into another. They never rested in a single place longer than a few days. At first, life on the road agreed with Anne. Strangely, it took the pressure off their period of adjustment, forcing them to work together. But in exchanging her "insulation of conventional upbringing" for his "insulation of fame, publicity, and constant travel," Anne felt that she and her husband were not breaking down the barriers of intimacy, allowing them to explore what she called the "real life" of human relationships.

There were the odd days when they were at least able to move into somebody's house; but even family visits were coordinated with professional duties. What appeared to be a social invitation from the White House, for example, resulted in Lindbergh's being appointed to the National Advisory Committee for Aeronautics. A trip to Cleveland to see Anne's grandmother was scheduled so that Charles could appear at the Cleveland Air Races, where he performed as a member of the Navy "High Hat" aerobatic team. At the races he also met Ernst Udet, the German flying ace, and Jerry Vultee, an engineer from Lockheed, with whom he placed an order for a low-wing monoplane for future survey flights.

After five months on the move together, Anne gave her husband good reason to settle down. "I have felt miserable for a week or more—nauseated all the time & throwing up," she wrote her mother from New York in late October. A week later, the Morrow family doctor confirmed that she was pregnant. "Charles is such a darling about it all," she assured her mother, "—I am terribly lucky to have him."

Their travel lessened over the next few months but hardly came to a standstill. They remained the most peripatetic couple on earth, their flights now having the additional purpose of finding a place to live. The Berkshire, on East Fifty-second Street in New York City, remained their base as they looked for permanent lodging—searches by air that took them to Long Island, the Blue Ridge mountains of Virginia, the Alleghenies in Pennsylvania, and upstate Connecticut. Like the rest of the Morrow family that year, they found themselves coming home to Next Day Hill to roost. At the urging of the Republican party, Dwight Morrow left his post in Mexico to run for the United States Senate, an election he won by two hundred thousand votes. His wife was thrilled to return to New Jersey, where she would reign over the social life of the community. Their son would also be joining them, still convalescing from his breakdown. And though she was often fatigued and at the mercy of her chronic heart disease, Elisabeth came back to Englewood as well, where she and a friend opened The Little School, a progressive nursery school for two- and three-year-olds in a white frame house behind a white picket fence on Linden Avenue.

During the queasy first months of her pregnancy, Anne was happy to be at Next Day Hill, grateful for the luxury of a staff serving her breakfast in bed and for afternoons reading and walking through the gardens. Charles appreciated the proximity to his business dealings in New York, but he never felt comfortable amid the grandeur of the Morrows' estate. By the start of 1930, the Lockheed company informed him that it had nearly completed the plane he had ordered at the Cleveland Air Races; and, after several weeks under the same roof as his in-laws, he eagerly left for Los Angeles. Surprisingly, so did Anne.

The Lindberghs spent the first months of the new year up and down the West Coast, making the Madduxes' house in Los Angeles their base. They visited Will Rogers and his family at his Pacific Palisades ranch. And in April, Lindbergh took delivery of his low-wing monoplane for $18,000.

All according to Lindbergh's specifications, the plane featured the latest developments in technology and comfort. He had requested a tandem cockpit to permit full vision to either side, the narrow fuselage allowing free use of parachutes in an emergency. An unpatented sliding isinglass canopy of Lindbergh and Vultee's design could be drawn to enclose the two cockpits, the first of its type to be used on an airplane. The plane had dual control, to permit flying, navigating, or photography from either cockpit. Lindbergh also had a small generator installed in the ship, so that they could plug in their new flying suits, which were electrified for warmth. After a few days of testing, Lindbergh pronounced the Lockheed Sirius ready for a transcontinental flight.

At sunrise on Easter Sunday, April 20, 1930, Lindbergh entered the front cockpit of the Sirius and revved the 450 h.p. Pratt & Whitney engine. His

wife—seven months pregnant—settled into the rear, organizing her navigation equipment. Most people expected Lindbergh to prove the value of his
new plane by filling the gas tanks and flying low and slowly across country.
Instead, he secretly made plans to stop once along the way to refuel, thus allowing him to carry less gas and fly at full speed the entire distance, above
the weather. "C. feels (very sensibly)," Anne wrote her mother, "that the object of such a flight is not the non-stop element but simply the speed across
the country." The Lindberghs left Los Angeles, stopped in Wichita and continued eastward at full throttle all the way, often as high as fourteen thousand feet, in search of the most favorable winds. They landed in New York
fourteen hours, forty-five minutes, and thirty-two seconds later—breaking
the transcontinental speed record by three hours.

Reporters awaited their arrival at Roosevelt Field. By the time the plane
came to a stop, however, the pregnant Anne was too nauseous—from the altitude, engine fumes, and an entire day of noise and vibration—to leave the
aircraft. Although her head had been throbbing with pain for the last four
hours of the trip, Anne had suffered in silence, afraid of spoiling the record
flight. Charles faced the press alone, covering as best he could for his wife's
remaining onboard. After the reporters had dispersed, however, she was
spotted being helped out of the plane and into a limousine, looking ashen except for her red, tear-stained eyes. Some reported that she had suffered a nervous breakdown.

The Lindberghs withdrew to Next Day Hill. Anne's seclusion prompted
more shocking canards. One day in May she answered the telephone, only
to have a reporter from the *London Daily News* ask about the "widespread
rumor in New York that the 'heir' was born in April and something happened to it!" Anne pretended to be the secretary and calmly responded,
"There is no information being given out." An army of reporters and photographers stood vigil at the Morrows' gate. "Their intrusiveness became so
objectionable," Lindbergh later commented, "that it became necessary to
employ special guards both day and night."

Charles and Anne imposed a news blackout for as long as possible. Because neither telephone nor telegraph operators were above accepting
bribes—indeed, Lindbergh heard of a new standing offer of $2,000 for any
"secrets of the household"—Charles devised a coded message to wire his
mother when the baby arrived: "Advise purchasing property" if it was a
boy; "advise accepting terms of contract" if it was a girl. Charles would
send the message using the name of an outlaw ancestor, Reuben Lloyd.

Next Day Hill practically became a sanitarium, what with doctors also
checking on Dwight Jr. and on Elisabeth, who, in the excitement of opening
The Little School, had suffered a mild heart attack. A delivery room and

nursery were set up for Anne, and Charles stepped up his search for a home-site, now focusing on New Jersey.

"PURCHASING PROPERTY," "Reuben Lloyd" wired Evangeline Lindbergh on June 22, 1930, Anne's twenty-fourth birthday. A nurse and three doctors had attended the birth. Charles stood by his wife during the entire eleven-hour labor, holding one of her hands while Betty Morrow held the other. When the pain became too excruciating for her to bear, the anesthetist put her completely under. For Charles's sake, Anne was happy to have delivered a son, even though he said the sex of the infant did not matter to him. When she first saw the healthy seven-pound, six-ounce newborn, she thought, "Oh dear, it's going to look like me—dark hair and a nose all over its face." Then she recognized Charles's mouth and the "*unmistakable*" cleft in the chin and happily fell asleep.

Lindbergh and his in-laws argued about releasing the news. Betty Morrow was able to wrest permission only to inform the household staff, so long as she did not reveal the baby's gender. After the diplomatic Dwight Morrow persuaded him to present the barest formal statement, Lindbergh dashed off a short script for Arthur Springer, Morrow's secretary, to read to the wire services. "Mr. Springer calling from the home of Ambassador Morrow," he was instructed to say. "A son was born today to Mr. and Mrs. Lindbergh. This is for your information. Mr. and Mrs. Lindbergh are issuing no announcement."

Telegrams and letters and flowers and presents and poems and songs poured in from all over the world—mostly from complete strangers. *Parents Magazine* sent the Lindberghs a free subscription; the director of the Florentine Choir of Italy composed a lullaby; chambers of commerce across the country sent silver cups and brushes. A Boston company printed special cards for the occasion—"Congratulations to the Happy Lindberghs"—hundreds of which arrived at Next Day Hill. Headlines referred to the infant as "Wee Lindy," "Baby Lindy," or simply "Eaglet." Countless editorial cartoons portrayed a baby eagle in flight with the stork. Numerologists and astrologers made public predictions, one pronouncing him a genius, another asserting, "The Lindbergh heir will earn a name for himself, through his own ability."

Desperate for information and a picture of the baby, the press knew how to smoke out the reluctant parents. Stories appeared that the baby was deformed or, worse, had been stillborn. Everybody walked around Next Day Hill in a state of anxiety, suspecting everybody else of selling out to the newspapers.

At last, Lindbergh called a formal press conference in New York. He barred five newspapers, including Hearst's, because of their "contemptible" journalistic practices. He called upon a policeman to eject one reporter from the room before he proceeded to give details about the baby—whose name, he announced, was Charles Augustus Lindbergh, Jr. When asked what career he might choose for his son, Lindbergh replied, "I don't want him to be anything or do anything that he himself has no taste or aptitude for. I believe that everybody should have complete freedom in the choice of his life's work. One thing I do hope for him, and that is when he is old enough to go to school there will be no reporters dogging his footsteps."

Lindbergh distributed a photograph of his son that he had taken himself. He told the "constructive press" to copyright the prints and asked them not to give them to the five newspapers he had excluded. Within a day, every newspaper in the world had a copy of the picture, including the five on the blacklist—one of which stole it from the Associated Press. When a journalist reported this fact to Lindbergh, he replied that that did not matter to him so much as the point that he had not cooperated with them. "My stand," he said, "is a matter of principle."

For the first time since he had become famous, Lindbergh received negative press. The masses still worshiped him. Indeed, New York's Governor Franklin D. Roosevelt had recently asked for an autographed picture of him, St. Louis wanted to erect a statue in his honor, and there were already whisperings of drafting him to run for President (even though he was Constitutionally underage). And the birth of his son uncapped a geyser of people with the best of intentions who also hoped to cash in on the Lindbergh name: an unemployed candymaker in Boston wanted permission to produce "Lindy Jr. Pure Honey Kisses"; the Magyar Evangelical Reformed Christian Church of Gary, Indiana, named their new church the Charles A. Lindbergh, Jr. Cathedral Chapel; and the stream of requests for interviews for articles and books had hardly abated since his flight. But now many members of the press who felt they had helped create this hero felt unfairly dismissed by him.

That summer *The New Yorker* suggested that for all Lindbergh's posturing on behalf of aviation, he had not contributed a single new idea other than his observation that the one light that penetrated fog was blue. "His technical advice to the companies which pay him bank president's salaries," wrote a columnist out of Toronto, "has been negligible. . . . He has cashed in on the name of Charles Lindbergh and the almost imbecile adoration of the American public." Although Lindbergh claimed the occasional spattering of mud onto people awaiting him on runways was the unintentional result of trying to avoid running into them, journalists were noting that it was happening all too often. Some spoke of his "violent temper." The writer from Toronto asked, "Does Lindbergh really dislike publicity, or does he realize that the best way to get it is to pretend that it is objectionable to him?"

Feeling the strains of the Depression, many did not think the Lindbergh baby should be afforded any special attention. Letters to newspaper editors reflected this shifting attitude of the shattered economy. "How much longer do your readers have to look at pictures of the Lindbergh family?" wrote a reader signed "Disgusted" to one newspaper. "It isn't enough to shove Lindbergh in every day, but now his baby has to cover the front page." Another reader concurred: ". . . the kid is no better than a longshoreman's, and perhaps not as good as some." Letters to the Lindberghs also reflected the hard times. What had once been requests for autographs became appeals for money. More than two hundred new parents asked for the baby's outgrown clothes.

That summer, Lindbergh found 425 acres for sale ten miles north of Princeton, New Jersey, in the Sourland Mountains. Supposedly so named because there was so little lime in the ground, this ridge of the Sourlands ran the intercounty line, separating the majority of the property in Hunterdon County from the front yard in Mercer County. Five hundred feet above sea level and one of the highest points in the state, the hill had its own brook, a few open fields, and woods of old oaks. This pocket of New Jersey was "practically inaccessible except by air," reported one wire service, and difficult even for locals to find. The town of Hopewell was less than three miles away; other than that, the area was uninhabited, except for a few poor farmers. Within weeks, the Lindberghs had bought the parcel, and he had ordered a quarter of the land to be cleared and leveled for a landing field. They engaged Chester Aldrich, the architect of Next Day Hill, to draw plans for a house.

As it would be another year before it would be erected, the Lindberghs rented an old farmhouse on ninety acres between their new property and Princeton. New York City was an hour away by train, two hours by car. White with green shutters, the three-story, eight-room house sat behind a white picket fence on Rosedale Road. It came furnished and had a field large enough to land the blue-winged Bird biplane in which Charles was still teaching Anne to fly. A butler, cook, and baby nurse moved in with them; but they ate their meals "farm-fashion," not served, just as Charles had as a boy. "Our own home—imagine it!" Anne exuberantly wrote her mother-in-law.

Anne settled into motherhood, though she did not feel that the motions came to her naturally. She read the latest books on child-rearing, which for all their modern theories of psychology still maintained a Victorian attitude against the display of affection. Lindbergh seemed too frightened of the baby to have any physical contact with him. By the end of the year, the child's hair was growing in curly and golden, and he took to lifting his arms to be picked up. Lindbergh at last gave in to taking him "ceiling flying," which would make "Little Charlie" laugh. The Lindberghs continued to go out almost every night, leaving the baby in servants' care. Charles seldom set foot in the nursery.

In February 1931, the Lindberghs hired a new baby nurse, Betty Gow, right off the boat from Scotland. She had heard about the position from another Scot, who worked at Next Day Hill. Betty was Anne's age, intelligent, and seemed responsible; and she moved in, along with Elsie and Aloysius "Olly" Whateley, the English couple. Anne's only concern about her staff was their inexperience with the press. "They have none of them been over here very long," she wrote Charles's mother, "and so are not so familiar with many U.S.A. customs. The baby is not quite in the same position as most other babies. I am thinking of the emergency situations that arise out of publicity. The house is rather unprotected. The baby sleeps outside. Unless he is watched every second, anyone could walk in and photograph him etc."

Anne worried that her family's movements could be followed by anybody who read a newspaper. Her sister Constance had already been the target of a failed kidnapping attempt at school; an insane woman had already come to their door insisting on seeing the baby as a matter of "life or death"; and another had been sending obscene letters before postal authorities arrested her in New York. Persistent rumors of the Lindberghs crashing somewhere put photographers on the alert at all times to capture the first picture of the "maybe orphan." Before spring, the foundation of their new, more private residence was being dug. Charles spent many afternoons chopping down trees around where the house would be built.

Until its completion, Anne felt most comfortable at Next Day Hill. But even there, legions of curiosity-seekers invaded their privacy. One day, a carload of sightseers sped into the front court, and, in haste, hit Anne's West Highland white terrier, Daffin, then screeched off, leaving the howling dog to die.

MORE THAN THE PRESSURES of fame—the omnipresence of the media and the masses—drove Lindbergh to more interior pursuits. Indirectly, his marriage had as much to do with his shifting aviation, as he put it, "from a primary to a secondary interest"—as he embarked on an intellectual journey into the realm of biology. In fact, Lindbergh had considered becoming a doctor in his youth, in the tradition of Lodges and Lands. "But," Lindbergh later wrote, "I was told that in carrying on his profession, a doctor had to be able to read and write Latin. My first contact with high-school Latin convinced me that the requirements of medicine lay beyond my intellectual desires and capacities." Still, Lindbergh used many of his flights to ask himself questions about the mysteries of life. If man could take to the skies, Lindbergh mused, why could he not remain on earth forever?

In 1928, he had become interested enough in biology to purchase several textbooks. "I decided then," he later recalled, "to reduce my activities in aviation sufficiently to permit the devotion of a reasonable amount of time to biological studies." In 1929, he bought a good microscope and thought about setting up a laboratory if he ever settled down. Once married, he could not help paying attention to his sister-in-law's deteriorating health. He even obtained permission from Princeton's president, John Grier Hibben, to visit the university's laboratories in his search for answers.

One day, Lindbergh asked Elisabeth's doctor why an operation could not be performed to repair her damaged heart. The physician replied that the organ could not be stopped long enough for the surgery to be performed. Lindbergh asked why a mechanical pump could not circulate the blood during an operation and was "astounded" that an eminent doctor could not answer the question. "Knowing nothing about the surgical problems involved," Lindbergh recalled, "it seemed to me it would be quite simple to design a mechanical pump capable of circulating blood through a body during the short period required for an operation." The prospect of this "artificial heart" spawned a new series of questions: "Why could not a part of the body be kept alive indefinitely if a mechanical heart was attached to it—an arm, or even a head? . . . Why would not a mechanical heart be valuable for certain surgical operations?"

Dr. Paluel Flagg, Anne's anesthesiologist, could not answer Lindbergh's questions either, but he said he knew a man at the Rockefeller Institute of Medical Research who could. On November 28, 1930, at the imposing complex of edifices built atop its own promontory between Avenue A (York Avenue) and the East River in the East Sixties, Charles Lindbergh and Dr. Flagg met the legendary Dr. Carrel, if not the Institute's most brilliant figure, certainly its most controversial.

Alexis Carrel was born in Lyons in 1873. The grandson of a linen merchant, he grew up learning the fine points of stitchery. Graduating from the local university at seventeen, he entered medical school there and proved himself unusually gifted, mentally and manually. He practiced sewing with a needle and thread on paper until he was able to make stitches that would not show on either side. In his twenties, he published his first paper on vascular surgery, a radical treatise at the time. He often espoused mystical views, which further alienated him from the scientific community. Temperamental and energetic, the small surgeon with penetrating eyes emigrated to Montreal, where he published a controversial paper on anastomosis (joining) of blood vessels. In 1905 he transplanted a puppy's kidney to the carotid and jugular of an adult dog and watched the kidney function for several hours.

Carrel's work attracted the attention of America's medical community, including Simon Flexner, the founding director of the Rockefeller Institute. This brilliant Jew from Louisville, Kentucky, who had little formal education, understood the importance of so unorthodox a mind as Carrel's to a facility interested in making quantum leaps in medical research. Carrel joined the Institute in 1906, becoming one of the new main building's first occupants. Designing his own very sharp, curved needle, and coating it as well as his thread with Vaseline, which rubbed off in the puncture holes, Carrel developed a new method of blood-vessel anastomosis which became standard operating procedure. For his work on the suturing of blood vessels and the transplantation of organs he became, in 1912, the first surgeon to receive the Nobel Prize.

A devout Roman Catholic, Carrel addressed each scientific problem from both the outside and from within, serving as metaphysician as much as physician. With his holistic approach, he linked the particles of the cosmos with the soul of man, always considering the balance between heredity and environment in his quest for enriching mankind. "The human body is placed, in the scale of magnitudes, halfway between the atom and the stars," Carrel would write. "Man is gigantic in comparison with an electron . . . when compared with a mountain . . . he is tiny." Genetic defects and man's adaptations to his environment fascinated him, leading him to spin numerous theories. One was the dangers to human beings of excessive light. "We must not forget," he wrote by way of illustration, "that the most highly civilized races—the Scandinavians, for example—are white, and have lived for many generations in a country where the atmospheric luminosity is weak during a great part of the year. In France, the populations of the north are far superior to those of the Mediterranean shores."

His work in the laboratory was as bodacious as many of his statements. While studying the healing of wounds in Lyons, he had considered the possibility of restoring and reconstructing injured tissues—by removing the unhealthy tissues, growing them successfully in a different medium, then substituting that new tissue for damaged tissue. Toward that end, on January 17, 1912, he removed a minute piece of heart muscle from an unhatched chicken embryo and placed it in fresh nutrient medium in a stoppered Pyrex flask of his design. He transferred the tissue every forty-eight hours, during which time it doubled in size and had to be trimmed before being moved to its new flask. Twenty years later, longer than the average lifetime of a chicken itself, the tissue was still growing. Every January seventeenth, the doctors and nurses at the Rockefeller Institute would celebrate with Carrel, singing "Happy Birthday" to the chicken tissue.

In 1913, on a visit to France, Carrel married Anne de la Motte, widow of a marquis. She was said to be blessed with mystical powers, and theirs was a spiritual—and childless—union. The following year, as war broke out, Carrel enlisted in the French Army Medical Corps, becoming a major. With chemist Henry D. Dakin, he developed the Carrel-Dakin germicidal technique for bathing infected wounds, which earned him the Cross of the Legion of Honor. After the armistice, Carrel returned to the Rockefeller Institute, leaving his wife in France for months at a time. Through the twenties, his work advanced from the problems of culturing pieces of tissue to whole organs.

Dr. Flagg could not have timed his introduction of Charles Lindbergh to Dr. Carrel any better. At one of the long tables in the Institute's dining room, Flagg witnessed the instantaneous connection between the surgeon and the aviator, each of whom was favorably predisposed toward the other. Carrel believed in the psychological importance of heroes, for they played a role in "promoting the optimum growth of the fit."

In Dr. Carrel, the hero found a hero—the first since his father; and Carrel found a son. Lindbergh promptly recognized that he was sitting with a Renaissance man dedicated to both enlightenment and the occult, a scholar who accepted the existence of powers unknown. "Carrel's mind," Lindbergh would later state, "flashed with the speed of light in space between the logical world of science and the mystical world of God."

Carrel listened to all of Lindbergh's questions. He patiently explained that a mechanical pump could not be used to circulate blood through the body while surgeons operated on Elisabeth Morrow because "blood soon coagulated in contact with surfaces of glass or metal . . . and its delicate cells could not withstand the hammering of mechanical valves."

After lunch, Carrel escorted Lindbergh and Flagg through the laboratories of his department of experimental surgery on the top two floors of the main building of the Institute. He explained that years before he had experimented with transplantation of limbs and organs, and he showed Lindbergh photographs and specimens of the work he had done in which the grafting had failed entirely. In no instance had a graft from one individual to another been successful. Dr. Flagg observed that as the three of them passed through each laboratory, activity stopped, the scientists standing in "silent tribute" to their special guest.

At last, Lindbergh asked if whole organs could be kept alive outside the body just as the fragment of chicken heart continued to pulsate with life. Upon hearing one of the very questions Carrel had been wrestling with himself, he opened a cabinet to show him an apparatus that had been built in his laboratory several years earlier. It was a perfusion pump—for circulating the nutrient media over tissue cultures, which was necessary to keep them alive. As Lindbergh looked at it, Carrel shook his head. "Infection," he said, "always infection." He had hoped to perform experiments on isolated living organs, but nobody had been able to build an operable perfusion pump that did not introduce infection.

Lindbergh gave this delicate but complicated contraption of glass tubes, electric wires, magnetic coils, and valves the once-over. It was so crudely designed that he felt he could improve upon it. Carrel said that if Lindbergh wished to design a new pump, he could have complete access to his facilities. The offer was irresistible. "Here was the possibility of working with a great surgeon and biologist, a man overflowing with ideas and philosophical concepts," Lindbergh later wrote of the opportunity, "in laboratories far better equipped than any I could dream of establishing in the basement of my New Jersey home." What was more, he would be able to pursue his work in private.

Lindbergh made sketches that night of a Pyrex perfusion pump. It was a simple design, which Carrel passed on to Otto Hopf, an extraordinary glass blower with a workshop in the basement of one of the Institute buildings. Carrel first experimented with this pump by inserting a section of a cat's carotid artery in the petri dish organ chamber. "We were for the first time in the history of experimental perfusion," Lindbergh proudly recalled, "able to avoid infection." They successfully perfused one tissue sample for a month. But when it came to perfusing whole organs, they discovered that the perfusing pressure was too low, and that when the organs were attached to the cannulae—the metal tubes used to introduce and draw off fluid—infection set in.

Lindbergh put in long weeks in Carrel's laboratory. He used the two-hour drive over New Jersey roads and through the Holland Tunnel "for contemplation on both conscious and subconscious levels," to rethink and redesign. If he could not put aside a day to get into the city, he would work in one of the laboratories at Princeton. (Although he continued to refuse offers of awards and honorary degrees, he did accept an honorary Master of Science degree that June sixteenth from Princeton University for "[leading] us in our conquest of the air.") Between his airline survey flights and business conferences, he often worked well past midnight with his microscope and textbooks, building and discarding one apparatus after another. "I learned," Lindbergh wrote, "about the problems of infection, the sensitivity of blood, the complicated character of living tissue, the hereditary qualities in every cell." He became absorbed watching through his microscope the slow movements of living cells—"especially after I had designed and constructed flasks containing tissue fragments embedded in quartz sand through which a nutrient fluid circulated, allowing individual cells to migrate or form group structures." One night, he examined his own sperm.

Carrel put each new apparatus Lindbergh designed to the test. The protégé found his mentor "untiring in his willingness to adopt surgical techniques to the requirements of my constantly changing apparatus. No matter how often infection developed or a mechanical breakdown occurred, he was ready to schedule another operation." For his part, Carrel was impressed with Lindbergh's industry as much as his ingenuity, marveling at the way this unschooled mind grasped this sophisticated discipline. "My friends," Carrel slyly said one evening to a former ambassador and an attorney, "the world will hear from this young man some day."

Lindbergh found Carrel himself "even more fascinating" than any of the projects he was pursuing in the Department of Experimental Surgery. "There seemed to be no limit to the breadth and penetration of his thought," Lindbergh recalled. He always looked forward to sitting at Carrel's lunch table in the large dining room, because of the stimulating conversation. "One day he might discuss the future of organ perfusion," Lindbergh would recall. "On another, he would be talking to a professional animal trainer about the relative intelligence of dogs and monkeys, and the difficulty of teaching a camel to walk backward." At another lunch, he expressed his concern over "the environmental effect of white bread on French peasants, and the effect of civilization in general on our human species. 'No one realizes,' he said, 'how many genetic defects modern man contains.' " One never knew if Carrel might launch into one of his tirades—ranting that "all surgeons are butchers" and that "all people are fools"—or if he might quietly withdraw to write—formulating some such notion as: "We must liberate ourselves from blind technology and grasp the complexity and the wealth of our own nature." Lindbergh once looked up from his work to see Carrel step into the room with Albert Einstein, discussing extrasensory perception.

Lindbergh recognized that Carrel had a "blunt tactlessness that created many enemies." But he also found in this fifty-seven-year-old doctor "character that attracted the love of those who knew him well." Nobody in Charles Lindbergh's adulthood affected his thinking more deeply than Alexis Carrel. Their relationship would intensify over the next decade; and Lindbergh would come to conclude at the end of his own life that Carrel had "the most stimulating mind I have known." And so it was that in recalling the winter of 1930–31, Lindbergh began to balance in his mind an "interest in aircraft" with an "interest in the bodies which designed and flew them."

IN THE THREE YEARS since Lindbergh's flight to Paris, teams of pilots had flown from northern California to Honolulu, the Fiji Islands, and Brisbane. Rear Admiral Byrd and pilot Bernt Balchen flew over the South Pole; Frenchmen Coste and Bellonte completed the first successful flight from Paris to

New York; and another team flew from Newfoundland to Tokyo, with stops across Europe and Asia. Falling for the first time into a commonplace routine of commuting between home and a job made Lindbergh itch for another great expedition of his own. Before he became tied down to his new work, and before Anne became too attached to their new baby, Charles plotted a journey that would take him and his wife to Japan by way of the northernmost reaches of the Pacific.

He had his new Lockheed land plane modified into a seaplane. At a cost of $4,000, he ordered two Duralumin pontoons—each with a 150-gallon fuel tank—from the Edo Aircraft Corporation in College Point, Long Island, to replace the landing gear. Because more power would be necessary to lift a heavier load, he asked the Wright Aeronautical Corporation for their new 575 h.p. Cyclone engine and a more effective propeller. For the first time, Lindbergh also installed a lightweight, long-range radio, one designed by the Communications Department of Pan American Airways. Anne—who had just received her pilot's license—would serve as radio operator.

From May to July 1930, the Lindberghs prepared for the trip, she putting their homelife in order while he nailed down the details of the flight. Fascinated, Anne watched Charles turn packing into a science of prioritizing. Mindful that every pound must equal its "value in usefulness," he stacked up the vitaminic benefits of canned tomatoes against the nutritionless but filling qualities of hardtack, warm bedding if they were forced to land in the North against an insect-proof tent if in the South. Using the baby's scale, Charles weighed the six pounds of a shotgun and two ounces for each shell against the birds they could kill if they needed food. Generally, a balance was found by packing a little of everything. He left the rifle at home, taking two revolvers instead. Lindbergh "conceived, organized, and financed" the flight personally; but as a consultant to Pan American, he intended to share all information and conclusions with them.

With an itinerary that included Eskimo villages as well as Asian capitals, Charles and Anne would have to pack for wilderness subsistence and embassy banquets. Each had an eighteen-pound personal allowance, suitcase included. The most "weight-expensive" item was footwear, and Anne found a pair of shoes that could double as slippers in both the bedroom and the ballroom. The Lindberghs spent their early July nights rearranging the three piles that covered their room at Next Day Hill—necessities, discards, and those items still being considered. While Charles corresponded with the Canadian Air Force about using their gasoline caches in northern Canada, with Nelson Rockefeller about Standard Oil providing fuel on their Siberian stops, with the Lomen Reindeer Corporation about supplies in the Northwest Territory of Canada, and with explorer Vilhjalmur Stefansson about the aberrations of weather in the Arctic, Anne brushed up her Morse code.

"I would have been content to stay home and do nothing else but care for my baby," Anne would later write of 1931. "But there were those survey flights that lured us to more adventures. I went on them proudly, taking my place as a crew member. The beauty and mystery of flying never palled, and I was deeply involved in my job of operating radio." The greater—unspoken—lure was the rush of being alongside her husband. "Oh, how she loved her Lindy!" remarked the baby nurse, Betty Gow, more than sixty years later. "She'd have gone anywhere and done anything for him . . . even leave that beautiful little baby behind."

After a year, Anne was warming up to motherhood. She felt more comfortable with little Charlie in her arms, and she delighted in his growing to look like his father. Two new dogs had joined the Lindbergh household, a fox terrier named Wahgoosh (after Charles's childhood dog) and a fearless Scotch terrier named Skean, neither of which strayed from the baby.

On a hot Monday, July 27, 1931, Charles and Anne arrived at College Point, Long Island, to begin their excursion. Their black Lockheed Sirius with orange wings sat upon its shiny pontoons at the end of a wharf in Flushing Bay. A small crowd pressed against the gates as the Lindberghs loaded their plane with its final provisions. Until their return, Charles and Anne would be in the world's newspapers almost every day, often on the front page. Sunday rotogravure sections were filled with photographs of their trip, practically turning their lives into comic-strip adventures.

They flew south for a day in Washington, gathering visas and clearances, before splashing down in The Thoroughfare at North Haven on the night of the twenty-ninth. The baby had already arrived by train with Betty Gow; and his parents had a few minutes to play with him before Anne put him to bed. Then she pulled Betty aside to give her special instructions: "I was told not to cuddle him," the baby nurse recalled, "—or to make him fond of me." The next afternoon, a little after two, the Lindberghs took off, heading over the pine trees toward the Camden hills.

From that moment on, Little Charlie became Betty Morrow's baby, with complete run of the place at North Haven. Before the Lindberghs departed, they had discussed Charlie's spending part of the summer with his other grandmother. But Evangeline reluctantly begged off, asserting, "Police protection is almost nil in Detroit; there is far too great a number of unemployed; conditions here are much like Chicago which, as you know, is in a bad way."

Surrounded by Morrows all summer, Charlie played on the beach, swam in the pool, and went on boating trips to neighboring islands. He took food only from his Grandma Bee or Betty Gow, both of whom recited poems, read books, and sang to him. When the baby's hair grew too long for a boy, they cut it, saving every "snip of gold." That summer little Charlie began putting words together, and he took his first steps. As the Morrows returned to Englewood at season's end, an epidemic of infantile paralysis struck New York City. It was decided that Charlie and Betty Gow should remain in Maine until the crisis had passed.

Meantime, Charles and Anne had flown from Ottawa up the western coast of Hudson's Bay, from Moose Factory to Churchill and onto Baker Lake. The country was barren there, except for a few houses and a church on the bare shore. At Baker Lake, a Canadian Mounted officer in his red coat, a few other white men, and some Eskimos greeted them. Two Eskimo boys could not take their eyes off Anne, for she was the first Caucasian woman they had ever seen.

The Lindberghs flew an entire night from Baker Lake to Aklavik, the northwesternmost point of the Northwest Territories. Throughout the flight—as they slipped between white cloud banks hovering over the Arctic ice pack to their right and the gray, treeless coast to their left—it never grew dark. They found a settlement of thirty houses and stayed with the region's only doctor, who made rounds on some of his patients just once a year by dogsled. They witnessed the excitement of the supply boat arriving the following afternoon.

Lindbergh piloted to Barrow through a storm, with Anne at the radio, securing the weather information they needed to land. They stayed for three days, enjoying a "Thanksgiving dinner" that ran into the early morning with most of the town in attendance—including the doctor, the minister, the nurse, the schoolteacher, and an old Scotch whaler. As cold in August as New England in November, this northernmost point in Alaska treated the Lindberghs to a banquet of reindeer meat, wild goose, cans of sweet potatoes, peas, and beets, even some canned celery. Charles and Anne left Point Barrow for Nome, a small mining town on the Bering coast.

Crossing the Bering Sea from North America to Asia—from Nome to Karaginski on the Russian island of Kamchatka—the Lindberghs felt as though they were returning to civilization. But only the most expert piloting enabled them to land in the fog at the harborless, uninhabited island of Ketoi. A typhoon also hit the area, grounding them for a day. Anne and Charles gave thanks throughout this trip for his training as an airmail pilot. After thrashing through seaweed, the Lockheed Sirius developed mechanical problems, which Anne broadcast on her radio, leading a Japanese naval vessel to come to their rescue, towing them into Buroton Bay.

One month after they had left New York, they arrived in Nemuro, Hokkaido, Japan, where they enjoyed their first bath since Nome. For over a week, they had been able to wash themselves only out of a basin; now they shared a tub, pouring basins of hot water over each other. The next day, they flew to Kasimigaura Naval Base in Tokyo. As the Lindberghs' journey was covered in front-page detail around the world, Japan had prepared for their arrival.

"Bouquets, cameras, reporters, crowds . . . ," recorded Anne, understanding for the first time what the throngs must have been like when her husband returned from Paris to New York. A car drove them to the Embassy in town, pushing its way through one hundred thousand people, most dressed in white, shouting "Banzai! Banzai!" The media reported that it was "one of the greatest demonstrations ever seen in the ancient capital." Scores of letters and cards in beautiful Oriental writing, attached to Embassy translations, awaited them. Most congratulated the Lindberghs on their safe arrival across the Pacific, assuring them that their visit would promote aviation as well as friendship between the United States and Japan. For many Japanese, Lindbergh's arrival was tantamount to a religious experience, thus furthering his cult following. Missionary groups of all sects throughout eastern Asia hoped he might visit them. The Prime Minister received them.

The Lindberghs spent more than two weeks in Tokyo—indulging in tea ceremonies and banquets when Charles was not inspecting air bases and roughing out the continuation of their expedition. They expected to fly to Nanking and Peking for two weeks, then on to the Philippines. Beyond that Charles was vague, though he was leaning toward returning home by way of Africa and South America. Not only was that the "best-weather route," but it had become traveled enough to have developed radio communication. It would also allow the Lindberghs to visit South American countries they had not yet seen—Argentina, Brazil, and Chile.

Anne was homesick. She had counted on returning by fall and confessed in a letter to her mother that she dreamed about "The Baby" every night— "almost." But she said little on the subject to her husband, feeling it was "such poor sportsmanship—when this *is* a marvelous experience." Besides, she had to admit, she did want to see Peking before returning. Mid-September they flew to the southern part of the main island of Japan.

After the Lindberghs said their sayonaras to the officials in Osaka, Charles made his final baggage check. He was so particular about the order of the equipment in the Sirius that Anne was not allowed to do the final packing. He noticed that the water canteens were out of place, and in setting things straight he discovered an eighteen-year-old Japanese boy stowed away, cramped into the space of the two two-gallon canteens. The Lindberghs asked the officials to be lenient with the boy, who had explained that life was not happy at home, and that he had hoped this great aviator from America would take him there.

After one more stop in Japan—in Fukuoka—the Lindberghs flew over the Yellow Sea. Miles before they reached the mainland, the color of the sea changed, mud from the Yangtze River besmirching the blue waters. The

Yangtze was in high flood, the worst it had been in decades, leaving an estimated fifty million people homeless. The Lindberghs landed in Lotus Lake,
just outside Nanking, where the river threatened the city's great wall.

As their plane was the only one in all of China with enough range to survey the outer limits of the floods, the Lindberghs offered their services to the
National Flood Relief Commission. They met with the Chinese president,
Generalissimo Chiang Kai-shek, and his Wellesley-educated wife for tea; but
they canceled all other social functions so that they could devote themselves
to the emergency at hand. The Lindberghs surveyed the lower Yangtze valley and found vast lakes among the narrow strips of rice fields, only to discover that those lakes were actually overflow from the river. Weighing the
value of each pound of supplies that they could carry, the Lindberghs decided
that medical supplies and a doctor who could service many were more valuable than food they might bring to a few.

On September twenty-first, while trying to carry out his mission, Lindbergh experienced one of the most terrifying moments of his life. He took off
from Nanking with Dr. J. Heng Liu, Director of the Department of Hygiene
and Sanitation, and Dr. J. B. Grant, from the Rockefeller Institute of Peking.
They were to inspect the larger cities in the flood area north of the Yangtze,
delivering packages of serum and vaccine.

Lindbergh splashed down on what had been rice fields, a few hundred
yards from the wall surrounding Hinghwa. The entire city seemed to be
sinking. A few sampans approached once they anchored, and Dr. Liu
boarded one of them. Suddenly, hundreds of sampans skittered toward them
from all directions. Lindbergh then made what he later realized was "the
fatal mistake" of handing Dr. Liu one of the medicine packets. The Chinese,
hungry and desperate, thought it contained food or money. An old woman
grabbed one of the foot-square packages wrapped in white cloth and sat
on it.

By then the boats were jammed so close that one could jump from one
to another—more than an acre of floating skiffs. Several Chinese bounded
their way toward the plane. Dr. Liu got lost among the hysterical throngs, as
Lindbergh turned all his attention to his plane. One boat with a partly open
fire pushed directly beneath the plane's left wing, which was made of wood.
Dr. Grant yelled to Lindbergh to get a gun. He grabbed the Smith & Wesson
.38 he had wedged beside his seat cushion, but he resisted showing it—"to
draw one gun against hundreds of sampans, crowded with desperate people," he thought, "seemed a fool's move." It would no doubt incite the mob,
which possibly included somebody who would shoot back. When at last
some Chinese, looking gaunt and grim, started to climb onto the pontoons
and wings of his plane, Lindbergh feared damage beyond repair.

He withdrew his revolver and fired once in the air. The people slowly pulled back, clearing a twenty-foot space around the plane. Dr. Liu was finally returned to the Sirius by sampan. As Dr. Grant pulled the anchor onto the wing, Lindbergh started the engine. He took off, with all the sampans attempting to follow. Fearing further episodes of uncontrollable hordes, Lindbergh and the doctors returned to Nanking. They all agreed not to mention the shooting, as "a false impression might have been given of the Chinese people."

Instead of dispensing medicine, the Lindberghs restricted the rest of their mission to gathering information. Anne flew while Charles sketched and mapped whole areas larger than the state of Massachusetts that were immersed. They moved upriver to Hankow, alongside the British airplane carrier *Hermes,* which served as their temporary home. Because the current of the river was too great for mooring the Sirius, the *Hermes* had offered to hoist the plane up from the water as they did their own seaplanes. On the day of their last survey flight, the Lindberghs sat in the plane as it was being lowered into the river. There proved to be too little slack in the cable to detach the hoisting hook as the current began to push the plane downstream. Lindbergh gunned his engine to maintain the plane's equilibrium while they tried to release it from the hook, but he could not correct the situation. In the struggle between the current and the cable, one of the plane's wings dipped into the water, flipping the plane onto its back. Charles shouted at Anne to jump in the river. After weeks of carefully brushing her teeth in boiled water, she found herself swallowing "buckets of this Yangtze mud." A lifeboat downstream rescued them both from the river.

The plane held up remarkably well, though its fuselage and one of its wings suffered enough damage to bring the Lindberghs' journey to a halt. The *Hermes* offered to take them and their plane to Shanghai, where they planned to have the Sirius repaired so that they could continue around the world.

On October fifth—sixth across the date line—while still aboard the carrier, Anne received a telegram from her sister Elisabeth that changed all their plans. Senator Dwight Morrow had died in his sleep of a cerebral hemorrhage. He had returned to Next Day Hill after speaking to the Federation for the Support of Jewish Philanthropic Societies of New York and had suffered a stroke in his sleep. He succumbed the next afternoon.

Betty Morrow wanted the funeral ceremonies as simple as possible—without a formal procession, honorary pallbearers, or even a eulogy. Even so, her husband's service at the First Presbyterian Church in Englewood, two days after his death, was attended by Vice President Curtis, along with Morrow's Amherst classmate Calvin Coolidge, a quarter of the United States Senate, Ambassador Harry Guggenheim, Judge Learned Hand, Adolph Ochs, and Bernard Baruch. Four thousand mourners stood outside the church. A graveside service included only family members, including Evangeline Lindbergh, who came to Englewood to represent her son and daughter-in-law. Newspapers ran laudatory editorials and reverential cartoons. Local schools closed, many stores shut, and flags were lowered to half-mast.

Elizabeth Morrow declined the Governor's offer to complete her husband's term in the Senate. After several large bequests to both Amherst and Smith and paying almost $1,000,000 in estate taxes (which reportedly put the debt-ridden state of New Jersey in the black), she inherited the bulk of the estate—close to $9,000,000, which yielded an annual income in interest and dividends from stocks and bonds of some $300,000. That was approximately what she needed to maintain the Morrow residences and to continue making extremely generous contributions to her favorite charities. With renewed vigor—often saying, "It's what Dwight would want"—Mrs. Morrow would emerge as a national figure, one of the prime exemplars of twentieth-century women who devoted their lives to public service through volunteerism.

Lindbergh arranged the return journey, sending a coded message (working back three words in a pre-designated dictionary) that he and Anne would arrive in three weeks. The Chinese government was so grateful for the Lindberghs' work in China that Chiang Kai-shek awarded them the National Medal, observing that they had been the first aviators to fly from the New World to China. Japan had been just as elated with the Lindberghs' visit. The American Ambassador wrote them, "Your coming at that time and the way that you and Mrs. Lindbergh comported yourselves as simple unassuming Americans left the happiest impression and made both of you, in the finest sense, ambassadors of good will." Over the next few weeks, the Lindberghs received hundreds of letters and gifts from the Orient, including kimonos, rare dolls, lacquerware, bronzes, swords, china, vases, scrolls, carved ivory, and carved bamboo. *The New York Times* praised them lavishly on its editorial page.

Instead of leaving their plane to be repaired in Shanghai, the Lindberghs had the China National Aviation company crate and ship it directly to Lockheed in Los Angeles. Meantime, they boarded a fast boat for Nagasaki, from where they trained across Japan to Yokohama. There they boarded the liner *President Jefferson,* which arrived at Vancouver on the evening of October twentieth. They flew commercially across country, arriving in New Jersey on October twenty-third.

"It is good to be home," Anne wrote her mother-in-law upon settling back into Next Day Hill, "—and oh, the baby! He is a boy, a strong independent boy swaggering around on his firm little legs." The toddler did not recognize either of his parents; but they made up for the time they had lost with him. Anne seemed surprised at how attentive her husband was to little Charlie—"playing with him, spoiling him by giving him cornflakes and toast and sugar and jam off his plate in the morning and tossing him up in the air. After he'd done that once or twice the boy came toward him with out-stretched arms," crying "Den!" ("Again!"). Charles went so far as to say he found his son "good-looking" and "pretty interesting."

Lindbergh was soon off on two weeks of Pan Am business again, flying in the southeast and Caribbean; but Anne decided to stay put for a while. She wanted to spend as much time as she could with Charlie. Even though he was six months younger than any of the other pupils at The Little School, the boy's aunt Elisabeth insisted on his enrolling. She took him to school for a few hours every day, where the other children were drawn to his golden curls.

While their new house still needed a few months of work, Anne and Charles took the baby on Halloween to spend their first night in Hopewell. Along unmarked, occasionally unpaved, roads they drove into the hills. It was a tricky route to navigate even in daylight. Approaching a little stone bridge over a brook, they turned left onto their property. The driveway ser-pentined for a kilometer to a clearing, where the house, with steep gables reaching three stories high, sat behind a low stone wall.

The whitewashed fieldstone house with its thick slate roof had two wings running perpendicular to and projecting slightly in front of the central sec-tion. Through the front hall, one entered the living room, paneled in dark wood. To the left were a library with a dark stone fireplace and a guest room; to the right were the dining room and kitchen, which led to servants' quarters and the large garage. Upstairs were the master bedroom, three guest rooms, and, in the back corner farthest from the entrance, the nursery. Pretty blue tiles decorated its fireplace; and a table, chair, and crib were already in place. The house had built-in closets and shelves and four bathrooms. There was enough architectural detail to make it attractive without being fancy. The electricity, plumbing, heating, and air conditioning in the house were all top-of-the-line, bringing its total cost to almost $80,000. For all that, none of the rooms had the spaciousness that the towering exterior suggested.

They spent the weekend there, playing with Charlie on the terrace, which looked onto woods. As construction would continue until the end of Janu-ary 1932, the Lindberghs continued living at Next Day Hill. But they drove to Hopewell almost every Saturday afternoon, returning to Englewood on Monday mornings. Although the idea of landscaping was still a few seasons off, Anne could not resist planting some special white tulip bulbs around the house before the ground froze.

The Lindberghs did not go to the Hopewell house at all in the last part of December. Charles's mother joined them in Englewood for Christmas, which everybody enjoyed. Charlie was especially happy with a present from Anne's mother, a Noah's Ark filled with pairs of animals. "He and Charles played with it for a long time," Betty Morrow recalled, "making a great procession of the animals across the floor." His father scarcely let a day go by after Christmas without testing him on their names; and by the new year, he could correctly select thirty animals from the ark.

The day after Christmas, Charlie was playing with rubber toys in the bathroom when Betty Morrow heard a splash and a "spluttering howl." He had fallen into the tub. Betty Morrow flew into a rage at Charles, sure that he had been ducking him "to test his courage." Although she learned otherwise, Mrs. Morrow was right to feel concerned. Nurse Betty Gow had gotten to the baby before his grandmother, and she found "Colonel Lindbergh laughing his head off. He saw that the baby wasn't hurt, just frightened. Still," she remarked decades later, "there was something about the Colonel—that little bit of sadism."

It was the same kind of toughening he had received from his own father. When the boy began to suck his thumb, Lindbergh insisted he wear specially made thumbguards at night, metal devices like wire hoods over the corks of champagne bottles, which had fasteners that were pinned to the crib's bedsheets. And one day that winter, Lindbergh built a huge pen of chicken wire outside their wing of Next Day Hill. When he had finished, he told Betty Gow to bundle Charlie up, to select one of his toys, and to place him in the pen "to fend for himself." For hours, the little boy stayed there alone, sometimes crying. Betty Gow went to Anne, insisting they rescue him. Although Anne was close to tears, she said, "Betty, there's nothing we can do."

On February 4, 1932, Charles Lindbergh celebrated his thirtieth birthday. The news about Lindbergh that week was that there was no news about Lindbergh—except that he was thankful to have slipped off the front page for a little while so that he could carry on with his business. "The world is left to guess whether there'll be a frosted cake at the Lindberghs' New Jersey home for Charles A. Lindbergh, Jr., now a toddling youngster, to admire," wrote one article. At last, Lindbergh felt that he was settling down to the kind of "real life" Anne had yearned for, the kind he had never known. While in the last year alone he had gathered twenty thousand miles' worth of adventure, his twenties closed on a note of calm.

After the trip to the Orient, Lindbergh's popularity had risen again. Fifteen thousand people a day still admired his trophies in St. Louis—which now included his recent acquisitions from the Orient; five million people had paraded through the exhibit since its opening five years earlier. More than ever, he preferred that the public's admiration remain from afar; and so he spent most of his days sequestered at the Rockefeller Institute. Despite the

Depression, the Lindberghs were receiving almost $65,000 a year from interest and dividends and his consultancy fees. They had so successfully brought the boiling publicity pot down to a simmer, the press had not yet suspected that Anne was pregnant again.

Anne had even housebroken her husband, ridding him of the only habits of his she could not abide—spitting and blowing his nose without a handkerchief. He now preferred to spend his evenings quietly at home, reading and listening to music. He adored being with his son, whom he addressed with a big "Hi! Buster" every time he saw him.

For the first time in his life, Charles Lindbergh found joy in his family and comfort at home.

10

SOURLAND

". . . a tragedy took place that was to affect our lives forever."
—C.A.L.

"GIVE THE LINDBERGH BABY A CHANCE!" BLARED A RECENT article in the National Affairs section of *Time*. The clarion call came in response to a widespread rumor in late 1931 that Charles Lindbergh, Jr., was deaf and had not learned to talk. "Cause of the affliction was supposed to have been the pre-natal drumming of airplane motors in his ears, causing a trauma, while his mother, Anne Morrow Lindbergh, continued to fly during her pregnancy," the article explained.

The rumor was completely unfounded but so widespread that some of America's most eminent journalists had to go on record to squelch it. Even Will Rogers felt compelled to write a column about a Sunday visit to Next Day Hill in late February, at which time he saw the Lindbergh baby:

> His dad was pitching a soft sofa pillow at him as he was toddling around. The weight of it would knock him over. I asked Lindy if he was rehearsing him for forced landings.

> After about the fourth time of being knocked over he did the cutest thing. He dropped of his own accord when he saw it coming. He was just stumbling and jabbering around like any kid 20 months old.

The Lindberghs still had not moved into their new house outside Hopewell. Completing an uncomfortable first trimester of her new pregnancy, Anne was just as happy to be waited on in their suite at Next Day Hill. With the first intimations of spring, she found herself up and around, engrossed in two projects that had been offered to her husband and which he had proposed she pursue. The first was a public address in behalf of flood relief in China; the second was a book about their recent journey to the Orient. Intimidated by the size of the latter task, she followed Charles's suggestion of breaking the journey into sections and jumping into the "Baker Lake" episode, that moment when they left civilization behind and Anne found herself the first white woman to appear in that region of Northern Canada. "If I get enough written, soon enough, & it isn't too bad," Anne thought, "then we'll talk to publishers."

For the most part, Anne devoted her time to little Charlie. She took to visiting the new house without nurse Betty Gow. "It is such a joy to hear him calling for 'Mummy'—instead of 'Betty' once in a while!" she confessed to her mother-in-law. To the little boy, Charles was known as "Hi." One day that February, while they were driving in New York, a car rear-ended them. Anne instinctively grabbed the baby, and Charles got out, while traffic stopped and irate drivers confronted each other. In the midst of the brouhaha, a small voice chirped, "Hi—all gone!"

On the afternoon of Saturday, February twenty-seventh, one of Mrs. Morrow's chauffeurs took Anne, the baby, and one of the maids from Englewood to Hopewell. Arriving at 5:30, they were met by Olly and Elsie Whateley, who had moved into the servants' quarters. Anne changed and fed the baby, putting him in bed by seven o'clock. He seemed to be coming down with a cold, sneezing several times. Anne checked on him a few minutes later; and at about eleven o'clock, both she and Charles entered the nursery, to medicate the baby's nose.

Monday the baby was still sick. After lunch, Anne called Next Day Hill and told Betty Gow that they would not be returning to Englewood, as had become their routine. Little Charlie did not leave his room all day and neither did Anne, except for a few short walks, during which time she left the baby in Elsie Whateley's care. Around seven, Lindbergh called from New York to say that he would be spending the night in town, not returning to Hopewell until the following night.

The next morning—Tuesday, March first—the baby was better but still croupy. Anne awoke with a cold as well. She called Betty Gow in Englewood and asked her to come to Hopewell and help out. There were still no definite plans as to where they would all spend the next few nights. Just before three o'clock, Anne and Betty went into the shuttered nursery, where Charlie had been napping; his health had noticeably improved. Anne took a walk down the long driveway and spent much of the afternoon with the baby downstairs in the living room. Around 5:30, he ran into the kitchen, where

Betty was sitting with the Whateleys. The nursemaid took the boy by the hand upstairs, where she read to him before feeding him some cereal. Anne entered the nursery at 6:15, by which time he had finished his dinner.

She and Betty Gow prepared the baby for bed. After rubbing Charlie's chest with Vicks VapoRub, they decided to make a flannel garment for him to wear beneath his nightclothes. A handy seamstress, Betty quickly ran up a little short-sleeved shirt from a remnant of cream-colored flannelette. The material had an embroidered hem in a scalloped pattern. She kept the left shoulder unsewn so that it could slip easily over the baby's head and be pinned; the rest was stitched in blue mercerized thread. Over this the baby wore a sleeveless fine-woolen shirt, which was attached to the two diapers under his rubber panties. Over all this, the baby wore a gray, size-2 Dr. Denton sleeping suit. Betty lay him down and affixed his thumbguards. Then Betty put the baby under the covers of his crib—a dark-wooded four-poster which stood behind a portable green and pink screen with pictures of farmyard animals.

Anne and Betty went to close the shutters; but as they had found on previous evenings, those at the corner window were too warped to close, even with both women pulling on them. Anne did not leave the room until 7:30; Betty remained another few minutes, during which time she went to the southern wall and pulled open the French window halfway. She put out the light, closed the door, and went into the bathroom, where she washed the baby's clothes. She reentered the room and found the baby fast asleep, breathing easily. She fastened the bedcovers to his mattress with two large safety pins and left the room, turning out the bathroom light. About ten minutes before eight, she went to the cellar to hang up the clothes she had washed, then joined Elsie Whateley for dinner in their sitting room.

Anne was in the living room waiting for Charles, who had called to say that he would be home a little late. Although his precise whereabouts that day were not recorded anywhere, he had been lost in his work at the Rockefeller Institute most of the week, completing experiments for a new technique of "washing" corpuscles, a method he was writing up for *Science* magazine. Some expected him at a dinner given by New York University at the Waldorf-Astoria, which was honoring Daniel Guggenheim among others; but there had, in fact, been a secretarial mix-up over his calendar, and he had planned all along to return to Hopewell.

Anne sat at her desk, writing. The lights in the corner library, directly below the nursery, were off; and the doors between that room and the living room were closed, shut off from the rest of the house. Outside, beneath a starless sky, a wuthering wind sent the temperature down into the thirties. For a moment, Anne thought she heard the sound of car wheels, but it was not for another fifteen minutes—at about 8:25—that Lindbergh came up the gravel driveway, parked the car in the garage, and entered the house through the connecting back hall and kitchen. After washing up, he joined Anne for dinner at 8:35.

They ate, then sat by the fire in the living room. A little after nine o'clock Charles heard a noise, which he attributed to somebody in the kitchen dropping something—"such as a wooden box." At about 9:15, the Lindberghs went upstairs and talked for a few minutes, before he bathed, dressed again, and settled into the library downstairs to read, sitting next to the window directly below the nursery window whose shutters would not close. Anne drew a bath for herself and prepared for bed. She had left her tooth powder in the baby's bathroom, which she retrieved without turning on the lights. After brushing her teeth in the master bath, she rang the bell for Elsie and requested a hot lemonade. It was approaching ten o'clock.

While the Lindberghs had been eating their supper, Whateley called Betty Gow to the telephone. Henry "Red" Johnson, a Norwegian seaman whom she had been seeing ever since their meeting at North Haven the preceding summer, was on the line. Johnson, in the country illegally, worked as a deckhand on Thomas Lamont's yacht. He and Betty had a date for that evening, which she had canceled when Anne Lindbergh summoned her to Hopewell. Sorry they could not get together, he announced that he was going to drive to Hartford to visit his brother. Upon hanging up, Betty went into the servants' sitting room and turned on the radio; the Whateleys joined her. After a few minutes, Betty went upstairs, where Elsie wanted to show her a dress she had just bought, then looked at her watch. "It's ten o'clock," she said, "I have got to go to the baby."

Betty went into the baby's bathroom and turned on a light. She thought of getting Mrs. Lindbergh so that they could check on the baby together, but Anne was still bathing. Betty entered the room, closed the French window, and plugged in the electric heater. Walking toward the baby's crib, she realized that she could not hear the baby breathing. "I thought that something had happened to him," Betty would later retell, "that perhaps the clothes were over his head. In the half light I saw he wasn't there and felt all over the bed for him."

Betty raced through the passageway into the master bedroom, just as Anne was exiting the bathroom. "Do you have the baby, Mrs. Lindbergh?" she asked. Bewildered, Anne said, "No."

"Perhaps Colonel Lindbergh has him then," she said. "Where is Colonel Lindbergh?" Anne instinctively went into the baby's room while Betty ran downstairs, through the living room and up to the door of the library, where Lindbergh was sitting at his desk. "Colonel Lindbergh," Betty said, trying to catch her breath, "have you got the baby? Please don't fool me."

"The baby?" he asked. "Isn't he in his crib?"

Before she could answer, he had jumped from his chair and run upstairs to the baby's room, Betty at his heels. Just from the look of the bedclothes, Lindbergh "felt sure that something was wrong."

He went to the master bedroom, brushing past Anne, who asked if he had the baby. "He did not answer me," she later recounted. "Someone had already told him." Charles went to his closet and loaded the rifle he kept there. He headed back toward the nursery, followed by Anne and Betty Gow. "Anne," he said, now looking right into his wife's eyes, "they have stolen our baby."

A chill came over the nursery. Lindbergh found its source, the southeast corner window, which was unlatched and open a crack. There, on top of the radiator case that formed the sill, he saw a small, white envelope—six and one-half by seven inches. He assumed it contained a ransom note, and he maintained enough composure not to touch it.

Lindbergh told Betty to get Olly Whateley, who ran upstairs. At Lindbergh's direction, the butler called the sheriff in Hopewell; then Lindbergh called Henry Breckinridge in New York and the State Police in Trenton.

Lieutenant Daniel J. Dunn answered that 10:25 P.M. call. "This is Charles Lindbergh," said the voice at the other end. "My son has just been kidnapped." The lieutenant asked what time he had been taken, and the caller said, "Sometime between seven-thirty and ten o'clock. He's twenty months old and is wearing a one-piece sleeping suit." With that, Lindbergh hung up. Detective Lewis J. Bornmann, also on duty that night, asked what that had been about. "I don't know," said Dunn. "Some guy said he was Lindbergh—said the baby was kidnapped. Jesus! Now what am I supposed to do?"

Bornmann worried that the call might not have been a prank. He suggested that Dunn call the Lindbergh house and that if the same voice answered the telephone, then they should follow up. Lieutenant Dunn called the operator, who put him through. "Hello, this is Charles Lindbergh," said the voice he had just heard. "This is Lieutenant Dunn, sir," he said. "Men are on their way."

Corporal J. A. Wolf was the first man in the field to be radioed, and he suggested the dispatcher also send Troopers Cain and Sullivan, who were on patrol that night as well. At 10:46 a teletype alarm was sent across the state: "COLONEL LINDBRGS BABY WAS KIDNAPPED . . . IS DRESSED IN SLEEPING SUIT REQUEST THAT ALL CARS BE INVESTIGATED BY POLICE PATROLS." By eleven o'clock, checkpoints had been established at the Holland Tunnel, the George Washington Bridge, and all ferry ports along the Hudson River. New Jersey streets were roadblocked and hospitals were alerted to report the admission of any children fitting the Lindbergh baby's general description. Police were notified in Pennsylvania, Delaware, and Connecticut.

Single-minded missions were Lindbergh's specialty. Now, with only the thought of his son's safe return in mind, he believed a coolheaded, methodical approach would bring him back. Refusing to allow panic to set in, he immediately asserted his authority. From that moment on, he acted as the man in charge of a situation that steadily proved to be beyond his control.

He issued orders that nobody was to enter the nursery or walk around the premises until the police had arrived. Betty Gow found herself searching the rest of the house, from cellar to attic, frantically opening closets and drawers along the way, finally dissolving in tears. Anne had already made one more brief check of the nursery before rushing back into her room. "Without realizing why I was doing it," she recalled, "I threw open the window and leaned far out." She heard what sounded like a cry, over to the right in the general direction of the wood pile. Before she could speak, Elsie Whateley said, "That was a cat, Mrs. Lindbergh." Stunned, Anne dressed and automatically searched the house. The wind howled.

Lindbergh and Whateley investigated the house as well, then scouted the grounds for fifteen minutes, turning up no trace of the child. Harry Wolfe and Charles Williamson, special officers of the Boro of Hopewell, Mercer County, arrived at 10:35. They glanced into the nursery, where they detected muddy clumps on a leather suitcase that sat beneath the presumed window of entry. That drew them outside, where they found impressions in the mud, indentations where a ladder had evidently been placed. About seventy-five feet southeast of the house, they discovered a wooden ladder in two sections. Ten feet beyond that they found a third ladder section. They left everything untouched and returned to the house.

Corporal Joseph A. Wolf of the New Jersey State Police arrived a few minutes before eleven. He announced that superintendent H. Norman Schwarzkopf himself—a thirty-seven-year-old West Point graduate, who was the first man to lead the decade-old New Jersey State Police—was on his way, along with several other troopers. The two officers from Hopewell were for all intents and purposes dismissed. While some of the Lindbergh property was just outside Hopewell in Mercer County, the Lindbergh house itself stood in Hunterdon County, technically beyond the Hopewell jurisdiction.

In command of his house and his emotions, Lindbergh calmly explained to Corporal Wolf that he suspected nobody and could recall no suspicious behavior. The dog, Wahgoosh, had been in the opposite wing of the house that night; and, as Anne later noted, he "couldn't have heard through the howling wind all that distance." Lindbergh pointed out the presumed ransom note to Wolf, who moved it with his penknife to the fireplace mantle. He too observed traces of yellowish clay on the suitcase and on the hardwood floor of the nursery. He questioned Lindbergh about those present in the house. Schwarzkopf arrived shortly before midnight. Because his training was in the military, he acted more as an administrator than a detective. He turned those duties over to Captain John J. Lamb, who headed New Jersey's investigative services, and his lieutenant, Arthur T. "Buster" Keaten, the local investigative bureau chief. Detective Bornmann began interrogating the household staff.

Students at nearby Princeton were just turning in for the night when word hit the airwaves—on WOR radio out of New York City. Henry Breckinridge's stepson, Oren Root—a Princeton junior who periodically weekended with the Lindberghs—was returning to his dormitory room when a friend told him that the Lindbergh baby had been kidnapped from the Hopewell house. "Forget it," Root told him. "The press is always distorting stories like that. Besides," he added, showing off some of his personal knowledge, "the Lindberghs leave every Monday for Englewood." A few hours later, Henry and Aida Breckinridge pounded on Root's door, awakening him from a sound sleep. Afraid they would not be able to find the house in the dead of night, they asked Oren to guide them.

The Breckinridges had been unnecessarily cautious. Had they just driven through the next town of Hopewell, they could not have missed the place. Through the winter-bared woodlands, the normally obscured Lindbergh house stood out for miles. "It was blazing with lights," remembered Oren Root more than sixty years later. "We arrived around two-thirty, and every light and lamp in the house was turned on. As we approached we could see flashlights, headlamps from police cars, even some men carrying torches all lighting the place up. Everyone was in a state of contained panic, with 'Slim' trying to be everywhere at once, keeping a lid on the excitement, keeping his voice down."

Through the night the troopers worked, waiting for daylight to permit them to extend their search into the surrounding woods. Until then, activity revolved around the nursery. Corporal Frank A. Kelly dusted the envelope for fingerprints but was able to procure only a worthless smudge. He slit open the envelope and carefully removed a single sheet of paper, folded once, which he handed to Lindbergh.

It was written in blue ink, in a strangely ornate but immature hand, full of eccentric embellishments and shaky penstrokes. "dear Sir!" it read:

> *Have 50.000 $ redy 25 000 $ in*
> *20 $ bills 1.5000 $ in 10$ bills and*
> *10000 $ in 5 $ bills. After 2-4 days*
> *we will inform you were to deliver*
> *the Mony.*
> *We warn you for making*
> *anyding public or for notify the Police*
> *the child is in gut care.*

> *Indication for all letters are*
> *singnature*
>   *and 3 holes.*

More difficult to decipher was an odd symbol in the lower-right corner of the note. The identifying mark consisted of two interlocking, silver-dollar-sized blue circles. In the oval formed by their intersection was a solid, penny-sized red circle. In each of the circles outside the oval was a wavy, vertical line. To the left, right, and center of these inked impressions were three square holes punched through the paper, in a straight line, one inch apart. The symbol would have to be kept secret if the Lindberghs wanted to ensure that any future correspondence was being conducted with the actual kidnappers.

Neither the notepaper nor a dusting of the room yielded a usable fingerprint, but the note itself offered enough peculiarities to provide clues about the kidnappers' identity. The handwriting, positioning of the dollar sign, and spelling all suggested someone of European origin, probably German or Scandinavian.

First light increased the activity outside the house. A half-dozen troopers searched the surrounding woods. After twelve hours on the scene, the police had found no trace of the baby and only three clues beyond the note. Beneath the nursery window, next to the impressions left where the ladder had stood, was a shoeprint in the mud. Closer examination revealed a textile pattern, suggesting that the culprit had worn a sock or cloth bag over his shoes, to avoid leaving footprints, just as his evidently wearing gloves had kept him from leaving fingerprints. Having no ruler with him, the detective at the scene estimated the size of the shoeprint—twelve and one-half inches long and four and one-quarter inches wide. Nobody thought to make a plaster-cast of the print.

The second piece of evidence was a nine-and-one-half-inch-long, wood-handled, three-quarter-inch chisel, made by the Buck Brothers Company. It was found near the third, and most crucial piece of evidence outside the house—the ladder—which the police had brought indoors to examine more closely. Fearing somebody might walk off with it as a souvenir, they thought it more important to preserve the integrity of the evidence than the crime scene.

Even to the untrained eye, the extension ladder was revealing. It was homemade, crude but cunning. Each of its three pieces measured eighty and one-half inches in length, producing a ladder of more than twenty feet when assembled. It weighed only thirty-eight pounds. Considerable craftsmanship and forethought could be seen in its construction. Each of the three pieces was of a different width, so that it could nest into another, collapsing to a portable unit of six and one-half feet.

5.18

Dear Sir!

Have 50.000 $ redy 25 000 $ in
20 $ bills 15000 $ in 10 $ bills and
10.000. $ in 5 $ bills. After 2-4 days
we will inform you were to deliver
the mony.

We warn you for making
anyding public or for notify the
the child is in gute care.

Indication for all letters are

singnature

and 3 holes.

Ex 9

Part of the ladder had broken. One of the side rails of the center section had split along the grain, suggesting that while the kidnapper had been successfully able to climb into the nursery, the added weight of his victim was enough to crack the wood. The location of the break indicated that the kidnapper and the baby might have fallen as much as five feet to the ground.

By the time Corporal Wolf left the scene to write the Major Initial Report of the crime, he believed it must have involved at least two perpetrators. "It is obvious," Wolf wrote, "that this crime has been carefully planned and the layout . . . [and] routine of the Lindbergh home studied."

It was equally obvious, to Oren Root at least, that Lindbergh felt the need to supervise the case. The New Jersey State Police, from its chief down, was not yet old enough to have much experience in solving major crimes. One of Schwarzkopf's detractors would later note that the only police experience he had was "as a floor-walker at Bamberger's Department Store." Few men on the scene that night had ever done more than write traffic citations. Corporal Kelly, dusting the ransom note for fingerprints, for example, had until recently been a road trooper. Efficient though all the police were trying to be, Root observed, "you could tell that every one of them was nervous just being in the presence of their local hero."

For the second time in less than five years, the world revolved around Charles Lindbergh. Radio programs everywhere were interrupted and front pages of newpapers were remade, shunting the Sino-Japanese War and Congressional attempts to repeal prohibition aside. "LINDBERGH BABY KIDNAPPED FROM HOME OF PARENTS ON FARM NEAR PRINCETON; TAKEN FROM HIS CRIB; WIDE SEARCH ON," read the headline in the *The New York Times,* which topped four columns on the right-hand side of page one. The back roads of central New Jersey were already crawling with reporters. Before dawn, one journalist pounded on the door of Paul T. Gebhart's general store and hotel in Hopewell. "Wake up, Pop!" he yelled. "You'll have three hundred here for breakfast."

Anticipating public reaction, Lindbergh emphasized to all those within the estate walls the cruciality of controlling everything that was said and not said to the press. "I hope you boys will excuse me," Lindbergh told the first wave of reporters, who had found their way to his secluded house in the predawn hours, "but I would rather the State Police answered all questions. I am sure you understand how I feel."

Lindbergh ordered the immediate conversion of the Hopewell house into an auxiliary police station. A twenty-line switchboard was installed in the garage, which became headquarters. Because three dozen peace officers had been pulled from three counties to guard every entrance of the house and property, all available bedding in the house was set down in the living room and dining room, turning the ground floor into a makeshift dormitory. Lindbergh designated the guestroom for informal meetings and reserved his study for private conferences. Betty Morrow's staff in Englewood cooked meals for forty men a day and delivered them to Hopewell.

Anne's assignment during these first terrifying hours was to stay out of the way. Amid the bedlam, she maintained her composure in her bedroom, comforted by her mother. She wrote a long letter to Charles's mother, and the mental exercise of setting down the details as best she knew them filled her with hope. The kidnappers' "knowledge of the baby's room, the lack of finger prints, the well fitted ladder," she wrote "—all point to *professionals* which is rather good—as it means they want only the money—& will not maliciously hurt the baby." That allayed her fears that a "lunatic" had taken the baby. Meantime, Anne noted, Charles, Henry Breckinridge, and the detectives appeared optimistic, thinking "the kidnappers have gotten themselves into a terrible jam—so *much* pressure—such a close net over the country—such sympathy for us—& the widespread publicity." Anne felt "dreadful" not to be able to "do *anything* to help"; but she found solace just in watching her "calm, clear, alert, and observing" husband.

Henry Breckinridge placed a call to a friend in Washington, J. Edgar Hoover, Director of the Federal Bureau of Investigation. Because of the initial suggestions that professionals had committed the crime, Hoover said his agents would tap into their underworld connections.

Official reaction to the crime was unprecedented, as every level of government joined forces in the most massive manhunt in history. Observed one reporter, "The world dropped its business, that day, to discuss in horrified and angry accents the most revolting crime of the century." President Hoover and his Attorney General offered Colonel Schwarzkopf the fullest cooperation of every law-enforcement agency of the federal government, including not only the FBI but also the Secret Service, the Internal Revenue Service, and the Postal Inspection Service. Coast Guard stations were put on special watch. The Department of Commerce ordered the policing of the nation's airports, and F. Trubee Davison, Assistant Secretary of War for aviation, placed the Army Air Corps at Lindbergh's disposal. The Army signal corps lined the shortest distance between Trenton and Hopewell with communications cable, sometimes right across farms and fields. Customs and immigration officials from Canada to Texas, New York harbor to California went on alert. New Jersey's Governor A. Harry Moore and New York's Franklin D. Roosevelt offered their police resources as well.

Congress moved to the top of its agenda the pending legislation that would make kidnapping a federal offense punishable by death when two or more states were involved. Its subsequent passage became known as the Lindbergh Law.

President Hibben of Princeton drove to Hopewell to offer the resources of the university, specifically a few thousand students who were prepared to scour the woods for any trace of the baby. Lindbergh and Schwarzkopf declined the offer, for fear that amateurs might contaminate a crime scene; but undergraduate troops took to the woods anyway. Within twenty-four hours of the baby's disappearance, it was estimated that one hundred thousand peace officers and cooperating citizens were involved in the nationwide dragnet. And that did not count the Boy Scouts of America, whose Chief Scout Executive, Dr. James E. West, called on his entire membership—past and present—"to be alert and watchful and cooperative in every way possible in seeking clues or information as to the Lindbergh baby." That put another 914,840 boys and young men—forty percent in rural areas—into the field. William Green, president of the American Federation of Labor, urged the thousands of members of the trade unions to organize search brigades and blanket New Jersey and its neighboring states. Daniel Sheaffer of the Pennsylvania Railroad wired Lindbergh that "OUR FACILITIES ARE AT YOUR COMMAND WE ARE HAVING ALL OUR TRAINS AND STATIONS COVERED AND OUR DETECTIVE TRAIN AND STATION FORCE ARE ACTIVE." Women's organizations, such as the White Plains Contemporary Club, refrained from their usual activities so that they could search boardinghouses for stray children; and they urged other ladies' groups to follow suit. Indeed, every baby in public was looked at twice by every passerby, and practically anyone seen with a blond tot was stopped and questioned. One solitary bank clerk from Trenton, driving home from a vacation out West, was pulled over 107 times just because of the New Jersey plates on his car.

"WE DONT NEED TO TELL YOU FOLKS HOW WE FEEL," Will and Betty Rogers wired the Lindberghs. Most of the world felt the same, but many declared their feelings nonetheless. Privately, President Hoover wrote, "My heart goes out to you in deepest sympathy in your distress, and I do pray that you may speedily have your son restored to you." Other heads of state, national legislatures, and the foreign press also expressed their sympathy. New York City's municipal radio station broadcast a special service, in which Catholic, Protestant, and Jewish clergymen prayed for the speedy return of the child. Several state legislatures passed resolutions offering sympathy and prayers to the Lindberghs. Even the new invention of television was called into play, when Station W2XAB atop the Columbia Broadcasting Building uninterruptedly broadcast the photograph of the Lindbergh baby during the afternoon and every fifteen minutes during the evening. There were only a few thousand television receivers within the thousand-mile broadcasting radius that could pick up the fuzzy transmission; but for the first time television had instantly broadcast the image of a kidnapped person over an extensive range.

When neither a trace of the baby nor word from the kidnappers surfaced after the first day, Lindbergh felt his most critical task was in opening lines of communication with the kidnappers. He believed the media should be told that a ransom note had been left and that the Lindberghs fully intended to pay it. Anne appealed to the kidnappers' hearts, releasing to the press the baby's diet, in hopes that "whoever has taken the baby may see and understand the necessity for care" in light of the child's recent illness.

On March second, a penny postcard arrived from Newark. It was addressed to "Chas. Linberg, Princeton, N. J.," with the "J" looping backward. It said: "BABY SAFE, INSTRUCTIONS LATER, ACT ACCORDINGLY." Even though the card bore neither the identifying symbol nor the same handwriting as the ransom note left on the window sill, its importance was in no way doubted. More than five hundred men—practically the entire Newark police force and several fire companies—were put on that one piece of potential evidence. A mail carrier had noticed it while emptying a box in the center of the rooming-house district of Newark; and he had brought it to the attention of the police, who searched two thousand homes within two square miles.

Meantime, law-enforcement officers nationwide traced countless drivers of cars that had been reported all day as appearing suspicious. Of particular interest was the observation of Benny Lupica, a student at Princeton Preparatory school, who lived a little more than a mile from the Lindberghs. On the afternoon of March first, he had gone to his R. F. D. mailbox on the road opposite the entrance to the Lindberghs' farm. He was standing on this remote lane when a car drove by—a Dodge with what appeared to be two sections of a ladder poking out the empty right-hand side. Lupica caught a glimpse of the driver, a man with "a thin face," wearing "a black overcoat and a fedora hat."

The rural mail carrier from Hopewell appeared at the Lindbergh house several times a day, bringing hundreds of letters at a time. Detectives screened every item, most of which came from strangers. A man from Pulaski, Virginia, offered his pack of bloodhounds, and a veteran postal inspector from Minneapolis offered his professional services. Tips came from around the world. Astrologers and seers, from as far off as Trieste, sent accounts of their visions, while thousands of people sent accounts of their dreams in which the baby appeared—often fatally so. Crank ransom notes arrived by the thousand, mostly from people who were Depression-desperate, trying to get their hands on some cash. Kidnapping had, in fact, become one of the "big money crimes" in which the rackets trafficked—with kidnapping syndicates springing up in every major city. Four hundred such crimes had been reported since 1930 in Chicago alone.

A New Jersey bootlegger, con-man, and sometime stool pigeon named Morris "Mickey" Rosner got Henry Breckinridge on the telephone the day after the Lindbergh kidnapping. Under indictment for grand larceny in a stock swindle, Rosner said he had the contacts to ascertain who committed this crime. The next morning, he sat in the corner library in the Hopewell house with the three colonels managing the case—Lindbergh, Breckinridge, and Schwarzkopf—suggesting that two of his henchmen act as intermediaries to the criminals.

Lindbergh had been involved in enough dangerous ventures to know the imperative of backup plans. And so he elected to proceed unofficially with Rosner. Schwarzkopf was against Breckinridge's giving this known criminal $2,500 "for expenses"; and he and "Buster" Keaten were aghast when Lindbergh also handed over the ransom note with its unusual identifying symbol of interlocking circles, the one touchstone they had to test the validity of any future communiqués from the kidnappers. But Lindbergh was so powerless that he felt obliged to follow every avenue, even down the most criminal alleys. His instincts told him there was a basic honor among thieves.

By the day after the kidnapping, there was already no question that Lindbergh was acting rashly and that he resented being forced into behaving that way. Keeping her distance, Anne thought he looked "like a desperate man"— so distraught that she was afraid even to speak to him. "It was probably the first time she realized her Lindy was not a god, but only a mortal," Betty Gow observed. "We were all so helpless." Anne confined her crying fits to the privacy of her bedroom.

The Lindbergh kidnapping affected every child and parent in America. The wealthy seemed prime targets, but fears did not stop there. If "Baby Lindy"—protected by servants within estate walls—could be abducted, then every child in America was vulnerable. Parents encouraged their children to come *inside* and play, and many were forbidden thereafter from walking even a block from home by themselves. For several generations the Lindbergh kidnapping became children's first cautionary tale. They were told never to talk to strangers, and any adults in the vicinity of schoolyards were stopped and questioned. The House of Morgan commissioned a private force of two hundred and fifty bodyguards to protect the families of its partners.

Numerous letters streamed in to Hopewell advancing theories worthy of Agatha Christie. Some suggested that the kidnapping was the work of one of the many female admirers of Lindbergh who resented his marrying Anne Morrow. Many actually accused Elisabeth Morrow.

The absence of Anne's older sister through most of the kidnapping crisis fueled speculation for more than sixty years that she was the perpetrator of the crime. Several people have suggested that she was mentally unstable and the family kept her locked up at Next Day Hill during this period. In truth, it was her physical, not mental, health that was failing. Her heart condition left her constantly fatigued. On top of that, on the night of the crime she was, in fact, in bed nursing an impacted wisdom tooth. Even madder theories sprang up and lingered to the end of this century. One propounded that

Lindbergh himself killed his baby, accidentally or otherwise, and could not face the consequences. Such theories were based on a lack of information rather than any evidence.

Agatha Christie herself was inspired to capture some of the hysteria created by this case in her classic thriller *Murder on the Orient Express*. Maurice Sendak, a poor boy in Brooklyn, was so traumatized by the event that he admitted to having spent a lifetime trying to exorcise his fears through his macabre children's books. The Lindbergh case inspired sculptor Isamu Noguchi to create his only "strictly industrial design," the "Radio Nurse"— an intercom that served as "a device for listening in to other rooms within a house, as a precaution against kidnapping."

"I am wondering if proper consideration has been given in the investigation . . . to the 'Epileptic Colony,' which . . . is located in the neighborhood," a doctor wrote from Chicago. He observed that "it is definitely established, by members of the medical profession, who have done work with epileptics, that the outstanding characteristics are pathological irritability and revenge." Even without the suggestion, the state home for epileptics four miles away, in Skillman, New Jersey, was investigated, as were all neighboring mental asylums and orphanages. The police obtained from the Lindberghs' building foreman a list of everyone who had worked on the house so that they and their families could be questioned.

They also interrogated a man named Millard Whited, one of the illiterate backwoodsmen living in a shack in the Sourland Mountains. He told Lindbergh and officers Keaten, Wolf, and Lamb that on three occasions in the past two weeks he had seen a strange man nosing around the Lindbergh property. He provided specific dates and a general description of the man. When a pair of detectives later called on Whited, he declared he had never seen any suspicious people on the Lindbergh property. At every turn, the case produced a similarly surreal twist.

"No story was too fantastic for investigation," reported *The New York Times* on March fourth. "No suspected place was too remote for search. The entire nation was aroused and there were stories of innocents being detained for questioning"—from Maryland to New Hampshire. A man in Long Branch, New Jersey, called the switchboard at the Lindberghs simply to present his suggestion that the famous flier use his influence with the government to obtain immunity for the kidnappers if they would return the baby unharmed. Before the conversation was completed, state troopers had the caller in custody for two hours of interrogation and another two days of investigation. Three suspicious characters who had been reported by a waitress in Pennington because they had asked for directions to the Lindbergh house the week before turned out to be newsreel photographers who simply wanted to photograph the house.

"It is impossible to describe the confusion," Anne wrote her mother-in-law on Saturday, March fifth, "—a police station downstairs by day—detectives, police, secret service men swarming in and out—mattresses all over the dining room and other rooms at night. At any time I may be routed out of my bed so that a group of detectives may have a conference in the room. It is so terrifically unreal that I do not feel anything."

At first, any reasonable-sounding person who telephoned the Hopewell house to say he had seen the baby was patched through to Lindbergh himself. But nobody described the baby to his satisfaction. Thousands of sightseers descended upon the Sourland Mountains, filling the streets of Hopewell from morning until night, and crowding around the entrance of the Lindbergh estate. One perfectly respectable-looking man insisted he had "a secret he would tell no one else but Anne Morrow Lindbergh." Even he was ushered into the Lindberghs' bedroom, where the anxious couple awaited his pronouncement. The man burst into some lines from Shakespeare, before the police carted him off.

After forty-eight hours with little sleep, insinuating himself in every aspect of solving the crime, Charles at last got a good night's rest. It made a great difference in his attitude and, as a result, Anne's. "He is tense and worried still," she wrote his mother, who carried on teaching her Chemistry classes at Cass Technical High School, "but excited and buoyant." Charles's optimism—constantly staving off his and Anne's worst fears by living in constant hope—dictated his every movement. Remaining active made him feel his baby remained alive.

In an attempt to nudge the abductors into making some kind of move, Lindbergh released a public statement urging them to "send any representatives that they desire to meet a representative of ours who will be suitable to them at any time and at any place that they may designate." If that was acceptable, Lindbergh pledged not only confidentiality but also "that we will not try to injure in any way those connected with the return of the child."

That very moment, the authorities apprehended a suspect whom they were convinced was the right man. "Red" Johnson, Betty Gow's suitor, was taken into custody in West Hartford, Connecticut, just as another postcard allegedly mailed by the kidnapper was found in the Hartford post office. It too had the backward J in New Jersey and read, "BABY STILL SAFE. GET THINGS QUIET." Because of his relationship with the Lindberghs' baby nurse, he had knowledge not only of the Lindbergh house but also of the movements of all the people therein. Pouncing on his being an illegal alien, the police proceeded to find everything about the Norwegian sailor suspect. All but clinching the case for several police officers was their finding in his green Chrysler coupé—a car several witnesses had said they had seen in the vicinity of the Lindberghs' house—an empty milk bottle! A milk-drinking sailor seemed beyond probability; and it took several people attesting to Johnson's often drinking a quart at a time before they accepted the possibility of his innocence. The sender of the postcards was soon discovered to be a mentally disturbed young man.

After several days of relentless "grilling and criticism," Betty Gow had also been cleared as a suspect. Because of her unusual opportunity to commit the crime, many considered her at least an accomplice if not the prime suspect. But Betty lacked motive altogether. She loved the baby as if it were her own and had been as desolated by his disappearance as the baby's mother. Ironically, she could not help blaming herself for the crime, repeating to herself for years statements that began, "If only . . ." Charles felt that she and all the Lindbergh servants were completely above suspicion.

On March 5, 1932, another ransom note arrived, this one genuine, validated by the identifying symbol of interlocking circles and punched holes. "We have warned you note to make anyding Public also notify the Police," said the note in the same wobbly hand, full of uncrossed T's and many other idiosyncrasies in spelling, handwriting, and diction. "Now you have to take the consequences." Because of the publicity, the note explained, their transaction would have to be postponed. "Dont by [sic] afraid about the baby," the note added, assuring the Lindberghs that they were feeding him according to the diet and wished "to send him back in gut health." This delay, however, meant they had to include another person in what they suggested was a conspiracy, thus necessitating an increase in their demands—to $70,000. A postscript added that this kidnapping had been prepared for years "so we are prepared for everything."

A virtual copy of the letter to Lindbergh arrived in care of Henry Breckinridge in New York City. While the syntax of this letter was as tentative as it had been in the first letter, the handwriting was noticeably steadier. The basic peculiarities of the cursive remained the same, but it was less crude in appearance, as if the writer was no longer trying to disguise his penmanship. This letter reiterated that the boy was being cared for; but it made clear that "We will not accept any go-between from your seid." The Lindberghs would have to await further notification as to how the money would be delivered, but that would not occur "before the Polise is out of this cace and the Pappers are quite."

These letters, kept from the public, thrilled Lindbergh, for they continued the dialogue that might lead to his son's rescue. He issued another public statement announcing that if the kidnappers were not willing to deal with him and his wife directly, "we fully authorize 'Salvy' Spitale and Irving Bitz to act as our go-betweens. We will also follow any other method suggested by the kidnappers that we can be sure will bring the return of our child." The newspapers explained that Bitz and Spitale were former associates of Jack

"Legs" Diamond, the recently murdered gangster. The press themselves, however, were not told that Mickey Rosner had brought them into the case, so that they could act as independent agents.

In Chicago, Al Capone issued a statement while waiting to be transferred from the Cook County jail to the federal penitentiary in Atlanta to serve an eleven-year sentence. "I know how Mrs. Capone and I would feel if our son were kidnapped, and I sympathize with the Lindberghs." To show the depth of his feelings, Capone offered $10,000 for information that would lead to the recovery of the child and the capture of the kidnappers. Amazingly, some of the nation's most reputable attorneys urged Henry Breckinridge to allow Capone to rescue the Lindbergh baby.

Debate over the ethics of dealing with criminals raged across the country; but after meeting the "underworld kings," Anne felt closer to them because of the sincerity of their sympathy than that which was offered by a lot of politicians, many of whom simply appeared on the Hopewell property for their own publicity, posing by the ladder, which had been releaned against the house to help the police reconstruct the crime. Charles continued to warn Anne, "never count on anything until you actually *have* it"; but having even miscreants on their side, she wrote her mother-in-law that the news was looking decidedly "good."

Charles was visibly "buoyant and alive," at last able to engage in what he considered a contest of wills, one which he believed he could win by making the right moves and by playing fairly. Feeding off his moods, Anne felt "*much* happier" herself, assured that their baby was safe. She wrote Charles's mother almost daily.

Anne appreciated the fact that she was surrounded by people who were not only hopeful but also disciplined. "The tradition of self-control and self-discipline was strong in my own family and also in that of my husband," she later wrote. "The people around me were courageous and I was upheld by their courage. It was also necessary to be disciplined, not only for the safety of the child I was carrying but in order to work toward the safe return of the stolen child." Despite the hundreds of "dedicated people" assisting in this great effort, the Lindberghs were still stuck in the painful position of waiting, having to avail themselves to even the most improbable accomplices.

In Washington, D.C., a porcine middle-aged man named Gaston Means sat in the living room of Mrs. Evalyn Walsh McLean, one of the richest women in the world. Although he came from a distinguished North Carolina family, Means spent much of his life straddling the law. After being fired as an investigator for the Department of Justice, he took up bootlegging and eventually served time in Atlanta. Mrs. McLean was the daughter of a Colorado mining magnate, the estranged wife of the publisher of *The Washington Post,* and the owner of the Hope Diamond. Deeply moved by the plight of the Lindberghs, she consented to meet with Gaston Means when he called her with extraordinary news about the Lindbergh case. No fool, Mrs. McLean asked her friend "Jerry" Land—Evangeline Lindbergh's cousin—to sit in.

During his criminal period, Means explained, he had met the leader of the ring that had kidnapped the Lindbergh baby. He said he could guarantee its safe return if he could deliver $100,000. His explanation was full of compelling detail, including the kidnappers' insisting that a Catholic priest be the go-between. Mrs. McLean selected a local pastor and agreed to come across with the money. Jerry Land left for Hopewell, where he vouched to Lindbergh for the apparent veracity of Gaston Means. As Means's suggestions of the underworld's part in the crime seemed to match those of Rosner, Bitz, and Spitale, Lindbergh ordered the plan to proceed—with the understanding that he would reimburse Mrs. McLean if the transaction proved successful. The heiress withdrew the money from her bank—in old bills—plus $4,000 to cover Means's expenses.

Meantime, in Norfolk, Virginia, John Hughes Curtis, president of the struggling Curtis Boat Building Corporation, went to the dean of Christ Episcopal Church, the Very Reverend Harold Dobson-Peacock, with an amazing story of his own. During the hard financial times, Curtis said, he had repaired the boat of a rum-runner who now claimed the kidnappers of the Lindbergh baby asked him to approach Curtis with the request that he serve as go-between. Curtis was a respected member of his community, but he did not have the credentials to reach the Lindberghs themselves. He knew, however, that Dobson-Peacock had become acquainted with the Morrows when he had been rector in Mexico City. Curtis's story convinced the Reverend to place a call to the Lindberghs. He proved unable to get past a personal secretary who identified himself as Morris Rosner. The inmates had taken over the asylum.

Undeterred, Curtis followed another path to the Lindberghs' door. Living in Norfolk was retired Admiral Guy Hamilton Burrage, the former commander of the *Memphis,* the cruiser that had carried Lindbergh home from Paris in 1927. Curtis convinced Burrage to reach Lindbergh. After proving his identity to him, Burrage put Curtis on the phone. But Lindbergh remained strangely noncommittal, leaving the puzzled Burrage to suggest to Curtis and Dobson-Peacock that they compose a letter requesting a meeting in New Jersey.

The reason for Lindbergh's hesitancy was the sudden entrance of an even more clownish character into what had become a three-ring circus—John F. Condon. A former school principal, Mathematics teacher, and a Doctor of Pedagogy, the seventy-one-year-old Condon was a walrus of a man, with a bristly white mustache and large torso. He usually dressed in dark, three-piece suits and a black bowler, which he replaced with a straw boater in the summer. He was a flag-waving patriot and an habitué of the YMCA, where he refereed local athletic events; he still coached students at Fordham University in swimming, boxing, and body-building. Condon was so incensed that his hero Charles Lindbergh had to consort with common criminals in order to get his son back that he decided to do something about it.

Unsolicited, this lifelong resident of the Bronx offered his services as a go-between by sending a letter to his local newspaper, the *Bronx Home News*. Bumptious, verging on the foolish, Condon wrote in purple ink in a hand-writing as flowery as his language, "I offer all that I can scrape together so a loving mother may again have her child and that Colonel Lindbergh may know that the American people are grateful for the honor bestowed upon them by his pluck and daring." He offered $1,000 of his own to garnish the suggested $50,000 ransom money demanded of the Lindberghs. "I stand ready at my own expense," he added, "to go anywhere, alone, to give the kidnapper the extra money and promise never to utter his name to any person."

Condon was a minor celebrity in the Bronx. A subsequent FBI investigation found that his neighbors considered him "an altruistic and honorable educator. . . . On the other hand he also has the reputation of being somewhat of an eccentric, some persons even going so far as to state that he is a 'nut.' " The Bronx *Home News,* with its circulation of 150,000 readers, had been running his letters, poems, and essays for years, often under his pseudonyms P. A. Triot and J. U. Stice. Many accused him of being a self-important wind-bag; others respected him for putting his money where his mouth was. Neither Lindbergh nor the New Jersey State troopers knew of his offer.

On the night of March ninth, Condon returned to his modest two-story house in the tree-lined Bedford Park section of the Bronx and found a personal letter addressed to him, printed in a neat but childlike scrawl. "dear Sir," it read:

> *If you are willing to act as go-between*
> *in Lindbergh cace pleace follow stricly*
> *instruction. Handel incloced letter personaly*
> *to Mr. Lindbergh. It will explan everyding. don't*
> *tell anyone about it as son we find out the Press*
> *or Police is notifyd everyding are cansell and it*
> *will be a further delay. Affter you gett the money*
> *from Mr. Lindbergh put these 3 words in the* New-York American

Mony is redy *Affter notise we will give you*
further instruction don't be affrait we are not
out fore your 1000$ keep it. Only act stricly. Be at
home every night between 6-12 by this time you will
hear from us.

Enclosed was another sealed envelope, addressed to Lindbergh. Because of the poor handwriting, Dr. Condon considered the note to him a "crank" letter. But he thought he should get a second opinion from a few friends.

Condon took a trolley to a restaurant he frequented on the Grand Concourse near Fordham Road. He showed his letter to Max Rosenhain, the proprietor, who suggested they confide in another friend, who had a car, a clothing salesman named Milton Gaglio. They persuaded Condon to call the Lindbergh estate in New Jersey. Robert Thayer, a young attorney, came on the line. He asked Condon to read the note addressed to Lindbergh; and upon his describing the strange hole-punched symbol at the bottom of the page, Thayer asked him to come immediately to Hopewell.

Around midnight, the three men left in Gaglio's car, stopping at the Baltimore Lunch Room in Princeton for a cup of coffee. They phoned the Lindbergh house to announce their imminent arrival and got directions to Hopewell from a policeman. Barely into the town, they were met by Colonel Breckinridge, who guided them to the house.

A little before three A.M., Breckinridge escorted Condon, Rosenhain, and Gaglio through the kitchen door of the Lindbergh house. Breckinridge took Condon to the nursery upstairs, which Lindbergh entered. Condon presented the two letters, the authenticity of which was obvious on sight. They agreed that Condon should serve as the official go-between.

Condon's rendition of the next few hours involved his insisting on meeting Mrs. Lindbergh and admonishing her against crying—"If one of those tears drops, I shall go off the case immediately." They did, in fact, meet, after Lindbergh suggested he spend the night there. There was not enough room to accommodate Gaglio and Rosenhain as well, so they departed. As it was, Condon spent the night on the floor in the baby's nursery, on a mattress covered in Army blankets.

The next morning, Condon removed the two safety pins which still held down the blankets in the baby's crib and a few of his toy animals—a lion, camel, and elephant. He told Lindbergh and Breckinridge that he wanted to use them as means of identifying both the kidnappers and the child, by asking the kidnappers where they last saw the pins and to watch the child's reaction to the toys. He asked if the baby could identify the animals; and Lindbergh said his reaction to the first two animals would reveal nothing, but that his son called the third animal an "elepunt."

After breakfast, Lindbergh entrusted the man from the Bronx with a one-sentence letter authorizing him to serve as go-between. Breckinridge drove Dr. Condon home—during which time he found his passenger fatuous but trustworthy. Condon placed the advertisement in the New York *American* as instructed, but because he was a well-known local figure, they agreed he should use an alias in the advertisement. John F. Condon suggested an acronym from his initials—Jafsie. With the appearance of the first "Jafsie" ad, hope returned to the Hopewell house.

"There *really* is definite progress. I feel *much* happier today. It does seem to be going ahead," Anne wrote Mrs. Lindbergh after a lachrymose week. Even though she had tried to stifle her sobs with her pillow, Charles had heard them more than once and upbraided her in "sharp" tones, suggesting that sorrow implied hopelessness.

Confident though he was about the Jafsie connection to the kidnappers, Lindbergh still desperately welcomed anyone claiming the vaguest connection to his child. In the middle of one night, he met with a manacled convict from a nearby prison, who claimed to have information about the baby. Under the third degree from Lindbergh and the police, he broke down, proving to be yet another fake who, in the words of Betty Morrow, "wanted a joyride & the fun of seeing Lindbergh." When the renowned psychic Edgar Cayce, of Virginia Beach, suddenly had a vision of the baby's whereabouts, the FBI sent two special agents to an address he had conjured in East Haven, Connecticut. This trail came to a dead end, as neither the street nor anybody by the name he mentioned even existed.

The New Jersey police continued investigating even more vaporous leads. And they aggressively interrogated all the members of the Lindbergh and Morrow staffs. One of the waitresses at Next Day Hill, Violet Sharpe, seemed pivotal because she had known that Mrs. Lindbergh had asked Betty Gow to come to Hopewell on March first. In her police interview she came across as unusually high-strung. When the police tried to pin her down on the details of her date on the night of the kidnapping, she turned forgetful and even a little truculent. A search of her room revealed nothing unusual other than a bank book that showed a balance that was more money than she earned in a year.

In the early afternoon of Friday, March eleventh—just hours after Jafsie's first ad appeared—Dr. Condon's telephone rang. He was out, lecturing at Fordham. Mrs. Condon told the caller—whom she said had "a thick, deep, guttural accent"—that her husband would be home at six o'clock. Sometime around seven the phone rang again, and a man with a German accent asked, "Did you *gotted* my letter with the *sing-nature,*" unwittingly revealing himself as the author of the original ransom note, which spelled the word as he mispronounced it. They conversed for a few minutes, with the German caller instructing Condon to be at home between six o'clock and midnight every night that week, at which time he would receive his next set of instructions. Condon heard voices in the background, including one shouting in Italian, *"State zitto,"* which meant "Shut up." Breckinridge spent the night at the Condons'. Between bouts in Madison Square Garden that night, the announcer asked the crowd of fifteen thousand to stand in silence for three minutes and "pray for the safe return" of the Lindbergh baby. "I think it is thrilling to have so many people moved by one thought," Anne wrote of the communal prayer, happily recalling that similar invocations had helped deliver her husband to Paris in 1927.

The next evening at six, Breckinridge and Al Reich returned to 2974 Decatur Avenue. At 8:30, a cab driver named Joseph Perrone rang the doorbell and handed a letter to Dr. Condon, whose name and address were written in what had become familiar scrawl. "We trust you but we will note come in your Haus it is to danger," it said. "even you can note know if Police or secret servise is watching you." The cabbie waited at the door while Condon and Breckinridge read the instructions that followed: Condon was told to drive to the last subway station along Jerome Avenue; one hundred feet beyond, on the left side, he would find a vacant hot-dog stand with an open porch surrounding it; in the center of the porch, he would find a stone; and under the stone, a notice would tell him where to go next. The note also told Condon to bring the money with him—in "¾ of a houer." It was validated with the strange symbol.

Breckinridge was taken aback. It was a Saturday, and he said it would be days before he could have the money in hand. Regardless, Condon said he must keep that appointment. As he got into Al Reich's Ford coupé, Breckinridge urged him to be careful, reminding him that he was dealing with criminals. Breckinridge questioned the driver and learned that he had been hailed on Gun Hill Road at Knox Place by a man in a brown topcoat and a brown felt hat. After asking in a pronounced German accent whether Perrone could find 2974 Decatur Avenue, he had handed him the letter and a dollar bill.

It was little more than a mile to the Woodlawn station at the end of the IRT's Jerome Avenue line. There was no confusion finding the next set of instructions. Heading back toward the car, Condon stood beneath a streetlamp to read the note aloud, so that Al Reich could hear it as well. "Cross the street and follow the fence from the cemetery direction to 233rd Street. I will meet you." The tall, heavy-iron fence staked the western border of the four-hundred-acre Woodlawn Cemetery, separating the historical graveyard from Van Cortlandt Park. As Al Reich drove Condon toward the main entrance of the cemetery, he nervously kidded, "When they shoot you, they won't have to carry you far to bury you."

Condon waited at the big front gate, rereading the instructions and checking his watch. It was 9:15. A man approached him on Jerome Avenue, but walked right by. After another fifteen minutes in the cold, Condon saw a white handkerchief being waved through the bars of the gate from inside the cemetery. Condon approached, as the man with the handkerchief darted among the gravestones. He was bundled in an overcoat, had the brim of his fedora pulled down over his eyes, and held the handkerchief over his nose and mouth. "Did you *gotted* my note?" he asked. "Have you *gotted* the money?" Condon, recognizing the voice from their telephone conversation, said no, that he could not bring the money until he saw the baby. Suddenly, both men heard footsteps inside the cemetery. The man in the shadows feared the police. Condon insisted that he had not involved them; but in an instant, the stranger climbed over the fence, said it was too dangerous to meet, and ran up Jerome Avenue.

It had been a uniformed cemetery security guard. After assuring the guard that everything was all right, Condon pursued the man himself. Well into Van Cortlandt Park, at the southern tip of its lake, the man let Condon catch up with him. "You should be ashamed of yourself," Condon reported having said. "No one will hurt you." But the man worried that he could be sentenced to thirty years if caught, that he might even "burn." And, he explained, he was only a messenger from the actual kidnappers.

With his hat pulled down and his coat collar turned up, the man walked with Dr. Condon to a bench near a tennis shack, where they sat. "What if the baby is dead?" the man asked, voicing a thought nobody in the case had yet uttered. "Would I burn if the baby is dead?" Taken aback, Condon asked why they were meeting if the baby was dead. The man with the concealed face assured him that the baby was not dead, that, in fact, he was being fed better than the diet in the newspaper had prescribed. Still he wondered, as he asked again, "Would I burn *if I did not kill it?*" He hastened to add that the Colonel need not worry, that "The baby is all right."

Condon tried to ascertain that he was speaking with someone in direct contact with the child. "You *gotted* my letter with the *singnature,*" he said. "It is the same like the letter with the *singnature* which was left in the baby's crib." Condon hesitated, because he understood the ransom note had been left on the windowsill. But it reminded him to produce the safety pins he had taken from the crib and to ask the man if he had ever seen them before. The man correctly identified them as the pins fastening the blankets to the mattress.

According to Condon, they entered into a friendly chat. The man imparted that his name was John, that he was from Boston, that he was a sailor, and that he was Scandinavian, not German. Condon did his best to engage "John," hoping to disarm him enough to provide information and perhaps a good look at his face.

They talked for more than an hour. John seldom lowered his guard, but Condon was at least able to discern that the man before him was probably in his mid-thirties, a lean five-foot-nine, a middleweight of 160 pounds, with a smooth, unblemished triangular face—high cheekbones and a small mouth, and deep-set, almond-shaped, blue-gray eyes. John said that the baby was on a "boad" some six hours away by air in the care of two nurses. He said the gang included a head man, who would take $20,000 of the ransom, while his three henchmen and two nurses would receive $10,000 each. He said neither "Red" Johnson nor Betty Gow was involved in the crime. Condon tried to get John to turn on the gang and come clean with the police, but he resisted. He said this crime had been planned for a year, and he stuck to his mission of convincing Dr. Condon to come forth with the money. To prove to his leader that he had performed his task, he told Condon to take another ad in the Bronx *Home News,* saying, "BABY IS ALIVE AND WELL. MONEY IS READY." Because Condon insisted on a "cash-and-delivery" deal, John said that on Monday he would send proof that his gang was holding the actual baby. The two men shook hands on their agreement. At 10:45 John stole off into the woods almost as mysteriously as he had appeared.

Reich drove Condon home to Decatur Avenue, where Henry Breckinridge waited to hear every detail. The attorney was struck by John's saying that the crime had been planned for a year, for that repeated what had been said in one of the ransom notes that Condon had never seen. Breckinridge was convinced that they were in touch with the actual kidnappers. Al Reich added that he got the distinct impression that the man who had walked by Condon on Jerome Avenue—whom he described as medium-sized and Italian—was in cahoots with "Cemetery John" and had probably signaled Condon's approach. Although he was never able to see John's face completely, Condon asserted that he could identify him if he saw him again.

Lindbergh refused to allow himself to believe the best, but he told his wife and mother-in-law that he considered the situation "very very good." During this crucial period of secret negotiations the press banged out new stories, which threatened to frighten the kidnappers back into hiding. Gangster Mickey Rosner was suddenly telling interviewers that the baby was all right. Then, without anyone's foreknowledge, the New York *Daily Mirror* anounced that prominent attorney Dudley Field Malone would act as an official intermediary delivering a $250,000 ransom. That seemed sure to stop the kidnappers from accepting the pittance they were about to settle on. Further rumors circulated that the *Daily News* itself may have engineered the kidnapping, because, as Betty Morrow noted in her diary, "the tabloids hate C. so!"

For several days everybody waited. As instructed, Condon placed an ad in the March thirteenth Bronx *Home News:* "BABY ALIVE AND WELL. MONEY IS

READY. CALL AND SEE US. JAFSIE." It brought no response. On March fourteenth, they ran another ad, stating: "MONEY IS READY. NO COPS. NO SECRET SERVICE. NO PRESS. I COME ALONE LIKE THE LAST TIME. PLEASE CALL. JAFSIE." Getting no reply, they ran it the next day. Still receiving no reply, they amplified the statement: "I ACCEPT. MONEY IS READY. YOU KNOW THEY WON'T LET ME DELIVER WITHOUT GETTING THE PACKAGE. PLEASE MAKE IT SOME SORT OF C.O.D. TRANSACTION . . . YOU KNOW YOU CAN TRUST JAFSIE."

The kidnappers might have had doubts. During those anxious days of waiting together, Condon and Breckinridge shared two minor suspicious incidents. One day a short, young Italian came to the house selling needles. The two men answered the door and Condon purchased some. When the Italian departed, Breckinridge observed that he left the block without stopping at a single other house. An hour later, another Italian appeared at the Condons', this one carrying grinding equipment. Breckinridge thought he "looked the part of a scissors grinder," and so they gave him a knife and a few household items to sharpen, for which Condon paid him a quarter. Like the needle salesman, the scissors-grinder left the block without soliciting any other business. Breckinridge believed one or both men were emissaries of the kidnappers, determining how guarded the house was.

Back in New Jersey, H. Norman Schwarzkopf was taking heat from the public. Having acceded to Lindbergh's demand that he say nothing of the covert operation in the Bronx, he appeared to be making no progress in the Lindbergh case. All the sources of his State Police—both legitimate and underground—were drying up. Spitale and Bitz and Rosner were coming up empty-handed. Police from New Jersey were being routinely dispatched to Maryland, Tennessee, and Kentucky to check on sightings of the Lindbergh baby, but none returned with encouraging news. Schwarzkopf even took to the radio, appealing for the nation's assistance. Lindbergh continued to trust him "absolutely," finding him wonderful to deal with despite "hundreds of complications and difficulties, pressure of the press, petty jealousies, interference of politics, etc. etc." With the first warm days of March, tourists flocked to the Lindbergh house. Barnstormers operating out of Hopewell's emergency airfield offered sightseers the opportunity of flying over the estate for $2.50.

On March 16, 1932, a package mailed from Brooklyn arrived at Dr. Condon's house. Recognizing the handwriting, he notified Breckinridge, who came from his office and opened it. Inside was a laundered, gray wool Dr. Denton sleeping suit, size 2. Breckinridge called Lindbergh and asked him to come to the Bronx to identify it. An accompanying note, complete with the signature of interlocking circles, said that circumstances now forbade the direct swap Condon had proposed, that the baby was well, and that eight hours after receiving their $70,000, the kidnappers would notify Condon where to find him. "If there is any trapp," it concluded, "you will be responsible what will follows." At 1:30 in the morning Lindbergh—in the hunter's cap and large glasses he had worn to slip by the reporters—arrived at Dr. Condon's. He examined the sleeping suit and said, "It looks like my son's garment."

Lindbergh was so excited he wanted to pay the ransom immediately. Condon asked if they should not see the baby before paying; but the boy's father felt time was becoming their greatest enemy, as it infuriated the kidnappers and gave the press the opportunity to discover these secret negotiations. They would have to take the kidnappers at their word. Condon proposed that their ad at least suggest the need for "some sort of C. O. D. transaction"; but Lindbergh was adamant. The March eighteenth edition of the Bronx *Home News* ran the simplest response possible: "I ACCEPT. MONEY IS READY. JOHN, YOUR PACKAGE IS DELIVERED AND IS O.K. DIRECT ME."

In his anxious efforts to move the "transaction" along, Lindbergh made a heartfelt plea to the press. He said that he believed the return of the baby was being delayed by the "vast amount of space devoted to the case by the press of the country." He asked, in this most sensitive moment, "that beginning at once the papers confine their accounts of the case to three hundred words each day, and that these brief stories be printed in single column form to effect a minimum of typographical display." The request was observed, for a while: "Telephone calls are fewer, letters are fewer—the reporters no longer trail us," Anne wrote her mother-in-law—"the publicity is dying down. . . . things are quieter every day—so we sit & wait & hope. C. is cheerful."

As for herself, Anne had been rendered virtually devoid of feeling and suspended in time. Since the night of March first, she had hardly experienced all the emotional ups and downs because she had entered a kind of trance state, for self-protection. Charles had kept her uninformed about most of the efforts being made to retrieve their baby and he still insisted she cry alone, whenever she found the energy. "I have a sustained feeling—like a high note on an organ that has got stuck—inside me," she wrote her sister Elisabeth. "The time since then has been all in one mood or color, no variation . . . It is just that night elongated. Of course, it has superficially been different. Every second, like a dream, the whole scene swings, melts, changes. Personalities change from black to white, faces look different, tones are different, the tempo of the activity speeds up and slows down, but always that high note that got stuck in the organ Tuesday night!"

On March twenty-second, at one o'clock in the morning, Lindbergh called his house from New York to say that someone was coming out in Colonel Breckinridge's car. He said the passenger especially wanted to see her and Betty Gow, and also Whateley and Elsie. He asked Anne to be awake and dressed and to admit the visitors at once. Although Charles spoke in his usual guarded tone, Anne could not help reading between the lines of her husband's message. She excitedly awakened her mother, who was staying at the house, and they prepared themselves, feeling their ordeal was almost over. They lay on Anne's bed until three in the morning, when they heard the car pull up the driveway.

But when they rushed down to see the baby, they found instead "a dark dreadful looking man"—one Murray Garsson of the Labor Department. He and his assistant were investigating the kidnapping, claiming they could solve the mystery in forty-eight hours. They vigorously questioned everybody in the house until dawn. The worst part, observed FBI Special Agent J. M. Keith, was when Garsson "ordered Mrs. Lindbergh to show him the furnace, accompanied her to the cellar, and in her presence began poking around in the ashes . . . leaving the plain inference that the Lindberghs themselves had killed the youngster and burned the body."

The Jafsie ads continued to run in the Bronx newspapers, but they elicited no response. Meantime, Condon picked up a wooden box he had ordered, made according to the specifications the kidnappers had dictated, while Lindbergh worked with the Morgan Bank on the box's contents. Speaking only to Morgan partner Thomas W. Lamont, then considered the most powerful man on Wall Street, Lindbergh had the bank bundle the first $50,000 worth of ransom as stipulated in the notes. For three restless days, Condon kept the money in his house. Then he took it to the Fordham Branch of the Corn Exchange Bank, where he learned that no special account had to be opened, that it was simply there subject to his call.

The case dragged toward its second excruciating month, with Lindbergh still calling all the shots. He listened to his inner circle of advisers, but the only man to effect any change in his behavior proved to be the unimposing head of the Law Enforcement Division of the Internal Revenue Service. Elmer Irey, who had the further distinction of being the man who had outfoxed Al Capone, understood Lindbergh's intention to hand over money without any guarantee that the baby would be returned. But he insisted that the serial numbers of the bills be recorded.

Irey further suggested that America would probably be going off the gold standard soon, calling in all its gold coins and currency. That being the case, he suggested that the ransom be paid in gold certificates, virtually identical to regular bills except for a round, yellow seal. Even if the country did not change standards, Irey suggested that the gold certificates would be easier to spot. Surely, Irey argued with Lindbergh, if the baby were returned, there was no reason the state should not exercise its duty to pursue the criminals. Lindbergh allowed the bundled money to be removed from the Bronx to J. P. Morgan & Company, where more than a dozen bank clerks and Treasury agents tied and banded another 5,150 bills, divided in two packets. They kept samples of the string and bands they used, for future identification in the event that the money should be recovered.

Seeing how any dealings forced Anne to face the reality of the crime, Charles continued to shield her as much as possible, excluding her from most of the details. She knew almost nothing, for example, of the meeting Charles held in the house with Admiral Burrage, Reverend Dobson-Peacock, and John Curtis, who arrived from Norfolk. Lindbergh did not believe that Curtis was in contact with the actual kidnappers; but, as always, he kept creating options for himself. He asked Curtis to obtain either a current photograph of the baby or a message with some kind of symbol that might suggest they were the right party. If nothing else, Lindbergh knew his meeting with the three men from Virginia would shift public attention to them and away from the secret negotiations in the Bronx.

Anne took part in a séance in the nursery with a medium from the New York Society for Psychical Research—who spoke intriguingly of three men and two women being involved, including Italians, Germans, and Scandinavians; but the episode only made her withdraw further from the specifics of the case. She chose to focus instead on the future. Mid-pregnancy, she realized that was the only way she could keep herself healthy for her second child. She thought of the white tulips she had planted—"so pure and clear and fresh"—and could hardly wait for them to flower, as though they harbingered happier times. As March came to an end, she resumed "regular life" as best she could. With the first tips of flowers poking through the warming ground, she exercised patience, even though the ad from Jafsie declaring "MONEY IS READY" had appeared every day for a week without a response. Anne's mother did not tell her that one afternoon a black crow had flown into the nursery and perched on the baby's crib.

The last day of March abounded with good omens, even though they were at cross purposes. In Washington, Gaston Means had given Evalyn Walsh McLean every reason to believe that the $100,000 she had surrendered was about to bring the Lindbergh baby home. Meantime, John Curtis was claiming that he had just received a letter from the gang with which he had been dealing, and they had lowered their demand to $25,000. That night Colonel Schwarzkopf told Anne and her mother that the police had made contact with a man who claimed to have seen the baby and that he was "safe & well," that they knew who the kidnapper was, and they were just waiting for the baby's return before apprehending him. And after a month of hundreds of people canvassing the Lindbergh estate, Betty Gow discovered one of the baby's thumbguards along the gravel driveway, which everybody grasped as a talisman. Lindbergh himself quietly left for a Morrow townhouse at 2 East Seventy-second Street, where he said he would be staying for several days, the surest sign to Anne that the exchange was at last imminent.

On Friday, April first, Condon received a letter which contained another addressed to Lindbergh. It instructed him to have the money ready—"in one bundle"—by the following evening, at which time he would be given further instructions. If this was acceptable, the note read, he should state in the New York *American*, "YES EVERYTHING O. K." The ad appeared the next morning. Lindbergh informed Colonel Schwarzkopf that the drop was about to occur, but he forbade the police chief from taking any part in the operation.

After spending Friday night in Hopewell, Lindbergh drove to the Bronx early Saturday afternoon, carrying $50,000 with him. As a security measure, he sent a package of $20,000 in another car. Lindbergh tried to pack all the ransom money into the wooden box Condon had ordered, but it would not fit. It could accommodate all $70,000 only by raising the lid and tying the box shut with cord. For the next six hours Lindbergh, Condon, Breckinridge, and Al Reich waited. Lindbergh, like Condon's wife, feared for the old man's life and assured him he no longer had to proceed with his duties. But Condon would not hear of backing out, saying, "I want to see those little arms around his mother's neck." Lindbergh, who intended to be his driver, was carrying a small handgun.

At 7:45 a letter arrived by cab—instructions to Condon to proceed to a flower shop at 3225 Tremont Avenue in the East Bronx, where further orders would be waiting under a rock. Lindbergh drove Al Reich's Ford to the address, J. A. Bergen Greenhouses, where Condon found the next message. He returned to the car and they read the note by flashlight. Several people walked by, but one of them—about thirty years of age, five-foot-nine, 155 pounds, with dark complexion—in a brown suit and brown felt hat with a snap brim caught Lindbergh's attention. "He walked with an unusual gait rather awkwardly and with a pronounced stoop," he later recalled in a confidential statement to the New Jersey police. "His hat was pulled down over his eyes. As he passed the car, he covered his mouth and the lower part of his face with a handkerchief, and looked at Dr. Condon and at me." The note told Condon to cross the street and walk to the next corner, following Whittemore Avenue.

Lindbergh wanted to accompany Condon, but the latter pointed out that the note said to come alone. Instructions to the contrary, Condon did not carry the money with him. He walked to Tremont and Whittemore, which marked the northern tip of St. Raymond's Cemetery. He spoke to a man with a little girl at the unmarked intersection, asking if that was Whittemore Avenue, but they did not know. Seeing nobody else around, he headed back to the car. Halfway across the street, a voice came from the cemetery.

"Ay, Doctor," he said. "I could hear the call distinctly," Lindbergh would later affirm, even though he was a few hundred feet away, "and the 'Doctor' was pronounced with a definite accent." Condon walked down Whittemore on the cemetery side of the street.

Condon could see the man cutting across a road within the cemetery. When they finally caught up with each other, the man cried, "Here I am, Doc." Standing just a few feet apart, Condon recognized the man as "John" from Woodlawn Cemetery. "Have you gotted the money?" he asked. "Yes, it is in the car," he replied.

John asked who was in the car, and Condon told him Colonel Lindbergh. John asked if he was alone, and Condon replied that he always kept his word. He asked John where they had met before, and John correctly said at Woodlawn Cemetery. When John asked for the $70,000, Condon explained that times were hard and Lindbergh had a difficult enough time raising the $50,000 the kidnappers had originally asked for. "Well, I suppose that we will be satisfied to take fifty thousand," John told Condon, "and in six hours I will send you the note telling where the baby is." Condon said he could not agree to that, that he would rather go with John as a hostage until they were satisfied with their money. Short of that, Condon suggested a simple exchange of the directions for the money.

Back at the car, Condon explained to Lindbergh that he had talked John out of the extra $20,000. Lindbergh appreciated the gesture but did not wish to upset the kidnappers in any way. Condon returned to the hedge where they had just met and waited for John. From his vantage point, Lindbergh could not see either man; but he did see, across the street, the same man he had seen earlier near the Bergen greenhouses. Using his handkerchief, the man blew his nose—loudly enough to be heard by Lindbergh and, he presumed, anyone else in the area.

Down Whittemore Avenue, Condon handed the box with $50,000 over the hedge to John with his left hand and accepted a sealed envelope with his right. John thanked him and said that "all were satisfied" with his work. He got down on his knees and inspected the money, pulling out a sheaf of bills from the middle of the box. He arose and told Condon not to open the note for six hours. He shook Condon's hand over the hedge, thanked him, and disappeared among the headstones in the dark. As Condon hastened back to the car, Lindbergh noticed the man blowing his nose did not put his handkerchief in his pocket but threw it down instead, beside the sidewalk. Then he disappeared.

"The baby—where is the baby?" the anxious father asked. Condon handed Lindbergh the sealed note and told him of his promise to wait before opening it. To Condon's surprise, Lindbergh resisted tearing the envelope open, even as they drove off. Not far from the cemetery, they approached

Westchester Square, with its Kiddy Corner. Condon suggested they pull to the
side of the road. He argued that while he had given *his* word not to open the
letter, Lindbergh had made no such promise. Out of the envelope he pulled
a six-by-five-inch scrap of paper with five short sentences—the first definitive
indication in thirty-two days of his son's whereabouts.

> *The boy is on Boad Nelly. It is a small boad*
> *28 feet long. Two person are on the Boad. The*
> *are innosent. you will find the Boad between*
> *Horseneck Beach and gay Head near Elizabeth*
>   *Island.*

Lindbergh knew those waters—between Martha's Vineyard and the Massachusetts mainland—from his honeymoon.

They returned to Condon's house in the Bronx, where they informed
Breckinridge and Al Reich of the transaction. Word was transmitted in code
to the house in New Jersey that the money had been handed over. But those
in Hopewell did not understand that "no tooth" meant they did not have the
baby.

Lindbergh, Breckinridge, Condon, and Reich drove to the Morrow townhouse on Seventy-second Street, where they met several investigators from
the IRS. A chuffed Condon boasted that he had saved Colonel Lindbergh
$20,000 by withholding the smaller packet of money. Elmer Irey, the IRS
crime-buster, explained how Condon had blundered, that the smaller packet
was composed of fifty-dollar bills which had purposely been banded together
because they would be easiest to spot.

Lindbergh went to the telephone to arrange for Navy airplanes to assist
in the search for the boat *Nelly*. He asked that a Sikorsky seaplane be
brought to the airport at Bridgeport. At two in the morning, Breckinridge,
Irey, Condon, and Reich drove with him to the Connecticut airstrip, from
which they took off at sunup. Al Reich remained on the ground, driving
Lindbergh's car to the Aviation Country Club on Long Island, where a trust-
ing Lindbergh intended to land with his baby.

All morning, Lindbergh buzzed the water, circling the tiny Elizabeth Islands low enough for his passengers to get a good look at every boat that
even approximated the description of the *Nelly*. A half-dozen Coast Guard
cutters joined in the search. As noon approached, they became less choosy
in their pursuit, chasing after anything afloat. As night fell, they landed on
Long Island and piled into the car, silent and empty-handed. Lindbergh deposited his passengers in New York before continuing alone to New Jersey.
As he dropped off Condon and Reich, he spoke at last—saying, "We've been
double-crossed."

Upon arriving in Hopewell, he spared Anne as much as possible, relating the last day's events in hopeful obfuscation. He suggested that the kidnappers invented the story about the *Nelly* as a ruse to buy them extra time to escape or perhaps as a lever to pry more money out of them.

The next day Lindbergh and Henry Breckinridge took off from Teterboro Airport in Lindbergh's Lockheed Vega. They returned to the area they had scoured the day before, widening the circumference of their scope with each hour. By dusk, they found themselves off the coast of Virginia.

After Charles's second day of futile searching, Anne's mood changed dramatically. For the first time in the five weeks that her baby had been missing, her mother observed, "she acts as if she had given up hope." With Lindbergh's approval, Dr. Condon placed a new ad in the Bronx *Home News,* which would run for the next two weeks: "WHAT IS WRONG? HAVE YOU CROSSED ME? PLEASE, BETTER DIRECTIONS. JAFSIE."

Since the kidnapping, the Lindberghs had received almost forty thousand letters. While some included contributions toward the ransom, most contained useless information and advice. The most preposterous of those who wrote were divided into several categories of their own, including "wheels" (mental cases, whose wheels one could see spinning) and "butterflies" (clues that led nowhere). The hundreds who claimed they would deliver the child if the Lindberghs would only pay them slowly awakened Anne from her nightmare—in anger. With the mail at last dropping to a few hundred letters a day, even the newspapers had run out of articles to write. "We have been rather gloomy lately," Anne wrote her mother-in-law in early April. "We are now living from day to day but realize we must look forward to weeks."

The press pieced together much of the preceding week's scenario. Reporters had sighted Lindbergh looking despondent; and people in the Bronx wondered if John F. Condon was not the Jafsie whose cryptic messages had been appearing in the paper all month.

Lindbergh felt a statement had to be released to the press. Colonel Schwarzkopf officially acknowledged that a $50,000 ransom had been paid and that the kidnappers had failed to return the baby or identify his whereabouts. Privately Lindbergh conferred with the major press services, asking them to soft-pedal the story, especially that the Treasury Department was actively hunting for the marked bills, distributing to banks a fifty-seven-page pamphlet listing the serial numbers. Within a day, the kidnapping was again front-page news. "That we can't keep anything private is most discouraging," Anne wrote Charles's mother. "Although things are bad they are not hopeless," she added, clinging to her husband's Gibraltar-like optimism.

The mysterious "Jafsie" came out of hiding, thriving on every minute in the limelight. To keep his phone from ringing off the hook, he had his number unlisted. While Lindbergh appreciated Condon's diverting attention from Hopewell, he regretted that it rendered him useless any longer as a go-between.

With little beyond stray clues to follow, the police returned to the Lindbergh and Morrow houses, where they again questioned members of the staff. They delved especially into the personal life of the evasive Violet Sharpe, but they came up with nothing.

Nobody followed the new barrage of stories more closely than Evalyn Walsh McLean. After reading of the Jafsie drop in the Bronx and hearing about John Curtis in Norfolk, she demanded that Gaston Means account for himself and her $100,000. Means told her that Curtis's gang, Jafsie's gang, and the one to which he was an intermediary, were all one and the same, and that the only reason the baby had not been returned was that the gang realized the money was "hot." Insisting he had actually held the Lindbergh baby in his arms, he offered to take Mrs. McLean on his next mission to recover him. After accompanying Means to South Carolina and El Paso, and being told that the gang was demanding another $35,000, she realized that she was being swindled. When she demanded her $100,000 back, he said that it was too late, that he had just given it to one of the kidnappers. Mrs. McLean called her attorney, who called J. Edgar Hoover. Means would soon be indicted.

For days, no important leads surfaced, and despondency engulfed the Lindbergh estate. Then, on April sixteenth, John Curtis of Norfolk announced that the baby was safe!

Two days later, Lindbergh received Curtis in his study in Hopewell and heard a new installment to his story of the gang—five Scandinavian men—with which he had been communicating. Like Gaston Means, he said there was but one gang, and the man named John, whom Dr. Condon had met, was its leader. The conspiracy also included a German woman, a trained nurse, who wrote the ransom notes. Curtis said he had met John at his house in Cape May, at the southern tip of New Jersey.

According to Curtis, John said the plot to kidnap the baby originated "in the household," with an employee, and that the kidnappers had been to the scene of the crime two or three times before March first. He said he and another man had climbed the ladder, chloroformed the baby, and carried him through the house and right out the front door. He said that the baby had been taken directly to Cape May and later by boat to the Martha's Vineyard area. When Curtis insisted to John that he would need some proof for Lindbergh, John showed him ransom money, comparing serial numbers to those printed in the newspaper. Curtis admitted he had no tangible evidence of either the child or the kidnappers. Furthermore, he said John wanted another $25,000 and that it had better come soon, because there was a new wrinkle in this plot.

As Lindbergh later wrote it down, "The kidnappers told Curtis that a very powerful underworld organization was attempting to get the baby and was offering huge sums of money." As a result, the baby was about to be transferred again, from a small boat near Martha's Vineyard to a larger one—an eighty-foot-long two-master closer to Block Island. Neither Schwarzkopf nor his men believed any of Curtis's story; neither did Colonel Breckinridge nor Anne. Lindbergh felt they had to play along.

On the night of April nineteenth, Lindbergh drove to a hotel in Cape May Court House. Curtis preceded him to arrange the meeting. Schwarzkopf, believing no harm could come from what he considered a bogus operation, agreed to hold his forces back, giving Lindbergh and Curtis as much elbow room as possible. Over the next three weeks this plan for Lindbergh to connect with the kidnappers and his son kept changing. After each disappointment, Curtis inflated Lindbergh's hopes with an abundance of credible details.

While Lindbergh fundamentally felt Curtis was lying, lack of any alternative impelled him to buy into his far-fetched story. Charles kept "expressing faith in it," Anne observed, "though *never absolute faith*. Still he has been rather encouraging, for him." Anne was starting to open her eyes to certain realities, but her trust in Charles was enough to sustain her a little longer. "I have, of course, great confidence in *his* judgment," she wrote Charles's mother, "but I do not dare hope too much, especially in the face of the tremendous body of evidence which seems to say, 'Don't trust these people.' In the meantime there is nothing else here."

In all this time Colonel Schwarzkopf's continuous investigation had turned up nothing of value in New Jersey. Nobody had heard another word from any of the gang in the Bronx. On May eighth, Mother's Day, Lindbergh spent the night in New York City at the Morrows' apartment with Anne— their first evening alone since the ordeal had begun. The next day, Anne went to her doctor who said both she and her baby, due in three months, seemed healthy. Charles left for the New Jersey shore, believing the meeting with the kidnappers was at hand.

In Atlantic City, Lindbergh met Curtis and a friend, who was lending them his eighty-five-foot ketch, the *Cachalot*. Curtis said his contact with the gang told him to meet them near Five Fathom Bank, off Cape May, and that the gang was aboard a black-hulled Gloucester fisherman called the *Mary B. Moss*. The *Cachalot* cast off at seven o'clock that Monday night. They reached the rendezvous point five hours later and spent the next six hours sailing in circles. When the *Cachalot* returned to port Tuesday morning, Lindbergh remained on board so that reporters would not see him.

He spent most of the next day, Wednesday, alone on the ship, waiting, while Curtis said he would try to reestablish contact. He reported that the gang-members were fighting among themselves over settling for so little money. Thursday, the twelfth, was rainy and windy. After lunching with Lindbergh on the *Cachalot*, Curtis left for Atlantic City. The weather showed signs of clearing, and he spoke of a rendezvous for that night. .

At 3:15 that drizzly afternoon—the seventy-second day into what the *Trenton State Gazette* called "the most widespread search ever conducted in police history"—two men were driving along the Hopewell–Mt. Rose Highway. It was a little-traveled, muddy road. At a particularly isolated spot near the summit of a hill—about a half-mile out of the hamlet of Mt. Rose and two miles southeast of Hopewell—the passenger, a forty-six-year-old man named William Allen, asked the driver, Orville Wilson, to pull to the side of the road so that he could relieve himself. Allen wandered into the thick, damp woods about sixty feet. "I went under a branch and looked down," Allen later recounted. "I saw a skull sticking up out of the dirt, which seemed to have been kicked up around it. I thought I saw a baby, with its foot sticking out of the ground."

Allen called Wilson over to the macabre sight. "Well," Wilson asked, "what are you going to do about it?" Allen said he was going to report it to the Hopewell police. They headed into town, where they found Patrolman Charles Williamson at the barber shop. Upon hearing Allen's account, Williamson leapt from the chair. Within minutes, Allen and Wilson had led a team of New Jersey policemen to the Mt. Rose road.

There at the edge of Mercer County was a clear view of the Lindbergh house, some four miles away—its white walls plainly visible by day as its lights would have been by night. Upon exiting their cars, two of the officers observed a burlap sack—worn and bloodstained—on the ground just off the side of the road. Allen guided them into the woods. The police took one look down and asked Allen to go home, where they would question him later.

The officers had a badly decomposed child's body before them, face down in the dirt. The size of the body, the shape of the skull, the still golden, curly hair all suggested the Lindbergh baby. More police were summoned to the makeshift gravesite. They carefully turned over what proved to be an incomplete corpse. Not only had the figure blackened severely, but its left leg was missing from the knee down as was the right arm below the elbow and the left hand. The body parts had probably been eaten by animals, as had most of its viscera. But the eyes, the nose, and the dimpled chin left little doubt as to the corpse's identity. The clothes were in bad condition, but intact.

Before imparting the news of their discovery to the Lindberghs, one of the inspectors suggested they get a description of the baby's outfit on the night of his disappearance. Two officers went to the Lindbergh house and questioned Betty Gow, who provided not only the details of every item he wore but also the remnant of flannel and the spool of blue thread with which she had sewn his undershirt.

The officers returned to the corpse with Colonel Schwarzkopf. Under his direction, an inspector cut and peeled off each layer of the baby's clothes, manipulating the body with a stick. He accidentally pierced the softened skull, leaving a small hole below the right earlobe. Each article of clothing was exactly as Betty Gow had described, down to the scalloped flannel undershirt with its blue thread. A visible skull fracture suggested a violent blow to the head had been the cause of death.

Back in his office at the Lindbergh house, Colonel Schwarzkopf called the coroner, then approached Betty Gow with the two undershirts they had just removed from the baby's body. Betty recognized them at once and asked from where they had come. He broke the news to her, which she fought hard against believing. A little before five o'clock, Schwarzkopf approached Anne's mother, who had buried her husband but six months prior. She took the news calmly, immediately realizing that the baby had been dead since that first night and that the kidnappers had kept his sleeping suit as a bargaining chip.

With Colonel Schwarzkopf, she went upstairs to find Anne in the master bedroom. "The baby," she said, approaching her daughter, "is with Daddy." Anne sat there bravely, as her mother comforted her. Then she confessed that since the first night she had thought he had been killed.

Lindbergh was still in the dark—alone on the *Cachalot* off Cape May awaiting word from John Curtis. Colonel Schwarzkopf told Anne that men were en route to southern New Jersey to deliver the news to him in person. Upon learning from two members of the Curtis party that his son had been found, dead, Lindbergh asked if his wife knew and if she was all right. Then he left for home.

Colonel Schwarzkopf summoned the reporters hanging out at Pop Gebhart's general store to the Lindbergh garage for an important announcement. It took the better part of an hour before their colleagues from Trenton arrived. Not until everybody had gathered did the somber police chief read his press release. He had not finished the first sentence before several of the men bolted for the door; but Schwarzkopf insisted that nobody leave the room until the entire statement had been read. Before dinner that night, the story had been broadcast across the country on all the major radio networks.

The baby's corpse was removed to 415 Greenwood Avenue in Trenton,

Swayze & Margerum, Funeral Directors. Walter H. Swayze was a mortician as well as the Mercer County coroner. Because the victim had met a violent death, state law required the county physician to perform an autopsy. While waiting for him to arrive, Betty Gow identified the remains in the embalming room. Although wholly unprepared for the grotesquerie of what she saw, she recognized the baby not only from his facial features and hair but also from his sixteen teeth, especially the eyeteeth, which had just cut through the gums, and the way in which the second toe almost overlapped the big toe. "There was absolutely no doubt," Betty Gow would recall sixty years later, "this was my Lindbergh baby." Dr. Philip Van Ingen, the pediatrician who had attended the child shortly before his kidnapping, also positively identified the body.

The autopsy by Dr. Charles H. Mitchell revealed no signs of strangulation or bullets. With so much decomposition to the body, there was little for him to add beyond the supposition that "the cause of death is a fractured skull due to external violence." Because blood had been found nowhere near the crime-scene, not even on the chisel left behind, it seemed logical that when the ladder had broken, the baby had met his death smashing against the side of the house or onto the ground.

Lindbergh did not reach home until two o'clock in the morning, and he went directly to his wife. By then raw emotion had overtaken her, and she wept uncontrollably. On this occasion, Charles made no effort to stop her. He said little, but Anne clung to every measured word. "He spoke so beautifully and calmly about death that it gave me great courage," she would write his mother afterward. He grasped any straw of consolation that he could find. That their baby was dead from the beginning meant that nothing they did could have made any difference in sparing his life. Learning that he suffered a blow to his head, Charles commented, "I don't think he knew anything about it."

Anne had a long sleepless night in bed, but she got more rest than her husband. Charles sat in a chair beside her the entire time, watching her. "His terrible patience and sweetness and silence—terrifying," she noted the next day.

In thinking of the immediate future, Lindbergh told Colonel Schwarzkopf that Friday the thirteenth that he wished his son to be cremated. With vendors already selling food to the parade of tourists on the Mt. Rose road, he knew a gravesite would become nothing less than a carnival sideshow. Most distressing of all, a photographer had broken into the morgue in Trenton and snapped a picture of the dead baby, copies of which were being peddled for five dollars each.

Lindbergh felt he should view the body. Colonel Schwarzkopf assured him that the corpse had been positively identified. But Lindbergh insisted.

That afternoon Colonels Schwarzkopf, Breckinridge, and Lindbergh drove up an alley to the back door of Swayze & Margerum, while a crowd of mourners congregated in front. Lindbergh ordered the sheet removed from the little body lying on the examining table, leaned over to inspect the teeth and toes, and walked out of the room in silence. A number of public officials were present when Lindbergh told the County Prosecutor, "I am perfectly satisfied that is my child."

The body was wrapped in a shroud, placed in a small oak coffin, and driven by hearse to the Rosehill Cemetery and Crematory in Linden, New Jersey. Rubberneckers strained to look in the window of the car, hoping to get a glimpse of Lindbergh; others merely touched the car as it pulled away. Lindbergh and Breckinridge stayed inside the mortuary until the crowd had dispersed, then went to the house of Rosehill's proprietor. Schwarzkopf followed the casket, to protect its contents. Until he could take to the air to scatter the ashes, Lindbergh requested that they remain at Rosehill.

For days, Anne could not help reliving her every minute with her child— "I am glad that I spoiled him that last weekend when he was sick and I took him on my lap and rocked him and sang to him. And glad that he wanted me those last days. . . ." She heeded Charles's words and considered it a blessing that the baby had not lived beyond that first night: "He was such a gay, lordly, assured little boy and had lived always loved and a king in our hearts. I could not bear to have him baffled, hurt, maimed by external forces. I hope he was killed immediately and did not struggle and cry for help—for me." She found it nearly impossible to speak without crying.

Charles's grief, Anne discovered, was different from hers. He kept talking about the bigger picture, how they must "find some way of making Time go backwards," so that they could reclaim who they were before this catastrophe. He felt diminished by the whole experience—deceived and degraded. "And the security we felt we were living in!" he remarked, resolving never to be so naïve again. "Everything is chance," he said. "You can guard against the high percentage of chance but not against chance itself." Perhaps, he thought, America had become so barbaric that Lindberghs could no longer live there. In a rare unguarded moment, he said to Anne, "I hoped so I would bring that baby back."

Charles insisted they start rebuilding their lives. Anne decided to concentrate on her new baby; Charles thought of returning to his scientific work. Future children, she believed, could not take little Charlie's place; but she felt that he had "made something tremendous out of our marriage that can't be changed now. And for the world, too, perhaps, the sacrifice will bring something." Anne and Charles had never been so close as they were at his birth— except, she now observed, at his death.

Two images from this abysmal period haunted Anne forever. The first was of her white tulips, which finally struggled through the packed ground—even though countless policemen had trampled the flower beds. What was terrible, Anne wrote years later, "was that they all came up crooked. . . . crooked and misshapen and wizened, half-formed, faceless—not one erect and perfect and whole."

The second image was even more chilling, a sight she regretted never witnessing. Anne Lindbergh never once saw her husband cry.

11

APPREHENSION

"Individuals are custodians of the life stream—temporal manifestations of far greater being, forming from and returning to their essence like so many dreams."

—C.A.L.

THERE WAS AN OUTPOURING OF SYMPATHY—SOME SAID THE greatest public display of grief since the assassination of Lincoln. Others, such as Henry Breckinridge, suggested that the sentiments cut deeper and wider than that because "Lindbergh's popularity knew no boundaries. This touched everybody—the most famous baby in the world had been brutally killed."

Over one hundred thousand telegrams and letters, plus hundreds of bouquets, arrived in Hopewell. The Lindberghs received official messages of sympathy from President and Mrs. Hoover, the Prince of Wales, General and Mrs. Chiang Kai-shek, Mexican President Ortíz Rubio, and Benito Mussolini. "IT IS WITH DEEPEST REGRET THAT THE PEOPLE OF LITTLE FALLS LEARNED OF YOUR GREATER SORROW," telegraphed their mayor, echoing the sentiments wired by the mayors of practically every major American city.

As civic organizations had rallied behind Lindbergh in 1927 with congratulations, so now they gathered with condolences—the B'nai B'rith of Atlantic City; the Dutch Girl Scouts in Ossterbeek, Holland; the Australian Motherscraft Society in Sydney; the Germiston Methodist Church in South Africa; the Kiwanis Club of Hope, Arkansas . . .

Lindbergh heard from his elderly aunts in Minnesota and even his estranged half-sister Eva, who wrote, "Father told me once 'no sorrow on earth is so great as the loss of a child'— And the needless loss of your beautiful little son seems to me the cruelest in history."

The general public felt the same. Thousands of strangers sent the Lindberghs letters and tributes, many suggesting that the baby had died for their sins. They included Biblical quotations, pictures of Jesus, and the suggestion that their son "offered himself as a helper of humanity, as the Christ did when he incarnated in the body of Jesus." One James Spink of Buffalo, New York, wrote, published, and distributed a pamphlet called "The Little Eaglet," in which he rendered the lad's tale, paralleling his Passion with appropriate citations from Scripture. *The Hungarian Jew,* a periodical published in New York, wrote in its next editorial that "not Lindbergh, but we were the sinners. We tolerated lawlessness in the land until it grew to diabolical proportions. . . . The baby's blood is upon our heads."

The next wave of Lindbergh poems—elegies and threnodies—appeared. Then came the songs—the Lindbergh marches and foxtrots of yesteryear replaced by such dirges as "Bring My Darling Baby Back" and "The Eaglet Is Dead." Popular novelist Kathleen Norris wrote a syndicated newspaper column urging every American woman to "build a monument to little Charles Lindbergh Jr."—not a monument of stone and marble but one of spirit, a promise to feed and clothe the thousands of desperate children in orphanages and tenements.

Without Miss Norris's provocation, entire communities enshrined the child: Jacksonville Beach, Florida, unveiled a memorial to the baby and dropped roses from airplanes onto the site; the Girl Scouts of Stonington, Connecticut, planted a five-foot weeping willow tree in his honor; the town of Charlotte, North Carolina, held a mass memorial service; the schoolchildren of San Juan, Puerto Rico, raised money for a wreath to be placed upon the baby's grave.

One woman living in Canada was moved enough to send the Lindberghs pictures of her one-year-old son—"who resembles the lost little angel almost 100%"—and to offer them the child for adoption!

The Lindberghs sleepwalked through the next few days, trying to ignore the New Jersey State Police, still stationed in their garage, spending hours each day working with a replica of the ladder up against the baby's window, trying to reconstruct the crime. While Anne could not stop replaying every moment she spent with her child—bringing him back by touching his clothes and imagining the feel of his curls—Charles could not keep from monitoring the police as they formulated an array of theories. He found the cold details therapeutic.

On Saturday, May 21, 1932, Charles and Anne drove to Long Island, to spend a weekend with the Harry Guggenheims. The serenity of Falaise produced a jumble of emotions for them. Exactly five years earlier, the young airmail pilot had arrived in Paris thirty-three hours after leaving Long Island; and on this very night Amelia Earhart recaptured the nation's attention by becoming the first woman to fly solo across the Atlantic, departing from Newfoundland and landing in Ireland. The choice of date was no accident. Earhart's husband and promoter, George Putnam, had evidently selected it to stoke the publicity fires.

Although they did not know her well, the Lindberghs liked Amelia Earhart, finding her lively company if not an especially able flier. Her success would only draw more attention to aviation and the advances in aeronautical technology since Lindbergh's more challenging crossing. While she was perhaps coiffed and costumed to look a little too much like Lindbergh, he was grateful to have "Lady Lindy," as the press called her, filling the front pages. He was incredulous that anybody would actually crave such attention. Charles relaxed enough that weekend to joke that he had "heard Amelia made a very good landing—once."

During long walks at Falaise, the Lindberghs spoke of their future. "We have an intense yearning for a quiet life, free from publicity—at any price," Anne wrote. "Nausea at the sight of newspapers. We are starting all over again—no ties, no hopes, no plans." After her own three years in the spotlight, albeit in her husband's shadow, she had come to share his aversion to fame and the toll it exacted. She wished her husband could detach himself from the kidnapping case. "I would like him to get back into the Institute work," Anne wrote his mother; "it would be a definitely constructive thing for his personal life. It is quiet, absorbing work and he is happiest now when he speaks of it." Charles needed no convincing. He was already talking of severing all his ties to aviation, because they inevitably led to publicity. Giving up $16,000 a year in salaries from TWA and Pan American seemed a small price for privacy.

Almost overnight, Charles and Anne's great attachment to their new house turned into a stronger repulsion. In addition to the constant reminders of Charlie, it had become a magnet for the morbidly curious. After several more weekends at Falaise, they found themselves returning not to Hopewell, but to Englewood—where misfortune followed them.

Elisabeth Morrow had been laying as low as possible for the past few months, but her heart began acting up. Charles had recommended a doctor at the Rockefeller Institute, who examined her, and his report was extremely discouraging. A second physician said the twenty-eight-year-old Elisabeth had lesions on her heart valves which would only worsen and that he doubted she would live to forty. For whatever time she had left, Elisabeth would have to curtail her activity so as never to exert herself. She decided to convalesce in England, where she had previously found peace and quiet among friends in Somerset.

Coming just six months after the death of her father and three months after the death of her son, the news stupefied Anne all over again. "There's nothing in this world can give me joy," she wrote in her diary, wondering what effect this "terrible apathy of mind, spirit, and body" must be having on her unborn child. Charles returned to his laboratory at the Rockefeller Institute, where he designed a new centrifuge.

Even though Charles had never felt comfortable amid his mother-in-law's hyperactive social life in Englewood, he and Anne appreciated the gates and security guards at Next Day Hill. Even there, however, the ramifications of the kidnapping followed them. Violet Sharpe, the English maid whose alibi at the time of the kidnapping always seemed suspect, was subjected to further interrogation. Extremely agitated, she refused to answer many questions, as the police probed into her personal life. On Friday, June tenth, she was told to prepare herself for another inquisition later that day. Before the officers could take her to the Hopewell police station, she went upstairs with some cleaning solvent—cyanide chlorine—and swallowed it. Upon returning to the pantry, she fainted and died.

Further investigation revealed that Violet was hiding nothing related to the kidnapping, only an embarrassing relationship with the Morrow butler. Within a year, forty-eight-year-old Olly Whateley, the Lindbergh butler, would die from a perforated duodenal ulcer, adding to the endless rumors surrounding the Lindbergh kidnapping. While no law-enforcement agency ever found a link between any of the Morrow or Lindbergh servants and the crime, their sudden deaths would stir future conjecture.

At the end of June 1932, the Lindberghs returned to Hopewell. Charles had been called to testify in the trial of John Curtis, which was being held in the small Hunterdon County courthouse in Flemington. It proved to be a brief but bizarre trial in which the prosecution had to refashion its argument to fit a peculiarity in New Jersey state law. Even though Curtis had broken down and confessed to Lindbergh of having fabricated the whole gang of kidnappers with whom he said he was in contact, it was not illegal to report false information to the police. Lindbergh testified for the prosecution. The jury found Curtis guilty of obstruction of justice, and the judge fined him $1,000 and sentenced him to one year in jail.

With that, the Lindbergh case disappeared from the newspapers. There were no suspects, no leads, and a poor economy, which forced New Jersey to lay off dozens of state troopers. Although the case was still active—the FBI working in conjunction with the New York City and New Jersey police forces—investigators were chasing phantoms. Colonel Schwarzkopf sent handwriting specimens from the ransom notes to law-enforcement officials and wardens of penal institutions across the country, asking them to compare the handwriting of all their prisoners. The Treasury Department tried to detect a pattern as some smaller bills of the Lindbergh ransom gradually surfaced in New York.

Schwarzkopf even pinned hopes on a studious man named Arthur Koehler, the head of the Forest Service Laboratory of the Department of Agriculture in Madison. Schwarzkopf had sent him splinters of the wood in the kidnap ladder, enough to allow Koehler to believe he could deduce the builder's identity. While Koehler's area of expertise was not considered an exact science, he had already proved himself a reliable court witness on several occasions. He had testified that lumber had specific markings as individualized as fingerprints, from which he could trace its history—where it was grown, where it was milled, where it was sold.

The Curtis trial over, the Lindberghs gave the house in Hopewell one more chance. Charles talked constantly about its virtues in design and construction as though trying to convince himself. Anne settled into a routine of piano lessons and walks, even writing—making attempts to chronicle their trip to the Orient. Every time they drove into town, however, they had to pass the spot on the hill where their baby's remains had been found.

Concerned with making the Hopewell house safe enough for his wife and expected baby, Lindbergh seized upon the idea of a police dog. He and Anne located a breeder of German shepherds, who singled out his most intelligent animal—named Pal. Charles, who had a way with dogs since childhood, approached the "wolf" and tried to pat him, which prompted Pal to bare his teeth and growl. Lindbergh was impressed.

The trainer said it would take a fortnight before Pal would accept Lindbergh as his master; and for the first few days, the breeder warned, Lindbergh must not approach him alone, for the dog would maul him. Each caveat pleased Lindbergh even more. The breeder drove up the next day in a small paddy wagon, with Pal bolted inside. They released him into one of the garages at Hopewell, which had been turned into a large cage with heavy wire. After the trainer left, Lindbergh let their two small dogs, Skean and Wahgoosh, run over to Pal so that they could get used to him. Charles followed. By the end of the day, he had the German shepherd obeying every signal. Lindbergh renamed the dog Thor.

More than security, Thor brought joy into the Hopewell house. Charles spent most of the next week teaching him new tricks and commands. He trained the dog to fetch specific items by name, including the leash which Lindbergh would put on Skean and Wahgoosh so that Thor could walk them. The dog became fiercely protective of Anne, awakening her in the mornings by putting his nose on her side of the bed and seldom leaving her side during the day. "The devotion of this dog following me everywhere is quite thrilling," Anne wrote in her diary, "like having a new beau."

By August 1932, the Lindberghs stopped pretending about their feelings toward the house in Hopewell and moved—at least temporarily—back to Next Day Hill. No sooner had they settled into their wing of the mansion, with their own staff, than their little dogs ran away. In his pursuit, Charles found eight reporters chasing after him. The episode made Anne adopt Charles's point of view, that were it not for the press attention that surrounded them, "we might still have him."

On the fifteenth of August, Lindbergh appeared at a New Jersey airfield and tested an all-metal low-winged Northrop monoplane. It was the first time in the three months since the discovery of his son's body that Lindbergh had flown. He went up for an hour, telling the inquiring press that his short flight was of "no particular significance." What he told nobody except his wife was that he flew over the Atlantic Ocean, several miles out to sea, where he strewed his firstborn's ashes.

Later that night, just after midnight, Anne's labor pains began. In light of the public hysteria of the last six months, the Lindberghs and their doctors had agreed that it was best for her to deliver the baby in the privacy of the Morrow apartment in the city. So, at 3:45 that morning, she and Charles and her mother drove from New Jersey through the deserted streets to 4 East Sixty-sixth Street. The obstetrician, Dr. E. M. Hawks, the anesthesiologist, Dr. Flagg, and a nurse arrived moments later.

Flagg immediately administered gas, but Anne suffered nonetheless for the next three and one-half hours. She seemed always conscious of Charles's presence, as he held her hand, stroking her wrist with his forefinger. She was not aware that she began to hemorrhage during the labor, and Dr. Hawks thought, "Oh my God, I've killed the second Lindbergh baby!" Flagg put her completely under, and a half hour later, she gave birth to a healthy seven-pound, fourteen-ounce baby—with big eyes, the Morrow nose, and the Lindbergh dimple in the chin.

All that day, Anne kept sighing that the baby was "all right," until Charles said, "He has a wart on his left toe." Such teasing was an obvious expression of his own relief. "You'll wear the baby out, looking at it," he said. But she did not want to dismiss her feelings of joy so readily. "The spell was broken by this real, tangible, perfect baby . . . a miracle," she wrote. "My faith had been reborn."

In an effort to see that the hysteria that surrounded his first child did not recur, Lindbergh issued an annnouncement of the birth of his second son to the press along with a request:

> Mrs. Lindbergh and I have made our home in New Jersey. It is naturally our wish to continue to live there near our friends and interests. Obviously, however, it is impossible for us to subject the life of our second son to the publicity which we feel was in a large measure responsible for the death of our first. We feel that our children have a right to grow up normally with other children. Continued publicity

will make this impossible. I am appealing to the press to permit our children to lead the lives of normal Americans.

Lindbergh let the press believe the baby had been born in Englewood. He filed the birth certificate with no name; and he diplomatically called the *Times* and the *Tribune* to inform them of this fact. He also said that there would be no photographs released.

Most of the reputable newspapers in the country honored Lindbergh's wishes for privacy. Some even wrote to assure the family that they would make no effort to obtain pictures of any of them and that they would write no stories on the Lindberghs other than those based on officially issued statements. Lindbergh was pleased to read several articles about Thor and his great ferocity.

One night after they had returned to the safety of Next Day Hill, however, a local half-wit appeared at the new baby nurse's upstairs window. Anne became as apprehensive as ever. Charles routinely called the police and calmly suggested that the baby not sleep alone, not even in the daytime on the porch. "We give in," Anne noted in her diary. "Will this haunt us forever?"

The following week, Anne went into the city to see Dr. Hawks and to treat herself to a new hat. At Macy's she walked by a mirror and could hardly believe how old, pale, and worried she looked. Suddenly other shoppers caught sight of her and literally mobbed her. Anne fled.

Charles refused to let his wife submit to her fears. He would accept a life of precaution but never one of paranoia. Although the season in North Haven was winding down, he thought it best to take Anne there, even though it meant leaving their one-month-old behind. He trained Thor to "Go mind the baby," which meant lying by his crib and accosting anyone who approached other than Elsie Whateley and the nurse, who slept with him every night. At least two males of the domestic staff were ordered to remain close to him at all times, and a watchman was hired. Anne was naturally reluctant to abandon the baby, still unnamed; but Dr. Van Ingen thought it best not to move him from Englewood. Charles flew his wife from the Long Island Country Club on the afternoon of September thirteenth in his Bird biplane.

They intended to be gone but ten days, but they stayed sixteen. When he and Anne were not playing tennis or hiking on their Big Garden Island, Charles flew, chopped trees, and read. Anne found added strength in her family—Dwight Jr., home from an archaeological trip to Europe before returning to Amherst, Con about to return to Smith, and Elisabeth, back from England to announce her engagement to a Welshman, Aubrey Niels Morgan, whose family owned David Morgan, Ltd, a department store in Cardiff. She planned to live in Wales. Without saying it outright, Lindbergh experienced for the first time the healing powers of a family in a time of distress. He filled his wife's heart with joy one night in North Haven when he commented, "I don't know any place I like as much as this now."

The Lindberghs returned to Englewood invigorated. They settled, at last, on a name for the new baby—Jon—which they came across in a book of Scandinavian history. It had no association to either of their families, was uncommon but not strange, and—as Charles liked to point out—"It is phonetic spelling!" He sarcastically added, "Let's see what people say about it! It will be a scream to hear them speculating about where we got it from."

The Lindberghs continued to reassemble the pieces of their lives. He returned to Dr. Carrel's laboratory at the Rockefeller Institute and to his work as technical adviser in the aviation industry. He also proposed donating the house in Hopewell to the state of New Jersey for use as some kind of children's home. It seemed the only way, Anne noted, "to make it up to the boy."

The dreadful year ended on a note of hope. The Lindberghs and Morrows gathered for a wedding three days after Christmas, on a Wednesday afternoon at 4:30, at which time Elisabeth Morrow married Aubrey Morgan. A thick fog settled over Englewood, but inside the candle-lit library at Next Day Hill, the few dozen guests felt warm and cheery. Charles liked the groom very much and appreciated the company of another man in the Morrow matriarchy. The newlyweds embarked on a honeymoon in the south of France before settling in Cardiff.

Several weeks of socializing made the Lindberghs feel they were returning to normal life. They attended a public banquet at which Charles accepted a belated decoration from the government of Romania, a dinner with George and Amelia Earhart Putnam, and another with Vita Sackville-West and her husband Harold Nicolson—whom the Morrow family was considering to write the official biography of Dwight Morrow. But all feelings of security were illusory. The barking of dogs in the night was enough to keep them both awake.

With the first anniversary of the kidnapping, newspapers recycled the story. Articles recapitulated the crime and editorials reprehended the New Jersey State Police. Concealed from the public, because they might interfere with attempts to crack the unclosed case, were kidnap threats against Jon, which the Lindberghs were receiving. In his fight to keep his wife from sinking into depression at Next Day Hill, Lindbergh resorted to his lifelong elixir—travel.

A successful ten-day car trip to Detroit—during which Anne disguised herself with glasses and a blond wig and he slicked down his hair with a washable black rinse—encouraged the Lindberghs to travel more. "C. felt entirely free for the first time in six years," Anne observed, "his freedom handed back to him. And to feel it is always there now, a hidden reserve. We *can* get away!" Charles made plans for their next trip.

Aviation had thus far weathered the Depression; and Lindbergh—as Technical Director of TWA, "The Lindbergh Line"—had not inspected any of its air routes in more than a year. On April 19, 1933, he and Anne left Newark for Burbank, where they intended to pick up their Lockheed Sirius, reconditioned after its 1931 spill into the Yangtze. They flew to Camden, Baltimore, Washington, Pittsburgh, and Columbus, discovering a trail of new transcontinental beacons. St. Louis felt like a homecoming for both of them, as friends as well as fans turned out to greet them. Lindbergh expressed great admiration for the city's new terminal building and glassed-in control tower; and he visited the exhibition of his decorations and trophies at the Missouri Historical Society, adding a few more to the collection and expressing concern over their security. They spent the night with Philip Love; and in front of his old flying mate, he reverted to an immature teenager, bullying Anne in front of him, dragging her up to bed by one ear. (She learned the only way to deal with such behavior was to play along—though she did once find him so exasperating that she dumped a pitcher of water on his head.)

Crowds once again welcomed the Lindberghs every time they landed, glorying in having the gods back in their Heaven. Charles and Anne enjoyed a week in Los Angeles, then headed east, happy to be in their familiar orange-red and black plane, fitted once again with wheels where the pontoons had been. On May sixth, they got caught in a dust storm over the Texas panhandle and spent the night inside the plane. Six planes searched for them while they were "missing." They hit page one of *The New York Times* when they were "found."

Once back in Englewood, Lindbergh planned their next trip, this one equal in scope to their trip to the Orient. The air routes of the world were "entering their final stage of development," Lindbergh noted. "The countries had already been crossed and the continents connected. It remained only for the oceans to be spanned. Their great over-water distances constituted the last major barrier to the commerce of the air." Thus, this trip's official purpose was to survey potential transatlantic air routes and bases between North America and Europe. There were three alternatives—the Greenland-Iceland route in the north, the Newfoundland-Ireland route in the center, and the Bermuda-Azores route in the south. The northern route was most "tantalizing" to Lindbergh, for it offered the greatest safety net of land below, never more than seven hundred miles over water.

At a factory in Caldwell, New Jersey, Lindbergh modified his Lockheed Sirius. Mechanics installed a new 710 h.p. Wright Cyclone F engine and a Hamilton Standard controllable pitch propeller with two positions. These changes increased the range of the plane and the load with which it could take off from water. After testing the plane on July first, Lindbergh flew to the Edo factory on Long Island, where the wheels were once again replaced with pontoons. As with their previous expedition, the Lindberghs financed the flight themselves. Pan American supplied the best radio available at the time and sent a ship to Greenland to serve as an operations base.

Selecting equipment for this trip was at least as difficult as their 1931 voyage to the Orient. Although they would be leaving New York in midsummer, the Lindberghs had no itinerary—only the probability that they would travel both farther north and south than ever before. Again they would have to prepare for the possibility of forced landings at sea as well as on the Greenland Ice Cap. They would carry two complete radio sets, one waterproof and fitted into a rubber sailboat. This time they also compromised the plane's performance by adding guns, a bug-proof tent, and extra food. The Sirius with full tanks would thus be so heavy as to demand both a good wind and a long runway of sheltered water to take off.

Lindbergh met with Fred C. Meier of the Bureau of Plant Industry and Weather Bureau in the Department of Agriculture to discuss the practical aspects of Lindbergh's newest invention. His "sky hook" was a piece of aluminum tubing that contained cartridges with petrolatum-smeared slides prepared to collect microorganisms from the atmosphere along the flight. The results of these experiments would prove valuable to scientists studying the movement of air currents in northern regions and even to physicians studying hay fever by tracking the aerial movement of pollen. He also packed a Leica camera with a fifty-millimeter lens to photograph prospective air bases. Once again, "the first couple of the sky," as the press referred to the Lindberghs, brought positive publicity to aeronautics.

Without fanfare, they began their expedition on July 9, 1933. Charles arrived at Glenn Curtiss Airport at eight o'clock that morning and spent much of the day putting his Sirius through its final tests. His presence quickly attracted the press and almost resulted in his crashing into a plane full of cameramen trying to get a closer shot of him.

After a thunderstorm passed through, Anne arrived at the airport with the Harry Guggenheims and Aida Breckinridge. Around 3:30, the big ship slid down its ramp into the water. After forty-five seconds of splashing forward, the plane took off, heading northeast. "The Lindberghs have set no definite route nor have they picked definite landing places and stopover points," wrote *The New York Times*. "Furthermore, they have set no time for their return. While the flight is being undertaken as a survey of what may some day be used as an air route to Europe for Pan-American Airways . . . the couple proposes to enjoy the trip without the worry of keeping to schedules." The *Jelling*, a Danish steamer Pan American had hired to serve as one of several support ships, had left Philadelphia the week before and had already placed gasoline and landing buoys for the Lindberghs at Halifax and St. John's. The boat would serve as their weather scout, primary radio contact, repair shop, and occasional hotel along their journey.

The Lindberghs stopped in North Haven to say good-bye to their son and their respective mothers. More than ever, Anne was apprehensive about abandoning her baby, but never enough to pass up an opportunity to fly with her husband. And Charles was not about to let past travails curtail his future travels. On the afternoon of July eleventh, they left for Nova Scotia. Over the next eleven days, they surveyed Newfoundland. Anne's diary recorded happy encounters with their hosts on board the support ships and on shore, while Charles's dwelt on the topography.

Over the next twenty-four days, the Lindberghs explored Greenland—Godthaab, Holsteinsborg, Ella Island, Eskimonaes, Angmagssalik, and Julianehaab. He fished and kayaked among the Greenlanders when the fog kept them from flying reconnaissance. They thrived in the island's little towns set among the rocky hills, fjords, and "iceberghs" (as Anne began spelling it). They flew across the ice cap—"a huge continent of ice," populated with prehistoric-looking musk ox and polar bears.

"In those tiny, isolated outposts of the North," Anne would later recollect, "the burden of fame fell from us and we achieved a measure of anonymity. We were strangers; we were guests; but we were not celebrities set apart from the human race." While they felt they were blending into the daily life, they had no idea to what extent the press still monitored their movements.

One day in August, when the Lindberghs were grounded, the media lost sight of their whereabouts altogether. By nightfall, rumors of their demise had spread. At ten o'clock, Reuters in London teletyped, "IT IS REPORTED HERE THAT LINDBERGH HAS CRASHED AND BEEN KILLED IN GREENLAND." The rumor avalanched into a global sensation, a major news item that had to be retracted, making the press themselves realize how reckless they became when writing about Lindbergh.

Another day in Holsteinsborg, where Charles was returning from a flight over the fjords, Anne watched a group of children run out to greet the plane as it descended from the sky onto the Davis Strait. "Tingmissartoq! Tingmissartoq!" they shouted, Inuit for "the one who flies like a big bird." On their last day in Greenland, after hearing the cry throughout their stay, the Lindberghs asked a young Eskimo to paint it on the fuselage of the Lockheed Sirius.

On August fifteenth the *Tingmissartoq* left Greenland's east coast for Reykjavik, Iceland. After the five-hour flight across the Denmark Strait, they found the waters in the harbor too rough to reach the capital city. A British aviator named John Grierson, then flying the northern route from England to America, came to their aid. He commandeered a ferryboat and brought the Lindberghs and their plane to a mooring near the hangar where his plane was lodged.

They spent a week in Iceland, circumnavigating the entire country before flying on to the Faroe and Shetland Islands. A five-hour flight over the North Sea brought them to Copenhagen. During their week in Denmark, mobs snowballed as word of their presence spread. Charles wanted to visit Sweden, but he knew the arrival of its favorite "son" would unloose festivities beyond his desires. To shake the press, he and Anne steered the *Tingmissartoq* south for several minutes before radically changing course and making their way for Stockholm.

After a few days in the city—where the Lindberghs were able to enjoy some of its restaurants, parks, and museums before photographers and crowds began following them—Charles quietly arranged to visit his ancestral home. On September seventeenth, they flew to the island of Karlskrona, in southern Sweden. A man met them in a motorboat, brought them ashore, and drove them into the Skåne countryside. They arrived in the village of Gårdlösa, a scattering of white houses with red roofs and green doors, as night was falling. There was still enough light to see green fields and windmills along the rolling hills in the distance. At last they arrived at a white house which made up one side of a cobblestoned courtyard; barns formed the other three sides. Far from any reporters, Lindbergh had reached the homesite of Ola Månsson.

Charles and Anne crossed the road to visit another farm, where they met a man whose grandfather had known Lindbergh's grandfather. He gave Charles a pair of Ola Månsson's eyeglasses, which Månsson had evidently sent seventy years earlier as payment on a debt. He also presented Lindbergh with papers written in Månsson's hand, complete with his signature. Lindbergh autographed a book for the family, and the matriarch hugged it. When it was time for the Lindberghs to leave, all the people in the neighborhood gathered around them in the dark courtyard. As one of them shone a light from a bicycle on Lindbergh's face, they broke into the Swedish national anthem.

The Lindberghs toured Europe for another two months, taking in Finland, Russia, Estonia, Norway, England, Ireland, Scotland, France, Holland, Switzerland, Spain, and Portugal—all potential airline gateways to the New World. Charles devoted much of his time to airport inspections and meetings with heads of foreign airlines, while Anne enjoyed the role of tourist. Together, they saw a ballet from the royal box at the opera house in Leningrad, attended a banquet in their honor in Moscow, and met the King of Norway in Oslo. They also spent a week in Wales with Anne's sister and Elisabeth's new husband, who were preparing for their imminent move to California for her health. At the Berkeley Hotel in London they bumped into Jean Monnet, an old Morrow friend, who spoke of his fears about America under the new president: "Roosevelt is trying to bring about social reforms in a period of reconstruction," the French economist said, "and that is fatal."

For Charles, the happiest moments abroad seemed to be when he was alone with his machinery. One night in Inverness he came in from having spent six hours in a cold rain, fixing a broken cable on the plane, which was anchored on the river Ness. Tired and soaked to the bone, he told Anne, "I'd a hundred times rather spend an evening like this than one in New York."

On October twenty-sixth the Lindberghs slipped into Les Mureau naval base on the Seine; but once they entered the lobby at the Crillon in Paris, there was hardly a moment during the next week when Charles did not go unnoticed. *"Tiens! C'est Lindbergh!"* cried Parisians on the boulevards. "They still regard him as a romantic young boy—the Fairy Prince," Anne wrote Elisabeth shortly after their arrival. "Women bang at the door of his car, crowds collect as he leaves the hotel." With mixed emotions, Anne found that she was often ignored, for the French did not connect her with Lindbergh. "They simply can't think of him as married," she observed. "It is like a famous movie actor. He is Romance." The constant hysteria surrounding him in France made Lindbergh talk seriously of giving up aviation and of never visiting another major city again.

He charted their journey home. The *Tingmissartoq* took them to the Azores, more than eight hours out to sea from Lisbon. Once there, however, Charles discovered that the harbor at Horta was too small for them to take off with the full load necessary to reach Newfoundland. He hoped to find a larger harbor on another of the islands, at Ponta Delgada. When it too proved inadequate, Lindbergh replotted their route, charting the equatorial waters between Africa and South America.

Anne had had enough. "I am homesick for my baby," she told the press at Horta. "It's time my husband took me home." But Lindbergh remained strangely noncommittal both to the reporters and to his wife. He would say only, "My time is my own." Ironically, once the Lindberghs had at last decided to conclude their journey, they encountered one unforeseen obstacle after another.

They turned southward and inland, toward the bulge of Africa that came closest to South America. They stopped in the Canary Islands and what was then the Spanish colony of Río de Oro on the African continent before proceeding to the Cape Verde Islands, two hundred miles closer than any port in Africa. Huge ocean rollers made landing extremely difficult; and Lindbergh realized that taking off from there for South America in their overloaded seaplane would be impossible.

He decided to forfeit their two-hundred-mile advantage and fly with a light load of fuel back to the West African coast—to Dakar, in Senegal. The Lindberghs were about to leave when they were informed by telegraph of an epidemic of yellow fever there. They learned of a safe port where they could land just one hundred miles south of Dakar—Bathurst, in British Gambia, where the Gambia River meets the ocean. They encountered absolutely no trouble putting the *Tingmissartoq* down on the river's gentle waters. That stillness would prove to be a curse.

As opposed to their predicament in Cape Verde, the *Tingmissartoq* would need more wind or wave chop to help lift the plane's pontoons "on their steps," especially with the added burden of extra fuel necessary for a sixteen-hour flight. Bathurst, during that season, typically provided no wind whatever. The Lindberghs lightened their load, leaving behind such nonessential Arctic items as sealskin boots and even their anchor.

They tried to take off from their glassy runway five times that day. During each attempt, Charles worked the controls in silent frustration, not even communicating to his wife. The stillness kept them from even an attempt the next day. Lindbergh spent the day after that, December fifth, jettisoning more of their load—food, tools, sleeping bags, practically all their clothes. He even went into the plane with metal shears to cut a gasoline tank out of the fuselage. Later that night, while out walking, Anne noticed her handkerchief fluttering in the wind. A few hours later, with the rising of the moon, they made what would have to be their last attempt before settling on another route home altogether. After an unusually long run in semidarkness, the plane splashed across the water, then spanked it many times, before the pontoons rose from the sea.

Sixteen hours later the Lindberghs spotted the Pan American barge at Natal, on the bulge of Brazil—1,875 miles from Bathurst. It was three o'-clock in the afternoon local time, and steaming hot. Feeling punch-drunk as she got off the plane, Anne let herself think of Christmas at home with her son Jon.

Lindbergh promptly learned, however, that Juan Trippe wanted him to return to New York by way of Rio de Janeiro, Montevideo, Buenos Aires, and all the other major Pan American stations along the way. Mindful of his wife's anxiety, Lindbergh told her he too wanted to go home directly and that they would stop only where necessary. At that, it would be almost another week just getting out of Brazil. Even though Anne was desperate for the travel to end, Charles announced that they would be going via Manáos, a thousand miles up the Amazon.

They might very well have lingered in the jungle were it not for an unpleasant encounter outside a rubber factory. An American approached the Lindberghs and thoughtlessly blurted, "You know, we were the first to hear of the kidnapping here!" It was an unpleasant smack of reality after nearly six months of living virtually unattached from the rest of the world.

The next day, the Lindberghs left Brazil for Port-of-Spain, Trinidad, despite a torrential rain. It was one of the few times even Charles conceded to Anne that it was "Bad stuff!"—the sort of weather through which he generally chose not to fly. Months later, he learned that their departure through cloud-covered mountains had given birth to a jungle myth: Just after the *Tingmissartoq* had passed over a band of Waiwai natives, a bolt of lightning had struck the chief's house, running down one of the hut's poles, singeing both his son's head and daughter's backside, melting the head of his hunting spear, and splintering a floorlog that they used as a ceremonial seat. Because, as one anthropologist explained, "There is no such thing in the jungle as coincidence," the tribal explanation for this phenomenon was that the god Makanaima, upset with the Waiwais, had created a great mosquito to buzz over them, inflicting this fiery sting.

Despite Anne's anxiety, Charles took another week getting them to Miami by way of Puerto Rico and Santo Domingo. They received a telegram from The White House within hours of their December sixteenth arrival on American soil. "WELCOME HOME AND CONGRATULATIONS UPON THE SUCCESSFUL COMPLETION OF THIS, ANOTHER FLIGHT MADE BY YOU IN THE INTEREST AND FOR THE PROMOTION OF AMERICAN AVIATION," wired Franklin D. Roosevelt. "I HOPE THAT OUT OF THE SURVEY YOU HAVE MADE NEW AND VALUABLE PRACTICAL AIDS TO AIR TRANSPORTATION AND COMMUNICATIONS WILL COME." The Lindberghs thanked the President for his surprising interest in their trip.

The *Tingmissartoq*'s pontoons splashed down into Flushing Bay, Long Island, at 7:37 on the evening of December 19, 1933; and the media blitz on the Lindberghs' lives resumed. A flotilla of speedboats carrying motion picture and still photographers, reporters, and radio interviewers closed in on them, one of the boats cutting so close that the plane rocked dangerously. Although they had been gone five months and ten days (to the minute)—during which time they had logged 29,781 miles and linked four continents—it was as if the Lindberghs had never left.

With the rapid advances in technology, the journey marked an end in a period of aviation, one which Lindbergh believed "was probably more interesting than any the future will bring." The perfection of machinery, he observed just a few years later, "tends to insulate man from contact with the elements in which he lives. The 'stratosphere' planes of the future will cross the ocean without any sense of the water below." Wind and heat and moonlight takeoffs would no longer concern the transatlantic passenger. Before the year had ended, Lindbergh called his friend F. Trubee Davison, president of the American Museum of Natural History in New York, to offer the *Tingmissartoq* and all its accoutrements—down to the Lindberghs' can of insect repellent. For years it hung in the museum's Hall of Ocean Life, where it became one of the museum's most popular attractions. After another few years at the Air Force Museum in Ohio, it found a permanent home as part of the Smithsonian Institute's collection of aircraft.

Despite his aversion to New York City, Charles had taken of late to saying, "The only place where I'd feel content leaving a baby" was in an apartment. And so, in January 1934, the Lindberghs moved to 530 East Eighty-sixth Street. Their penthouse had two terraces, a river view, and a feeling of privacy and security. Jon, then sixteen months old, slept but a room away from his parents. Around the corner, Anne located a nursery school, to which she walked Jon and the dogs every morning. Jon was young, even for this playgroup; and yet Anne felt that she and Charles lived in a strange world "where we are 'different,' " and the sooner Jon was sent "into it . . . and with the youngest possible children, the easier it will be for him." She found the apartment conducive for finishing her book about their expedition to the Orient and for starting a *National Geographic* article about their trip to Greenland. Busy settling in, the Lindberghs refused an invitation to a large informal reception on the night of February first at the White House. Had Charles been more politically savvy, he might have attended the event, for the President evidently had aviation on his mind those days. One week after the event, he realized just how much.

On February 9, 1934—without any warning—President Roosevelt annulled all domestic airmail contracts between the government and more than thirty airlines. He claimed that there had been criminal conspiracy in awarding the contracts, and he ordered the Army to assume responsibility for carrying the mail. The root of the problem lay in the spoils system—specifically, the New Dealers suggested, the payoffs of their Republican predecessors.

In anticipation of Roosevelt's taking office, the lame-duck Congress had established a special Senate committee under Senator Hugo Black, Democrat from Alabama, to investigate airmail and ocean-mail contracts. In his preliminary investigations, Black learned that former Postmaster General Walter Folger Brown had dispensed numerous contracts at a "clandestine conference," capriciously and corruptly. While most people in aviation recognized Brown's vision had done as much to galvanize the industry as any other force, his unilateral, dogmatic practices left much to criticize.

The Black Committee went into session in September 1933, requesting the financial records of every important player in aviation. Even before the Lindberghs had returned from their recent tour, he had been asked to submit itemized statements of all his cash and stock transactions with airlines since 1924. Audits of some companies' books revealed that certain contracts had been awarded to the least desirable bidder—United Aircraft and American Airways among them. As a result, a United executive testified that his

$253 investment in the company was now worth $35,000,000; a TWA executive testified that his company had paid a competitor over $1,000,000 not
to bid on an airmail award. After hearing a few such gross examples, and assured that Army pilots were capable of flying the mail, Roosevelt revoked all
the existing contracts.

The results were devastating. The aviation industry on the whole, many
argued, had solidified during the Depression because of Brown's work,
though most of the companies were still struggling, paying down their initial
debts. Transcontinental & Western Air, Inc., for one, was still posting losses
after more than three years of operation—$1,270,973 since incorporation,
and over $5,000,000 if its predecessor companies were counted. In all that
time, nobody had received a bonus nor had any stockholders received dividends. Company salaries had never exceeded $20,000. What the Black Com-
mittee was overlooking, TWA President Richard Robbins wrote the new
Postmaster General, James A. Farley, was that "there has been created in the
United States of America the greatest air transport system in the world. In
this development our company has played a leading part." TWA, he said,
was still committed to that development, prepared to spend another
$3,500,000 purchasing the newest and finest flying equipment. All their fi-
nancial planning was predicated on their government contracts. In the name
of his employees and over twenty thousand stockholders, he asked the administration to reconsider its decision.

The company's most famous employee and stockholder was incensed,
convinced that the President had thrown the baby out with the bathwater.
Lindbergh believed in the integrity of the people who ran TWA and knew
how they had sacrificed to get the company off the ground. He had never
taken part in any contract negotiations, but he felt he could not "remain
silent in the face of action so unconsidered, drastic, and unfair."

"Your action of yesterday affects fundamentally the industry to which I
have devoted the last twelve years of my life," Anne wrote, starting off a
draft of a telegram Lindbergh would complete. In it, he insisted on a point
greater than TWA's or his own benefits—the right to a fair trial, where honest parties could assert their innocence. "THE CONDEMNATION OF COMMERCIAL AVI-
ATION BY CANCELLATION OF ALL MAIL CONTRACTS AND THE USE OF THE ARMY ON
COMMERCIAL AIR LINES," Lindbergh concluded with certainty, "WILL UNNECES-
SARILY AND GREATLY DAMAGE ALL AMERICAN AVIATION." Lindbergh sent his 275-
word telegram to the President, simultaneously releasing a copy of the text
to the press.

Stephen T. Early, secretary to the President, was dispatched to attack the
messenger not the message. He told the press that the President first read
Lindbergh's telegram in that morning's newspaper, before it had even reached
his desk, and that Lindbergh had thus violated the usual courtesy of allow-

ing the President to receive communications before the media. Because there was little the Roosevelt administration could dispute in Lindbergh's argument, Early accused Lindbergh of sending the message strictly for "publicity purposes."

Initially, most of Washington sided with the power of the presidency. Even a Farmer-Laborite congressman from Minnesota said Lindbergh was "like a small boy trying to aggravate the President with a beanshooter"; Senator George Norris, a Nebraska Republican, referred to the signing bonus Lindbergh had received when he first joined TWA, and declared, "At last Colonel Lindbergh is earning the $250,000 stock fee and other fees he received from the aviation industry for use of his name. The public long has wondered just what Colonel Lindbergh really did for the tremendous payment revealed as going to him by the airmail investigating committee. Now we know." Despite these early efforts to dismiss Lindbergh's attack as the work of a lobbyist, nobody challenged the truth of what he had to say.

The Lindbergh rebuke became the talk of the nation. As one "plain citizen" wired Stephen Early, "TO CHARGE LINDBERGH WITH SEEKING PUBLICITY WILL CERTAINLY TICKLE THE AMERICAN SENSE OF HUMOR." Over the radio Will Rogers spoke highly of Lindbergh's knowledge of aviation and urged him and the President—whom Rogers described as the two best-loved men in America—to come together to sort out the problem. But Roosevelt would not back away from his position.

On February 18, 1934, the president of TWA furloughed all its personnel and attempted to develop a minimal schedule for passengers that would keep the company alive. Other major airlines suffered similarly. The Army had even worse problems.

As Lindbergh had tried to explain, they were not prepared to handle the mail. Although the Army had close to one thousand planes available at the time, fewer than 150 of them were suitable mail carriers, and they could transport only a fraction of the load that the commercial planes could. But a bigger problem, Lindbergh knew, was that flying the mail required special skills.

Three days before the Army took over the airmail schedule, three of its pilots were killed on practice runs, two crashing in a snowstorm over Utah, another over Idaho. Another Army pilot barely escaped death crashing near Linden, New Jersey. By the end of the Army's first week with its new assignment, another three pilots were killed, five more critically injured, and eight planes had washed out, accounting for property damage of $300,000. Lindbergh feared more disaster would follow "as the Army spirit is to push on in spite of everything and that is just what kills pilots in bad weather."

The final weeks of that year's winter turned unusually inclement, one of the most foggy, rainy, and snowy in the nation's history. Each day brought another horror story. Superintendent of the Aerial Mail Service Benjamin Lipsner tried for days to speak to the President, and when he finally got through, on March eighth, he begged him to "stop those airmail deaths." Roosevelt agreed to curtail the airmail service, but he would not hear of returning the mail to the commercial airlines. The next day four more Army mail pilots were killed. Roosevelt held his ground, calling a moratorium on airmail service. As the bodies of Army pilots mounted, so did pressure against the administration.

Secretary of War George H. Dern assembled a special committee to study and report upon Army aviation in relation to national defense, and he invited Lindbergh to serve on it. Lindbergh sensed this was an administration ploy to enlist his support. He replied to Dern that he stood ready to contribute whatever he could toward the maintenance of an adequate national defense, but he would not join this committee because he believed "that the use of the Army Air Corps to carry the air mail was unwarranted and contrary to American principle."

The next day, March 16, 1934, both the Black Committee and the Department of Justice tried to induce Lindbergh's support. For more than two hours, Lindbergh sat in the big red leather witness chair in the largest caucus room in the Senate Office Building. The room was packed with cameras and microphones and scores of people who wanted a glimpse of their hero. In answering even the toughest questions about commercial irregularities, he remained measured and articulate, insistent that "these contractors should have been given the right to trial before being convicted." *The New York Times* reported, "Whenever his face flashed in the familiar, winsome smile, a murmur of approval ran through the hall. He seemed still to be one of the world's most fascinating figures."

The same day he testified, Carl L. Ristine, Special Assistant to the Attorney General, asked Lindbergh to confer privately with him "about some matters pertaining to air mail contracts and controversial subjects." Lindbergh appeared in his office at the Post Office Department Building in Washington that evening. Upon his arrival, Lindbergh found not only Ristine, but also A. G. Patterson, chief investigator for the Black Committee, and a stenographer. Sensing that he was being set up, Lindbergh placed a call to Henry Breckinridge in New York.

Breckinridge advised his client to make no statement and to have no conversation before anyone representing the Black Committee without a subpoena, witnesses, and counsel present. He also told Lindbergh that if the inquiry were by an accredited representative of the Attorney General of the United States, it was his duty "to give freely any facts in his possession that had to do with any offense against the laws of the United States." Lindbergh replied, "Check." Breckinridge asked to speak to Ristine, who explained that Patterson had only stopped by and that the stenographer was, in fact, a personal secretary of the Attorney General. If Ristine would agree to furnish a transcript of the proceedings promptly, Breckinridge said he did not object to Lindbergh's being questioned.

The interrogation quickly turned testy, full of hypothetical questions and hostile insinuations. Lindbergh felt that Ristine was not interested in an investigation of facts so much as a confirmation of his opinions that laws had been violated. But he also felt so confident about his position that he answered questions for close to three and one-half hours, thwarting Ristine at every turn. At times he seemed to enjoy toying with him, making him lose his temper by restraining his own. In the end, Ristine learned nothing that advanced his cause. Almost a month later, Lindbergh telegraphed Ristine reminding him that he still had not received the transcript of their conference.

By then it would have been imprudent for the Department of Justice not to comply. The Army was delivering the mail on a greatly reduced schedule, and a twelfth pilot had just crashed. Radio, newspapers, and newsreels all offered Lindbergh platforms from which to address the nation.

An editorial in the *New York Times* asserted that Lindbergh was "as fine a witness as one could find searching the whole world over." Everyone from the man on the street to William Randolph Hearst concurred. Congressman Hamilton Fish, who represented the President's home district, said his constituents' mail had been running ninety-seven percent in favor of Lindbergh ever since the "discourteous treatment" shown by Stephen Early in replying to the Colonel's initial telegram. Walter Lippmann, like many other Washington pundits, found it "shocking" the way in which "overzealous partisans of the Administration" set out to discredit Lindbergh—"to investigate his earnings, to make out that he was a vulgar profiteer who was disqualified and had no right to be heard."

On April 20, 1934, Postmaster General Farley—the unwitting appointee who took the fall for the Administration's political blunder—called a conference of commercial airlines for the purpose of accepting new bids for the old airmail routes. To save face, Farley said that no line would be granted a contract if it had been represented at the "Spoils Conference" of 1930, at which Walter Brown had parceled out the original contracts. The major airlines responded by reorganizing, mostly by changing their names: American Airways became American Airlines; Eastern Air Transport became Eastern Airlines; United Aircraft became United Airlines; and Transcontinental and Western Air became Trans World Airlines. Lindbergh found the solution "reminiscent of something to be found in *Alice in Wonderland*."

Some of the leading personnel at each company had to be sacrificed in the "purge," including Lindbergh's friend Richard Robbins at TWA. Lindbergh himself wrote a letter of resignation, because he did not want to be part of a company "based on injustice and which necessitates the resignation of officers who have contributed so greatly to its development"; but management persuaded him to stay. On May 8, 1934, TWA was flying the mail again, and Charles Lindbergh had emerged as the one figure both the public and the industry believed they could turn to serve as their watchdog.

The "Air-Mail Fiasco," as Lippmann referred to it, had deep repercussions for the President. For the first time since he had taken office, his authority had been effectively challenged, making him appear both fallible and impenitent. Neither Roosevelt nor Lindbergh would ever forget the other's behavior during that skirmish, nor would either forgive.

By summer, Lindbergh was restless again. He let the New York apartment go and placed an order for a new plane, a single-engine, 125 h.p., two-place high-wing monoplane built by the Monocoupe Corporation in St. Louis. In August, the Lindberghs picked it up and proceeded to the West Coast to visit Anne's invalid sister.

The Lindberghs joined the Morgans at Will Rogers's 250-acre ranch in Pacific Palisades. Away on a trip, Rogers had made the spread available to Elisabeth, then desperately trying to recuperate. On Wednesday, September 19, 1934—after only three days together—the Lindberghs were abruptly summoned East again. Colonel Norman Schwarzkopf telephoned from New Jersey to tell Lindbergh that the kidnapping case had been cracked and a man he believed for certain had been involved in the crime had been apprehended—a German carpenter from the Bronx. "Oh God," Anne said upon hearing the news, "it's starting all over again." "Yes," Charles replied, "but they've got him at last."

The Lindberghs moved back to Next Day Hill, still their safest refuge from the press. The media was so frenzied in its reporting on "the crime of the century" that each new revelation ignited a wildfire of rumor, in some cases forever clouding aspects of the story. But as the smoke cleared, certain tangible truths about this case revealed themselves:

Since the spring of 1932, the wood technologist Arthur Koehler had been analyzing the kidnap ladder. He began by completely disassembling it, numbering each rail and rung. Several types of wood—pine, birch, fir—went into the ladder's construction, each with its own internal markings of rings and knots and its own external markings from the machinery that milled the raw timber into lumber and from the tools used to build the ladder. One piece of wood—identified as "rail number 16"—was especially interesting because it had four nail holes in it that had no connection with the making of the ladder, thus suggesting prior usage. Of low-grade sapwood, with no signs of weathering, it suggested that the rail had been previously nailed down indoors and used for rough construction, perhaps in the interior of a garage or attic.

There were dozens of other clues that kept Kochler on the investigative trail. The rungs of this homemade ladder, for example, were of soft Ponderosa pine but showed no signs of wear, indicating that the ladder had been built for this particular job. The marks on those rungs from the planer that dressed the wood revealed an unusual combination of cutter heads. Koehler mailed a form letter to 1,600 lumber mills on the East Coast, asking if their lumber planers shared the same characteristics. Positive replies came from twenty-five mills, which were asked to send sample boards. From them, Koehler was able to identify the Dorn Lumber Mill in McCormick, South Carolina, as the source of the boards that became the ladder's siderails. Twenty-five lumberyards had received shipments of Dorn's southern pine since the fall of 1929. Through scientific deduction, Koehler whittled the list down to the National Lumber and Millwork Company in the Bronx, which had bought its shipment in December 1931, three months before the kidnapping.

In November 1933, after eighteen months of investigation, Koehler needed only the sales records of the Bronx lumberyard to close in on the likely builder of the ladder. Unfortunately, National Lumber was largely a cash business and kept no such accounts. There, in the middle of the Bronx, Koehler's investigation reached an apparent dead end.

Meantime, the FBI, New Jersey State Police, and New York City Police Department had continued to follow every lead. Gradually, a cluster of clues surfaced in the form of ransom bills, which began appearing within two weeks of their having been paid in St. Raymond's Cemetery in the Bronx. Each was traced as far back as possible—usually from a New York bank to a shop to a customer, who was then investigated. On April 5, 1933, a Presidential Order increased the flow of Lindbergh ransom money: To combat the growing Depression practice of hoarding gold, Roosevelt directed that all gold coin and certificates valued at more than one hundred dollars be deposited or exchanged at a Federal Reserve Bank by May first. It would not become a crime to save or spend gold certificates, for the crime lay only in possessing more than one hundred dollars' worth; but they suddenly became less common and thus easier to spot.

On May first the Federal Reserve Bank of New York at Liberty and Nassau received $2,980 from a man who signed his name as J. J. Faulkner. When the bank realized that it was Lindbergh ransom money, the police searched the address on his deposit slip. But Faulkner was never found. Another ten bills turned up during the year, most of them in Manhattan. On the occasions when the recipients of the bills could recall who had passed them, they repeated the same characteristics—a white male of average height, blue eyes, high cheekbones and pointed chin, a German accent.

On September 18, 1934, a teller at the Corn Exchange Bank in the Bronx

checked a ten-dollar gold certificate against the list of Lindbergh ransom
money and found a match. He notified the authorities, who noticed writing
in the margin of the bill—"4U-13-14 N.Y." The police investigators speculated that the bill came from a nearby gas station. One of the bank's clients
was the Warren-Quinlan service station on Lexington Avenue and 127th
Street. The manager there, Walter Lyle, remembered the customer who had
paid for ninety-eight cents' worth of gasoline with the bill. When Lyle had
looked askance at the gold certificate, the customer had said in a decidedly
German accent that the money was good—that, in fact, he had about one
hundred more just like it at home. The New York Motor Vehicle Bureau provided the police with the name of the owner of that car—Bruno Richard
Hauptmann of 1279 East 222nd Street, the Bronx. In addition to information about his dark blue 1930 Dodge sedan, the registration card indicated
that he was German-born and a carpenter.

The police staked out his house, which was within minutes of Woodlawn
Cemetery, St. Raymond's, Dr. Condon's house, the National Lumber and
Millwork Company, and the area in which most of the ransom money had
been passed.

On the morning of September nineteenth, three black sedans carrying
Special Agent Thomas Sisk from the FBI, "Buster" Keaten of the New Jersey State Police, and James Finn of the New York Police Department, among
others, parked down his street. The officers watched Hauptmann through
binoculars as he left his house and walked around the corner to his locked
garage, from which he removed his car. They tailed him as he drove up
Tremont Avenue; and, before losing him in traffic, one of the officers pulled
him over. In an instant, the suspect was surrounded by police brandishing
guns. They removed his wallet and found that this was Bruno Richard
Hauptmann and that he was carrying a twenty-dollar gold certificate, the serial number of which they instantly found on the master list. When they
asked where he got the gold note, he said from his house, where he had another three hundred of them. The police asked if he had not recently told a
gas station attendant that he had *one* hundred such bills at home, and Hauptmann admitted that he had lied to the attendant.

In an apparent attempt to display his honesty, Hauptmann quickly revealed that he had entered the country illegally, on his third attempt as a
stowaway. Since his arrival, he had worked at various jobs before marrying
a German-born waitress, fathering their child, and finding regular work as
a carpenter.

Although Hauptmann had suggested he was a crooked man gone
straight, once the police got him back to his second-floor, five-room apartment, they developed a growing sense of his guilt. Most of the Hauptmanns'
furniture looked new and expensive, incongruous in its humble surround-

ings. The centerpiece of the room, for example, was a luxurious floor-model Stromberg-Carlson radio, worth hundreds of dollars. When Hauptmann's wife, Anna, entered the apartment and saw her husband in handcuffs, he tried to calm her in German, saying that the police were there because of an incident involving his gambling. An officer who spoke German picked up on the fib. An inspection of their bedroom turned up hundreds of dollars worth of promissory notes, new ladies' shoes, five twenty-dollar gold pieces, and an expensive pair of field glasses. The police asked Hauptmann point-blank where he had the rest of the Lindbergh ransom money. The suspect denied knowledge of the money or the case, other than what he had read in the newspaper. The police ripped open his mattress but found only stuffing inside.

Hauptmann explained that his fortunes had recently changed, that he had not been a carpenter for several years and that successful Wall Street investments had allowed him to purchase his few luxury items. In the living room, the police found ledger sheets of stock transactions—as well as road maps of New Jersey and other states along the Eastern seaboard. Hauptmann's landlady was ushered upstairs with two ten-dollar gold notes that Hauptmann had given her toward his current rent. They were Lindbergh ransom bills. While the police turned his apartment inside-out, Hauptmann sat impassively—occasionally stealing a glance out the window.

Sisk of the FBI walked to the window. There was nothing of interest outside, just the small, crude garage fifty feet away. "Is that where you have the money?" he asked. Hauptmann said that he had no money. Sisk, Keaten, and Finn went to investigate the garage anyway.

Finn noticed that two of the floorboards there were loose, and when they pried them up they noticed fresh dirt. Grabbing a shovel, he dug until he hit a jar. Inside was nothing except water. Convinced that it had once contained ransom money, Finn confronted Hauptmann with his accusation again. Hauptmann reiterated that he had no ransom money, that he did not know what Finn was talking about. With that, they collected some of Hauptmann's papers, with specimens of his handwriting, and carted him off to the 2nd Precinct police station on the lower West Side for questioning. A few hours later, they brought in Anna Hauptmann.

She was released within a few hours, appearing to know nothing of any criminal activity on her husband's part. On her return home, she saw police still combing her apartment for clues. They had made two significant discoveries. In one of Hauptmann's notebooks, they found a sketch of a ladder, of the same crude design as the one left on the Lindbergh property. They also found that Hauptmann's toolchest was complete except for the standard three-quarter-inch chisel, which was one of the few pieces of evidence left at the scene.

The police subjected Hauptmann to twenty-four hours of punishing examination. He consistently denied any participation or knowledge of the Lindbergh kidnapping. He said he had worked on a construction crew at the Majestic Apartments on March 1, 1932—the day of the kidnapping—and remained on the job through the following month, at which time he quit carpentry. Later that night, Joseph Perrone, the cab driver in the Bronx who had delivered one of the ransom notes to Dr. Condon, was brought into the interrogation room at the 2nd Precinct. Pressed by the police, he identified Hauptmann as the man who had dispatched him to Dr. Condon's house two years earlier.

Close to one o'clock in the morning—when Hauptmann was hungry and weary—they asked if he would provide samples of his handwriting. He agreed, offering specimens of both his printing and cursive. The writing varied in style, as though Hauptmann were trying to disguise it. Even so, dozens of idiosyncrasies in the spelling of words and the shapes of letters, which bore startling similarities to the Lindbergh ransom notes, kept appearing. After a solid day and night of relentless investigation, the suspect slumped over the writing table.

A fresh team of FBI agents and New York and New Jersey police arrived in the Bronx that morning to dismantle the Hauptmann garage. Behind a board nailed across two joists above the workbench, a detective found two newspaper-wrapped packets. One contained one hundred ten-dollar gold notes, the other eighty-three bills. All their serial numbers were on the ransom list. Removing more boards from the joists, the police found another hidden shelf, this one with a one-gallon shellac can. Inside, beneath some rags, were a dozen packages of gold notes, tens and twenties—another $11,930 of ransom money. Anna Hauptmann was shown the money and was dumbstruck. Downtown, the police were informed of the discovery and asked Hauptmann if he had any gold notes hidden away. Three times he denied having any, until they told him of their discovery.

Caught in another lie, Hauptmann proceeded to explain the presence of more than a quarter of the Lindbergh ransom in his garage. He said a tubercular friend of his from Germany named Isidor Fisch, with whom he had invested in the stock market and in a sideline business trading furs, had gone home to his parents in Leipzig the previous winter. Before leaving, he had stowed several containers of belongings for safekeeping, including a shoe box, which Hauptmann said he placed on the top shelf of a broom closet in his kitchen. During a recent rain, water leaked through the kitchen ceiling and into the closet. While inspecting it for damage, he discovered the forgotten shoe box, which he opened—only to discover $40,000 in gold certificates. Hauptmann said he hastily removed the money to his garage to dry it out. Because Fisch had owed him $7,000, he had no qualms spending that much. Unfortunately, Fisch could not confirm the story. He had died the preceding March. Fisch's family later reported that not only had Isidor returned to them penniless, but over the next year they heard from several people from whom he had borrowed money.

After listening to the story, the police obtained several more incriminating details, which refuted other Hauptmann assertions. The suspect had claimed to have worked at the Majestic Apartments on Central Park West and Seventy-second Street for two or three months in 1932, starting on March first, the day of the Lindbergh kidnapping. The New York police investigation uncovered that Hauptmann did not begin his work at the Majestic until the twenty-first of March . . . and that he had quit the job on April second, only hours before the ransom money had been passed at St. Raymond's. It was the last date on which Hauptmann worked as a carpenter before becoming a Wall Street investor.

Almost simultaneously, Albert S. Osborne, the eminent "questioned documents examiner," who had been studying the handwriting of the ransom notes since May of 1932, confirmed what seemed obvious to many who casually compared the ransom notes to Hauptmann's handwriting, samples written before and after his arrest. He said they were written by one and the same person. His colleague-son concurred.

Several secondary witnesses paraded through the 2nd Precinct, each picking Hauptmann out of a lineup, though the one on whom the police counted most did not pull through. John F. Condon spent hours at the police station, much of it in the immediate presence of Hauptmann. While he felt strongly that this was "Cemetery John," Jafsie was reluctant to assert as much. Condon insisted that he had to be careful, that a "man's life is in jeopardy." He might have meant more than Hauptmann's, as he revealed to Agent L. G. Turrou. Upon fingering a suspect, Condon said, he felt his own life "wasn't worth five cents" because "They" would "kill him."

Hauptmann's character came further into question on Thursday afternoon, when the police received information from authorities abroad. Contrary to Hauptmann's insistence that he had no criminal record prior to his arrival in America, German police reported that he had been convicted of grand larceny and armed robbery. In one instance, he had entered a house through a second-story window by way of a ladder. In another, he had held up two women at gunpoint, seizing groceries they were carting in baby carriages. He had served close to four years in a German prison. Shortly after his release, while still on probation, he was arrested for another series of burglaries. He had barely been reincarcerated when he escaped from prison grounds and attempted to stow away to America.

Still lacking a confession to the Lindbergh kidnapping, the police handcuffed a weakened Hauptmann in a chair, turned out the lights, and threat-

ened to "knock [his] brains out." They almost made good on the threat, kick-
ing him and beating him, probably with a hammer, delivering blows to the
shoulders, arms, abdomen, and head. More questioning followed; but he
never confessed to any knowledge of or participation in the Lindbergh kidnapping.

While teams of police tore his story apart, others did the same to his
house. Back at 222nd Street in the Bronx, more evidence piled up. On the
doortrim inside a closet in the Hauptmann baby's room, a detective discovered some writing in pencil: "2974 Decatur" and "Sedgwick 3-7154." They
were the address and former phone number of Jafsie. The board was pried
loose and presented to Hauptmann, still in custody. More than once he admitted that the writing was his, and he provided an explanation for writing
Condon's address that was as peculiar as his admission had been unexpected.
"I must have read it in the paper about the story," he said. "I was a little bit
interest, and keep a little bit record of it and maybe I was just in the closet
and was reading the paper and put down the address."

Then another discovery was made at the house. Although the lead detective from New Jersey had been in Hauptmann's attic several times, he had
not previously noticed one of the pine planks in its southwest corner was
shorter than the other boards by a good eight feet. This detective suddenly
recalled the wood expert, Arthur Koehler, commenting that rail 16 of the ladder had some prior use. Rail 16 was brought to the Bronx and laid across the
crossbeams of the attic floor. Four holes in the rail lined up exactly with
four nailholes in the floor joists.

Arthur Koehler was summoned. Although a little more than an inch of
wood had been cut away between the rail and the original floor plank, the
number, color, dimension, and pattern of the rings indicated to him that the
one piece of the wood had been cut from the other. Koehler also examined
a hand plane taken from Hauptmann's garage, whose blade markings, he
said, revealed that it had been used in making the ladder.

The police searched for some implement that might have been used to
punch the holes in the strange design of interlocking circles on the ransom
notes; but no such tool nor the symbol's significance was ever discovered.
They did find, however, yet another stash of money in the garage, this one
in a two-by-four, which had been pounded between two wall joists and
drilled with six holes. In five of them were rolls of ransom money. In the
larger sixth hole they found a small, loaded pistol. Again authorities asked
Hauptmann if he was concealing any more money before they confronted
him with the goods.

Upon the Lindberghs' return to New Jersey, Colonel Schwarzkopf informed them of the evidence being marshaled against Hauptmann. For two

and one-half years, the police and the press had referred to the unknown perpetrators of the crime in the plural. With the apprehension of Hauptmann, all such references changed to the singular. Although Anna Hauptmann claimed not to have known that her husband's first name was anything other than Richard, the press now spoke of him as Bruno.

On Wednesday, September 26, 1934, Lindbergh appeared before a grand jury in the Bronx County Courthouse. He had little to add to the evidence against Hauptmann, but his mere presence reminded the twenty-three jurors why it was so important that they serve justice. After fifteen minutes answering questions—mostly about the ransom money—a juror asked if Lindbergh would recognize the voice of "Cemetery John" if he heard it again. "It would be very difficult to sit here and say that I could pick a man by that voice," Lindbergh said of the few syllables he had heard shouted from a distance of some two hundred feet over two and one-half years earlier. Upon completing his testimony, however, District Attorney James Foley asked if he wished to see the man they had arrested and hear his voice. Lindbergh said yes.

Hauptmann was indicted for extortion that afternoon. The next morning he was brought to the D.A.'s office in the Bronx, where a group of detectives were waiting. Hauptmann was ordered to stand in various parts of the room and say, "Hey, Doctor! Here, Doctor! Over here!" After Hauptmann was ordered back to his prison cell, the tall man wearing a cap and sunglasses huddled among the detectives went to Foley's desk and averred, "That is the voice I heard that night."

In October 1934, a grand jury sat in the Hunterdon County Courthouse in Flemington, New Jersey, to determine if there was enough evidence to indict Hauptmann on murder charges. New Jersey law stated that if a death occurred during the commission of a felony, the felon was responsible for the taking of that life even if it were accidental or taken by somebody else. The State had only to prove that Hauptmann had entered the house to commit a theft and that the baby had been killed as a result of that crime. Instead of five to thirty years for kidnapping, the state's Attorney General, David Wilentz, could ask for the death penalty. Under Wilentz's direction, most of the case's leading players faced the grand jury, including a cameo appearance by Charles Lindbergh. He attested to his recognizing Bruno Richard Hauptmann's voice.

Hauptmann was indicted for murder in the first degree, and the dozens who had gathered outside the courthouse in the small town cheered. A crowd of one thousand stood in silence beneath their lit torches the night of October nineteenth, when he was extradited to New Jersey and incarcerated in the new Flemington jail, just behind the courthouse. He pled not guilty at his arraignment, and his trial was set for January 2, 1935. Until that time, round-the-clock guards were forbidden to speak to him. The overhead light in his cell burned day and night so long as he was in custody.

Primarily for financial reasons, Hauptmann changed attorneys. His wife had retained a sympathetic but ineffectual noncriminal lawyer to represent him until a reporter from the *New York Journal* approached her with an intriguing offer. For the exclusive rights to Anna Hauptmann's story, the *Journal* agreed to hire well-known criminal attorney Edward J. Reilly to defend her husband. The Hearst paper would also pick up such miscellaneous expenses as Anna Hauptmann's lodging in New Jersey during the trial. The deal seemed irresistible, even though the former "Bull of Brooklyn," as he had been called, was now referred to as "Death House Reilly," for defending so many murder suspects. Unknown to the Hauptmanns, the fifty-two-year-old Reilly was a syphilitic alcoholic, loud of voice and dress. In other ways, he was even worse suited for the role of defending a man the press had already convicted. Reilly not only kept a photograph of his hero Charles Lindbergh on his desk but also believed, as he told an FBI agent, "that he knew Hauptmann was guilty, didn't like him, and was anxious to see him get the chair." On being named Hauptmann's counsel, Reilly printed special stationery for the case, which featured a ladder embossed in red.

Reilly mounted his basic defense—gathering witnesses to support Hauptmann's alibis: that he had been in New York picking up his wife at work on the night of the kidnapping; that he had been at a party with friends in the Bronx the night the ransom had been paid; and that the money in his garage had come from Isidor Fisch. Meanwhile, the Lindberghs tried to resume their lives at Next Day Hill. Fortunately for Anne and Charles, just as the case threatened to consume them all over again, a houseguest arrived.

Harold Nicolson—whom the Lindberghs had met the previous year—had been engaged as the official biographer of Dwight Morrow. He moved into Next Day Hill for ten weeks so that he could peruse his subject's papers and interview his friends and relatives. Although trying to concentrate on Morrow, Nicolson was suddenly in a position to have greater access to Lindbergh than almost anybody outside his family had ever had. And while Nicolson was meant to be recording the past, it was impossible not to be drawn into the current controversy.

"This is the only household in the United States in which the L. baby is not discussed," Nicolson wrote his wife, Vita Sackville-West. Although Nicolson had heard that Lindbergh was silent and aloof, he was surprised to find him affable and even garrulous. His somewhat nervous "chatter, chatter, chatter" at breakfast allowed him to keep his mind off the one forbidden topic. "I daresay I shall get the whole tragic story one day in a flood of confidence," Nicolson reported to his wife. "But one has the feeling that the wound is still terribly raw and cannot be touched. He is interesting about America, which he knows very well. I find him, apart from his actual physical charm, a really delightful companion." Nicolson was one of the few to detect his host's humor from the start, as when Lindbergh warned him about his dog, telling Nicolson that if he tried to pass him, Thor might grab hold of him. "By the throat?" Nicolson asked. "Not necessarily," Lindbergh replied. "And if he does that, you must just stay still and holler all you can."

Nicolson surprised himself, succumbing to Lindbergh's personality as he did. Anne's former mentor from Smith, Mina Curtiss, for one, initially found him "really no more than a mechanic, and that had it not been for the lone eagle flight, he would now be in charge of a gasoline station on the outskirts at St. Louis." Nicolson, on the other hand, discovered "a sensible man, without unthoughtful prejudices and with a direct approach to things." His admiration only deepened as he observed Lindbergh's uncommon decency. He was repeatedly impressed with the hero's sense of proportion, how he "never shows off and never talks big." He found Lindbergh's reputation for sulkiness and bad manners entirely the result of the public's desire to pick at his public image. "What I loathe most," Lindbergh told Nicolson one day, "are the silly women who bring their kids up to shake hands with me at railway stations. It is embarrassing for me, and embarrassing for the kids. It makes me fair sick." After ten days in his company, the rather particular houseguest was finding Lindbergh "as simple and refreshing as a stream in the woods." Another month, and he decided that Lindbergh was nothing less than American royalty, that he "really is a hero in this continent and he never cheapens himself."

He admired Anne as well. Nicolson read her article "Flying Around the North Atlantic" in the latest *National Geographic* and pronounced it "excellent." He turned to Charles and said, "You should take another trip so that she can write another story, for the writing instinct, once it is started, is much stronger than the flying one!" Anne was flattered, further encouraged a few weeks later when Nicolson reported that his wife also liked the article.

Before daybreak on the morning of December 3, 1934, the night watchman at Next Day Hill knocked on the Lindberghs' bedroom door. "Colonel, Pasadena calling," he said. Mrs. Morrow was in California, where Elisabeth had recently been operated on for appendicitis, so this predawn call did not bode well. Lindbergh took the phone and said, "I'm afraid that's bad news." Anne stood by his side, scribbling on a pad, "Tell her I'll come out." Charles had only to shake his head. They returned to their bed, where he tried to comfort her. After all Anne had been through in the past two years, it was difficult to accept yet another family tragedy. The pain only increased when Mrs. Morrow returned to Englewood and, in an utterly thoughtless moment, blurted to Anne, "Of all my children, why did it have to be Elisabeth?"

Her sister's death increased Anne's devotion to her husband. While he took charge of the burial arrangements, she realized "how I must be good to Charles and love him always, and the things I must cherish and the things I must crush." Like him, Anne began to steel her emotions, realizing she could not "count on anything." She vowed to rededicate her life to Charles, as she resolved "to finish the book for him, to give him a home and a sense of freedom and power and fulfillment." But first of all, she resigned herself "not to disappoint C. at the Trial."

The Lindberghs had little time to mourn, only a few weeks before they had to present themselves to the public again. Hundreds of reporters, photographers, columnists, radio announcers, and technicians were already converging upon the little courthouse in Flemington. The fifty rooms at the town's Union Hotel had not had a vacancy in a month, forcing the majority of visitors to scramble for places to sleep. Half the houses in Flemington opened their doors to strangers, including one where Anna Hauptmann stayed. Country clubs, taverns, and poolhalls rented rooms and floorspace. By New Year's Eve, thousands of tourists were angling for ringside seats. There was carousing in the streets.

Within earshot of the uproar, Bruno Richard Hauptmann tried to remain calm as he lay upon his cot, smoking cigarettes and reading. But he spent most of his time pacing the prison bull pen. "His reading has been confined to short periods, then the pacing would resume," observed one of the guards. "He also has a worried expression."

12

CIRCUS MAXIMUS

"The newspaper idea of not surrounding oneself with
mystery was to tell them everything they wanted to know.
I had no intention of doing this."

—C.A.L.

"OYEZ! OYEZ! OYEZ! OYEZ!" SANG OUT THE COURT crier at 10:10 o'clock on the Wednesday morning of January 2, 1935.

Microphones and cameras were banned from the courtroom so long as the trial was in session, but a telegraph pole at the slushy corner of Main and Court streets in the center of Flemington, New Jersey, radiated a dense network of wires in every direction, connecting the entire world to the proceedings in the snow-covered, century-old courthouse.

Up the seven stone steps from Main Street and past the four thick Doric columns, practically every square inch of the two-and-one-half-story, white neo-colonial building was requisitioned for purposes of communication. The Associated Press had installed four teletypes, each capable of sending an astonishing 3,600 words an hour. Western Union had installed 132 wires, enough to transmit three million words a day. The Postal Telegraph and Cable Company had fifty operators manning thirty-six wires, providing a capability of one million words a day.

Direct broadcasting of the court proceedings may have been prohibited, but many of the nation's leading news commentators came to Flemington to deliver their nightly reports of the day's events in court. Gabriel Heatter, for one, also intended to issue live reports every day during the noon recess. The leading stations in New York City hired famous attorneys and legal scholars to deliver commentary.

Newspapers assembled teams to cover the trial from every

angle. The New York *Mirror,* for example, sent its editor in chief and lead columnist, Arthur Brisbane, for commentary, Damon Runyon for reportage, and the nation's most powerful columnist and popular radio commentator, Walter Winchell, for his staccato personal impressions. The New York *Evening Journal,* another Hearst paper, had two young "sob sisters" vying for scoops, Dorothy Kilgallen and Sheilah Graham. Both played second fiddle to Hearst's star reporter, Adela Rogers St. Johns, who showed up every day in a different Hattie Carnegie outfit paid for out of her expense account. The *Herald Tribune* placed no limitations on the length of the pieces Joseph Alsop submitted. For the duration of the trial, many of the nation's most famous authors could be seen in town, reporting on what everyone agreed was "The Trial of the Century." With but a touch of irony, H. L. Mencken went even farther, calling the trial the biggest story "since the Resurrection."

"His Honor Justice Trenchard," announced the court crier; and the seventy-one-year-old Thomas W. Trenchard of Trenton entered the courtroom. Ordinarily the thirty-by-forty-five-foot room—with its high ceiling, large windows, and electric lights suspended from the ceiling—gave a capacious feeling. But some five hundred people were sardined into space meant to accommodate a third that number. Trenchard, with his gray hair and mustache, was known to most of those present for never having had one of his decisions in a murder trial reversed.

At nine o'clock that morning, several dozen members of the public had been permitted up the narrow winding stairs and into the courtroom. Some were sent to seats in the upstairs gallery—supported by four white pillars—on a first-come, first-serve basis. After a few minutes, the courthouse doors were closed and admission was by ticket only—red for journalists and photographers, white for officials and members of the bar, yellow for telegraphers, who were allowed into the top-story wire room but not the courtroom itself. The county sheriff himself signed every one of the 150 press tickets, each of which had a number that corresponded to a place at one of the unpainted benches and tables behind a low chestnut balustrade or off to the side. No typewriters were allowed in the court, so most reporters scribbled in notebooks. One reporter estimated that a million words a day would spew out of that small room, not counting the court transcripts, which would be released to the press as fast as they could be reproduced.

Shortly before ten o'clock that morning the supporting players had taken their places. The prosecution lawyers entered first, seating themselves around a table in front of the balustrade close to the jury box. The short and lean Attorney General, David T. Wilentz, not yet forty but already a star in the state of New Jersey, led them in. The son of Latvian Jews, he had come to America when he was four, at which time his father established a cigar factory in Perth Amboy. David did not attend college but read law at New York

A pioneer in commercial aviation, Charles Lindbergh surveys South American routes in 1929 with Juan Trippe, founder of Pan American.

The beginnings of America's rocket program—physicist Robert H. Goddard, flanked by his two strongest supporters, Harry Guggenheim and Charles Lindbergh.

Dr. Alexis Carrel, Nobel laureate. Lindbergh's mentor and hero.

Dr. Carrel and Lindbergh lunching at the Rockefeller Institute, where they developed a perfusion pump, soon known worldwide as an artificial heart.

"The Lindbergh Baby" on his first birthday, June 22, 1931.

March 1932. Outside the baby's room of the Lindbergh house near Hopewell, New Jersey. For two and a half years, the authorities had no idea as to who climbed the ladder. (New Jersey State Police Museum)

The Lindberghs escaped
the hysteria that
followed their son's fatal
kidnapping by traveling
to remote regions.
Greenland, summer
1933.

Cape Verde Islands,
repairing sun damage.

Anne at Porto Praia.

Leaving the Shetland Islands.

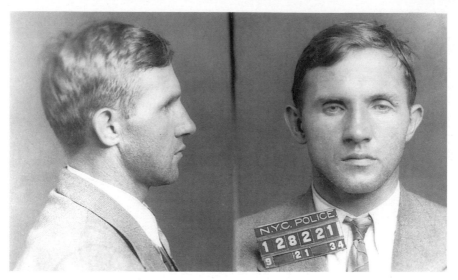

Bruno Richard Hauptmann. Arrested for committing "The Crime of the Century."
(New Jersey State Police Museum)

In January 1935, the entire world was plugged into the courthouse in Flemington, New
Jersey. (UPI/Corbis-Bettmann)

Lindbergh with the chief of the New Jersey State Police, H. Norman Schwarzkopf, whose son would distinguish himself a half-century later in the Persian Gulf War. (UPI/Corbis-Bettmann)

The "Baby's Mother" comes to testify.

For the prosecution: New Jersey Attorney General David T. Wilentz and "Jafsie," John F. Condon, the go-between who paid the Lindbergh ransom money in a Bronx cemetery. (UPI/Corbis-Bettmann)

Hauptmann and his attorney, Edward "Death House" Reilly. (New Jersey State Police Museum)

Lindbergh on the stand. Once he testified, his attorney said afterward, the trial was over. (UPI/Corbis-Bettmann)

"The Trial of the Century." While both teams of attorneys shared a light moment, Hauptmann (far right) warily looked on and Lindbergh (six seats to his right) studiously looked away. (UPI/Corbis-Bettmann)

Anne, coping with tragedy.

Charles, Anne, and their second son, Jon, could never appear in public without being photographed. Threats were already being made on Jon's life.

Flight. The Lindberghs became exiles—arriving in Liverpool, December 31, 1935.

The Lindberghs found security at Long Barn in England. Jon and Anne with their dogs Skean and Thor.

The Lindberghs take to the skies again. In Ireland, he took Irish Prime Minister Eamon De Valera for his first flight.

Refueling at Raipur, 1937.

Illiec. The private island the Lindberghs bought off the Brittany coast, 1938.

Lindbergh visited
Germany six times
between 1936 and 1938,
a fascination that
plagued him for the rest
of his life. Below, he and
Anne meet Hermann
Goering. (Goering
photo Bayerische
Staatsbibliothek
München)

After three years abroad, Lindbergh returned to speak against U.S. intervention in World War II. He became the leading spokesman for America First—a big political tent that also included such diverse personalities as Burton K. Wheeler, Democratic Senator from Montana, Mrs. Kathleen Norris, popular novelist, and American socialist leader Norman Thomas. New York City, 1941. (Brown Brothers)

Lindbergh at the podium. Fort Wayne, Indiana, 1941. (AP/Wide World Photos)

Charles with sons Land and Jon. Lloyd Neck, Long Island, 1940.

On holiday. Florida, 1941.

Because of Lindbergh's prewar speeches, FDR would not allow him into the armed forces; but after Pearl Harbor, Lindbergh found other ways to serve. He became a human guinea pig, testing the effects of altitude at the Mayo Clinic, September 1942.

He also served as a "technical representative" in the South Pacific—where he unofficially flew on fifty bombing missions. Emirau Island, May 1944.

Law School. A smooth talker, he became a leading attorney in his hometown. Active in Democratic politics in Middlesex County, he attracted the attention of the party bosses. After helping elect A. Harry Moore governor of New Jersey, he was named Attorney General. A devotee of the racetrack, Wilentz—with his snazzy suits, turned-down hat brims, and ever-present cigar—was a press favorite, always good for a dramatic photograph and a ready quote. His son Robert later held that his father was personally against the death penalty and probably would not have prosecuted Hauptmann himself had he not been completely convinced of his guilt.

Colleagues just as sure surrounded him: his chief assistant, Anthony Hauck, Jr., the district attorney of Hunterdon County, who had prosecuted John Hughes Curtis; Joseph Lanigan, who worked out of the state attorney general's office; and George K. Large, a former judge and Flemington attorney.

Close behind them entered the attorneys for the defense. The voluminous and florid chief attorney, Edward J. Reilly, and his assistant Frederick Pope wore dark-gray morning coats and gray striped trousers. The rest of their team—Egbert Rosecrans of Blairstown and C. Lloyd Fisher, who had defended John Curtis—wore business suits.

Seconds after Judge Trenchard had mounted the U-shaped bench and settled into his high-backed chair, a murmur spread through the courtroom. Bruno Richard Hauptmann entered, wearing a grayish-brown, double-breasted suit, a handkerchief in his breast pocket. He was not handcuffed. Pale but neatly groomed, he walked slowly to his chair near the middle of the row just inside the rail. After a brief word with his counsel, Hauptmann looked up to find a thousand eyes staring at him.

Before the audience could ponder his blank expression, their attention was drawn to the most anticipated entrance of the morning. Although the rumor was that he would appear only to testify, Charles Lindbergh—in a gray suit without a vest—strode into the courtroom, walking between the attorneys' desks and the rail, right past Hauptmann. Without making any eye contact with him, he sat four chairs away. Whenever Lindbergh leaned forward to confer with the state's attorneys, some could see that he was carrying a pistol in a shoulder holster. Sun streamed through the dozen large windows of the courtroom. Outside in the January cold, hundreds filled Main Street, many pressing their noses against the windows of the courthouse.

The once quiet town, which served as the marketplace for the surrounding chicken farmers, had become nothing less than an amusement park devoted to the Hauptmann trial. The press dominated the social activity, turning a salon at the back of the four-story, red-brick Union Hotel into "Nellie's Tap Room," their private saloon, at which they drank, swapped stories, and discussed every detail of the case. Tourists swarmed about the New Jersey town, and vendors hawked autographed pictures of the Lindberghs—with forged signatures—along with courthouse bookends and replicas of the kidnap ladder, with green ribbons, to be worn around the neck. One entrepreneurial towhead snipped his own curls and sold packages of them at five dollars each as the Lindbergh Baby's locks. Over the ensuing weeks, the level of tastelessness would only increase.

Normally the sidewalks of Flemington rolled up at sundown, and the proprietors of the Union Hotel served fifty meals a day. Now they kept their dining room open from seven o'clock in the morning until midnight, offering such specialties as Lamb Chops Jafsie, Baked Beans Wilentz, and, for dessert, ice cream sundaes called "Lindys," to as many as a thousand people. Even the Women's Council of the Methodist Church learned to turn tidy profits, serving as many as one hundred lunches every weekday to the overflow of attorneys and writers. With the arrival of the trial, the Mayor of Flemington proudly announced, not a single townsman was on relief, as any local could find a job as a waitress or messenger boy.

Lindbergh's businesslike demeanor that first morning made it clear that he had no intention of interacting with the press or public. In fact, he and Schwarzkopf, who had driven with him, had parked the car on Main Street and walked openly through the crowd into the courthouse with great solemnity. For Lindbergh, more than Hauptmann's fate rested in the balance that month; he was judging America.

"For several weeks it will be necessary for me to devote most of my time to the trial at Flemington," he wrote in a memorandum to himself. "After it is completed," he added, "I feel that it may be advisable to take my family away from the New York area for an indefinite period. Under the circumstances which now exist I doubt that it is possible for us to live near New York in reasonable safety or peace. The combination of our present-day press and the uncontrolled crime situation necessitates our leading such a guarded and restricted life that among other reasons I feel is detrimental for my son to grow up under its environment." Lindbergh hoped time might improve living conditions for him and his family; but, he added, "until it does I must find a home where my family can live in safety and under conditions which better permit constructive thought and action." The pandemonium aside, Lindbergh hoped the citizens of Flemington could conduct a fair trial. Without that, he feared, the case would never die.

With rapt attention, Lindbergh leaned forward in his chair and rested his chin on his hand, as Judge Trenchard ordered the Sheriff to begin jury selection. The names of local citizens were written on pieces of paper and placed in a glass-and-wooden box, from which the Sheriff pulled one name at a time. Each person was sworn in, then seated in what visiting English author Ford Madox Ford described as "a common kitchen chair." Then the lawyers tested the integrity of each by asking about the influence of the press, specifically the most notorious member of its corps, who had already served as "Bruno" Hauptmann's judge and hangman. Time and again the defense asked potential jurors, "Have you read the Winchell column in *The Daily Mirror?* Or heard his broadcast? And from what you have heard, have you formed any opinion?" Nobody familiar with Winchell's position claimed to have been influenced by it.

Six men and four women, most in their thirties and forties, were selected. They were a cross-section of the town—a machinist, an insurance salesman, a worker at a CCC camp, a railroad worker, two farmers, a widow, a stenographer, and two housewives.

Judge Trenchard had intended to adjourn that day at four o'clock, but the old clock suspended on the front of the gallery had stopped ten minutes before the hour. It was almost another hour before he realized what had happened. Then Trenchard ordered four constables to escort the jurors to the Union Hotel, where they would be quartered on the fourth floor for the duration of the trial. He remanded Hauptmann back across the "Bridge of Sighs" to his cell.

On the town's streets one could literally hear the clacking of typewriters, as journalists filed their reports for their morning papers. As novelist Kathleen Norris noted in an article for *The New York Times,* "The big story is on its way to every corner of the world. In Africa, in China, in Soviet Russia and Fascist Italy they will be reading what American justice has done here today. . . . history is to be written in these next few weeks, never to be obliterated from our records."

The second-day crowd in Flemington was even larger than the first, with hundreds queuing up in the predawn cold for admission tickets. The mob hoped for a glimpse of Lindbergh. When they broke ranks to rush his arriving car, Lindbergh and Schwarzkopf drove to the rear of the jail and entered the courthouse through the back.

Before noon a retired carpenter and an unemployed bookkeeper had joined the jury. The only interruption in the procedure occurred during voir dire, when Anne Morrow Lindbergh, long sequestered from the public, entered the courtroom.

Wearing a black silk suit, a shell-pink blouse, a simple black satin beret, and a blue fox fur, the diminutive figure briskly entered the room from behind the bench with Mrs. Norman Schwarzkopf. As they found their seats in the second row of chairs, behind their husbands, the audience audibly whispered her name. Many actually stood to get a better look. Judge Trenchard had to tap his gavel and raise his hand to bring the spectators back to their seats. Charles watched her until he realized she was perfectly composed, then returned his gaze to the jury selection.

Once the twelfth juror was chosen, the judge dismissed the dozens of others in the pool, leaving a block of vacant seats in the courtroom. When the Sheriff opened the doors to fill them, hundreds flooded past him—filling the aisles, standing against the back walls, hanging over the balcony.

Judge Trenchard turned to the jury, admonishing the eight men and four women to refrain from reading newspapers, listening to the radio, and attending public assemblages of any type, "more particularly where public addresses of one kind or another are to be made." With that, he ordered the case to commence.

Attorney General Wilentz's opening statement explained the New Jersey law that stated that the death of anyone during the commission of a burglary is considered murder in the first degree. "Now, on the first day of March 1932," Wilentz asserted, "the State will prove to you that a very distinguished citizen of this country" was a resident of Hunterdon County and that his son—"a happy, normal, jovial, delightful little tot"—was killed by "the gentleman in the custody of the sheriff's guards right in the rear of the distinguished members of the Bar who make up the defense counsel."

For the next forty-five minutes, Wilentz detailed the crime as he believed Hauptmann had committed it. "He came there with his ladder, placed it against that house. He broke into and entered at night the Lindbergh home with the intent to steal the child and its clothing. And he did. Not only with the intent, but he actually committed a battery upon the child and did steal it and did steal its clothing. . . . Then as he went out that window and down that ladder of his, the ladder broke. He had more weight going down than he had when he was coming up. And down he went with this child. In the commission of that burglary that child was instantaneously killed when it received that first blow. It received a horrible fracture, the dimensions of which, when you hear about it will convince you that death was instantaneous." Wilentz proceeded to describe Hauptmann's subsequent flight with his "dead package," the hasty burial after removing the baby's sleeping suit, the Lindberghs' shocking discovery that their child had been taken, the ransom notes, the role of Dr. Condon, the meetings at Woodlawn Cemetery and St. Raymond's, where the ransom money was exchanged for false instructions to the missing child. He told of Lindbergh, Dr. Condon, and Colonel Breckinridge getting into a plane and how "Lindy, who could find a speck at the end of the earth, couldn't find his child because Hauptmann had murdered it." He described Lindbergh's having to return empty-handed "to the home of sorrow." He graphically described the accidental discovery of the baby's corpse in the woods off a New Jersey backroad. As he did, Lindbergh showed no emotion, fixing his gaze on Wilentz. His pallid wife lowered her head, casting her eyes down. By the time she looked up, she had blanched further.

By then, Wilentz was describing Hauptmann's capture. He explained how the defendant had spent the ransom money and how he had lied about how much he had hidden in his house and garage; how he had written Dr. Condon's address and telephone inside his child's closet; how the government had traced the wood of the ladder to the very lumberyard at which Hauptmann had purchased his own lumber. Not only that, Wilentz said, "he has got this ladder right around his neck; he took part of that attic of his and built the ladder with it—and we will prove that to you beyond any doubt."

Wilentz concluded his opening remarks insisting that Hauptmann had "committed this crime, he had planned it for months, because he wanted money—money—money—lots of money he wanted, and he got it." He said Hauptmann wanted that money so that he could "live a life of luxury and ease so he would not have to work." Indeed, Wilentz noted, he quit his job the very day he collected the $50,000 . . . and in "the midst of the worst depression of this land, in May 1932, he spends four hundred dollars for a radio," thousands of dollars more in the stock market. After assuring the jury that the State would prove all these "facts" to them, Wilentz demanded the ultimate penalty for murder in the first degree. Hauptmann sat through most of the formal accusation with his arms across his chest, watching Wilentz as he paced before the jury. When Wilentz finished, a few spectators applauded.

Edward Reilly rose to move for a mistrial "on the grounds that the impassioned appeal of the attorney general was not a proper opening. It was a summation intended to inflame the minds of this jury against this defendant before the trial starts." Judge Trenchard denied the motion, though he cautioned the jury to "keep their minds open until the last word has been said in this courtroom."

With a few minutes until the lunch break, Wilentz called his first witness, a civil engineer and surveyor who described the precise location of the Lindbergh house and property. The Lindberghs lunched with the Schwarzkopfs at the nearby home of prosecuting attorney George Large.

An hour into the afternoon session, Wilentz called Anne Lindbergh to the stand. She nervously sat in the witness chair even before being sworn in. She stepped down to take her oath then returned to the wooden chair. While her testimony was not crucial to the case, the State knew that the presence of the baby's young mother would be powerful. She was able to identify her son's sleeping garment, the undershirt Betty Gow had sewn, which had been found on the corpse in the woods, and the baby's thumbguard. She detailed her last day with her son, including how she had stood beneath his window, thus explaining the set of woman's footprints found in the mud. With great composure, she looked at a photograph of her child, smiling slightly as she identified it. Then she told of the frantic search through the house for the baby that night. Anne's voice was faint but firm, commanding the attention of everybody in the room—including Hauptmann, who almost never took his eyes off her. Charles took obvious pride in his wife's "perfect self-control" during her forty minutes on the stand.

Edward Reilly approached the bench, only to say, "that the grief of Mrs. Lindbergh requires no cross-examination."

At 3:30, Wilentz called his next witness. In a gray suit and gray shirt and tie, Charles Lindbergh's tall, lanky frame practically seemed too big for the witness chair. He was no longer armed. Wilentz walked him through the first days of the crime, up until receiving the second ransom note, which arrived through the mail. It being the close of an already impactful day, Wilentz kept his star witness from dropping any bombshells.

Gathering from the reaction in court that the media would be swaying public sentiment against his client during the next few hours, Defense Attorney Reilly went to Trenton, where he spoke over Station WNEW. He told the public that he was preparing a powerful defense, one which would establish that Hauptmann had nothing to do with the crime and that the kidnapping had been planned and executed by a gang. Knowing that Lindbergh would be moving public opinion even more the next day, Reilly asserted that he had "an awful lot of questions to ask Colonel Lindbergh, an awful lot of things I want answers to. An awful lot of questions."

The next morning, Lindbergh returned to the stand, where, prompted by David Wilentz's questions, he continued his narration. When he reached the night of April 2, 1932, at St. Raymond's Cemetery in the Bronx, he spoke of seeing Dr. Condon cross Whittemore Avenue and hearing "very clearly a voice coming from the cemetery, to the best of my belief calling Dr. Condon." Lindbergh said he heard, "in a foreign accent, 'Hey, Doctor!' " Wilentz quickly moved Lindbergh through the rest of his testimony—another fifty questions—before bringing him back to the night of April second. Then he asked, ". . . since that time, have you heard the same voice?"

"Yes, I have," Lindbergh replied.

"Whose voice was it, Colonel, that you heard in the vicinity of St. Raymond's Cemetery that night, saying 'Hey, Doctor'?"

Lindbergh turned from the Attorney General and, for the first time, looked directly at the defendant. "That was Hauptmann's voice," he declaimed loudly and clearly. The accused stared right back at him, with a stone-cold expression. A hush fell over the courtroom, then an audible communal gasp. A few more questions followed about Lindbergh's hearing the voice a second time in District Attorney Foley's office in the Bronx and about viewing his son's corpse in the Trenton morgue.

Colonel Breckinridge was present for his client's testimony and later told his stepson, Oren Root, "The minute Lindbergh 'pointed his finger' at Hauptmann, the trial was over. 'Jesus Christ' himself said he was *convinced* this was the man who killed his son. Who was anybody to doubt him or deny him justice?" Another month of testimony remained.

In the next hour before lunch, Edward Reilly tried to regain some ground. Instead of challenging Lindbergh's testimony, however, he attempted only to plant doubts. He asked about the Lindbergh and Morrow servants and some of their mysterious demises, about Betty Gow's relationship with "Red" Johnson, about the failure of Wahgoosh the dog to bark, about any hostility from neighbors in the Sourland Mountains, about the possibility that the kidnapper abducted the baby and exited through the front door of the house. None of it seemed to matter. At one point, Reilly tried to impugn the fallibility of the police; and when Lindbergh replied, "I think we have very good police," many in the court broke into laughter and applause.

At another point, Reilly tried to set a trap for Lindbergh but fell into it himself. Reilly asked the witness if he had not, in fact, believed that John Curtis had been in contact with the gang that had kidnapped his child. The court interrupted, pointing out to Reilly that he was assuming that the people with whom Lindbergh was negotiating had possession of the child. Prosecutor Wilentz said that he did not object to the witness answering the question so long as Lindbergh was asked his present belief. Reilly accepted the condition, and the jury was allowed to hear Lindbergh state that he currently believed that the defendant was guilty of the kidnapping. Lindbergh's opinion was no doubt as prejudicial as it was immaterial.

Furthermore, Reilly never attacked the part of Lindbergh's testimony which was as vulnerable as it had been damaging. He did not ask one question about the three syllables—"Hey, Doctor"—Lindbergh claimed to have heard. In fact, Lindbergh had testified before the grand jury that the voice he had heard had uttered two syllables—"Hey, Doc"; and Wilentz had said in his opening that Lindbergh had heard the phrase twice, not once, as Lindbergh now testified. Even overlooking these variances, Reilly did not raise the issue of Lindbergh's reliability, his ability to recall three distant syllables over three years.

President Roosevelt delivered his State of the Union Address that day, but *The New York Times* relegated it to its far left-hand column, making room for a four-column headline on the right: COL. LINDBERGH NAMES HAUPTMANN AS KIDNAPPER AND TAKER OF RANSOM; COOL IN 3-HOUR CROSS-EXAMINATION. In a letter to her mother-in-law, Anne Lindbergh passed along the observation of one reporter: "I think *Reilly* withstood the cross-examination very well."

The Lindberghs spent the weekend at Next Day Hill, but it was impossible to keep the subject of the trial out of the house. The topic filled the papers and the airwaves; and the Lindberghs were hosting Betty Gow, who had returned from Scotland for the sole purpose of testifying, knowing her absence would only fuel further speculation as to her involvement in the crime. Although Lindbergh had scrupulously avoided discussing the case, except in court, on Sunday he granted a special interview to Lauren "Deak" Lyman of *The New York Times,* a reporter he liked and trusted, expressing his wish that the trial be conducted as fairly as possible. The article contained no quotes from Lindbergh, but it stated that he did not view the case as the battle the press had been depicting. Lyman said Lindbergh wanted "to bring out the truth regardless of whether it should create doubt or conviction of the defendant's guilt, and regardless of whether the facts were brought out by the defense or the prosecution." Toward that end, Lindbergh said he deliberately avoided ever looking at the jury for fear of prejudicing them.

More than sixty thousand tourists descended upon Flemington that Sunday. Many drove to the narrow Mount Rose Highway, where the baby's body had been discovered. More than five thousand people visited the courthouse, and local peace officers admitted groups of two hundred at a time into the courtroom, allowing them to sit in the jury box, the witness stand, and the judge's chair. The most awesome sight on the tour, however, was of the connecting building. The light that glowed through one of its windows came from the bulb that hung over Hauptmann's prison cot.

The featured witness during the trial's second week was Betty Gow. In three hours of testimony, the thirty-year-old nurse corroborated the Lindberghs' accounts of the events of March 1, 1932. She identified the undershirt she had made for the baby, establishing that the kidnapper had committed a burglary by breaking and entering and stealing these articles of clothing. Betty Gow's further identification of the baby's sleeping suit suggested that the kidnapper and the ransom collector were one and the same person.

Edward Reilly tried both to implicate and imprecate Betty, failing in each attempt. He asked about her relationship with "Red" Johnson, which she described as an innocent friendship with an innocent man. When Reilly tried to discredit her because the State was paying $650 for her testimony, Betty explained that she was being paid only for her passage between America and Scotland and compensation for lost wages. "Mr. Reilly got very short change out of Betty," Kathleen Norris added in her column in the *Times* that day. Upon leaving the stand, Miss Gow collapsed in an anteroom of the courthouse.

The next day, two witnesses identified Hauptmann. The first was Amandus Hochmuth, an eighty-six-year-old man who lived near the Lindbergh property and claimed to have seen a man in a green car with a ladder turn toward the Lindbergh estate on the morning of March 1, 1932. When asked if he could identify the man in the car that day, Hochmuth pointed a trembling finger at Hauptmann. Suddenly the lights in the courtroom went out, and Reilly thundered, "It's the Lord's wrath over a lying witness." The crowd laughed, but Trenchard brought order to the court. Wilentz re-posed his question, and this time, the old man trudged from the witness chair to Hauptmann and touched his knee. Hauptmann only shook his head, then turned to his wife and said, *"Der Alte ist verrückt!"* ("The old man is crazy.")

He may have been, and then some. The bespectacled octogenarian apparently had cataracts. But during cross-examination, Reilly questioned the witness's sanity, not his vision. The spry old man came across as credible, thus placing Hauptmann in the vicinity of the Lindberghs' estate on the day of the crime.

The second identification came from Joseph Perrone, the Bronx taxicab driver, who had delivered the letter directing Dr. Condon to his first meeting with "Cemetery John." When the prosecution asked if that man was present in the court, Perrone walked over to Hauptmann, slapped his shoulder, and said loudly to the jury, "That is the man." Hauptmann stared at him, then snarled, "You're a liar."

Six hundred people packed into the courtroom the following morning, anticipating a dramatic day of testimony. Jafsie was taking the stand. A natural ham, the corpulent Dr. John F. Condon strutted slowly to the witness chair and proved incapable of responding to the plainest question without gilding his answer. When asked, for example, where he had lived his seventy-four years, Condon replied: "In the most beautiful borough in the world."

For five hours, David Wilentz had to prod Condon through his bombast, trying to get the witness to limit his responses. Edward Reilly, no stranger to grandiloquence himself, encouraged him to blather, hoping to trip him up in his own testimony. With great fervor Condon described advertising to be the go-between, hearing from the kidnapper, meeting Lindbergh, and his subsequent encounters with "John" at the two cemeteries. Although he had a few moments of confusion—as when he mistestified about the first time he had seen the unusual hole-punched signature—nobody got the better of Jafsie, whose appearance on the stand included extravagant hand gestures and re-enacted dialogue, complete with an imitation of "Cemetery John"'s German accent. At day's end, three moments from the performance lingered in everybody's memory, the three occasions when Wilentz asked Condon to identify John.

"John," Condon bellowed each time in stentorian tones, articulating each syllable as he stared into the sleepless eyes of the defendant, "is Bruno Richard Hauptmann!" Hauptmann sat with his arms and legs crossed and stared right back. Lindbergh leaned forward, resting his elbows on his knees, fixing his eyes on the witness. After court that afternoon, the defense attorneys suggested to the press that Condon's few fumbled answers indicated that he was both unreliable and possibly an accomplice to the crime. But the general consensus was that Condon had been a powerful witness.

Over the next week, the trial settled into the presentation of evidence. Even though the expert testimony occasionally lapsed into scientific jargon, the Lindbergh trial maintained its primacy in the media. *The New York Times* ran nearly complete transcripts of each day's sessions. Wilentz noticed that the jury seemed to be able to tolerate only two hours at a time of scholarly explication. He goaded his witnesses into making their points as quickly as possible. He broke the monotony by interrupting the experts with other witnesses.

His choreography proved effective. Looking at large charts placed on a rack near the jury box and at eleven-by-fourteen-inch photostats that were passed among them, the jurors were able to understand Albert Osborn's explanation of the remarkable similarities between Hauptmann's handwriting samples and the handwriting in the ransom notes. He pointed out similar misspellings—"haus" for "house," "note" for "not," "anyding" for "anything," "gut" for "good," and "boad" for "boat," for example, as well as similar Germanic formations of certain letters. Even more incriminating were "inventions" in forming certain letters—such as the inverted capital "N"s and "y"s that looked like "j"s. There were literally dozens of matches.

Reilly spoke to the press every day. Although the prosecution had another week of witnesses, the defense attorney felt impelled to present his upcoming strategy, issuing the questions he would be asking Hauptmann, including those about his friendship with Isidor Fisch, whom Reilly insisted was the man Jafsie had met in the cemeteries. In realizing that he might be biting off more than he could chew, he hastened to add, "our purpose is not to try to solve the crime or to prove who did it, but to prove that Hauptmann is not guilty." In Trenton, Reilly posed a panel of eight handwriting experts for pictures, a team that he said would affirm that Richard Hauptmann could not have written the ransom notes.

The picture was seen around the world—almost everywhere except the top floor of the Union Hotel in Flemington, where the twelve jurors were sequestered. According to the constables, the jurors were not allowed to see any newspapers, because after clipping all the articles pertaining to the Hauptmann case, little remained. Besides the Hauptmann trial, the big news that week was a jailbreak at San Quentin resulting in the death of the warden, a bank heist in Ottawa, Illinois, in which a bank officer and sheriff were killed, and the killing of two notorious murderers and kidnappers, "Ma" Barker and her son.

The Lindberghs rested that weekend at Next Day Hill. Anne was not much company, as the trial dragged her into a deep depression. While

Charles, with Nordic sangfroid, could show up for the trial every day and observe it with objectivity, Anne could not. Many days she walked around the estate's fenced grounds and sat on a tree stump to cry. Many nights she whimpered herself to sleep. She had frequent nightmares, not just about her firstborn, but about her father and Elisabeth as well. She often awoke in tears.

Although Anne seemed to be suffering an emotional setback, she would later realize that she had entered a painful but salutary period. The trial had churned up feelings of remorse, self-pity, and nostalgia, which proved to be normal, healthy stages of grief.

Charles, on the other hand, remained rigid in his refusal to acknowledge his pain. Anne would come to believe that such stoicism was "courageous" but that it was only a halfway house on the long road to recovery. "It is a shield, permissible for a short time only," she would write years later, clearly thinking of him. "In the end one has to discard shields and remain open and vulnerable. Otherwise, scar tissue will seal off the wound and no growth will follow. To grow, to be reborn, one must remain vulnerable—open to love but also hideously open to the possibility of more suffering."

Writing during this dismal period saved Anne's sanity. "If I could write out moods which could be admitted to no one, they became more manageable, as though neatly stacked on a high shelf," she would recall several decades later. "Brought to the aseptic light of the diary's white page, the giant toadstools withered." It was a turning point in her growth as an artist, her self-confidence increasing as she found her literary voice.

Entering the third week of the trial, the prosecution persisted in what they considered a case of "identifications." They would continue to place Hauptmann at every twist in the kidnapping story. As a surprise witness, Wilentz called Hildegarde Alexander to the stand. Swathed in fur, this twenty-six-year-old model and evening-gown saleswoman cut a glamorous figure. She testified that one evening in March 1932, in the Fordham Station of the New York Central Railroad in the Bronx, she had seen Dr. Condon, whom she knew slightly. Curiously, she added, she noticed another man in that Bronx station that night "watching him very significantly." That man was Hauptmann, whom she subsequently recognized in a photograph after he had been arrested. There was little way of refuting her recollection.

Reilly fared just as poorly trying to impugn the handwriting experts that followed—two that day, two more the day after. As another four followed, two of the defense's handwriting experts announced that they were walking off the case. Reilly explained to the press that he had been unable to pay them; but each of them was quoted the next day as saying his analysis would not have been favorable to the defense.

The trial continued to take its toll on Richard Hauptmann. Guard reports revealed that he was pacing more and crying in his cell. After the appearance of the men who discovered the baby's corpse and the doctors who examined the body, Hauptmann's case took another turn for the worse. Edward Reilly announced in court that he did not intend to claim that the body was other than that of Colonel Lindbergh's child. Members of his own team felt he should not have allowed any Achilles heel in the case to go unattacked. Lloyd Fisher, for one, leapt to his feet and said, "You are conceding this man to the electric chair!" As he stormed out of the room, the defendant said to his attorney, "You are killing me."

Hauptmann was furious. After two dozen witnesses testified that day, he finally blew his top. Special Agent Thomas Sisk had described Hauptmann's capture and how his furtive glances out the window of his house led to the discovery of the ransom money in his garage. The normally sphinxlike defendant scowled, shaking his head from side to side. Then Sisk talked about the jug containing water, which he had unearthed inside the garage. He said he found no money in the jug, but that the next day, when questioning Hauptmann, the defendant "admitted that he had that money in there three weeks before he was arrested." That provided a neat explanation for the dampness of the money when it was discovered; but Hauptmann had consistently maintained that the money had got wet from the leak in his closet, where he claimed it had sat for years.

"Mister, Mister, you stop lying," he shouted, springing toward the stand, brandishing his finger. Guards restrained him, but he lurched forward and cried, "You are telling a story." For the second time in all the hours court had been in session, Lindbergh looked at Hauptmann. Even before Judge Trenchard had restored order, Lindbergh was looking back at the witness stand.

Hauptmann's contempt was contagious. The next morning, the prosecution called Ella Achenbach, a former neighbor of the Hauptmanns, to the stand. She testified that a day or two after the Lindbergh kidnapping, the Hauptmanns had called on her, saying they had just returned from a trip. Anna Hauptmann shrieked from her chair at the defense table, "Mrs. Achenbach, you are lying!"

Attorney General Wilentz seized the situation, objecting "to these demonstrations, whether they are staged or otherwise." A legal tussle ensued as the defense objected to Wilentz's implication. When Judge Trenchard restored order, Mrs. Achenbach went on to reveal that Mrs. Hauptmann had also told her that Richard had recently sprained his ankle and that she had even seen her neighbor limp. "Lies, lies—all lies," Mrs. Hauptmann muttered throughout the testimony.

The week ended with even more incriminating evidence. The jury saw the board from Hauptmann's closet with Dr. Condon's telephone number written on it; and they heard the stenographer of Bronx District Attorney Foley read the testimony of Hauptmann in which he admitted that the handwriting was his and that he had written the information down because he had been interested in the case. "Everybody is against us now," Anna Hauptmann told the press after court had recessed. "Nobody has a good word to say. They lie—lie—lie."

A cold snap struck the East the fourth week in January, and with it came some of the most chilling testimony in the Hauptmann trial. Unfortunately for the accused, his lead attorney's faith in him seemed to dwindle along with most of the public's. Either through insufficient preparation or a simple desire to get to the next phase of the trial, Reilly let whole chunks of testimony go unchallenged:

The first witness that Monday was an agent of the Intelligence Unit of the Treasury Department of the United States government. He had computed Hauptmann's finances between the dates of the ransom payment and his apprehension. Transaction by transaction, he showed how during that time, the unemployed Hauptmann's assets had increased by $44,486. Reilly asked nothing about Hauptmann's possible earnings from freelance carpentry or from his business dealings with Isidor Fisch, to say nothing of cash he might have kept in the house before April 2, 1932.

The timekeeper for the Reliance Property Management Company took the stand with records from 1932. He attested that Richard Hauptmann did not start working for the company until March twenty-first, that he did not show up for work the day the ransom was paid, and that he worked for the company only one day more after it had been paid. Reilly asked nothing of other company records that showed Hauptmann had worked for the company as early as March first, or about possible tampering of the books. He made no attempt to test the character of the witness, called a liar by many in the years since his testimony.

A theater cashier identified Hauptmann as the man who gave her a strangely folded five-dollar bill on November 26, 1933—which happened to be Hauptmann's birthday, a night he insisted he celebrated with his wife and friends. Reilly asked the cashier nothing about her original statement to the police, in which she said the man who passed the money was an "American."

The next day saw two more people identify Hauptmann in and around Hopewell. Then Hauptmann's landlord testified that after the arrest, he noticed that part of a board was missing from the attic floor above his tenant's apartment. This heralded the arrival of the prosecution's eighty-seventh and final witness.

"It's a long story," asserted Arthur Koehler, who took the stand on Wednesday and whose testimony would spill over to the next day. "We want the long story, let's have it," Wilentz said. Technical though Koehler's testimony was, the jury, gallery, and even the prisoner sat spellbound. Lindbergh, with his infinite faith in scientific scrutiny, was riveted. The middle-aged man detailed the eighteen months he spent deconstructing the "kidnap ladder," narrowing down the forty thousand mills and yards in the country in which wood was dressed and sold to the National Millwork and Lumber Company in the Bronx. Thus, more than a year before the police had apprehended Richard Hauptmann, Arthur Koehler had found himself standing in the very yard where Hauptmann used to buy his wood.

After Hauptmann was captured, Koehler was able to examine his tools as well as lumber used in building his attic floor. As a result of his study, Koehler swore that one of the uprights in the ladder had originally been part of a plank in the flooring of Hauptmann's attic, fitting right down to the nail-holes. The rest of the lumber in the attic, he maintained, also came from the very yard at which his search had ended. Furthermore, a study of the tools found in Hauptmann's garage revealed that the plank from the attic had been planed down by one of his tools.

Hammering a final nail into Hauptmann's coffin, Koehler said that a three-quarter-inch chisel was used in making the recesses for the rungs of the ladder, and that upon inspecting the Hauptmann toolchest he found no such tool, one that would be standard equipment in an ordinary carpenter's kit. That was the exact tool found at the Lindbergh house. Hauptmann returned to his cell with his head bowed and eyes cast down.

The trial in Flemington had become the hottest ticket in the world. Sheriff Curtis declared that he had five thousand applications for seats from all over the country and from a dozen foreign nations. "The trial should have been held in Madison Square Garden," he said. The general public could not help noticing the number of famous faces increasing every day. On this last full day of the prosecution's case, Flemington's largest crowd in weeks was rewarded for waiting in a blizzard by getting glimpses of Mrs. James Farley, wife of the Postmaster General, author Ford Madox Ford, and actress Lynn Fontanne, sporting a leopard-skin coat.

Temperatures dropped into single digits that night, producing four-foot snowdrifts throughout the state of New Jersey. Charles took Anne for a walk in the storm, and she felt exhilarated by the touch of his hand, pulling her up the hill. The next morning, making his customary drive from Englewood to Flemington, he got stuck between drifts. State troopers came to his rescue, allowing him to abandon his car, as they drove him to the courthouse. Even arriving a half-hour late, he had not missed much. Judge Trenchard was similarly delayed; and the first few minutes of business that morning were given to some final observations of Arthur Koehler under direct examination. In the end, Koehler's testimony had been so dumbfounding in its precision that there was little for the defense to challenge. As Ford Madox Ford observed in a column for *The New York Times,* Koehler "was like the instrument of a blind and atrociously menacing destiny. You shuddered at the thought of what might happen to you if such a mind and such an inconceivable industry should get to work upon your own remote past—a man who searched 1,900 factories for the traces of the scratches of your plane on a piece of wood. It was fantastic and horrifying."

Defense attorney Fred Pope at least got Koehler to agree that the ladder had been poorly constructed, from which he hoped the jury would infer it was hardly the work of a professional carpenter. After a few more questions from each side, the State rested.

Egbert Rosecrans for the defense moved for a verdict of acquittal. He held that no evidence had shown that the crime was even committed in the county in which court was convened (the corpus delicti having been discovered in Mercer County), that the State had failed to show proper intent to commit a felony ("Stealing clothes of the child, the sleeping garments?"), and that there was a paucity of evidence placing his client at the scene of the crime. Trying not to deliver his summation, Wilentz addressed every one of Rosecrans's points, insisting that "there is not only sufficient evidence but overwhelming evidence . . . which requires this defendant to answer." He argued statutory definitions, maintaining that "murder . . . which shall be committed in perpetrating or attempting to perpetrate any . . . burglary . . . [or] robbery . . . shall be murder in the first degree." The Court concurred.

That afternoon, Lloyd Fisher took center stage for half an hour, presenting the defense's opening argument. Everybody in town suspected that this was to be the most startling day of the trial. Rows of observers stood shoulder-to-shoulder, right up to the edge of the Judge's bench. Fisher promised the capacity crowd that the defense would provide alibis for Richard Hauptmann on three significant nights in the case—March 1, 1932, April 2, 1932, and April 26, 1932, the night the theater cashier swore he gave her a five-dollar-note that turned out to be ransom money. He also promised handwriting experts of their own—not as many as the prosecution, he said, because of lack of funds—and further compromising information on Isidor Fisch. Fisher maintained that the ladder had been so manhandled since the crime that it had been rendered a worthless piece of evidence and that many of the prosecution's most important witnesses were impeachable.

Then, at 3:09, Edward Reilly boomed, "Bruno Richard Hauptmann, take the stand!"

Guards on either side stood with him, then allowed the man in the brownish-gray sack suit to step forward. For all his sleeplessness, there was spring in his walk, an animal magnetism about his muscular body and chiseled face. He spoke in a low, often guttural voice. Reilly coaxed the thirty-five-year-old witness to speak up as he limned his background. After describing being wounded and gassed during the war, serving time in prison, and illegally entering the country, Hauptmann's counsel interrupted him in order to bring forth two other witnesses. The owner of the bakery at which Anna Hauptmann worked and his wife were sworn in to testify that they recalled Hauptmann's presence in their shop on the night of March 1, 1932. They proved to be of little help to the defendant, as Wilentz's cross-examination reduced their recollections to vague suppositions.

Hauptmann resumed his testimony, laying the groundwork for his alibis. He discussed his employment in 1932, but he offered a scanty account of his time on March 1, 1932, other than the morning. He stumbled over the date on which he started work at the Majestic Apartments, having to be corrected by his attorney.

The next day—Friday, January 25, 1935—should have seen Hauptmann's best testimony. Six hours were given to his batting answers to his attorney's lobbed questions, so that he could account for himself under oath. But he made two grave errors. One was over the misspelling of the word "signature," which had appeared in the ransom notes. Reilly got Hauptmann to tell the jury that the police had directed him to misspell the word when they asked him to write it. In truth, the police had never asked Hauptmann to write that word. Even worse, when Reilly asked him to spell it on the stand, he got it wrong. The second mistake came toward the end of his direct-examination when Hauptmann described how the police had roughed him up—a "couple of knocks . . . in the ribs, when I refused to write." That he had been beaten was never challenged; but Hauptmann had previously asserted that he was "glad" to give writing samples, for they would clear him.

The day ended with thirty minutes of cross-examination by Wilentz, who wasted no time hurling questions at Hauptmann about his illegal entry into the United States, the extradition hearings in the Bronx at which he admitted telling the truth only "to a certain extent," his criminal record in Germany, his business dealings with Fisch, his hiding the ransom money and a pistol in his garage. Then the Attorney General confronted Hauptmann with one of his old notebooks which contained the word "boat"—spelled "boad."

Reporters noticed more than once that Hauptmann used his handkerchief to pat his face and wipe his hands, and that whenever he heard the word "baby," his hands fluttered and his lips trembled. "What Bruno needs," commented Jack Benny, after visiting the courtroom, "is a second act."

By this time, most of Flemington was convinced of Hauptmann's guilt. At Nellie's Tap, the press sang their version of the Schnitzelbank song, each new verse spilling onto the streets, where locals took up the chorus:

> *Is das nicht ein singnature?*
> *Ja, das ist ein singnature!*
> *Is das nicht peculiar?*

> *Ja, ist damn peculiar!*
> *Singnature?*
> *Peculiar!*
>
> *Is das nicht ein ransom note?*
> *Ja, das ist ein ransom note!*
> *Is das nicht ein Nelly boad?*
> *Ja, das ist ein Nelly boad!*
> *Ransom note?*
> *Nelly boad!*

After one day in Flemington, Edna Ferber became disgusted with herself for joining the fashionable crowd, talking about how "divine" and "wonderful" it all was. She admitted that it was thrilling theater. But she left town so sickened by what she had seen, she wrote that "it made you want to resign as member of the human race and cable Hitler saying, Well Butch, you win."

"There is a steadily deepening tension and a steadily increasing horror in the Flemington courthouse as the most unfortunate man in the world makes his fight for his life," wrote novelist Kathleen Norris for *The New York Times* that evening. "For no matter what may be proved against him, nor how intense the detestation in which the American people may hold him, there is no doubt that Bruno Richard Hauptmann is unfortunate—pitiful. Menace gathers like a storm-cloud over him, the central figure of a living drama that will be known throughout all our history as the great kidnapping trial . . ." In an adjacent column, Alexander Woollcott dropped all pretense of neutrality. While commenting on the number of "lonely and itching women who find him so physically attractive as to be above all suspicion," he believed: "The most recurrent imbecility is the little notion cherished by those who say that, whereas they suppose Hauptmann was naughty enough to take the ransom money, they still doubt if he had anything to do with the kidnapping." He said that if both Dr. Condon and Colonel Lindbergh have been willing to swear that Hauptmann was the man they recognized from the cemetery, then it was certainly Hauptmann.

The SRO crowd on Monday caught the best show of all—when Wilentz subjected Hauptmann to five hours of intense interrogation. At several points, Hauptmann's waxen face came to life, his jaw jutting and his eyes blazing. His monotone erupted into sarcastic laughs and angry shouts. But Hauptmann maintained his control, never breaking down and confessing as the prosecution hoped and the audience expected. At times, he appeared to enjoy the sparring, occasionally smiling when Wilentz failed to land a blow. But he did have to concede a number of damaging points.

The jury heard Hauptmann admit to several untruths and to withholding information. He confessed that he had lied to the police upon his arrest when he told them that the twenty-dollar gold certificate in his wallet was part of his innocent hedge against inflation. Then he asked the jury to believe that the $15,000 the police found had belonged to his friend Fisch. He admitted that he had lied when he told the police that the first cache of ransom money they found in his garage was all that he had, only to have the police discover another $840. He admitted that he had lied in the Bronx court about having met Fisch in the Bronx in May 1932, and now asked the jury to believe that he had met him through a friend in March or April of that year. He admitted that upon Fisch's death he had withheld from Fisch's family the fact that he had left a bundle of money behind.

When confronted with the piece of wood from his closet with Jafsie's address and telephone number written on it—pencil markings he had admitted in the Bronx County Court were his—Hauptmann now said he had not written them. Wilentz tried to get Hauptmann to explain his contradictory answers, but he kept evading them. At last he explained that he had been "quite excited" when first presented with the evidence (which some have long held was falsified, possibly by a journalist playing a prank) and so wrongly admitted that the writing was his. Now he went so far as to say that the handwriting did look like his but that he could not remember "putting them numbers on" and that he was "positively sure I wouldn't write anything in the inside of a closet."

Fed up with Hauptmann's obduracy, Wilentz said, "You are having a lot of fun with me, aren't you?" Hauptmann said no, but Wilentz pointed out that every few minutes the defendant smiled at him. Then, interjecting some theories he had acquired from the State psychiatrist, who had drawn a psychological profile of the criminal, Wilentz said, "You think you are a big shot, don't you?"

"No," Hauptmann replied. "Should I cry?"

"No, certainly you shouldn't. You think you are bigger than everybody, don't you?"

"No, but I know I am innocent."

Although he was seated and further shackled by his imperfect English, Hauptmann did not shrink before Wilentz's obvious posturing for the crowd. "Lying, when you swear to God that you will tell the truth. Telling lies doesn't mean anything," the Attorney General said with disgust, milking the scene.

"Stop that!" the defendant shouted.

The day also contained more damaging evidence. There were peculiarities in Hauptmann's handwriting that matched those in the ransom notes—

hyphenating "New York," reversing the "g" and "h" in words such as "Wright" and "light." And then there was Hauptmann's small ledger book with its sketch of a ladder similar to the one left at the Lindbergh house.

And there was more. Some of Hauptmann's explanations of his financial affairs seemed so outlandish that they prompted bursts of laughter from the spectators. By the end of the day, the defense told the press that it intended to use both the laughter and Wilentz's improper questions as points on which they would appeal if Hauptmann were convicted. Judge Trenchard announced that he would thenceforth disallow people to stand in the courtroom, thus limiting the number of spectators.

The next day, the State caught the defendant in another lie. While Hauptmann had earlier testified that he and Isidor Fisch had begun their partnership speculating in the stock market in 1932, staked by Fisch, Wilentz produced two letters Hauptmann wrote Fisch's brother, which described their partnership beginning in 1933, with Hauptmann contributing most of the cash. The rest of the day was devoted to Hauptmann's "sudden wealth" in the spring of 1932. He had to admit that he had lied to Fisch's brother about $5,500, which he said had come from a private bank account. During his seventeen and a half hours on the stand, eleven under cross-examination, Hauptmann's memory failed him too many times. "Hauptmann made a good witness," Wilentz told the press upon the conclusion of his cross-examination, "considering the fact that he has told so many different stories and has had to admit both damaging truths and untruth."

Hauptmann's wife, who had already invoked considerable public sympathy, followed him on the stand. But her plight would ultimately work against him. "How long should a woman stick to a man, anyway?" wrote Kathleen Norris, marveling at the faith of Anna Hauptmann. By the time the "thin, fuzzy-headed woman, plain, long-nosed, [and] pale," testified, the world had already heard her husband admit that he concealed most of his financial affairs from her, "that he deceived his wife even when she was working hard to help him save."

In two hours of testimony, Anna Schoeffler Hauptmann supported her husband's three alibis—accounting for him on the nights of the kidnapping, the ransom payment, and the money being passed at the movie theater. She also refuted Mrs. Achenbach, denying that she had told her that she and Richard had just returned from a trip during which he had sprained his ankle. Under cross-examination, a polite Wilentz challenged her never having seen the box of money that was allegedly resting on the top shelf of her broom closet. Then he reminded her of her testimony in the hearing in the Bronx just a few months earlier in which she claimed that she could not remember whether her husband had been with her on the night of March 1,

1932. During the next short recess, Mrs. Hauptmann walked toward her husband, who wagged his finger at her, saying, "Cut out that don't remember stuff."

The next several days of trial saw a ragtag assortment of defense witnesses, who harmed the defendant more than they helped. Elvert Carlstrom claimed to have seen Hauptmann in Fredericksen's Bakery on the night of March 1, 1932; but in rebuttal the prosecution presented a witness who asserted that Carlstrom had been with him that night, in Dunellen, New Jersey. August von Henke said he met Hauptmann that night as well; though he turned out to be a shady character who had changed his name twice and who ran a speakeasy. Louis Kiss said he was also in Fredericksen's that night and claimed to have seen Hauptmann; he remembered because he was supposed to deliver two pints of rum he had just made that night and got lost. He was later refuted as well, as the friend purchasing the rum testified that the delivery occurred more than a week later. The gallery became amused at the popularity of Fredericksen's Bakery—busier, one lawyer derided, than Grand Central Station.

So impeachable were many of the other defense witnesses, it was often difficult to keep track of who was on trial. Reilly brought forth an ex-convict, a "professional witness," a mental patient, and several others whose testimonies were easily challenged. While on the stand to testify that he had seen a group of people at St. Raymond's the night the ransom money was paid, a cab driver with theatrical aspirations broke into an impersonation of Will Rogers. Back in his cell, Hauptmann asked Lloyd Fisher, "Where are they getting these witnesses from? They're really hurting me."

A few did help Hauptmann's case. Two people credibly supported his alibi for the night of his birthday in 1933. And Dr. Erastus Mead Hudson, a physician who made a hobby of fingerprinting, testified that he had shown the New Jersey State Police his new method of silver-nitrate fingerprinting, which allowed him to lift more than five hundred usable prints from the kidnap ladder. None of them was Hauptmann's. And though the defense's team of handwriting analysts had shrunk to one, John M. Trendley acquitted himself well, suggesting that Hauptmann's handwriting resembled that of many Germans for whom English was a second language.

The defense knew it would not be enough to refute charges against the accused, that it would have to introduce alternatives scenarios. Reilly did everything he could to suggest the guilt of Isidor Fisch. Unfortunately, at least a dozen defense witnesses who might have helped make that case ignored their subpoenas, failing to show up at the last minute. Most of those who still put faith in the defense's "Fisch story" were quieted by several prosecution rebuttal witnesses, including Isidor Fisch's sister, who testified that he had died with only 1500 marks—$500—to his name.

As the trial concluded its fifth week, the proceedings appeared in news-reels one night at most of the first-run theaters in New York City. Audiences saw both Lindberghs and Dr. Condon as well as Hauptmann and Wilentz during one of their testy exchanges. The films were the product of Fox Movietone News, who along with Universal, Paramount, Hearst Metrotone, and Pathé, had housed a large motion-picture camera in a muffled box in the gallery, its lens fixed on the witness stand. They had also rigged a microphone halfway up one of the courtroom windows, about thirty-five feet from the witness stand.

Although it seemed unlikely that the attorneys, the judge, and the police had no knowledge of the setup—indeed, a state trooper was stationed right next to the camera to make sure it could not be heard—all officials denied sanctioning the filming. While the few minutes of film presented to the public were sympathetic toward the prosecution, the Attorney General blew the whistle on further exhibition of the newsreels. The judge ordered the equipment removed from the court for the rest of the trial and indicated that there would be no legal action taken provided none of the twelve thousand feet of film was exhibited again so long as the case was being tried. As a result of motion pictures' ability to sway emotions in the Lindbergh case—both in the performances they encouraged within the courtroom and in the reactions they could manipulate outside the courtroom—cameras were banned from virtually every trial in America for the next sixty years.

When the defense took a final stab at implicating Morrow and Lindbergh servants in the crime, Lindbergh informed the prosecution that he wished to retake the stand in their defense. Wilentz felt further testimony on the subject was unnecessary, especially as he had what he considered a more dramatic final witness. On Saturday, February 9, 1935, he called Elizabeth Morrow to the stand. There was little information Anne's mother could supply; but her presence in court provided a gracious finale to the pageant. Anne accompanied her to court and found the day more harrowing than when she had testified, for this time she allowed herself to observe the surrounding hysteria. With Betty Morrow's appearance, Wilentz had only to mention "the late Senator" to remind the jury how New Jersey's first family had suffered.

The trial took its toll on the Lindberghs. Anne was as distraught as ever, but Charles would not allow her to express as much in his presence. Having to put on her best face for her husband as well as the public rendered her "completely frustrated," boxed in and climbing walls. She rambled about the grounds depressed, miserable except for the time she spent with Jon. She but pecked at her book. Only to her diary, she felt, could she express her feelings. "I must not talk. I must not cry. . . . I must not dream," she wrote on January 20, 1935. "I must control my mind—I must control my body—I must control my emotions—I must finish the book—I must put up an appearance, at least, of calm for C." At night, she shrank into a corner of their bed, "trying not to cry . . . not to wake C., trying not to toss or turn, trying to be like a stone, heavy and still and rigid, except for my tears." Other diary entries from that year were even more morose, so dark that Charles later urged her to burn them. Persuaded that their immolation would help eradicate her pain, she did.

Meantime, Charles continued to focus completely on the case, still bottling all his anguish. Although he thought he never revealed as much, he was as grief-stricken as his wife. Having been his family's emotional pillar since adolescence, he nonetheless needed somebody to lean on and felt unable to express such human frailty. His sorrow and self-pity surfaced in the form of anger. Because Anne was closest to him, it was inevitable that she would become the ultimate victim of his distress.

Early in the morning of Monday, February eleventh, Charles snapped. Before leaving for the start of summations in court, he lost his temper and dumped years of frustration on his wife. He told Anne she had been living too much within herself and was controlled by her feelings. He showed no mercy for her fragile state of mind; in fact, he chastised her for not using her mind, for neglecting work on her book. He called her a "failure," then left for Flemington. For one of the few times in her life, Anne found solace from her mother.

"Talk to Mother, and strength pouring into me," is all Anne would impart to her diary that day. But Betty Morrow's diary is more revealing. "Anne came into my room with tears in her eyes," she wrote before citing her husband's verbal abuse. "Oh! Mother," Anne continued, "Elisabeth helped me so much with Charles." For the first time Mrs. Morrow saw that "Charles isn't capable of understanding her—the beauty of her soul and mind," and that for years she had been forced to become two people, the person she was and the person Charles wanted her to be. "He loves her," Mrs. Morrow realized, "but he wants to *reform* her—make her over into his own practical scientific mold. Poor Charles! What a condemnation of him!" Betty Morrow realized she must support Anne now more than she ever had. But she felt hampered, knowing she could not quarrel with her son-in-law—"no matter how stupid he is."

Charles spent his thirtieth day in the Flemington courthouse, listening to the first round of summations. Anthony Hauck delivered a forty-five-minute "opening" of the State's closing argument, ultimately reminding the jurors: ". . . we are not required to have a picture of this man coming down the ladder with the Lindbergh baby. But we have shown you conclusively, overwhelmingly, beyond a reasonable doubt, that Bruno Richard Hauptmann is guilty of the murder of Charles A. Lindbergh, Jr."

Edward Reilly, in his old-fashioned black coat and striped trousers, began his summation by raising a Bible and quoting St. Matthew: "Judge not," he said, "lest ye be judged." Then in a deliberate (and slightly patronizing) manner, his hands often clasped behind his back, the New York lawyer asked the jury to rely on "horse-sense" and "motherly intuition," not the testimony of hired "technicians and experts." He wondered aloud how one man alone could have pulled off such a crime. Toward that end, he suggested a conspiracy, one which might have included any number of people, starting with the "disloyal" servants of the Morrows and Lindberghs. He implicated Violet Sharpe and Olly Whateley and Betty Gow. Then he suggested the complicity of Isidor Fisch, "Red" Johnson, and Dr. Condon. He moved on to accuse the police of doctoring and planting evidence—the attic board that fit too conveniently with the ladder rail, the board from Hauptmann's closet with Dr. Condon's address, the payroll record that indicated that Hauptmann did not work the day of the ransom payment. He stacked his handwriting and wood experts alongside the prosecution's. He finally got around to challenging Charles Lindbergh himself, asserting:

> Colonel, I say to you it is impossible that you, having lived for years in airplanes, with the hum of the motor in your ears for years, with the noise of the motor and the change of climatic conditions that you have lived under since you made your wonderful flight, to say with any degree of stability that you can ever remember the voice of a man two and a half or three years afterwards, a voice you never heard before . . .

"I feel sure in closing," Reilly said, "even Colonel Lindbergh wouldn't expect you and doesn't expect you to do anything but your duty under the law and under the evidence."

The next day, Attorney General Wilentz delivered a summation that United Press reporter Sidney Whipple said "made up in vituperation what it may have lacked in logical argument." Over four and one-half hours, he pleaded with the jury to throw the book at Hauptmann, because since his apprehension, nothing "has come to the surface or light that has indicated anything but the guilt of this defendant . . . and no one else. Every avenue of evidence, every little thoroughfare that we traveled along, every one leads to the same door."

Then he pelted Hauptmann with insults—calling him "a fellow that had ice water in his veins, not blood," an "egomaniac who thought he was omnipotent," a "secretive fellow . . . that wouldn't tell anybody anything," the "filthiest and vilest snake that ever crept through the grass," an "animal . . .

lower than the lowest form in the animal kingdom, Public Enemy Number One of this world."

In response to the defense's suggestions of police improprieties, the Attorney General asked Colonel Schwarzkopf to stand up. "Does he look like a crook?" Wilentz asked. "Does he deserve that sort of treatment for this burglar, this murderer, and convict?" Whipped up by his own frenzy, he even launched into a description of the killing of the baby that he had not mentioned before, one at complete variance with the murder he described six weeks earlier in his opening argument. Wilentz had originally stated that the baby died when the ladder broke. Now he suggested the baby was killed prior to that—"What else was the chisel there for? To knock that child into insensibility right there in that room."

Wilentz spent most of the day effectively recapitulating the evidence. He said that a parade of living witnesses had come to testify against Hauptmann, while the defense conveniently blamed people who were dead. To accept their argument, Wilentz argued, one had to accept a "grave conspiracy." Late in the day, he played his trump card: "Colonel Lindbergh's identification of his voice," Wilentz said plainly, "—if it is good enough for Colonel Lindbergh under oath, if Colonel Lindbergh says to you, 'That is the man who murdered my child,' men and women, that is good enough."

The next morning, Judge Trenchard delivered a seventy-minute charge to the jury. Lindbergh lunched in town at attorney George Large's house with Colonels Breckinridge and Schwarzkopf, then drove home to Englewood. Fortunately, the tension was lessened by another visit from Harold Nicolson.

After spending two months in England, Nicolson returned to Englewood that very morning to continue his research on Dwight Morrow. He spent the afternoon sipping sherry with Betty Morrow, Aubrey Morgan, and Anne Lindbergh. Shortly after Charles returned from Flemington, dinner was served. They turned on two radios as they sat, one in the pantry, the other in the drawing room. "Thus there were jazz and jokes while we had dinner and one ear strained the whole time for the announcer from the courthouse," Nicolson would later write his wife. After dinner, Nicolson withdrew to the library, the Morrows and Lindberghs to another room.

Close to seven thousand people gathered around the Hunterdon County Courthouse, completely blocking Flemington's Main Street. At 10:27, an assistant to the Sheriff was sent up the courthouse stairs to the belfry, where he tolled the bell. The crowd shouted for several minutes in anticipation of the verdict—chanting "Kill Hauptmann! Kill Hauptmann!"

At 10:31, Hauptmann was ushered in from his cell, manacled to a state trooper and accompanied by five other policemen. The jurors entered, none of them looking his way. It was not until 10:45 that Judge Trenchard returned to the bench, asking the jury, then the defendant, to rise. "Mr. Foreman, what say you?" the judge asked. "Do you find the defendant guilty or not guilty?" The foreman replied that they found him "guilty of murder in the first degree."

Messenger boys bolted toward the door, but Judge Trenchard forbade anybody from leaving until the business of the court was done. The jury was polled, and at the court's suggestion, Attorney General Wilentz moved for immediate sentencing. Looking at the convicted man through his horn-rimmed glasses, Trenchard pronounced that he "suffer death at the time and place, and in the manner provided by law." At 10:50, the condemned man was led out of the courtroom, his face "white as a death mask, his eyes sunken," observed one reporter. Anna Hauptmann sat looking at the floor, not lifting her head until her husband had left the room—at which time she began to cry. A few minutes later, Hauptmann fell facedown on his cot and sobbed uncontrollably. By then word had reached the street, shouted from a second-story window by a messenger boy. The crowd roared.

Betty Morrow poked her head into the library at Next Day Hill to tell Harold Nicolson, "Hauptmann has been condemned to death without mercy." By the time he joined the others around the radio in the drawing room, he could hear what Anne remembered as "the howling mob" over the radio. They sat in silence, listening to the newscaster declare, "You have now heard the verdict in the most famous trial in all history. Bruno Hauptmann now stands guilty of one of the foulest . . ." Anne at last spoke up and said, "Turn that off, Charles, turn that off."

They all went to the pantry for ginger beer. Charles perched himself upon a countertop and began to speak to Nicolson about the trial. "There is no doubt at all that Hauptmann did the thing," he said. "My one dread all these years has been that they would get hold of someone as a victim about whom I wasn't sure. I am sure about this—quite sure." Then he analyzed the case, point by point. "He pretended to address his remarks to me only," Nicolson observed. "But I could see that he was really trying to ease the ag-onised tension through which Betty and Anne had passed. It was very well done. It made one feel that here was no personal desire for vengeance or jus-tification; here was the solemn process of law inexorably and impersonally punishing a culprit." They all went to bed, Charles commenting on his way out, "That was a lynching crowd."

"The long trial at Flemington, the charge of the judge and the verdict of the jury established a crime," wrote *The New York Times* the next day in its lead editorial, "but did not clear away a mystery." Indeed, the newspaper suggested, part of the public fascination with the case was the daily hope that "either the evidence of the police or the admissions of Hauptmann would show precisely who the kidnapper was and what were his preparations and methods of operation." Because of that lack of tangible proof, debate about the case has never stopped.

Because apparently nobody witnessed the kidnapping of the Lindbergh baby, some questions can never be answered with absolute certainty. Nobody will ever *know* who removed the baby from his crib. Even if Hauptmann's guilt were a certainty, one will never know whether or not he acted alone, whether or not Fisch or others (what about the Italian-speaking voice in the background of one of the phone calls to Condon?) were involved, whether or not it was Hauptmann who climbed the ladder (or even used the ladder at all), whether or not the baby was killed accidentally or intentionally. But the weakness of the defense's case and the strength of the prosecution's left little room for a juror to vote other than he did. Even on the first ballot, they were unanimous as to Hauptmann's guilt, disagreeing only about the penalty. Over another four ballots, the seven-to-five vote for the death penalty reached unanimity. As Ethel Stockton, the last of the jurors to die, said more than fifty years after the fact, "The evidence submitted to the jury was overwhelming . . ."

The power of Lindbergh's testimony was undeniable. If he had expressed even the slightest uncertainty, the jury might have had reasonable doubts of their own. He had none. To the end of his life, on the rare occasions when he discussed the trial—either with family or a few intimate friends—he never wavered in his conviction.

In the sixty years since "The Lindbergh Case," countless theories suggesting Hauptmann's innocence have surfaced. There is room for such hypotheses because there was never any evidence placing Hauptmann on the Lindbergh property, either outside on the ladder or inside the baby's bedroom. But even if several witnesses had been coerced or had convinced themselves that Hauptmann was guilty and worth perjuring themselves for, even if evidence had been faked or tampered with, even if law-enforcement agencies had botched their work, even if all the expert testimony from both sides nullifed each other, even if Richard Hauptmann had been a more sympathetic witness, more at ease with the English language and less a target for a hostile press corps, even if the Court had been biased against him—there remained a veritable mountain of undisputed evidence against him, a man so chronically secretive that his own wife declared she did not even know his first name was Bruno until the tabloids smeared it across their front pages.

"Few today deny that the trial was unfair," wrote attorney and law professor Alan M. Dershowitz in 1988, "—not only by current standards, but by the far less rigorous standards of the 1930s. But many who acknowledge the trial's unfairness insist that Hauptmann was plainly guilty." Six points in the case allowed Lindbergh to sleep at night secure in the feeling that the sole offender had been brought to justice. Not only did five handwriting experts state there was no doubt that Hauptmann had written the ransom notes, but it appeared as much to the layman's eye. There was no disputing that Arthur Koehler's detective work had brought him to Hauptmann's lumberyard in the Bronx more than a year before the carpenter had become a suspect. Hauptmann was never able to explain satisfactorily why Dr. Condon's address and telephone number were written in his closet. Hauptmann had been throwing around great sums of Lindbergh ransom money at a time when he was barely earning a living. All of Hauptmann's alibis appeared flimsy. And finally, Condon, the taxidriver Perrone, and Lindbergh himself all identified Hauptmann's voice, which Lindbergh maintained was "a very strange voice," and "unmistakable."

In his closing remarks, Reilly had tried to put the fear of God into the jury. "Hang this man and cover up our sins," he had said. "Hang him and ten years from now, after he is dead, have somebody on their deathbed just about to meet their Maker, turn over and say, 'I want to make a confession, I was part of the Lindbergh gang,' and then where is our conscience, where are our feelings when we have sent an innocent man to his death, and we think about the real culprit—he must be somewhere in the world. There must be two or three of them still alive, because no one man could do this." And yet, the next sixty years brought forth not a single confession, not a shred of evidence or testimony connecting anybody but Bruno Richard Hauptmann to the crime.

"The trial is over. We must start our life again, try to build it securely— C. and Jon and I," Anne wrote on Valentine Day, 1935. "I must start again, without Elisabeth, with my eyes open, without confusion or fooling myself, honestly and patiently, keeping clear what matters. Charles and a home and Jon—and work."

A "MOST ASTOUNDING LETTER" from Smith College the next week, offering Anne an honorary Master of Arts degree, lifted her spirits. She was reluctant to accept, thinking Smith ought to reward "people who have done things in their own rights, on their own responsibilities—women who have held a career by themselves." But her proud husband insisted she accept it.

With resolve that had eluded her for months, Anne returned to her writing. Ever since her article in *National Geographic,* publishers had been inviting her to submit books to them. One was Harcourt, Brace, with whom Harold Nicolson had been working. At the end of April 1935, she met with Alfred Harcourt and explained that she felt the time had come for a professional editor to read her first full-length manuscript, *North to the Orient.* Charles copy-edited each page before Anne sent it off. A few days later, Harcourt telephoned to say, "I would take it if it were written by Jane Smith. It's a good story, it's moving, it's well constructed, and parts of it border on poetry." His acceptance was one of the most satisfying moments in her life. When Charles learned the news that evening, he *"beamed* with pride" . . . and subsequently placed an advance order for nine hundred copies.

The manuscript required minimal editing and was scheduled for publication that summer. Advance word was so positive that rumors spread that the book must have been ghost-written. Fifteen thousand copies were in the bookstores on publication day, August fifteenth. Within four months, Harcourt, Brace had 185,000 copies of the book in print, making it the number-one nonfiction bestseller of 1935. Its success encouraged her to reread her diaries of the trip to Greenland, Europe, and Africa and to make notes for a second book.

The spring and summer of 1935 proved at least as productive for Charles, and as rewarding. He returned to his laboratory at the Rockefeller Institute and his medical experiments with Dr. Carrel. Out of the public eye, Lindbergh had designed in late 1934 a pump "by which a pulsatile circulation of nutrient fluid, properly oxygenated, could be maintained through an organ." Using Lindbergh's machine, Dr. Carrel performed surgeries that showed that circulation, even in such vital organs as the kidneys, could be interrupted for as long as two hours without causing permanent damage. However, despite rigorous standards and conditions, bacterial infection still invaded the apparatus and the organs.

In the spring of 1935, Lindbergh perfected his invention, designing a new type of organ chamber. It was an intricate modern sculpture of glass—bulbs and tubes that vaguely resembled a saxophone fused on top of a wine bottle. On April 5, 1935—using the Lindbergh Pump—a whole organ was successfully cultivated *in vitro* for the first time. Dr. Carrel bled an etherized cat to death, removed its thyroid gland, and placed it in the organ chamber. It was perfused for eighteen days, permitting for the first time an entire organ to live outside of the body. The idea dating at least as far back as 1812—when French physiologist Le Gallois wrote of "artificially circulating a fluid through an organ"—had, thanks to the Lindbergh Pump, at last been realized.

Over the next two months, Carrel and Lindbergh performed more than two dozen experiments with the pump. They tested spleens, ovaries, kidneys, and hearts. In almost all instances, they succeeded in keeping them fully viable and free of infection. This work brought two new medical facts to light: cultivated organs remain alive; and their structure and functions vary according to the composition of the perfusing liquids.

"A new era has opened," Carrel declared. "Physiology and medicine have acquired . . . a powerful tool for the investigation of the intricate rela-

tions between organs and blood . . . Now anatomy is capable of apprehending bodily structures in the fulness of their reality, of understanding
how the organs form the organism, and how the organism grows, ages, heals
its wounds, resists disease and adapts itself with marvelous ease to changing
environment." The ramifications of these experiments were endless, extending into the worlds of pathology, physiology, and anatomy. Organs affected
with malignant tumors, for example, could be studied while being kept alive
although separated from the human body. The effects of different perfusing
solutions could be evaluated. Faulty organs might be removed from the body
and repaired, to be replanted. Perhaps a similar pump could keep an entire
body alive while organs from another body—perhaps even artificial organs—
could be implanted!

"Not one of the 22 great medical scientists who are members of the
Rockefeller Institute for Medical Research in Manhattan has a reputation
with the man-in-the-street equal to that of a minor volunteer worker at the
Institute named Charles Augustus Lindbergh," wrote *Time* in the late summer of 1935. "Lindbergh is considered . . . exclusively as a flyer," Dr. Carrel
said in the article, ". . . but he is much more than that. He is a great savant.
Men who achieve such things are capable of accomplishments in all do-
mains." These new accomplishments, of course, drew even more publicity,
giving the media a new angle on the nation's top-drawing headliner. Reporters staked out the Rockefeller Institute as well as Next Day Hill; and it
became nearly impossible for Lindbergh to walk the streets anywhere in between.

Lindbergh was sorry the public had been made aware of his only refuge,
but he was pleased that Dr. Carrel was at last receiving what Lindbergh considered his due. Later in the year, Carrel published an American edition of
Man, the Unknown, a subjective discourse on the human body and soul, full
of scientific fact and metaphysical opinions. For the first time, the public at
large got a sense of the controversial thoughts long kept confined to the select few who came in contact with him. No doubt because of his close association with Lindbergh, the book became an immediate success that year
alongside Anne's. By the following year, his book had bumped *North to the
Orient* off the top of the charts, becoming the nonfiction bestseller of 1936.

Having decided to put New Jersey behind him, Lindbergh spent much of
the summer in the air, trying to find his bearings and a new place to settle.
Poulticing their bruised marriage, he took Anne twice to Little Falls, which
was not much different from when he lived there, except for the sign on the
water tower that bragged, "Charles A. Lindbergh's home town welcomes
you." He took Anne around his farm and house, which sat abandoned on
what had become public parkland. He introduced her to old friends, neighbors, and relatives, including his half-sister Eva, with whom he had not spo-

ken in years. It was a cautious meeting, devoid of bitterness. A visit with Charles's mother in Detroit elicited a flood of memories, though he saw no reason ever to live there. They also went to Long Island several times, where Lindbergh momentarily considered Harry Guggenheim's offer to sell some of his land at Port Washington.

That August, while the Lindberghs were in North Haven, Henry Breckinridge's office wired that Will Rogers had been killed, along with pilot Wiley Post, when their seaplane crashed on takeoff from a lagoon near Point Barrow, Alaska. Charles was on the telephone all day—"suddenly electrified into steely usefulness," noted Anne. For the next three days, he pulled every string necessary to transport Rogers's body from Alaska to Los Angeles for burial at Forest Lawn—all according to the widow's wishes. "OF ALL THE LOVING KINDNESS SHOWN MOTHER THE WONDERFUL THING YOU DID HAS BEEN HER GREATEST COMFORT," wired Rogers's son Bill. The press could not resist mentioning Lindbergh in all the obituaries, linking the nation's two greatest folk heroes.

Lindbergh remained part of the nation's daily conversation even when he was not generating the news, as stories related to the trial continued to consume the public. Hauptmann's fractured defense team began the appeals process; an exhausted Edward Reilly was taken to a hospital in a straitjacket, suffering from a "breakdown"; Jafsie took to the vaudeville circuit; and Mrs. Hauptmann went on the stump, giving speeches to raise money for her husband's defense, for which she hired Lloyd Fisher. His appeal contested 193 points in the original trial. The Flemington jury announced that they were writing a book, each juror contributing a chapter; Hauptmann wrote a brief autobiography, but the prison in Flemington would not allow him to release it while the Appeals Court was considering his case. Lloyd Fisher's investigators claimed to have found a child on Long Island who was "the Lindbergh Baby."

On October 9, 1935, the New Jersey Court of Errors and Appeals unanimously upheld the lower court's first-degree murder conviction, thus adding to the controversy about the fate of Richard Hauptmann. The arguments raged all the way into the office of Governor Harold G. Hoffman. A detective named Ellis Parker aroused the thirty-nine-year-old governor's interest enough to get him to call upon Hauptmann. While getting no answers about the crime, the secret meeting did raise enough new questions for Hoffman to investigate further. Word of the meeting leaked, and the New York *Daily News* announced, "LINDBERGH CASE REOPENED." In early December the *Daily Mirror* began publishing installments of "HAUPTMANN'S OWN STORY!" While Hauptmann's attorneys prepared their brief for the New Jersey Court of Pardons, Hauptmann wrote a personal letter to Hoffman, pleading his innocence and his willingness to take either a lie detector test or a truth serum. (The handwriting in both this and subsequent Hauptmann letters for mercy displayed similarities to the Lindbergh ransom notes.) Judge Trenchard set the date for Hauptmann's execution—January 17, 1936.

Supporters for Hauptmann rallied—some opposed to the death penalty in general, others believing Hauptmann received an unfair trial. ("There are millions of people all over the world waiting for you to come forward and save this man that you condemned with your erring words," an anonymous resident of Port Chester, New York, wrote Charles Lindbergh. "Well Lindy," wrote another anonymous New Yorker, ". . . here is hoping when you and your China-faced wife go up in a plane you will both come down in flames.") Lindbergh became a target for a whole new set of irrational assailants. He received scores of letters that threatened the life of his second son. According to Lindbergh's count, Post Office authorities arrested fourteen people in connection with them.

Even though Next Day Hill was fenced and a night watchman had been hired to make rounds, Lindbergh heard a shout from outside one night, while he was sitting in an upstairs bedroom. He opened the window and looked down upon the pasty face of a babbling mental patient, whom the police came to arrest. Another night, the Lindberghs were returning from Manhattan to Englewood when a car tried to force them into an alley. Lindbergh quickly braked, then sharply turned left, while the other car shot ahead. Local and state police assisted the Lindberghs in these offenses as much as they could, he later wrote, "but alarming incidents still occurred."

Jon was attending The Little School in Englewood (the innovative nursery school Elisabeth Morrow Morgan had started and on whose board Charles sat). One morning, a teacher called Anne to tell her a "suspicious-looking truck," covered with canvas, was parked outside the schoolyard. When the children were called in from recess, the truck left. State troopers found the truck a few miles away—full of newspaper photographers, who had snapped pictures of Jon Lindbergh through slits in the canvas. "No arrests were made," Lindbergh noted, "because no clear violation of the law existed, and the press was so powerful politically that police authorities had to proceed cautiously. The arrest of a photographer or reporter invariably brought claims that freedom of the press was being suppressed."

Then one day late that fall, while one of Jon's teachers was driving him home from school, another car full of men sped up, forcing them into the curb. The terrified teacher clutched Jon, who began to cry. A man jumped out of the car and rushed toward them, thrusting a camera in the boy's face. It was not the first such incident. Lindbergh kept his son from returning to school and hired a retired detective with a sawed-off shotgun to shadow the boy.

That latest incursion by the media, Charles wrote his mother, was "trivial in comparison to the whole situation." There were no laws to protect him from the American press; and fighting back would only enhance his family's visibility, making them even more vulnerable to the ongoing kidnapping threats. On top of that, he felt a number of New Jersey officials had taken to using the Hauptmann case for political gain—specifically Governor Hoffman, who seemed to be considering clemency for Hauptmann and was eager to remove Colonel Schwarzkopf from his post. Lindbergh could no longer concentrate on his work; and leaving his family behind while he was on business trips had become unthinkable. "Between the politician, the tabloid press, and the criminal," he wrote his mother in mid-December, "a condition exists which is intolerable for us."

Lindbergh secretly prepared to move his family away. On December seventh, Charles told Anne to ready herself and Jon to live abroad for the entire winter, if not longer—on twenty-four-hours' notice. Over the next fortnight he quietly obtained passports in Washington and completed travel plans to England, because he believed "the English have greater regard for law and order in their own land than the people of any other nation in the world." Dr. Carrel gave him a letter of introduction to an eminent surgeon there, who could open doors to England's medical community. Aubrey Morgan sailed ahead on a fast boat, so that he could meet them when they arrived and take them to his home in Wales. And on December nineteenth, Lindbergh placed a call to Deak Lyman in the city room at *The New York Times*. He invited the reporter to Englewood, to discuss a matter too confidential for the telephone.

At Next Day Hill, Lindbergh revealed that he was taking his family to England because of the threats against their lives. He had no intention of changing his citizenship, he asserted, merely his residence. Lyman recognized the gravity of this story and asked why Lindbergh had not called any number of other respectable journalists. Lindbergh explained that he wanted the story to be "as dignified and accurate as possible" and that the *Times* had given him the most cooperation during the difficult past few years. He offered Lyman this exclusive, complete with details of his flight from America, on the condition that the *Times* hold the story until the Lindberghs' ship was twenty-four hours at sea. The reporter agreed.

On Saturday, December 21, 1935, Lindbergh called Lyman to say his ship was sailing at midnight. Later that evening, when the reporter was sure the paper had been put to bed, he revealed his scoop to the city editor. The editor wanted to run the story immediately, but Lyman got him to accept the terms to which he had agreed with Lindbergh.

At 10:30 P.M. that Saturday night, Charles, Anne, and Jon said good-bye to Grandma Bee, Constance Morrow, and the staff at Next Day Hill and got into the chauffeured limousine. Accompanied only by Anne's new secretary, Margaret Bartlett "Monte" Millar, they rode in silence to a mostly deserted dock at West Twentieth Street in Manhattan, their ghostly faces flashing in and out of the dark under the streetlamps. Not even the crew of the *American Importer* knew the identity of its only passengers as the Lindberghs marched in absolute silence up the gangplank and down the corridors of the forward deck to their rooms.

Monte Millar shook hands with the Lindberghs and left them to settle into their home for the next ten days. As she disembarked, she could not help thinking, "There was something holy about it all . . ." Not for several more hours, during which Anne lay awake listening to the noise of other ships, did the *American Importer* set sail.

Deak Lyman remained in the city room until he learned that the ship had departed. He returned the next day to write his story. The only man who could explain why the nation's hero felt compelled to leave his homeland, Lyman wrote that the threats against Lindbergh since his flight to Paris had severely escalated over the years. His story omitted only the specifics of the Lindberghs' "flight" plan. Lyman's pages were handled with the utmost secrecy, bypassing copyboys as they went directly to the paper's most trustworthy typesetter. It was later reported that no outgoing telephone calls from the *Times* had been permitted while the story was going to press.

The Lindberghs had enjoyed their first day at sea—sitting on the sunny deck and taking their meals in their cabin—when the Monday issue of *The New York Times* hit the streets.

LINDBERGH FAMILY SAILS FOR ENGLAND
TO SEEK A SAFE, SECLUDED RESIDENCE;
THREATS ON SON'S LIFE FORCE DECISION

read the front-page, four-column headline that crowned Deak Lyman's description of the Lindberghs' passage. "The letters are coming once more, the demands for money, the threats of kidnapping and murder," concluded the eloquent 1,750-word article, which would win Lyman the Pulitzer Prize; "and so the man who eight years ago was hailed as an international hero and a good-will ambassador between the peoples of the world is taking his wife and son to establish, if he can, a secure haven for them in a foreign land."

PART THREE

13

RISING TIDES

"Western civilization—how I had taken it for granted before I came to Europe! It had seemed as immortal as life does to early youth."
—C.A.L.

THE LINDBERGHS WERE AT SEA.

Their crossing would take nine days; beyond that, their future was virtually uncharted.

The *American Importer* encountered a bad storm mid-Atlantic, reconciling the ship's three passengers to a largely cabin-bound journey and a quiet Christmas. Charles did not look back for a moment. As he wrote Henry Breckinridge, he had no intention of returning Stateside until he felt that his three-and-a-half-year-old son could live there "in safety and under reasonably normal conditions at home and at school."

The tempest the Lindberghs faced mid-ocean was not as great as the one they left behind. Deak Lyman's account of the cloaked departure of America's hero launched a massive public discussion about the dismal state of the nation. "I should say that the reaction . . . was overwhelmingly one of consternation and sympathy," wrote Lindbergh's friend Harry Guggenheim. "Your leaving America as you did, so quietly and so suddenly, just seemed to cast a gloom on our nation," wrote a mother from Syracuse, one of countless people he had never met who wished him Godspeed. Journalists and their readers decried how they had forced Lindbergh into exile. Even William Randolph Hearst, whose newspapers had been among the most offensive, proclaimed that "it is extremely distressing and discouraging that this grand country of ours is so overrun with cranks, criminals, and Communists that a splendid citizen like Colonel Lindbergh must take his family abroad to protect them against violence."

The Lindberghs rose early on December 31, 1935, in Liverpool's harbor. It suddenly seemed as though this hegira might be for naught, as a frenzied gauntlet of photographers gathered at the gangplank. Anne descended a few paces ahead of Charles, who carried Jon in one arm—the boy's hat brim pulled down, partially covering his face. On their way to the Adelphi Hotel in town, where they would spend the night, Anne heard newsboys in the streets crying, "Lindbergh in Liverpool!"

The next day, Aubrey Morgan motored the Lindberghs to Brynderwen, Llandaff, Wales, just west of Cardiff. In the privacy of their own apartment in the Morgan manse, surrounded by gardens, they promptly acclimated to their new surroundings. "No fear of the press trespassing on the grounds— or eavesdropping—no fear at night putting Jon up to bed—& then running up to see if he is all right," Anne wrote Charles's mother after but a few days in the Welsh countryside. "We have been bothered very little and seem to be left quietly alone here, both by people & press."

For weeks, the Lindberghs' plans remained indefinite, as Charles talked vaguely of living in England or perhaps Sweden or France. They received unsolicited offers from strangers and friends to stay with them, some from as far off as the Archduke Joseph Francis in Budapest. From Aberdeenshire alone came two proposals—one from Lord Sempill offering his Craigevar Castle, the other from a "poor fisher woman" offering the "warmest corner of our home and heart."

Charles and Anne spent a few nights in London, where Lindbergh found to his amazement that he could walk the streets unmolested. One day, they watched the funeral procession of King George V from their window at the Ritz Hotel; on another occasion they dined with Harold Nicolson, who mentioned that he owned a property not an hour outside London that he was looking to lease. Lindbergh was reluctant to live so close to the city; but London's apparent lack of violent crime opened his mind to that possibility. After several discouraging weeks house-hunting in the countryside, they agreed to inspect Long Barn, the Nicolsons' "tumbled-down . . . cottage" in The Weald of Kent.

Their twenty-five-mile drive to the southeast that last week of February was not as pastoral as they had hoped. But upon passing through Sevenoaks, their outlook brightened. Only the sound of singing birds greeted them as they opened the gate of the old, rambling house, "screened from the road by low feathery trees." Anne and Charles walked to the back where they discovered the two main blocks of the house created a court. Looking down the hill on which they stood, they beheld beautiful gardens and fields and farms as well as a tennis court and swimming pool—"all quiet, all country, all still."

Harold and Vita Sackville-West had lived in Long Barn for almost twenty years before their recent move to nearby Sissinghurst Castle, which they had restored from a pile of Elizabethan ruins into one of England's showplaces. Long Barn displayed their renovative powers as well. A melding of three cottages and a barn, this two-story house rambled without plan. First built in 1380 of oak beams from salvaged ships, its roof sagged from age; its floors sloped, its walls slanted, and its passageways staggered between steep spiral staircases. There was no hall upstairs, so that each of the seven bedrooms opened into the next, often at odd angles.

The Lindberghs giggled upon entering each room, wondering what irregularity they would encounter next. Charles joked that he would enjoy bringing a drunk through the house, for it was without any two lines that were either parallel or perpendicular. Layers of dust had settled on the broken lamp shades and the old palm-leaf fans; and visible cracks in the windows and walls created drafts everywhere. Water had obviously leaked in as well, for several pictures were stained and the paint on the walls was curling. Before they left the house, Charles had only to nod to Anne and say, "Of course there's no question about it—it'll do!"

Within two weeks, the Lindberghs had signed a half-year's lease—for £45.15s a month—and made themselves at home. The only setback at first, Anne noted, was that it was all "too beautiful and I woke up each morning feeling detached and weekendy—like a guest." They arranged for two of their dogs—Thor, the German shepherd, and Skean, the Scottish terrier—to be shipped overseas, on the *Queen Mary*. "I am afraid they have not appreciated the honor," Charles wrote his mother.

Although the lamp-plugs did not fit into the sockets, doors did not lock, toilet chains seldom functioned, and worms had eaten away at much of the furniture—the Lindberghs quickly adjusted to their house. William Caxton, England's first printer, was reputed to have been born at Long Barn in the 1420s, and it was rumored that his ghost could be heard at night, clanking away at his printing press. But Vita Sackville-West assured them that she had not had a single supernatural encounter in the house in her two decades there. The Lindberghs realized that those noises they heard in the night were just mice living in the walls or bats in the bedrooms.

Rearranging furniture and moving in some of their personal belongings, Charles and Anne made Long Barn their own. They hired a small staff, including a plain-looking, red-haired nurse, who, Charles kidded, "lowers our standard." Harold Nicolson assured him that they would live there undisturbed by any of the local citizenry, except for the Chief Constable of Kent himself, who would occasionally drop by for a cup of tea, simply to ascertain whether or not they were "being bothered by curious and vulgar people and whether he can give you more police protection." There was no need. Except for one scuffle with photographers, the press left them alone.

Winston Churchill asked Nicolson to tell Lindbergh that he would be welcome to lunch with him at Chartwell, his nearby estate, whenever he wished.
But the Lindberghs never pursued the invitation.

Not since he quit college to take up flying had Lindbergh felt the opportunity to make such a "fresh start" in life. Cut off from most of his former
business and social connections, he hired a secretary and winnowed away
many of the commitments from his past. In his study at Long Barn, Lindbergh sometimes went weeks doing little else but dictating letters for hours
at a time. Late at night, he often went to Anne's smaller study to catch up on
more mail, handwriting personal letters—on blue onionskin paper from
Smythson's. He continued to make and file carbon copies of even his most
trivial dispatches, as he instinctively felt the need to keep a complete record
of his thoughts and activities. He asked Henry Breckinridge not to destroy
any of the mail, not even the envelopes, sitting in sacks in the attorney's
New York office. "Sometimes the most unimportant looking scrap of paper
turns out to be of great value to the police," Lindbergh explained. "They tell
me that they quite frequently find that seriously threatening letters are preceded by other communications."

While Lindbergh's relationship with Henry Breckinridge waned—especially after the lawyer entered politics and never made good on a $20,000
personal loan from Lindbergh—three friendships deepened in his absence
from America, all with men he felt were involved in nothing less than advancing civilization. He conducted a massive correspondence with Harry
Guggenheim, for one, writing about the citizens' committee against crime in
New York, which Guggenheim had been asked to chair. The two men also
continued their epistolary conversation about rockets. Several institutions, including the California Institute of Technology, were trying to win the support
Guggenheim had been lavishing solely on Professor Goddard. Lindbergh,
however, persuaded his friend that Goddard alone would develop the rocket
better than any team could.

Believing the rocket had entered its most interesting period of discovery,
Lindbergh also corresponded as much as ever with Goddard. After but a
short time abroad, he saw enough political unrest to suggest the possibility
of war in Europe. And so Lindbergh asked Goddard to consider the martial
applications of the rocket, for it could "carry explosives faster than the airplanes, farther than the projectile." In their unguarded correspondence, Lindbergh and Goddard agreed that "the rocket is inherently an offensive rather
than a defensive weapon," specifically in the areas of long-range shelling
and high-speed planes. In no time, Goddard shared with Lindbergh his vision
of "liquid propellant rockets of high speed such as we are testing here [in
Roswell], capable of being directed to air craft from the ground by radio, or

automatically in flight by infra red rays, the explosive charge consisting of the remainder of the propelling charge."

The third great relationship that sustained Lindbergh while he was abroad was with Dr. Carrel. As management of the Rockefeller Institute passed from Simon Flexner to a more bureaucratic Dr. Herbert Gasser, Carrel was being nudged into retirement. Gasser disapproved of the research scientist's high profile, a public image that became sullied by new interpretations of his writings. Carrel's admiration of Mussolini for his "building up of a great nation," for example, read differently now that Mussolini had invaded Ethiopia. Other comments about civilization collapsing, modern nations saving themselves "by developing the strong," not "by protecting the weak," and his concern for the "salvation of the white races" sounded alarmingly like statements being uttered by Hitler.

Carrel liked to display his boldness in almost everything he said, sometimes just for their shock value. (According to one of his colleagues at the Rockefeller Institute, Carrel once kidded that "if he had to live his life over, he would have become a dictator in South America.") In truth, Carrel was an elitist who believed in a disciplined society; but he was appalled by both genocide and anti-Semitism. He was simply alarmed by what he considered the rapid decay of the democracies of the world, which he attributed to a diminution of faith. "He had no love for Nazism, Fascism, or Communism," wrote a friend of Carrel, "but he knew that their ideologies gave those nations an ever-flowing source of energy. By contrast, the democracies seemed to have discarded faith, and there lay the cause of their weakness and inefficiency."

Carrel wrote to Lindbergh about creating a foundation devoted to "the study of man." It was meant to consider: the use of voluntary eugenics in the building up of a stronger human race; procedures to increase the nervous resistance of the individual; psychological, physiological, and chemical factors of spiritual growth; the problems of longevity; social and economic conditions that are "indispensable to the life of an elite"; the possibility of raising human intelligence above its present level; the genesis of great leaders. The outline of Carrel's plans—as broad-scoped as it was high-minded—appealed immensely to Lindbergh, giving him license to take a scattered-fire approach to science for a while and see if he hit anything worth pursuing.

Upon his departure from the Rockefeller Institute, Carrel would return to his native France, maintaining an apartment in Paris but preferring to live on an island off the Brittany coast. In letters, he and Lindbergh discussed the Institute for Man, and everything else under the sun; one of Lindbergh's epistles grew to fifty-six pages. As Lindbergh dabbled in a series of scientific studies, he never failed to rush to Carrel with his results.

Lindbergh's latest scientific work spanned a broad spectrum. He modified his organ perfusion apparatus; he studied infra-red rays so that he might develop an instrument for their projection and measurement; and he read up on genetics. With a growing interest in immunology, he studied gibbons and gorillas, which drew him to texts about animal life in Africa. Combining his interests in aviation and medicine, Lindbergh corresponded with doctors, hospitals, and government agencies around the world, as he considered the possible uses of aircraft in connection with the control of locust on the savanna, tsetse fly research in Tanganyika, and yellow fever research in Entebbe. His original work in organ perfusion got him to thinking about "artificial hibernation"—reducing the respiration and pulse rate of an animal, producing different states of consciousness. He read up on sleep, hypnosis, anesthesia, even Indian mysticism and yogic meditation.

So transfixed was Lindbergh by all his new study, he was virtually oblivious to the topic dominating the news at home. In the months following the October 1935 rejection of his appeal, Bruno Richard Hauptmann found swelling public support for his case. Such champions of justice as Clarence Darrow, H. L. Mencken, and Eleanor Roosevelt all issued public statements—not asserting his innocence so much as questioning his guilt. After studying the eleven volumes of trial transcripts, Governor Harold Hoffman launched his own investigation of the case.

The day before Hauptmann was to be electrocuted, Hoffman granted a reprieve of thirty days. In so doing, he wrote Colonel Schwarzkopf and announced to the press, he was not expressing an opinion as to the guilt or innocence of Hauptmann. It was more, he asserted, that "I am impressed by the evident anxiety of so many people to hurry him to his death when too many questions are still unanswered which he may help to solve." Hoffman focused his action on one aspect of the crime—the complicity of others. "I do not believe," he said, "that this crime was committed by any one man, and there is ample evidence, direct from the record, that the chief witnesses and those who were engaged in the prosecution share my belief. The fact that others are implicated does not provide an excuse for Hauptmann," he added, "but neither does it excuse any official from doing his full duty in bringing every other participant to the bar of justice." Hoffman ordered Colonel Schwarzkopf "to continue a thorough and impartial search for the detection and apprehension of every person connected with the crime."

The next month brought forth no new information, only louder arguments about evidence and witnesses that had already been examined. The execution was rescheduled for the week of March 30, 1936. The confession from Hauptmann, which so many had expected since his capture, never came—not even when a newspaper offered him close to $100,000 for his wife's future security nor when the Governor offered to commute his sentence to life imprisonment for the same confession.

Then, at the eleventh hour, a confession did come—but not from Hauptmann. On March twenty-seventh, each of the eight members of the New Jersey Court of Pardons received a copy of a twenty-five-page typed statement admitting to the crime. It was written by one Paul Wendel, a convicted perjuror, disbarred attorney, and sometime mental patient. It proved to be fraudulent, but for several days it warranted close scrutiny; and with only minutes to go, Hauptmann's execution was postponed for another forty-eight hours. When Governor Hoffman told the Attorney General he believed another reprieve might induce the long-awaited confession, Wilentz convinced him that Hauptmann had been given plenty of last-minute opportunities and that this man would never confess. When Hoffman asked about the possibility of accomplices, Wilentz contended that Hauptmann's naming them would first require incriminating himself, which he would never do.

"What a miserable mess New Jersey had made of the Bruno Hauptmann case!" read the lead editorial in *The Boston Herald* on April second. It echoed the sentiments of most of the nation, that the trial of Hauptmann had been a "shocking exhibition"—with a judge who "exercised little control over his courtroom," where "[y]ellow journalism reached its malodorous climax," in an environment "which suggested the ballyhooed sideshow of a circus." But like most of the nation, the editorial did not call for any mercy for Hauptmann. Harold Hoffman became a symbol of politics interfering with justice. "It may be that at first the Governor had some grounds for doubting the correctness of the verdict," continued the editorial from Boston. "But he has not revealed them. He has not brought forth a shred of evidence to justify his dilatory tactics. The people know as much now about the facts as before he intervened." A movement was launched to impeach him.

After another day, the best case that could be presented for Hauptmann came from André Maurois, who raged at the cruelty of preparing a man for his execution three times. "Whether Hauptmann is guilty or not is no longer the question," he wrote in an article for *Le Figaro,* which made its way around the world. "The death of a guilty man may be necessary for the good of society. But all civilized people ought to admit that a man who has had the order of his execution countermanded at the last moment, should not then be forced to die."

At 8:44 P.M. on Friday, April 3, 1936, Bruno Richard Hauptmann was strapped in a chair in the brightly lit execution chamber at the state prison in Trenton and received three electrical shocks of 2,000 volts. At 8:47 the prison physician pronounced him dead. "HAUPTMANN . . . REMAINS SILENT TO THE END," read *The New York Times* headline the following morning, though, in fact, the executed man left behind a statement he wanted published after his death. It repeated his "innocence of the crime for which I was convicted" and asserted: "Should . . . my death serve for the purpose of abolishing capital punishment—such a punishment being arrived at only by circumstantial evidence—I feel that my death has not been in vain."

Because the Lindbergh kidnapping case ended on an unresolved note, discord over the case will forever linger. Until her death sixty years later, Mrs. Hauptmann petitioned the state to reopen the case; but she found support from neither future governors nor state supreme court justices—one of whom was Attorney General David Wilentz's son.

"WHILE APOLOGIZING FOR THIS INTRUDING YOUR PRIVACY WOULD LIKE TO OFFER FULL FACILITIES OF UNITED PRESS OF AMERICA IF YOU SHOULD DESIRE TO MAKE ANY STATEMENT WHATSOEVER IN CONNECTION HAUPTMANNS EXECUTION," the wire service informed Lindbergh. He made none. Harold Hoffman would persist in privately investigating the case, long after he was voted out of office. He enjoyed some revenge in June 1936, when he chose not to reappoint Colonel Norman Schwarzkopf as head of the New Jersey State Police, believing he had been responsible for the "worst bungled police job in history."

Many in the United States thought the execution might trigger Lindbergh's return; but the postmortems only repelled him further. "There has never been any question in our minds about returning to America," Lindbergh wrote Abraham Flexner later that year. "I do not want to live under conditions similar to those which existed at the time we left. The crime situation is probably a little better, but the newspapers have improved little, if at all, and I believe it would be difficult for the political situation in New Jersey to be much worse. When Colonel Schwarzkopf was head of the State Police, I had complete confidence in that organization at least. Since it has now become involved in New Jersey politics, we have no longer even that element of stability."

"We are very happy in England," Lindbergh asserted. "At least we are able to read and think about things which are both pleasant and interesting." So secure did they feel at Long Barn, the Lindberghs ventured into public. Since their arrival there had been invitations from leaders in aviation, medicine, and government. American Ambassador Robert Bingham's dinner offers usually included the option of spending the night at the Embassy. The Lindberghs became frequent guests of Lady Astor, who took to inviting them for tea or dinner at 4 St. James's Square and for weekends at their magnificent country estate, Cliveden.

The Lindberghs' landlords provided the greatest entrée of all. A friend of the new king, Harold Nicolson informed Lindbergh that His Royal Highness "would be very glad" to resume the acquaintanceship they had formed during two meetings in 1927, after the flight to Paris. Pleased with the invitation,

Lindbergh hoped to arrange for a private audience; but he insisted on one condition: "I have spent a large portion of my life in a country where such a thing [as a top hat] would be immediately shot off," he wrote Nicolson, "and while I wish as far as possible to conform with the customs of England, I still feel quite strongly about this particular item. I did once, under pressure, wear one of these things, but fortunately none of my friends ever found out about it."

On May 12, 1936, the Lindberghs met the King at a "tea" given by the assistant Military Attaché for Air in the United States Embassy in London. Edward VIII arrived with a lady friend, Mrs. Ernest Simpson, an American, whom Anne felt was "not beautiful and yet vital and real to watch," one of "the few authentic characters in a social world—one of those who *start* fashions, not one of those who follow them." Lindbergh and the King had but a few minutes to speak privately before a circle of all the other guests had formed around them. Three days later, a message arrived from St. James's Palace, inviting the Lindberghs to dinner.

May twenty-seventh was Derby night, and the King celebrated with a party for eighteen—including Lord and Lady Mountbatten, Prime Minister and Mrs. Stanley Baldwin, and Mr. and Mrs. Simpson. Although Anne was easily the most accomplished woman at York House that night, she reverted to her insecure self, feeling, "Nothing I said mattered." Charles, utterly relaxed despite having to wear a tail coat and white tie, said little and, as usual, became a center of attention. Afterward, Charles told Anne he got a strong sense from Edward VIII "that he frequently wishes that he could stop being King and have some of the freedom which other men can have."

These occasional sips of the high life reminded Lindbergh why he preferred to abstain. Enjoying more privacy in their marriage than they had ever known, Charles and Anne felt that they had awakened from their four-year nightmare. Holding hands, they walked for miles across their fields each evening, delighting in the flowers and the birds. His dry but corny sense of humor returned. He and Anne ate all their meals with Jon; and Charles taught him the first stanza of Robert Service's "The Shooting of Dan McGrew."

Long Barn became everything Hopewell had been meant to be. Anne settled into a new book, an account of their 1933 journey from Africa to America. Charles became more interested in aviation than he had been in several years. While the business had suffered because of the airmail crisis in 1934, technology had surged. The companies that regained their footing were already taking their planes to new heights, speeds, and destinations.

Both Pan American Airways and Trans World Airlines asked Lindbergh to return to their payrolls as Technical Adviser. He refused them both, feeling he could not accept such a position so long as he saw "no possibility of maintaining a home in the United States to which I am willing to take my family." His participation with both companies, however, hardly diminished. If anything, his correspondence about aviation increased while he was in Europe—especially with Pan Am, whose officers he kept apprised of the latest European developments in aircraft, air routes, and airports. He also got Pan Am and TWA to work together in solving the problems of pressure cabins. And by the end of the following year—only ten years after the *Spirit* flew the Atlantic—Lindbergh was reviewing bids from eight manufacturers for the construction of one-hundred-passenger airplanes that could make the same crossing—aircraft whose cruising speed would be two hundred miles an hour with a range of five thousand miles or more, and a payload capacity of twenty-five thousand pounds.

In addition to his other scientific interests, Lindbergh used his time in England to visit aircraft manufacturers and landing fields. He was appalled that "the country which produced the Industrial Revolution" had allowed much of its aviation industry to rust as it had. It appeared to be a country looking back at the glory of its Navy instead of ahead to the importance of an Air Force. And yet Lindbergh found pockets of progress, especially in military designs, some of which surpassed American planes. That spring, Lindbergh placed an £1800 order with Phillips & Powis Aircraft Ltd. in Reading to build a low-wing monoplane with an American Menasco engine of 250 h.p. A redesign of an existing model—with modifications by Lindbergh—it would have two cockpits in tandem with a sliding roof, orange wings, a black fuselage, a cruising speed of 170 miles per hour, and a range of one thousand miles. The manufacturers promised delivery in August.

For the weekend of April twenty-third through the twenty-sixth and again for a long weekend starting June fifth, the Lindberghs visited Pierre Lecomte du Noüy—a biophysicist, philosopher, and former colleague of Dr. Carrel—at his country house outside Paris. There they also met Carrel's wife, Anne, a large woman with thick gray hair parted in the middle and pulled back off her strong face. Both Lindberghs felt an instant kinship with her— "She has a woman's emotion, quick intuition and understanding," Anne wrote in her journal, "and yet a man's breadth of mind, breadth of view, clarity of vision, impersonality of attitude (the scientific attitude)."

Charles was even more impressed, however, with Mme. Carrel's unexpected interest in the occult. Going outside for a walk that Sunday, he found her looking for her wedding ring, which she had lost. In order to find it, Mme. Carrel sketched a map of the grounds where she had been walking earlier; then she held over the paper a small pendulum—a weight on a string— which kept zeroing in on one particular area. Lindbergh and Anne Carrel walked along the path in the direction of that spot. "Soon Mme. Carrel took the lead," Lindbergh would later record of the event, "with the pendulum in her hand which she held in front of her. About 200 yards from the house, and in the area which she had located, the pendulum began to swing in circles." Mme. Carrel said that the ring was near. Within two minutes the pendulum was "swinging violently," and when they looked down, there it was. That afternoon Mme. Carrel instructed Lindbergh in the ways of the pendulum; and by the end of their visit, he proved to be unusually gifted in its use. He found himself increasingly drawn to mystical phenomena.

Other than the Carrels and their friends, however, little in France impressed Lindbergh positively. The flourishing nation that had apotheosized him a decade earlier had gone to seed. "I have never before been in a country which has so definitely given me the impression that a change of some kind must take place," he wrote Henry Breckinridge. "There is an air of discouragement and neglect on every hand, and people seem to be waiting almost from day to day for something to happen." French cities showed obvious physical disrepair, political corruption, labor unrest, fuel shortages, store closures, and overall lack of leadership. "There is a wonderful feeling of peace and stability in England," Lindbergh wrote a former colleague at the Rockefeller Institute on July 4, 1936, "but it is shaken a little when one crosses to France and finds, in a country so near, such fear of military invasion, such depression and such instability. England now seems to need an ocean instead of a channel on the East." Greater danger lay beyond France.

SHORTLY BEFORE the Lindberghs had moved abroad, the United States Army had appointed Major Truman Smith—a Yale graduate and career officer with a longtime interest in German history—to be Military Attaché to the American Embassy in Berlin. The chief responsibility of the handsome six-foot-four career soldier was "to report to Washington about the growth of the German army, including the development of new weapons and new battle tactics." Smith was soon alarmed, for he recognized that Germany was erecting a new military force in the air—the Luftwaffe—and that American intelligence had gathered little information about it. To make matters worse, the Ambassador—an academician, William Dodd—displayed little interest in military matters; and Washington, accordingly, did not appreciate the magnitude of the German buildup. An infantryman, Smith realized he needed an aviation expert to help him size up the Luftwaffe.

One Sunday morning in May 1936, Smith's wife pointed out a squib on the front page of the *Paris Herald* about Charles Lindbergh's having just visited a French airplane factory. It occurred to Smith that Lindbergh might be just as willing to inspect German air factories.

Smith broached the subject of such a tour to the German Air Ministry and was informed within the day that approval for such a visit had come from the highest levels, Hitler's number-two man and Air Minister, Hermann Goering, and his chief assistant, State Secretary Erhard Milch. Fearing that the Germans might use the visit for their own propagandistic purposes, without revealing anything new, Major Smith asked his German counterpart to specify what combat units, factories, and bases they would show such a distinguished visitor as Lindbergh. The list included a number of air installations not yet seen by any American. Never having met Lindbergh, Smith mailed his invitation in care of the assistant air attaché in London, assuring Lindbergh that his visit would be interesting, private, and "of high patriotic benefit."

Lindbergh was intrigued. "Comparatively little is known about the present status of Aviation in Germany," he wrote his mother of the unique opportunity, "so I am looking forward, with great interest, to going there. Even under the difficulties she has encountered since the war, Germany has taken a leading part in a number of aviation developments, including metal construction, low-wing designs, dirigibles, and Diesel engines. If it had not been for the war she would probably have produced a great deal more. On the other hand, if it had not been for the war it is doubtful whether aviation would be as far advanced as it is today."

Lindbergh requested only that the proposed dates of the visit be changed, so that he could keep appointments he had already with Carrel and a Frenchman who was reputed to have exceptional powers in the use of a pendulum. The Germans complied, suggesting the last week of July and insisting that the Lindberghs attend the August first opening ceremonies of the Olympic Games in Berlin, as Goering's special guest.

Only in the last month had Lindbergh requested a reappointment in the Air Corps Reserve, so that he could become "immediately effective in case our country is ever involved in war." Because of that military status, he was being invited as a civil guest of Lufthansa, the German commercial airline, rather than as a guest of the Luftwaffe. Much of the program the Air Ministry assembled for Lindbergh pertained to commercial aviation; but according to the man who initiated Lindbergh's visit, there was no mistaking this as anything but a military mission.

Borrowing a Miles Whitney Straight from Phillips & Powis, Lindbergh and his wife flew on July twenty-second from England to Berlin, landing at Staaken—the military airport. Fifteen huge German bombers and a phalanx of heel-clicking officers were on hand to greet them. The president of the Air Club of Germany welcomed Lindbergh in the name of the entire German aviation community. The Lindberghs were driven into town separately—Charles in an open car with Truman Smith, to the reminiscent sound of a cheering crowd, while Anne rode with his wife, Kay. Germany appeared recovered from the Great War. A sense of festivity, even superiority filled the streets, which were draped with the red-and-black Nazi flags. Past the Brandenburg Gate, Anne noticed young slips of trees planted in perfect rows. The Lindberghs stayed with the Smiths in their apartment; and Charles found his host an unusually "able and perceptive army officer."

While Anne enjoyed a week of deluxe tours around Berlin, Charles followed a rigid military schedule, a succession of inspections. Accompanied by an assistant air attaché, Theodore Koenig, Lindbergh visited the Tempelhof civil airport, where he was permitted to pilot a Junkers (JU) 52, the Luftwaffe's standard bombardment plane, and the Hindenburg, a large four-motored experimental passenger plane. He spent a day with the Richthofen *Geschwader* (Wing), the elite fighter group of the Luftwaffe. One day he visited two Heinkel factories and saw their latest dive-bomber, medium bomber, fighter, and observation planes—all, Lindbergh found, of superb design. He spent another day at the Junker works at Dessau, where he saw their new JU 210 engine, a liquid-cooled engine far more advanced than he or Koenig had expected, and a JU 86, a low-wing, all-metal medium bomber already in mass production. Lindbergh spent another day at the German air research institute of Adlershof, where the scientists spoke freely of their work until he steered the conversation to the subject of rockets.

In light of all the new construction he saw, Lindbergh concluded that Germany was "now able to produce military aircraft faster than any European country. Possibly even faster than we could in the States for the first few weeks after we started competitions. Certainly we have nothing to compare in size to either the Heinkel or Junkers factories," he wrote Harry Davison. Even greater than the size of the plants and their crews was "a spirit in Germany which I have not seen in any other country. There is certainly great ability, and I am inclined to think more intelligent leadership than is generally recognized. A person would have to be blind not to realize that they have already built up tremendous strength," he wrote Henry Breckinridge.

Lindbergh participated in three important social events during his week in Germany. The first came the day after his arrival at an Air Club luncheon in his honor. Before a crowd of aviators and diplomats, Lindbergh delivered a speech, which he had worked on for weeks. Its text ran longer than anybody had expected, prolonged by its having to be translated into German, sentence by sentence. Its subtext lingered long after it had been delivered. "We who are in aviation carry a heavy responsibility on our shoulders," Lindbergh said, "for while we have been drawing the world closer together in peace we have stripped the armor of every nation in war. It is no longer possible to shield the heart of a country with its army. Armies can no more stop an air attack than a suit of mail can stop a rifle bullet. . . . Our libraries, our museums, every institution we value most, are laid bare to our bombardment."

With his unique diplomatic status, Lindbergh seized this opportunity to express a simple sentiment theretofore unspoken. "In making the address," he would later explain, "I tried to issue a warning of the dangers involved in the Nazi military development, and, at the same time, keep in mind that I was a guest of Germany on an invitation issued through the military branch of an American Embassy." In straddling that line, he drew his lunchtime remarks to a close by saying: "Aviation has brought a revolutionary change to a world already staggering from changes. It is our responsibility to make sure that in doing so we do not destroy the very things which we wish to protect."

The reaction in the hall and in the German press was measured. While Hitler himself was said to have insisted that the newspapers print the speech in its entirety, no papers commented editorially.

The reaction elsewhere was far less repressed. Speaking of a "new" Charles A. Lindbergh, *The Literary Digest* observed, "He was Lindbergh in full maturity, no longer shy, ready to take his place as a world citizen, among the influential of the planet. In a ten-minute speech . . . and at the age of thirty-four, he had thoughtfully and deliberately abandoned forever, the role of private citizen to which he had clung with desperate futility since he stepped out of 'The Spirit of St. Louis' at Paris at twenty-five." "Colonel Lindbergh's frank, truthful and courageous words have rendered a notable service to Europe and perhaps to the entire world," wrote British pundit Henry Wickham Steed. The speech deeply moved Dorothy Thompson, columnist in the *New York Herald Tribune,* as well. It reminded her of another brave oration, one she had heard as a young woman just out of college, when the recently defeated Congressman C. A. Lindbergh had argued against American intervention into the European war. "The colonel spoke bravely in the midst of the quicksands, with the backing and aid of world prestige and world renown," Thompson wrote on July 28, 1936. "But it was from his father, whom the war drove into obscurity, that he inherited both the courage and the right to speak as he did and where he did. There is some justice in history. And 'as the twig is bent, so is the tree inclined.' " Editorial reaction at home was almost unanimously favorable.

Some Jews, however, wished Lindbergh had never gone to Germany. "I AM CONVINCED THAT THE GERMAN PROPAGANDA DEPARTMENT WILL TRY TO INTERPRET YOUR VISIT AS AN APPROVAL OF THEIR REGIME," cabled Harry Guggenheim's brother-in-law Roger Straus. "I EARNESTLY REQUEST THAT YOU DO WHATEVER YOU CAN TO PREVENT SUCH AN INTERPRETATION BEING MADE EITHER WITHIN OR WITHOUT GERMANY." The world was already aware of overt public acts of anti-Semitism in Germany—the Nuremberg Laws of 1935 stripped the Jews of German citizenship and forbade their marrying Aryans, while earlier laws had already restricted their employment and excluded them from public office, participation in any of the mass media, or sitting on the stock exchanges. But Guggenheim himself wrote Lindbergh that he had "every confidence that you would so conduct yourself as to give no aid to anti-Semitism."

Lindbergh's second important social occasion in Berlin was on July 28, 1936, when Hermann Goering hosted a formal luncheon in his honor at his opulent official residence on the Wilhelm Strasse. Past a line of bows and salutes, the Lindberghs were taken upstairs into a long hall, where Frau Goering—dressed in green velvet and wearing a dazzling pin, a diamond swastika set in emeralds—greeted them. The most important figures in German aviation—including Chief of the Technical Bureau of the Luftwaffe, Colonel Ernst Udet, whom Lindbergh had met years earlier at air races in America—suddenly fell silent when a pair of doors at one end of the room opened and an imposing figure appeared.

General Goering wore a white uniform bedecked with gold braid and medals. His body was turning to schlag, but the visage was still worthy of marble—strong, good-looking, and youthful. "There were few people in Berlin in 1936 who doubted that Goering was dangerous and a 'killer,' " observed Truman Smith of the Führer's most faithful adjutant—for he had undoubtedly been involved in the "blood purge" of June 30, 1934, and other internecine atrocities. But Goering also presented himself as the Third Reich's renaissance man—the one with an eye for masterworks of art, antique furniture, precious stones, as well as the German crafts of handwrought silver, porcelain, and weaving tapestries. "My paladin," Hitler called him, appointing him not only Air Minister but also the presiding officer of the Reichstag, Commissioner for the Four-Year Plan for economic recovery, Director of the state theaters of Prussia, and Minister of forests.

Goering made charming conversation with Anne during lunch—about the opera at Bayreuth, the fine wine, and her role in aviation; but he was most interested in her husband. Long fascinated with all things Swedish, Goering wanted time with Lindbergh alone.

After their meal, Goering and the Lindberghs walked through art-filled galleries to a less formal room, where he sat on a couch and played with his pet lion until the beast urinated on his white pant leg. While Goering changed into a pair of golf knickers, the Lindberghs were granted the further honor of visiting Goering's study, a long, book-lined drawing room decorated in scarlet and gold, with tapestries, Madonnas, and other *objets d'art* he had "borrowed" from German museums. Now reeking of cologne, Goering rejoined them, showing off his possessions, including a fine sword. He handed it to Lindbergh to test, but Lindbergh courteously refused. At last, Goering took Lindbergh off alone to a side table on which sat a photograph album. "Here are our first seventy," he said turning the pages, each of which contained a picture of a military airfield. "From the inspection trips I had made through German factories," Lindbergh would later note, "I knew warplanes were being built to fill those fields."

"Beyond question," Truman Smith would later write of that afternoon, "the 'state' luncheon of Goering's was an important milestone in the air intelligence progress of the office of the American attaché. From this day on, an even closer liaison developed between the American officers and the Air Ministry." Had it not been for Lindbergh's visit to Germany in 1936, "it is likely that the American air attachés would never have obtained the privileged position that was soon theirs in the Berlin attaché corps."

At the third important social event, on his last full day in Germany, Lindbergh got a glimpse of Adolf Hitler himself. On August first, both Lindberghs joined a crowd of one hundred thousand for the colorful opening ceremonies of the Olympic Games. The predominantly German crowd cheered wildly when Hitler arrived in the stadium and received a bouquet of roses from a young blonde girl. Lindbergh had a choice seat from which to view the proceedings. Although Truman Smith, with the approval of the Embassy, had hoped to arrange for a meeting between Lindbergh and Hitler, Lindbergh's place on one of the gray stone benches of the grandstand that day was the closest he would ever get to the Führer.

The following afternoon, the Lindberghs flew to Copenhagen, where Charles and Dr. Carrel addressed the International Congress of Experimental Cytology. They remained for two weeks, during which time Lindbergh and his mentor demonstrated their pump—perfusing a cat's thyroid gland—in a small room of the Carlsbad Biological Institute for ten scientists at a time. In this, Lindbergh's debut before a scientific body, he explained each part of the apparatus, while Dr. Carrel translated into French. After viewing the mechanism, many of the two hundred fifty scientists who saw the pump in action declared that "Lindbergh's work as a scientist would probably be remembered long after his flight to Paris is only a dimly recalled event in aviation history."

Lindbergh himself had, in fact, become more concerned with the immediate future; and in the middle of his stay in Copenhagen, he committed to paper some thoughts. "As I travel in Europe," he wrote, "I become more concerned about the power of destruction which is being built in aircraft; yet it is not so much the power I think is dangerous, as the suddenness with which it can be used. There has been great military power assembled before but it could only be expended with comparative slowness. The flame of war has never been difficult to light, but while it has burned in the past it is more likely to explode in the future."

For all his fears, Lindbergh could not help feeling Germany was "the most interesting nation in the world today, and that she is attempting to find a solution for some of our most fundamental problems." Some solutions he had trouble accepting, as with the case of a brilliant young doctor he met in Copenhagen: Richard Bing, a half-Jewish German citizen, was just then coming "under the Jewish stigma." Lindbergh and Carrel rushed to Bing's aid, helping him secure a grant from the Rockefeller Foundation, which enabled him to move to New York and become an American citizen. But Lindbergh could not open his eyes to the fact that Nazi anti-Semitism was much more difficult to deal with than that.

"There is no need for me to tell you that I am not in accord with the Jewish situation in Germany," he wrote Harry Guggenheim after his visit to Germany. And while he was not yet able to accept what he heard as anything but rumor or propaganda, the "undercurrent of feeling" was "that the German Jews had been on the side of the Communists."

"While I still have many reservations," Lindbergh wrote Truman Smith from Denmark, "I have come away with a feeling of great admiration for the German people. The condition of the country, and the appearance of the average person whom I saw, leaves with me the impression that Hitler must have far more character and vision than I thought existed in the German leader who has been painted in so many different ways by the accounts in America and England."

"With all the things we criticise," Lindbergh added, this time to Harry Davison at J. P. Morgan, "he is undoubtedly a great man, and I believe has done much for the German people. He is a fanatic in many ways, and anyone can see that there is a certain amount of fanaticism in Germany today. It is less than I expected, but it is there. On the other hand, Hitler has accomplished results (good in addition to bad), which could hardly have been accomplished without some fanaticism."

In thanking General Goering for his visit, Lindbergh offered nothing but praise. "It is always a pleasure to see good workmanship combined with vision in design and great technical ability," he wrote on August 20, 1936. "I have never been more impressed than I was with the aviation organizations I saw in Germany. I believe that the experimental laboratories which are being constructed will undoubtedly contribute very greatly to the progress of aviation throughout the world."

In the afterglow of the Berlin Olympics, Lindbergh's feelings toward Germany were hardly unique. Anne, even more than Charles, found herself shocked by the "strictly puritanical view at home that dictatorships are of necessity wrong, evil, unstable and no good can come of them—combined with our funny-paper view of Hitler as a clown—combined with the very strong (naturally) Jewish propaganda in the Jewish owned papers." While Anne's published papers would later reveal her enthusiasm for the new vitality in Germany, she would take her editor's advice and expurgate some of her gushier effusions about her ten "perfectly thrilling" days in Berlin. "Hitler," she wrote her mother on August 5, 1936, "I am beginning to feel, is a very great man, like an inspired religious leader—and as such rather fanatical—but not scheming, not selfish, not greedy for power, but a mystic, a visionary who really wants the best for his country and *on the whole* has rather a broad view."

The Lindberghs were hardly alone in being swayed by Hitler's magnetism. Arnold Toynbee and Lloyd George had recently formed similar opinions. From Lindbergh's vantage point, "Europe, and the entire world, is fortunate that a Nazi Germany lies, at present, between Communistic Russia and a demoralized France. With the extremes of government which now exist, it is more desirable than ever to keep any one of them from sweeping over Europe. But if the choice must be made it can not be Communism." In the end, Lindbergh felt the Germans were "especially anxious to maintain a friendly relationship with England," they had no "intention of attacking France for many years to come, if at all," and they seemed "to have a sincere desire for friendly relations with the United States, but of course that is much less vital to them."

"I don't believe anybody else in the world could have succeeded in doing what you did," Major Smith wrote Colonel Lindbergh after his visit: "pleasing everybody, both the German public and the American public." After that visit, Truman Smith observed, "Captain Koenig found himself in a privileged position in the attaché corps. In the ensuing twelve months, he visited more factories and airfields than any other foreign attaché, with the possible exception of the Swedes and the Italians." Of even greater benefit, Smith added, by the end of that year, Air Corps headquarters in Washington awakened at last to the "imposing rearmament program in Germany."

Something reawakened in Lindbergh as well, a spirit that had lain dormant since his son's kidnapping. His wanderlust had returned. Over the next year he would spend more than two hundred hours in the air, most of it piloting his new Miles Mohawk with its Menasco B6 engine, across three continents. These flights—always in the name of professional aviation but just as much for his personal edification—had not lost their power to enthrall the world.

In November 1936, he flew alone to Ireland to inspect a landing field for Pan American. What was meant to be a three-day trip stretched to ten, as a stubborn fog created the longest delay Lindbergh had ever faced on account of weather. He made the most of his time in the home of his forefathers, the Lodges and Kissanes. "It has always had a strange attraction for me," Charles wrote his mother of Ireland. "Possibly because I shall never forget the first sight of the hills of Kerry from the *Spirit of St. Louis;* possibly because a love of the old country is passed on even to the distant descendants of all Irishmen."

Lindbergh gave Eamon de Valera, the Prime Minister of the Republic of Ireland, his first airplane ride; and the thrilled passenger invited Lindbergh to a dinner he was giving for U. S. Postmaster General Farley. En route to the dinner, Lindbergh thought it might amuse his host, the Minister of Defence, to know that he and Farley had been on opposite sides of the recent airmail controversy. "Oh! Don't let that worry you," he replied in his lilting brogue. "The leader of the opposition will be present tonight. He executed seventy-nine of us a few years ago. We haven't forgotten it, but we don't bring politics into affairs for people from other countries." Anne was happy to have sat this trip out, for she had recently discovered she was pregnant for the third time, her baby due in May.

The Lindberghs spent Christmas at Long Barn, preparing for a major trip on which his wife would accompany him. During the many stops they would make in Asia, Africa, and Europe in early 1937, the Lindberghs observed what Charles would later record were "the early symptoms of the breakup of the British Empire and of Western civilization's waning power in the East":

In Rome, Lindbergh was startled by the omnipresence of Mussolini's soldiers and intrigued by the massive excavation within the city, exposing its great past in building its future. "The twentieth-century dictator prophesied that Italy would return for a third time to be the directing force of Western civilization," Lindbergh observed. "He would electrify railways, drain the Pontine Marshes, increase the birth rate, and reclaim the Italian Empire. How imitative it was! A dictatorship, conquest, and power, armies marching off for Africa and Spain, great structures rising—one might be describing ancient Rome instead of modern Italy."

The Lindberghs flew down the Tyrrhenian coast, over the ruins of Pompeii. Charles looked at the skeleton of the magnificent Grecian temple of Jupiter at Segesta in Sicily and could not help feeling "that a people who had hewn such mystic beauty from the material of stone could have risen above the morbidity of war and human quarreling. Yet," he realized, "the Greek city-states were in constant disagreement, and the civilization they had developed gave way to the centralized power of Rome."

Flying over what had once been a Roman triumphal arch in Carthage, the remnants of ancient Alexandria and Cairo, an old wall from Biblical Jerusalem, and the site of Babylon, Lindbergh saw reminders of once glorious civilizations, all fitting together in his mind like pieces of a jigsaw puzzle.

Into March, they crossed India just above its mid-section, from Gwadar to Calcutta, stopping in Karachi, Jodhpur, Udaipur, Bombay, Nagpur, and

Raipur. They would have toured the country from Kashmir in the north to Ceylon in the south as well, had an engine part not failed, grounding their plane for more than two weeks. They spent most of that time in Calcutta, which had been Lindbergh's ultimate destination anyway. His purpose in traveling this distance was in part to advance aviation—"On the one hand," he would later write, "it was time to establish air routes around the entire earth and I wanted to gain first-hand experience in the area lying between eastern Europe and China."

On the other, he was interested in Indian mystical phenomena. In London libraries Lindbergh had read medical reports of yogis "who controlled their pulse and breath, of an Indian who drank sulphuric acid and still lived, of others who had themselves buried alive for days or walked uninjured over beds of glowing coals. There were publications from more doubtful sources which described miracles of levitation and clairvoyance." In India he hoped to "learn secrets as yet undiscovered by Western science . . . even find bridges between the physical and spiritual worlds. After all, radio was unknown not many years before. Why mightn't there be some way of recording emanations from the human spirit?"

Lindbergh also hoped to meet up with one of his English neighbors, Sir Francis Younghusband—a British soldier, explorer, author, and mystic—who had led the British expedition into the forbidden city of Lhasa in 1904 and who was attending a Parliament of Religions organized in honor of the Eastern saint and mystic Ramakrishna.

During several sessions the Lindberghs sat in the front row of a Calcutta auditorium, before a large picture of Ramakrishna. Charles listened intently to Sir Francis "advocate the unity of faiths under a brotherhood of man," the audience "striving hard to break down the religious barriers between them." Anne could barely keep a straight face, seeing her agnostic husband in front of banners declaring "Religion is the highest expression of man," as he sat among "crowds of barefoot Indian monks, holy men, students, and a few stray, wispy people from Pasadena, London, Boston, following an Indian swami in an orange turban." She had to bite her lip when the alarm on Charles's wristwatch alarm sounded in the middle of a prayer. At another session an Indian poetess noticed the famous visitor from the West and compared him to "Buddha, Galileo, and other spiritual figures of the world." Lindbergh's embarrassment was visible. "What other man on earth today could have his blush reported on five continents?" *The New York Times* asked in an editorial. "Not STALIN, MUSSOLINI, nor HITLER. They are past the blushing stage."

Lindbergh also got to explore Calcutta, observing its poverty, filth, and disease. He could hardly believe this same country had "once produced a civilization of art and architecture and religion—or that conditions were in fact worse before the British government took over." On March 18, 1937, the Lindberghs flew their repaired plane over Fatehpur Sikri, the former capital of Akbar, descendant of the Mogul khans. "These were once great buildings," Lindbergh noted, "now a mass of ruins."

They arrived in Athens at the start of April. Wandering among the broken columns of the Acropolis after having seen the remains of a dozen other civilizations, Lindbergh reached an epiphany. "In these ruins," he realized, "lay a timeless warning. At the same moment, one sensed the heights of Western achievement and the depths of Western failure. One realized how easily strength was perverted to decay, how human wisdom was more essential to a temple's walls than the rock on which it stood." Lindbergh thought of Athens and Sparta warring with each other until all of Greece collapsed. Now he thought of England and Germany assuming those same positions. "War! War!" he would later write. "What useless conflicts there had been through those intervening centuries!" Seeing that cycle gearing up anew, Lindbergh became consumed with the idea of stopping it.

Anne and Charles returned to Long Barn on April 9, 1937. His travels had led him to see England in a new light. The impending coronation of George VI, who had ascended to the throne upon the abdication of Edward VIII the preceding December, depressed him. "The life of the monarch should be an example to his subjects," Lindbergh wrote. "A good king must either have great strength or a good reputation." He felt the monarchy had lost much of its prestige as a result of the whole affair: "There is no example of true romance, and no clear principle has been established—unless it be that the King of England may have his mistresses, but must not marry a twice divorced woman. However, the majority of the Empire carries on with cowlike placidity and satisfaction in the knowledge that they now have a king who will do the proper thing."

Lindbergh appreciated all that England had offered him and his family. He and his family had lived "without worry from politics, press, or fanaticism," he wrote Colonel Schwarzkopf back in New Jersey. And yet, England now struck him as a backward nation, another crumbling empire. "It was as though the Englishman's accomplishments, century after century, had become a cumulative burden on his shoulders until his traditions, his possessions, and his pride overweighed his buoyancy of spirit," he would later write. "I felt that England, aged, saw not the future but the past and had resigned herself to the gardens of her greatness year by year. She was satisfied with her empire and a legal status quo enforced by her warships' guns. It was as though her desires blocked out the knowledge of her mind that life is not stabilized for long by conquest, and that wings fly over land and sea and gun batteries." It troubled Lindbergh that the best propeller he could get for his Miles Mohawk in England was of the type he had used on the St. Louis-

Chicago airmail in 1926, one already obsolete in America by the time the *Spirit of St. Louis* had been built.

The night of May 11, 1937—Coronation Eve—Charles drove Anne into the city. She had felt labor pains for two days, and she suffered more in the car, just as they found Oxford Street blocked off for the next day's procession. Pulling out of a huge traffic jam on Wigmore Street, Lindbergh was asked if he had a permit to drive through. "I have something better than a pass," he told the constable. "I have my wife, who is going to have a baby." They registered Anne in The London Clinic as "Mrs. Charles," and she lay there quietly through another night and day. Doctors and nurses agreed the baby would not be arriving on Coronation Day; but around eleven that night, Anne went into labor. Charles, gowned and masked, was present for the birth, forty-five minutes later. "A Coronation baby, after all!" Anne would record in her diary. He had blue eyes, what Anne called the Morrow "pug," and the unmistakable Lindbergh cleft in his chin.

Because public attention had been diverted, it was several days before the press caught wind of the birth. One night while reporters staked out the main entrance of the clinic, Charles slipped Anne and their new son out the doctors' entrance and into a waiting car. They enjoyed another several days of quiet at Long Barn before the press discovered them there. Charles had arranged to bypass normal governmental regulations on the registering of births; and it was May twenty-fourth before he submitted a press release of the event to the American Embassy. Not until June twenty-first did Lindbergh register his son's name—Land, Evangeline Lindbergh's maiden name.

All that spring, several joyous Morrow events made Anne feel the gentle tug of her family. Her mother received an honorary Doctorate of Humane Letters from Smith College; her sister Constance, upon turning twenty-one, married Aubrey Morgan, their late sister Elisabeth's widower; and her brother, Dwight Jr., after many years of treatment for mental disorders, was well enough to marry Margot Loines, a friend of Constance. But Anne knew it would be the worst time for Charles to return to New York, for that May twentieth to the twenty-first would mark the tenth anniversary of his flight. A committee of college presidents, ambassadors, military leaders, and captains of industry, headed by General Pershing, Governor Lehman, Mayor LaGuardia, and Orville Wright joined forces for the occasion. "I am embarrassed to think of your being asked to devote your time and energy to preparing a speech for the anniversary of my flight to Paris," Lindbergh wrote Morgan partner Thomas W. Lamont. "I believe that the past should not be turned into an obligation for the future; and ceremonies for celebrating past events almost invariably become an obligation for those taking part in them. It seems to me that the past should be used to simplify rather than to complicate our lives. At this time, especially, there are too many serious problems which require concentrated attention to justify our spending very much time celebrating the accomplishments of another period."

The guest of honor's absence notwithstanding, a day of encomiastic ceremonies and intercontinental broadcasts took place in both New York and Paris, culminating in a banquet for hundreds at the Waldorf-Astoria. *The New York Times* noted in its editorial that day that "When this age is viewed in retrospect the monument to Colonel LINDBERGH . . . will more probably be for his impetus and continuing contribution in bringing about the air transport era than even for his heroic deed of May 20–21, 1927." Indeed, in St. Louis alone—where 165,000 people turned out for a three-day air meet celebrating the 1927 flight—airline and airmail service had doubled in the last eighteen months.

Lindbergh spent the day quietly in England, refusing all invitations to speak to reporters or over the radio. He acknowledged the anniversary only by placing an order with Tiffany & Company in London for eight silver boxes—the lids engraved with maps showing the route of his famous plane—one for each of his St. Louis backers.

The Lindberghs continued to explore Europe, making two trips that summer to the Carrels' private island off the Brittany coast; and in October they accepted a second invitation from Germany, officially to attend the Lilienthal Aeronautical Society Congress in Munich and unofficially to gather more intelligence about the Luftwaffe for the United States Army.

"What a life you have had!" Ambassador Dodd wrote Lindbergh in advance of his visit. "There is not a match for it in all our history; but what dangerous plans lie ahead for poor old Europe. I hope you may render some service in the direction of peace." Lindbergh could not help feeling the same, that he was singularly able to visit any country in the world and collect information about its air forces. Such information, he believed, was crucial for the avoidance of war, for, as he wrote the Ambassador, "It is not sufficient for people to desire peace. It is necessary to be able to enforce peace, and to do away with the advantages which may be obtained by war." To Lindbergh, that meant "preparing" for it.

Charles and Anne flew their Miles Mohawk to Munich on October 11, 1937, and spent the next five days in and around the city. During the Lilienthal Congress the Lindberghs were lodged in a thirteenth-century castle nestled in the Bavarian Alps as guests of an anti-Nazi baron. Lindbergh met no leaders of the Third Reich this trip; and he left Germany even more impressed than he had the last time. "Hitler is apparently more popular than ever in Germany," Lindbergh wrote Dr. Carrel, "and, much as I disagree with some of the things which have been done, I can understand his popularity.

He has done much for Germany." Charles wrote Anne's friend Amey Aldrich that he saw "youth, hope and vigor in Germany today—and a strength . . . based on one of the strongest of foundations—defeat."

As before, Lindbergh visited factories and airfields. Even more impressive than the array of shiny planes he saw was the large decentralized system of small factories ready to mint many more of them. Lindbergh was the first American to visit the Focke-Wulf factory in Bremen, where the Germans demonstrated a model of a flying machine that landed and took off vertically and was able to hover without any apparent movement; it could also fly backward or forward with good maneuverability in turning. "I have never seen a more successful demonstration of an experimental machine," he would write of the helicopter.

Most important, Ernst Udet of the Luftwaffe was authorized to show Lindbergh alone the Rechlin air testing station in Pomerania. "This," Truman Smith commented, "was one of the most secret establishments in Germany, and so far as was then known, foreign attachés were barred." Lindbergh thus became the first American to examine in detail the Messerschmitt (ME) 109, the Luftwaffe's leading single-engine fighter, as well as the Dornier (DO) 17, its latest light bomber-reconnaissance airplane. From his visits, he gathered that the Luftwaffe was developing a Messerschmitt 110, a twin-engined fighter with 1200 h.p. Daimler-Benz engines—which turned out to be the case. Before Lindbergh's departure, he helped Truman Smith prepare Report no. 15540, "General Estimate (of Germany's Air Power) of November 1, 1937."

"Germany is once more a world power in the air," announced the four-page survey. "Her air force and her air industry have emerged from the kindergarten stage. Full manhood will still not be reached for three years." The report detailed the planes Lindbergh had seen and estimated the strength of the entire air force which he had not seen. He said that Germany had already outdistanced France in its technical development and had all but closed the gap on Great Britain. "A highly competent observer," Truman wrote in conclusion, referring to Lindbergh, estimated that "if the present progress curves of [America and Germany] should continue as they have in the past two years, Germany should obtain technical parity with the USA by 1941 or 1942." At the end of the year, Truman Smith returned to America on leave and discovered his report had been photostatted and circulated widely. He was, therefore, disappointed to see Congress cut rather than increase War Department requests for appropriations for the Army Air Corps.

Other American embassies wrote Lindbergh, inviting him to inspect air bases in their countries. But at the end of 1937, he was most anxious to see what strides America was making in aviation. So mindful was Lindbergh of his position in these obviously historical times, he began to keep a journal.

For the first time in his life, he would write daily entries for more than a few weeks; in fact, he would maintain the habit for most of the next seven years.

The Lindberghs celebrated a quiet—and early—Christmas at Long Barn, with their two children, on the twenty-fifth of November. Charles and Anne were sailing on the S. S. *President Harding* on the twenty-seventh, and they planned to be gone several months. Charles had clearly developed a pattern of embarking on a long trip after the birth of each child, as though weaning his wife from their children.

They stuck to themselves during the crossing, mostly writing. Anne progressed on *Listen! The Wind,* her account of their Africa-to-America journey; and Charles prepared chapters of a medical book he was cowriting with Dr. Carrel, *The Culture of Organs*. Before their ship had docked, the Lindberghs learned that reporters had flocked to meet them. Charles took Anne to the third-class gangplank and down a freight elevator, thereby evading the army of photographers and journalists waiting at the foot of the first-class gangplank. The newsmen ran after them, but they escaped to Mrs. Morrow's waiting car.

No sooner had they reached Next Day Hill than the press cars had returned to wait outside the gate. A sentry had to be put on duty, which the media soon exaggerated, reporting twelve policemen on guard, as well as a direct telephone wire to the state police headquarters. "Suppose we will have constant trouble with press now," Lindbergh wrote in his new journal. "Rumors, lies & all the sensation of American journalism at its worst."

"Let's leave Colonel Lindbergh alone," Frank E. Gannett urged the editors of the papers that comprised his chain. "I believe firmly that it is a newspaper's duty to print the news, but I am utterly opposed to the invasion of the privacy of a citizen." Other major media announced a similar policy, in an effort to prove that the Lindberghs' fleeing America had taught them a lesson. But within days, the press coverage was as bad as ever.

Most of the Lindberghs' trip was spent catching up with old friends and business associates. Other than sitting for Robert Brackman, who painted oil portraits of both Charles and Anne, the most consequential encounter was with a good-looking, bespectacled thirty-two-year-old named James Newton. An entrepreneurial real-estate developer from Fort Myers, Florida—and a friend of Thomas Edison and Henry Ford—Newton moved on to a strenuous career working for Harvey Firestone, until he collapsed from overwork. Then he found himself attracted to the Oxford Group, "an informal association of men and women, started by an American, Frank Buchman, who were committed to creating sound homes, teamwork in industry, and unity within and between nations, based on moral and spiritual change." Introduced by Dr. Carrel, Newton—a powerful personality with a gentle soul— would become Lindbergh's most constant friend for the rest of his life.

Lindbergh did not get to survey American developments in aviation on this trip, as he had hoped; but what little he saw convinced him, as he wrote Major General Frank Ross McCoy, "that Germany is rapidly surpassing us in air strength."

On February 20, 1938, Hitler spoke to the Reichstag of the ten million Germans living just beyond his borders, suggesting his vision of an Anschluss. By the time the Lindberghs boarded the England-bound *Bremen,* less than three weeks later, the Nazis had marched into Austria. Lindbergh was already dreading the possibility that America and Germany might end up crossing swords. "If we fight, our countries will only lose their best men," Lindbergh noted, echoing his late father's sentiments. "We can gain nothing. . . . It must not happen."

Lindbergh found such thinking lost on the English. To him, they seemed worried about Germany but just as incapable of doing anything about it. Except for a few people he met at Cliveden, he found the conversation at tea parties centered on grouse hunting and the indomitability of the Royal Navy. "And the people show little sign of changing," he wrote. "They need an entirely new spirit if British greatness is to endure." Literally choking on the smoke-filled fog of London, Lindbergh craved fresh air.

THE MOST STIMULATING CONFLUENCE of earth, water, and sky Lindbergh had ever seen lay not two hundred miles across the English Channel, where Brittany's Côtes-du-Nord forms the Inlet of Pellinec. On this northwestern spur of France, huge cumulonimbus clouds roiling off the Atlantic play with the light, flooding a tiny archipelago of miniature islands below in pinks, oranges, and purples. Most of the time, these rock formations sit as islands dotting the coastline; but twice a day the tide recedes, pulling so much water out of the inlet that the islands stand as weird, craggy hills among tidal pools—a wet desert, dead-quiet except for the birds and the constant winds.

It was no wonder that the Carrels had settled on the Île Saint-Gildas, the largest member of this mystical archipelago. Since the eleventh century, a chapel has towered over the small compound of buildings that came to be erected behind protective walls on the hundred-acre island—"a combination of an old French farm and a Maine island and the moon." Lindbergh had enjoyed nothing more in Europe than his visits there, savoring the arrival as much as the stay.

When traveling alone to Saint-Gildas, Lindbergh flew over the island and dropped a message tied to a streamer and weighted with a stone to announce his approach. Then he parked his plane at the airdrome at either Morlaix or Dinan, where a car and driver navigated the sinuous Brittany roads and dropped him off at the edge of the small town of Port-Blanc, where the pavement dead-ended at the water. Lindbergh did not reach this point on his first visit until close to midnight and high tide, which would have consigned most visitors to the mainland for the night. But along with his personal bag, Lindbergh carried an emergency rubber raft, which he inflated and paddled through the phosphorescent water to the island.

A few islands away—ten minutes by boat, a kilometer walk at low tide— was Illiec. Barely four acres, it was smaller but higher than any of the surrounding islets, completely at one with the elements—"a part of the sea," Lindbergh wrote in his diary, "—like a boat in a storm." Anomalously, in the middle of this bizarre natural granite sculpture, jammed up against a towering rock with one sheer side that dropped to the water, sat a majestic, three-story Breton manor house. Beneath its slate roof, the stone structure had a dozen rooms, including a tiny chapel and two conical towers. It was built in the 1860s by Ambroise Thomas, who composed his opera *Mignon* there. It lacked all the modern conveniences—heating, electricity, and plumbing, though it had cistern drinking water.

The moment Lindbergh learned that it might be for sale, he deputized Madame Carrel to negotiate its purchase. For the asking price of $16,000, it became the Lindberghs'. He knew it was a folly, seeing "only too well that the conditions in France are bad—that they may even lead to revolution." But, he admitted to his journal on March 31, 1938, "even one summer at Illiec would almost justify buying it. The very memory of such a summer would strengthen the rest of life. I have never seen a place where I wanted to live so much."

Within a week, Charles and Anne flew to Brittany, to inspect the pig they had bought in a poke. Anne was as taken by the scenery as her husband, but the interior of the house was drearier than she feared—dark walls covered with matting, heavy Victorian furniture, cheap tapestries. By the end of the the day, however, Anne had planted some cuttings from Long Barn among the heather and gorse, and her head was swimming with plans for redecorating, building cupboards, buying chemical toilets. Off to one side of the house was a cottage, where a caretaker, cook, and their thirteen-year-old son lived. The next day, men began work on the property, inside and out.

The Lindberghs returned to England for the balance of the spring, during which time Charles completed his work on *The Culture of Organs* and Anne all but completed hers on *Listen! The Wind,* for which Charles wrote a foreword and drew several maps. They also spent these six weeks cramming in as much social activity as possible.

The Lindberghs discussed politics at Sissinghurst with Vita Sackville-West and Harold Nicolson ("Lindbergh is most pessimistic," Nicolson wrote in his diary a few weeks later, erroneously ascribing Lindbergh's suggestion that England "should just give way and then make an alliance with Germany" to what he assumed was his belief "in the Nazi theology, all tied up with his hatred of degeneracy and his hatred of democracy as represented by the free Press and the American public.") That same week they also stayed with the Astors at Cliveden, where Anne found Charles "shocking the life out of everyone by describing Germany's strength"; and they rejoined Lady Astor at 4 St. James's Square for luncheon with George Bernard Shaw. The other guests included the American Ambassador to France, William C. Bullitt, Ambassador Joseph Kennedy, and Thomas Jones, Lloyd George's confidant and Secretary to the British Cabinet. The conversation that day turned mostly to a provocative mimeographed newsletter being published in London called *The Week,* whose editor, Claud Cockburn, had coined the term "Cliveden Set," a disparaging term he used to suggest the pro-Nazi leanings of the Astors and their friends. (The American Embassy had long since discredited the bulletins, finding them riddled with gossip, scandal, and unreliable information.)

The Astors also invited the Lindberghs to a ball at the end of the month for the King and Queen. Charles wore a new set of tails, his first since Paris in 1927. The Queen conversed with Anne, noting that she had heard that the Lindberghs' child had been born on Coronation Day. "I think it's very nice," Queen Elizabeth said, "when something big is happening to you, to think that something big is happening to someone else, too."

Later in the evening, the Queen sent word that she wished Lindbergh to dance with her. Lindbergh explained to the attendant that he had never danced a step in his life and was told it would be acceptable to sit out the dance and talk. And so for twenty minutes they conversed about the troubles of the world and the perils of the American press. Lindbergh liked Queen Elizabeth, finding her natural and dignified, "but not at all stiff." After the party, when Anne asked what they had talked about, Charles explained that he felt the Queen was terribly tired, showing the strain of her new regal life, and that he just went on prattling because he thought "it was the easiest thing for her."

Two days later, an invitation arrived from Buckingham Palace, inviting the Lindberghs to a ball on June first. The Lindberghs booked a room at Claridge's for the evening, where they could dress for the formal event, which was called for 10:30 P.M. Shortly before leaving for the palace, Anne and Charles sat opposite each other at a small table in their room, sipping sherry and eating melba toast—he in his knee breeches and white waistcoat, and she with a tiara—laughing at each other.

Anne danced until three. Charles sat out all the dances, finding the event less of an ordeal than he had anticipated, thanks in large measure to Lady Astor's conversation. He granted that nobody pulled off formal occasions with more dignity than the English. Through it all, he could not help noticing that his wife looked positively "drunk with happiness," happier than he had ever seen her. For a moment it seemed to dawn on him that had he not swept her away a decade earlier, this would probably have been the sort of life Ambassador Morrow's daughter would have led.

Instead, on June seventh, Lindbergh flew his wife and their two sons to their private island—where heat came only from the fireplace, light from kerosene lamps, and water from a well in front of the house. By the twenty-third, they were able to move out of their guest quarters on Saint-Gildas and into their own house on Illiec. Work continued all summer, with five hundred cypress trees getting planted on the east side of the island and five hundred pines on the west.

Illiec proved to be the haven of Lindbergh's imaginings, a physical and mental challenge. He and Anne found it conducive for walking and working. Although Jon was deprived of any friends his own age, he was already growing up enormously independent, fascinated by marine life. He spent most of his time swimming, shell-collecting, and often gathering their dinner from the sea—shrimp, crab, even abalone, which he pried from underneath rocks.

Illiec's greatest attraction remained Dr. Carrel. Lindbergh spent every available minute with his mentor; and for months his mind was Carrel's to mold. Sitting in the doctor's high-walled garden or by the fireplace late into the night, the two men discussed improving qualities within the human species and the population at large, through diet and reproduction. "Eugenics," Carrel wrote in *Man, the Unknown,* "is indispensable for the perpetuation of the strong. A great race must propagate its best elements." He and Lindbergh carried on such discussions over the course of the summer, delving into the subject of "race betterment." Unfortunately, similar discussions were raging throughout the Third Reich, a coincidence that would not be lost on future detractors of either Carrel or Lindbergh.

Lindbergh planned to continue his quest for life's answers that summer in Brittany and beyond. He had hoped to study the local folklore and its superstitions in the neighboring islands and provinces; and he wanted to return to India and see the Himalayas. But along with "the maritime tides of Saint-Gildas," he found, "there was a rising world-wide tide of war." Increasingly, letters requesting his participation in more earthly affairs arrived for him at the Penvénan post office on the mainland. "Problems of civilization and survival towered above my fascination with phenomena that sometimes lay exposed in the tidelands of rationality and life," he wrote of those days. "Why spend time on biological experiments when our very civilization was at stake, when one of history's great cataclysms impended?"

At the suggestion of Colonel Raymond L. Lee, military attaché for air in the U.S. Embassy in London, Lindbergh agreed to undertake a survey of aviation in the Soviet Union. He and Anne spent the last two weeks of August 1938 in Russia, following an itinerary prescribed by the Soviet government—Mogilev, Kiev, Odessa, Rostov, and Moscow.

What Lindbergh did not see on the trip impressed him more than what he did. It quickly became apparent that "Stalin's Russia did not wish to expose her Air Force to foreign eyes"—mostly, Lindbergh realized, out of embarrassment. The few aeronautical sites he was shown were far inferior to the many other sights they showed off—the new subway, the new theater built in the form of a huge tractor, the new ice-cream factory, and a collective farm. While Lindbergh could not observe enough to estimate the nation's production capacity, he concluded that "the Russian Air Force probably consisted of several thousand planes which would be effective in a modern war but were no match for the Luftwaffe in either quality or quantity." He found Russian life bleak—marked by secrecy, scarcity, and suppression.

They left the Soviet Union by way of Czechoslovakia, where Lindbergh met with President Eduard Beneš and his military staff and visited their aviation establishments. "This country is prepared for a German invasion at any moment," he wrote his mother. He found their army strong and modern but "not well equipped in the air."

On September 8, they flew to Paris and checked into the Crillon. The press quickly gathered outside the hotel. The Lindberghs delayed their return to Illiec by a day in response to a private invitation from Ambassador Bullitt. At dinner the next night, with French Minister of Air Guy La Chambre also in attendance, they talked for hours about aviation. Lindbergh tried to make La Chambre see, as he would write in his journal, "The French situation is desperate. Impossible to catch up to Germany for years, if at all." France was producing fifty warplanes per month, about one-tenth Germany's output.

Charles and Anne had only a few days in Illiec before they flew to England. They spent the third week of September in London, often in the company of Ambassador Kennedy. More than ever, Lindbergh felt that "the English are in no shape for war. . . . They have always before had a fleet between themselves and their enemy, and they can't realize the change aviation has made."

At Kennedy's request, Lindbergh committed to paper the next day some of his comments regarding military aviation in Europe, so that they could be transmitted to both the White House and Whitehall. Kennedy promptly wired the bulk of the letter to Secretary of State Cordell Hull—including Lindbergh's estimates of German production and his conviction that "Germany now has the means of destroying London, Paris, and Prague if she wishes to do so. England and France together have not enough modern war planes for effective defence or counter-attack." That being the case, Lindbergh added, "I am convinced that it is wiser to permit Germany's eastward expansion than to throw England and France, unprepared, into a war at this time."

Germany felt less bold. Although Lindbergh would have no way of knowing it, that very day Goering received a secret report from his own General Helmuth Felmy, who informed him that none of their bombers or fighters could "operate meaningfully" over England. "Given our present means," the report stated, "we can hope at best for a nuisance effect. . . . A war of annihilation against Britain appears to be out of the question."

The Lindberghs spent the night of September twenty-sixth at Cliveden, where they listened to Hitler on the radio. It was a spellbinding oration, even to those who did not understand German—one that brought the aggressive nation to the brink of war. The Astors and their guests debated the issue all night. Charles and Lady Astor argued that England should steer clear of the fray, while Lord Astor and the others got caught in what Lindbergh called "the spirit of the 'Light Brigade,' " insisting that Germany must be stopped now before getting any stronger. Charles and Anne retired for the night in the "Tapestry Room," which afforded them a view of the gardens and beyond to the Thames.

The next day, Lindbergh went into London, where he noticed trenches being dug in parks, sandbags surrounding doors and windows of buildings, and lines of people waiting for gas masks. He had tea with David Lloyd George, who told him that war seemed inevitable and that the Nazi system was as bad as the Russian system. Having visited both countries recently, Lindbergh became exasperated that the former Prime Minister did not "recognize any difference to England between an alliance with European Germany and Asiatic Russia. He apparently does not worry about the effect of Asia on European civilization."

Lindbergh spent much of the next two days at the Embassy with Joseph Kennedy, who, in turn, preached appeasement to an already persuaded Neville Chamberlain. The Prime Minister left for a conference in Munich—where he would meet Hitler, Mussolini, and Daladier of France. Chamberlain returned to his jubilant nation with the promise of "peace for our time."

As much as any diplomat in the world, Lindbergh spent the next month globe trotting among the capitals of Europe on government missions. A minister without portfolio, his sole motivation was public service. He had no thirst for power or attention, and he paid for all his flights out of his own pocket. At Ambassador Bullitt's beckoning, he went first to Paris, where he was asked to help supply military aircraft to France. The goal was to purchase warplanes from the United States, which the Neutrality Act of 1935 made impossible. Bullitt suggested, however, that American factories be built in Canada, where they could circumvent the law and produce the planes.

This private meeting—which included Daladier, La Chambre, Bullitt, and Jean Monnet—thrust Lindbergh into a crisis of conscience. "Aside from the personal problems involved," Lindbergh would later retell, "there were serious questions relating to loyalty to my own country and to the civilization of which it was a part. I loved France second only to America, and I had fallen in love with Europe as a whole. From the time the Canadian Plan was first outlined to me, I had reservations about the effect it would have on both America and Europe." It seemed to Lindbergh "a roundabout way of getting the United States again involved in Europe's wars—against the wishes of Congress and the American people."

Lindbergh believed England and France were viewing the gameboard in the wrong way, looking only at short-term moves. To him, totalitarianism was the ultimate enemy, and that if England and France would draw back, "a westward expansion by Hitler might still be prevented through a combination of diplomacy, strategic convenience, and the use of defensive power." Lindbergh's worst fear was that "the potentially gigantic power of America, guided by uninformed and impractical idealism, might crusade into Europe to destroy Hitler without realizing that Hitler's destruction would lay Europe open to the rape, loot, and barbarism of Soviet Russia's forces, causing possibly the fatal wounding of Western civilization."

"I was far from being in accord with the philosophy, policy, and actions of the Nazi government," Lindbergh would later write of his position, "but it seemed to me essential to France and England, and even to America, that Germany be maintained as a bulwark against the Soviet Union." Lindbergh astounded his confreres at the private meeting by suggesting that France purchase bombers not from Canada but from Germany! He argued that Hitler might actually "welcome the opportunity to make a gesture to protect his western frontier."

Lindbergh went to Illiec to ponder his role in the Canadian Plan. After three days of climbing the rocks and wandering among the tidal pools, he patriotically recommended men in American aviation whom the French could contact in confidence. After writing letters of introduction, he excused himself from further meetings on the plan, which soon dissolved. He flew to Berlin, where the military attaché of the American Embassy had invited him for the third time, ostensibly to attend the Lilienthal Society's Aeronautic Congress. Before his arrival, Lindbergh received his first slap in the face over his new role in world affairs.

Delayed in Rotterdam for a night because of weather, he learned in a telephone conversation with Truman Smith that trouble had flared up in Moscow over an article published in the mimeographed London newssheet *The Week*. It claimed that Lindbergh had told members of "the Cliveden Set" that "the German air force could take on and defeat, single handed, the

British, French, Soviet and Czechoslovak air fleets," and that "he knew all about the Russian air force because, when in Moscow recently, he had been offered the post of head of the Soviet civil aviation administration." The latter remark was sheer invention on somebody's part, and the rest was a simplification of Lindbergh's feelings about the strength of the Luftwaffe—which had not been uttered at Cliveden but at a luncheon Thomas Jones hosted in London.

Pravda reprinted the article as though it had come from a reputable news source, allowing the Russian government to denounce Lindbergh as a liar. Lindbergh's hosts from the Russian Embassy wired that it was "imperative" that he set the record straight. But Lindbergh adhered to his longtime policy of offering no comment—which only created greater concern.

Flying into Berlin the next day, Charles was immediately struck by the changes in the country since his visit a year earlier. Berlin showed every sign of "a healthy, busy, modern city." The aviation community seemed more ebullient than usual, willing to show off their latest planes and factories not only to Lindbergh but also to many distinguished guests who had flown in for the conference, Lindbergh's friend Igor Sikorsky among them. For a solid week, Lindbergh inspected sites.

On Tuesday, October 18, 1938—after a long day visiting the Junkers engine factory at Magdeburg, flying to Dessau to visit the Junkers factory, then back to Berlin—Lindbergh left Truman Smith's apartment for a stag dinner at the American Embassy. The new Ambassador, Hugh Wilson, saw in Lindbergh's presence the opportunity to establish friendly personal relations with Hermann Goering, thereby improving American-German relations. Furthermore, unknown to Lindbergh, Wilson had told Truman Smith that he also "hoped to obtain at such a dinner Goering's support for certain measures especially desired by the State Department concerning the easing of the financial plight of the large number of Jews who were being forced to emigrate from Germany in a penniless condition."

Lindbergh joined a distinguished group of gentlemen that night—Generals Milch and Udet, the Italian and Belgian ambassadors, several American military attachés, and three of the greatest minds in German aviation, Ernst Heinkel, Adolf Baeumker, and Dr. Willy E. Messerschmitt. Goering was the last to arrive. Lindbergh was standing in the back of the reception room as the Marshal made his way toward him. Before he had even reached Lindbergh, Goering accepted a red leather box from his chief aide-de-camp and began a speech.

Nobody was prepared for the moment. Because Lindbergh did not speak German, the American Consul-General in Berlin, Raymond Geist, stepped forward to translate. To the surprise of at least every American in the room, Lindbergh was being decorated with the Verdienstkreuz Deutscher Adler—

the Service Cross of the German Eagle—a decoration for his services to the aviation of the world and particularly for his 1927 flight, which postwar Germany had never acknowledged. "By order of der Führer," Goering said, opening the box.

Inside was a golden cross with four small swastikas, finished in white enamel, strung on a red ribbon with white and black borders. Accompanying the medal was a proclamation on parchment signed by Hitler. Lindbergh was surprised by the honor but thought little of it, only that it "was given with the best of intent and with no more political motif in the background than was usual with the presentation of decorations in Europe." (In fact, the French Ambassador and Henry Ford had recently received the same award.) Lindbergh accepted the decoration as unceremoniously as it had been presented, and the men all took their seats for dinner.

Ambassador Wilson sat at the head of one of the two tables, Lindbergh at the other. Through the meal, Lindbergh spoke mostly to Air Minister Milch about aviation, though Milch did ask why Lindbergh should not winter in Berlin. In fact, Anne had been house-hunting that week, as Charles believed Berlin would be the most interesting city in the world during the next few months. Privately, Ambassador Wilson had told Lindbergh that such a move would prove "helpful" to him.

After dinner, Goering approached Lindbergh again, leading him into a room for a personal talk. Ambassador Wilson accompanied them to translate. Goering immediately asked about Lindbergh's trip to Russia; and before a second question on the subject could be raised, Wilson diplomatically offered the translating services of Consul-General Geist, knowing that an ambassador's presence during a private conversation about world affairs could prove inhibiting if not embarrassing. Lindbergh spoke frankly, saying that he did not think the conditions in Russia were good and that the people did not seem well-fed or happy.

Goering steered the conversation to German aviation. While the American diplomats were grateful for whatever information they could glean, they also had to consider the possibility that the Germans were using Lindbergh, pulling the wool over his eyes by filling him with false impressions of German strength. (Later, people told stories of the Germans secretly moving planes by night from one airfield on Lindbergh's itinerary to another, to impress him with the size of their fleet. The stories were both untrue and unnecessary, as Lindbergh was less concerned at that moment with the potency of the Luftwaffe than with its potential. He was more interested in their research and development than the existing number of planes.) And when Goering spoke of a new Junkers 88 bomber, which no American had seen, Lindbergh did not doubt the Air Marshal's boasts of its ability to fly at five hundred kilometers an hour. (In fact, the JU 88 would quickly become the nucleus of the Luftwaffe's fleet of bomb-carriers, with Germany producing fifteen thousand of them over the next six years.) Lindbergh left the Embassy a few minutes after Goering. It was the second, and last, time they ever conversed.

Anne Lindbergh and Kay Smith were chatting when their husbands returned from the Embassy. Neither of the men had attached much importance to the Goering medal; and Charles showed it to Anne without comment. "She gave it but a fleeting glance," Truman Smith observed, "and then—without the slightest trace of emotion—remarked, 'The Albatross.'"

Lindbergh never saw it that way, insisting almost twenty years later that the decoration "never caused me any worry, and I doubt that it caused me much additional difficulty." But Kay Smith went to bed that night prophesying to her husband, "This medal will surely do Lindbergh much harm."

Two weeks later, Lindbergh wrote General H. H. "Hap" Arnold, Chief of the Air Corps, urging him to visit Germany immediately to assess the military situation there for himself. Arnold wrote back that he was "100% in favor of making the trip just as you outlined." Lindbergh himself prepared to return there for his own enlightenment. "I am extremely anxious to learn more about Germany and I believe a few months spent in that country would be interesting from many standpoints," Lindbergh wrote Joseph Kennedy on November 9, 1938. Anne found a house in the Berlin suburb of Wannsee, which she thought would "do perfectly." They returned to France to pack up Illiec and collect their children.

The very night of Lindbergh's letter to Kennedy, Germany staged the worst pogrom that the Third Reich had witnessed, a nationwide series of "spontaneous" demonstrations. More than one hundred synagogues were burned, thousands of shops and houses owned by Jews were destroyed, tens of thousands of Jews were arrested and carted off to confinement camps, and dozens of Jews were killed. *"Kristallnacht,"* as that night of mayhem came to be known, opened the world's eyes to the barbarism on which the Third Reich was built. "My admiration for the Germans is constantly being dashed against some rock such as this," Lindbergh wrote in his journal back on Illiec. Then he confessed an utter inability to understand such persecution.

The Service Cross of the German Eagle suddenly reflected badly on its recipient. The press, which had grown to resent Lindbergh's uncooperative attitude, instantly revised history. In December, for example, *Liberty Magazine* reported Lindbergh's having flown to Berlin especially to receive the medal; *The New York Times* wrote of his proudly wearing the medal all evening. "With confused emotions," wrote *The New Yorker* on November 26, 1938, "we say goodbye to Colonel Charles A. Lindbergh, who wants to go and live in Berlin, presumably occupying a house that once belonged to Jews. . . . If he wants to experiment further with the artificial heart, his surroundings there should be ideal." FDR's Secretary of the Interior, Harold Ickes, lashed out against Lindbergh in a speech before a Zionist meeting in Cleveland that December, asserting that anyone who accepts a decoration from Germany also "forfeits his right to be an American."

For more than ten years, Lindbergh had been a universal symbol, an *Übermensch* whose accomplishments had been in the name of mankind, not any single class of people. And though he had been for three years a man without a country, many at home now hoped he would end his exile and lead the fight against Fascistic oppression.

As a long-festering resentment of Germany surfaced in the United States, it became increasingly difficult for Lindbergh not to take a stand against the Third Reich. "Now," theorized Aubrey Morgan in a letter to Lindbergh at year's end, that boiling population had "found a convenient channel to explode their pent-up wrath by stoning a fellow American. So you have become the scapegoat. The press certainly went out of their way to make you the real villain and Machiavellian intriguer behind the European scenes."

"People in this country have stopped thinking," Dr. Carrel wrote Lindbergh from New York—where, he noted, gentiles almost as much as Jews had become agitated by the German attacks against its Jews. "The papers have published misleading articles about your plan to stay in Berlin," he added, noting their terrible effect. "There is a good deal of ill feeling against you." Friends and relatives wrote the Lindberghs, urging them not to live in Berlin and to return the medal. "We know Charles never denies anything the newspapers print and we know too that some outrageous things have been printed about him," the wife of one of Anne's cousins wrote her. "But this thing seems to us to be different. For the first time, it actually puts Charles on a side, it allies him with something this country believes is wrong and bad, and it may give impetus and encouragement to some weaker men who lean to the wrong side."

Lindbergh needed nobody to tell him to abandon his plans to move to Berlin. Wanting immediate access to the diplomatic corridors of a city (and a proper school for his son Jon), Anne and Charles decided on their own to leave Illiec for an apartment at number 11 bis Avenue Maréchal Maunoury in Paris's 16th arrondissement. "I am not very much concerned by the stories printed in the newspapers, and I have neither desire nor respect for a popularity which is dependent on the press," he explained to Dr. Carrel in early December. The move to Paris, he explained, was for one basic reason: "the fact that I do not wish to make a move which would seem to support the German action in regard to the Jews." He admitted that he still did not understand the Germans' methods; and until he did, he wrote, "I do not wish to cause embarrassment to our Government, or to the German Government. Moving to Berlin under present circumstances might easily do this."

As for returning the medal, Lindbergh would write almost three years later, after it assumed even greater significance in the public eye: "It seems to me that the returning of decorations which were given in times of peace, and as a gesture of friendship, can have no constructive effect. If I were to return the German medal, it seems to me that it would be an unnecessary insult. Even if war develops between us, I can see no gain in indulging in a spitting contest before that war begins." And, Lindbergh wondered, what of medals from other nations that might become enemies. All those decorations were part of the past, the property of the Missouri Historical Society.

With Paris as his base, Lindbergh spent the next four months continuing his shuttle diplomacy. He paid several visits to England, where he conferred with Ambassador Kennedy, the Astors, and the aviation officials of the United Kingdom. At the requests of the air ministers of France and Germany, he embarked on two secret missions to Berlin—a week in mid-December and three days in mid-January—during which he advanced the same notion he had during the Canadian Plan conferences. Recognizing the need to fortify their air force, Daladier and La Chambre at last told Lindbergh that they were prepared to buy engines at least, if not planes, from Germany, if the Third Reich was willing to sell them. Lindbergh never learned whether or not the plan was agreed to by Hitler himself, but Air Minister Milch told Lindbergh that they could proceed with a deal. His work done, Lindbergh withdrew from the project. He subsequently learned the French did as well, for tensions between the countries were mounting again.

During his visits to Berlin, Lindbergh persistently sought answers to what was euphemistically being called "the Jewish question." Raising the subject whenever possible, he did not find a single German who did not seem ashamed of the recent lawlessness against the Jews. Nor did he encounter a single German who did not want the country rid of the Jews. He felt the entire nation had bought into the Nazi propaganda that the Jew "is largely responsible for the internal collapse and revolution following the war. At the time of the inflation the Jews are said to have obtained the ownership of a large percentage of property in Berlin and other cities—lived in the best houses, drove the best automobiles, and mixed with the prettiest German girls." Lindbergh met with George Rublee, an old friend of Dwight Morrow who had become Chairman of the Inter-governmental Refugee Committee and was in Berlin lobbying for Germans to moderate their attitude toward the Jews. Lindbergh extolled Rublee's virtues to Milch and Udet and introduced him to Otto Merkel, of Lufthansa, whom he thought might prove sympathetic to Rublee's mission.

Nazi Germany, a rising monument to technocracy, was an ideal Lindbergh kept hoping to embrace. So long as he was able to intellectualize his feelings, he was able to believe some new system of government—a new order—might save a degenerating world. "I shared the repulsion that democratic peoples felt in viewing the demagoguery of Hitler, the controlled elections, the secret police," he would later reveal. "Yet I felt that I was seeing in Germany, despite the crudeness of its form, the inevitable alternative to decline—a challenge based more on the drive to achieve success despite established 'right' and law." Rather than look at the price being paid for that "success," Lindbergh buried his head in the sand when confronted with the crimes of inhumanity that repelled so many others.

In Lindbergh's mind, the final shootout in Europe would not be between Fascism and democracy but between two dictators—Stalin and Hitler. Nothing he had heard attributed to the Nazis even approached the "ruthlessness and terror" of the Russians, who were rumored to have slaughtered forty million people since their revolution. "My greatest hope," Lindbergh would write, explaining the political policy that would guide him over the next few years, "lay in the possibility that a war would be confined to fighting between Hitler and Stalin. It seemed probable that Germany would be victorious in such a conflict; and by that time France and England would be stronger. Under any circumstances, I believed that a victory by Germany's European people would be preferable to one by Russia's semi-Asiatic Soviet Union. Hitler would not live forever, and I felt sure the Germans would eventually moderate the excesses of his Nazi regime."

As late as April 1939—after Germany overtook Czechoslovakia—Lindbergh was willing to make excuses for Hitler. "Much as I disappove of many things Germany has done," he wrote in his diary on April 2, 1939, "I believe she has pursued the only consistent policy in Europe in recent years. I cannot support her broken promises, but she has only moved a little faster than other nations have in breaking promises. The question of right and wrong is one thing by law and another thing by history." After his January 1939 mission, Lindbergh did not set foot on German soil until the Third Reich had fallen.

The Lindberghs took advantage of their winter in Paris, frequenting museums and galleries. They posed for sculptors—Jo Davidson did a bust of him, and Charles Despiau one of her; and they bought several oil paintings by Vlaminck. They also dined with the likes of Gertrude Stein and Alice B. Toklas, Lin Yutang, and the Duke and Duchess of Windsor. (Lindbergh now wrote him off as an utter bore, noting of his private conversation with the ex-King, "The entire time was spent in talking about two subjects: the flavor of wines and how much higher the Étoile is than the Place de la Concorde.")

One night Anne and Charles went to the Tour d'Argent on the Seine. Their beautiful dinner was spoiled by a group of Americans and French at the next table, who recognized them. They spoke too loudly about Lindbergh's hostile relationship with the press—"about newspaper rumors, about the kidnapping of our baby, about the trial at Flemington, about all the things that discretion should have prevented their mentioning at an adjoining table," Lindbergh wrote in his journal. He was no longer an unequivocal hero.

Indeed, some held him in contempt. In the Lindberghs' absence, many Americans wearied of feeling guilty for their departure and wondered why they were reluctant to return. Family and friends informed them that there was a campaign afoot against them. Audiences in motion-picture houses hissed when Lindbergh appeared in the newsreels; many Jewish booksellers boycotted Anne's critically acclaimed bestseller *Listen! The Wind;* and, in December 1938, advertisements from TWA appeared without its slogan "The Lindbergh Line." These rumblings distressed Anne deeply, because she felt, "C. is not and never has been anti-Semitic." She hoped this moment of unpopularity would prove fleeting, but she knew the "ball of rumor and criticism, once it starts rolling, is difficult to stop."

After three years abroad, Lindbergh questioned what further contribution he could make toward improving relations among the countries of Europe. If there was to be a war, he thought, "then my place was back in my own country. I felt I could exercise a constructive influence in America by warning people of the danger of the Soviet Union and by explaining that the destruction of Hitler, even if it could be accomplished through using American resources, would probably result in enhancing the still-greater menace of Stalin." As one of the few people to have visited the world's political hot spots, he felt compelled to argue for an American policy of "strength and neutrality, one that would encourage European nations to take the responsibility for their own relationships and destinies. If they prostrated themselves once again in internecine war, then at least one strong Western nation would remain to protect Western civilization."

Lindbergh booked passage on the *Aquitania*. His decision to summon his family to America, he noted in his journal, would depend on "what I may find I may be able to do if I spend the summer there."

14

THE GREAT DEBATE

"My father had opposed the United States's entering
World War I. . . . I was not old enough to understand
the war's basic issues, yet I felt pride in the
realization that my country was now powerful and
influential enough to take a major part in world crises."

—C.A.L.

MUCH OF YESTERDAY'S HEARSAY BECAME TODAY'S HISTORY.
On January 1, 1939, for example, Walter Winchell
stretched some comments of Joseph P. Kennedy and told his
newspaper and radio audience that it was Lindbergh's "now
famous report on Germany's power in the air, which was to
prove a final factor in Prime Minister Neville Chamberlain's
policy at Munich." An estimated fifty million people received
that "information." More than one historian later quoted
Winchell in asserting that the terms at Munich might never
have been conceded were it not for Lindbergh's miscalcula-
tions of German strength. Another compounded that error,
connecting it with the statement of an eminent British historian
who said it had been "very well known" that the Germans
had shuttled the same planes from one field to another during
Lindbergh's inspection tours—another piece of gossip. Some
went so far as to suggest there might not have been a second
World War had Lindbergh never gone to Germany!

Into 1939, as Hitler expanded his empire, "Munich" and
"Chamberlain" entered the lexicon as terms of appeasement
and fecklessness. In America, some referred to Lindbergh as a
doomsayer, a Nazi dupe, even a "collaborator."

After months of conflicting reports about Lindbergh's travels in Europe, Washington correspondent Arthur Krock tried

to set the record straight. With the United States government at last modernizing its flying fleet, the esteemed *New York Times* commentator explained that it owed much of its new size and efficiency to him, as they were at last responding to his alarm. "[C]riticism of any of his activities—in Germany or elsewhere—" Krock wrote, "is as ignorant as it is unfair."

In his column of February 1, 1939, Krock detailed the results of Lindbergh's missions to Berlin, stressing for his critics that Lindbergh "throughout has been an official American reporter and adviser on aviation," and that the American government had been the chief beneficiary of his information and technical appraisal. "Colonel Lindbergh is no usual man," Krock concluded, "and that applied to his temperament and methods. This individualism has earned him some personal unpopularity. But any founded on belief he has not been a patriot, and most valuably one, is ill-founded indeed." Not everybody read the *Times*.

ON SATURDAY, April 8, 1939, Lindbergh bid adieu to his wife and their two children in Paris and trained to Cherbourg, where he boarded the *Aquitania* and sailed for New York. He confined himself to his stateroom as much as possible during the crossing, working on a new book, another rendering of his flight to Paris. The first night of the crossing he went to the dining room early, hoping to avoid the crowd. He was joined by one other passenger, one of many Jewish refugees on board. She was a pretty Romanian of twenty, and that presented problems of its own. He made polite conversation and enjoyed her company; but he knew he would have to change tables for the rest of the voyage, or else "the newspapers in America will grab her, photograph her, interview her, and then throw her in the gutter according to their usual procedure." And yet, Lindbergh presumed, in changing tables she would probably think it was on account of her being Jewish.

In his introduction of Lindbergh's *Wartime Journals,* which would be published in 1970, William Jovanovich noted that the entries were printed exactly as written, except in the cases of certain personal references to living people, repetitions or material deemed "not important enough to warrant adding to the length of the work as a whole." That was, for the most part, true. But there were exceptions, several omissions in the published texts that were substantive in nature. As with the later publication of Anne's diaries, the bulk of these omissions centered on one subject: the Jews.

None of the cuts contains any overt denigrations of Jews. In fact, most of the references express Lindbergh's affinity and admiration for them. But in so writing about a single tribe, he was segregating them in his mind from the rest of the nation; and to that extent he was, like many of his countrymen, anti-Semitic. The following paragraph from Lindbergh's journal entry of April 10, 1939, for example—after a day or two of rough waters, which kept most of the passengers from leaving their cabins—was never published:

> The steward tells me that most of the Jewish passengers are sick. Imagine the United States taking these Jews in in addition to those we already have. There are too many in places like New York already. A few Jews add strength and character to a country, but too many create chaos. And we are getting too many. This present immigration will have its reaction.

Lindbergh was not singling Jews out for persecution; indeed, he could just as easily have written the same about any other minority. But it is difficult to imagine his making the same comment about White Anglo-Saxon Protestants.

After more than three years abroad, Lindbergh was convinced that the world was tumbling toward chaos. He only hoped it was not too late to avert a major war—for that would "be more likely to destroy Western civilization than to solve either our problems or those of European nations." With his return, Lindbergh resolved "to take whatever part I could in preventing a war in Europe, and to campaign against my country taking part if war broke out."

America awaited his arrival, especially those with an interest in aviation—including policy-makers in Washington. General Henry H. "Hap" Arnold, Chief of the Air Corps, radioed while Lindbergh was in transit, asking him to contact him as soon after arriving as possible.

Before the *Aquitania* had even docked, tugboatloads of newspapermen hopped on board. Lindbergh locked himself in his cabin, permitting nobody to enter except three unexpected callers—the Carrels and Jim Newton, who had anticipated the press and had obtained permission to go out on the pilot boat with the customs men, in order to help Lindbergh off the ship. In no time, reporters were pounding on the cabin door. At one point a photographer who had bribed a steward burst into the cabin from an adjoining stateroom, flashed a photograph, and ran. "It is a ridiculous situation when one cannot return to one's own country without having to go through the roughhousing of photographers and the lies and insults of the press," Lindbergh mused. "It takes the sweetness from the freedom of democracy and makes one wonder where freedom ends and disorder begins."

After the gangway had been let down, two New York police officers came to Lindbergh's cabin to suggest they form a cordon around him. Lindbergh said he preferred to exit alone if possible, and after all the other passengers had disembarked, he made a run for it. One hundred fifty reporters and photographers lined both sides of the corridor, popping flashbulbs in his eyes as they shoved toward him. "All the way along the deck the photographers ran in front of us and behind us, jamming the way, being pushed aside by the police yelling, falling over each other on the deck," Lindbergh wrote of the arrival. He and his escorts crunched across the broken glass of hundreds of discarded flashbulbs. The Morrow chauffeur, waiting at the bottom of the gangplank, whisked him away, along the new Henry Hudson Parkway and across the George Washington Bridge to Englewood. Once at Next Day Hill, Lindbergh telephoned General Arnold.

The next morning, he borrowed the Morrow De Soto and drove to West Point. There Lindbergh and Arnold discussed the European situation. Acknowledging that Lindbergh had already supplied what Arnold called "the most accurate picture of the Luftwaffe, its equipment leaders, apparent plans, training methods, and present defects" that he had received, the General spoke of a new mission for Lindbergh. Meeting again two days later in Washington, Arnold asked if Lindbergh would go on active duty and "make a study of an attempt to increase the efficiency of American [aeronautical] research organizations." The next morning Lindbergh accepted the call to active duty, as a Colonel in the Army Air Corps. He wrote Dr. Carrel that he would have to discontinue indefinitely their medical research together; and he cabled Anne in Paris to sail with the children on the next available boat.

On the morning of April 20, 1939, Lindbergh spent half an hour with Harry Hines Woodring, Secretary of War, discussing military aviation in Europe and America, before arriving at the White House for an appointment with his Commander in Chief. Although the two most famous living Americans had dueled over the airmail in 1934, this was Lindbergh's first face-to-face encounter with Franklin D. Roosevelt.

The President was seated at his desk at one end of a large room. "He leaned forward from his chair to meet me as I entered," Lindbergh would later write in his journal, "and it is only now that I stop to think that he is crippled. I did not notice it and had no thought of it during our meeting." Roosevelt immediately asked about Anne, who had known his daughter at Miss Chapin's School. "He is an accomplished, suave, interesting conversationalist," Lindbergh noted. "I liked him and feel that I could get along with him well. Acquaintanceship would be pleasant and interesting."

"But," he added with equal conviction, "there was something about him I did not trust, something a little too suave, too pleasant, too easy. Still, he is our President, and there is no reason for any antagonism between us in the work I am now doing." While he found FDR "mostly politician" and felt they "would never get along on many fundamentals," Lindbergh was pleased to serve him and their country. "It is better to work together as long as we can," Lindbergh told himself; "yet somehow I have a feeling that it may not be for long."

After fifteen minutes with the President, Lindbergh left one pack of press photographers on the White House steps for another at the offices of the National Advisory Committee for Aeronautics. Lindbergh told the committee secretary that he would enter the room for their board meeting only after the photographers had finished taking pictures. They said they did not want any pictures without Lindbergh in them. At last the photographers proposed— on their "word of honor"—that they would leave him alone in the future if they could get just one picture of him. "Imagine a press photographer talking about his word of honor!" Lindbergh thought, flashing back seven years to one image from the past he could never shake. "The type of men who broke through the window of the Trenton morgue to open my baby's casket and photograph its body—they talk to me of honor." He waited in seclusion until the last photographer had left the room, and only then did the meeting commence.

That afternoon, Roosevelt told the press corps of his conversation with Lindbergh, asserting that Lindbergh's figures about German air power "were the same that we knew at the time of Munich." Furthermore, the President added, he had "corroborated what our people had accepted as fact last September in regard to the construction possibilities."

The next day, Lindbergh drove to Bolling Field, where he was assigned a Curtiss P-36A, a single-seater monoplane, the Air Corps' most modern fighter. He spent a few hours getting the feel of the plane. The next day, he embarked on a three-week inspection tour with twenty-three stops. Through the summer he traveled, visiting laboratories, educational facilities, factories, and airfields from coast to coast. During an overnight detour to Roswell, he saw Robert Goddard and discovered that the rocketeer had "accomplished more this year than during any similar period in the past"—making advancements with lightweight pumps, tube-wound combustion chambers, gyroscopic controls, and moveable vanes. Lindbergh told Goddard of what he had seen in Germany and how his every mention of rockets was quickly deflected. "Yes," Goddard said, "they must have plans for the rocket. When will our own people in Washington listen to reason?"

"Obviously, the American potential was tremendous," Lindbergh would later recall of his survey trip, "but existing factories and research facilities were inadequate in comparison with those existing in Germany." He devoted the next several months to ameliorating the situation however he could. One way was in chairing a NACA committee formed to coordinate the two dozen separate organizations in America then engaged in aeronautical research. At General Arnold's request, he also sat on a board charged with revising the Air Corps' research-and-development program and proposing specifications for military aircraft that could be procured within the next five years. And for the rest of 1939, as Lindbergh later recorded, "I talked to Senators, Congressmen, diplomats, executives, scientists, and engineers about steps necessary for the development of American aviation and, inevitably, about the danger of war in Europe and the attitude America should take." He excited *National Geographic* enough about Dr. Goddard to prepare an article about his work in Roswell. As had been his overriding mission for a decade, he pushed America to be the leading air power in the world. Lindbergh accepted only two weeks of pay for his months of government work.

The President soon recommended that $300,000,000 be budgeted for the expansion of the Army and Navy air forces. And, as Arthur Krock noted, "When the new flying fleet of the United States begins to take the air, among those who will have been responsible for its size, its modernness and its efficiency is Colonel Charles A. Lindbergh."

Lindbergh's new military duties kept him from meeting Anne at the dock when she returned to America at dawn on April 28, 1939. Besides, he suggested to her in a note which reached her on board the *Champlain,* his presence would only attract greater attention. With customs agents, a police guard of close to one hundred men, and a chauffeur for protection, Anne and the children disembarked with relative ease. When she arrived at Next Day Hill, she found Charles asleep upstairs, having driven from Washington through the night. He immediately awoke; and she delighted in finding her husband so chipper because of his new duties. "It is wonderful to see him like that," she wrote in her diary, "—absorbed, active, putting his energy into something successfully."

On May 27, 1939, the Morrows gathered around the dining table at Next Day Hill for Anne and Charles's tenth wedding anniversary. "[A]ll went merrily till I asked for more champagne to drink a health," Betty Morrow wrote in her diary that night. "I didn't say to whom—but C. shook his head & said—in a low decided voice to me—'No—no—or we'll never have another anniversary here.' " His mother-in-law suddenly remembered that threatening tone from a decade earlier, when she had started to get a sharper knife to cut their wedding cake. "Of course I didn't go on with the toast," she recorded further, "but afterwards in the evening I had a chance to say that I had not meant to go against his known feelings about anniversaries." Later that night, Charles came into her room and apologized for speaking as he had. It was involuntary, he explained; he had been wrong and he was sorry. "He was very sweet about it," Mrs. Morrow wrote of his apology, the first from him in her memory. "Oh! How he has changed in ten years!"

Three days later—between government trips—Charles and Anne went house-hunting. They got lucky with the first rental they looked at, a big, white clapboard house on a hill in Lloyd Neck, on the north shore of Long Island. It sat high, overlooking the Sound—a situation reminiscent of Little

Falls and Illiec; and Charles appreciated that it was "neither too accessible nor too isolated," with several airfields close by. They leased it until November first in the name of their secretary, Christine Gawne, for $2,000; and they moved right in—with Miss Gawne and Soeur Lisi, a governess for the children from Switzerland. But it would be almost two months before Charles would be able to spend an entire weekend there.

Recognizing the seriousness with which Lindbergh was taking his new governmental work, the mainstream press gave him some elbow room in which to perform his duties. *Time* even wrote a piece sympathetic to his side in his "long dark years of war" with the public and the press. "For twelve years Charles Lindbergh has been a hero, and twelve years is too much," the article read. ". . . For the fact is that the relation of Charles Lindbergh to the U. S. people is a tragic failure chalked up against the institution of hero worship. . . . Either the pursuit of the public will drive him to lead an almost monastic life, abandoning the world which other men enjoy, or perhaps now at last hero worship will die a natural death." Eating its cake and having it, *Time* put his picture on their cover.

Lindbergh paid no attention to the war *Time* spoke of, only to the saber-rattling along Europe's borders. Before he had even returned home, Italy had conquered Albania. Days later, Hungary withdrew from the League of Nations and, in its alliance with Germany, instituted anti-Semitic laws. Lindbergh's fears steadily grew as France, England, and Russia deadlocked in their attempts to form a "peace front" against Germany. He worried even more when the Nazis revoked nonaggression pacts with Poland and a naval agreement with England only to sign a nonaggression pact with the Soviets. Meantime, President Roosevelt hosted King George VI and Queen Elizabeth of England, in an overt display of amity. Shortly after their visit to America, FDR called for a repeal of the arms embargo to belligerents, so that the United States might come to the aid of Britain, and he asked Congress to revise the Neutrality Law. Lindbergh turned all his thoughts to the world situation.

Anne had never seen her husband so galvanized. She watched with envy and awe as he plotted a course of political action for himself; and she sometimes questioned why she did not feel equally passionate. Because their marriage had made Anne so utterly dependent upon Charles for most of her feelings and actions, she hardly allowed herself to see that she did not actually share all his political views. Living less *with* Charles than *through* him, she only knew that she was feeling incomplete and unfulfilled—and mildly depressed. That summer, most unexpectedly, Anne found inspiration, and even more, as she fell in love with another man.

Antoine de Saint-Exupéry was not yet forty but already an international legend. A pioneering airmail pilot, his yearning for adventure had led him across the cities of Europe, the mountains of South America, and the deserts of Africa. Born to a notable family without money, he had grown up without a father and become unusually close to his mother. This nomad who appreciated nature was six-foot-two, shy but exuding sex appeal. Anne Lindbergh had never met anybody like him.

Unlike Charles Lindbergh, "Saint-Ex," was not only a man of action and science but also of philosophy and art—an aviator unafraid of expressing emotion. He was lauded in his native France as the first prose-poet laureate of the skies—the celebrated author of *Night Flight* and *Wind, Sand and Stars*. (He would soon write and illustrate *The Little Prince,* a perennial bestseller that would make him France's most widely translated author.) And he liked to perform card tricks.

Anne read *Wind, Sand and Stars* upon its American publication in the summer of 1939 and found it contained all she "ever wanted to say and more of flying and time and human relationships." Seeing a kinship between their books, her French publishers enlisted Saint-Exupéry to write a one-page preface to their forthcoming edition of *Listen! The Wind.* Upon reading Mrs. Lindbergh's book, however, Saint-Exupéry wrote nine pages, a penetrating analysis of both the work and the author. When she learned that he was then in New York City, she found the nerve to invite him to Lloyd Neck for dinner and the night.

With Charles off at a meeting, she picked him up at the Ritz and was surprised to find him stooped and balding and "not at all good looking." Nonetheless, she fell instantly under the spell of his "inscrutable" face and intense dark eyes. Anne drove just a block from his hotel when her car stalled and refused to restart. They pulled over to a repair shop, then took a taxi to Pennsylvania Station. Waiting for a train to Long Island, they sat on high stools at a counter and drank orangeade, like a pair of teenagers on a date. They nattered in French all the way to Huntington, about everything from aviation to their mutual admiration of Rilke. Despite Anne's rusty French, they spoke the same language. Before long, they were finishing each other's sentences.

"It was very exciting," Anne would write in one of the longest entries to be found among decades of diaries.

Perhaps it was only because it was almost the first time anyone had talked to me purely on my *craft*. Not because I was a woman to be polite to, to charm with superficials, not because I was my father's daughter or C.'s wife; no, simply because of my book, my mind, my *craft*. I have a *craft!* And someone who is master of that craft, who writes beautifully, thinks I know enough about my craft to want to compare notes about it, to want to fence with my *mind,* steel against steel.

More than sparks filled the air. "Summer lightning," she wrote in her diary.

Charles was not waiting for them at the station nor back at the house. Peculiarly, he got caught in traffic that night and did not return home until ten o'clock. Anne and Saint-Exupéry carried on their spirited conversation, barely interrupting its flow when he returned, for Lindbergh hardly spoke a word of French. They sat up until midnight, with Anne summing up her two-thousand-word entry exclaiming, "What an incredible day!"

The next morning Charles steered the conversation to the war—Germany's strength, England's strategy, France's struggle. After dropping Saint-Exupéry off at a friend's house for lunch, Anne commented to Charles that she feared the Frenchman would be killed if he continued flying.

They picked him up at five and brought him home for a swim, supper, and a walk along the beach. Conversation continued for hours. By the time they all retired, again at midnight, Anne was practically beside herself. "When one finds a person who has the same thought as yours," she wrote in the most uninhibitedly jubilant pages she had written in years, "you cry out for joy, you go and shake him by the hand. Your heart leaps as though you were walking in a street in a foreign land and you heard your own language spoken, or your name in a room full of strangers." It had been a most unusual weekend, one of the few times in the Lindbergh marriage in which Charles was not the center of attention.

The next day, the Lindberghs drove their guest into the city. Charles became so engrossed in a fable Saint-Exupéry was relating that, until his engine began to sputter, he did not notice that he had run out of gas. Lindbergh was plainly embarrassed; but, fortunately, they stalled on a downgrade just before the Fifty-ninth Street Bridge and coasted into a gas station just ahead. At last they parted. Charles was pleased to have made his acquaintance. Anne was changed forever.

"In Saint-Exupéry," one of her oldest friends would later confide, "Anne saw that a man of machinery could also be a man of poetry. Oh, there's no doubt, she fell in love—not just with Saint-Exupéry . . . but with all the possibilities he embodied. For the first time she understood that she did not have to remain trapped under her husband's foot forever and that her marriage contract contained an escape clause."

Anne was hardly about to leave her husband; and, indeed, Saint-Exupéry already had a wife and mistress. Instead, she reinvested her new feelings into her decade-old marriage, renewing the vows she had made to herself to become an artist. "My mind has quickened, and my sight and feelings," she wrote in her diary while his memory was still fresh. "For a week now the world has been almost unbearably beautiful. It cries out everywhere I turn. A twisted branch tears at the heart. The tendril of a dried vine is infinitely pathetic. A driving white rainstorm gives me wings, and trees steeped in the drowsy dark of evening stand up like rooted gods, reaching for the sky."

Charles did not yet realize the impact Saint-Exupéry had made, absorbed as he was in his own work. During his frequent visits to Washington—staying in a small pied-à-terre he rented in an apartment house called The Anchorage—Lindbergh renewed an old acquaintanceship with William R. Castle. Both a former Ambassador to Japan and Undersecretary of State, Castle had helped the Lindberghs with diplomatic arrangements when they had made their trip to the Orient. A rock-solid conservative, Castle was then working with the Republican National Committee. Dining with him that summer, Lindbergh spoke of "having a small group ready to jump in if a war begins in Europe, with the purpose of keeping this country out of trouble."

Castle could not have been more sympathetic, writing him afterward that he wished to share Lindbergh's thoughts with another friend, the conservative news commentator Fulton Lewis, Jr. The three men met alone for dinner at Castle's house on August twenty-third and found themselves in accord over the need for action should war break out in Europe, as seemed imminent.

Privately, they agreed on another subject as well. "We are disturbed about the effect of the Jewish influence in our press, radio, and motion pictures," Lindbergh confided to his journal that night. "It may become very serious. Lewis told us of one instance where the Jewish advertising firms threatened to remove all their advertising from the Mutual system if a certain feature were permitted to go on the air. The threat was powerful enough to have the feature removed. I do not blame the Jews so much for their attitude, although I think it unwise from their own standpoint."

An expurgated portion of that evening's entry revealed that the three men had more to say on the subject.

> We must, however, limit to a reasonable amount the Jewish influence in the Educational agencies in this country—ie. press, radio, and pictures. I fear that trouble lies ahead in this regard. Whenever the Jewish percentage of total population becomes too high, a reaction seems to invariably occur. It is too bad because a few Jews of the right type are, I believe, an asset to any country, adding to rather than detracting from its strength. If an anti-Semitic movement starts in the United States, it may go far. It will certainly affect the good Jews along with the others. When such a movement starts, moderation ends.

On the first of September, Germany invaded Poland. "What stand should America take in this war?" Lindbergh asked his diary the next day. "This is now our most pressing issue. We have enough internal problems without confusing them with war. I see trouble ahead even in times of peace. War would leave affairs chaotic—and always the best men lost." The next day Roosevelt addressed the nation, pledging American neutrality. Lindbergh liked the speech but said to himself, "I wish I trusted him more."

After three years of observing conditions in Europe firsthand, Lindbergh did not intend "to stand by and see this country pushed into war if it is not absolutely essential to the future welfare of the nation." To his journal, he announced, "Much as I dislike taking part in politics and public life, I intend to do so if necessary to stop the trend which is now going on in this country." He considered the radio and magazines the most effective forums in which to air his views.

Lindbergh began thinking about the effect aviation had already had on the world—not only in augmenting military strength but also in decreasing the size of the planet. With his Olympian view of the earth—in which populations of continents appeared to him as masses of people—Lindbergh wrote: "We, the heirs of European culture, are on the verge of a disastrous war, a war within our own family of nations, a war which will reduce the strength and destroy the treasures of the White race, a war which may even lead to the end of our civilization." Dr. Carrel had no doubt contributed to his thinking; but the words were all Lindbergh's—handwritten in pencil, then edited on secretary-typed drafts.

Peace, Lindbergh felt, could exist only so long as "we band together to preserve that most priceless possession, our inheritance of European blood, only so long as we guard ourselves against attack by foreign armies and dilution by foreign races." He viewed aviation as "a gift from heaven to those Western nations who were already the leaders of their era . . . a tool specially shaped for Western hands, a scientific art which others only copy in a mediocre fashion, another barrier between the teeming millions of Asia and the Grecian inheritance of Europe—one of those priceless possessions which permit the White race to live at all in a pressing sea of Yellow, Black, and Brown."

Lindbergh believed the Soviet Union had become the most evil empire on earth and that Western civilization depended on repelling it and the Asiatic powers that lay beyond its borders—the "Mongol and Persian and Moor." He wrote that it also depended on "a united strength among ourselves; on a strength too great for foreign armies to challenge; on a Western Wall of race and arms which can hold back either a Genghis Khan or the infiltration of inferior blood; on an English fleet, a German air force, a French army, an

American nation, standing together as guardians of our common heritage, sharing strength, dividing influence." He did not believe the nations of the West should "commit racial suicide by internal conflict," but must look instead to earlier fratricidal conflicts, such as the Peloponnesian War, in which Athens and Sparta battled, leaving much of Greece in ruins.

Lindbergh incorporated these thoughts into an article for the November *Reader's Digest,* which he called "Aviation, Geography, and Race." DeWitt Wallace, the magazine's founding editor, was proud to publish it. Sending Lindbergh a check for $2,500, he wrote, "No one in the country is able to exert a deeper influence on public opinion than yourself." The following March, *The Atlantic Monthly* published a continuation of Lindbergh's thinking, a piece called "What Substitute For War?"

In that second article, he pointed out that the "history of Europe has always been interwoven with conflict . . . the Ethiopian war, the World War, the Boer War, the Franco-Prussian War, the war between Germany and Austria, the war between Prussia and Denmark, the Franco-Sardinian war against Austria, the Crimean War, the British opium war; revolutions and uprisings in Spain, Germany, Italy, France, Ireland, and the Balkans; British actions in Africa, India, China, Afghanistan, Palestine, and elsewhere; French action in Africa, Indo-China, and Mexico" all taking place within the last century. This new confrontation, Lindbergh believed, was but another convolution in the great coil of history.

From his perspective, "This present war is a continuation of the old struggle among western nations for the material benefits of the world. It is a struggle by the German people to gain territory and power. It is a struggle by the English and French to prevent another European nation from becoming strong enough to demand a share in influence and empire." A strong Germany, he asserted, was as essential to a strong Europe as England and France, "for she alone can either dam the Asiatic hordes or form the spearhead of their penetration into Europe."

"Europe divided in war," Lindbergh believed, "reduces the stature of our civilization and lessens the security of all western nations. It destroys life, and art, and the spiritual growth that spring from peaceful intercourse among men." He was reminded of his great flying trip to India in 1937, when he and Anne saw only "the bones of marble and of bronze that represent the greatness of Rome, and Greece, and Egypt, and Babylon."

Lindbergh saved more trenchant rhetoric for his first radio address, the text of which would conjure up Washington's Farewell Address—warning the people of America against becoming "entangled in European alliances"— and the Monroe Doctrine, opposing further European interference in the Western hemisphere. He intended to urge his audience to view the world sit-

uation as he did, with utter detachment—without permitting "our sentiment, our pity, or our personal feelings of sympathy, to obscure the issue, to
affect our children's lives. We must be as impersonal as a surgeon with his
knife." Incisively, Lindbergh asserted, "We should never enter a war unless
it is absolutely essential to the future welfare of our nation." He saw nothing essential in our participation in this one. "We must either keep out of European wars entirely," he warned, "or stay in European affairs permanently."

Lindbergh intended to call on Americans to accept his synthesis of years
of xenophobic thinking. "[T]hese wars in Europe are not wars in which our
civilization is defending itself against some Asiatic intruder," he wrote, in
what would prove to be the speech's most memorable excerpt. "There is no
Genghis Khan or Xerxes marching against our Western nations. This is not
a question of banding together to defend the White race against foreign invasion. This is simply one more of those age old quarrels within our own
family of nations—a quarrel arising from the errors of the last war—from the
failure of the victors of that war to follow a consistent policy either of fair-
ness or of force." Lindbergh believed nothing less than Western civilization
itself was at stake in this war, and that "as long as America does not decay
within, we need fear no invasion of this country."

Anne approved of the speech, but she feared "it will be confused, it will
be smeared politically and brought down to the level of the Neutrality Act
issue." She worried that her husband would come under "heavy-fire criticism
from many quarters," friends as well as enemies. "He knows this & does not
mind it," Anne wrote Charles's mother, for he felt "sure that he sees the
right course."

On Wednesday, September thirteenth, Lindbergh took the milk train out
of New York's Pennsylvania Station to Washington. "Won't it be strange,"
Anne wrote Mrs. Lindbergh, "if Charles will be fighting the same fight as his
father, years ago!"

Thursday morning, Lindbergh went to see General Arnold and told him
of his intention to take to the airwaves. Arnold recognized the strength of
Lindbergh's commitment and therefore suggested that he discontinue his
current "inactive-active" status in the Air Corps so long as he was taking an
active role in politics. Lindbergh concurred. Anxious not to embarrass the
Air Corps, he offered a copy of his speech for Arnold to read. The General
found that "it contained nothing which could in any way be construed as un-
ethical" due to Lindbergh's connection with the Air Corps; and he felt that
Lindbergh was "fully within [his] rights as an American citizen" to broadcast the remarks. Arnold and Lindbergh discussed whether or not they
should show the address to Secretary of War Woodring. Lindbergh said he
preferred not to, unless it was absolutely necessary.

The next day, Lindbergh met with Truman Smith, then active in G-2

(General Staff, Military Intelligence Division), at Smith's request. Colonel Smith said he had an urgent message to deliver, even though he knew what Lindbergh's response would be. Smith said the Administration was "very much worried" by Lindbergh's intention to broadcast his opposition to their country's entry into a European war . . . and that a cabinet position of Secretary of Air would be created for Lindbergh if he would refrain. "So you see," Smith said, laughing, "they're worried."

At 8:30, the Lindberghs and the Fulton Lewises went to the Carlton Hotel, where they walked through a lobby full of photographers. Upstairs they found a room filled with radio equipment and twenty people. At 9:45, Lindbergh stood before six microphones—two each from the National Broadcasting Company, the Columbia Broadcasting System, and the Mutual Broadcasting System—and spoke. He was not happy with his high-pitched and flat delivery; but, strangely, his unimpassioned tone accentuated his sincerity. As soon as he was finished, everybody in the room congratulated him; Jim Newton sat in the corner and beamed. One step ahead of the press, the Lindberghs raced outside the hotel and down several blocks, escaping to Fulton Lewis's house, where they listened to a rebroadcast of the speech. Commentators were already signaling the speech's political significance. The Lindberghs boarded the two A.M. train to New York.

By the time they arrived, Lindbergh had once again grabbed the morning headlines. By noon, hundreds of telegrams and letters—most from strangers—were arriving in Lloyd Neck. The vast majority of them were favorable—calling Lindbergh brave and patriotic. One likened his speech to the Sermon on the Mount. General Arnold wrote that Secretary Woodring thought "it was very well worded and very well delivered" (as did Arnold himself). Anne shared the general response with her mother-in-law, saying how heartening it was to receive support "from all kinds and types of people—grateful mothers & fathers, school professors and teachers, businessmen, and also farmers, ranchers, small shop keepers . . . as though C's speech has answered a real need, a clear call in the confusion."

Philippics followed. Hardest-hitting was Dorothy Thompson, who only months earlier had praised Lindbergh for following the courageous path of his father. In her syndicated column she dismissed this speech as the rantings of a "somber cretin," a man "without human feeling," a "pro-Nazi recipient of a German medal." Furthermore, she got the bee in her bonnet that Lindbergh "has a notion to be the American Fuchrer." She admitted that she had no proof of her theory; but she would attack him in three more columns that year, six in 1940, and four in 1941—all aimed at getting readers to see him as more than just "America's number one problem child." She believed he was a Nazi.

Less than one month after his first speech—on October 13, 1939—Lindbergh addressed the nation a second time. "Neutrality and War," as he titled the speech, was less philosophical and more pragmatic in its content, with a specific program. American policy, he said, should not be directed toward Europe so much as America, and the United States should "draw a sharp line between neutrality and war." That meant refusing credit to belligerent nations or their agents. Like his father before him, Lindbergh believed that once American money was invested in a warring country's economy, "many interests will feel that it is more important for that country to win than for our own to avoid the war. It is unfortunate but true that there are interests in America who would rather lose American lives than their own dollars."

"This talk is going to create more criticism than the last one," Lindbergh predicted the day of its delivery. "It is more detailed and more controversial. However, I think it is desirable to get people thinking about fundamental problems and to speak clearly on this present issue of 'neutrality.' The criticism which arises is of very secondary importance." By the following Monday, letters were arriving at radio stations by the sackload. Nearly ninety percent of the mail seemed to be in Lindbergh's favor, though he was level-headed enough to know "the people who like what you say are more likely to write than those who don't—at least that is true in the intelligent classes." He would never be able to get through them all, but Lindbergh saved what would grow into a collection of tens of thousands of letters, many of them never opened.

Days later, threatening letters began to arrive at the Lindberghs' house. "It is a fine state of affairs in a country which feels it is civilized," Lindbergh complained to his journal; "people dislike what you do, so they threaten to kill your children." Lindbergh considered his options, but laying down his pen was never one of them. "I feel I must do this," he wrote of his new political role, "even if we have to put an armed guard in the house."

"I have taken the stand that this country should not enter the war," Lindbergh wrote Madame Carrel after his second speech, feeling that any rational Frenchman would disagree with his position; "and that peace in the near future is the only way of preserving the quality, the prestige, and the influence of our western civilization."

As a result of Lindbergh's conviction, the Carrels and the Lindberghs did not stop communicating with each other, but their letters and time together decreased. Even though the doors of the Rockefeller Institute had closed to him, Carrel would have liked to continue working in America. But one evening, talking to Lindbergh and Jim Newton, he said, "It's becoming more and more difficult for me to sit in New York and know that my country is sliding into hunger and disease. I feel I must go back. There must be more that I can do in France than here." He thought he might even prove to be a "lifeline" for France, a link in getting whatever aid from America might be necessary.

Meantime, Lindbergh became the nation's symbol of neutrality. His stand, Anne wrote Madame Carrel, "has been gravely misunderstood, misquoted, and as usual smeared with false accusations and motives." She "felt very badly about this," finding it difficult "to be arbitrarily labelled and shelved on a side so opposite to all one's friends and feelings." She was not surprised to find him as unconcerned as ever about public opinion. "Personally, I rather enjoy the situation," Lindbergh admitted to his mother in November 1939, "for I feel that the goal ahead is well worth the effort necessary to atain [sic] it."

Toward that end, Lindbergh met government figures of every stripe in Washington, aligning himself with no political party or organization. He spent one afternoon with a half-dozen Democratic senators who advocated language in the pending neutrality legislation that would minimize the chances of American involvement in the war. He spent another day with ex-President Herbert Hoover, William Castle, and Carl W. Ackerman, the influential Dean of the Columbia University Graduate School of Journalism—all Republicans who supported Lindbergh's position wholeheartedly. Lindbergh knew his growing antipathy toward Roosevelt would lead most people to assume that he and the President were of opposite parties; but the labels meant nothing to him. "As far as I am concerned personally," Lindbergh wrote in his journal, "I have but little fear of being classed as a Republican for long. I have too little interest in either politics or popularity. One of the dearest of rights to me is being able to say what I think and act as I wish. I intend to do this, and I know it will cause trouble. As soon as it does, the politicians will disown me quickly enough . . . I have no intention of bending my ideas or my ideals to conform to the platform of either party. One must make certain compromises in life—that is a part of living together with other men—but compromise is justified only when the goal to be gained is of greater importance than what is lost in compromising."

When Senator William E. Borah, Republican from Idaho, suggested that Lindbergh would make a good candidate for President, Lindbergh explained that he enjoyed too much "the ability to do and say what I wish to ever be a successful candidate for President. I prefer intellectual and personal freedom to the honors and accomplishments of political office—even that of President."

On November 4, 1939, FDR signed the Neutrality Act. It allowed sale of arms to belligerents as long as they paid cash and transported them in non-American ships. While this appeared to represent a policy of impartiality,

Lindbergh saw it as an American effort to aid Britain and France. Except for his article "What Substitute for War?"—in the March 1940 issue of *The Atlantic Monthly*—he would not address the public for a half-year.

His silence coincided with a lull in the fighting abroad—what people called "the phony war." When he was not brooding about foreign affairs, Lindbergh attended to his own domestic agenda, starting with the "ceaseless problem for us" of where to live—"how best to fit our unique set of circumstances to this changing world." He wondered where Jon and Land could lead normal lives, where Anne could write, where they could be away from the "deadly life of a modern city, and yet not isolate ourselves from those contacts and associations that made up civilized life." Complicating matters was the increase in terrifying letters arriving at his door—calling him a Nazi, threatening to kidnap his two sons. When the Lindberghs' lease in Lloyd Harbor expired, they moved back to Next Day Hill.

On January 21, 1940, Charles and Anne stole away for a vacation on the "Florida West Coast Special." They were ticketed to Tampa, but they hopped off the train in Haines City, centerstate, in order to evade the press. Only their host, Jim Newton, was there to meet them and to drive them through Fort Myers on the Gulf coast and just beyond to Punta Massa. There they boarded a one-horse ferry to Sanibel Island, drove its length, and crossed a small bridge to Captiva, where a shell road led to the Newton family's cottage set in a grove of palms and pines. The three-bedroom house sat on a strip of land so narrow that the Gulf was visible from the front door and the bay from the back.

The next ten days were magical. Unusually cold weather descended upon this tropical haven, but that did not keep the Lindberghs away from the water. Newton borrowed a thirty-foot cabin cruiser; and along with him and an Audubon Society game warden named Charlie Green, Anne and Charles sailed down the coast into the Everglades, along the Shark River, and among the Keys. For the better part of a week, they explored exotic bayous and mangrove swamps, completely unnoticed except for the eyes of hundreds of pelicans, egrets, buzzards, ducks, and ibises.

Charles was rejuvenated, Anne transported. "Wilderness," he blurted to Jim Newton one day. "People need it and miss it. It's frightening to think that in a few years our children and their children may not be able to experience it. It feeds the soul." Then he startled Jim Newton by claiming to have contributed to its gradual disappearance. While Lindbergh had hoped aviation might "unify the world," he could not help seeing the trouble it was creating, enabling man to penetrate remote places, perhaps to trespass where he did not belong. At night in Florida, he rowed his wife out onto the still waters, and they soaked in the "beauty and quiet . . . and isolation" of their surroundings. Anne realized the importance of responding to her husband, whenever he pulled her into adventure: "I should always go when C. calls," she wrote during this romantic interlude, "—break through my crust of inertia or fear—because life lies behind it." By the time the Lindberghs returned to New Jersey, Anne was pregnant.

The thought of a fourth child forced Anne to confront feelings she had been avoiding for years. "Isn't it possible for a woman to be a woman and yet produce something tangible beside children—something that stands up in a man's world?" Anne had written a cousin during her last pregnancy. Even entering the new decade, such thoughts were bold. Now reaching her thirties, she heard a psychological clock ticking—one which made her feel "it's time I did 'get down to' something, 'too old' to be 'promising.' " She was struggling with feminism.

More than ever, Anne yearned to write—"not because I feel I have anything to give . . . not because being an artist comes first (it doesn't) not because it matters to anyone else what I say." She simply felt that the thread of her life "will not be strong without that strand." All the imagery of Captiva and its environs had renewed her; and for the rest of her life, she would find herself drawn to that region, in search of metaphors. But unlike her feminist heroines—Virginia Woolf, Vita Sackville-West, and Rebecca West—Anne wanted to define new roles for women without sacrificing the traditional ones, those of wife and mother.

She had already become a magnet for similarly striving women all over the country, many of whom poured their hearts out to her. Although few of these women were her intellectual or social equals, Anne found comfort in their letters. They filled an emotional void her husband never could. For decades, she engaged in lengthy correspondences with many of these needy women. "Perhaps my job right now," she wrote one such suppliant, "is not to write books but to have my baby, keep a peaceful home and try to give my husband the kind of atmosphere, and thought and encouragement, and balance that will help him to deal with some of the problems he feels so disturbed about in the world today."

She and Charles moved into another house in Lloyd Neck, one more substantial than their first—a three-story wooden farmhouse dating back to 1714, full of charm and history. It overlooked a tidal inlet and Cold Spring Harbor. Anne suffered through the early spring there, as her morning sickness coincided with the disheartening news of Germany's conquering Denmark, Norway, Holland, and Belgium. The Nazis now approached Paris.

Alone in bed, Anne did "a lot of *mental* writing and a soaking up of old trains of thought." She found that she could not bring herself to blame Europe's current ills entirely on Hitler, as though he were some *"accidental scourge* unconnected to other world events—alone responsible for all," that if he were wiped out, all would be well. "Nazism," Anne wrote in her diary in April 1940, "seems to me scum which happens to be on the wave of the future. I agree with people's condemnation of Nazi methods but I do not think they *are* the wave. They happen to be riding on it."

With pressure mounting for America to enter the war, Lindbergh felt impelled to address the nation again. He wrote a speech called "The Air Defense of America" on May fifteenth, which he arranged to deliver from the Columbia Broadcasting System's Washington studios on the nineteenth, a Sunday, at 9:30 in the evening. His simple message required only twelve minutes of airtime. "We are in danger of war today not because European people have attempted to interfere with the internal affairs of America," he said, "but because American people have attempted to interfere with the internal affairs of Europe." He called on his nation to prepare itself for war, suggesting that the best offense was a proper defense. Without naming the faction, Lindbergh told his audience, "The only reason that we are in danger of becoming involved in this war is because there are powerful elements in America who desire us to take part. They represent a small minority of the American people, but they control much of the machinery of influence and propaganda. They seize every opportunity to push us closer to the edge." A month later, Lindbergh spoke again, calling on the nation to resist the propaganda spurring America into battle.

With his mail running 20 to 1 in his favor, Anne felt that her husband was giving voice to the silent majority of the nation. "[H]e speaks for inarticulate America," commented one of Anne's friends. Increasingly, Lindbergh found himself speaking for intolerant America as well.

Lindbergh had no supporter more ardent than Father Charles Edward Coughlin, a Catholic priest with a large following on the radio and through a national weekly tabloid called "Social Justice," which he published in Royal Oak, Michigan. With a definitely anti-Semitic agenda, he appropriated Lindbergh's likeness to help sell his own message, putting him on the front of his national weekly, quoting him in his suggestion as to who were the unnamed "war-breeding *clique*." The more Lindbergh attracted such bigots, the more people judged him by his followers.

On Monday, May 27, 1940, their wedding anniversary, Anne and Charles drove along Huntington Bay and found the spot where they had rowed out to their honeymoon boat eleven years earlier. It was a clear night, with dogwood and chestnut flowers in full bloom. Later they drove to the beach at Lloyd Neck, where they had summered the preceding year. Charles left for a walk alone down the beach, while Anne sat on a raft. Even in this peaceful moment, she could not help feeling depressed, thinking of all the people she cared about in England and France. And then she caught sight of her husband's figure in the distance, an approaching silhouette, and she instinctively felt hope. "And I think, yes—*that* is what keeps one going in times like these," she wrote in her diary, "the thought, the realization that there are a few men in the world, here and there—one has met them—who are on top of fate. And I do not mean just that they always win, but they are not downed by their circumstances in spite of everything."

When Charles reached his pregnant wife after his walk, Anne told him of her thoughts, of her belief that there were strong people in Europe, survivors who "will not be embittered, will get something from it, make something of it—if they are not killed." Even though Anne and Charles had never discussed the depth of her unrequited romance the preceding year, he saw his wife's pain. After a quiet moment, he tried to comfort her by saying, "I hope Saint-Exupéry survives."

Anne had followed Saint-Exupéry through the press—his return to France, his testing planes and training pilots. A Dorothy Thompson column the first week of June 1940 praised his flying missions against the Germans and moved Anne to tears. "Nobody has the right to write a word today who does not participate to the fullest in the agony of his fellow human beings," Saint-Exupéry told Miss Thompson. "If I did not resist with my life, I should be unable to write. . . . The Christian idea has got to be served; that the word is made Flesh. One must write with one's body." Saint-Exupéry, a reserve officer, was demobilized from his flying group just weeks after France's hasty capitulation to the Germans, which placed the government in the hands of elderly Marshal Henri Pétain in Vichy. Anne and Charles could not help thinking of their second home, as they often listened to a recording of *Mignon,* the opera that had been composed on Illiec. Their neighbors in France, the Carrels, were in their prayers.

Instead of resisting himself, or even hiding out on Saint-Gildas, the sixty-seven-year-old Alexis Carrel thought it in the best interests of his countrymen if he cooperated with the new Vichy government as much as necessary to help secure the authority, personnel, and equipment he would need to address the problems of "war medicine"—wound infection, hemorrhage, shock, gas burns, and poisoning that would soon plague his nation. As the "phony war" of the winter turned real, Carrel spent most of his time studying "the conditions which have brought about the degeneration of modern men"—moral, intellectual, anatomical, and racial. "The problem of remaking society is extremely complex on account of the multiplicity of the factor of deterioration," he wrote a medical colleague. "In France, the main trouble is moral corruption." When Carrel approached Pétain with his vision of an "Institute of Man," Jim Newton would later recall, "Pétain offered to subsidize it. Carrel accepted and went to work, despite the obstructions placed in his way by the medical profession."

Carrel's pursuit of his humanitarian work in association with Pétain's Vichy government would later provoke severe criticism from the Resistance forces backing de Gaulle. While suffering from wartime deprivation—refusing extra rations of food and fuel, which he could have procured—Carrel was observed one day at the German Embassy. He had arrived, in fact, to request help in feeding starving French children; but he happened to appear when a party was in full swing. Although the Carrels retreated as quickly as possible, rumors spread that the Germans had entertained them. "You know how Alexis felt about the Nazis when he was in New York," Madame Carrel would later explain to Jim Newton. "He felt much more strongly, living in Occupied France. Why, many of our staff at the institute were members of the Resistance, and we protected them." Accused of being a collaborator, the septuagenarian's health declined.

Saint-Exupéry was conflicted about the German occupation of France as well. With only ill-will for the anti-Jewish Vichy government, and not much kinder feelings for the egomaniacal de Gaulle, he sought perspective on the situation in New York City. "Did you see?" Anne remarked to Charles one morning, "Saint-Exupéry is here, but he is going back again!"

"Yes," Charles replied, "I see, with jealousy." Taken aback, Anne asked why with jealousy. "Because," he responded, "you seem to be so interested in him."

Anne quickly interjected that she had a purely literary interest in him, that she admired him—"and because I keep looking for someone to be left like that from *my* world, my world of writing."

Charles had long attempted to be his wife's muse, but his methods usually failed. "He goes over the record," Anne wrote in her diary, "—nine years, and only two books and wonders why it is. Has he not given me the right kind of environment?" As if shaming her was not enough, he further subjected her to a loyalty test. While Anne's mother parceled Bundles for Britain and broadcast pro-Ally speeches on the radio, and Anne's sister Constance, married to a Welshman, supported pro-British causes, Lindbergh kept pressing his wife to demonstrate whether she was more Morrow or Lindbergh.

Then Anne had a breakthrough. She found a way of making a literary offering to Saint-Exupéry, all the while affirming her loyalty to her husband. An article gushed from her in a few days.

It represented, she wrote her mother by way of preparing her for its publication, "all the winter's mental strife—all the arguments—& counter arguments . . . building of a bridge between C.'s beliefs & my own & not least, my deep sense of the injustice to him & to his side." But that was not its sole raison d'être. "I wouldn't do it if I didn't feel convinced of his integrity & the integrity of his stand," she wrote. ". . . And I wouldn't do it if I didn't feel that there are things he has not—& probably *could* not present well. If

I did not feel there were things I could present better than he. And that the presentation of these things might help both him & his cause." In trying to be too many things to too many people, the article never congealed as either accurate history or sound philosophy. It remained a moving hodgepodge of an admittedly confused woman trying to make sense of contradictory feelings.

"I think the clearest definition of the article is that it attempts to give a *moral* argument for Isolationism," Anne wrote her mother on September 4, 1940, "—which I think no one has yet presented." Upon reading Anne's description, Betty Morrow—whose lifelong devotion to Smith College had just been capped by being named her alma mater's Acting President—broke into tears.

The five-thousand-word piece was hardly on paper before Lindbergh took a copy of it to her publisher, Alfred Harcourt. He read it on the spot, pronounced it "beautiful," and said he was eager to publish it. In less than a month, the Lindberghs had copies of the forty-one-page, pocket-sized book in hand. Anne decided to tender all her income from the tract to the American Friends Service Committee to assist them in their war-relief efforts in Europe, especially France.

The book's central metaphor became its title—*The Wave of the Future*. As Anne explained at the text's core, the war in Europe did not strike her as a struggle between the "Forces of Good" and the "Forces of Evil" so much as a conflict between the "Forces of the Past" fighting against the "Forces of the Future." Far from siding with the new totalitarian regimes, she suggested that "somehow the leaders in Germany, Italy and Russia have discovered how to use new social and economic forces; very often they have used them badly," she wrote, "but nevertheless, they have recognized and used them. They had sensed the changes and they have exploited them. They have felt the wave of the future and they have leapt upon it. The evils we deplore in these systems are not in themselves the future; they are scum on the wave of the future."

Anne condemned the tyrannies of Nazism and asserted that she could not "pledge my personal allegiance to those systems I disapprove of, or those barbarisms I oppose from the bottom of my heart, even if they *are* on the wave of the future." But she did suggest "that it is futile to get into a hopeless 'crusade' to 'save' civilization," for that task could not be accomplished by going to war. Instead, she thought America's task was less in fostering a revolution in Europe than in fomenting a reformation at home, in protecting and preserving "our own family and nation."

"There is no fighting the wave of the future," she wrote toward the end of her essay, "any more than as a child you could fight against the gigantic roller that loomed up ahead of you suddenly." In conclusion, Anne could only offer vague platitudes expressing the need for America to reaffirm its basic beliefs. Constance Morrow Morgan suggested that her sister's prewar book was an obvious illustration of her identity crisis, "torn as she was between being Anne Morrow and Mrs. Charles Lindbergh."

Few books in the history of publishing have encountered a reception like the one that greeted Anne Morrow Lindbergh's *The Wave of the Future: A Confession of Faith*. It immediately became the number-one nonfiction best-seller across the country—fifty thousand copies in its first two months alone—and received prominent reviews everywhere. The book had many admirers, including the growing numbers of Americans who opposed intervention into the European war. DeWitt Wallace of *Reader's Digest* condensed the book for his readers and called it *"the* article of the year." Even English-born poet W. H. Auden pronounced it a "beautiful book." He reminded her that "everything one writes goes out helpless into the world to be turned to evil as well as good, that every work of art is powerless against misuse."

Such was the case with *The Wave of the Future*, which overnight became the book people loved to hate. Surpassed in modern literary history perhaps only by *Mein Kampf,* it was one of the most despised books of its day. Anne's hopeful message, innocently intended to bind the opposing sides with its universal images, only wedged them farther apart. It was promptly quoted and persistently misquoted. Ironically, it resulted in rallying greater support for the side she had meant to oppose by offering a weak stalking horse. Store owners as well as book buyers boycotted it, sending copies back to the publisher. One dealer wrote Alfred Harcourt that he thought both Lindberghs "should be put behind barbed wires!" Half a century later, *The Wave of the Future* remained a book nobody remembered with affection—not even the author, who later recanted much of its contents, which she ascribed to her naïveté.

Dorothy Thompson lashed out at Anne Lindbergh in the pages of *Look,* accusing her (as most readers did) of calling Communism, Fascism, and Nazism the "wave of the future," accosting her for saying there was no way of fighting it. In her syndicated columns, Thompson repeatedly misrepresented Anne Lindbergh's metaphor and distorted the record even further by suggesting that the Lindberghs supported several "American Fascists" just because they had endorsed the writings of the Lindberghs. (These rabble-rousers included William Dudley Pelley, who had organized the openly anti-Semitic "Silver Shirt" brigades, and the more intellectual Lawrence Dennis, who contended that Fascism was America's best hope against the rising tide of Communism.) FDR's outspoken Secretary of the Interior, Harold L. Ickes, went farther than that, publicly calling Lindbergh a Nazi and calling *The*

Wave of the Future "the Bible of every American Nazi, Fascist, Bundist and Appeaser."

Franklin Roosevelt campaigned for a third term on a non-interventionist platform. Days before the 1940 election, he assured voters that American boys would not be sent into any foreign wars. Two months later, after his landslide election over Wendell Willkie—for whom Lindbergh voted—he spoke in a Fireside Chat of making America "the great arsenal of democracy." At his inauguration, three weeks later, he invoked Anne Lindbergh's book, chiseling her metaphor into the public consciousness. "There are men who believe that . . . tyranny and slavery have become the surging wave of the future—and that freedom is an ebbing tide," he proclaimed. "But we Americans know that this is not true."

The increasing attacks made Anne recoil, not only from further political statements but from publishing at all. "I find I am hurt, not by the reviews exactly," Anne wrote in her diary, "but by the growing rift I see between myself and those people I thought I belonged to. The artists, the writers, the intellectuals, the sensitive, the idealistic—I feel exiled from them. I have become exiled for good, accidentally, really. My marriage has stretched me out of my world, changed me so it is no longer possible to change back." Anne's few intimates—her family and a scattering of friends—all recognized the new isolation she had created for herself by aligning herself so publicly with her now controversial husband. "You know, Anne," her former suitor Corliss Lamont wrote her, "some of your old friends hesitate even to suggest meeting with you, for fear it might embarrass you in some way; though no doubt *you* may feel that you might embarrass them." When Charles encouraged Anne to call on Saint-Exupéry during his visit to New York in January 1941, she refused for that very reason. She was distressed from not seeing him; but, alas, she wrote in her diary, "I am now the bubonic plague among writers and C. is the anti-Christ!"

Although politics strained many of Anne's relationships, her family never abandoned her. When newspaperman William Allen White suggested conflict between Lindbergh and his mother-in-law, Betty Morrow fired a handwritten letter off to him in Emporia, Kansas, insisting "Colonel Lindbergh and I differ about what our country's attitude towards the war should be, but each honors the sincerity of the other's opinions and there is no misunderstanding between us." Anne's sister Constance and her husband, Aubrey, said that they and the Lindberghs had all "agreed to disagree."

A few months later Anne would write an article, "Reaffirmation," for *The Atlantic Monthly*, in which she tried to clarify the thesis of *The Wave of the Future*. Even though she reasserted her definition that the evils of Fascism were but the "scum on the surface of the wave," and that she opposed the way in which the dictator-governed nations met the wave, there was no erasing what had been stamped into the public consciousness.

In the midst of this debate, Anne was presented with yet another reason to withdraw from the public. At two o'clock in the morning of October 2, 1940—within days of her book's publication—she awoke at Lloyd Manor with labor pains. Charles rushed her to Doctors Hospital in Manhattan, where she gave birth a few hours later. Both Charles and Anne had hoped for a girl; and getting their wish, the father insisted on naming the child after her mother. To avoid confusion, the newborn—Anne Spencer Lindbergh—would be called Ansy. With reporters already staking out the Lindbergh house, and so much unpopular undertow from *The Wave of the Future,* Lindbergh thought it best for Anne to cloister herself in the hospital with their daughter for more than two weeks.

He visited the healthy mother and daughter almost every evening; but he spent his days working to keep America out of the war. His wife's "confession of faith"—to both the anti-intervention effort and to him—refortified him for his mission. Charles reread his father's book *Why Is Your Country at War?*

GRASS-ROOTS anti-intervention movements sprouted across the country. Even though veterans groups found their membership divided on the issue, most—like the Veterans of Foreign Wars and the American Legion—strongly supported Lindbergh's position of building up America's defenses. When legionnaire Bennett Champ Clark, Democratic senator from Missouri, invited Lindbergh to address an antiwar rally in Chicago, he agreed, for the first time, to address the issue at a public gathering. Although fronted by veterans, the assembly was backed by a local organization called Citizens Keep America Out of War Committee, led by a Chicago builder named Avery Brundage, who also headed the American Olympic Association.

On August 3, 1940, Lindbergh flew to Chicago on one of TWA's new Boeing "stratoliners." He was met by the chauffeur of Colonel Robert R. McCormick, the publisher of the *Chicago Tribune,* who showed his support of Lindbergh's cause by offering extensive publicity for the rally in his newspaper. The next day Lindbergh drove to Soldier Field, where a respectable half-capacity crowd of forty thousand people gathered. Under a broiling sun, Lindbergh spoke for twenty minutes. "I do not offer my opinion as an expert," he insisted, "but rather as a citizen who is alarmed at the position our country has reached in this era of experts." And unpopular though some of his opinions might prove, he proclaimed, "I prefer to say what I believe, or not to speak at all. I would far rather have your respect for the sincerity of what I say, than attempt to win your applause by confining my discussion to popular concepts."

As the first rumblings of the Battle of Britain were being felt, he asked his audience to consider "a Europe dominated by Germany," insisting that no matter who won the war, Western civilization would depend on a strong America and that cooperation with a victorious Germany need not be impossible. To keep America out of the war, Lindbergh urged "an impregnable system of defense." The crowd, eager to applaud at every opportunity, threw Lindbergh slightly off his rhythm; but in the end, he found it "much easier to speak to an audience than to microphones alone." While a houseguest of the McCormicks, Lindbergh met other like-minded citizens, who urged him to continue speaking out.

Choosing public arenas over guarded radio studios made him a bigger public target; and it became open season on Lindbergh. The "attack launched against Lindbergh has gone far beyond the ordinary canons of debate," observed *The Christian Century* not three weeks after his Chicago address. "It has pulsed with venom. If this man who was once the nation's shining hero had been proved another Benedict Arnold he could not have been subjected to more defamation and calumny." Indeed, Ralph Ingersoll, publisher of *PM,* filled the front page of his new daily tabloid with a signed editorial censuring Lindbergh. Illustrated with only a photograph of a grinning Lindbergh sharing a jolly moment with Hermann Goering, Ingersoll declared, "Lindbergh is a political novice. His speech was post-graduate work. Obviously, he was helped in writing it. Who are the people who did his thinking and helped in his writing? Who are his gang?" Ingersoll concluded by denouncing "Colonel Charles A. Lindbergh as the spokesman of the fascist fifth column in America." Walter Winchell called "The Lone Eagle" the "Lone Ostrich." Lindbergh's FBI file, quiet since the Hauptmann trial, was reactivated, as the agency gathered information that might bear upon "his nationalistic sympathies." The most treasonous behavior investigators could uncover were sketchy reports of Lindbergh's smiling on the streets of Berlin in 1936 or of Lindbergh's associating with the likes of Merwin K. Hart, the head of the New York State Economic Council and an alleged promoter of an American Fascist movement who was assumed to have ties with more reactionary fringe groups.

Publicly, FDR let others in the White House speak for him. Pulitzer Prize–winning playwright and speechwriter Robert Sherwood delivered a radio address in which he attacked Lindbergh and Henry Ford, another anti-interventionist long considered anti-Semitic. Ford was partially excused because he was a genius; Lindbergh, on the other hand, was accused of having a "poisoned mind," of being a traitor—an "unwitting [purveyor] of Nazi propaganda." The Lindberghs were receiving so many obscene letters—generally unsigned—that the Post Office took the precaution of inspecting their mail.

At the same time, Lindbergh was not blind to his legions of supporters. "The sheer number of the unsolicited letters and telegrams is little short of astounding," observed Paul Palmer, a *Reader's Digest* editor who wrote an article that August on America's apparent shift in attitude toward its living legend. He stated that more mail followed a Lindbergh radio address than that of any other person in America, including FDR, thus making this reluctant orator "one of the great radio voices of all time." Even Robert Sherwood called Lindbergh an "extremely eloquent crusader for the cause of isolationism. . . . undoubtedly Roosevelt's most formidable competitor on the radio." What Palmer found most striking was "the amazing fact that over 94% of these thousands of letters and telegrams express ardent approval of the Colonel's anti-war position."

In covering America's reaction to the new public Lindbergh for *Scribner's Commentator*, C. B. Allen found many people asking why Lindbergh had chosen to step up to the microphones and wondering who was getting him to do it. "From the beginning," Allen assured his readers, "it has been his own idea. No diplomat or former diplomat has been 'advising' him. He has not sought and even repels those who would be his special advocates or advisers. No word painter or ghost writer has been helping him prepare his speeches; they are as wholly and typically Lindbergh as his amazing flying career."

While the Lindberghs' controversial position ruptured several old friendships, it fostered as many new ones. Norman Thomas, America's leading Socialist, disagreed with Lindbergh's occasional bluntness; but, he wrote him, "I applaud your stand and deplore the rather vicious type of attack that has been made upon you." New York attorney John Foster Dulles did not buy all Lindbergh's arguments, but he too said he was "very glad you spoke as you did," for he concurred with his feeling of "grave danger" should the United States continue its apparent foreign policy. Chester Bowles, then an advertising executive, congratulated Lindbergh for his courage and expressed his hope that "you will keep on talking and talking in spite of all the criticism and innuendos that will undoubtedly be fired in your direction." Frank Lloyd Wright wrote, "We all knew you could fly straight. Now we know you can think straight. When talk is quite generally cheap and unreliable, you are brave enough to talk straight."

With Americans from all walks of life hoping Lindbergh would become the spokesman for their anti-interventionist cause—including Senators Bennett Champ Clark of Missouri, Ernest Lundeen and Henrik Shipstead from Minnesota, Burton K. Wheeler of Montana, Gerald P. Nye of North Dakota,

Patrick McCarran from Nevada, and William E. Borah of Idaho, university presidents Alan Valentine of the University of Rochester and Robert Maynard Hutchins of the University of Chicago, and even John Cudahy, who had served in the New Deal's diplomatic corps—Lindbergh found himself drawn to a group of young men in New Haven, Connecticut, mostly law students at Yale.

R. Douglas "Bob" Stuart, Jr.—a good-looking, go-getting graduate of Princeton, the son of the first vice president of the Quaker Oats Company, then studying law—had contacted Lindbergh back in November 1939, after Lindbergh's first antiwar address to the nation. Along with Potter Stewart and Sargent Shriver, Stuart had been one of six Yale students who had invited him to the campus to speak. In the spring of 1940, Stuart and Stewart and two other Yale University law students—Eugene Locke of Texas and Gerald R. Ford of Grand Rapids, Michigan—circulated a mimeographed letter and petition to students and recent graduates of universities throughout the country "to enlist the support of those who feel, as we do, that the policy of the United States should be hemisphere defense rather than European intervention, and who are willing to work for the adoption of that policy." This introductory letter asserted that they were neither pacifists nor affiliated with any political party. On four military matters, these young bulldogs were firmly committed:

1. The United States must build an impregnable defense for America.
2. No foreign power, nor group of powers, can successfully attack a *prepared* America.
3. American democracy can be preserved only by keeping out of the European war.
4. Aid short of war weakens national defense at home and threatens to involve America in war abroad.

Stuart had gone to Chicago in search of backing for his organization; and he enlisted a family friend, General Robert S. Wood, the chairman of Sears-Roebuck, to act as chairman. Stuart postponed his third year of law school in order to serve as the full-time director of this group, the Committee to Defend America First. The movement's name got shortened in daily parlance to its last two words.

"The early members of its governing body," wrote Richard Moore—a young attorney who would soon leave his firm to become America First's Assistant National Director— ". . . included a mixture of conservatives and liberals, Republicans and Democrats and independents." From the Roosevelt Administration itself they included General Hugh Johnson, who had headed the National Recovery Administration, Stuart Chase, an economist credited

with coining the phrase "New Deal," and George N. Peek, the former head
of the Agricultural Adjustment Administration. Two senatorial wives, both
Democrats—Mrs. Burton K. Wheeler and Mrs. Bennett Champ Clark—and
two daughters of famous men—Alice Roosevelt Longworth (daughter of
T.R.) and Kathryn Lewis (daughter of labor leader John L. Lewis) also served
on the national committee. Liberal journalists John T. Flynn and Oswald
Garrison Villard, popular novelist Kathleen Norris, humorist Irvin S. Cobb,
and World War I ace Eddie Rickenbacker, then head of Eastern Airlines,
rounded out the list.

Lindbergh was so impressed with the campaign the twenty-five-year-old
Stuart had mounted in just a few months—complete with platform, personalities, and financing—he was considering his invitation to speak before a
student gathering at Yale University. On October 22, 1940, Jim Newton and
Lindbergh went to a Trans-Lux newsreel theater to watch the footage of a
speech he had delivered eight nights earlier. That had been the first time he
had not refused to allow the film companies to photograph him—a great risk,
he believed, "because of the Jewish influence in the newsreels and the antagonism I know exists towards me. . . . I take the chance that they will cut
my talk badly and sandwich it between scenes of homeless refugees and
bombed cathedrals." As Lindbergh's picture came up on the screen, many in
the theater hissed. The editing of the newsreels that night was not as distorted
as Lindbergh had feared; and he was encouraged at the end when a larger
number of people in the audience applauded. The next day, he accepted the
invitation of the America First Committee, telephoning one of its leaders,
Kingman Brewster—the student chairman of the Yale News, who would one
day become president of the university.

Lindbergh drove himself from Long Island to New Haven on October 30,
1940. After dining with several students at the home of Professor A. Whitney Griswold, another future Yale president, they all drove to Woolsey Hall.
The imposing marble building was filled beyond capacity—close to three
thousand people. Lindbergh spoke for half an hour, his longest speech yet.
His first ten minutes were professorial in tone, a brief history of the events
in Europe that had led to the current war. Then he articulated his message
for the "generation which is taking over the problems of life during the
greatest period of mutation that man has ever known": "We must either
keep out of European wars entirely," he said, repeating his familiar refrain,
"or participate in European politics permanently." In making that decision
he asked his audience, "Do we intend to attempt an invasion of the continent
of Europe. Do we intend to fight a war in the Orient? Do we intend to try
both at the same time?" If the answer to the latter questions was yes, he said,
"it is long past time for us to begin the construction of bases in the Pacific,
and to stop our wavering policy in the Philippines—we should either fortify

these islands adequately, or get out of them entirely." He confined his remarks that night to Europe, because, he said, "no nation in Asia has developed their aviation sufficiently to be a serious menace to the United States at this time . . ."

Lindbergh expected heckling during his speech but encountered only rapt attention. He received a tremendous ovation, enough for him to note in his journal that the meeting "was by far the most successful and satisfying . . . of this kind in which I have ever taken part." It encouraged him not only to continue speaking publicly but to do so under the aegis of this impressive "youth group." While many of the other antiwar organizations had distinctly reactionary—often anti-Semitic—taints to them, America First seemed to attract men and women of all ages, political persuasions, and religions—including a number of influential Jews. These included Sidney Hertzberg, their publicity director, and Lessing Rosenwald, one of the Sears-Roebuck heirs. Furthermore, noted an FBI report on the organization, there was "a tremendous Jewish group" subsidizing the movement, using the Guggenheim Foundation as its front.

During the next year, millions of words would be spoken and written on the subject of intervention. As each side fought for the soul of the nation, the argument boiled down to eleven months of oratory between Franklin Roosevelt and Charles Lindbergh. The latter would prove to be the biggest draw for the America First movement, making thirteen public appearances as its featured speaker in practically every region of the country. Contrary to persistent rumor, Lindbergh wrote all his own speeches—with only minor editing from Anne. He received no compensation from any organization or individual for his efforts; and he paid for all his own transportation and lodging.

In January 1941, President Roosevelt asked for "all-out aid" for the democracies; and the Congress introduced a bill that would give him almost unlimited war powers. In his State of the Union address on January sixth, he gave the still-isolationist nation a big push toward war when he asked Congress for a lend-lease bill—one empowering the President to transfer war material to any country deemed vital to U. S. interests, deferring payments for those ships and arms. Four days later, Congress opened debate on the subject, one of the hottest in its history. Four days after that, Lindbergh received a telegram from Hamilton Fish, the President's congressman, who actively opposed the bill in the House. "THIS IS MOST IMPORTANT AND FAR REACHING ADMINISTRATION BILL EVER PRESENTED TO CONGRESS," Fish wired Lindbergh, asking him to testify before the Committee on Foreign Affairs.

Lindbergh arrived at Capitol Hill early on Thursday, January 23, 1941, and walked through some of the buildings that had been his childhood playground. When he approached the Ways and Means Committee Room of the new House Office Building—at 9:55 as scheduled—he encountered a huge crowd. Police had to escort him into the room, which was jammed with a thousand people. Motion-picture cameras and lights were already in place, and dozens of still photographers swarmed around the table at which Lindbergh sat. He faced the committee—twenty-five-strong. Although he was as charismatic as ever, the public got its first hard look at a Lindbergh just shy of forty, his hair thinning and graying at the temples, with age lines in the alabaster skin. The hero famous for his perfect smile sat solemnly in a dark suit, eager to talk.

For the next two and one-half hours he testified without pausing even for a drink of water. For the pro-intervention representatives, the hearing proved to be something of a joust, in which they attempted to knock Lindbergh off his horse of staunch neutrality. One such attempt came in answering questions from Rep. Luther A. Johnson of Texas:

You are not, then, in sympathy with England's efforts to defeat Hitler?
I am in sympathy with the people on both sides, but I think that it would be disadvantageous for England herself, if a conclusive victory is sought.

I think you are evading the question—not intentionally; but the question is very simple, whether or not you are in sympathy with England's defense against Hitler?
I am in sympathy with the people and not with their aims.

You do not think that it is to the best interests of the United States economically as well as in the matter of defense for England to win?
No sir. I think that a complete victory, as I say, would mean prostration in Europe, and would be one of the worst things that could happen there and here. . . . I believe we have an interest in the outcome of the war.

On which side?
In a negotiated peace; we have the greatest interest.

. . . Which side would it be to our interest to win?
Neither.

After a lunch break, the tournament continued, as Rep. Wirt Courtney of Tennessee asked, "Do you think that either Germany or England is the more to blame for the present conflict?" Lindbergh replied: "Over a period of years, no."

Lindbergh expressed his belief that American aid to England would only prolong the war. He urged America to arm itself and defend its own borders;

and he suggested that American entry into this war "would be the greatest disaster this country has ever passed through." Several times during his four and one-half hours of testimony, the crowd burst into applause. Before dismissing the witness, even Chairman Sol Bloom noted, "you have made one of the best witnesses that this committee could possibly ever hear. You answered all the questions only as a Colonel Lindbergh could answer them . . ."

A fortnight later, Lindbergh was back in Washington, testifying before the Senate. He found this hearing conducted with more dignity but also more acrimony. He used his opening statement to amplify some of the comments he had made before the House, particularly to explain that when he had refused to say he favored an English victory it was because "an English victory, if it were possible at all, would necessitate years of war and an invasion of the Continent of Europe," which he believed "would create prostration, famine, and disease in Europe—and probably in America—such as the world has never experienced before." That was why he preferred a negotiated peace to a complete victory by either side. Senate Bill 275, he believed, pursued a "policy which attempts to obtain security for America by controlling internal conditions in Europe." It troubled Lindbergh that America was sending a large portion of its armament production abroad, while its own defense systems—especially the air forces—were in "deplorable condition."

Senator Claude Pepper of Florida got the inquiry off to an unintentionally amusing start when he tried to put Lindbergh's comments in some historical context. "Colonel," he asked, "when did you first go to Europe?"

"Nineteen twenty-seven, sir," he replied, which brought the house down in a prolonged demonstration of laughter and applause.

Pepper soon made it clear that he wanted to show that Lindbergh was pro-German. He asked Lindbergh to comment on the fact that many people "have been puzzled by the absence of any indication on your part of any moral indignation at what they consider outrageous wrongs which have been perpetrated and are being perpetrated by the German Government." Lindbergh asserted his belief "that nothing is gained by publicly commenting on your feeling in regard to one side of a war in which your country is not taking part." Instead, he suggested, he felt "very strongly that the attitude of this country should be receptive to a negotiated peace." He further asserted his belief that America should not "police the world."

While Lindbergh's testimony may have sounded logical in theory, many Americans were incensed at the coldness of his responses. "[Y]our failure to denounce the perversions of Nazi doctrine, the shocking cruelty and destruction of which they are guilty," wrote one stranger who expressed the sentiments of millions, "is an eloquent declaration of where you stand." Cornelius Vanderbilt, Jr., expressed his sentiments more succinctly, when he wired Lindbergh: "WHAT AN UNPATRIOTIC DUMB BELL YOU ARE." *The Richmond*

News Leader, edited by biographer D. S. Freeman, observed on its editorial page that "Millions would vote today to hang LINDBERGH or to exile him—as enthusiastically as they cheered and extolled him. Half the letters that have come to newspapers during the past few days have been abuse of him. Some of the communications have been so scurrilous that they could not be printed, though the writers doubtless sealed them with satisfaction and then sat down by the fire to plume themselves as patriots." Whether one agreed with Lindbergh's view of the world or not, Freeman thought it surely demonstrated Lindbergh's patriotism, that if he was trying to aid the Nazis he could achieve that "much more readily by keeping away from the committee room and plotting in the background." Within the week, the House passed Lend-Lease by a vote of 260–165; the Senate followed suit in early March by a margin of 60–31. In London, the blitz continued.

A case of chicken pox ran through the Lindbergh house, first putting Anne in bed and ultimately downing Charles for ten days. They both recovered in time to stick to plans they had made to revisit Florida. As before, they eluded the press. On March 6, 1941, Jim Newton met them in Haines City, then drove them to Fort Myers, where he had outfitted the Lindberghs with a large sailboat with an engine and a small dory. Because he knew the coastal waters so well, he would be their only guide.

"Occasionally we camped under twisted sea-grape trees on shore in a bugproof tent," Anne would later write. "We explored Shark River again, silently this time, sailing before the wind with jib and jigger, into the timeless world of wilderness and wild life. Pushing through the maze of streams and rivers opening up before us, between bare ghostly arms of mangrove roots, we scarcely made a ripple, occasionally startling a great white heron, or a pink ibis, or water turkeys. Swallow-tailed kites circled slowly above our heads. At sunset we put the sails down and poled through small bayous under arching bushes."

The centerpiece of their trip was a voyage to Dry Tortugas, one of the outermost keys off Florida's southwest coast. Charles took command of the twenty-four-hour crossing, ordering watches on deck for everybody—"two hours apiece until nightfall, then four on and eight below." Over the next few days, they explored the island—which boasted an enormous nineteenth-century fortress, Fort Jefferson—and the neighboring keys. In the calm waters they swam and dove, each trying for the first time a helmet attached by a forty-foot hose to an air pump. They were thrilled to enter this strange world of silence and exotic sights—"purple sea fans, luminous blue fish, yellow, black-and-white striped, gliding in and out of ferns, coral branches, all moving to a rhythm we did not know or feel." Although they had set out for ten days, the Lindberghs floated off the tip of the United States for almost three weeks, all but completely detached from newspaper and radio reports. A refreshed Lindbergh returned to Long Island to resume his crusade.

Working through young Bob Stuart, Lindbergh spent the next two weeks writing an address for a meeting in the Chicago Arena on April seventeenth. General Wood introduced him to the crowd of more than ten thousand, announcing that Lindbergh had officially joined the national America First Committee. Over the next twenty-five minutes, Lindbergh explained why. "The America First Committee is a purely American organization formed to give voice to the hundred-odd million people in our country who oppose sending our soldiers to Europe again," he said. "Our objective is to make America impregnable at home, and to keep out of these wars across the sea. Some of us, including myself, believe that the sending of arms to Europe was a mistake—that it has weakened our position in America, that it has added bloodshed in European countries, and that it has not changed the trend of the war."

The plainspoken Lindbergh incited thirty interruptions of applause and almost no opposition within the hall. "War is not inevitable for this country," he proclaimed. "Whether or not America enters the war is within our control." While many took his clarity for clairvoyance, the future would later prove some of his pronouncements just plain wrong. "Personally, I believe it will be a tragedy to the world—a tragedy even to Germany—if the British Empire collapses," he said. "But I must tell you frankly that I believe this war was lost by England and France even before it was declared, and that it is not within our power in America today to win the war for England, even though we throw the entire resources of our nation into the conflict. With all our organization and industry, we are not, and will not be able to transport an army across the ocean, large enough to invade the continent of Europe successfully as long as strong European armies are there for its defense."

Six nights later, Lindbergh addressed another capacity crowd, filling ten thousand seats in New York's Manhattan Center. Outside, among another ten thousand people milling on Thirty-fourth Street, were members of a watchdog organization called Friends of Democracy. Its national director, Leon M. Birkhead, had recently informed Lindbergh that his group had discovered "that the America First Committee is being used by Hitler's propagandists to advance a doctrine which is anti-American and anti-democratic." His supporters picketed the event, calling it "the largest gathering of pro-Nazi and pro-Fascists, of both domestic and imported brands, since the German American bund rallies in Madison Square Garden." The Non-Sectarian Anti-Nazi League distributed handbills headlined "What One Hitler Medal Can Do." *PM* characterized the gathering as "a liberal sprinkling of Nazis, Fascists, anti-Semites, crackpots and just people" in which the "just people seemed out of place." Walter Winchell announced that "every hate spreader they could find showed up for that meeting." Meantime Interior Secretary Ickes said the America First Committee's ties to "professional Fascists and anti-Semites" had become "clear and scandalous"; and he named Lindbergh "the No. 1 United States Nazi fellow traveler."

With so many others denouncing his opponent, President Roosevelt remained above the fray. But on April twenty-fifth, he could not resist a zinger or two of his own. At a press conference, a reporter asked, "How is it that the Army, which needs now distinguished fliers . . . has not asked Colonel Lindbergh to rejoin his rank as Colonel?" As though waiting for the question, Roosevelt launched into a folksy history lesson about Clement L. Vallandigham, leader of the "Copperheads," those Yankees during the Civil War who were sympathetic to the Confederates. "Well, Vallandigham, as you know, was an appeaser," Roosevelt said, getting a laugh from his audience. "He wanted to make peace from 1863 on because the North 'couldn't win.' Once upon a time there was a place called Valley Forge," he continued in making his point, "and there were an awful lot of appeasers that pleaded with Washington to quit, because he 'couldn't win.' " When another reporter asked the President if he was still talking about Lindbergh, FDR said, "Yes," drawing another round of laughter as well as the next day's headlines.

Lindbergh was not amused. Had FDR's attack been strictly political, he would have paid little attention to it. Because the President of the United States had spoken specifically to Lindbergh's commission in the Army, however, he felt his "loyalty, character, and motives" were being questioned and his honor impugned. Lindbergh handwrote a draft of his response, in which he stated, "I had hoped that I might exercise my rights as an American citizen, to place my viewpoint before the people of my country in time of peace, without giving up the privilege of serving my country as an Air Corps officer in the event of war." But since his Commander in Chief had clearly implied "that I am no longer of use to this country as a reserve officer," Lindbergh said he saw "no honorable alternative" to tendering his resignation as Colonel in the United States Army Air Corps Reserve. "Here I am stumping the country with pacifists and considering resigning as a colonel in the Army Air Corps," he wrote ruefully in his journals, "when there is no philosophy I disagree with more than that of the pacifist, and nothing I would rather be doing than flying in the Air Corps." He showed his letter to Anne, who suggested a coda: "I will continue to serve my country to the best of my ability as a private citizen."

Miss Gawne typed the letter, which Lindbergh sent to the White House while his formal resignation went to the Secretary of War. "If I did not tender my resignation," Lindbergh was forced to recognize, "I would lose something in my own character that means even more to me than my commission in the Air Corps. No one else might know it, but I would. And if I take this insult from Roosevelt, more, and worse, will probably be forthcoming."

On May 3, 1941, at an America First rally of fifteen thousand at the Arena in St. Louis, Lindbergh hammered away at his new theme—that "no matter how many planes we build in America and send to England, we cannot make the British Isles stronger than Germany in military aviation." One week later, he spoke to ten thousand people in Minneapolis, in his most personal and hard-hitting speech to date. After summoning up his father's fight against American entry into the first World War, he attacked the President for misleading the nation, keeping it uninformed as to where it was being led. He asserted that he had never wanted Germany to win this war, but that the only way Germany could be defeated was by an invasion. "Even if an invasion were possible, which I do not believe," Lindbergh averred, "the resulting devastation would be so great that Europe could not recover for generations if it could recover at all."

When Lindbergh returned to New York City for his next address, on May twenty-third, the rally required Madison Square Garden. The night was charged with political energy, as some twenty-five thousand people filled the flag-festooned stadium. Almost as many stood on the street, listening to the speeches over loudspeakers. The Committee to Defend America by Aiding the Allies heckled that those who entered the stadium would "mingle with Nazis, Fascists and Communists."

The charge was true, as many recognizable extremists had shown up for the meeting—including disciples of Father Coughlin and of Joseph McWilliams, leader of the pro-Fascist American Destiny Party. Furthermore, there were rumors (secretly substantiated by FBI reports) that Senator Burton K. Wheeler's wife was "bitterly anti-Semitic," as was one of Colonel McCormick's key men, Harry Jung, who headed the American Vigilante Intelligence Federation, another purportedly pro-Nazi group. Talk of Colonel McCormick's and General Wood's anti-Semitism was rampant.

Arriving with a police escort, the Lindberghs were shunted past the crowd into a quiet room with the night's other featured speakers. While waiting, John T. Flynn—columnist for *The New Republic* and leader of the liberal flank of the America First movement—was informed that Joe McWilliams himself was sitting in the front of the hall. Flynn said he was going to denounce McWilliams from the platform. Lindbergh advised disclaiming "any connection between America First and McWilliams" but stressed that "it should be done with dignity and moderation."

At last the speakers paraded onto the stage into a flood of lights and a torrential ovation. Shouts of "Lindy!" and "Our next President!" went up. Photographers rushed toward him. The hysteria made Anne fearful that somebody might shoot her husband.

Flynn opened the meeting by attacking those who had smeared America First's purpose and whose support they rejected—namely Communists, Fascists, Bundists, and Christian Frontists . . . and specifically, Joe McWilliams. The audience booed and threatened to turn unruly, until police stepped into the breach. The crowd settled down to listen to short addresses by Mrs. John P. Marquand, wife of one of the most celebrated novelists of the day; Kathleen Norris, a popular writer herself, who spoke of mothers losing their boys in times of war; and Norman Thomas, who simply believed, "This is not our war."

The introduction of citizen Lindbergh set off a wave of applause that practically shook the Garden. He stood in silence—slightly stooped, grinning—until the crowd quieted. He spoke that night of the United States as a civilization of mixed races, religions, and beliefs, and he inquired why the country had to jeopardize all that "by injecting the wars and the hatreds of Europe into our midst?" The audience cheered wildly. "With adequate leadership we can be the strongest and most influential nation in the world," he told the crowd. But first, he said, they must "demand an accounting from a government that has led us into war while it promised peace."

The occasion offered the press enough material to skew their stories in any direction they wanted. The anti-isolationists played up the support that night for Joe McWilliams and his followers. Dorothy Thompson and *PM* wrote of Lindbergh's becoming the leader of the pro-Nazi movement. Henry Luce's *Time* and *Life* ran photographs of Lindbergh and his colleagues with their arms held high as they were reciting the Pledge of Allegiance, looking for all the world as though they were *Sieg Heil*-ing. Rumors of Lindbergh's heading the German underground in America became rife.

In truth, Charles Lindbergh was never associated with any pro-Nazi or anti-Semitic organization; he never attended any Bund meetings; and since more than four months before the outbreak of war in Europe, he had neither consorted nor consulted with anyone known to have any connections with the Third Reich. When Truman Smith invited him to meet a visiting German dignitary, Lindbergh declined, noting: "I have had no communication with Germany, or with German citizens, since I left Europe in April 1939, and I think it is important for me to be able to say this whenever the question arises. It is a stupid situation, and I do not intend to govern my actions by such considerations indefinitely, but I do not want to give my enemies any unnecessary opportunity to cause confusion in the public mind at this time." He even stopped writing to the Carrels so that he could attest, if ever necessary, to having had no direct communication with the Continent whatever.

In a speech at the Arena in Philadelphia on the night of May 29, 1941, Lindbergh traced the foreign policy the President had pursued, one which subtly but steadily engaged America in the European war. "First they said, 'sell us the arms and we will win.' Then it was 'lend us the arms and we will win.' Now it is 'bring us the arms and we will win.' Tomorrow it will be 'fight our war for us and we will win,' " Lindbergh told the crowd of fifteen thousand, which spilled out into the street. Lindbergh reported that America First's membership was increasing by thousands every day, as chapters were being formed across the country—each of which hoped for a "Lindbergh rally." "If you can just arrange to divide yourself into 118 equal parts," Bob Stuart wrote their top draw, "all the America First representatives will be happy."

The movement gained momentum through the summer; and those who believed in it took pride in Lindbergh's giving voice to their feelings. In response to a Dorothy Thompson column stating that many army officers disapproved of Lindbergh, Major A. C. Wedemeyer wrote Lindbergh that the opposite was true, "that most of the officers highly approve of you as an individual and as a clear thinking realist with the most unselfish motives." Indeed, whether one agreed with Lindbergh's position or not, most conceded that he was not appearing in public for personal gain. One man wrote a letter to the editor of the Dayton *Journal-Herald* likening Lindbergh to the prophet Isaiah, who sacrificed "his favored position in high places to warn his people against alliances that will destroy much that is good in the land." A poll in FDR's home district showed that more than ninety percent of the constituents were against American entry into the war.

But Lindbergh had never been subjected to such personal attack. Libraries across America pulled his books from their shelves; in Ottawa, Ontario, a group asked the Mayor to burn Lindbergh's books in a public square. Charlotte, North Carolina, changed the name of Lindbergh Drive to Avon Avenue. The Kansas City Liberty Memorial removed Lindbergh's name from its list of honorary members. And the town of Little Falls repainted its water tower so that it no longer boasted a favorite son. A Gallup poll published April twenty-seventh said while "there were still 81% of the people opposed to U.S. war entry now, if it appeared that the only way to beat Germany and Italy was for the U. S. to go to war, 68% would now say 'Go.' "

Lindbergh went back on the warpath for peace, arguing his case on the West Coast. On June 18, 1941, he and Anne boarded a TWA DC-3. Riding in the "silvered limousine of a plane," with its "soft seats, small curtained windows, muffled noise, air conditioning, [and] sky hostesses" hardly seemed like flying, so removed were they from the elements. With fueling stops along the way, they crossed the country in less than eighteen hours.

Two days later, Lindbergh spoke at the Hollywood Bowl to his largest live audience yet. Lindbergh said it was "the most beautiful and inspiring meeting place I have ever seen—open sky and stars above, and hills dimly outlined in the background, so that the rows of people merge into the hills themselves"—an estimated eighty thousand flowing onto the surrounding roads. After speeches by Kathleen Norris, Senator Worth Clark, a Democrat from Idaho, and actress Lillian Gish (who pled for a referendum on the war), the special guest star himself spoke. Because Japan had formed a military alliance with the Axis powers, Lindbergh said, America's entering the war would probably mean "we must be prepared to fight Japan in the Pacific at the same time that we are convoying our troops and supplies across the Atlantic." In its current state of unpreparedness for war, Lindbergh asserted that the "alternative to a negotiated peace is either a Hitler victory or a prostrate Europe, and possibly a prostrate America as well." Cries of "Our next President!" went up again. "No," Kathleen Norris said privately, "he is more like a Joan of Arc."

Eleven nights later, Lindbergh spoke at San Francisco's Civic Auditorium. Because of the fickleness of the European nations toward each other, Lindbergh underscored the folly of America's allying with any of the belligerents. When the war started, he pointed out, "Germany and Russia were lined up against England and France. Now, less than two years later, we find Russia and England fighting France and Germany. . . . The murderers and plunderers of yesterday are accepted as the valiant defenders of civilization today." Furthermore, he observed, "A refugee who steps from the gangplanks and advocates war is acclaimed as a defender of freedom. A native born American who opposes war is called a fifth-columnist." Then he fell back on his own personal bugbear: "I tell you," he said, "that I would a hundred times rather see my country ally herself with England, or even with Germany with all of her faults, than with the cruelty, the godlessness, and the barbarism that exist in Soviet Russia. An alliance between the United States and Russia should be opposed by every American, by every Christian, and by every humanitarian in this country."

Before leaving California, the Lindberghs spent three days with William Randolph Hearst at his Wyntoon ranch, a veritable Alpine village he had constructed at the foot of Mount Shasta. Although Lindbergh still disapproved of Hearst's journalistic practices, he appreciated the anti-intervention message that his newspapers spread. "A period of crisis is the real test of character and leadership," Lindbergh wrote him afterward. "I believe that you have done something for this country in the crisis we are going through, for which our people will be forever grateful."

In August, the great debate heated up. Opposition to Lindbergh had grown so vocal before his appearance in Cleveland, the police insisted on "X-raying" the furniture of the apartment in which he was staying and posting police guards all along his route, from his room to the podium. When he ventured to Oklahoma City on August twenty-eighth, to lecture on Air Power, he learned there had been threats of shooting. Worse, the city council unanimously voted to revoke America First's lease with the Municipal Auditorium, forcing the organization to seek a new venue. Upon hearing this news, Lindbergh said, "if we could not rent a hall we could hold our meeting in a cow pasture." They settled instead on a ballpark just outside the city. Fifteen thousand people weathered the blizzard of publicity, further convincing Lindbergh that American citizens were "definitely opposed" to intervention. "But what has Roosevelt in his mind," Lindbergh asked in his journals, "and how far will he be able to take us? How close can we skate to the edge of war without falling in?" Closer, Lindbergh realized, if the President could somehow discredit him.

For months, Harold Ickes publicly hectored Lindbergh, now referring to him as a "Knight of the German Eagle"; and Lindbergh generally ignored him. On July 14, 1941, however, Ickes got his goat. At a Bastille Day meeting sponsored by France Forever, the Secretary of the Interior built his rousing speech at Manhattan Center on the subject of liberating France largely around the image of "ex-Colonel Lindbergh" and "what a menace he and those like him are to this country and its free institutions." He said he could tell Lindbergh "where he could readily locate an artificial heart with the aid of an x-ray machine." Beyond the name-calling, Ickes raised a point many Americans had thought but few had spoken: "No one has ever heard Lindbergh utter a word of horror at, or even aversion to, the bloody career that the Nazis are following," Ickes said, "nor a word of pity for the innocent men, women and children, who have been deliberately murdered by the Nazis in practically every country in Europe." For all Lindbergh's repudiation of Communism, Ickes said, "I have never heard this Knight of the German Eagle denounce Hitler or Nazism or Mussolini or Fascism."

> No, [Ickes continued] *I* have never heard Lindbergh utter a word of pity for Belgium or Holland or Norway or England. *I* have never heard him express a word of pity for the Poles or the Jews who have been slaughtered by the hundreds of thousands by Hitler's savages. *I* have never heard Lindbergh say a word of encouragement to the English for the fight they are so bravely making for Lindbergh's right to live his own life in his own way, as well as for their own right to do so.

For months, Lindbergh had ignored such attacks. In this last speech, however, Lindbergh naively felt Ickes had been hoist with his own petard, placing both the Secretary and his president in a position Lindbergh could "attack with dignity and effectiveness."

On July 16, 1941, Lindbergh wrote Roosevelt. His short letter called Ickes on his unfair behavior, specifically for criticizing him for accepting a decoration from the German Government in 1938. He asked the President to inform his cabinet member that he had received the decoration in the American Embassy in the presence of their own ambassador and that he was there at that ambassador's request. Lindbergh offered his word that he had "no connection with any foreign government" and that he would willingly present himself and all his files for investigation to prove as much. Lindbergh felt he was owed an apology from him. Upon mailing the letter, he also released a copy to the press.

Lindbergh heard from neither the President nor his Interior Secretary. Instead, he received a nine-sentence note from FDR's secretary Stephen Early, who dismissed the letter as an obvious publicity stunt, as demonstrated by the fact that the newspapers had received their copies a full day before the President. In his own reply to the press, Ickes chided Lindbergh for this breach of political etiquette and challenged him to reveal his true colors. "If Mr. Lindbergh feels like cringing when he is correctly referred to as a knight of the German Eagle," Ickes wrote, "why doesn't he send back the disgraceful decoration and be done with it? Americans remember that he had no hesitation about sending back to the President his commission in the United States Army Air Corps Reserve. In fact, Mr. Lindbergh returned his commission with suspicious alacrity and with a total lack of graciousness. But he still hangs on to the Nazi medal!"

Even Lindbergh's supporters had to ask themselves some of the questions Ickes raised. General Wood gently suggested that Lindbergh publicly condemn totalitarianism in any form, thus silencing the whispering campaign that he was pro-Nazi. Billy Rose sent him a long telegram that same day, enumerating some of the Third Reich's known atrocities to date. "IF YOU ARE WILLING TO CONDEMN HITLER AND HIS GANG AND THEIR UNSPEAKABLE BARBARITIES," the theater impresario added, "I WILL ENGAGE MADISON SQUARE GARDEN AT MY EXPENSE AND GIVE YOU AN OPPORTUNITY TO AIR YOUR VIEWS. MY ONLY CONDITION IS THAT THE PUBLIC MELTING DOWN OR HAMMERING OUT OF SHAPE OF YOUR NAZI MEDAL BE MADE A FEATURE OF THE RALLY." Lindbergh had "slipped badly," Ickes noted in his diary. "He has now made it clear to the whole country that he still clings to this German decoration. . . . For the first time he has allowed himself to be put on the defensive and that is always a weak position for anyone." The Great Debate was deteriorating into a more simplistic question, one which became the title of a pamphlet distributed by Birkhead's Friends of Democracy: "Is Lindbergh a Nazi?"

THE LINDBERGHS could bear Long Island no longer. "[W]e are so sick of the atmosphere that surrounds New York & gets thicker all the time," Anne wrote Kay Smith that summer, thinking of the "bitterness, suspicion, hate, pressure etc." The Lindberghs' unlisted telephone seldom stopped ringing—with requests and threats—keeping Charles and Anne from getting much work done there. They fled to Martha's Vineyard, where they rented a small house at Seven Gates Farm in Vineyard Haven. It was smaller than they would have liked, so that children and secretaries would have to double up; but it sat in serene isolation, surrounded by wild hills, private beaches, trees and berry bushes, and endless vistas of rocks, distant islands, and the sea. It reminded Charles of Illiec. In a hillside hollow overlooking the water, he had two men erect a cabin-sized tent, in which he and Anne could bunk and she could write.

Lindbergh had long told himself that the moment American entry into the war seemed inevitable, he would drop a bombshell. He would publicly name "the groups that were most powerful and effective in pushing the United States toward involvement in the war." Having agreed to speak at another America First meeting, in Des Moines, he realized his engagement there would provide that moment. He penciled draft after draft of his most provocative speech yet, one he bluntly titled "Who Are the War Agitators?"

In it, he pointed out that Americans had solidly opposed entering the war when it began, and that three groups had been "pressing this country toward war" ever since—the Roosevelt administration, the British, and the Jews. Behind those groups, he added, were "a number of capitalists, anglophiles, and intellectuals, who believe that their future, and the future of mankind, depend upon the domination of the British Empire." He wrote that the first group was encouraging American participation so that it could accrue more power. The second group, he said, saw it as a way of lightening its military and financial load. But the core of his thesis rested on the third group, for whom he reserved his sharpest comments.

This portion of the speech threw Anne into "black gloom." She did not disagree with anything he wrote. In fact, she found "what he says is as far as I can tell true and moderately stated," without "bitterness or rancor." Her desperation, she confided to her diary, came because "I hate to have him touch the Jews at all. For I dread the reaction on him." She could already envision the next morning's headlines—LINDBERGH ATTACKS JEWS—knowing that many people would read no further, "being only too eager to believe the worst of C." The "ugly cry of anti-Semitism will be joyfully pounced upon and waved about [his] name," she thought, as it was "so much simpler to brand someone with a bad label than to take the trouble to read what he says." She tried to express as much to her husband, that the meaning of his words were not the same as the effect they would have, that the speech would be taken as "Jew-baiting."

Lindbergh said the point was not what the effect would be on him but "whether or not what he said is *true* and whether it will help to keep us out of war." Feeling that the perception was as important as the reality, Anne anxiously rewrote several paragraphs, making them less accusatory and more understanding. She hoped, for example, that he might say: "I call you people before me tonight to witness that I am not anti-Semitic nor have I attacked the Jews." But he would not. He departed for Des Moines, leaving his wife with "a sinking of heart." Instead of snuffing the inflammatory reaction she foresaw, she feared his words would prove to be "a match lit near a pile of excelsior."

For the first time Lindbergh felt that he was "fighting a losing battle," that Roosevelt had cleverly rigged the American psyche "so that just a small incident could draw us into a declaration of war." The week before he was to deliver his fiery speech, the nation moved another step in that direction, when the U. S. destroyer *Greer* was attacked near Iceland on September fourth. Roosevelt did not address the nation on the subject until the evening of the eleventh, the very moment before Lindbergh was to speak, thus delaying the start of the America First rally. The President's speech was piped into the Des Moines Coliseum, filled with eight thousand Iowans. They all listened to Roosevelt declare that he had ordered the U. S. Navy to "shoot on sight" any German or Italian ships in the American Defense Zone, which he said stretched from Iceland to the west coast of Africa. Less than a minute after the President had finished, Lindbergh and his colleagues walked onstage, to loud applause mixed with boos.

Although the loudspeakers did not function properly for the first few minutes, the other speakers warmed the crowd up enough so that by the time Lindbergh reached the microphone, the audience was ready to listen—even the hecklers. Six minutes into his speech, when he reached the point at which he named the three war-agitating groups, most of the crowd stood and cheered. For the rest of his speech, the Iowans drowned out the opposition that occasionally erupted.

In the end, Lindbergh had reduced his comments about the Jews to three paragraphs. They were the only public comments he ever made during the Great Debate in which he mentioned them. Although he felt he was showing his sympathy for a long-persecuted tribe, each additional sentence would be used to burn the brand of anti-Semite deeper into his public persona.

"It is not difficult to understand why Jewish people desire the overthrow of Nazi Germany," Lindbergh said. "The persecution they suffered in Germany would be sufficient to make bitter enemies of any race. No person with a sense of the dignity of mankind can condone the persecution of the Jewish race in Germany. But no person of honesty and vision can look on their pro-war policy here today without seeing the dangers involved in such a policy, both for us and for them."

Instead of agitating for war, the Jewish groups in this country should be opposing it in every possible way, for they will be among the first to feel its consequences. Tolerance is a virtue that depends upon peace and strength. History shows that it cannot survive war and devastation. A few far-sighted Jewish people realize this, and stand opposed to intervention. But the majority still do not. Their greatest danger to this country lies in their large ownership and influence in our motion pictures, our press, our radio, and our Government.

Ironically, it was in his third paragraph about the Jews, in what he intended to be his most compassionate words on the subject, that Lindbergh incurred the most wrath:

I am not attacking either the Jewish or the British people [he said]. Both races, I admire. But I am saying that the leaders of both the British and Jewish races, for reasons which are understandable from their viewpoint as they are inadvisable from ours, for reasons which are not American, wish to involve us in the war. We cannot blame them for looking out for what they believe to be their own interests, but we also must look out for ours. We cannot allow the natural passions and prejudices of other peoples to lead our country to destruction.

Lindbergh had bent over backward to be kind about the Jews; but in suggesting the American Jews were "other" people and that their interests were "not American," he implied exclusion, thus undermining the very foundation of the United States.

Because he spent all the next day in seclusion on the train home, it was not until his arrival in New York on Saturday morning that Lindbergh learned how despised he had become. Most of the nation's newspapers carried vituperative denunciations of his speech.

"He is attacked on all sides," Anne noted in her diary, "Administration, pressure groups, and Jews, as now openly a Nazi, following a Nazi doctrine." Thinking about the national response, Anne wondered why nobody minded his naming the British or the Administration as pro-war, but "to name 'Jew' is un-American—even if it is done without hate or bitterness or even criticism." She asked her diary why.

By the time Charles arrived home, she could answer her own question, recognizing that the implied segregation was "setting the ground for anti-Semitism." Her husband never saw that. When she told him that she would rather see the country at war than "shaken by violent anti-Semitism," he rigidly held that those were not the options. For him the choice was "whether or not you are going to let your country go into a completely disastrous war for lack of courage to name the groups leading that country to war—at the risk of being called 'anti-Semitic' simply by *naming* them." Happy to be re-united, Anne and Charles pitched a pup tent in the hills west of the house and slept together under the stars in the cool, clear night.

He awoke the next morning to a Niagara of invective. Few men in American history had ever been so reviled. One columnist stated that the Lone Eagle had plummeted from "Public Hero No. 1" to "Public Enemy No. 1." Anne noted that he had become nothing less than "the symbol of anti-Semitism in this country & looked to as the leader of it." Presidential Secretary Stephen Early commented only that Lindbergh's words sounded like those pouring out of Berlin. He left prominent Republicans to issue harsher denunciations, and they did. Wendell Willkie called the Des Moines speech "the most un-American talk made in my time by any person of national reputation"; New York Governor Thomas E. Dewey, on his way to becoming the party's new standard-bearer, called it "an inexcusable abuse of the right of freedom of speech." Jewish groups demanded retractions, as did Catholics and Protestants; Christian theologian Reinhold Niebuhr called upon America First to "divorce itself from the stand taken by Lindbergh and clean its ranks of those who would incite to racial and religious strife in this country." *Time* wrote, "The America First Committee had touched the pitch of anti-Semitism and its fingers were tarred." *Liberty* went even farther, calling Lindbergh "the most dangerous man in America." Before him, they observed, "leaders of anti-Semitism were shoddy little crooks and fanatics sending scurrilous circulars through the mails. . . . But now all that is changed . . . He, the famous one, he who was once illustrious, has stood up in public and given brazen tongue to what obscure malcontents have only whispered behind the back." Rabbi Irving F. Reichart of Temple Emanu-El of San Francisco commented that "Hitler himself could not have delivered a more *diabolical* speech."

One Sol Schwartz of Brooklyn, who introduced himself in a letter to Lindbergh as a Jewish anti-interventionist, said the Des Moines speech had become "a tragic event in my life." He explained that his gentile friends now regarded him differently, that to the man in the street, Lindbergh had suggested that all Jews were "INTERNATIONAL BANKERS, WARMONGERS, BOLSHEVIKS . . . whether he lives on Riverside Drive or in the slums of the east side." Norman Thomas asserted that the speech "did great harm." He told his friends that Lindbergh was no anti-Semite but that this speech was "by no means the whole truth or free from error." By way of instruction, he wrote Lindbergh, "There are lots of forces, for instance, impersonal economic forces, which make for war beside the groups which you mention."

He also censured him for exaggerating "the solidarity of the Jews in this matter and their power," a common misconception.

In fact, statistics revealed less Jewish domination of the media than Lindbergh supposed. A study in 1941 by a Notre Dame philosophy professor pointed out that Jews controlled only about three percent of the American press. The government departments most responsible for foreign policy were largely in the hands of non-Jews; and only one Cabinet member was Jewish. In radio NBC's twenty-six member advisory council contained but two Jews; the president of CBS was Jewish, but the majority of its board of directors was non-Jewish; Mutual was a co-operative organization, the *Chicago Tribune* chief among its stockholders. And though most of the American motion-picture studios were owned by Jews, most were virtually paranoid about keeping pro-Jewish sentiment off the screen.

To anyone who asked, Lindbergh's longtime friend Harry Guggenheim insisted that "Slim has never had the slightest anti-Semitic feeling." But during the years surrounding the America First movement, their friendship undeniably eroded. Walter Winchell gleefully announced that Lindbergh's "halo has become his noose." And the President continued to say nothing, allowing the rest of the populace to kick his rival now that he was down. Although eighty-five percent of the mail pouring into the offices of America First backed Lindbergh, thousands of letters excoriated him. Lindbergh read only occasional samples, but he instructed the secretaries of the local chapters not to destroy any of it—"no matter how unfavorable or blasphemous it may be"—explaining, "I am holding all mail as a matter of record, and I want the bad as well as the good." Ultimately, these tens of thousands of letters went to Yale University, which began housing his archives shortly after he had delivered his America First address on its campus.

Lindbergh's few public defenders tended to be names that harmed more than they helped—Alf Landon, Father Coughlin, Merwin K. Hart, and Herbert Hoover. While maintaining that his "remarks at Des Moines were true, and moderately stated," Lindbergh intended to suggest that the most practical solution to the crisis was for him to resign from the America First Committee. He left for Chicago, where General Wood had called an emergency meeting to discuss the possibility of adjourning the committee altogether.

At breakfast the next morning, Lindbergh told Wood he did not feel it was time to adjourn, and that while he was "not willing to repudiate or modify any portion" of his statement, he would announce that his Des Moines speech expressed his opinion and not necessarily that of America First.

Lindbergh absented himself from the lunch meeting, so that the committee members could freely discuss the Des Moines speech and how to repair its damage. Several hours later, Bob Stuart called Lindbergh and asked him to join them. The committee had decided to issue a statement asserting that neither Lindbergh nor America First was anti-Semitic and that the interventionists, "by twisting and distorting what Colonel Lindbergh said at Des Moines, have tried to label that address as anti-Semitic." America First was remaining in business, its doors open to "all patriotic Americans, whatever their race, color or creed." While continuing the policy of not imposing restrictions on America First speakers, General Wood suggested to Lindbergh that he make no reference to Des Moines at his next speaking engagement.

On October 3, 1941, at Fort Wayne, he took Wood's advice and spoke of the many violations of the Administration against the "will of the people." Before concluding, however, he did interject a few personal remarks, the closest he ever came to pleading for sympathy. "In making these addresses," he reminded his audience of eight thousand in the Gospel Temple, and millions more listening on their radios, "I have no motive in mind other than the welfare of my country and my civilization. This is not a life that I enjoy. Speaking is not my vocation, and political life is not my ambition. For the past several years, I have given up my normal life and interests . . . because I believe my country is in mortal danger, and because I could not stand by and see her going to destruction without putting everything I had against that trend." After the speech, Lindbergh was feeling "written out" on the subject of isolationism. He explained to General Wood that it seemed advisable to him for the committee to "avoiding building up any one man to a position of too great importance in the organization."

Just when it sounded as though Lindbergh was throwing in the towel, FDR revived him. The President asked Congress to revise the Neutrality Act, which had prevented the arming of American merchant ships and kept them from entering the war zones. To America Firsters, such as Richard Moore, this reversal seemed the last step before "the final straw which would turn America into a full belligerent." Lindbergh agreed to speak at the next meeting at the end of October in Manhattan and another in early December in Boston.

Because Anne was busy moving the family into another house—one with heat—at Seven Gates Farm, Charles left for New York alone. "The most fundamental issue today is not one of war or peace, but one of integrity. Whether we go to war or whether we stay out, we have the right to demand integrity in the leadership of this nation," he told a crowd of twenty thousand at Madison Square Garden on October 30, 1941. "The enthusiasm generated by the New York rally was contagious and gave an important lift to the rank and file members just when it was needed most," Richard Moore later recalled. But the "man on the street" felt different. Lyle Leverich, then a copy boy on the New York *Daily News,* attended the rally and remembered it fifty years later as one of the most "awesome sights" of his life. "There, in the midst of many, open Nazi-sympathizers was the hero of my childhood, Lindy, and I was literally sickened by the spectacle," he recalled. "I felt betrayed." Millions felt the same.

On November 7, 1941, the Senate passed FDR's neutrality bill amendment by a vote of 50 to 37. Six days later, the House did the same by the slightly narrower margin of 212 to 194. America First refused to say die. By December first, it was going public with a new policy called "We Will Meet You at the Polls!" by which they would target swing Congressional votes and support only those candidates who would "oppose further steps to involve us in war."

Anne spent the first week of December in New York and New Jersey. In her absence, Charles repitched her tent by the side of the new house and camped out. He divided his time there between the book he had started in Paris two years earlier—a detailed account of his 1927 flight—and writing his next America First address, which he had agreed to deliver in Boston on the tenth.

It promised to be his strongest speech yet. In it he would ask the audience to consider "how ridiculous it is that this democratic nation has twice, within a generation, been carried to war by Presidents who were elected because they promised peace." Before crusading for four freedoms across the seas, Lindbergh wrote, "let us make sure that the roots of freedom and democracy are firmly planted in our own country"—starting, he added, with "the Negro . . . in our southern states."

Anne was still away on Sunday, the seventh, when the radio announced that Japan had attacked the Philippines and the Hawaiian Islands. Lindbergh was shocked. "An attack in the Philippines was to be expected," he wrote in his journal, "although I did not think it would come quite so soon. But Pearl Harbor! How did the Japs get close enough, and where is our Navy?" He anxiously waited for confirmation of the story, that this was not just a hit-and-run raid being exaggerated by radio commentators into a major attack. "If C. speaks again," Anne thought on her way home, "they'll put him in prison."

Details of the events unraveled slowly, but by the next morning there was no doubt that the attack on Hawaii had been heavy. Lindbergh telephoned Bob Stuart in Chicago to recommend canceling their meeting in Boston. Then he phoned General Wood, who said, "Well, he got us in through the back door."

Realizing his two-year crusade had come to an end, Lindbergh composed a statement for the America First Committee to release on his behalf that December eighth. "We have been stepping closer to war for many months," he wrote. "Now it has come and we must meet it as united Americans regardless of our attitude in the past toward the policy our government has followed. Whether or not that policy has been wise, our country has been attacked by force of arms, and by force of arms we must retaliate." He urged the nation to build its neglected military forces into the mightiest in the world. He wired his message to Bob Stuart, then fell publicly silent on the subject of the war, or anything else for that matter, for several years to come. He took Anne for a walk across their isolated beach, during which he pronounced the bombing in Hawaii "the most important event in our lives."

Over lunch, the Lindberghs listened to the radio, as the President addressed a special joint session of Congress, calling for a declaration of war against Japan. "What else was there to do?" Lindbergh mused. "We have been asking for war for months. If the President had asked for a declaration of war before, I think Congress would have turned him down with a big majority. But now we have been attacked, and attacked in home waters. We have brought it on our own shoulders; but I can see nothing to do under these circumstances except to fight."

Lindbergh wrote in his journal that day—for posterity—"If I had been in Congress, I certainly would have voted for a declaration of war."

Anne concurred, but she approached the day's events with more practical incertitude. "Where," she wondered, "will we be thrown in the maelstrom—our private lives?"

15

CLIPPED WINGS

"There are occasions when incidents combine to outline basic laws
of life and nature with extraordinary clearness—incidents of birth and
death, of peace and war, of beauty and hardship."

—C.A.L.

OTHER DEBATES IN AMERICAN HISTORY WOULD LATER BE recalled with at least an appreciation for the high-mindedness of their ideas; and other members of America First would bear no stigma for having been allied with that particular cause. But America First swiftly entered the annals of public discourse tainted; and Charles Lindbergh would thenceforth be contaminated, considered by many wrong-headed at best and traitorous at worst. "Imagine," Anne's sister Constance would later comment on Lindbergh's reputation, "in just fifteen years he had gone from Jesus to Judas!"

Lindbergh himself wanted little more than to spend a year or two in quiet contemplation—"thinking and reading and writing"—alone with his wife and three children. But his own sense of duty got the better of him. "Now that we are at war I want to contribute as best I can to my country's war effort," Lindbergh wrote in his journal on December 12, 1941. "It is vital for us to carry on this war as intelligently, as constructively, and as successfully as we can, and I want to do my part."

America First's National Committee called a meeting to determine the organization's future, which included the possibility of opposing entry into the European war. Hours before the meeting was held in Chicago, that option was made moot, as Germany and Italy declared war on the United States. The committee dissolved; and Lindbergh hoped to follow most of its leadership into the armed services. General Robert Wood volunteered as soon as war was declared and was accepted by the Ordnance District in Chicago; Bob Stuart had an ROTC commission and reported to Fort Sill as an artillery officer. Most of his contemporaries from the original committee at Yale also volunteered for active duty. Having surrendered his Army Air Corps commission in a most public display, Lindbergh lacked the luxury of so easy a decision.

His first inclination was to write directly to the President, explaining "that while I had opposed him in the past and had not changed my convictions, I was ready in time of war to submerge my personal viewpoint in the general welfare and unity of the country." He demurred, however. "If I wrote to him at this time," Lindbergh entered in his journal less than a week after Pearl Harbor, "he would probably make what use he could of my offer from a standpoint of politics and publicity and assign me to some position where I would be completely ineffective and out of the way." Lindbergh regretted having resigned his commission; "but whenever I turn the circumstances over in my mind," he noted, "I feel I took the right action. There was, I think, no honorable alternative."

In late December 1941, Lindbergh decided to approach his highest-ranking military friend, General "Hap" Arnold, Chief of the Army Air Forces. After failing to get past his aide, Major Eugene Beebe, just to schedule an appointment, Lindbergh sent a handwritten note to the General himself. He offered his services to the Air Corps, all the while understanding the "complications" created by his recent political stand.

Lindbergh received a courteous reply, appreciation for his overture but nothing more. A week later, General Arnold made public Lindbergh's offer over the radio, which made Lindbergh hopeful. "Is it an indication that my offer will be accepted?" he asked his journal. "And if so, will it be as a civilian or as an officer?" Even *The New York Times* was supportive, writing on its editorial page, "There cannot be the slightest doubt that Mr. Lindbergh's offer should be and will be accepted. It will be accepted not only as a symbol of our newfound unity and an effective means of burying the dead past; it will be accepted also because Mr. Lindbergh can be useful to his country. He is a superb air man, and this is primarily and essentially an air war. Whether he has passed the age when he can be used for active service in the field is a matter for competent authorities to decide. But there can be no question of his great knowledge of aircraft and his immense experience as a flier. Nor have we any doubt that he will serve in the line of duty with credit to himself and to his country."

The rest of the American press was not that kindly disposed. Lindbergh attended a dinner party in New York at the home of Edwin Webster, whom he had known from America First, just days after the organization had dissolved. Although Lindbergh did not wish to make a speech, the other guests—mostly America Firsters—imposed upon him to say a few words.

Lindbergh held forth for five minutes, trying to explain that the recent decision to disband was "really to the best interests of the country, and that no matter what we did or advocated or stood for, we would have been viciously and bitterly attacked if we had continued our activities after the start of the war." He added that it was "unfortunate that the white race was divided in this war."

As a result of Lindbergh's offhanded comments, many newspapers reported that the America First movement was alive and well. *The New York Post* said that "its nucleus of native fascist, anti-Semitic and, in some cases, pro-German organizations, continue to speak and publish material close to the line of treason, if not across it." Washington columnists Drew Pearson and Robert S. Allen wrote that Lindbergh was still blaming Britain for the war, while a radio broadcaster said that Lindbergh was still insisting that "Germany should have been appeased and tied to us as an ally against Japan and China." The *New York World-Telegram* reported that Lindbergh said "it was too bad that we were divided on the question of the yellow race," and *PM* ran a series of provocative quotations plucked from Lindbergh's America First speeches under the headline: "Do You Want the Man Who Said These Things . . . To Have a Hand in Your Fight Against Fascism?"

The next day, Lindbergh tried to reach General Arnold but again got the runaround from Major Beebe, who advised his going directly to the Secretary of War. Beebe's tone of voice made Lindbergh realize that the matter of his future military service had been discussed at the highest levels of U.S. government and that "everything had been arranged" for Lindbergh to have a showdown with Secretary Henry L. Stimson.

Spending the weekend in Washington, he telephoned Stimson's office on Monday, January twelfth, and was given an appointment for that afternoon. After a few minutes of pleasantries, Lindbergh told Stimson outright that with his country at war, he hoped to find the way in which he could "make the greatest personal contribution." He said he had been considering the possibility of working in the aviation industry, but not without first seeing if there was any way he could assist the Army Air Corps. Stimson replied in diplomatic double-talk until Lindbergh pressed him to talk turkey.

Stimson told Lindbergh outright that he was loath to put him in any position of command because of his public prewar opinions. He said he did not think anyone of such persuasion should be in a position of command in the war because he did not believe such a person "could carry on the war with sufficient aggressiveness!" And he said he doubted that Lindbergh had changed his views since.

Lindbergh replied that he felt it had been a mistake for America to enter the war; but that decision now made, he stood behind it—eager to help in whatever way he could be most effective. Stimson said he had no idea what that might be, as Lindbergh's speeches raised a question of loyalty. He proceeded to misstate Lindbergh's positions, saying they included his advocating an alliance with Germany and his expressing antagonism toward China—two opinions Lindbergh had never espoused.

Stimson called in his Assistant Secretary of War for Air, Robert A. Lovett, to discuss the possibilities of Lindbergh's helping the government in a position of non-command. At their suggestion, Lindbergh met with General Arnold the next day in Lovett's office in the Munitions Building. Arnold and Lovett said there were many ways in which Lindbergh could serve the Air Corps, but they were "not sure what the public and press reaction" would be at that time. After talking in circles for half an hour, Lindbergh said he was "not sure that the situation which worried them could be straightened out satisfactorily," because he "was not willing to retract" what he had said in his addresses. Before leaving, Lindbergh asked Lovett whether he thought the Administration would object to his working with a commercial company. Lovett said he did not think so, and "that as far as the War Department was concerned he thought they would support such a move." Encouragingly, Arnold told his friend, "I think you *can* find some way to straighten all this out."

Lindbergh had no idea to what extent politics had been the controlling factor in his Washington meetings. He was not privy to memoranda about him that were circulating through the executive branch of the government. The same day Lindbergh volunteered for the Air Corps, for example, his old foe Harold Ickes wrote the President, "it is of the utmost importance that his offer should not be accepted." Poring over Lindbergh's speeches and articles had convinced him, he wrote FDR, "that he is a ruthless and conscious fascist, motivated by a hatred for you personally and a contempt for democracy in general. . . . His actions have been coldly calculated with a view to attaining ultimate power for himself—what he calls 'new leadership.' Hence it is important for him to have a military service record." Ickes said accepting Lindbergh's offer would be granting "this loyal friend of Hitler's a precious opportunity on a golden platter. It would be . . . a tragic disservice to American democracy to give one of its bitterest and most ruthless enemies a chance to gain a military record. I ardently hope that this convinced fascist will not be given the opportunity to wear the uniform of the United States. He should be buried in merciful oblivion." Secretary of the Navy Frank Knox felt the same. "If it were . . . put up to me," he wrote the President, "I would offer Lindberg [sic] an opportunity to enlist as an air cadet, like anybody else would have to do. He has had no training as an officer and ought to earn his commission." Roosevelt concurred with both men, especially Ickes, whom he wrote, "What you say about Lindbergh and the potential danger of the man, I agree with wholeheartedly."

Anne and Charles in Bavaria. Their marriage was not the storybook romance the world imagined.

The two Anne Lindberghs. Westport.

Never able to stay long in a single place, Lindbergh continued to tour the world, fighting for environmental issues. Luzon, 1969.

Indonesia, 1967.

Saigon, 1967.

President Lyndon B. Johnson and Vice President Hubert H. Humphrey look on as
Lindbergh signs autographs for the *Apollo* astronauts at the White House, 1968.

Brazil, 1969.

Lindbergh and President Richard M. Nixon, with whom he was willing to pose for pictures to help the cause of conservation, 1972.

Tree-hugger.

October 1969. Anne Morrow Lindbergh in her "Little House," where she wrote her perennial bestseller *Gift from the Sea* and several volumes of bestselling diaries.

Jon Lindbergh's career has been mostly around or under water. (New Jersey State Police Museum)

Land Lindbergh became a rancher; his sister Ansy (Anne S. Lindbergh) wrote children's books.

Scott Lindbergh, outside the family chalet in Switzerland, pursued the study of animal behavior.

Lindbergh giving away in marriage his youngest child, Reeve, also a writer, 1968.

Grandfather Charles
with Reeve's daughter
Elizabeth.

Tonga, 1972. (copyright Tom Nebbia)

Stimson wrote the President after his meeting with Lindbergh that despite the "really valuable service" he had rendered the government when he had been assessing German air power, he had told Lindbergh that he was "unwilling to place in command of our troops as a commissioned officer any man who had such a lack of faith in our cause as he had shown in his speeches." The next day, the Secretary disingenuously told the press that Lindbergh would be doing "research on a commercial project in which the War Department is interested." He also announced the Air Corps' goal of enlisting two million men in 1942. Lindbergh would not be one of them.

Searching for his first job in almost twenty years, Lindbergh proved as naïve in war as he had been in peace. "I believe my difference in outlook would make me of more value rather than less," he wrote General Wood while he was figuring out his future. "It seems to me that the unity and strength necessary for a successful war, demand that all viewpoints be represented in Washington. However, the discussions I have had to date indicate that definite limits exist to the Administration's desire for 'unity', and that those limits do not extend very far into the group of people who have disagreed with the policies of the President." In January, he turned to what he considered his fallback—a position in the aviation industry. Having spent considerable effort over the years trying to avoid just such a situation, he found this new pursuit "rather strange," all the harder having to "stand by and do nothing while one's country is at war." Only later did Lindbergh learn that his name had come up at a recent meeting between the President and several senators, and FDR had said, "I'll clip that young man's wings."

Lindbergh wasted no time in contacting his friends Juan Trippe at Pan American and Guy Vaughan at Curtiss-Wright. Although Lindbergh had not drawn his retainer as an adviser from Pan Am for many years, he had never severed his connection with either the company or its management. At a meeting in the Chrysler Building in New York City on January nineteenth, Trippe enthusiastically told him there were many things he could do for the company. Vaughan responded similarly, offering Lindbergh any position he wanted, hoping he would study their prototype aircraft.

Within days of each meeting, both prospects evaporated. Trippe telephoned Lindbergh that "obstacles had been put in the way"; and in person the next day, he privately explained, "The White House was angry with him for even bringing up the subject and told him 'they' did not want [Lindbergh] to be connected with Pan American in any capacity." Vaughan informed Lindbergh that the situation there was suddenly "loaded with dynamite." Lindbergh knew that no company with a government contract could afford to take him on without getting clearance from the Administration. "I am beginning to wonder whether I will be blocked in every attempt I make to take part in this war," Lindbergh mused in his diary.

He put out more feelers. His cousin Rear Admiral Emory Scott "Jerry" Land, Chairman of the U. S. Maritime Commission, brokered for him a fifteen-minute meeting with Colonel William A. Donovan, who was about to become Director of the Office of Strategic Services. They discussed the possibilities of Lindbergh's studying international air transportation, but nothing more came of the meeting. At the same time, Phil Love, his friend since Kelly Field, offered to investigate the possibilities of bringing Lindbergh back into the Air Corps through its Fiftieth Wing, which Love would be commanding. Love's superior officer dismissed the very notion.

Then another friend in high aviation circles leapt at the chance of hiring Lindbergh. Over dinner at his house in Hartford, Eugene Wilson, president of United Aircraft, outlined several projects in which he thought Lindbergh could take part, particularly a study of comparative aircraft performances. Ten days later, it came to the public's attention that United had sold aviation equipment to Japan and Germany before the war; and Wilson now felt that it would be "inadvisable" for Lindbergh to join the company. Lindbergh agreed. "The war is going badly for us," he noted, "and people will be looking for a scapegoat."

Nine months earlier, Major Reuben Fleet—a pioneer airmail pilot who had organized the Consolidated Aircraft Corporation—had tried to lure Lindbergh to his company by offering him an annual salary of $100,000 and a research facility built anywhere in the southwest that Lindbergh pleased. On March 12, 1942, Lindbergh met with Fleet in New York City, hat in hand. He hoped the research and development position was still available, which he would accept only if the salary were not more than $10,000. Fleet was thrilled to present the proposition to his company's new management board, only to have the embarrassing task, not two weeks later, of withdrawing the offer. As Fleet would later explain, they were simply unwilling to employ him for fear of reprisal from Roosevelt. With billions of dollars in defense contracts waiting to be dispensed, no manufacturing company in America could afford to offend the Administration. Except one.

Before receiving Reuben Fleet's regrets, Lindbergh heard from Harry Bennett, director of personnel, labor relations, and plant security for Ford Motor Company. After learning of Lindbergh's futile attempts at securing a job, Bennett reported, Henry Ford wanted to discuss the possibility of Lindbergh's working at his bomber factory. On March twenty-third, Lindbergh boarded a seven P.M. train from Boston to Detroit.

After lunch the next day with Ford and Bennett at the Dearborn plant, they drove a few minutes to the west, where Ford had performed a minor manufacturing miracle. Four miles to the southeast of Ypsilanti, Ford owned acres of forest and farmland, through which trickled a stream called Willow Run. In early 1941, on Ford's promise to produce one B-24 Liberator bomber—a four-engine, high-wing monoplane—per hour, the government had agreed to spend some $200,000,000 on a plant and equipment. Three square miles were cleared in three weeks; and in a year's time, the manufactory for the B-24 was built. It included what was called "the most enormous room in the history of man"—an L-shaped structure that ran 3,200 feet before elbowing another 1,279 feet—plus almost five million square feet of hangars and 850 acres of landing field, complete with seven concrete runways. At that, the new operation at Willow Run was but one cog in the gigantic Ford wheel, which included three main plants in the Detroit area and another sixty branches spread across the country. Modifying its ability to produce cars for civilian use toward meeting the demand for engines and planes and tanks and jeeps and staff cars necessary to fight the war, Ford Motor Company adopted a twenty-four-hour/seven-day workweek.

While driving from Willow Run to the company's River Rouge plant, Ford and Charles Sorenson, one of his production chiefs, asked Lindbergh if he would "come out to Detroit and help them with their aviation program." Lindbergh grabbed the offer, though he advised their first clearing it with the War Department. The very suggestion that he should have to ask anyone about what he did in his own factory irritated Ford; but Lindbergh reasoned "that we would have to have much contact with them in the future and that a good start would be of great advantage." Neither Ford nor Lindbergh feared that this job offer would be rescinded; and, after spending the night with his mother and uncle, Lindbergh returned to Willow Run to acquaint himself with designs, procurement programs, and the layout of the factory. The next day he trained to Washington, where he met with Air Secretary Lovett, who expressed his approval of Lindbergh's plan to work for Ford.

Lindbergh proceeded to Martha's Vineyard for a long weekend, to pack his bags, play with his children, and discuss the immediate future with his wife. She was torn between following her husband and setting up another home or remaining in Martha's Vineyard with her three children. Having just learned that another baby was on the way, they agreed that Charles should get situated in Detroit and return for visits until he had found a proper place for all of them to live. "Another husband would assume that I would come with him to Detroit," she wrote in her diary, "but he sees my side too clearly. He wants too much for me. He wants me to live my own life. He wants this so passionately that it angers him when he sees anything frustrating it. Household duties, cooks that can't cook, nurses that won't leave me alone. Friends and family obligations which take my time. Depressions which rob me of confidence. I think almost all our quarrels arise from this passionate desire of his to see me freed to fulfill what there is in me."

Lindbergh rose at 4:30 on the morning of April 1, 1942, crossed on the

5:45 ferry and just kept driving, stopping only for gasoline and sandwiches, which he ate in the car. Twenty-eight and a half hours later, he arrived at the Dearborn Inn. After bathing, Lindbergh drove to Willow Run and spent most of the day meeting personnel and inspecting the plant—"acres upon acres of machinery and jigs and tarred wood floors and busy workmen. . . . a sort of Grand Canyon of a mechanized world." That afternoon he made an hour-long test flight in a B-24C, the Liberator bomber which they would mass-produce and which Lindbergh already saw ways of improving. He spent the next day acquainting himself with the Willow Run and River Rouge plants—"studying production and procurement data, drawings of plane assembly, going through the plane itself, and in general getting to know the Ford organization and its methods."

The government's attempts to stifle Lindbergh's wartime career increased his desire to prove himself a good soldier. He shifted his high-octane work ethic into an even higher gear, never allowing anybody to accuse him of goldbricking. He usually left for work before daybreak and did not return home until long after dark. He became his own harsh taskmaster, creating assignments for himself when he had exhausted those put before him.

Lindbergh could have asked Ford for almost any salary he wanted; and he did—$666.66 per month, which he would have earned as a colonel in the Air Corps. Except when work demanded, he never took advantage of his access to priority flights, generally insisting on riding the train or driving himself. Although he had not marched to the beat of anyone else's drum since leaving the Air Mail in 1926, Lindbergh put on his best face, grateful for even this mundane opportunity to serve. After little more than a week on the job—which had already included a trip to Washington to meet with Merrill Meigs, director of the aircraft section of the War Production Board—Lindbergh told himself that "this change is probably good for me, and there are elements that I enjoy—getting to know the inside of a great industrial organization, for instance." He kept his nose to the grindstone, avoiding eye contact with the public whenever possible. He refused newspaper interviews.

Shortly after his new job began, a false rumor circulated that Lindbergh was being hissed and booed when he walked through the aisles of the assembly line. When the University of Michigan's student newspaper ran an editorial, "People Should Prohibit Lindbergh From Defense," based on the fiction, Lindbergh chose to ignore it, though others wrote to the editor in his defense. *Liberty* ran an open letter to Lindbergh in July 1942 entitled "Have You Changed Your Mind?" challenging him to affirm that he was "publicly and wholeheartedly behind our government and the President in the struggle to win this war!" The editor in chief even sent Lindbergh a suggested outline for his reply.

Lindbergh handwrote his own response to the article, refusing to retract any of his prewar statements and, in fact, reiterating his belief that the alternative to a negotiated peace in Europe was "either a Hitler victory or a prostrate Europe and possibly a prostrate America as well." He believed the Roosevelt administration had thus far pursued a course which had "led to a series of failures and disasters almost unparalleled in history." Upon rereading his reply, Lindbergh chose to ignore the article, retreating to his policy of refusing to deny rumors or answer critics. He politely rejected offers from news services around the world to write similar articles; and he continued to ignore all calls upon him to return medals he had received from Germany, Japan, and other Axis nations. He sent the Missouri Historical Society a check for increased protection at the museum; but, with the rising war hysteria, he instructed the curator to do nothing that "draws unusual attention to the Collection."

Suffering more than he expected from the end of the public's great love affair with him, Lindbergh found himself drawn deeper into his marriage. His immediate family (and friend Jim Newton) remained his emotional spars; his wife became his mainstay. As a result of their separations, which would lengthen as the war continued, Lindbergh had never been so emotionally needy. In his hotel room, when he was not making the most of an unfulfilling job, he lived for Anne's letters. "You have in your pen a touch of divinity that I cannot describe beyond saying that it is there," he wrote her in April 1942. "But in your writing you take one above the ordinary levels of the earth. You show not only the best of life but something above life, something better than life. And for ordinary people you form a bridge to that something—a bridge for people who could not otherwise approach it. . . . In writing and in living, you are the only person I have ever known in whom lies the ability to be in contact with life and with what lies beyond it at the same time—to gain the one you have not found it necessary to turn your back on the other. By what gift or effort you have accomplished this, I do not know, but in your writing you help other people to do what you have done."

For the first time, Lindbergh found himself articulating some of his deepest feelings. In June, he told Anne that her letters brought nothing less than "calmness and beauty and spirit to a life in which these elements are hardly known. And in bringing these elements, they carry great strength and encouragement. They create a spiritual horizon that is all too easily lost, and without which life loses more than half its values. Your letters tell me, over and over again, like the ringing of clear bells on a spring evening, that love exists and always will, that there is something to look forward to beyond this war, something far greater, infinitely more worth while." Some of his replies ran on for more than twenty pages.

In his spare time that spring, Charles house-hunted in Detroit. Despite the scarcity of large family dwellings for rent, Lindbergh remained as choosy as

possible, mindful that his wife "has already spent too much of her time fixing up the many houses we have rented in our nomadic existence. . . . Anne
has books to write, children to take care of, a baby to bear, a move to make,"
he told himself. "To refurnish a house now is just too much."

The best he could find was a large house in the Bloomfield Hills area,
north of the city and a long drive to Willow Run, but literally in the backyard of Detroit's artistic colony, the Cranbrook Academy of Art. The house
was not decorated according to either of their tastes, in golds and greens and
various shades of pink, with thick carpets, satin and velvet upholstery, and
faux-Impressionist paintings in gilded frames—all set amid manicured lawns
and formal hedges. But it came equipped with the most modern conveniences—a sprinkler system for the garden, a water-softening system, a fan-
cooling system, an intercommunication system, even lights on the porch that
attracted insects then electrocuted them. Charles thought the house made up
in convenience what it lacked in style and would allow Anne to function
comfortably, especially during the absences his war work would demand.
After living alone for three months on the second floor of the Dearborn Inn,
he found the three wooded acres "exceptionally attractive." He signed a
one-year lease, at $300 per month.

"Very Hollywood!" Anne thought, when she saw the house for the first
time in July. The "ersatz elegance" of the place depressed her at first, making her long for the severity of Illiec. But Charles told her it was "mental
prostitution" even to dwell on the subject of the house, that she must settle
in to these temporary quarters and proceed with life, extinguishing any negative thoughts with "mental discipline." He stressed that they must "learn to
live lightly." To prove his point, he removed all his clothes from his bureau
and put them in a suitcase he kept in the closet.

Charles was in New York on August 12, 1942—after a trip to Washing-
ton, where he had discussed with General Arnold the merits of the B-17 (a
Boeing four-engine bomber) over the B-24s Ford was producing—when
Anne went into labor. He rushed home to Detroit and was by her side at the
Henry Ford Hospital at 5:12 the following morning, when she gave birth to
a seven-and-a-half-pound boy.

It would be four months before they completed his birth certificate. In this
instance it was Anne who kept stalling—not just because she was waiting for
the "perfect name" to present itself, but also because it marked in her mind
the end of an era. "The age of child bearing is over," she wrote her sister
Constance; "& I think I realize with some reluctance that though I have
Jon, Land, Anne and (?) Mark, I shall never have Christopher, Michael and
Peter; Hylla, Reeve, Ursula and Fidelity will not be my little girls." Shortly
before Christmas, they selected Scott, a name that had passed through the
Land family tree for two centuries.

With the birth of the fifth Lindbergh baby came the death of a family member who had been with them longer than any of the other children. Thor, the great German shepherd Charles had bought to protect his family shortly after the body of young Charlie was found dead, had been faltering from age for weeks. In the dog's final days, Lindbergh noticed its sole interest in life had been reduced to squiring Anne. "He struggles pitifully to get up and follow her whenever she goes by," Lindbergh wrote in his journals; "and sometimes he is able to get to his feet and walk along behind her—dragging his rear legs stiffly over the grass—but with an expression of great joy in his eyes at being near her. When he is lying down, his eyes follow her as long as she is in sight."

He died quietly under a hickory tree on the lawn in Bloomfield Hills and was buried in a grave Lindbergh dug. "He had no pain, and I think he died as the old should die, not lingering so long that all joy is gone from the living," Lindbergh wrote in his journal that night. It is among the most moving passages in all his years of diaries, more emotional than anything he ever wrote about a human being. "I think Thor found something worth while in life to the very day he died, and yet I think he was ready and willing to go. But now, for us, there is a great empty, lonely feeling in the places he used to be." The death reduced Anne to tears. She could not think of Englewood, New York, Long Barn, Illiec, Lloyd Neck, or Martha's Vineyard without thinking of her brave "wolf" galloping to the family's protection. "Thor was a symbol of something," she wrote, "—of devotion and love and family unity. A great unity of my life—the child-bearing years. His going ends a chapter."

The Lindberghs settled into suburban life. Charles went to his office or on business trips every weekday, while his wife cared for the house and children; weekends, they visited Charles's sixty-six-year-old mother, who had recently developed a tremor. Lindbergh would use this early symptom of Parkinson's disease to persuade her that, after a quarter-century of teaching, she should retire. For the next few months, however, Evangeline Lindbergh would persist in commuting by bus to downtown Detroit, all the while caring for herself, her house, and her brother, who continued to tinker with new inventions.

Lindbergh made the move to Detroit complete with one unusual addition. Shortly after mentioning to Harry Bennett at Ford that he was interested in purchasing a trailer, Lindbergh was asked to the company garage in Dearborn to inspect a seven-year-old (but practically unused) trailer Henry Ford himself had bought for his Edison Institute Museum. It was a Stagecoach Model, built by the Ideal Manufacturing Company, a "huge brown elephant" on wheels, outfitted with a divan that doubled as a bed, a combination icebox unit and kitchen sink, a dining area, lavatory, draped windows, electric lamps, and a linoleum floor. Lindbergh wanted to buy it on the spot; but Ford insisted that he simply take it. He explained that he had put the trailer in his museum to "show the future of road transportation, and that since the future was 'here,' there was no use keeping it in the Museum any longer. He said that someday they might want to show the past of road transportation, and in that case the trailer would be worth more if it had been used." A week later, Lindbergh attached the trailer to his car and drove it home, parking it in their back woods. The Lindberghs would use the trailer for its intended purpose on several road trips; but over the next fifteen years it would follow them wherever they moved, its primary function becoming a quiet place for Anne to write, her "room of one's own."

A few months later, Lindbergh sent Ford's production chief, Charles Sorenson, a confidential letter in which he questioned his own job performance. "I came here in the hope that I might offer suggestions and advice, based on some years of experience in various fields of aviation, which would be of assistance in the Ford Company's aeronautical activities," Lindbergh wrote. "I find, however, that the Company's policies and methods are so different from those I have followed in the past that until I learn to understand them better I must consider myself more a student than an adviser." Lindbergh's discontent stemmed from more than his inexperience playing on a large team or from his first encounters with office politics. (One day he witnessed Ford executives Bennett and Sorenson literally come to blows.) Lindbergh's greater frustration came in seeing Ford mass-producing planes that were inferior to those they should have been producing, simply because it would be too costly to retool the factories. "I feel quite sure that Ford officers did not realize the mediocrity of the B-24 when they set up such elaborate jigs and machinery for its production," Lindbergh would later tell a Ford Company historian. "However, even if they had shared my personal estimate of the B-24, I am not sure they would have made any change in their procedure—or that they should have. A very high production of bombers was desired at the earliest possible date . . ."

In an effort to spread his wings, Lindbergh suggested a relationship with Ford similar to those he had maintained in the past with Pan American and TWA. He wished to be struck from the payroll so that he might engage in "aviation developments elsewhere in the country." While he would continue to devote much of his time to Ford—testing planes and representing the company at meetings across the country—he would allow himself to be reimbursed only for company-related expenses. He refused Ford's offer to cover his rent while he was living in Detroit, and he came to accept Ford's gift of the trailer only by justifying it in his mind as payment for the work he was doing at Willow Run.

In the summer of 1942, before Lindbergh could find new outlets for his energy and expertise, he got dragged into the news. William Dudley Pelley, organizer of the Fascistic Silver Shirts storm troopers, went on trial in August for sedition; and the defense subpoenaed Lindbergh to testify. Lindbergh had no idea why, as he had never had any contact with Pelley or any member of his organization. He appeared at the courthouse on August 4, 1942, where a crowd of reporters and photographers met him at the door. He said nothing to them and almost as little under oath. The defense attorneys proved to have no good reason for having summoned him; and Lindbergh could testify little more than that "the majority of the people of this country were opposed to getting into war—that is, before we were attacked." The government chose not even to cross-examine him, and Lindbergh was off the stand within twelve minutes.

From those paying close attention to the trial, Lindbergh picked up public sympathy. Newspapers that had not supported his prewar positions rushed to his defense. *The Roanoke Times,* for example, editorialized: "The effort of Pelley's counsel to drag Lindbergh into the proceedings was unfair to Lindbergh and does not seem to have helped their client in the least. We have taken the view all along that Lindbergh was a misguided and mistaken young man, but we have never had the slightest reason to doubt the patriotism or to feel that he would for one moment put any other country's interests above that of his own country." Even the crotchety Theodore Dreiser observed that Lindbergh was "a babe at politics & finance and gets his foot in something of a political or socio-economic trap every time he opens his mouth." And yet, he added, "all this has nothing to do with my admiration for Lindbergh for what he is and has done. He offered his services to our Army, didn't he? And I am not one to assume that they would have been disloyal services. Rather, I think he would have fought the enemy to the death-line—his own or its." But alongside news of Germany bombing England and threatening Stalingrad, and first reports of the planned extermination of all Jews in Europe, the Pelley story never commanded great public attention, just enough for people to remember yet another headline linking Lindbergh to Fascists.

Lindbergh remained a bogy to the nation at large and anathema to Jews, who would instinctively recoil at the mention of his name for generations to come. During the war, to cite but one example, the John P. Marquands were staying with the George S. Kaufmans at their country house in Bucks County. One morning Anne Lindbergh called, hoping to reach her longtime friend Adelaide Marquand. When the message was delivered a few hours later, Beatrice Kaufman said to her guest, "You may call her back if you wish, but you may not do so from this house." Mrs. Marquand, who strongly supported both Lindberghs, asked her husband to drive her to the train station, which he did.

In September 1942, President Roosevelt visited Willow Run. The company product line—from jeeps to planes—was put on display for his inspection. Lindbergh thought it best to absent himself from work that afternoon. Only days later, he set his sights on a new aspect of military aviation, which would allow him to combine his interests in aviation and medicine, taxing both his mind and body. On September 22, 1942, Lindbergh and a half-dozen colleagues from Ford flew to Rochester, Minnesota—in one of the company's B-24 "clunkers," which sprang a near-fatal gasoline leak along the way.

Dr. Walter M. Boothby, a Harvard-educated pioneer in aviation medicine, welcomed them. He chaired the Aeromedical Unit for Research in Aviation Medicine at the Mayo Clinic, where Lindbergh hoped to advance the practice of high-altitude test flying. With new planes reaching altitudes over forty thousand feet, aviatic warfare encountered unexplored medical problems, particularly hypoxia—inadequte oxygenation of the blood. Lindbergh was eager to examine the altitude chamber the Mayo experimental laboratories had built.

The large steel chamber had two compartments—one in which the tests were conducted, the other an air lock, which permitted entrance, exit, and observation without changing the pressure within the test chamber. Lindbergh sat right down and strapped on oxygen hoses and a mask that had microphones attached. A motor-driven vacuum pump changed the cabin pressure to simulate an altitude of forty thousand feet. The relatively small body of conflicting statistics as to the point at which "blood vapor pressure becomes dangerous and the effect of frequent and prolonged anoxia on brain tissue" made Lindbergh think that he could contribute to this increasingly important study.

For the next ten days, he became a human guinea pig. The experiments in which he partook at the aeromedical laboratory required intense physical activity and mental acuity. Before entering the chamber he had to "desaturate" for half an hour—riding an exercise bicycle or walking on a treadmill while breathing pure oxygen through a rubber face mask—to wash the nitrogen out of his body and prevent the formation of nitrogen bubbles under decreased pressure. Inside the chamber, measuring temperature changes against alertness, he performed numerous tests, simulating parachute jumps from high altitudes. More than once he strained himself to unconsciousness. During his stay in Rochester, he attempted one especially dangerous test of a descent at a speed twice that of any prior attempts. He determined that the Army's emergency-oxygen equipment was inadequate.

Before Lindbergh's tests, the prevailing opinion among flying personnel in 1942 was that "you could not train your senses to become aware of a hypoxic condition in time to take conscious action to overcome it." Lindbergh challenged that supposition. Working with Dr. Boothby and his staff, he devised a system whereby the oxygen supply to his mask would be cut off without his knowledge, while another mask with a full supply of oxygen was laid at his side in the chamber. "It was my job to learn to detect hypoxia quickly enough to change the masks without assistance," he would later write. "Several trials taught me to make the change with a number of the originally available seconds of consciousness still in reserve." Lindbergh's subsequent report would affect the future of high-altitude flying, as he recommended that the use of emergency bailout oxygen equipment in a low-pressure chamber become a part of the indoctrination program for all high-altitude aviators.

Upon his return to Ford, Lindbergh put his study to practical use. He flew P-47s—the single-engine, low-wing "Thunderbolts"—Air Force fighters capable of reaching forty thousand feet at a speed of 430 m.p.h., with their Ford-built 2000 h.p. Pratt & Whitney engines. For weeks he tested the planes so that he could formulate emergency procedures. Then he ordered changes in the design of the plane's hatch, and he instructed other test pilots as to how they might reach higher altitudes. As a result of Lindbergh's study, Ford modified its oxygen equipment, thereby saving countless lives.

On one of his flights, Lindbergh ran short of oxygen without warning— at thirty-six thousand feet. The gages indicated otherwise; but he sensed too late that something was happening "to clarity of air, to pulse of life, perception of eye." He grew aware, he would later write, "of that vagueness of mind and emptiness of breath which warn a pilot of serious lack of oxygen."

As the dials in front of him faded and he began to black out, he shoved the stick forward, diving as quickly as possible. Senseless, except for a vague awareness of a shriek outside his cockpit, he fell twenty thousand feet before full consciousness returned and his thought process was restored with the increasing density of air. Shortly after landing, a mechanic informed Lindbergh that the plane's pressure gage was reading fifty pounds too high and that his oxygen tank had simply run empty at thirty-six thousand feet. "That had caused all my trouble—a quarter-inch error of a needle," Lindbergh would note and never forget.

Lindbergh's interest in high-altitude flying brought him to East Hartford, to inspect United Aircraft's new twenty-eight-cylinder engine. After his visit, Eugene Wilson, president of the company, wrote Lindbergh that "considerable water has gone under the bridge since we last talked with you," and he wondered if Lindbergh might be "in a position to help us in the direction of research and development." Lindbergh pounced upon the invitation, explaining that his only commitments to Ford were of a personal nature, once he finished a few more weeks of tests and modifications on the P-47s.

As those Thunderbolts entered production—becoming the most effective bomber escort planes in the European Theater—Lindbergh steadily devoted more time to United's development of the Navy Marine Corsair (Vought F4U), which would be used as both a carrier fighter and a land-based plane. Between December 1942 and July 1943, Lindbergh made eight trips to Hartford, where he taught pilots the fine points of flying the plane, with its unique, upturned-wing design. Trained as a fighter pilot and frustrated at not having seen action, Lindbergh participated in maneuvers and mock combat. Deak Lyman, formerly of *The New York Times,* then working as an executive for United Aircraft, recalled Lindbergh's taking his plane up and engaging in a high-altitude gunnery contest against two of the Marines' best pilots. Lyman said the forty-one-year-old civilian "outguessed, outflew, and outshot" both his opponents, each practically half his age.

Lyman visited Anne Lindbergh in Detroit during one of her husband's trips to Connecticut; and she commented that Charles's new work "had made a new man of him, made him boyish again and had done much to remove the sting of his relations with Washington just following the declaration." His work at United had become so engrossing, he even gave up the diary he had scrupulously maintained for almost five years. "If it weren't for his family," Anne said, "I am sure he would never come to Detroit. He would like to devote every minute seven days a week to United." Or even better . . .

On January 5, 1944, Lindbergh conferred with Brigadier General Louis E. Wood of the Marines, in Washington, about the possibility of going to the South Pacific for a survey of Corsair operating bases in the combat zone. United was receiving conflicting reports regarding the relative value of single- versus twin-engine fighters; and Lindbergh wanted to gather facts that would assist in designing the next generation of such planes. He had a personal agenda as well: After two years being sidelined, he yearned to see action at the front. The General said he would take the matter up with his superiors; and the next day Lindbergh was told he could proceed.

Until the arrangements were made, Lindbergh continued to test planes, mostly single-seater or two-place planes at military bases. The work was dangerous, as some of the planes were experimental and others were obsolete, many with untried or overworked parts. During four days in January at Eglin Field in Florida, Lindbergh flew eight different planes—including the Boeing B-29, which America was about to release into the skies. This superfortress—capable of flying 350 m.p.h., with a radius of over two thousand miles, and a maximum bomb-load of twenty thousand pounds—was the pride of the nearly one hundred thousand planes the United States would produce that year, a vast improvement in speed, range, and load over any of the 2,200 planes America had produced in 1939, when Lindbergh had first sounded his alarm.

Largely because of the exponential growth of American aviation, and the resultant superiority in the air, the war turned in favor of the Allies. Germany was all but ejected from Russia and Africa; and the Allies had bombed the daylights out of the industrial Ruhr Valley and Hamburg and were beginning to raid Berlin. In the Pacific, Japan was retreating as well, losing control of the steppingstones to her borders—the Solomon Islands, Kwajalein Island, and the Gilberts. The Allies moved on to the Marshall Islands and then the Kurile Islands.

Lindbergh spent the first days of April 1944 in New York City. He went to Brooks Brothers to buy his uniforms, which were required in combat areas. Traveling on "technician status," former-Colonel Lindbergh would be required to wear a Naval officer's uniform but without any insignia or rank. In the event of his capture, he would be a man without a country.

On April 22, 1944, the Allies invaded Hollandia, New Guinea, catching the Japanese offguard and allowing eighty-four thousand Allied troops to establish themselves there. Two days later, just as that news made the American headlines, "tech rep" Lindbergh left from North Island, San Diego, on the first leg of his trip to that precise dot on the map.

It would take two months for him to reach the north coast of New Guinea, as he stopped in Hawaii, Midway, Palmyra, Funafuti, Bougainville, and Green Island en route. Approaching the war zones, Lindbergh kept redefining the duties of his singular job. He flew on dawn patrols and joined rescue missions into the jungle and over the seas; wherever he went, he asked to go to the front lines. Upon learning that Lindbergh had actually fired his guns when he was over Japanese-held Rabaul, a Marine colonel dressed him down. "You have a right to observe combat as a technician, but not to fire guns," he told the unranked civilian. "Of course," another Marine officer chimed in, with a wink, "it would be all right for him to engage in target practice on the way home." From then on, the military looked the other way whenever Lindbergh chose to assert himself as a soldier.

"The more I see of the Marines the more I like them," Lindbergh wrote in his journal. The obverse was just as true. Grumblings among the troops were heard whenever Lindbergh's presence was detected, men questioning his loyalty if not his competence. But just as often he would encounter former members of America First; and he invariably left everybody impressed with his skill, fortitude, and modesty.

On May twenty-ninth, Lindbergh dropped a five-hundred-pound high-explosive bomb on Kavieng, hitting a strip of buildings along the beach where anti-aircraft guns had been reported. "I don't like this bombing and machine-gunning of unknown targets," he had to admit to his diary. "You press a button and death flies down. One second the bomb is hanging harmlessly in your racks, completely under your control. The next it is hurtling down through the air, and nothing in your power can revoke what you have done. The cards are dealt. If there is life where that bomb will hit, you have taken it." He flew more than a dozen combat missions with Marine squadrons against Japanese targets on New Ireland and New Britain. "The missions," reported one Army Air Force Colonel, "consisted of strafing and dive bombing Japanese troops remaining at the once strong bases of Rabaul and Kavieng." Although Lindbergh had yet to encounter enemy planes in the air, he had become an expert bombardier.

Effective though the single-engine Corsairs had been, many were beginning to act up. And so, before returning Stateside, Lindbergh wanted combat experience with the twin-engine P-38s, which the Army Air Force was flying, so that he could compare them. An old friend, General Ennis Whitehead, waved him on to Hollandia, where P-38s were being flown.

On the afternoon of June twenty-sixth, Lindbergh knocked on the shack door of Colonel Charles MacDonald, the commander of "Satan's Angels," the celebrated 475th Fighter Group of the Fifth Air Force. Entering the Colonel's quarters, Lindbergh offered his name; but MacDonald, engrossed in a game of checkers, did not catch it. Lindbergh explained that he was interested in learning about combat operations with P-38s, and that General Donald Hutchinson, the Task Force Commander, had said MacDonald was the man to see. The Colonel and the Deputy Commander remained guarded in their conversation and focused on their game, while the tall intruder dressed in khakis just stood there. At last MacDonald asked, "What did you say your name was, and what phases of operations are you particularly interested in?"

"Lindbergh," he replied, "and I'm very much interested in comparing range, fire power and your airplane's general characteristics with those of single engine fighters." His eyes still on the checkerboard, MacDonald realized that the only way the intruder could get his answers was by flying the plane; and the tall man was not wearing any kind of wings. After a few more moves, he asked, "Are you a pilot?"

"Yes," he said, which prompted MacDonald to take a closer look at the forty-two-year-old man with the receding hairline standing there. "Not Charles Lindbergh?"

"That's my name," he replied. MacDonald forgot his checkerboard and began talking airplanes. The men quickly became friends; and Lindbergh, who had but eight hours of flying time in a P-38, was invited on a "four-plane anti-boredom flight" the next day to Jefman and Samate. Once Lindbergh left the shack, MacDonald's deputy said, "My God! He shouldn't go on a combat mission. When did he fly the Atlantic? . . . [He's] too old for this kind of stuff." MacDonald thought their visitor seemed fit; besides, commented Major Thomas B. McGuire, Jr., the Air Force's second-leading ace, who would be flying on his wing, "I'd like to see how the old boy does."

The next day they all saw, as Lindbergh not only mastered his plane but, four hundred miles deep into Japanese territory—weaving through black puffs of ack-ack—also successfully strafed an enemy barge in Kaiboes Bay.

After several more days of bombing missions, the crew chief of the 475th had noticed that Lindbergh's plane invariably returned with much more fuel than any of the others. One evening, MacDonald introduced the new recruit to the rest of the pilots at a briefing in the thatch-roofed group recreation hut; and he asked Lindbergh to explain why that was the case. In his flat Midwestern tones, Lindbergh said that by raising manifold pressure and lowering revolutions per minute, the engines would consume less gasoline, gallons that could be translated into time in the air and an increase in combat radius. The initial reaction from his young audience was of disbelief and disrespect, cracks about grinding their engines down. "These are military engines," Lindbergh replied, "built to take punishments. So punish them." Then he added that if any man felt uncomfortable about adopting his methods, he should not. "You're the captains of your own ships," he said. "You must make the decisions. After all, you know more about flying your planes than I do." But over the next few weeks, the three squadrons of Satan's Angels learned otherwise, as they stretched their six-to-eight-hour missions to ten hours, allowing them to surprise the Japanese with attacks deeper into their territory than expected.

"In the days that followed," MacDonald would later recount, "Lindbergh was indefatigable. He flew more missions than was normally expected of a regular combat pilot. He dive-bombed enemy positions, sank barges and patrolled our landing forces on Noemfoor Island. He was shot at by almost every anti-aircraft gun the Nips had in western New Guinea." By then Lindbergh had logged more than twenty-five combat missions and close to ninety hours of combat time. On July 10, 1944, Lindbergh received a message from Australia requesting his presence. It was signed "MacArthur."

He left two mornings later and was met at American Army headquarters in Brisbane by General George C. Kenney, who commanded the Allied Air Forces in the Southwest Pacific. Kenney had heard rumors that Lindbergh had been flying combat with Army squadrons, which was against regulations. Lindbergh said he did not want to create any embarrassment, but he did not want to "go back up to New Guinea and sit on the ground while the other pilots were flying combat." He asked if there was not some way around the regulations. "Well," the General replied, his eyes lighting up, "it might be possible to put you on observer's status . . . [which still] would not make it legal for you to do any shooting. But if you are on observer's status, no one back in the States will know whether you use your guns or not."

Lindbergh was introduced to General Richard K. Sutherland, MacArthur's Chief of Staff, with whom he discussed his method for increasing the combat radius of the P-38s. Sutherland was so astonished by Lindbergh's report—that a radius of seven hundred miles could be reached— he insisted that Lindbergh talk immediately to General MacArthur himself. After exchanging cordial salutations, MacArthur—looking younger than Lindbergh expected—asked if what Sutherland had just told him was true. Lindbergh replied that only instruction and training were necessary. "MacArthur said it would be a gift from heaven if that could be done," Lindbergh wrote in that day's journal entry, "and asked me if I were in a position to go back up to New Guinea to instruct the squadrons in the methods of fuel economy which would make such a radius possible." MacArthur also said Lindbergh could do any kind of flying in any plane he wanted. He showed Lindbergh his map of the South Pacific and outlined his general plan of action—the immediate steps, the future steps, "and the limitations which were imposed by present fighter combat radii."

Lindbergh returned to New Guinea, where he spent much of his time teaching fuel consumption. He reteamed with some of his friends from the 475th the following week on Biak, a Japanese stronghold three miles across the water. When weather kept him grounded, Lindbergh explored the brilliant coral reefs surrounding the islands.

Biak also provided Lindbergh with the most grotesque images of war he had ever seen, visions that would haunt him forever. On Monday, July 24, 1944, Lindbergh and several officers drove a jeep to the Mokmer west caves, where the enemy had waged one of its most stubborn stands. They went as far as they could up a crude military road, then walked the next few hundred feet toward the caves. Going down a hill, they came to a pass with bodies of a Japanese officer and a dozen soldiers "lying sprawled about in the gruesome positions which only mangled bodies can take." Several weeks of weather and ants had eaten most of the flesh from the skeletons. The sight of skulls smashed to fragments prompted one officer to say, "I see that the infantry have been up to their favorite occupation," namely, knocking out gold-filled teeth for souvenirs.

At the side of the road, they passed a bomb crater in which lay the bodies of another half-dozen Japanese soldiers, partly covered with a truckload of garbage Allied troops had dumped on top of them. "I have never felt more ashamed of my people," Lindbergh wrote in his journal. "To kill, I understand; that is an essential part of war. Whatever method of killing your enemy is most effective is, I believe, justified. But for our people to kill by torture and to descend to throwing the bodies of our enemies into a bomb crater and dumping garbage on top of them nauseates me." The caves themselves looked and smelled so hideous—what with burned bodies of Japanese soldiers scattered among mud and filth—that Lindbergh and the other men lasted there but a moment. Two days later, Lindbergh drove to another cliff cave, where he encountered the standing body of a Japanese soldier in uniform, roped tightly to a post set in the ground, headless.

On July 28, 1944, Lindbergh joined up with the 433rd Fighter Squadron, as observer in the No. 3 position of an eight-plane sweep. Their mission was to bomb and strafe "targets of opportunity" on Amboina, a small, Japanese-held island off the southwest coast of Ceram. As the horizon brightened, Lindbergh took off with other P-38s on Mission #3-407. One of his fellow combat pilots could not help noticing that he had been slow in retracting his wheels upon takeoff. "Lindbergh from Doakes," those on the mission heard over their radios. "Get your wheels up! You're not flying the *Spirit of St. Louis.*"

Although the Japanese were rumored to have strong flying forces in the area, the skies were clear. Suddenly, the radio squawked that another fighter group had spotted enemy aircraft nearby, a "Sonia" that was successfully eluding two American P-38s, whose pilots had run out of ammunition. As Lindbergh, Colonel MacDonald, and Captain Danforth Miller dove through a white cloud and black anti-aircraft bursts of smoke, Lindbergh got his first sight of a Japanese plane in the air—closing in head-on, with their combined speed close to six hundred miles per hour. "Of all the attacks it is possible to make on a Japanese plane," MacDonald would later explain, "the one liked least is the head-on pass, for here you and the enemy approach with tremendous speed, each with guns blazing. There is always a good chance for collision, even though both of you try to avoid it, and against a Japanese one could never be sure to what lengths his suicidal tendencies would push him." Lindbergh fired for several seconds, seeing his machine gun tracer bullets and 20 mm. cannon shells pelt the Sonia; but a collision seemed unavoidable. As the Sonia zoomed closer to Lindbergh, he pulled back on his controls with as much force as he could exert. There was a violent jolt, with but a five-foot cushion of air between them, as Lindbergh successfully banked to safety and the Sonia succumbed to a vertical dive into the sea.

Not long after the Americans had returned to Mokmer strip on Biak Island, word spread that "Lindbergh got a Jap." Lindbergh himself never made much of the story. If anybody brought it up, he would merely explain, "I shot in self-defense." Other soldiers remembered gathering in the lantern-lit mess tent to listen to Lindbergh speak that night. Expecting to hear a good war story from this "god-figure of all pilots everywhere," the men only heard a soft, Midwestern voice droning on about throttle setting and r.p.m.

Missions were canceled on August 1, 1944, because weather was bad in all enemy directions except north toward the Palau Islands. Before Lindbergh's arrival, that next step toward Japan, across the equator into the North Pacific, had been routinely considered beyond range. Armed with Lindbergh's instruction, Colonel MacDonald asked him and two others if they wanted to fly there. Their enthusiasm overcame MacDonald's warning that the mission would be dangerous, what with enemy fighter strength far outnumbering theirs.

They announced their arrival in the hostile area by strafing a ship. The men soon sighted three enemy planes, which Colonel MacDonald and Lieutenant Colonel Meryl Smith destroyed. Suddenly Lindbergh noticed an enemy fighter diving on Smith; and by the time he had turned back in Smith's defense, that same Japanese Zero had shifted its attack toward Lindbergh, then within gun range. As the Zero dove down, firing on Lindbergh's tail, MacDonald tried to force it off with a deflection burst, as did the mission's two other planes. Too low to dive, Lindbergh could only bank toward MacDonald, who saw him crouching in front of the plane's armor plate, waiting for bullets to hit, as he "commended his soul to God."

"I think of Anne—of the children," Lindbergh would later write of the moment. "My body is braced and tense. There is an eternity of time. The world was never clearer. But there is no sputtering of an engine, no fragments flying off a wing, no shattering of glass on the instrument board in front of me." One of the deflection shots had set fire to the Zero, whose pilot had simply proved to be a blessedly poor shot. All four Americans returned to Biak unharmed.

Bombers had been requesting fighter cover over Palau for some time, but they had repeatedly been refused on the grounds "that the distance was too great and the weather too bad." This mission with Lindbergh refuted such excuses. Within days, the top brass had done an about-face on sending other fighters there; within weeks United States forces landed at Palau; and within three months, MacArthur would wade ashore at Leyte, his triumphal return to the Philippines.

Shortly after the mission to Palau, MacDonald was granted a leave to the States. He tried to talk Lindbergh into returning with him—now that he had tempted fate twice. But Lindbergh refused, saying, "I haven't finished yet." He rejoined the Marines on Biak, where he shared a tent with Major McGuire. From New Guinea, Lindbergh moved on to Kwajalein and Roi Island, where he instructed fighter squadrons in long-range cruising procedures and, despite admonitions, flew on combat missions. Several officers talked to Lindbergh about resecuring his colonelcy and returning to the Pacific to serve with MacArthur; but Lindbergh said he wanted to complete his present study first. Besides, he intimated to his diary, "There are political complications, and I am hesitant to accept a commission under Roosevelt, even if I could obtain one."

At another private meeting with MacArthur in Brisbane, the General told Lindbergh of his recent conference with the President in Hawaii. MacArthur said Roosevelt's mind and voice were as commanding as ever, but he was amazed at how sickly he looked. He said that FDR would almost certainly be reelected that fall, "unless the people learned of his actual state of health." MacArthur was otherwise interested in all Lindbergh had to say about his mission to the Pacific, especially in his success increasing the combat radius of the P-38 by almost two hundred miles. MacArthur asked how many Japanese planes he had shot down, and Lindbergh told him of his experience off the south coast of Ceram. "Good," said the swaggering commander of the Pacific, "I'm glad you got one."

On his way home, Lindbergh conducted one more series of tests at Kwajalein and Roi islands. Flying again in the F4Us that had brought him to the Pacific, Lindbergh wanted to see how heavy a bombload the Corsairs could carry. The first week of September 1944, he engaged in exercises over the Japanese-held atolls of Taroa, Maloelap, and Wotje. He began his trials by carrying the standard thousand-pound bomb, and over the next week trebled that weight. He even built a special belly rack for a large bomb. By the end of his second week, Lindbergh navigated his Corsair through tricky winds while carrying a two-thousand-pound bomb and two thousand-pound bombs—the heaviest bombload ever attached to an F4U. On September thirteenth, he dropped that load on Wotje Island, completely wiping out the southern portion of a Japanese gun position. "The take-off and drop with 4,000 lbs. of bombs completes the test program I laid out several days ago," Lindbergh told his journal. After flying fifty combat missions, he was ready to return home. In the end, Lindbergh considered the F4U "the best Navy fighter built during the war."

That afternoon he flew to Kwajalein, and the next day to Hawaii, where he arranged his return to California. Late on the night of Saturday, September 16, 1944—after stops in San Francisco and Los Angeles—Lindbergh taxied to the Hotel del Coronado in San Diego for the night. The next morning, he telephoned his wife and his mother, to tell them he would be making the final leg of his trip home as soon as transportation came available.

As was the case for millions of women "left behind," the war had at least as deep an impact on Anne as it did on Charles. During those years, she had moved into two different houses in Bloomfield Hills and raised four children, living with shortages and ration coupons. Without robbing her of her tenderness, the war had toughened her—forcing her to build her own "world of people." Fortunately, the local artistic community offered a number of stimulating minds—Lily and Eero Saarinen, the Finnish architect, whose father Eliel Saarinen had built and directed the Cranbrook Academy of Art; Carl Milles, the Swedish sculptor; and several teachers from Cranbrook, including sculptors Svea Kline and Janet de Coux. She enjoyed her art classes, especially sculpting; and she spent as much time as possible in her trailer, writing.

While recuperating after the birth of Scott, in August 1942, Anne recalled an outline of a flying episode she had written before the war. One year
later, it had become a thirty-thousand-word novella about the ordeal of a
pregnant wife flying in a two-seater across the Alps with her husband, a daring English pilot. While she was in the middle of writing it, Charles expressed his cold opinion that he did not believe the story could be published
for some time, because of the way the public still felt about them. Her publisher, Alfred Harcourt, felt otherwise.

In some ways, Lindbergh proved to be right. The Book-of-the-Month
Club turned down *The Steep Ascent,* citing a number of fanatical letters
from members who, upon reading its announcement, said they would resign
if the club endorsed it; *Reader's Digest* said it was too difficult to excerpt; and
Harcourt, Brace set its first printing at twenty-five thousand copies, half that
of *Listen! The Wind.* The first reviews confirmed the publishers' cautious position. While they were largely positive, enough of them dipped into personal
criticism—"It is no accident that these two fliers dangerously lost in the Alps
found safety on Mussolini's soil"—to hurt the book's sales. Immersing herself in her diaries and ever-widening correspondences with new friends—
which included many lonely, worshipful women—Anne Lindbergh would
not publish another book for eleven years.

Just as Anne was adapting to Bloomfield Hills, she learned that their
landlord was unable to renew their lease. She wrote Charles that they would
have to be packed up and moved into a new house by September 1, 1944,
even though he would still be away. "I do not like to leave the decision about
the winter on your shoulders," he had written her while in New Guinea, "but
there seems no wise alternative, and you know there is no one I trust as
much."

"As far as the Ford Company is concerned," he told her, "I have done
about all I can in that connection. Their aviation problems are now primarily connected with mass production, in which I am only secondarily interested, and which they understand far better than I." As a result of his work
in the South Pacific, Lindbergh said he would have to spend much of his time
in Connecticut, in connection with United Aircraft's fighter program. "This
is work I *am* interested in," he said, "but which I have no intention of carrying on indefinitely. I entered it because of the war, and I remain in it for that
reason only." That said, Lindbergh was prepared to move to any section of
the country that appealed to Anne; "there is nothing I would rather do than
spend a few months studying and writing in a beautiful and quiet place," he
wrote, echoing his sentiments of three years earlier.

She found such a place in Westport, Connecticut—just an hour by train
from New York and twenty minutes from the United factory in Bridgeport.
It came unfurnished, but Anne felt "it looks rather like us—settled down

among trees and a field and a brook," with good schools, swimming, and boats nearby. She toiled for weeks to make Charles's homecoming as perfect as possible.

Amid her packing, Anne's eyes had almost passed over a short paragraph in the Detroit *Free Press:* "AUTHOR-PILOT MISSING OVER SOUTHERN FRANCE—SAINT-EXUPÉRY." After months on the ground teaching pilots, the forty-four-year-old writer had just returned to action and had been alone on this reconnaissance flight.

Anne had fearfully combed the newspapers for years, always half expecting to find such a headline. Throughout the war she had carried him in her thoughts, poring over every article and book he wrote. She even considered *The Steep Ascent* an offering to him, which might somehow reunite them. "I am sad we never met again," Anne admitted to her diary. "I am sad he never tried to see us, though I understand it; I am sad that politics and the fierceness of the anti-war fight and the glare of publicity and the calumny and mixed-up pain and hurt and wrong of my book kept us from meeting again. I am sad that I never had the luxury of knowing whether or not he forgave us for our stand, forgave me for my book [*The Wave of the Future*]." Anne could hardly bear the irony that Saint-Exupéry had been called upon to make "the supreme sacrifice" for his country just as France was being liberated. Anne had felt such grief only twice before, upon the deaths of her sister Elisabeth and her first baby.

She counted her blessings. "I have a husband I love," she wrote. "Nowhere could I find, could I have found, a better husband—a husband to whom I could give so much, who gives me so much—no marriage as good. A husband, a good marriage, is earth. Charles is earth to me, the whole world, life." And yet, she had to confess, Saint-Exupéry was "a sun or a moon or stars which light earth, which make the whole world and life more beautiful. Now the earth is unlit and it is no longer so beautiful. I go ahead in it stumbling and without joy."

On the night of September 18, 1944, Lindbergh left San Diego on TWA Flight 40. After almost a dozen stops, he reached Pittsburgh the following afternoon and boarded the night train to New York. When he arrived at the station the next morning a group of photographers and reporters were waiting on the platform. He put on his lensless eyeglasses and walked past them with the rest of the passengers until someone called out "that old, familiar, and annoying cry: 'There he is.' " They chased him up the escalators, onto the street, and even opened his taxi door after he had closed himself in—so they could snap one more picture as he leaned out to shut it. He insisted he had nothing to say about his trip.

He taxied into the city, breakfasted at the Engineers Club, and called Anne at Next Day Hill. She would go directly to Westport to make at least one room in the house ready; and the children would join them two days later. Then he caught the next train to Hartford. After spending the day with the officers of United Aircraft, he took the train to Westport. The cabdriver had to stop twice to get precise directions to the "Tompkins House" on Long Lots Road. Lindbergh liked what he saw—a large house set back from the road, surrounded by trees.

Before she had a chance to prepare herself, Anne heard the taxi and then her husband's familiar fast steps. "And there he was, lean and brown, very young and taut looking, bursting into the room," she would record, "—like life always."

Despite the differences in their experiences, Anne liked to think that the war had not separated her from her husband so much as drawn them closer. "Is this just a miracle of understanding?" she wondered. "Or simply love. Or do we really both of us now stand at the same point, at the end of something, at the beginning of something?"

She was not sure, knowing only, "Both of us are groping and a little lost—but we are together."

PART FOUR

16

PHOENIX

"To me in youth, science was more important than either man or God.
The one I took for granted; the other was too intangible
for me to understand."

—C.A.L.

BECAUSE THE WAR NEVER HAD AN OFFICIAL BEGINNING FOR Lindbergh, it never had an official ending either.

He had not been in his Westport house an entire morning before he began commuting regularly either to the United Aircraft offices in Hartford or the Chance Vought factory in Stratford to discuss fighter design, new jet projects, fuel range, climb, speed, and firepower—still for no pay. At forty-two, he continued to work as a test pilot.

"[T]here's no denying the fact," Lindbergh would later write Colonel Charles MacDonald, "that I never had a more fascinating time in my life than on those combat flights in the South Pacific." But he never shook some of the horrifying memories he carried back from the war zones—the destruction, degradation, and deaths. For years he prayed for the soul of the Japanese pilot he had shot down at Amahai Strip; and like everybody else who lived through the war years, Lindbergh lost many who were dear to him: Philip Love, whom he had met at Kelly Field and drafted into the Air Mail Service, was killed in a transport plane crash; William Robertson, who had run the company that hired Lindbergh and Love to fly the mail and became a backer of the *Spirit*, was killed in a glider accident; and flying ace Major Thomas McGuire, who had recently shared his tent on Biak with Lindbergh, went down in the Southwest Pacific. The hardest blow for Lindbergh, however, came at what should have been a moment of jubilation, as the last German forces in France were surrendering.

Dr. Alexis Carrel died on November 5, 1944. The man

who had been a father-figure to Lindbergh for fifteen years had returned to wartime France to display his patriotism by serving his countrymen. In so doing, he subjected himself to four years of hardship as well as ostracism for collaborating with the enemy forces. "Cold, privations and isolation," he had recently written a friend, had brought suffering to him and his wife. Another friend of the Nobel laureate eulogized, "He died really of a broken heart; he could not stand the accusations made against him and his sensitive soul broke under them."

"It is distressing," Lindbergh noted upon Carrel's death, "that a man who cared as deeply for his country and who was as much concerned about the welfare of mankind as Carrel should die under such a cloud of accusations. I suppose that it is to be expected in revolutionary times, and I feel sure that in the more objective future his actual accomplishments and character will show these accusations in their true light." While many, including Corliss Lamont, had long found much of Carrel's thinking "indescribably muddled, banal, and prejudiced"—particularly his belief in "the superiority of the white race"—Lindbergh considered Carrel one of the great figures of his time. "Regardless of whether his philosophy was right or wrong in instances," he wrote, "it was carefully thought out and courageously stated. Many of the men who now accuse him are those whose shortsightedness and political indifference, if not actual dishonesty, brought about the conditions in which France now finds herself."

For the rest of his life, Lindbergh would contribute time, energy, and money wherever he thought it might restore the reputation of his mentor. Toward that end, Lindbergh helped establish a Carrel Foundation. Its objective was "to promote the study and dissemination of the ideas expounded during his lifetime by the late Alexis Carrel; to preserve manuscripts, records, apparatus, and other memorabilia left by or which relate to the late Alexis Carrel; to sponsor research projects which shall deal with subjects in which the late Alexis Carrel was interested; and the advancement and diffusion of knowledge concerning science, religion, and humanity."

The following year, Lindbergh and Madame Carrel themselves would pack fifty-eight wooden crates with the artifacts of this extraordinary life— everything from unpublished manuscripts to an Egyptian mummy. Lindbergh would supervise moving the bulk of the Carrel collection to Georgetown University. And in 1949, he would contribute an introduction to *A Trip to Lourdes,* an account of a miracle Carrel witnessed, which he had not wanted published in his lifetime. While the loss of other friends sensitized Lindbergh, Carrel's death spiritualized him, leading him to question, as Carrel had most of his life, the relationship between science and religion.

By the spring of 1945, battle fatigue had exhausted the nation. Anne Lindbergh, for one, felt an air of desperation overtaking her friends and family. The Lindberghs and Morrows had been luckier than most, losing no immediate family members in the war; but she sensed a virtual epidemic of depression. After years of relative calm, her brother, Dwight Jr., was displaying signs of mental disorder again; and George Vaillant, the husband of one of her oldest friends, the former Susanna Beck, committed suicide. "Obviously," she wrote in a letter as the end of the war was in sight, "this winter & spring people are going through profound disillusionments & despairs." On April 12, 1945, the nation's leader for the last twelve years died.

The passing of Franklin Roosevelt did not affect Washington's official attitude toward Lindbergh overnight. It took a week. While Allied forces surrounded Berlin, Lindbergh was called to the capital to discuss his joining a Naval Technical Mission expedition to Europe. He would travel, as he had in the South Pacific, as a civilian representative of United Aircraft, to study the enemy's development in high-speed aircraft. The nature of this mission was far more sensitive than Lindbergh's recent military venture and required State Department clearances, authorization he felt he would have theretofore been denied. But, as he wrote a friend from America First in the second week of the Truman administration, "I . . . found a general feeling that there will be a definite turn in the direction of constitutional government from now on." And, he would later report to General Wood, "the vindictiveness in Washington [has] practically disappeared as far as I was concerned."

"Conflicting reports have been coming in in regard to the effectiveness of German jet and rocket fighters—some say their value is greatly exaggerated," Lindbergh wrote his mother, as he was waiting for his final clearances; "some say the Germans would have held supremacy of the air if they had been a year farther ahead with their jet and rocket development. It is important for us to find out what the real facts are, and that is my primary mission."

On Friday, May 11, 1945—four days after the Germans surrendered—Lindbergh left Washington on a Navy transport plane for Europe, via Newfoundland and the Azores. The Captain invited Lindbergh to take the controls for part of the journey; but he was just as happy spending the bulk of the flight lying on the cabin floor. "One might as well sleep," Lindbergh wrote elegiacally in his journal, "for the modern military plane is usually uninteresting from the passengers' standpoint—high above the earth—often above the clouds, so that no details can be seen (even if bucket seats and badly placed windows didn't make it so difficult to see anyway). Every year, transport planes seem to get more like subway trains."

Sunday, he awoke to see the soft morning light bathing Mont-Saint-Michel outside one of the cabin portholes, seven thousand feet below. "What wouldn't I give to spend a day on Illiec and watch and listen to its tides!" he wrote of his own magical island. "Illiec," he wrote, "a half hour's flight away, six years away, a war away, and God knows how much more."

Arriving the Sunday morning after V-E Day, Lindbergh found few officers at the Paris headquarters of Naval Force France with whom he could conduct business. Reacquainting himself with the city that had once thrown itself at his feet, he spent most of the day touring familiar sites, unrecognized. At first glance, everything seemed unchanged. Second looks revealed pockmarks of machine-gun bullets in the Arc de Triomphe and an entire column felled by a tank shell at the Hotel Crillon. Even so, Paris seemed to have escaped the war relatively unscathed. Over the next three days, Lindbergh studied secret intelligence data and met with U. S. Ambassador Jefferson Caffery and General Carl Spaatz. Admiral Alan G. Kirk informed Lindbergh that France had been harmed in ways not necessarily visible—the harbors were destroyed, the country was slow to reorganize, and there persisted the threat of its turning Communist.

It was not until the Naval Mission penetrated deeper into the Continent that Lindbergh could take full measure of the war's effects. At times over the next week, he felt as though he were walking through a sequence of dreams, each more surreal than the last. The visions were all the more disturbing for Lindbergh, who clearly remembered all that he had admired in the Third Reich just six years earlier.

In a G. I. uniform, Lindbergh flew into Germany along with several Technical Mission officers. Despite the armistice, they were armed with pistols because resistance activity was still being reported. The destruction he saw in Mannheim, where they landed, reminded Lindbergh of a Dali painting—"which in its feel of hellish death so typifies the excessive abnormality of our age—death without dignity, creation without God." He found Munich also in ruins.

Worse than any demolition of buildings for Lindbergh was the breakdown of human behavior. The French, Russians, and Poles, he learned, had looted and murdered; and the next day, in Zell-am-See, headquarters for the German Air Force, he learned that the Americans had as well. As Lindbergh's party drove within a few miles of Berchtesgaden, they could not resist detouring to Hitler's fabled mountain headquarters, which had been heavily bombed. Walking through rubble, Lindbergh entered Hitler's inner sanctum and was rendered speechless. Standing at a vast space in a wall, which once held a plate-glass window, he looked onto one of the most beautiful sights he had ever seen—"sharp gray crags, white fields of snow, sawtooth peaks against a blue sky, sunlight on the boulders, a storm forming up the valley." Through a gap in the mountains, he could see Bavarian plains all the way to the horizon. "It was in this setting," Lindbergh saw further, "that the man Hitler, now the myth Hitler, contemplated and laid his plans—the man who in a few years threw the human world into the greatest convulsion it has ever known and from which it will be recuperating for generations."

"Hitler," he would write in his journal that night, "a man who controlled such power, who might have turned it to human good, who used it to such resulting evil: the best youth of his country dead; the cities destroyed; the population homeless and hungry; Germany overrun by the forces he feared most, the forces of Bolshevism, the armies of Soviet Russia; much of his country, like his own room and quarters, rubble—flame-blacked ruins. I think of the strength of prewar Germany." The 1970 publication of this journal entry would be one of the few times Lindbergh ever came close to admitting that he might have misjudged Hitler, his first suggestion of a condemnation.

Lindbergh was billeted that night in Zell-am-See, in a house that had been seized from a German family. As he carried his barracks bag through the door, he passed a forlorn woman lugging her belongings out. Three young children followed, looking "angry and a little frightened." Later that night he discussed the German Air Force with the commanding officer of the 506th Parachute Infantry over dinner, at which the American soldiers proudly drank "Goering's wine"—from his private cellar, which had been "liberated" when he had been captured nearby. Lindbergh could not help thinking of his earlier private audiences with the second-most powerful man in the Third Reich. Although he seldom imbibed, Lindbergh sampled the wine.

Moving on to Oberammergau, Lindbergh hoped to locate an old acquaintance, Dr. Willy E. Messerschmitt, who had engineered many of Germany's most effective flying machines and had ushered aviation into a new age. His Me262 was the world's first jet-propelled combat airplane, and his Me163 Komet the first practical rocket-powered airplane—capable of speeds close to six hundred miles per hour. Both of these jet aircraft had been unleashed on the Allies too late to change the course of the war. Lindbergh learned the once-revered designer's large country house had been "liberated" by American troops; and he found him living with his sister's family in a village farther into the country, reduced to sleeping on a pallet in a barn.

Speaking through Messerschmitt's bilingual brother-in-law, Lindbergh conducted a technical conversation with the jet-age pioneer. Messerschmitt propounded the development of rocket-type planes for both military and commercial use and prophesied that within twenty years supersonic aircraft would need only a few hours to carry passengers between Europe and America. A visibly broken man, he told Lindbergh that he had been concerned about defeat as early as 1941, when he saw America's estimates for its own aircraft production. Lindbergh further learned that Messerschmitt had only recently returned from England, where he had been a prisoner of war. Both the British and the French had asked him to serve as a technical adviser.

When Lindbergh asked whether he would be interested in working in America if an opportunity arose, he said he would have to hear the conditions. Wernher von Braun—who had helped develop the V-1 (a robot bomb that could be ground-launched on a 150-mile predetermined course) and the V-2 (a liquid-fuel rocket used as a ballistic missile)—was about to accept such an offer from the United States government. Messerschmitt would remain in Germany, dying in 1978, never recovering financially or emotionally from the war. Von Braun, on the other hand, became celebrated as America's most outspoken proponent of rocket development and helped thrust America ahead of its new competitor, Soviet Russia, in the space race.

At every turn, Lindbergh saw destroyed buildings, dispossessed people, and hungry children. "I feel ashamed, of myself, of my people," Lindbergh wrote in his diary, trying to sort out his feelings, "as I eat and watch those children. They are not to blame for the war. They are hungry children. What right have we to stuff ourselves, while they look on—well-fed men eating, leaving unwanted food on plates, while hungry children look on. What right have to we to damn the Nazi and the Jap while we carry on with such callousness and hatred in our hearts." Lindbergh felt the worst was still to come once winter set in. "Yes, I know," Lindbergh told himself; "Hitler and the Nazis are the cause. But we in America are supposed to stand for different things."

Over the next three weeks, Lindbergh gathered information and collected grievances. "We stopped at demobilization centers; we confiscated documents, interrogated engineers and scientists, and picked our way through litter in looted laboratories," Lindbergh would later write of the task. In Heilbronn he learned that German prisoners were being held in camps, exposed to the elements. Near Wiesbaden he learned that American troops had given a building full of pregnant women one hour to evacuate. He heard that in Stuttgart the French and the Senegalese were responsible for three thousand cases of rape that resulted in hospitalization—for physical injury. At a detention camp at Freising, he was told that German prisoners were fed only whatever other Germans brought them. Lindbergh considered such behavior not only morally base but also politically unsound, as the camps contained many with experience in rocket development who were hearing Russian radio broadcasts promising better conditions to those who would relocate to the Russian zone of occupation.

On the Sunday afternoon of June 10, 1945, in the company of Navy Lieutenant E. H. Uellendahl, Lindbergh arrived at the underground tunnels of Nordhausen, dug deep into a spur of the Harz Mountains. There the Third Reich had built its factory for the V-2 rockets, a thousand of which had exploded on England.

They approached the tunnels through Camp Dora, part of the notorious Bergen-Belsen concentration camp. Displaced persons of many nationalities inhabited the vast prison grounds, residing in the crude wooden barracks, from which emanated the stench of inadequate sanitation and rotting garbage. Amid the squalor gleamed hundreds of parts for the V-2 rockets, which refugees had fashioned into shelter. The camp had until recently supplied labor for the assembly lines inside; and Lindbergh was told the only way the souls condemned there would ever come out "was in smoke."

Lindbergh and Uellendahl entered the massive cavern, driving beside a railroad track. Along the opposite wall of the tunnel sat lathes and jigs, a production line for V-1 buzz bombs. Every so often another tunnel branched off the main artery, leading to a workshop that produced engines or turbo-superchargers. Eerily, while every tunnel of this industrial anthill was devoid of life, it was fully illuminated—"as though," Lindbergh noted, "waiting only for a change in shift." The two men explored the tunnels, finding a small hospital here, an office there, V-2s in various stages of assembly everywhere. After exploring for miles, they returned to civilization, spending the night in a large house near the center of Nordhausen.

The next day was even more phantasmagoric. Intimations of what lay ahead came at breakfast, as members of Lindbergh's party discussed alleged savageries at Camp Dora. "That's where the Germans had furnaces that were too small to take a whole body, so they used to cut the arms and legs off and stuff 'em in that way," said one man. "The prisoners were so badly starved that hundreds of them were beyond saving when the Americans came," added another.

A short time later, Lindbergh and his party had made their way up the mountainside above the camp, off the road so that they might reach a low, factory-like building. The diameter of its brick smokestack was disproportionately large for its height. At one end of the building, he saw two dozen stretchers, soiled and bloodstained—"one of them showing the dark red outline of a human body which had lain upon it." Upon entering the building they saw a plain black coffin with a white cross painted on it. Beside that, covered in canvas on the concrete floor, lay what was unmistakably a human body. In a moment, Lindbergh realized exactly what kind of "factory" he had entered.

Moving into the main room of the building, Lindbergh saw two large furnaces, side by side, with steel stretchers for holding the bodies protruding through the open doors. "The fact that two furnaces were required added to the depressing mass-production horror of the place," Lindbergh would note. The sight appalled him. "Here was a place where men and life and death had reached the lowest form of degradation," he wrote. "How could any reward in national progress even faintly justify the establishment and operation of such a place. When the value of life and the dignity of death are removed, what is left for man?"

A figure walked through the door, something between a young boy and an old man. It was a seventeen-year-old Pole, wearing a striped prison uniform, cinched at the waist but otherwise much too large for his skeleton of a body. Speaking German to Lieutenant Uellendahl, he pointed to the furnaces and said, "Twenty-five thousand in a year and a half." Then he ushered the two Americans into the room they had first entered, and he lifted the canvas from the corpse on the floor.

"It was terrible," the boy said, his face contorted in anguish. "Three years of it." Pointing to the bony cadaver, he added, "He was my friend— and he [was] *fat.*" As though sleepwalking, Lindbergh followed the boy outside, his mind "still dwelling on those furnaces, on that body, on the people and the system which let such things arise." He was jerked back to reality by Uellendahl's translating again: "Twenty-five thousand in a year and a half. And from each one there is only so much." The boy cupped his hands together, then looked down. Lindbergh followed his gaze and realized they were standing at the edge of a pit, eight feet by six feet, and possibly six feet deep. It was filled to overflowing with ashes and bone chips. Lindbergh noticed two oblong mounds of clay nearby, evidently pits that had been capped. The boy reached down and picked up a knee joint, which he held out for Lindbergh's inspection.

The horrors were not lost on Lindbergh. "Of course, I knew these things were going on," he would write in his journal on June 11, 1945; "but it is one thing to have the intellectual knowledge, even to look at photographs someone else has taken, and quite another to stand on the scene yourself, seeing, hearing, feeling with your own senses." His mind flashed back to the rotting Japanese bodies he had discovered in the Biak caves and the load of garbage he had seen dumped on dead soldiers in a bomb crater. He thought in rapid succession of stories he had heard of Americans machine-gunning prisoners on a Hollandia airstrip, of Australians pushing Japanese captives out of transport planes, of American soldiers probing the mouths of Japanese soldiers for gold-filled teeth, of pictures of Mussolini and his mistress hanging by the feet. "As far back as one can go in history," he told himself, "these atrocities have been going on, not only in Germany with its Dachaus and its Buchenwalds and its Camp Doras, but in Russia, in the Pacific, in the riotings and lynchings at home, in the less-publicized uprisings in Central and South America, the cruelties of China, a few years ago in Spain, in pogroms of the past, the burning of witches in New England, tearing people apart on the English racks, burnings at the stake for the benefit of Christ and God."

Lindbergh never considered that his ignoring—or his ignorance of—the

Nazi slaughter was tantamount to condoning it. Instead, he stood ready to accept only collective blame, as an American and a member of the human race. "It seemed impossible that men—civilized men—could degenerate to such a level," he wrote. "Yet they had. Here at Camp Dora in Germany; there in the coral caves of Biak. But there, it was we, Americans, who had done such things, we who claimed to stand for something different. We, who claimed that the German was defiling humanity in his treatment of the Jew, were doing the same thing in our treatment of the Jap."

Lindbergh could reckon with the horror of this systematic mass genocide only by equating it with other human atrocities. Looking down at the pit of ashes at Camp Dora, he concluded, "What is barbaric on one side of the earth is still barbaric on the other. 'Judge not that ye be not judged.' It is not the Germans alone, or the Japs, but the men of all nations to whom this war has brought shame and degradation." To the end of his life he clung to his impression "that in World War II Japanese and German atrocities averaged worse than ours, but everything considered I don't feel at all certain about it." In a letter to a professor who later analyzed his political position before the war, Lindbergh contended that he had no "vengeful wish against the Germans in general," feeling that "they had suffered enough by the end of the war." But he was adamant that "we could not let atrocities such as those of the concentration camps go unpunished." He strongly supported the trials against war criminals that opened in Nuremberg that November.

Lindbergh descended the mountain and spent the next three hours walking through the whitewashed tunnels of Nordhausen, inspecting V-1 and V-2 parts, marvelling at the technology and trying to reconcile the way in which the forces of evil had harnessed it. "The V-2s," he concluded, "were the last symbol of the mystical drive and dictatorial power of the Nazi Führer, used to advance 'Nordic civilization' and his political doctrines." He thought back to that day in 1936 when he watched Hitler walk across the grass of the Olympic stadium in Berlin while one hundred thousand people cheered, investing their hopes in what he now regarded as "a strange mixture of blindness and vision, patriotism and hatred, ignorance and knowledge."

"Some irrational quality of the man, his actions, and his oratory enticed the entire German nation to support his ideas," Lindbergh would write of Hitler with twenty-five years of hindsight. Nowhere did Lindbergh acknowledge, either in the spring of 1945 or anytime after that, that the promise of Hitler had seduced him as well. Anne Morrow Lindbergh would later note that "the worst crimes of the Nazis were not known until after Pearl Harbor and some not until the end of the war or even until the Nuremberg Trials"; but she was also as quick to admit, "we were both very blind, especially in the beginning, to the worst evils of the Nazi system." Lindbergh never made any such concession. His observations about Camp Dora were his only public acknowledgment that he had misjudged the Third Reich.

Having covered almost two thousand miles during his last two weeks in Germany, Lindbergh returned to Paris. After two days of conferences with military personnel and the American Ambassador, he arranged his journey home. With that, he brought seven years of diary-keeping to an end, closing the book on his wartime experiences.

He returned from his two months in Europe more alarmed about the state of the world than ever. But he knew that the American public no longer gave a hoot for his opinions. In fact, many delighted in rubbing Lindbergh's nose in news clippings—old ones full of his defeatist predictions, new ones detailing Nazi atrocities. As the extent of Germany's evils was steadily revealed to the world, letters to newspaper editors invited the Lindberghs to gaze upon the "wave of the future" that had fascinated them so. Bernard DeVoto, in a long column in *Harper's* magazine, had recently reminded his readers that "It didn't seem to matter to Charles A. Lindbergh that the Jews were being exterminated. The Jews didn't seem to matter nor the Poles nor the Czechs nor the Greeks. The destruction of France didn't seem to matter, nor the invasion of Russia, nor Holland, Belgium, Norway, Denmark. Massacre, the bombing of Coventry or Warsaw or Rotterdam didn't seem to matter, the enslavement of millions, the starvation of millions, the slaughter of millions. What the hell? It was just the same old game about the balance of power. If we would only mind our own business we'd be able to get along with the Germans."

For the rest of his life, Lindbergh cleaved to his theories, insisting that he had been right in his noninterventionist position. More than once he qualified his prewar statements, emphasizing the "vast difference" between vanquishing Germany and winning the war. "Seldom in history has a nation been defeated as completely as Germany," Lindbergh granted. "Most of her cities are in ruins; millions of her people are dead. Yet the disturbing fact remains that while our soldiers have been victorious in arms, we have not so far accomplished the objectives for which we went to war. We have not established peace or liberty in Europe. There is less security there now than perhaps ever before, and less democracy. The value of truth has never been so low. The ideals of justice and tolerance have practically vanished from a continent. Freedom of speech and action is suppressed over a large portion of the world, especially in the so-called 'liberated nations,' many of whom have simply exchanged the Nazi form of dictatorship for the Communist form. Poland is not free, nor the Baltic states, nor the Balkans. Fear, hatred, and mistrust are breeding on a scale that never existed before. In fact, a whole civilization is in disintegration."

As he had for the better part of a decade, Lindbergh feared the rising power of Soviet Russia. That, coupled with chaos reigning in Europe, made America's withdrawing its influence on the Continent in the foreseeable future seem impossible. "We have taken a leading part in this war," he said, "and we are responsible for its outcome. We cannot retire now and leave Europe to the destructive forces which it has let loose. Honor, self respect, and our own national interests prevent that." He further believed, "No peace will last which is not based on Christian principles, on justice, on compassion allied with strength, and on a sense of the dignity of man. Without such principles, there can be no lasting strength; no matter how great the technical advancement or how large the armies. The Germans found that out."

Not long after his return to America, Lindbergh visited his mother in Detroit. His letter to her from the train home revealed a changed man. He wrote of "spiritual awareness" and the importance of spending time in the garden, enjoying the sun, listening to the birds. He copied page after page for her of Lao-tzu, a philosopher Anne had given him to read years earlier but whose words had taken on new resonance for him since his trip to Germany. "Think what a different world we would be living in if Hitler had read and understood him," Charles wrote his mother, quoting the following passage:

> One who would guide a leader of men
> > in the uses of life
> Will warn him against the use of arms
> > for conquest.
> Weapons often turn upon the wielder . . .
> A good general daring to march,
> > dares also to halt,
> Will never press his triumph beyond
> > need. . . .

He now counted Lao-tzu "among the greatest of philosophers"—next only to Christ as a mystic—and quoted him for the rest of his life.

Lindbergh's report of his European mission, which he submitted to Admiral H. B. Sallada, urged the United States government to immerse itself immediately in all the written material "liberated" from Germany, to bring selected German personnel to America, and to construct research facilities for the development of high-speed aircraft. "German plans for increasing accuracy through radio and television, for increasing range through high-speed catapults, larger rockets, and more efficient design, and for the incorporation of wings and cockpit," he said, "all indicate the tremendous development rocket aircraft will probably go through in coming years."

While Lindbergh's political opinions may have been arguable, his acumen regarding rockets had long proved prescient. It frustrated him to discover

that the German V-2 design of 1943 was virtually identical to Robert Goddard's rocket of 1939, and that even after the bombing of Pearl Harbor, the
government did not appreciate the value of Goddard's work. Ironically, the
enemy had taken greater interest in Goddard's accomplishments than had his
own countrymen. Indeed, when one German technical officer was being de-
briefed in May 1945, he blurted out, "Why don't you ask your own Dr.
Goddard?"

Battling cancer along with his chronic tubercular condition, Goddard
was eventually employed by the Navy. He worked under a government contract at Annapolis, developing small rocket motors less sophisticated than he
had designed years earlier. More than a decade would pass before Washington would grasp the significance of his work, two hundred patents that
would radically affect defense systems and help launch America into space.
Back in 1945, however, the government was evidently funneling its resources
into secret weaponry of another kind. Goddard died on August tenth, living
just long enough to learn what it was.

Lindbergh had long predicted that atomic energy would be used to attain
much greater speeds in all mechanical modes of transportation; but he was
taken aback when, in early August, he learned unofficially that the United
States had split the atom and harnessed enough of its power to allow America to drop an "atomic bomb" somewhere over Japan. A group of scientists
asked Lindbergh to join them in their attempt to persuade the government
not to drop the bomb, "because of its terrible power and the precedent of
ruthlessness that would be set." Lindbergh declined to participate, because
he felt, as he later explained, "that under the political circumstances that existed at the time, my participation would do more harm than good."

On August 6, 1945, a B-29 Superfortress flew over Hiroshima and
dropped one of the new bombs, killing almost eighty thousand Japanese.
"Nothing before so revolutionary had impacted on the lives of men so suddenly," Lindbergh would later reflect. "The announcement . . . that the entire center of a large Japanese city had been leveled by one bomb, bursting
as a secret of intellectual development, seemed too fantastic to be earthly."
Lindbergh considered the act a "mistake." He believed that releasing the
bomb "in the way we did will forever remain a blot on American history."
Years later he explained, "I would not have objected to dropping the bomb
had it been necesssary to win the war, or even if we had informed the Japanese of its existence and they had thereafter refused to surrender." Three days
later the United States Air Force dropped a second bomb on Nagasaki, and
within a week the Japanese had surrendered. The old game boards on which
international policy had theretofore been played had to be discarded, as
those two blasts completely redefined all concepts of war and power, indeed
the modern world itself.

On a visit to the Midwest in September 1945, Lindbergh dined with Robert M. Hutchins, Chancellor of the University of Chicago, whom he had befriended years earlier during their fight against intervention. Hearing Lindbergh's present concerns, he invited him to stay for an Atomic Energy Control conference which the university was hosting. It was a gathering of both atomic and social scientists—the former group having created this doomsday weapon, the latter discussing its future uses.

Lindbergh considered the issues discussed at the conference the most pressing of their time; and despite all his instincts to avoid reentering the public arena, he would not be able to contain his newfound insights for long. The splitting of the atom had placed science in what he called "the unique position of having challenged God, threatened the existence of man, and scared its own disciples out of their wits all at the same time." He considered "asinine" the assertions of many that weapons had become "so terrible that World War II would be the last war fought."

Not two months after the Chicago conference, on November 8, 1945, Lindbergh confidentially addressed fifteen Republican congressmen in a private dining room of a Washington hotel. Although everybody present was sworn to secrecy, his remarks reached the press within a few days, complete with inaccuracies. *The New York Times* reported that Lindbergh had advised "keeping the atomic bomb a complete American military secret," that he had advocated "maintaining American air power superior to that of all the rest of the world," and that he had expressed strong mistrust of Russia: all that was true. But the article proceeded to state that Lindbergh said "he had changed his views about isolationism during the war" and that he had suggested that he did not feel "America should place confidence in the United Nations Organization but should rely on her own armed strength."

In the past, Lindbergh had allowed misquotations to go unchallenged, at the cost of further inflaming the national debate and injuring his personal reputation. But now he felt, "These times are too critical and too dangerous to justifying unnecessary division of opinion among Americans on vital international policies." He telephoned the Associated Press and read them a statement he had handwritten. "I have not changed my belief that World War II could have been avoided," he said, "but the issue between so-called Interventionists and Isolationists is past except from an academic standpoint. We fought the war together and we face the future together as Americans—a future that is more fraught with danger than the war itself." With that in mind, Lindbergh emphasized his second point: "In an era which has developed the Atomic bomb, and which will develop trans-oceanic rockets capable of carrying atomic bombs, the necessity for world organization for the control of destructive forces is imperative. The only alternative is constant fear and eventual chaos." He advocated a world organization backed by military power, "an organization led by the western peoples who developed modern science with its aviation and its atomic bomb."

One month later, Lindbergh further expounded upon some of his ideas. Invited to address the Forty-second Aviation Anniversary Dinner of the Aero Club of Washington, he thought at first that he might discuss such subjects as turbo jet transports, high-altitude rocket flights, and landing on other planets. But as he composed his thoughts, "such questions became dwarfed by the basic problem of how to keep aircraft from destroying the civilization which creates them."

"The developments of science, improperly guided, can result in more evil than they bring good. What peaceful men take a thousand years to build, fools can now destroy in few seconds," he said in the admonitory tones the public had come to expect from him. For the rest of his speech, Lindbergh was less doctrinaire than he had been in the past. "[P]ower alone has limited life," he said. "History is full of its misuse. There is no better example than Nazi Germany. Power without a moral force to guide it invariably ends in the destruction of the people who wield it. Power, to be ultimately successful, must be backed by morality, just as morality, must be backed by power." Lindbergh concluded by saying, "We are a Christian people. The ideals we profess are high. We have all the necessary elements to lead the world through this period of crisis." But, he asked, "can we combine these elements in our daily policies and lives? Whether our civilization is facing new heights of human accomplishment or whether it is doomed to extinction depends not as much on technical progress as on the answer we make to this question."

The following summer, Lindbergh was asked to join a committee charged with addressing some of the new questions of the nuclear age. As part of the fallout after the atomic bombing of Japan, the Ordnance Department of the United States Army initiated a secret project at the University of Chicago—Chicago Ordnance Research, acronymed CHORE—under the direction of Walter Bartky, Dean of the Department of Applied Mathematics. CHORE's activities consisted largely of evaluating weapons—machines guns, missiles, and bombs—and their uses. The work was so confidential Bartky hand-delivered his invitation to Lindbergh to become a consultant to the panel. Even CHORE's name was kept secret . . . until somebody pointed out that it was printed on the guarded door of its windowless offices on the Chicago campus. Believing "the United States should remain dominant in weapons development," Lindbergh accepted the offer.

Over the next several years, Lindbergh traveled constantly, gathering information and testing equipment, investigating "potential staging bases for our strategic bombers," remaining at the vanguard of aviation development. He even flew a Lockheed P-80 jet fighter, the first American jet to enter squadron service.

In the CHORE briefing room, the likes of Fermi, Zillard, and Urey scribbled formulae across the chalkboard walls. "There," Lindbergh later summed up, "I listened to a mathematics of combat effectiveness and destruction that seemed to leave the human being devoid of his senses. I studied graphs showing the value of 'scatter effect' for machine guns, and others indicating probabilities of kill for existing and for improved weapons. There, hour after hour, we discussed calibers, explosives, muzzle velocities, measures of aggression, defense, counterdefense, and counter-counterdefense." They played war games in which "[m]athematical calculations informed us that future jet-powered warplanes would fly too fast for bullet interception, that pilots of supersonic fighters would not have time to aim and fire in a head-on pass and still avoid colliding with each other, that guns would become obsolete for airplanes and have to be replaced by 'homing' missiles, that human eyes and muscles and cognition were too slow for the reaction times essential to success—concepts startling to the experience of a World War II combat pilot. In the next major conflict, electronic devices would be set loose in combat with each other. They would be maintained and monitored by men who would have no sense of wielding weapons, whose very existence would be preserved or snuffed out by the result of the competing intelligence of the synthetic brains to which the human brain would relinquish control of its destiny. In mathematical war games, men were already referred to as 'bodies,' and were moved like chessmen according to directions issued by analog computers."

The mathematics at these colloquiums often went over Lindbergh's head; but he was riveted by the level of thinking, the extrapolations upon extrapolations. Lindbergh felt his major contribution to the discussions lay in his trying to maintain "a connection between mathematical theory and practical fact." He would periodically interrupt to say, "Let's get a check in the field." Often bringing the most humanistic perspective into the room, one whose actual war experience remained fresh in his memory, Lindbergh argued "that even military aviators are human, that when a bullet hits your airplane some emotional effect takes place, that a coefficient relating to the senses must be included in some combat-effectiveness formulas."

Lindbergh appreciated both the humor and horror of a story one of the CHORE scientists told at dinner one night about testing the first atomic bomb at Alamogordo. Just before setting off the blast, Enrico Fermi had said, "Now when I press this button, there is a chance in ten thousand it will be the end of the world."

After the war, the American military engaged in a contentious battle of "unification," from which a single Department of Defense emerged with a new branch. The Air Force—no longer part of the Army—was eager to secure adequate government funding; and its first secretary, W. Stuart Symington, had hardly moved into his new office before soliciting Lindbergh's advice.

Lindbergh became a consultant to Secretary Symington and his successor, Harold Talbott, often reporting through Generals Hoyt Vandenberg and Lauris Norstad. His primary mission was to assist in the reorganization of the Strategic Air Command. In his first few months on the job, for which he insisted on neither pay nor publicity, he spent weeks inspecting and conferring with personnel at Andrews, MacDill, Carswell, Walker, Davis-Monthan, and McChord Bases; and he flew one hundred hours in Strategic Air Command bombers. Afterwards, he wrote in his first report to General Vandenberg, it was obvious to him that "the standards of performance, experience, and skill which were satisfactory for the 'mass' air forces of World War II are inadequate for the specialized atomic forces we have today. Since a single atomic bomber has destructive power comparable to a battle fleet, a ground army, or an air force in the past, its crew should represent the best in experience, character, and skill that the United States can furnish."

Lindbergh "believed it essential for SAC to have enough power to win an atomic war," he later wrote. "Still more important, it should prevent one." That goal in mind, he refused no Air Force assignment. As each mission paved the way for the next, he was constantly crossing the country or circling the world—sometimes as part of a committee, often alone. He was authorized to fly as a passenger in any Air Force aircraft and to pilot any such plane in which he could demonstrate proficiency; he was granted access to all classified data, up to and including TOP SECRET. His recommendations that "SAC be given top priority in the selection of its officers and crews, that its personnel receive improved terms of tenure, that the construction of air-refueling tankers be accelerated to increase practical bombing ranges, that monthly periods of flight training in emergency procedures be inaugurated to cut down accident rates, and that every SAC pilot fly a basic trainer on occasion in order to maintain proficiency in the ABCs of flying technique" were all adopted, save the last.

Lindbergh flew with the 509th Atomic Bomb Group out of Walker Air Force Base, New Mexico, on simulated bombing missions over Canada, Greenland, the North Magnetic Pole, and various cities in the United States. SAC work combined with a general mission on Air Force morale and proficiency, brought him to Alaska, Guam, Tokyo, Nagoya, Manila, Germany, France, and England, flying P-80s and P-51s.

On January 5, 1948, Lindbergh flew in an Air Force transport plane, a C-47 Dakota, to Japan. At three thousand feet, he circled Hiroshima and marveled at its tranquil beauty, settled between plum-tinted mountain ranges and the inland sea. Lindbergh found it difficult to imagine the hellfire that had devastated it. "There is no sign," he recorded, "to mark the gigantic mushroom cloud that once towered in the sky, no sign, except, when I look more carefully, the shades on earth below. . . . the blasted, radiated, and heat-shriveled earth of Hiroshima." He tried to imagine eighty thousand people inside the gray saucer who perished in the blast and as many again burned and mangled. The visit "forced" Lindbergh, as he wrote his wife, to four conclusions:

1. I do not see how civilization can survive a major atomic war.
2. If Russia continues unchecked, there is almost certain to be one.
3. We must find some way to prevent a second atomic power rising.
4. That this can be prevented by peaceful means is improbable.

Within a few years, Lindbergh would be attending secret meetings in a briefing room at Strategic Air Command headquarters at Offutt Air Force Base near Omaha, Nebraska, looking at large-scale maps of major cities, on which a general would place tinted plastic discs and calmly describe the level of obliteration they represented.

"If Soviet armies overrun Europe," Lindbergh reported to Secretary Symington in November 1949, "much more of Western civilization will be destroyed, and the American military position greatly weakened." For that reason he felt it was essential to help rebuild Germany, which he considered "the best and possibly the only source from which a major increase in European fighting strength can be obtained quickly." He further defended his position by pointing out: "her geographical position makes her the natural buffer against a Soviet invasion. Her people understand better than any others the terror of Soviet occupation. Her Communist vote is relatively low. Most of her men above 22 years of age are trained soldiers. Given the opportunity, they would fight bitterly to protect their homes if Soviet armies attempt to move farther westward."

Lindbergh issued a public statement supporting the anti-Communist Truman Doctrine. As opposed to his prewar stance, Lindbergh now "advocated continued American participation in international affairs, with a consistent foreign policy involving economic aid and the use of military force, if necessary to safeguard peace." He maintained that the policy he had formerly advocated—"that England, France, and America build their strength but refrain from war while Nazi Germany and Communist Russia fought out their totalitarian ideas"—was sound, and that he had correctly predicted the outcome of the war—"with Western civilization greatly weakened in a world full of famine, hatred and despair," with a "strengthened Communist Russia, behind whose 'iron curtain' lies a record of bloodshed and oppression never equaled."

Lindbergh's copious letters home during his Air Force, CHORE, and Pan

American inspection flights revealed another change in his attitudes, a diminishing thrill from aviation. "I can't get used to the ease with which one covers the world today," he wrote Anne after another polar crossing. "It's no longer an effort—Pole—equator—oceans—continents—it's just a question of which way you point the nose of your plane." Planes flew people, not the other way around. In fact, Lindbergh observed, "The pure joy of flight as an art has given way to the pure efficiency of flight as a science. . . . Science is insulating man from life—separating his mind from his senses. The worst of it is that it soon anaesthetises his senses so that he doesn't know what he's missing." Hardly a letter to Anne failed to mention how much he missed her, especially when he revisited places they had been the first to survey.

ALONG WITH much of postwar America—then experiencing a baby boom and a move to the suburbs—the still-expanding Lindbergh family settled down for the first time. On October 2, 1945—after a long labor—Anne Lindbergh gave birth to her sixth child, a girl, at Doctors Hospital in New York. Charles was, as with all her previous deliveries, at her side. Anne had been considering non-family names for the baby, born on her sister Ansy's birthday; but after two months of deliberation, she acceded to Charles's desire to delineate his children's background. She was named Reeve, the middle name of both her deceased aunt, Elisabeth, and her Morrow grandmother.

While still renting the Tompkins house in Westport, the Lindberghs decided to make Connecticut their "permanent" home. Just a few miles closer to the city than their present location, the Lindberghs spent $25,000 on a parcel of land and water at the east side of Scott's Cove, near Darien. The two and one-half acres of undeveloped property, screened from the nearest house by pine, spruce, and hemlock, also included three small islands, connected to each other and to the mainland at low tide by a sandbar. While looking for an interim house to rent, they found an ideal property for sale.

In an area called Tokeneke, on a four-and-one-half-acre promontory jutting into Scott's Cove, sat a large but unpretentious three-story, Tudor-influenced house. Looking down on the island-dotted coast, the rambling seven-bedroom structure was reminiscent of Illiec. Complete with a foyer opening into a large living room with a fireplace and picture window, a den, library, and sewing room, a screened sleeping porch off the master bedroom, an ample servants' wing, and a toolhouse, the property was theirs for $41,250.

Lindbergh hired an architect, Charles DuBose, to make alterations, adding a heavy slate roof, fieldstone siding, and a playroom on the second floor. For privacy as much as aesthetics, the Lindberghs paid special atten-

tion to the landscaping, planting tall trees, spreading yews, and banks of rho-
dodendrons around the house and its circular drive. Charles transplanted
cuttings from his mother's lilac bushes in Detroit, which had come from her
parents' house at 64 West Elizabeth Street. He parked Anne's office-trailer
deep into their woods.

In Charles's mind, he and Anne were entering the best years of their lives.
With five healthy children and a beautiful house to accommodate them all,
they could settle down to their various pursuits. Unfortunately, Charles and
Anne's notions of a home were at odds with one another. "We were
'nesters,' " Anne's sister Constance said of the Morrows; "we found our
places, and we returned to them year after year, generation after generation." Charles, on the other hand, commented another family intimate, "was
only interested in houses so that he'd have a place to 'park' Anne and the
children. Once he felt they were safely parked, he felt it was all right for him
to fly the coop."

"C. will always move!" noted Betty Morrow; and that transience kept her
daughter unsettled, always wondering in the back of her mind when her
husband would, without warning, pack them all up again. Ironic as it was
predictable, once the Lindberghs had a place in which to settle down, he absented himself more than ever.

"Take off your coat—are you going to stay?" little Ansy asked her father
on one of his returns. Fifty years later, that same daughter commented, "We
never really knew whether Father was coming or going; and it didn't really
matter, because whether he was there or not, he always made his presence
felt."

He was in many ways a model father. When he was home, Lindbergh
read to his children every night, and he encouraged those old enough to
write stories and poems—which he typed and kept. He invented games; and
he paid rewards for work he assigned and challenges he issued. The house at
Darien was a summer camp unto itself. He taught the children to fish, sail,
swim, and hike (with candies "left by elves" along the trail for the younger
children to follow). He even rigged up a trapeze. He told his older boys,
"Don't you let me catch either of you coming back [from school] perfect in
deportment!" Every Sunday night all the children queued up by the telephone to talk to their ailing grandmother in Detroit, whom they called "Farmor," Swedish for "father's mother."

All that said, he imposed a deliberateness to the playtime, which often de-
pleted much of its joy. Everything required a purpose. He provided little understanding when challenges went unmet, and he would not listen to excuses
for work left undone. The creative writing exercises became nagging assignments. As his father had with him, Lindbergh often teased his children to
tears. There were hugs but no kisses. And, remembered Ansy of the endless

lists of chores and rules left for everybody in the household to fulfill and fol-low, "There were only two ways of doing things—Father's way and the wrong way."

For Anne there were no loud demands, only quiet expectations and com-plaints when they were not fulfilled. Her duties included keeping precise household books, accounting for the pettiest cash expenditures. It was not strictly a question of being cheap. Indeed, Anne Morrow Lindbergh, with her healthy trust fund, enjoyed shopping for new clothes; and, on occasions, her husband was not above buying her a piece of jewelry from Tiffany's. It was just that her purchase of a $300 black Karakul coat had to be entered in the small notebooks alongside the thirty-five cents spent on shoe repair, fifteen cents on rubber bands, or the twenty cents on tinsel for the Christmas tree. Each month the accounts were tallied and typed along with the amounts spent on food and domestic wages, then transferred to larger balance sheets, on which they were categorized for grand totaling at the end of the year. Be-cause they had lived in so many different houses, Anne was periodically re-quired to compile household inventories, listing every article of clothing, item of furniture, book title, blanket, and piece of silver they possessed. Their kitchen inventory was always kept up-to-date, down to the tea strainer and the "8 glasses with black design"—which had been cottage-cheese con-tainers.

Anne was a far gentler parent than Charles, ruling by kind example rather than intimidation. In his absences, there was a palpable relaxation at home. "He must control everything," Betty Morrow observed in her diary, "every act in the house." Each of the children learned to deal differently with his despotism, as their personalities reflected. Jon was the most deferential, almost always following his father's rules; as a result, his grandmother ob-served, "he withdraws into himself." Land learned to anticipate his father's demands, finding it easier than rebelling; and his mind often wandered. Even as a preschooler, Scott often escaped into his own world. Ansy was already expressing defiance and exhibiting nervous tics. One of Jon's schoolteachers commented in a report card on his behavior, which, in fact, summarized the way all the Lindbergh children felt about their father: "The children like him," she wrote, "but are puzzled by his dreaminess, abruptness, and peri-odic indifference to them when he is involved in his own plans."

"They are all apprehensive," Betty Morrow wrote of her Lindbergh grandchildren, "—never knowing when their father will fall upon them. The atmosphere—the tension in the house is so terrible—that when C. goes off for a day or two—everybody sings!" Increasingly, Anne found herself alone in her room, crying.

Lindbergh hired a series of secretaries, each of whom was given a "pol-icy" statement to study before starting work. "I want to create the impression that I am difficult to reach and away much of the time" was its basic premise. "I will leave posted, by the telephone, the policy to be followed for the day in regard to calls by phone or door, business details, etc." it read. Even when he was at home, he had what he called "away" days, on which he was to be considered "out" except for those people on the prescribed list.

In late 1946—at age forty—Anne became pregnant for the seventh time. But her morning sickness did not seem the same as with her prior children. Upon the recommendation of her friends Mrs. John Marquand and Mrs. Philip Barry, she visited their physician, a doctor from Englewood who practiced in the city. Renowned as much for his bedside manner as for his medical ability, Dr. Dana W. Atchley discovered that Anne had gallstones. He said the remedial operation was perfectly routine but that it could affect her pregnancy. In the gentlest way, Dr. Atchley asked her to consider an abortion.

After discussing the situation with Charles, Anne elected to proceed with her pregnancy, postponing any surgery until such time that it became mandatory. Then shortly before Christmas—"apparently for no reason at all"— Anne miscarried. "I did nothing consciously to cause it," Anne confided to her sister Con, "—though I suppose one could make out a good case for it being the subconscious just simply rejecting it. But I cannot help but taking it as an act of mercy." On Valentine's Day, 1947, she underwent the necessary surgery—suddenly panicking, thinking she might die.

The operation went without incident, but the experience proved profound in unexpected ways. Anne had discussed her preoperative fears with Dr. Atchley, and he displayed rare qualities of wisdom, humor, and "dry compassion." When Anne tried to describe these conversations with her husband, he found them difficult to comprehend. "But you're not the kind of person who needs to go to anyone for help," he said. "You're the kind of person *other* people go to for help." Anne agreed with him only to end the conversation, for she had long felt otherwise.

During the next few weeks of recuperation, Anne and Dr. Atchley continued their dialogue, which became more intimate—often about Anne's role as an artist and a woman. He told her that she had "every attribute of an artist except one—& that was the conviction that it was more important to cultivate one's own garden than anyone else's." She countered that she felt that was true of most women; but Dr. Atchley begged to differ, suggesting that this was not about gender so much as about her upbringing—that, as Anne realized, "I had been made to feel that what I did for others was all right but what I did for myself was wrong." Anne had never met anybody with such piercing insight.

These conversations—usually held during Charles's long absences—made Anne realize how much she could not discuss with her husband. Having bottled up most of her sorrow and anger for decades, Anne reached out for confidantes. She had long maintained regular correspondences with her mother, sister, sister-in-law, and a handful of old friends. She wrote regularly to her mentor from Smith, Mina Curtiss, and from Cranbrook, Janet de Coux. Like Charles, she kept all their letters and made carbon copies of all her penned replies, which supplemented the diaries she maintained. She received fan letters every week, picking up new followers every time she published a book, article, or poem. Some admirers proved so persistent in either their praise or their pleas that Anne simply could not resist replying. Every now and then, Anne would select one of them and reveal an aspect of her personality long submerged, a doleful little girl who needed a shoulder to cry on.

Shortly after her release from the hospital, Anne left for Phoenix, where she stayed alone in an inn and relaxed. A few weeks later, in April 1947, Charles joined her, and they enjoyed several happy days together. One night, they were invited to Taliesin West, Frank Lloyd Wright's desert estate, by the eighty-year-old master himself. In his *Autobiography,* Wright had recently called Lindbergh "a square American," praising his integrity and forthrightness during the prewar years. "And," he added, "this goes for his brave little wife." Anne spent her time in Phoenix in constructive thought, sitting at night on top of the flat roof of her cottage, thinking of the mirador in Cuernavaca and how her life had "catapulted" since then. She wondered, "what have I made of it? & will I ever write again? & what I have learned this winter?"

Charles tried to answer her questions by challenging her to write about the changing world. After engaging her with the idea that "contact with post-war Europe was essential to an understanding of all life today, that Europe gave something vital but intangible"—without which nothing less than Christianity, Western Civilization, and Democracy were at stake—he suggested to both Anne and *Reader's Digest,* with its ten million readers, that she write a series of articles on postwar Europe, pieces that would require her traveling abroad for a month or two.

Shortly after they returned to Connecticut, the assignment came through. "It is, of course, a wonderful offer—I can go anywhere I want, write what I want, & they take care of all transportation, expenses, etc.—and facilitate everything. It is an ideal way to go," Anne wrote Farmor. "And yet it is such a decision for me to go & has taken a lot of courage. I hate to leave Charles & the . . . children . . . and I feel so shy meeting strange people." But she knew Charles wanted her to go.

On August 1, 1947, Anne sallied forth, traveling across France, Germany, and England—big cities as well as small towns—for the next nine weeks. It was a depressing journey, as she witnessed destruction and deprivation on a scale worse than she had imagined. "The basic values of our civilization," she observed in one piece, "are crumbling away like this rubble." Anne often wrote home of the difficulties of the trip, but her newsy letters revealed a growing inner strength at being able to take care of herself. "I have been lonely," she wrote Charles just days before boarding the boat home, "it has been difficult. I have made mistakes & yet it has been one of the big things in my life. Of all the things you have given me in life—& you have given me so much—perhaps this is one of the biggest. Your sending me out on this mission alone. (For I should not have done it if you had not pushed me a little & told me I *could* do it!) I am grateful to you for it. You are always giving me *life,* life itself. May I make something of it!"

Upon her return, Charles was delighted to see Anne spending so much time in the trailer. She wrote five pieces, which were published in *Life, Harper's,* and *Reader's Digest.* She even published a poem called "Second Sowing" in *The Atlantic Monthly,* which drew considerable notice, including a note of praise from Edna St. Vincent Millay. Charles lauded her as well, pleased to see that his plan had helped her flourish as an artist. But he still did not understand his wife's demons any better than he did before her European trip. He found her subsequent writer's block—aborting two novels and abandoning her poetry—utterly incomprehensible.

His nagging and all its attendant tension returned, which only set Anne back further. Melancholy often sent her rushing to Next Day Hill, where she divulged to her mother, for the first time, "the difficulties of her life—being married to such a powerful man as Charles who had never known a woman till he married." Things had been different when Anne did not assert herself. But her growing independence—which, ironically, came from his encouraging her to find her own voice—provoked greater intolerance. Over the next year, conditions worsened. The love Charles professed in his letters when he was away on his many trips for the Air Force, SAC, CHORE, and Pan American was as constant as the criticism he expressed when he was at home. Having missed the last two Christmases himself, Charles had taken to discouraging his sons from attending birthday celebrations at Next Day Hill, on the grounds that "all family celebrations are sentimental."

In Charles's absence, Anne sometimes allowed herself to cry through entire days. When he was home, he monitored her so closely as to infantilize her. "I want so much for you to think me a 'good girl,' " she would admit to him on days she was so frozen with panic that she could not write. That all his efforts were not enough to inspire her frustrated him even more; and he alternated between being her comforting muse and a cruel scourge. Worst of all, he became a shining example:

In Anne's absence and the months after her return from Europe, Charles committed to paper some of his thoughts of the past few years. "There are times in life when one feels an overwhelming desire to communicate belief to others, to band together with one's fellow-men in support of a common cause," he wrote of his latest impulse. Twice in the past he had felt such a desire—when he had been a young pilot and preached aviation, and a decade later when he spoke against American intervention in "Europe's internal wars." In 1948, with mankind "in the grip of a scientific materialism, caught in a vicious cycle where our security today seems to depend on regimentation and weapons which will ruin us tomorrow," he felt compelled to speak out for a third time.

He wrote close to twelve thousand words, which he divided into two parts. The first contained vignettes from his life, each with a moral. The day at Willow Run in 1943 when he almost went down testing a P-47 fighter because of a faulty pressure gage taught him that "in worshipping science man gains power but loses the quality of life." The day over the South Pacific in 1944 when he almost went down in his P-38 while confronting a Japanese Zero taught him that "without a highly developed science, modern man lacks the power to survive." And visiting Germany in 1945 taught him that "if his civilization is to continue, modern man must direct the material power of his science by the spiritual truths of his God." These experiences led to conclusions in the second part of the book, an essay aimed at breaking that grip of a scientific materialism whose values and standards "will lead to the end of our civilization."

The core of Lindbergh's argument was that "the quality of a civilization depends on a balance of body, mind, and spirit in its people, measured on a scale less human than divine." He warned that science had become as much a victim of its technologists as religion had of its fanatics, that just as the "spiritual truths of Christ and Lao-tzu were perverted by the temporal exploitation of Christian and Taoist creeds, the intellectual truths of great scientists are being perverted by the material exploitation of industry and war. Hiroshima was as far from the intention of the pure scientist as the Inquisition was from the Sermon on the Mount."

Besides preaching his brand of apocalypticism, Lindbergh had other compelling reasons to publish his tract. It would show that he had served in the war, that he had come to recognize the evils of Nazi Germany, and that he had found religion—a sect of his own culled from his understanding of "the sermons of Christ, the wisdom of Lao-tzu, the teachings of Buddha . . . the Bible of the Hebrews . . . the philosophy of Greece . . . the Indian Vedas . . . the writings of saints and mystics." He also used the book to preach against "the godless philosophy and armies of the Soviet." The man once hailed as a deity appeared eager to claim his place as a human entity and nothing more.

Upon completing his manuscript, Lindbergh asked his friend John P. Marquand, the most successful novelist of the day, to recommend publishers who might be open-minded enough to accept the work from a still controversial figure. Lindbergh sent his manuscript to Marquand's first choice, the firm of Charles Scribner's Sons. Within a few days, he received a telegram from Charles Scribner himself, expressing his eagerness to publish it. The contract required the author to accept a low ten percent royalty because of the costs involved in manufacturing so small a book without raising its price beyond the $1.50 they hoped to charge.

In consenting to the terms, Lindbergh asked that one clause be added to the contract, the extraordinary stipulation that twenty-five thousand copies of the book be exempt from royalty. He asked that the amount he would normally earn on those copies be added to Scribner's promotion budget. Unsure as to the prospects of so unusual a book from so recently reviled an author, Scribner's printed a cautious ten thousand copies.

Of Flight and Life was published on August 23, 1948, and its first edition sold out within a day. Another forty thousand copies were rushed into print and were gone in a few weeks. The overwhelming majority of the reviews were favorable, including mild astonishment at the quality of Lindbergh's prose; but the book did not completely rehabilitate him. *The New York Times Book Review,* while praising the book, could not help quarreling with a few sentences in his three-page preface, which suggested that Lindbergh had been less "partisan" during the America First period than he actually was. And so, reviewer John W. Chase concluded, *Of Flight and Life* "is the honest expression of one man's evolving responsibility and his new faith in a time of crisis. It carries emotional currents of high tension. For this reason, it should, perhaps, be approached not only with respect but with caution."

John P. Marquand, who had never been impressed with Lindbergh's intellect, wrote him that the book "has filled me with respect and amazement—respect for what you have said and for the clarity of your thought and amazement for your literary skill." Even one Bernhard Goldfarb wrote to tell him that for years, "I hated you like many others," but that upon reading *Of Flight and Life* he said to himself, "maybe after all he must be a great man." Tens of thousands had their faith in Lindbergh restored, thus readmitting him to America's pantheon. He would forever have his detractors; but so long as he avoided certain sensitive subjects, people generally kept a lid on their sentiments about him, silently deifying him or demonizing him. His mail turned decidedly friendly again.

Honors and favors also came his way. The Secretaries of the Armed Forces reminded Lindbergh that as a Congressional Medal of Honor winner, he was authorized to ride as a passenger on any scheduled military flight "as a further token of the appreciation of your country for the outstanding service you have rendered the Nation." The Order of the Daedalians, an organization dedicated to "serving the country and the cause of Air Power," elected Lindbergh an honorary member. The American Ordnance Association, comprised of industrialists who supported national defense, voted to give Lindbergh its highest award, the Crozier Medal. When General of the Air Force H. H. "Hap" Arnold died in January 1950, Air Force Secretary Symington requested that Lindbergh serve as one of a half-dozen honorary pallbearers at Arlington National Cemetery. The Smithsonian asked Lindbergh how he felt about moving the *Spirit of St. Louis* toward the opposite end of the North Hall of its Arts and Industries Building to make room for the newly arrived Wright brothers' plane; Lindbergh had helped settle the dispute between Orville Wright and the museum over its place in the timeline of aviation, and so he considered it nothing less than an "honor" for his plane to share airspace with its progenitor.

The Girl Scouts in New Canaan wrote Lindbergh that they wished to name their local "Wing Flight" after him—though he replied that he felt "strongly that it is best not to name such an organization after a living person." Lindbergh Junior High School in Long Beach, California, wrote that it wished to dedicate its 1947 yearbook to him. In 1951 Little Falls informed him that its newest educational facility was being named Charles Lindbergh Elementary School. Offers of honorary degrees, which he refused, once again streamed in—from such prestigious institutions as Dartmouth College and the University of Notre Dame.

This Lindbergh revival coincided with the twenty-fifth anniversary of his flight. Predictably, Lindbergh refused to participate in any commemorations of 1927; and he declined the many requests for interviews that year. "I hope you will understand," he politely explained to one reporter, "when I say that I am anxious to continue living quietly with my family, and therefore wish to avoid personal publicity wherever possible." To the journalist's executive editor at the Associated Press, he elaborated, "I doubt that it is possible for anyone who has not lived through long periods of intense personal publicity to realize fully the problems it creates and the difficulties involved. I believe that over the years I have come to value the freedoms of privacy as highly as you value the freedoms of the press."

There was, once again, talk of drafting Lindbergh to run for political office. He could not have been less interested, though politics still concerned him deeply. The night before the 1952 elections, in which General Dwight Eisenhower was expected to walk off with the Presidency, Anne Lindbergh gave her husband copies of several speeches by Ike's opponent. Lindbergh was so impressed with what he read that he cast his ballot for Adlai Stevenson, the first Presidential vote he had ever cast for a Democrat.

While Lindbergh refused most interviews, he did agree in 1949 to speak with Richard Davis of *Newsweek* after learning that the writer was favorably predisposed toward him. Davis's "Special Report" ran three pages, the bulk of which detailed Lindbergh's war record. That same year, Lindbergh corresponded with Wayne S. Cole, then a doctoral candidate at the University of Wisconsin, who was writing a history of the America First Committee. Cole would write several books on the subject, including one a quarter-century later entitled *Charles A. Lindbergh and the Battle Against American Intervention in World War II,* which took no sides in discussing the debate but which fully aired Lindbergh's views.

Lindbergh also accepted two of aviation's most prestigious awards. The first was the Wright Brothers Memorial Trophy, which he received in 1949 at the Annual Wright Dinner at the Aero Club of Washington. He used the occasion to speak about man's need to "balance science with other qualities of life, qualities of body and spirit as well as those of mind—qualities he cannot develop when he lets mechanics and luxury insulate him too greatly from the earth to which he was born." In this lyrical address, he applauded the pioneer spirit of the men they were actually celebrating that night: "The Wright brothers," he said, "balanced success with modesty; science, with simplicity. At Kitty Hawk, their intellects and senses worked in mutual support. They represented man in balance. And from that balance came wings to lift a world."

The other prize was the Daniel Guggenheim Medal, awarded to Lindbergh for "pioneering achievement in flight and air navigation" at the Honors Night Dinner of the Institute of the Aeronautical Sciences in New York on January 25, 1954. Lindbergh doubly appreciated the gold medal—first because he admired Daniel Guggenheim's crucial support of early aviation and rocketry, and second because it was presented by Harry Guggenheim, who was able to demonstrate that their recent political differences had not destroyed their "fast friendship." Again Lindbergh harped on the themes of materialism in the modern age. "Short-term survival may depend on the knowledge of nuclear physicists and the performance of supersonic aircraft," he said in accepting the medal, "but long-term survival depends alone on the character of man."

Weeks later, Lindbergh was notified of an even more startling honor. Air Force Secretary Harold Talbott had recently been considering ways of ensuring his own place in history, of being "remembered by the American people." His chief of Information Services, Colonel Robert Lee Scott, Jr., suggested, "Sir, it's very simple. There's a great man who made the greatest single flight that's ever been made in this world. . . . He became a Colonel in the reserves and they hadn't taken him any higher because he offended President Roosevelt when he came back and told the truth about what the Nazis had ready in the Luftwaffe. . . . All you gotta do," Scott said of Lindbergh, "is make him a General." The awarding of such rank required Presidential

nomination and Senate approval. Eisenhower seemed only too pleased to announce the appointment; and with even former enemies in the press supporting it, the Senate followed suit. On April 7, 1954, in a private ceremony
in his Washington office, Secretary Talbott swore him in as a Brigadier General.

Later that year, Lindbergh added even more to his prestige when he completed another book. "I have been working a little each day lately on an outline of an autobiography which I hope someday to complete," Lindbergh had
noted in his journals back in January 1939, when he and his family had
been living in Paris. "We," his own hastily composed rendition of his 1927
flight, had never sat right with him; and Lindbergh had been determined
ever since to "create a record that was as accurate" as he could make it
"without the pressure of time." In every spare moment across the next
decade—aboard transatlantic ships, on commuter trains, in a tent in the
New Guinea jungles, in a bomber returning from the North Magnetic Pole,
on an air base in Arabia, in a trailer on the Florida Keys, in the Carrels' house
on Saint-Gildas—he crafted the manuscript. He wrote at least six complete
drafts of the story, which opened with the historic flight's moment of conception—while flying the airmail in the skies south of Peoria—and closed
with his tumultuous arrival—sitting on the ground at Le Bourget and seeing
"the entire field ahead . . . covered with running figures!"

Parts of the book were rewritten as many as ten times. In the penultimate
draft, the manuscript took its most dramatic turn, as the author transposed
260,000 words of memoir in the past tense into a pulsing narrative in the
present indicative. Even two dozen sequences that preceded the central story
of the memoir and which were scattered throughout—his Minnesota and
Washington boyhood, his army and barnstorming experiences—were recast
as flashbacks in the new tense.

Not until the 1950s did Lindbergh show a word of the manuscript to anyone. Anne was the first to read it, and her criticisms were of "tremendous
help." Reminding him to maintain his own style by "remaining in character,"
she indicated his occasional lapses into overwriting. "Your style," she told
her husband, "is clipped—short sentences, precise—not careless. . . . Imagine you are speaking to me, not writing at all." By the fall of 1951, Anne was
putting in countless hours of her own editing the manuscript.

Pleased with the way they published *Of Flight and Life,* Lindbergh submitted *The Spirit of St. Louis* to Scribner's. While he had agreed to a lower
royalty than usual on the former book, he did not hesitate to ask for a higher
percentage than usual on this surefire bestseller. "I know that during the
early period of sales, advertising costs are a major item for the publisher," he
wrote young Charles Scribner, who had recently succeeded his father as head
of the company. "But if sales are high," he noted, as was the case with the

Lindberghs' other books about flying, "it is due in part to the reputation of the author entirely aside from money spent by the publisher in advertising. Here, I think that the author has a right to a share in the indirect results of his previous accomplishments." Lindbergh sportily agreed to a $25,000 advance and a fifteen percent royalty from the first copy sold, all proceeds of the book being entered into a trust for his children, with Anne serving as trustee. He knew it was less than he could have received on the open market.

Lindbergh's editor, John Hall Wheelock, was extremely enthusiastic about the manuscript, even more moved after a second reading—"not only by the way you have unfolded your story," he wrote the author, "but by the extraordinary beauty of the descriptions of sea and air, of cloud and sky. That passage through canyons of storm, fighting off sleep and death, haunted by voices out of some super-sensory world, is conveyed with the immediacy of reality itself." He responded to Lindbergh's request for "severe" criticism by recommending "fairly drastic cutting." Over the next two months, the author excised seventy pages, mostly from the flashbacks, which Wheelock felt distracted from the central story. Lindbergh did, however, reject Wheelock's suggestion to omit both a brief afterword that chronicled the rest of the events that occurred on the night of his arrival, and a comprehensive appendix comprised of the log of the *Spirit of St. Louis*'s subsequent flights and all the engineering data related to the plane's construction.

By the end of 1952, Lindbergh had engaged a literary agent, George T. Bye, to negotiate the first serialization and motion-picture rights to the book. With little effort, Bye procured a whopping $100,000 from *The Saturday Evening Post,* which condensed and serialized the work in ten installments under the title "33 Hours to Paris." The Lindbergh articles generated the largest sales in the magazine's history, selling out the expanded printings in most cities within two days—gathering almost two hundred thousand readers a week more than usual. The Book-of-the-Month Club chose *The Spirit of St. Louis* as its main selection for September 1953. And some of the biggest names in Hollywood began bidding for the film rights—Howard Hughes, King Vidor, Hal Wallis, George Stevens, and a hotshot young writer-producer-director named Sidney Sheldon. Samuel Goldwyn wined and dined the Lindberghs, then suddenly withdrew from the competition, never revealing why. In fact, his friend Arthur Sulzberger had warned him that negative press would probably surround the project because of Lindbergh's purported anti-Semitism.

In the few months before publication, Anne and Charles toiled over the galley proofs. "He was the most fussy of authors, living or dead," recalled Charles Scribner. "He would measure the difference between a semicolon and a colon to make sure each was what it ought to be. To him, every detail in the book has as much significance as if it were a moving part in his air-plane." Despite all the tinkering, the book never lost its magic.

Up to the end, Anne found she could not read it "without feeling a rush of tears to my eyes and throat." She asked herself why that should be and concluded, "There is something in the directness—simplicity—innocence of that boy arriving after that terrific flight—completely unaware of the world interest—the wild crowds below. The rush of the crowds to the plane is symbolic of life rushing at him—a new life—new responsibilities—he was completely unaware of & unprepared for. I feel for him—mingled excitement & apprehension—a little what one feels when a child is born & you look at his fresh untouched . . . little face & know he will meet joy—but sorrow too—struggle—pain—frustration." Just before publication, Lindbergh dedicated the book: "To A.M.L.—Who will never realize how much of this book she has written."

Scribner's wrapped the six hundred pages in a dark-blue jacket that depicted a starry night sky. The book also included maps, fifteen photographs, and endpapers which had been reproduced from an original aquatint by Burnell Poole entitled "The Epic of the Air." It depicted a mountainous range of ocean waves beneath a forbidding sky, in the midst of which one could discern the familiar lines of Lindbergh's little plane, appearing as little more than a speck.

The Spirit of St. Louis became an overwhelming bestseller and received only favorable reviews everywhere. By the end of the year, the Book-of-the-Month Club alone had sold one hundred thousand copies. Dominating sales lists everywhere, it sold another several hundred thousand copies in its first twelve months on sale. "A great ovation," Anne noted in her journals. While she had feared brickbats in the way of personal attacks thrown at him, he received only bouquets. "In consequence," she added, "there is a wave of excitement about him again."

The Lindberghs enjoyed their happiest Christmas in years. Charles's resurrection led to an "expansiveness" that Anne could hardly recall. The following spring, he received another unexpected feather in his already well-plumed cap. The Trustees of Columbia University informed General Lindbergh that he had been awarded the Pulitzer Prize. Another wave of congratulations ensued.

"Boom days are here again," a jubilant Anne wrote in her diary. "The Great Man—the Great Epic—the Great Author etc. etc. I am living in the aura of 1929 again. Only I am different. . . ."

17

DOUBLE SUNRISE

"I first heard the term 'double sunrise' during World War II, when
I was on islands of the South Pacific. . . . While the sun is still below the
horizon, clouds color in both east and west. If you are not certain of
your directions, you sometimes have to look carefully to be sure
whether the sun is going to rise on your right hand or your left."
—C.A.L. (in a letter) December 17, 1968

"JEALOUSY," ANNE HAD ONCE WRITTEN IN HER DIARIES, "is the unlived life in you crying out to be spent."

Four months after *The Spirit of St. Louis* took off, she confided to her private pages, "I envy C. his terrific drive though often I suffer the consequences of it. That terrific drive which he applies without discrimination to crossing the Atlantic, writing a book . . . or finding out the price of butter!"

Charles's winning the Pulitzer Prize in the spring of 1954 gnawed at her. She felt he deserved the award and that she should have joined him in his happiness. And yet, she confessed, "it inevitably caused me pain"—mostly because "I helped him write the book. I helped it to be that perfect. I know it never would have been that perfect without my help."

Anne found even more painful the likening of her husband's work to that of Saint-Exupéry. She could not bear to see her French idol diminished, not even by her husband. "The motivation of one was love, understanding, insight, compassion for human beings," she wrote of the Frenchman. "The motivation of the other is conquest—success—achievement. Both the act itself and the writing about the act—was an act of conquest over the impossible. This is noble, this is courageous, heroic, exciting, also very beautiful, worthy of praise, fame—success. But it is not everything."

And yet, Anne had to admit, Charles had written "HIS book"—"And this *is His* book no matter how much of me is in it—it is his book. He has put all of himself into it. Personality—emotions—thought—hours of work. He has written HIS book & I have never written *mine*. I know this." For that she blamed only herself—"*my* cowardice—*my* inhibitions—*my* laziness—*my* lack of centeredness & sureness—*my* unhappiness & gropings—that have kept me from writing it." After almost ten years of dabbling, Anne admitted to herself that she was not sure "her" book would ever be written. She was smarting too much to realize that most of it had, in fact, been put down on paper—in her diaries and letters and chapters she had abandoned over the years. She had only to stop struggling with the idea of writing it so that she could at last pull it all together.

Ever since Jim Newton had exposed the Lindberghs to Florida's west coast, Anne made a point of getting there every year during the final weeks of winter, often alone. As early as March 1948, on the unspoiled island of Captiva, she had begun to let her mind wander, collecting imagery. Shells, especially, captured her attention, as she began to see how each variety was a different kind of dwelling and could symbolize a different phase of life. Staying in a shabby, rambling house of an inn, she wrote Charles that she felt like a hermit crab, leading an extremely simple life in this "deserted shell." She said she also realized that the Florida beach "is not the place to work."

That phrase would become the opening of her book, a group of essays she began to compose in 1950 in order to "think out" her own "particular pattern of living," her own "individual balance of life, work and human relationships." She was calling her collection *The Shells,* each piece composed of observations drawn from a different shell. As she tentatively shared the first pieces with intimate friends and family, she realized that these discussions she was having with herself on paper spoke to other women, "young and old, with different lives and experiences—those who supported themselves, those who wished careers, those who were hard-working housewives and mothers, and those with more ease." Anne gradually discovered "that many women, and men, too, were grappling with essentially the same questions as I, and were hungry to discuss and argue and hammer out possible answers. Even those whose lives had appeared to be ticking imperturbably under their smiling clock-faces were often trying, like me, to evolve another rhythm with more creatives pauses in it, more adjustment to their individual needs, and new and more alive relationships to themselves as well as others."

Anne got especially involved writing about a shell that had been given to her, that of a double-sunrise—a delicate bivalve, each side of which "is marked with the same pattern; translucent white, except for three rosy rays that fan out from the golden hinge binding the two together." It made Anne think about relationships and how each half gets drawn apart into its more specialized and functional role. Considering all the angst she had endured in her own marriage, she wondered if the two increasingly disparate halves could ever be rejoined—"can the pure relationship of the sunrise shell be re-found once it has become obscured?"

She got a chance to answer her own question in March 1951, during a marital rough patch, when Charles and Anne accepted an invitation together from John and Adelaide Marquand to visit them at their winter getaway, Treasure Island, four miles out to sea from Nassau. With a new war brewing in Korea, Marquand enticed Charles with the many advantages of the house they had rented: "There is no telephone," he boasted, "and there is no radio, except one that belongs to the . . . help. There are no electric lights and no power gadgets. The rudimentary plumbing is supplied by rain water pumped by hand into the tanks. There are two good bathing beaches, and the reefs on the northern part of the island are excellent for spear fishing. We also have a boat with a motor, so we are not entirely out of touch from everything." Also staying in the sprawling Great House on the private, narrow island would be Ellen Barry and Dr. Dana Atchley.

It was one of the most important weeks in Anne's life, one which validated much of her recent work on *The Shells*. It also allowed Anne to observe her husband alongside her new physician friend and to draw comparisons. While Atchley had both a probing mind and a compassionate soul, Anne could not help agreeing with Charles that he was "the perfect example of the intellectual who has neglected the life of the body!" Meantime Anne watched Treasure Island bring out the boy in Charles, as he spent long sunny days in the water. "I have rarely seen C. as happy, as free—as released—as gay with people as this week," Anne observed. At night, he held his own, talking science with Atchley and books with Marquand—even though the host did find "the Lone Eagle pretty tough to converse with as he does not understand the light approach to anything." The Lindberghs took long walks together and sat alone under the stars; and seeing his "bronzed body in his tan shorts . . . on the brilliant white beach—with a long sword on his belt almost the length of his shorts—& a spear in his other hand"—reconnected her to the feelings for the shy golden boy with whom she had first fallen in love. Anne realized that relationships are in constant flux; but she could at last write with surety, "The sunrise shell has the eternal validity of all beautiful and fleeting things."

Anne's week came to a perfect end during her final afternoon's walk. Roaming out to the far beach, she turned over a piece of dried seaweed and uncovered an argonauta—a rare, transparent, feather-light mollusk shell. She had just used that very object as the symbol for the next stage of relationships in *The Shells*—that period after the double-sunrise and the oyster bed of home and children—when "Woman must come of age by herself."

Anne had recently tried to buy an argonauta but could not find one for sale. "And here," she wrote in her diary, "was one given to me—at the moment I had ceased to look—or to want. Here was a gift from the sea—tossed up at my feet. Something I had never expected to find."

The holiday glow did not linger. Back home, the Lindberghs promptly reverted to their roles of victim and critic, as she returned to the oyster bed and he to his life as an argonaut. Anne was further beset by her brother's persistent struggle with mental illness—"a shattering problem," Anne divulged to one of her adoring correspondents, "which continues & has absorbed so much of my time & my emotional capacity for the last two years. It has taken all the extra emotional reservoir left over from my children & my husband." As much as anything, it kept Anne from completing her book. And then, Dwight Jr.'s severe condition unexpectedly solved many of Anne's problems.

Morrow had been diagnosed as schizophrenic. Believing he was a lighthouse having trouble beaming his light (or, other times, that he was all the saints rolled into one), he was sent to a closed hospital, where doctors believed his condition would only worsen. Although separated from her husband, Margot Morrow was determined to continue her search for someone who might aid in his recovery.

She heard about a controversial psychiatrist in Pennsylvania named Dr. John N. Rosen, who reputedly saved hopeless patients through radical treatments. Anne and her mother interviewed him and were greatly impressed. "It was really breath-taking," Betty Morrow wrote of the meeting, "—his confidence—his unprofessionalism & his sympathy. We came out gasping—but convinced that here was someone whom we must have work w. Dwight."

The maverick doctor insisted on Morrow's being checked out of the hospital and set up in an apartment with a couple who would see that all his needs were met. Rosen said he would work with him every day for six weeks. The patient was far from cured after a month and a half of therapy, but after two years he stopped hallucinating. From then on he was able to reintegrate his mind, ultimately earning a Ph.D., securing a teaching position, and remarrying.

During this period, Rosen recognized Anne's fragile mental state and suggested he treat her depressions as well. She cautiously agreed, reared like the rest of her clan to resist admitting to imperfection. But her unhappiness was undeniable, and she came to crave the appointments, which she attended every day of the summer of 1952. "I spent a year or two in therapy just crying," she would later admit.

The sessions caused a series of "storms" at home all summer, arguments with Charles about everything from the way she undercooked the asparagus to her failure to complete her book. The unspoken subtext of his anger seemed to be her growing need for analysis. While Charles had long been sympathetic to his brother-in-law's plight—"He put all his name and fame at my disposal," recalled Margot Morrow of that period when she was desperately searching for somebody who could help Dwight—he failed to understand why Anne would want to discuss her most personal problems with a stranger. He suggested that it was a sign of weakness. Charles would never admit that he was afraid of what she might say about him or, worse, that he was losing control over her—that she might truly become, as her chapter on the argonauta suggested, a creature of her own free will, learning "how to stand alone."

Anne began to welcome Charles's absences, finding them a relief from his relentlessness. His departures were hard on her, because she found herself "a quiver of anxiety," wondering if she would "be able to do it all without him—*as he wants?*" But the days his trips got canceled and he was stuck in Darien with his pent-up energy were harder. He would spend hours at a time fussing over legal matters, insurance policies, and finance. He compiled lists of "Things to Do," which he divided into three categories—Current, Immediate, and Near Future. Those done, he might busy himself with household inventories or making lists of all the planes he had ever flown, places the house trailer had been, books he had read. Or he might refine the packing list for his trips, sorting and weighing each item until he had reduced his standard load to a mere twenty pounds—and that included a dark-blue dacron suit, shoe polish, medical supplies (carried in a sock), stationery, dictionary, maps, his disguise of a beret and eyeglasses, even emergency food.

There was always mail to catch up on, most of which he never read, responding only to envelopes from recognizable senders or those letters which his secretary deemed important. A few biographies of him were in the works, in which he took no part except in discouraging friends from speaking to any of the authors. On the other hand, he made himself available to authors writing about Robert Goddard, Dwight Morrow, his grandfather Dr. Land, Henry Ford, and the Isolationist movement. And he was always in the middle of a new book himself. Even stopping for a red light, his children observed, he would instinctively reach for a knife-sharpened pencil and the blue paper pads he ordered from Bristol-Streeter in New York to scribble fragments of his life.

His papers in order, he filled folders with pages of tasks for everybody in the house to perform, lists he would carry to meals and bark out to Anne and the children. It made everybody in the family uncomfortable, "as if the dentist were picking your mouth trying to find cavities," Anne wrote. She began to grasp Dr. Rosen's observation about "compulsive *outward* orderliness being a compensation for *inward* dis-orderliness."

Lindbergh's obsession with the Cold War distracted him from his internal strife, and trivial matters assumed grave importance. He sometimes got so worked up over the eventuality of a third World War that his mother-in-law thought he was "a madman!" Because he was away from home so often, he went so far as to prepare Anne to act alone in the event of a nuclear attack. Scott's Cove was very safe, he said, but should war break out, Maine would be safer. New York should be avoided at all costs as it was "a key target, and vulnerable both by air and sea"; and dental appointments should be canceled, as there was the Soviet threat of sabotaging the water supply. When Anne said the kitchen needed a new stove, Charles told her to postpone the decision on this "important and complicated subject" until they could analyze the purchase "from personal, economic, and military standpoints." Charles, Mrs. Morrow wrote in her diary, "needs a steady job."

There was no want of offers, most of which he refused—everything from teaching at M.I.T. to General Wedemeyer's recommending to President Eisenhower that Lindbergh serve as Secretary of Air. He did, however, maintain a series of positions on several boards, at which he worked indefatigably:

In April 1954, Lindbergh served on a commission created by Congress to select a permanent location for a United States Air Force Academy. The five members traveled eight thousand miles, inspecting twenty-one sites from the air and fifteen on the ground, before deciding on a location eight miles north of Colorado Springs. The selection prompted eighty-seven-year-old Frank Lloyd Wright to wire Lindbergh, "YOUR EYE FOR A SITE IS AS GOOD AS YOUR EYE FOR A FLIGHT."

For six years, Lindbergh served on scientific committees whose mission was to develop ballistic missiles. Well into the fifties, America assigned low priorities to such programs, while the Russians saw their value, achieving what Lindbergh considered "extraordinary results with spatial missiles— the first satellite in orbit, the first missile to the moon, the first photograph of the moon's back face." Among the dozen other members of the Intercontinental Ballistic Missiles Scientific Advisory Committee, a distressed Lindbergh became a vocal supporter of the development of long-range, nuclear-warhead ballistic missiles and an ardent spokesman for "the establishment and consistent support of a long-range space policy." Meetings of these Air Force Management committees kept Lindbergh on the go—from discussions with senior Air Force officials at the Pentagon to talks with senior officials of aircraft companies, RAND Military Advisory Group, and the technological giant Thompson-Ramo-Wooldridge in Southern California.

Turning to more mundane matters, Lindbergh filled stretches of unscheduled time with inspection tours on behalf of Pan American, trips almost entirely of his own devising. When he was not at office meetings in Manhattan on company business, Lindbergh inspected Pan Am flights and facilities around the world, taking several major trips a year. In 1953, he focused on the Caribbean; 1954, South America; 1956, the mid-East; 1959, South

Africa. During three weeks in 1955, he flew from Port of Spain in the West Indies to Rome, via San Francisco, Tokyo, Bangkok, Rangoon, Karachi, and Istanbul. With each trip, Lindbergh became less concerned with the cockpit than the cabin—meal service, the size of the PAA flight bag, hot versus cold towels. Lindbergh admitted that he was not the best judge of first-class amenities, as he preferred sitting in the "tourist" section of the plane, the less elaborate service granting him more time to sleep. Lindbergh accepted but one dollar a year (plus expenses) from Pan Am for all his work, until Juan Trippe insisted on a $500-a-month retainer. By the end of the decade, Lind-bergh's time away from home increased.

For Anne, their marriage had become something of a sham. She wrote page after page about the "agonies of mind & emotions—spirit" and the "banked bitterness" she felt toward her husband for not being there for her. Fortunately, Dr. Atchley always was. "Dana pulled me through," she wrote in her diary, ". . . kept me alive." Trapped in his own difficult marriage, with a quarrelsome wife, the physician made time for Anne in his office after his scheduled appointments. Between visits, he dashed off short notes to her on prescription-size slips of yellow paper, which he folded in half and mailed in plain envelopes. He found her replies, on cerulean stationery, fortifying enough to call "blue vitamins." By the end of 1953, he admitted that the most cheering thought during his dark hours that year had been the emer-gence of Anne waving "goodbye to [her] lifelong pal, guilt" and realizing her potential. Anne completed *The Shells*; and in the spring of 1954, when a let-ter from a publisher she had met five years earlier invited her to submit her manuscript, she did.

Kurt Wolff had been a publisher in Germany before he found much of his inventory being tossed into the Nazi bonfires of 1933. This half-Jewish bib-liophile found refuge in France and Italy before emigrating to America in 1941. Within a year, he had started Pantheon Books, which began in his Washington Square apartment. Pantheon quickly distinguished itself not only as the translators and publishers of André Gide, Paul Valéry, and C. G. Jung, but also as the creators of physically beautiful books, featuring the work of such artists as Alexander Calder, Ben Shahn, and Marc Chagall. Publishing "world literature" in the American marketplace had kept Pan-theon a small and financially modest house; and Anne felt the courtly Wolff—a friend of her favorite author, Rainer Maria Rilke—would be a sympathetic reader, the first publisher to whom she would expose her fifteen-thousand-word manuscript.

The day after reading it, Wolff wrote the author, "I need not tell you that it is a lovely and touching book—written with that scrupulous care and workmanship which distinguishes you . . . I think you have made the case of women in this country, in our times, poignantly clear." With few suggestions to offer, he said, "if you see any way of confiding this book to us, we would try to translate it into a printed shape appropriate to its contents. I would be both proud and happy to have this privilege. But I will bring no pressure to bear on a conscience as delicate as yours." He did not have to.

By fall, Anne was correcting galleys of her retitled book, announced in Pantheon's Spring 1955 catalogue as *Gift from the Sea*. Anne's expectations for so personal and slender a book—not even one hundred undersized pages of text—were naturally low. She was resigned to its quiet publication in the shadow of Charles's persisting success with *The Spirit of St. Louis*.

Gift from the Sea blossomed into one of the most phenomenal triumphs in publishing history. It sold six hundred thousand copies in hardback, ranking number one on the bestseller list for a year; paperback sales exceeded two million copies. Pantheon enjoyed its first great financial windfall, paving the way for such future bestselling authors as Pasternak, Lampedusa, and Günter Grass. But it was this small American book that put the internationally celebrated publishing house on the map, continually requiring new editions and translations, continuing to make "religious" bestseller lists forty years after its publication.

Anne Morrow Lindbergh's book spoke to a century of women. It bridged the "victories" attained by feminists of her mother's generation with those of the Women's Liberationists of her daughters' generation. "Perhaps the great progress, humanly speaking, in these past twenty years, for both women and men, is in the growth of consciousness," she would observe on the book's twentieth anniversary. That, she believed, was largely the result of men and women talking to each other, "openly and honestly, often arguing and challenging, but at least trying to explain what they felt could never be explained." For the generation of postwar housewives and mothers—whom she called "the great vacationless class"—*Gift from the Sea* opened that dialogue.

Sadly, the two foremost feminists in Anne's life did not live to see the publication of her book. On September 7, 1954, after years of suffering from Parkinson's disease, Evangeline Lodge Land Lindbergh died at the age of seventy-eight. Unhappy in her youth and in her marriage, she had struck out on her own as a teacher in the wilds of Minnesota, and later in the Detroit school system, never allowing herself to be trapped. And yet Anne puzzled for a long time over her years of peculiar behavior, realizing decades later that Evangeline had been, no doubt, chemically imbalanced. Anne and Charles met in Detroit for her simple funeral service in the old country church on Orchard Lake, where Evangeline's grandfather Lodge used to preach and where she and "Brother" worshipped as children. She was buried in Pine Lake Cemetery, amongst her kin. Charles never delved into the sources of his mother's troubles, for it would have meant prying into his parents' marriage—a Pandora's box he chose never to open.

Three months later, Anne's mother suffered a stroke, which took her speech and left her partially paralyzed. A few weeks after that, she suffered a second stroke and her condition deteriorated. After a life of service—to family, schools, community, and church—Elizabeth Cutter Morrow died at the age of eighty-one.

While Charles took enormous pride in the success of his wife's book, he was not present to witness it. He traveled more that year than any in his life—eleven times across the Atlantic and once across the Pacific, in addition to various trips within the Americas. His repeated abandonments made Anne question her own book's sincerity. "There is a terrible irony in it with *Gift from the Sea* heading the best-sellers week after week, preaching 'Solitude—Solitude!' she wrote in her diary. "Here I am, having *just what I say I want* & it does not seem to be the answer! Then is the book all 'hooey' as I sometimes feel? I don't think so, but the truth of it is not relevant to me at this moment in my life."

Having become the nation's most popular author emboldened Anne to publish the book she had dreamed of since childhood, a collection of her poetry. Pantheon released *The Unicorn and Other Poems: 1935–1955,* thirty-five selections, in September 1956. Most of the poems bespoke the artist's loneliness—images of barren trees, bolted doors, abandoned roads, broken shells. The book's final poem concluded with a couplet that revealed something of what her marriage had both cost her and provided her:

> *Blow through me, Life, pared down at last to bone,*
> *So fragile and so fearless have I grown!*

Anne's book was published to prominent reviews of considerable acclaim. Volumes of poetry seldom sold more than a few thousand copies; but Pantheon had printed twenty-five thousand copies before its September publication, and another forty thousand for the Christmas rush. It was not until January 1957 that anybody took serious issue with the book; and the result was a literary flap the likes of which had hardly been seen since *The Wave of the Future.*

Poet John Ciardi, poetry editor of *The Saturday Review of Literature,* came out of his corner swinging. "As a reviewer not of Mrs. Lindbergh but of her poems," he wrote, "I have, in duty, nothing but contempt to offer. I am compelled to believe that Mrs. Lindbergh has written an offensively bad book—inept, jingling, slovenly, illiterate even, and puffed up with the foolish afflatus of a stereotyped high-seriousness, that species of esthetic and human failure that will accept any shirk as a true high-C. If there is judgment it must go by standards. I cannot apologize for this judgment." He proceeded to lacerate her poems, practically line by line. Nobody had ever treated Anne Lindbergh that way. Even in the hysteria over *The Wave of the Future,* reviewers had gone out of their way to be polite.

The response from the *Saturday Review*'s readership was overwhelming. On February ninth, the magazine published a small sample of the hundreds of irate letters its editors had received, with demands for Ciardi to apologize if not resign. The debate grew into what the magazine's founding editor, Norman Cousins, would later call "the biggest storm of reader protest in the thirty-three-year history of the *Saturday Review.*" It swept into classrooms, cocktail parties, libraries, even onto the pages of other periodicals. Cousins himself felt compelled to take his critic to task, chiding him for applying the word "illiterate" to Mrs. Lindbergh or her books. "There are few living authors who are using the English language more sensitively or with more genuine appeal," he wrote. "There is in her books a respect for human responses to beauty and for the great connections between humankind and nature that gives her work rare distinction and that earns her the gratitude and loyalty of her readers, as the present episode makes clear." But he would take no action against Ciardi, standing instead by the independence of his reviewers' opinions.

In a subsequent essay, "The Reviewer's Duty to Damn: A Letter to an Avalanche," Ciardi explained that he had not written in anger. He simply felt that *The Unicorn* "was about to be taken seriously as poetry, whereas my conviction was that it had not taken itself seriously . . . *as poetry.*" Anne maintained public silence, letting her fans speak for her. She wrote one of them that she did not think much of the poems herself, and she thought they were "not worth his attack." She was hurt not so much by what Ciardi said as "by his *intention* to hurt—to tear down, to destroy." She believed he was actually attacking "the false overly sweet image of me in the public mind—a kind of 'Whistler's Mother,' complete with lace cap—rocking chair—folded hands & smile of acceptance." Anne hated that picture too. But, she had to accept, "the American public seem to like it & defend it to the teeth. Unfortunately he did not destroy it—only shellaced me more tightly in the frame." Except for one verse in the following December's *Atlantic Monthly,* Anne Morrow Lindbergh never published another poem.

While this latest encounter with fame sent Anne scuttling back to the privacy of her home and diaries, Charles found himself the object of attention all over again, in CinemaScope no less. After several years in development, the motion-picture version of *The Spirit of St. Louis* was released.

A Jewish émigré known for the sophistication, and often cynicism, of his films, Billy Wilder seemed an unlikely candidate to translate the innocent story of a Minnesota farmboy's flight to Paris. But even though the writer-director had difficulty understanding Lindbergh's earlier isolationism and his accepting a medal from the very country Wilder had fled, the "Lone Eagle" had remained one of his heroes since 1927. If nothing else, making a film whose primary action consisted of a man sitting alone in a cockpit for thirty-three hours presented a creative challenge. Impressed with the seriousness of Wilder's work as a filmmaker, Lindbergh had sold the rights to him and his producing partner, Leland Hayward, for $200,000 plus ten percent of the gross from the first dollar of receipts. In Hollywood hyperbole, the press announced that Lindbergh had sold the rights for a million dollars.

During the months he worked on the screenplay, Wilder frequently sent his subject letters full of questions, the specificity of which only reassured him that Wilder intended to produce as accurate a reenactment as possible. With that in mind, Lindbergh convinced Hayward and Wilder to hire his old barnstorming friend Bud Gurney, then flying DC-6's for United, to serve as the film's technical adviser. Gurney got to take a lucrative leave from his commercial flying, and Lindbergh had his oldest friend shepherding the filmmakers if ever they strayed too far from the truth.

Knowing Wilder's need for details, Lindbergh agreed to accompany him on a specially arranged visit to the *Spirit of St. Louis* at the Smithsonian. They flew together on a commercial flight, during which they encountered terrible turbulence. In their prior meetings, the generally voluble Wilder found Lindbergh so cold and dry that he restrained himself from dropping his fabled one-liners. But with the plane shaking so badly, he could not refrain from leaning over and saying, "Mr. Lindbergh, would it not be embarrassing if we crashed and the headlines said, 'Lone Eagle and Jewish Friend in Plane Crash'?"

Leland Hayward and his wife (like Lindbergh, known to her friends as "Slim") joined them at the Smithsonian, where the museum had erected scaffolding, with a stairway up to a platform right alongside the *Spirit*. It was an eye-opening visit for the filmmakers to see how crude the plane was—with an instrument panel, Slim Hayward noticed, "about as complicated as the dashboard of a Model T Ford." She got a peek at Lindbergh's character when he stepped into the plane and noticed the engine fuel primer knob was pulled out. "This is not supposed to be in this position, it should be thrust in," he muttered, as he gently pushed it.

Back in California, adviser Gurney wrote Lindbergh that he had become most concerned as to whom should be cast in the lead. "I haven't the remotest idea who should," he confessed, "but I feel most strongly that whoever he is—he should be able to reflect to some extent, the way you impressed those who knew you at that time." Gurney did not just mean tall and lanky but also decent and modest. Because it was the only role of any importance in the entire picture, it warranted a movie star. Closest to fulfilling all those qualifications was James Stewart, a decorated pilot and lifelong admirer of Lindbergh, who lobbied for the role. For all his qualities, however, casting Stewart forced the filmmakers to sacrifice one of the essential elements of the Lindbergh story—for no matter how effectively Hollywood's makeup men worked their magic, nobody could disguise the fact that the twenty-five-year-old "Lone Eagle" was being portrayed by a forty-seven-year-old.

The film's only other serious deviation from the truth was a dramatic device of Wilder's. Before he had met Lindbergh, Wilder had toyed with the idea of showing Lindbergh spending the night before his flight, as had been falsely rumored in 1927, with a waitress of easy virtue. It would provide the story with a love interest, thus allowing the audience to follow another character anticipating his return and giving Lindbergh someone to whom he could soliloquize during the flight. Realizing how untrue to character such an addition would be, Wilder dropped the idea. Still facing the problem of dramatizing a man alone in a plane, he decided to break the monotony as Lindbergh had in his book, by flashing back to earlier events in Lindbergh's life which led to his flight. The rest, he decided, could be helped by a fly— an insect that stows away and buzzes around Lindbergh's sandwiches—to which Lindbergh could speak during his journey.

Wilder insisted the fly was dramatically necessary to carry Lindbergh from New York to Paris. But once filming began, Stewart found its falseness so irritating that he said either the fly left the picture or he did. Hayward said it was too expensive to reshoot the scenes already "in the can," and so they struck a compromise: the fly could travel as far as Newfoundland. The rest of the shoot was fairly typical, plagued with bad weather and cost overruns. Building three replicas of Lindbergh's plane and capturing the aerial footage that comprises much of the film amounted to more than $1,000,000 of the picture's $6,000,000 budget.

Although nobody involved was fully satisfied with the finished product, Warner Brothers pulled out all the stops in promoting the film. The studio threw a gala premiere at the Hollywood Egyptian Theatre in Hollywood on April 11, 1957, and they released it across the country throughout the spring, hoping to capitalize on publicity for the thirtieth anniversary of the flight. In its extensive advertising and promotion, the studio struck a deal with Kellogg's, which agreed to pack a three-inch replica of the *Spirit* into each of twenty million boxes of Rice Krispies. Standard Oil, Wright Aeronautical, Goodrich, Pioneer Instruments, and several other companies boosted the film with their own "tie-in" advertising.

Most of it proved to be for naught. Jack Warner was reputed to have called *The Spirit of St. Louis* the "most disastrous failure" his studio ever had, and he could not figure out why. Much of the problem seemed to be that the phenomenon of Lindbergh had subsided. Beside the many who had grown indifferent or hostile toward him, baby-boomers were more interested in rocket ships and outer space than in some antique plane. Despite several striking vignettes, especially those capturing the moments before takeoff, the contained action of the drama could not offer the kind of widescreen thrills—or even an antagonist—that movie audiences had come to expect.

And there was, it turned out, difficulty getting the film booked into several theaters because of Lindbergh's anti-Semitic reputation. In fact, shortly before it was released, a Warner Brothers attorney contacted Lindbergh's lawyer and suggested that the general don his Air Force uniform, fly to Israel, and officially review their troops. Lindbergh, of course, refrained from participating in any of the film's promotion, including his appearance at the opening. He ignored the requests for him to speak at banquets, to grand-marshal parades, to reminisce on the radio, or to appear on television game shows.

Trying to attract as little attention as possible, he and Anne and their three youngest children quietly slipped into Radio City one afternoon that March to see the film. Despite the few deviations from the truth for dramatic or comic effect, Lindbergh found it true to the spirit of his journey. The audience surrounding him that day was enthralled. And about halfway through the film, during one particularly tense moment in the flight, eleven-year-old Reeve clutched her mother's arm and whispered, "He *is* going to get there, isn't he?"

While their father's monumental flight was occasionally discussed at home, the equally famous subject of the Lindbergh kidnapping was strictly taboo. It pervaded the air they all breathed, but it was never remarked upon . . . until that day when each Lindbergh child would come home from school confused for having learned about a brother who was never discussed. "Father," Ansy later related of her conversation, "took me aside, told me the story in just enough words to satisfy my curiosity, and never discussed it again. He made it very clear, however, that 'they caught the right man.' "

Every few years, the unmentionable topic surfaced within the family, as a young man claiming to be the long-lost "Lindbergh Baby" would write or simply appear in Scott's Cove. The letters went unanswered; the impromptu visitors were not permitted entry into the house. Charles would quietly walk the pretenders back to their cars, the children not knowing exactly what he said as he sent them on their way. With such insanity always lingering just around the corner, the Lindbergh children were raised knowing more than not to talk to strangers. From the time they were old enough to travel alone, they were trained in the ways of traveling incognito—using assumed names, disclosing their itineraries only to those who had to know, never drawing attention to themselves. More than sixty years after the crime, the Lindbergh family continued to receive communiqués from "the Baby."

The five surviving Lindbergh children grew up practical but naïve, generous but cautious, industrious but self-critical. Each was nurtured to be uncommonly kind and polite; and each developed, by nature, a strong sense of privacy. They all inherited their mother's sensitivity and their father's vitality; the boys were quietly virile, the girls vigorously feminine. Growing up in a home with much love but little affection, the Lindbergh children saw a marriage so strong that it often excluded them. They were all encouraged at early ages to get on with their own lives, to leave the nest. Eager to achieve, they instinctively entered arenas that interested their father but in which they would not have to compete against him or his memory.

Coming of age in the Lindbergh family meant subjection to a barrage of letters from the paterfamilias, lectures on everything from finance and sexuality to career and press relations. Although Jon left for Stanford University a skilled pilot, his passion since his youth at Illiec was the sea. Charles removed any burden of his own career from his son's shoulders by telling him, "I don't believe I'd take up aviation as a career. Many of the elements which attracted me to flying no longer exist. Thirty years ago, piloting an airplane was an art. The air was as full of adventure and the unknown as North America was a hundred years after Columbus. . . . I think I would follow your footprints to the oceans, with confidence that chance and imagination would combine to justify the course I set." In addition to his studies, Jon pursued mountain-climbing and skydiving, and joined the Naval Reserve. He seriously considered leaving Stanford after his second year, as his father had at Wisconsin; but Lindbergh reminded his son that his grades at Wisconsin had not left him any choice.

Jon remained at Stanford but moved out of his dormitory and into a tent he pitched in the Coast Range foothills a few miles from campus. After completing his degree in Biology, he did postgraduate work at the University of California at La Jolla and spent three years as a "frogman"—an Ensign with the U. S. Navy Underwater Demolition Teams who worked with explosive charges. Three months before graduating, he married a schoolmate, Barbara Robbins, the daughter of a Chicago mining engineer. Charles and Anne were thrilled with his choice and even more elated the following year when they became grandparents.

Shortly before the birth, Lindbergh offered an unsolicited opinion, that should the newborn be a boy it not be named Charles. "As you know," he wrote, "your older brother was named Charles, Jr. The naming of your first boy 'Charles' would, without doubt, create undesirable and dangerous newspaper publicity connecting him with the tragedy of 1932—which was probably itself caused by excessive publicity." The advice was not necessary. The young Lindberghs named the girl Christine. She was less than a month old before Charles had sent Jon a letter about setting up trust funds for his children.

Land followed Jon to Stanford and spent his summers working on ranches—jobs his father arranged—one in British Columbia, another in Liberia. A hard worker, he always declined invitations for special sleeping and eating privileges so that he could bunk and chow down with the cowboys and farmhands. By the time he graduated, he had decided to turn his passion into a profession. When he and Jon announced that they wanted to become partners in a ranch, which Land would run, their father supported it wholeheartedly. Lindbergh knew the attractions of that life but warned his two eldest sons, "You both have deep, reasoning, and penetrating minds that will probably become restless if you try to keep them inside the barbed wire of a cow pasture, even a big cow pasture." After debating both sides of the issue in a long letter—and asking the boys to consider a location far from a "major fallout area" in the event of an atomic war—Lindbergh asked to participate in the venture as well.

Growing up in less solitude than the elder siblings, the three youngest Lindbergh children paid a price for being celebrities' children. Young Anne was most sensitive to the problems of having a famous father, that feeling of being "different." A captivating, petite blonde, Ansy maintained an air of modesty, even as she excelled in her studies, athletics, and music, playing both flute and piano; but she often felt all eyes were on her because she was a Lindbergh. "I wish I were the daughter of a shoemaker!" she angrily said to her father one day, explaining that a reporter from *McCall's* was writing up a dinner her Latin class was giving, only because the first Lindbergh daughter was part of the event.

Worse for her than her father's apparent omnipresence was his repeated absence. Years later, Ansy reread diaries she had kept in the 1950s and was astonished at how little there was about him, even though, she later noted, "I remember clearly that I never stopped thinking about him." For two of those years, she used to write letters to an imaginary friend named Carolyn, the salutations of which she shortened to "Dear Cal." It did not occur to her until many years later that she was actually writing to Charles A. Lindbergh—C.A.L. In 1958, she left for Radcliffe.

Scott Lindbergh was the most complicated of the Lindbergh children, the most sensitive of the boys. The stories he used to write as a child were invariably full of magic and exotic backgrounds; at the same time, he was always intrigued by practical problems. With great admiration, Charles wrote of him to Anne, "I have never known anyone, adult or child, with his ability to pull up out of what seem hopeless depths—he starts right in at times I would have said, 'To Hell with it, there's another morning coming tomorrow, and I'm going to get a night's sleep'—and he usually ends up successfully." And yet there was a growing restlessness within Scott, spurts of quiet defiance that Charles felt he had to squelch. He came down hardest on him.

Anne took up his cause. For one of the first times, she stood up to Charles, insisting that it was detrimental to denigrate Scott so relentlessly. "Did your Father . . . treat you like this?" she asked rhetorically, not knowing that C.A. had been worse. Anne insisted that "Scott needs support & not knocking down all the time." Charles countered that "Scott must learn to think—not to be careless. . . . His life may depend on it," especially in this dangerous new age. "Machinery," he said, "doesn't forgive."

"Neither," Anne snapped back, "does the unconscious." In great anger she asked, "What do you think it does to a person to have everything he does called wrong?" In Scott's case, it became something of a self-fulfilling prophecy, as he was always losing wallets and articles of clothing, showing up late, procrastinating. He felt he was not popular at school, that he was considered a "card," yet another reputation he had to live up to.

The youngest child, Reeve, fought a losing battle all her life. With big blue eyes and blonde ringlets, hyperarticulate from the moment she could speak, her primary task seemed to be in corraling her straying family members. As a toddler, she once told her mother, "When you . . . find Father, you tell him he must come back *sometime*." Her attitude hardly changed over the years.

Lindbergh related better to his children as they became adults, finding them more interesting as they grew more independent. Such was not always the case with his wife. The new social life Anne was creating for herself hardly engaged him. It seemed stuffy, full of overly refined friends with little practical experience in the world, people prone to analyzing the subtext of everything and talking endlessly about "relationships." "You have so many orchids in your life," he once complained to her. "You should collect a few cabbages."

Anne did not disagree. She was aware that she found solace playing analyst and nursemaid to a lot of effusive women. She also found herself, for the first time, opening up to men. Several of her repressed gentlemen friends found this sudden emotional availability like catnip. The husband of one of Anne's best friends launched into his own private correspondence with her, pouring out his heart; and Corliss Lamont, who had been carrying the torch for Anne since childhood, resurfaced in her life, professing his undying love for her. Failing to see his wife's need for admirers, Charles had little use for these people who, he felt, were wasting Anne's time with their problems. He called them "lame ducks."

Lindbergh even lumped Dr. Atchley into that category. And so he paid no attention to the regular exchange of Atchley's little yellow notes for Anne's "blue vitamins." He did not know they spoke almost every morning, quietly ministering to each other's loneliness. On top of her frequent visits to his office, they began to appear in public together, at dinner parties, restaurants, and the theater. Katharine Hepburn, a friend and patient of Dr. Atchley, occasionally saw them on the town together. "But, of course," she presumed, "they were both too respectable to do anything about their feelings." Miss Hepburn was wrong.

Englewood society buzzed that Atchley's marriage had soured because his wife had taken to mistreating him in public in retaliation for a secret affair in which he was engaged. "Nobody ever knew with whom," corroborated writer James Lord, who had been raised in the New Jersey town. While the doctor's Manhattan waiting room had become a harem of admirers—including such desirable women as Hepburn, Garbo, and Nancy "Slim" Hayward—Dr. Atchley had fallen in love with Anne Lindbergh.

The friendship of these two longing souls blossomed into a love affair in 1956 and continued for the next few years. "I wish I could take a nice long walk in the dry cold air and come back to a warm fire and a martini (or two), and then talk, talk, talk," he wrote in one of his missives at the peak of their relationship. "I am so full of people in trouble . . . and your wit, warmth and wisdom would solve everything." Most of his notes during this period were discreet effusions about how much he craved her company and was frustrated when they were apart. "I found myself urging you not to be late tomorrow," he wrote her in March 1956. "I am going to join A. A. (only the A. isn't for alcoholics)."

Anne divulged her adultery only to her sister and a handful of other confidantes. Her daughter Ansy stumbled across it one day shortly before starting Radcliffe and always wondered whether her discovery had been accidental. She noticed an unopened letter on a table addressed to "Anne Lindbergh" and assumed that she was the addressee. "I was in the middle of reading what was obviously a love letter," she later recounted, "when Mother came in and said, 'I believe that's mine.' " Only afterward did her unembarrassed mother comment, "You should not have seen that."

Many years later, Reeve Lindbergh would comment on the difficulty it must have been for Ansy to grow up in her mother's shadow while carrying the same name. It was perhaps more difficult for their mother, going through menopause, to see her beautiful and brilliant young daughter come of age. "I always felt," Ansy recalled, "that it was important to Mother that I know about her affair with Dr. Atchley. My sense," Ansy said, "is that Father never knew . . . or, rather, never chose to know. He knew that Mother loved him and would never leave him. And that was all he needed to know."

In the heat of the relationship, during the summer of 1956, Anne lost her wedding ring; and the Freudian implications were not lost on her. "There are no accidents in Psychiatry," she wrote her sister Constance.

A few months later Anne rented an apartment in New York City, two small rooms at 146 East Nineteenth Street, between Third Avenue and Irving Place. She was abandoning neither her house nor her family in Connecticut; it simply provided her "the new frame for seeing people & a place to escape to for a night." Dr. Atchley became a frequent visitor, for quiet dinners and martinis as well as the occasional breakfast they might host for their most intimate friends. The notes that continued to pass between them suggest deep, fulfilling love, what Atchley wrote was "one outstanding reason why I am glad I was born . . . a wonderful thing to happen to a human being—and so few are so lucky." After they saw the motion-picture version of *The King and I* together, Atchley found himself humming the song "Hello Young Lovers," a wistful recollection of one in middle age recounting, "All of my memories are happy tonight, for I've had a love of my own." The Rodgers and Hammerstein musical moved Anne as well and seemed to play a role in her making a decision about her domestic situation.

By late 1958, Anne's life was considerably brighter than it had been at the start of the decade. She was even back at work, trying her hand at fiction again. Only her marriage remained problematic, and to a few friends, such as Alan and Lucia Valentine, she raised the option of divorce. But another ballad from *The King and I* kept playing in her ear, a song in which Lady Thiang, the mother of the King's oldest son, describes Anna Leonowens's feelings for the self-contained King of Siam.

> *The thoughtless things he'll do*
> *Will hurt and worry you*
> *Then, all at once, he'll do*
> *Something wonderful.*
>
> *You'll always go along,*
> *Defend him when he's wrong*
> *And tell him when he's strong,*
> *He is wonderful.*
>
> *He'll always need your love*
> *And so he'll get your love*
> *A man who needs your love*
> *Can be wonderful.*

Anne recommitted herself to her husband. It was not the song, of course, that changed her thinking. It was more, as her daughter Reeve commented on Anne's general behavior, that "Mother enjoyed wearing her hairshirt—finding pleasure in the misery of situations." Although her marriage continued to cause her considerable pain and unrest—literally, headaches, indigestion, and sleeplessness—she wrote her sister, "I must accept the fact that my husband is as completely different from me as he can be—gets his stimulus differently, his contacts with people differently, his refreshment differently." She realized that in some ways they were "badly mated." But looking back on thirty years of marriage, she realized not only that she did not want it to end but also that she evidently had the kind of marriage she wanted. She tamped her affair with Dana Atchley down to a warm friendship.

"There were two suns in our solar system," Reeve once remarked of the experience of growing up Lindbergh. From the end of 1958 forward, as often as not, those two suns would rise on any given day over two separate continents.

18

ALONE TOGETHER

"Real freedom lies in wildness, not in civilization."
—C.A.L.

"C. IS NOT GOING TO CHANGE HIS PATTERN OF BEING AWAY from home most of the time," Anne explained to her diary on February 12, 1959. "I must plan—as a widow—to augment my life." She realized this meant more than gardening, shopping, and spending additional time with her family to "gay up life." She would have to get a new dog for protection and start collecting single men who could escort her to dinner, the theater, and ski slopes. "It is all rather hollow," Anne admitted, facing her Hobson's choice of an occasional husband or none at all. Since the beginning of their storybook romance, the Lindberghs had never been so estranged.

As each of the children left his dominion, Charles became increasingly independent, footloose. Barnstorming the world, he had not seemed so vigorous since his youth. Psychiatrist John Rosen believed he was "running away from old age" and "intimacy." Having completed her therapy with Dr. Rosen, Anne felt generations of Lindberghs had kept themselves in perpetual motion to keep from examining their feelings. She believed Charles's compulsive need to travel was related to the loss of their firstborn, whose death he never fully mourned.

In the spring of 1959, Anne considered an offer from Kurt and Helen Wolff, who were then being eased out of Pantheon Books. Temporarily retiring to Zurich, they asked Anne to spend a quiet summer with them. "One should be pampered from time to time," Helen wrote her, "the soul needs it as much as the body." Before she could commit, Charles coopted the plan. He proposed instead that they rent their own chalet together in Switzerland, which had become central to his European inspection tours for Pan American. Anne figured she stood a greater chance of being with her husband away than at home.

On July ninth, Lindbergh met his wife at the Geneva airport in a Volkswagen he had bought, then drove almost four hours, north around the lake through Lausanne and Montreux and down the Rhone Valley into the mountain village of Les Paccots sur Châtel St. Denis in the canton of Vaud. It was too dark for Anne to see much as they twisted through vineyards, orchards, and dark streets of tiny Swiss villages. Then Charles took an even more obscure back road to their house through a barnyard, getting stuck in a manure pile. Exhausted from a long day of travel and a wilting European heatwave, Anne squeezed out of the car into a new cement "apartment-house" of a chalet. The Lindberghs were on the third floor, a few simple rooms with a modern bath across the hall. It all seemed a high price to pay just to spend some time with her husband; but when Anne woke at noon her mood instantly brightened. The breathtaking view out her window revealed the deep valley in which they were nestled, between the Rhone below and snow-capped mountains above. Before the day had ended, Anne had visited the castle where Rilke had written his final poems and the little churchyard in which he was buried.

The Lindberghs had not been ensconced in "balcony living" a week before the Wolffs invited them to meet one of their authors, the renowned Swiss psychologist Carl Gustav Jung. "The great old man rather likes distinguished visitors, particularly Americans," they wrote Anne. "And I am sure you and Charles would find him fascinating." Both Lindberghs eagerly accepted the invitation. Anne was especially interested in his departure from Freudian analysis and his theories of the collective unconscious as manifested in archetypal images and symbols.

They met the "old wizard," as Anne described him, at his lakeside home in Bolligen. Charles at once felt "elements of mysticism and greatness about him—even though they may have been mixed, at times, with elements of charlatanism." Sitting in his small drawing room, Lindbergh asked the seventy-five-year-old Jung why he chose to live down by the water instead of up in the mountains. Jung explained his connection to the lake at their side, how its depths brought to mind different levels of the human subconscious. Helen Wolff was as interested in the question as in the answer. She thought to herself: "the eagle and the fish."

Jung abruptly changed the subject to flying saucers. "I had expected a fascinating discussion about psychological aspects of the numerous and recurring flying-saucer reports," Lindbergh later recorded. But he found, to his astonishment, that Jung believed all the reports and was no more interested in the psychology of the phenomenon than he was in learning any facts about it. When Lindbergh told him that the United States Air Force had investigated hundreds of reported sightings without finding a shred of evidence of supernatural phenomena, Jung indicated he did not wish to pursue the discussion much further. He referred to a book about flying saucers by Donald Keyhoe, the very pilot who had flown alongside Lindbergh on his forty-eight-state tour of the United States in 1927, which reported numerous sightings of unidentified flying objects. When Lindbergh said he had heard recently that Keyhoe had, in fact, experienced several nervous breakdowns, Jung replied, "I dare say he has."

Lindbergh added that he had discussed with Chief of the United States Air Force General Spaatz the recent flurry of UFO reports. "Slim," Spaatz had said, "don't you suppose that if there was anything true about this flying-saucer business, you and I would have heard about it by this time?" Jung was not impressed. "There are," he said, ending their conversation, "a great many things going on around this earth that you and General Spaatz don't know about."

Although Anne saw only a little more of her husband that summer than she would have had she stayed in Connecticut, the Helvetian getaway at least prepared her for Charles's startling suggestion that they temporarily abandon their house in Darien for a chalet of their own in Vaud. With two children married and the next two college-bound, Anne had come to see the increasing impracticality of their big suburban home. She hoped that the "unfamiliar setting of a foreign land" might provide her with "a fresh perspective on our lives, and the next turning of the road, life without children." She agreed to put the Darien house in the hands of a caretaker and return to Vaud for much of 1960.

The Lindberghs still spent much of their year apart, seeing each other only on the occasions when their separate itineraries crisscrossed. As a result, he missed several tormented romantic relationships in Ansy's life; and he failed to appreciate her need to rush off to emergency sessions with Dr. Rosen or to study the flute in France before returning to Radcliffe. He missed Scott's graduation from Darien High School and the decisions regarding his higher education, which resulted in his entering Amherst College. And he missed his son Land's wedding to Susan Miller, a cousin of Jon's wife.

Despite his poor attendance record, Anne had always assumed Charles would be there for her in sickness if not in health. In the spring of 1960, she learned otherwise. She had to undergo knee surgery, which proved to be more complicated than anticipated, and she was bedridden for several weeks at Harkness Pavilion under Dr. Atchley's watchful eye. Although Charles knew about the operation, he never showed up. "Where are you?" she cried out in a pathetic letter to her husband two weeks after the procedure. "I know I made light of the operation but I did hope you'd get here in time to take me home. Of course, I can arrange . . . a limousine but I wanted it to be you. It would help so. . . . Please come home as soon as you can. This is a time when I need you."

Lindbergh returned weeks later, "astonished" not to find his wife in Darien. The next morning, he called the hospital, asking only, "Aren't you ever coming home?!" She was two months on crutches and several more on a cane, during which time he lent almost no support. His rages returned, as he repeatedly exploded in irritation at her for "making mountains out of molehills," at her "heavy way of doing everything," at how badly she managed her life, at how much time she wasted. His "sermons" contained enough truth to muzzle her. But she bristled at his insensitivity to the fact that it was her constant presence at home that enabled him to lead his supercharged life orbiting the globe. He had all the time in the world, for example, to tend to his dying uncle, Charles Land.

While placing eighty-two-year-old "Brother" in a sanitarium in Luzern, Charles had, in fact, searched for a place to build a chalet in Switzerland for Anne. Ten days after inspecting an unsatisfactory site recommended by some Swiss friends, he saw several acres on the southern slope of Monts de Corsier, not twenty minutes above the town of Vevey, and bought them on the spot for $20,000. More than eight hundred meters above sea level, the secluded site offered a commanding view of Lac Leman, the Rhone valley, and the Alps. The property, surrounded by fields full of crops and cattle, backed onto a green pasture, which ran to the base of a steep cliff and was topped by a forest of beech and fir. "I need your help in . . . designing a chalet," Charles enthusiastically wrote Anne back in Darien, though he had, in fact, already drawn it in his mind and consulted with a builder.

Construction of the simple two-story structure began in the summer of 1962. The twenty-three-by-twenty-four-foot main floor consisted of a bedroom, bath, and a combination living room-kitchen; below were the garage, two small bedrooms, and a half-bath. Renting a chalet in the neighboring canton of Fribourg while their own was being built, they watched their new house progress.

Lindbergh's blueprints did not end there. Consumed with streamlining his life, he had recently written old General Wood, "the less I have, the most satisfied I am." In that spirit, he wanted to divide his four and one-half acres at Scott's Cove, sell the house, and build a smaller one for himself and Anne next door. He drafted two pages of specifications, the essence of which was: "emphasis on smallness of appearance, simplicity of construction and upkeep, proportion, texture of materials, appropriateness to woods, tides, and informal surroundings." His checklist was detailed enough to include cork stoppers in the tubs and basins instead of mechanisms that would wear out and a hook on the roof for block and tackle, for hoisting large pieces of furniture upstairs.

Anne tried to sort out what these sudden changes might mean to their lives. "We can't all move back to Europe," she thought, "when we've just come home to America. This is no family homestead we are contemplating, not even a summer one. It would be too small and too far away. Is it our old-age home, when the children leave us? Is it a European perch for C.? A place to write for me?" Just when she thought she was being forced to enter a phase of "living for oneself," she went along with the Swiss plans, buying into a dream that she and Charles might reclaim a part of their marriage that they had obviously lost. Moving from the present house in Scott's Cove into a smaller one seemed only a scaling down of her old life. "The chalet," she wrote, "sounds like an extension of life—perhaps even a new life."

By the spring of 1963, the chalet was habitable. Charles and Anne moved in with sleeping bags and air mattresses, two card tables and four wooden chairs. Within weeks some basic furniture arrived. Charles marveled at Anne's transforming the plaster-and-wood lodge into a cozy home—with books on the shelves, weavings by Land's wife on the wall, and objets d'art carefully placed among antique chests and cabinets. She soon had geraniums and petunias blooming in pots on the balcony. (In a few years, the Lindberghs would build another one-room chalet higher up their cliff, an even simpler, thick-planked abode to which Anne could retreat and write.)

By the end of the year, the Darien house was finished as well. With its three small bedrooms, a modest living room, and an efficient kitchen, it cost $60,000, plus another $20,000 for its only extravagance—a bomb shelter, which Lindbergh had spent weeks researching and designing, right down to a drainpipe large enough to accommodate any tidal waves caused by a mega-tonnage underwater burst along the coastline.

"For a man who wanted a simple life," Land Lindbergh later observed, "it kept getting so complicated. Father was so busy setting up these little houses—enclaves really . . . but he found he couldn't stay in them. After a few weeks at most, he'd have to take off. The life he set up for his family just didn't work for him." While the new chalet afforded everybody in the family a European base, it only encouraged the instability that made Anne feel insecure. "Chalet living," she wrote, "showed us how free life can be in the smaller, barer setting: how burdened we had become at home by the accumulations and traditions of 20 years in our old family house." But the addition of this small house further subjected her to that aspect of her husband's routine that she detested most, having to uproot herself whenever she felt she was settling in.

Leading lives on two continents increased the lack of communication between them. Although they now made two carbon copies of every letter they still regularly wrote to each other—one sent to each house—the Lindberghs seemed to miss more signals than they received. "I can see that in a few years I shall be living alone most of the time," Anne wrote her friend Mina Curtiss in 1961. She was already adjusting by looking out for herself. Charles called from Germany one night hoping to spend the weekend skiing with Anne, then in Switzerland; but she had already booked herself into a hotel in Locarno for two weeks. Though she was disappointed to tears over the "dream of a shared joy," she did not change her plans. "It was quite sad to come back & find you gone," Anne wrote Charles during one of her returns to Connecticut, "with only the suit-to-be-cleaned sitting on your side of the bed!"

In late 1963, young Anne sorted out her romantic life enough to leave Radcliffe and return to France, where she had fallen in love with a French student, the son of a Paris university professor. She and Julien Feydy married in a civil ceremony in the town hall of Douzillac, in the Dordogne, where Professor Feydy owned a castle. Although Lindbergh had great reservations about his twenty-three-year-old daughter's marriage—what with her history of unstable love affairs—he stood at his wife's side at the wedding. After the young couple had settled into married life in France, the bride's mother presented some provocative new thoughts on marriage, specifically her own. "I do not really think happiness is the point of marriage," she wrote Ansy, emphasizing other qualities, such as challenging one another and never being bored. "Actually, I think I am just beginning to understand your father, after all these years, & he perhaps, me. (Understanding is a very different thing from the deep bond between us which has always been there.)" Now that he was living his life completely by his own rules, even their friends who were privy to their marital strains found Charles more at ease than they had seen in years. Anne, having stopped trying to conform to his every wish, exuded a new sense of equanimity as well.

Lindbergh had long since concluded that "the only way I could concentrate on my fundamental interests, and live the type of life I believed in," required him to stop giving addresses or taking part in public ceremonies. His new itinerancy, on top of his penchant for privacy, made it all the easier to reject invitations of any kind, especially the institutional affairs—a gala celebrating the fortieth anniversary of *Time* from Henry Luce, a dinner honoring fifty years of Pulitzer Prize winners, and Senator Barry Goldwater's personal invitation to attend a rally sponsored by the Young Americans for Freedom, whose theme was "world liberation from Communism." When Adlai Stevenson invited Lindbergh to serve on the host committee of a tribute for their mutual friend Robert Hutchins, Lindbergh replied, "I like and admire Bob Hutchins too much to be willing to take part in inflicting a formal dinner upon him."

Nobody was more eager to entertain the Lindberghs than John F. Kennedy, whose father had held him in such high regard. Although Lindbergh had halfheartedly voted for Richard Nixon in the 1960 election, the young President issued Lindbergh a blanket invitation to visit the Oval Office. In April 1962, he formally invited the Lindberghs to a state dinner in honor of the French Minister of State in charge of Cultural Affairs, André Malraux. So eager was the President to have Lindbergh attend, the Kennedys asked him and his wife to spend the night at the White House. At Anne's insistence, they accepted. Charles grumbled not only that he had to buy a tuxedo but that he would no longer be able to answer invitations saying, "[I]t is seven years since I have gone to a formal dinner!"

Anne and Charles flew from New York and took a taxi to the White House. Their bags were whisked away at the pillared entrance, and they were escorted upstairs. At the end of a long corridor filled with historical pictures and mementoes, Mrs. Kennedy's secretary threw open a door and said, "The Queen's room for Mrs. Lindbergh"; then gesturing across the hall, "and the Lincoln room for Mr. Lindbergh." Anne cried out, "So far away!"

They were both put into the Queen's room, which they found plenty spacious, "sunny and welcoming." A maid entered with tea; and the Lindberghs perused the list of guests they would be joining that night, more than a hundred people from the worlds of art, music, theater, dance, and literature. They also received a penciled note from Mrs. Kennedy, asking them to cocktails before dinner.

Ushered down the hall to the Oval Room, they joined the Vice President and Lady Bird Johnson, members of the French Embassy, and the Malrauxs for drinks. They could not help being impressed by the easy charm of the President and the regal beauty of Mrs. Kennedy, who swept into the room in a long stiff pink gown, bare-shouldered, her hair done up high with a diamond star. A few minutes later, the Lindberghs and the other guests were escorted to the main reception hall, which was filled with the cultural elite. Many they knew—Archibald MacLeish, David Rockefeller, and Thornton Wilder; many more they but recognized—Leonard Bernstein, Tennessee Williams, Arthur Miller, and Julie Harris. Anne had not been so giddy at a social affair in years, gushing in admiration as she was introduced to Adlai Stevenson and suddenly seeing his jaw muscles freeze, the same paralysis she had seen countless times as people had rushed to her husband over the years. Lindbergh adopted his standard party air, reserved but polite. He was as famous as anybody in the room but unrecognized by many who had no idea that the tall, lean gentleman with the wisps of white hair combed over his mostly bald head was Charles Lindbergh. He was seated at the President's table, next to the French Ambassador's wife, along with Madame Malraux, Agnes de Mille, Edmund Wilson, Andrew Wyeth, Geraldine Page, and Irwin Shaw.

After dinner, toasts were exchanged—Kennedy saying this would be the first speech in the White House about French-American relationships that would not mention Lafayette. The guests then withdrew to the large reception room which had been transformed into a concert chamber, with rows of chairs. Amid the nation's most famous names, Lindbergh was suddenly swarmed by members of the press. He politely explained that he never gave interviews and that he had no comments; but many persisted, and he grew uncomfortable. Upon learning from an usher that they had been assigned front-row seats—facing a battery of cameras—for a performances of Isaac Stern's trio, Lindbergh balked. He arranged for a pair of seats several rows back. Anne found it difficult to lose herself in the Schubert that evening, feeling "too conscious of C.'s tense alertness beside me."

After the concert, as the guests dispersed, the Lindberghs were taken upstairs to rejoin the small group that had assembled before dinner. Charles conversed with Malraux, who spoke of his days as a military pilot and how he used to shoot from an open cockpit with a pistol. After a few minutes, the Lindberghs excused themselves, learning the next day that Isaac Stern had played the violin late into the night for those who had stayed.

After breakfast in their room, the Lindberghs met Mrs. Kennedy in the informal alcove at the end of the hall. She brought her two young children. "Although talking chiefly to us," Anne wrote in her diary, "she never forgot or brushed them aside. . . . This kind of confidence and closeness between mother and child cannot be faked. I was impressed that Mrs. Kennedy could maintain it in the midst of her public life and surroundings." At the President's suggestion, the Lindberghs departed by way of his office. Not only did it save them from the gauntlet of photographers waiting at the front door, but it allowed them to have a few private words with him.

"We left with a deep feeling of gratitude and—even more—with encouragement," Lindbergh wrote in his bread-and-butter letter. "There was a quality to the occasion, and the character you managed to weave through it, that brought out fundamental values at a time when such values seem to be disappearing in modern ways of life." The whole occasion, and rereading parts of Kennedy's *Profiles in Courage*, gave Lindbergh "confidence that the presidency of our country is held by someone who senses well beyond the more obvious problems of the days and year." Anne sent an autographed copy of *North to the Orient* to young Caroline Kennedy, and Charles inscribed a copy of *The Spirit of St. Louis*—"in memory of an early meeting"—for her eighteen-month-old brother.

As he suspected, that one public appearance prompted invitations for dozens more. Lindbergh withdrew into his shell. He refused to appear at the Fiftieth Anniversary dinner for the Boeing Company ("Many years ago I found that time consumed by dinner, ceremonies, etc., made it impossible for me to carry on the kind of life I wanted to lead . . ."); a reunion of his fellow Missouri National Guardsmen in the 110th Observation Squadron ("To me, reunions are pretty awful; they always detract from qualities of memory which I prefer to leave to the past where I think they belong and have the greatest value"); the American Astronautical Society's award presentation ("I am deeply appreciative of the honors I have received in the past; but I feel that I have had far more than my share of them"); being installed in the Aviation Hall of Fame (". . . personally I do not like the idea of enshrinement— it seems to me to separate one too much from the earth and its people"). He continued to ignore the commemorations of his flight to Paris which the National Air and Space Museum held every five years. He steadily declined offers for print interviews and was more resistant than ever to the pressure from television networks to appear on their programs. ("I am most anxious to continue living and working quietly, and I can think of nothing that would prevent this more than my appearance on television . . ."). Except to see occasional news events, he never even watched television.

He still received thousands of fan letters each year, mostly from autograph-seekers. One day he calculated that if he handled one letter a minute, working eight hours a day, it would take him over five years just to handle such correspondence. As a result, during his layovers in Darien, Lindbergh gave himself time only to flip through the return addresses on the envelopes that had arrived, opening but one out of every ten or twenty letters. The rest would be opened by a secretary and filed, ultimately sent to Sterling Memorial Library at Yale University, where his papers would become permanently housed. Even a mimeographed letter from the Easter Seals campaign would be placed in his archives . . . and, in the next folder, the sheets of Easter Seals themselves.

Anne became less shy about accepting invitations on her own. Having struck up a friendship with Lady Bird Johnson at the Malraux dinner, she received several invitations from the Vice President's wife for luncheons in Washington, which she attended. When the Johnsons moved into the White House, the Lindberghs remained high on Presidential guest lists. In 1964, Lindbergh voted for LBJ, marking the second time he had cast a Presidential ballot for a Democrat. (While he considered Goldwater "a well-intentioned, courageous, and honest man," he found in his political rhetoric "a basic naiveté that I think would be highly dangerous, especially in international affairs.") Lindbergh was "on the road" when two invitations from the LBJ White House arrived—one to meet Princess Margaret, the other the Shah of

Iran. Anne sent their regrets to both—"because of the absence of Mr. Lindbergh from the country and Mrs. Lindbergh's lack of knowledge of the date of his return or where to reach him."

By the mid-sixties, Lindbergh was roaming freer than ever. He let lapse his membership on most of his boards—including the Ballistic Missile Committee of the Department of Defense, which helped develop the Atlas, Titan, Thor, Minuteman, Polaris, and Jupiter missiles. He even turned down an invitation from Najeeb E. Halaby, Administrator of the Federal Aviation Agency, to assist the aviation industry in the development of an economically competitive, commercial supersonic transport aircraft. Not only did he not wish to be pinned down to fixed dates for committee meetings, he was also apprehensive about the wisdom of developing such a plane. "I have never before felt as little enthusiasm about a forward step in transport design," he wrote Secretary of Defense Robert S. McNamara in 1966; "and yet, under existing circumstances, I see no wise alternative to taking it." Calling himself a "low-cost, mass-transportation man," Lindbergh hoped the developers of an SST might make its seat-mile cost feasible; but he was more disturbed by the potential problem of sonic booms. "I think we have enough noises and distractions without filling the sky with louder ones," he said. "I am literally alarmed about our civilization's infatuation with scientific developments, and the delicate complication of life thereby created."

Lindbergh felt that commercial aviation had already found the right balance of speed, safety, and passenger comfort. The trip from New York to Paris that had taken him thirty-three and a half hours was then being flown in Boeing 707-331s in six hours, forty-five minutes, sometimes an hour faster. The single-engine *Spirit of St. Louis* with its 450 gallons of gasoline had been replaced by Super Jets powered by four Pratt & Whitney JT4A-9 turbojet engines—with a gross weight of 302,000 pounds, sixty times their predecessor. Where one man had filled cockpit and cabin, squeezing in a sack of sandwiches and some emergency equipment, the 707 could accommodate twenty first-class passengers and 120 economy passengers—who were treated to hot gourmet meals and cocktails—a crew of twelve, 18,000 pounds of baggage, freight, and mail. Before the end of the decade, the Boeing 747, the first of the jumbo jets, would begin transporting five hundred passengers at a time. Its fuselage was 231 feet long, almost twice the distance covered by the Wright brothers' first flight.

On May 16, 1965, Lindbergh was elected to the Board of Directors of Pan American World Airways. He had served the company as a technical consultant for so many years that he had never considered the possibility of taking a directorship; but when his old friend Juan Trippe had asked if he might propose him for the position, he realized how perfectly it fit in with his vagabond life. The regular board meetings in New York and the frequent directors' trips—two-week, round-the-world steeplechases—became the only appointments by which he fixed his calendar and set his watch. Increasingly, however, his global inspections disturbed him. As he confessed that year to Father Joseph T. Durkin, S. J. of Georgetown University, with whom he worked in collecting Dr. Carrel's papers, "My recent trip, involving, mostly, discussions about coming types of transport aircraft, does not leave me less apprehensive about the complexity, tempo, and standards of success our civilization is achieving."

Nobody had a broader perspective on the earth's physical changes over the past four decades than Charles Lindbergh. In making his forty-eight-state tour in 1927, he had seen the expanses of North American wilderness in a way no man had before. "The crushing impact of modern science and industry was only getting under way," he would later note; but "civilization" rapidly encroached upon the land and the sea. What was more, Lindbergh increasingly shouldered the blame: "The primitive was at the mercy of the civilized in our twentieth-century times," he would write, "and nothing had made it more so than the airplane I had helped develop. I had helped to change the environment of our lives."

As bad as the expansion which had overtaken most of the world's great cities, Lindbergh found, was the standardization. "New buildings in Beirut, Rio, and Chicago looked the same," he wrote. "Riots and crime in Washington were not unlike riots and crime in Manila." He became "alarmed by the exponentially mounting complication, luxury, and cost of cities—not by the cost in money, but by the cost in irreplaceable resources of the earth."

"In the midst of the fascinating life I have led," Lindbergh wrote in his early sixties, "taking part in man's conquest of air and space, I have often asked myself whether aeronautics and astronautics were actually a boon to the human race." To date, he concluded in a letter to Secretary of the Interior Stewart Udall, "I have been forced to the negative conclusion. While aircraft have brought peoples closer together in peaceful intercourse and understanding, they have more than counteracted this accomplishment through their ruthless bombardments in war—a killing that seems to have little or no relationship to evolution's selectivity. While missiles have opened to our knowledge unexplored reaches of space, they have made our civilization subject to extermination within hours."

Believing that "an overemphasis of science weakens human character and upsets life's essential balance," the boy who had once worshiped technology admitted that were he just now entering adulthood, he would choose a career that kept him in contact with nature more than science. His new god became Thoreau, all of whose works he read and whose most inspiring passages he copied out. One phrase from Thoreau especially resonated for him: ". . . in wildness is the preservation of the World." Lindbergh would thenceforth dedicate all his future journeys to his growing obsession with the survival of the planet. Increasingly, these voyages would take him into more primitive realms.

Lindbergh's longtime friend Jim Newton unwittingly set some of his new pursuits into motion. During the late spring of 1961, while the Lindberghs were in the mountains above Vevey, Newton was just across the valley in Caux-sur-Montreux, at the international conference center of Moral Re-Armament. A devout adherent of the movement, Newton invited Lindbergh to a number of its meetings, plays, and panel discussions. After attending several MRA functions, Lindbergh found himself in utter disagreement with what he considered a fanatical ideology and got in a long, unresolved argument with Newton saying as much—a healthy debate that only deepened their respect for each other. "But sometimes," Newton would later note, "the Almighty works in unusual ways."

While Lindbergh had no interest in any future MRA events, a meeting on Sunday, June eleventh, at Caux, affected him deeply. Delegates from Africa were on the platform that day—businessmen, white planters, a leader of forty thousand Mau Mau, and a striking ebony-colored member of the Legislative Council in Kenya, dressed in a business suit, who belonged to a tribe whose "admission to manhood" required killing a lion with a spear. Newton introduced Lindbergh to the delegate, Jilin ole "John" Konchellah, a warrior of the Masai tribe. The following Thursday evening, in the salon of the hotel in Caux, Lindbergh met alone with the imposing African—with his black moustache and beard and enlarged, contorted ear lobes, which were pierced for disc ornaments. Konchellah had never heard of Lindbergh before Newton briefed him.

Lindbergh wanted to learn everything he could about civilization's impact on Konchellah's semi-nomadic tribe, which roamed the Rift Valley along the Kenya-Tanzania border, in the shadow of Mt. Kilimanjaro. Konchellah said civilization had brought his "pastoral" tribe of three hundred thousand medicine, wheels, and literacy, which allowed them to read history and send letters to each other; but he emphasized that there had been education before the white man came. He knew, for example, the different kinds of trees and their uses, the rivers, animals, trails, and jungles. "That," said Konchellah, who had been taught in African mission schools and from correspondence courses, "is education." A modern primitive, Konchellah—thirty-two and the father of five—became secretary of the Masai United Front and a member of Kenya's parliament.

Konchellah told Lindbergh that the Masai prayed to their own god, (which did not have human form), worshiped the mountains, and sang to the sun and moon. Warriors rose at dawn to thank God for the light. These young men of the tribe were meant to protect the others from animals and human enemies, who often raided for oxen. When Lindbergh asked if he thought the promise of future products of civilization would make life better, Konchellah hesitated, then replied that he thought the traditional tribal way of life was best. He invited "the great white flyer" to visit him in Kenya, where Lindbergh had never been.

At the end of 1962, Lindbergh cleared enough time to make such a trek worthwhile. He had no intention of going on an organized safari, but of renting a car and driving himself. As this promised to be the most exotic location he had ever visited, Lindbergh was grateful for a friend's letter of introduction to Major Ian Grimwood, the Chief Game Warden in Kenya. "I like to travel quietly so I can see, think, and write," he wrote Grimwood. "I can shoot fairly well, but I don't like to kill things. I hate tourist procedures and first-class hotels. I can live on most any kind of food, and enjoy sleeping on the ground."

Grimwood permitted Lindbergh to make rounds with Denis Zaphiro, the warden in the Southern Game Preserve in the Kajiado District. Flying and camping together for close to two weeks at the end of 1962, they traveled most of the Kenya-Tanzania border, inspecting parks from Mara in the west to Lake Amboseli.

Lindbergh's greatest thrill, however, came when he drove into Tanzania and arrived at a Masai *boma* as the guest of John Konchellah. For several days he lived as one of the tribe. According to custom, he was assigned to the small thatched hut of the oldest woman, who entertained him at night, singing and dancing, shaking her necklaces. He did not figure out how far her favors extended; but he charmed her by fashioning earrings for her out of paper clips. The gray-haired woman prepared his meals, which included a kind of yoghurt—milk and blood from the same cow mixed in a gourd that had been rinsed with its urine, which served as a coagulant; the concoction was placed near a wood fire, from which it drew a smoky flavor. For days, Lindbergh joined a Masai cowherd, several men and boys with dark-red blankets slung over their naked bodies, carrying long-bladed spears. Another day he drove John Konchellah to a political meeting in a clearing a few miles north of Mount Kilimanjaro, where he was the only white man standing among several hundred blacks, their spears planted in the ground while they conducted tribal business in Swahili and Masai. After only two weeks in Africa, Lindbergh found it difficult to leave.

In parting, Konchellah presented Lindbergh with a shield he had specially made for him. Although they had known each other a short time, Konchellah had discerned the basic elements of Lindbergh's character; and, accordingly, he had the shield painted with a design reserved for the bravest Masai warriors. "A man carrying such a shield could never turn back in battle," Konchellah informed him, "regardless of the odds against him." Lindbergh treasured the gift.

He returned to Nairobi in February 1964, again alone. During this visit, Ian Grimwood guided him in his Land Rover through Masai country near Selengai. While driving one day, they passed another Land Rover with a flat tire, which turned out to belong to Dr. Louis S. B. Leakey, the British archaeologist and anthropologist. They loaned Leakey their spare; and the grateful scientist suggested that he and Lindbergh arrange a more proper meeting. Days later, Lindbergh arrived at Leakey's Centre for Prehistory and Palaeontology in Nairobi, where he spoke of his recent excavations in the Olduvai Gorge. He showed Lindbergh a cast of the skull of a "pre-man" two and a half million years old, which he had recently discovered and was about to make public. That week Leakey's wife, Mary, guided Lindbergh through their Tanganyikan excavations; and two months later the Leakeys visited the Lindberghs in Connecticut. Having difficulty raising funds for the many projects they supervised—which included work in India and Israel as well as research in primate behavior by Jane Goodall and Dian Fossey—Leakey hoped to enlist Lindbergh's support in encouraging Pan American to promote travel to Africa, where the Leakeys were organizing "caravan trips." Lindbergh urged Juan Trippe to make Nairobi one of their gateways.

One year later, Lindbergh heard the call of the wild again. By this, his third, trip to East Africa, he felt capable of serving as guide to his wife. He and Anne met in Paris, where Charles attended a conference on jet-powered civil aircraft, then escorted her to a formal dinner worthy of Louis XVI. From there they flew to Nairobi, rented a four-wheel-drive Land Rover and drove into Masai country. They pitched their tent that first night between acacia trees near the edge of a ten-foot cliff, while elephants across the dry riverbed watched. Animal noises—howling hyenas, galloping zebra, clomping rhinos, and roaring lions—filled the air. "That night," Lindbergh would write afterward, "we became a part of the jungle, living as primitive man lived in ages past. I felt as separate from my civilization as I had felt from East African animals at the formal Paris dinner a few days before." The next morning, the night-prowlers had been replaced by a docile herd of cattle at the nearby water hole, tended by Masai spearmen wearing only their red shoulder blankets. The Lindberghs spent close to two weeks alone in this animal kingdom. Then Charles lingered in Europe for two weeks of business before joining his wife back in America.

When he returned to Darien on April 3, 1965, he found his wife running a 105-degree fever. He rushed Anne to Harkness Pavilion in New York and put her in the hands of Dr. Atchley, who diagnosed that she was suffering from viral pneumonia. During her hospitalization, Charles read to her each evening; and after three weeks he drove her home, where he served her breakfast in bed. His attentiveness surprised Anne and underscored a great lesson she had extracted from the last few months. "This Spring is one of the first times in my life that I have been able to live next to C.A.L. and not get drawn into his rhythm or feel guilty about staying outside of it," she wrote in her diary. Then she made an admission that was thirty-five years in coming: "The illness and convalescence gave me the excuse to stay in my own rhythm and live at my own pace (for the most part). And I must preserve this integrity of rhythm in health—for though I will—I hope—be able to do more than I can today—I will never be able to keep up to his rhythm again—in fact, I never really *was* able to—but I tried."

In October 1965, Lindbergh invited each of his children and their spouses to join him for several weeks camping in southern Kenya. He and Anne offered to cover most of the costs. Lindbergh flew ahead, on the new weekly Pan American flight from New York to Nairobi, arriving on December eleventh. Over the next few weeks, Jon and his wife, Barbara, left their five children behind on Bainbridge Island, Washington, where they had settled; Anne and Julien Feydy flew down from Paris with Scott, who had transferred to Cambridge University; and Anne arrived with Reeve, a student at Radcliffe. Only Land—with his wife and two children on their four-thousand-acre ranch on the Blackfoot River in Montana—politely declined the offer, anticipating several strained weeks marching to the relentless beat of his father's drum. "I'm not going," he told his wife, "—too many people and too tight a schedule."

The "patriarchal safari" was as rigorous as it was wondrous. For a month, the Lindberghs lived out of their two Land Rovers, meticulously packed with four tents, forty gallons of drinking water, and enough preserved food to last ten days at a time. After leaving Nairobi, they spent two nights on the Dry Selengai, a week in the Kimana swamp area, and two days in the Shimba Hills, where Denis Zaphiro joined them. They traveled as far east as the Indian Ocean, where they spent three sweltering days on a beach north of Mombasa. With special permission from John Owen, the Director of the Tanzania National Parks, the Lindberghs spent some of their nights at Lake Manyara, in the Ngorongoro Crater, and on the Serengeti—where they drove twenty miles across the plains right through the heart of the great animal migration. "It was so strenuous," a weary Anne later reported to her friend Lucia Valentine, "that we all lost weight but Charles who seems to be impervious to heat, flies, dust, bad roads, long hours, canned food, ticks, and lack of washing water!"

Charles exulted in all the challenges, becoming physically and mentally stimulated by the powerful forces of nature he saw at work. The struggles for survival he witnessed in East Africa would provide him with more material for his next decade of autobiographical writing than anything else he experienced. "For me, in East Africa, more than any other place on earth," he would later write, "the strange and the familiar interweave. Nowhere else do I gain a comparable perspective on evolution, time, and space."

In September 1962, Lindbergh had received a form letter from a board member of the recently established World Wildlife Fund in Washington, which articulated many of his current feelings. "Too few people realize that hundreds of species of living creatures are in danger of extermination," it read. "Modern processes are destroying the natural habitat of many birds and mammals. Wildlife is menaced through the development of towns and cities which cover the land, through the multiplication of roads and industrial installations, through the pollution of streams due to industrial and human wastes, and through the destruction of wetlands." It spoke of two hundred species already extinct because of man and another two hundred fifty on the "Danger List"—including the American whooping crane, the Asian rhinoceros, and the Arabian oryx.

Lindbergh met with the head of its parent organization, the International Union for Conservation of Nature and Natural Resources (IUCN)—which oversaw some two hundred sixty organizations in more than sixty countries—at their offices in Morges, on Lac Leman, not fifty miles upshore from the Lindberghs' chalet. During subsequent visits to Switzerland, Lindbergh offered his services to the organization's leadership, volunteering to birddog endangered species during his global rovings. Circling the world as many as six times a year, Lindbergh found new purpose in all his travels, a reason to penetrate each country. Less than a year after the World Wildlife Fund's initial solicitation, Lindbergh was sending reports to the IUCN, cataloguing each country's exotic fauna and the names of people in the government who were sympathetic to the cause of protecting it. By the following year, ecological matters consumed practically all his reading and writing time.

Lindbergh debuted as an advocate for conservation in July 1964 with an article he wrote for *Reader's Digest* called "Is Civilization Progress?" With the Atlantic's having been crossed tens of thousands of times since 1927, Lindbergh asserted that flying no longer represented adventure to him, only progress. Now he questioned the very yardsticks—such as speed—by which he had long measured progress. He could offer "no proof whatever that the five or six thousand years of civilization, here and there on earth, have improved man's fundamental qualities, or that in his essence civilized man is a being superior to primitive man." He came to believe certain fundamental truths, "facts that man should never overlook: that the construction of an airplane, for instance, is simple when compared to the evolutionary achievement of a bird; that airplanes depend upon an advanced civilization; and that where civilization is most advanced, few birds exist. I realized that if I had to choose," he proclaimed, "I would rather have birds than airplanes."

Over the next few years, Lindbergh's involvement with the IUCN and the World Wildlife Fund intensified. Even more than his and Anne's generous contributions—five-figure donations each year and all the earnings from his writings on conservation—Lindbergh lent his name. He wrote his own solicitation letters, targeting people who could "exercise an influence on conservation activities" as well as write checks. In 1965, he suggested sending a letter to every federal and state legislator, every governor, several dozen foundations, and several hundred selected individuals. Although he knew the number of letters could run as high as ten thousand, the man who refused to give autographs to strangers intended to sign each one personally.

Some, particularly Jews, found Lindbergh's newfound passion disconcerting, especially when he flung around such phrases as, "I don't want history to record my generation as being responsible for the extermination of any form of life." Longtime editorial writer Max Lerner, for one, wondered, "Where the hell was he when Hitler was trying to exterminate an entire race of human beings?"

Lindbergh immersed himself in the movement. He accepted membership on the WWF board; he presented "sales talks" on behalf of the cause; and he used his pull to get articles published by like-minded authors. With access to transportation—anywhere Pan American flew—and powerful people, Lindbergh became the conservation movement's most effective roving ambassador. Dealing with heads of state or birdwatchers trying to save their local woodpecker, Lindbergh also became ombudsman for the movement, the one name to whom even complete strangers felt they could turn.

Whales were the first animals Lindbergh helped save. Upon learning in 1964 that only a few hundred great blue whales remained in the earth's oceans, and that there were not many more great finbacks, Lindbergh began fighting this "depressing example of man's destructiveness." He engaged the interest of the editors of Reader's Digest in the gigantic mammals; he attended meetings of the International Whaling Commission as the official representative of IUCN; and he wrote Prime Minister Eisaku Sato of Japan and President Fernando Belaunde Terry of Peru, warning them that even one more season of harpooning could result in extinction. He wrote ambassadors and cabinet members urging the United States government to apply pressure on these countries, encouraging a ban until such a time as the whales had a chance to reproduce in sufficient numbers. In order to get publicity for the cause, he even permitted a photographer from Life to accompany him and his son Jon on a two-week, gray-whale-watching voyage along the coasts of Baja California.

When he learned that the company killing blue and humpback whales off the Peruvian coast was actually owned by Archer Daniels Midland, headquartered in Minneapolis, he fired off a letter to Erwin A. Olson, the chairman of the ADM board. Lindbergh's argument was economic as well as ecological; and Olson issued a ban against catching the endangered species for two years.

Other animals and their habitats soon commanded his attention. When Lindbergh learned that the island of Aldabra—one of the great breeding grounds in the Indian Ocean of such rare species as the giant land tortoise, the green turtle, and the flightless rail—was being considered as a site for an air base, he wrote the Secretary of Defense, urging an alternate location. Upon hearing that American soldiers in Vietnam were sending ivory and animal skins back to the United States, Lindbergh telephoned the Army Chief of Staff, who told him that General Westmoreland was issuing orders that "no wild game was to be shot." So impressed was High Chief Tufele-Faia-oga with Lindbergh's concern for his island of Ta'u in Samoa, he bestowed upon him the ancient supreme title TUIAANA-TAMA-a-le-LAGI, "a Son of Heaven."

The wider he traveled, the deeper Lindbergh delved into primitive life. Accordingly, no place intrigued Lindbergh more than Indonesia. His passion for the developing island nation drew him there three times in 1967 alone. While in Jakarta in February, Lindbergh met with members of the Indonesian government and found they failed to realize the significance of the Udjung Kulon, an extraordinary game-filled peninsula on the southwestern tip of Java. Returning in May on Pan American business, Lindbergh met with Presidium Minister of Political Affairs Adam Malik, who arranged for Lindbergh to visit the area along with the Indonesian directors of forestry, nature conservation, and wildlife management. All the way down the coast, Lindbergh spoke of the importance of conservation in Indonesia in general and in the Udjung Kulon in particular, where the last two dozen Javan rhinoceroses remained. Before the boat turned around for its return on Sunday evening, Lindbergh swam ashore to Peutjang Island to talk to a Swiss professor and his physician wife doing research there. They invited him to stay with them.

For the next two weeks, Lindbergh remained off the coast of the Udjung Kulon. His ground base, where he slept on a split-bamboo floor of a guardhouse at night, was a two-minute walk to a white-sand beach and a three-minute swim to a coral bed of spectacular forms and colors. Immediately inland, Lindbergh entered tropical jungle, where python-thick vines and densely leafed branches crawled over multi-trunked trees. Besides the multitude of strange screeching birds, he was surrounded by wild pigs, giant lizards, bats, swinging monkeys, herds of banteng—wild oxen—and the occasional leopard. By the time he had returned to Jakarta, Lindbergh was informed that the government had issued orders increasing penalties for poaching and that further conservation measures were already under discussion. "I have never visited a more attractive area of jungle, sea, and wild life," Lindbergh wrote the Minister of Economical Affairs and Finance afterward, noting that his fortnight in the jungle had given him the feeling "that I existed not in the 20th century but in epochs past."

Thus, Lindbergh spent the sixties in a time warp of his own making, in a primeval forest one week and ultramodern laboratories the next. For no sooner would he be back in civilization than the medical community would call on him to discuss the future. When Dr. Theodore I. Malinin and Lieutenant Vernon Perry, who were expanding the study of organ perfusion, informed Lindbergh that his 1935 pump was still practical but limited in the new field of cryobiological perfusion research, Lindbergh developed a new machine of glass and plastic which could accommodate larger organs and withstand colder temperatures—a necessary step in developing a storage bank of human organs for transplantation. Dr. William W. L. Glenn of Yale University demonstrated for Lindbergh the most modern heart-lung machines at his hospital as well as some of the latest work on the remote stimulation of tissue by radiofrequency in exchange for his addressing a small group of doctors about his work with Carrel. Dr. Denton A. Cooley invited Lindbergh to the Texas Medical Center in Houston to watch him perform heart surgery and solicited his suggestions and advice.

"Diseases have been conquered, suffering minimized, infant mortality reduced, longevity extended," Lindbergh wrote of the physical sciences; but mindful of an overpopulated world, he urged new technologies to develop "agricultural machinery, hybrid crops, synthetic foods, artificial fertilizers, oceanic products—a lengthening list of techniques for increasing the world's . . . productivity." Increasingly, Lindbergh found the answers lay in maintaining balance. As he wrote in an article in the Christmas 1967 issue of *Life*, "The primitive emphasizes factors of survival and the mysteries beyond them. Modern civilization places emphasis on increasing knowledge and the application of technology to man's way of life. The human future depends on our ability to combine the knowledge of science with the wisdom of wildness."

Lindbergh sorted out many of his thoughts about "balance" in a voluminous correspondence with Harry Guggenheim on such sociological topics as leadership, dominance, competition, and the abolition of war—all as part of a "Man's Relation to Man Project" sponsored by Guggenheim's foundation. Inevitably, his thinking kept rebounding to the single issue he believed underlay most of the world's concerns—eugenics. It was a loaded word; but he believed in its literal meaning and positive possibilities. Guggenheim's friends periodically dredged up the old charges of racism and anti-Semitism against Lindbergh; but Guggenheim found them ridiculous. He took Lindbergh at his word when he wrote, "the idea of racial inferiority or superiority is foreign to me." One of the few men on earth to live among primitive people of all skin colors, Lindbergh asserted, "I can't feel inferior or superior to another man because of race, or in any way antagonistic to him. I judge by the individual, not by his race, and have always done so. I would rather have one of my children marry into a good family of any race than into a bad family of any other race."

Obsessed with improving the quality of life for future generations, Lindbergh never tired of discussing reproduction. He encouraged all his children to have healthy sex lives, which included understanding the "critical importance of genetic inheritance." Coming of age in the Lindbergh family involved numerous lectures about natural selection: the boys heard countless warnings about women who might entrap them by becoming pregnant; the girls were cautioned not to let emotions blind them to the qualities they really sought in men.

"If I had to choose but one thing I could impress on my children from whatever wisdom I have gained in life," he wrote his youngest, Reeve, in 1966, shortly before she became engaged to a Harvard-educated photographer named Richard Brown, "it would be the importance of genetics in mating." Overlooking the facts that at least two generations of Lodges and Morrows had been afflicted with mental illness, and that both Reeve's grandfathers had died prematurely of natural causes, he wrote her, "You have a good inheritance both physically and mentally. Preserve it and pass it on to your children, together with the realization of the importance of passing it on to them. Nothing attainable by man has as great value." That included the trust funds Lindbergh had established for his children, to which he had by then surrendered more of his wealth than he had maintained for himself.

"Advice should always be listened to and seldom followed," Lindbergh often told his children. But it generally proved easier to heed their father's words than to defy them. The sheer relentlessness of his ensuing arguments on matters of finance, romance, careers, or politics was usually enough to silence his family members though not necessarily convert them. ("I am most anxious that you don't become one of those Cambridge intellectual and scatter-brained faddists who talk so intensely and loosely about important subjects with which they have neither had much personal contact nor spent much time objectively investigating," he wrote Reeve as Vietnam was flaring up—one of the few issues in his lifetime which he did not see in black-and-white terms. Off the record, Lindbergh called Vietnam a "bad battlefield badly chosen," an engagement America should have avoided, despite his belief in "any operations which prevent the spread of Communism in Asia."

Once committed, however, he believed America should have invaded with full force, even though he deplored the defoliation of the country.) Lindbergh invariably imposed his will on all his children—except one.

Through the sixties, Lindbergh and his youngest son seemed to disagree on everything, except their means of argument. At that, Scott inherited his father's ability to bore in on a matter without letting go of a point until the other had conceded. In practically every visit and letter, Lindbergh took Scott to task for some infraction involving his money, his sports car, his education, or the condition in which he left the chalet. Scott responded with letters longer than he received, matching his father point by point, often with disarming candor. "Granted I have been, I still am, irresponsible," he wrote in 1963. "I follow the prompting of my dreams to an excess. I assert immature statements, sometimes out of genuine belief, sometimes out of pure perversity. I have made a thousand suggestions, procreated dozens of plans, most of which I have been unable to fulfill." Over the next four years, tensions only mounted, as Scott's behavior became increasingly provocative. With the threat of fighting in Vietnam hanging over every young American male, General Lindbergh's youngest son told his family in 1967 that he was renouncing his American citizenship.

His father reacted with predictable anger, his dialectics becoming diatribes. "At twenty-five," he wrote his son, "you are a man. Unlike your brothers, you have not shown much realization of the fact. You claim to stand on your ideals; but you have conducted yourself in anything but an idealistic manner. You accept your living income from the United States; but you refuse to take your part in the support of your country. You have made of yourself an example that argues for increasing the legal minimum age for drivers, witholding [sic] the outright gift of money from parents to their children; and the enactment of laws in relation to a country's support of individuals who refuse to support their country. As far as I am concerned, you convince me that I gave you too much confidence and freedom before you were of legal age, and that it was a mistake for me to arrange that you be financially independent thereafter." He called his son an "ass."

"You are not the first, but the fourth generation of Lindbergh 'rebels,' " Lindbergh wrote Scott in January 1968. "I actively opposed ways of life my country was establishing, and my father before me, and his father before him. I like and admire your rebellion, and up to a point it makes me feel even closer to you. What worries me most is that I feel elements of irrationality in your rebellion that can destroy both your effectiveness and you." Scott maintained his citizenship but withdrew into a life of his own in Europe, studying animal behavior in France, and falling in love with Alika Watteau, a Belgian writer-painter-actress—fifteen years his senior—who was also an animal-rights activist with two rare pet monkeys. (Charles had not met her, but had gathered from family members who had that she was not an ideal mate for Scott.)

After sending letters to his son every few weeks for several months without a reply, Lindbergh conceded "there is not much use in my continuing to write to you." He reminded him of the jams he had helped him through and the independence he had created for him. "What strikes me hardest is my loss of confidence in you and respect for you," he wrote Scott that March, "and my realization that if you were not my son you would be the kind of a fellow I wouldn't want to have much to do with. . . . It seems to me you are already in the early stages of disaster as far as your life is concerned."

Scott responded with a volley of letters that spring. "I am going to marry Alika in a few days," he announced on April 1, 1968, not giving his father time to respond or even to meet the bride. Lindbergh took this sudden action as a personal slight, which initiated a period of estrangement between father and son.

Anne felt she had failed Scott in not protecting him more from Charles, that she should have supported him more in his choice of schools and in his desire to seek psychiatric help. She also knew she never could have succeeded in countermanding his father. Scott "prefers to learn from the world than to learn from you," Anne had tried to explain to Charles. "It may be the harsher way to learn but it may be the best way for Scott to learn." And so the rift not only put a strain on all the Lindbergh children but it also wedged their parents further apart. Anne's heart still melted whenever her husband telephoned from some distant land to announce his return home; but she came to find his presence an intrusion and his absence an insult.

Abandoning the one family house that had felt like hers and moving into two new houses, seeing her children marry and her grandchildren born, Anne had further lost the ability to concentrate on her literary work. The last decade had allowed her to publish but one thin novel—*Dearly Beloved,* an occasionally forlorn look at marriage—and a few articles. Often feeling at loose ends while her husband patrolled the world, she felt up for little more than traipsing through her diaries and contemplating a book on middle age. "No news from C.A.L.!" she wrote her sister in January 1968. "I now am beginning to feel harassed—not knowing what I'm doing . . . I wish I knew. It makes everything else uncertain & wavery & unreal to not know. I have been expecting him every day for a week." She felt taken for granted, useless—depressed, as she wrote in her diary, by "the sense of getting older, the slowing down of my writing . . . and a general sense of not being needed by anyone—child or husband."

Charles had long planned to take Anne on a three-week vacation at winter's end to the Hawaiian Islands, as guests of his friend Sam Pryor, a retired Pan American executive. Once at Pryor's garden spot on Maui, both Lindberghs found themselves caught up in efforts to preserve a park on the island and in discussions relating to the establishment of ocean wilderness and park areas in the Pacific. Charles planned to go from there to Japan to address the whale crisis.

Just when they hoped to settle down for a few days of rest, Lindbergh overheard a telephone conversation between Pryor and his daughter in Alaska. She was lamenting the fact that a bill protecting Arctic wolves, which her husband, State Senator Lowell Thomas, Jr., was trying to get the legislature to pass, appeared headed for defeat. When Lindbergh learned the entire contents of the conversation, he turned to Pryor and said, "Let's go up and help him." Because Lindbergh had not made a public speech in nearly fifteen years, Pryor puzzledly looked at his guest and asked when. Lindbergh said, "Let's go tomorrow."

They flew into Juneau on March seventeenth, keeping Lindbergh's appearance secret from all but the state's top officials. Governor Walter J. Hickel invited Lindbergh to be his guest in a private upstairs apartment at the Governor's Mansion. Rumors of his presence circulated around the capital the next day, but few believed them. At 10:15 on the morning of the nineteenth, Thomas and House Speaker Ted Stevens escorted him into the House chamber. The startled legislators and spectators welcomed him with a standing ovation, and he offered a shy smile in return.

Lindbergh spoke extemporaneously that morning, apologizing for being a little "rusty" at speech-making. His humility quickly won the crowd over. After recalling his first visit to Alaska in 1931, in the *Sirius* with Anne, he proceeded to the purpose of his address, the importance of conservation in Alaska—because "what you do here," he said, "is going to be watched closely by the entire world." He spoke of pollution and erosion in the south of the state and the need to protect the animals in the north, even if that meant the elimination of bounties on predator animals. The brief appearance electrified the audience and received extensive press coverage. Representative Thomas described his guest's impact on conservation in the state as nothing short of a "miracle." He wrote Lindbergh that his presence inspired the legislature to pass immediate protective legislation. One of his colleagues said, "Seeing him today was like seeing someone come back from the dead. I'll never forget it. This was one of the most important moments of my life."

The next day, Lindbergh left for Tokyo, keeping an eye on the calendar because of a Pan American board meeting in New York in early April and engagements in Europe shortly after that. He would stop first in Hawaii, however, not only to collect his wife but also because he had fallen in love anew there—with Hana.

19

ALOHA

". . . a life stream is like a mountain river—springing from hidden
sources, born out of the earth, touched by stars, merging, blending
evolving in the shape momentarily seen. . . . Now it ends,
apparently, at a lava brink, a precipitous fall."
—C.A.L.

ISOLATED FROM ANY CONTINENT BY MORE THAN TWO THOU-
sand miles of Pacific Ocean bask the Hawaiian Islands. The
second largest bit of land in this volcanic archipelago, only
some seven hundred square miles, is named for the Hawaiian
demigod credited in Polynesian lore with fishing these islands,
shoals, and reefs up from the sea—Maui. The most popular
areas of Maui lie to the north and west. Some people are thus
attracted to its opposite side, several hours away by car.

The two-lane Hana Highway parallels the tortuous lava-
formed coastline, passing through forests and over streams
and past waterfalls. After more than six hundred hard turns
and fifty-six single-lane bridges, palm-bordered ranches,
pineapple and sugarcane fields, red- and black-sand beaches,
jungle and volcanic craters all converge at Hana. The town
even boasts its own concrete strip of an airport. From his first
visit in 1968, the warmth of Hana—the gentle moist air, the
mild water, the aloha spirit—soothed Lindbergh's soul as well
as his body.

By that time, Hana had become a second home to several
wealthy Americans. A few, like Sam Pryor, were especially en-
tranced by a corner of this Shangri-la farther south, down the
unpaved continuation of the coast road. Over the course of the
ten miles of mud and potholes and moss-covered concrete
bridges, past the waterfall-fed pools in Ohe'o Gulch (which,
for publicity purposes, the local hotel christened the Seven Sa-

cred Pools), the setting grew more lush. Orchids, hydrangea, anthuriums, hibiscus, and bougainvillea in shocking colors blossomed everywhere; and the sweet fragrance of plumeria, papaya, mango, and guava clung to the air. Here in Kipahulu a few houses were perched on the cliffs, with sudden drop-offs to the rock-crashing water below.

Amid dense foliage in this distant corner of this far-off island, Sam and Mary Taylor Pryor carved out a simple estate, a large A-frame on one hundred acres of rolling grassland—with plenty of room for his pet gibbons, which he dressed up as children. An influential figure in town, Pryor strove to maintain the purity of Kipahulu by seeing that electricity never extended that far south. Lindbergh was enthralled by the remote location, the rugged landscape, and the rustic living. "I have never seen a more attractive place to live," he wrote Pryor upon returning to Darien. Lindbergh asked his friend to look out for any land in the area that might come up for sale, a plot on the coast where he could build a small house.

Pryor did better than that. He offered the Lindberghs five of his own acres, which they purchased for $25,000. Charles immediately drew plans and met with the builder who would construct their two-story A-frame, a modest boulder-and-concrete house with three small bedrooms and two baths. Work on the property began in the summer of 1969.

After spending a few weeks that rainy spring in the Pryors' guesthouse, waiting for her husband's arrival, Anne had soured on the idea of building there. "It is a beautiful coast—wild & beautiful—like a tropical Illiec," she granted, "but not the kind of place I want to be in alone—difficult of access—isolated—inconvenient to run—¾ hour away on a terrible washed out road from the nearest general store or settlement—no electricity . . . no help—and a damp climate." Worse than the inconvenience was the fact that Hana would contribute to her transience. "While C.A.L. can be himself anywhere & seems to find his roots in flight itself—in change—in action," Anne wrote in her diary, "I, who long to feel rooted more & more as I grow older—. . . am more and more 'déséquilibrée' by great leaps of air-travel—time-change—& new habitats." She tried to talk herself into liking Maui, but she kept coming back to the question of her ability to put down any roots there. "And if I do," she wondered, "won't they just be torn up again?"

As though demonstrating loyalty to his marriage, Lindbergh insisted on naming their houses—in honor of the shells in *Gift from the Sea*. The house in Darien became "Tellina," the genus of the Double Sunrise; and the Swiss chalet was christened "Planorbe," the French word for the snail-like Moon Shell. Touched by Charles's gesture, Anne went along with the plan, suggesting that the "Argonauta"—a mother who leaves her shell and starts another life—be affixed to the new house in Hawaii.

Charles assured Anne that she would come to care for Hawaii once Argonauta was completed and that he intended to spend more time with his wife there. He misled her on both counts. It rained steadily the first week in January 1971, when they returned to Hawaii to move into their newly completed house; and they quickly discovered that the roof leaked. Worse than that, despite Charles's admonitions, the architect and contractor had failed to create proper drainage for the house. A torrential downpour awakened them their first night; and muddy streams, just as Charles had foretold, sluiced through the house. They spent the next few hours out in the storm, he digging channels with a bucket while she built a mud dam. The house had not even dried out when they were invaded by armies of ants, spiders, cockroaches, lizards, rats, even a mongoose. And then Lindbergh was summoned to an emergency meeting of the Pan American board in New York.

Anne was, as she scratched in her diary, "furious to be left at this point in this place in this state. A place which is not of my choosing. I do not have friends, family, or interests here. It is not a place I would normally choose to live in alone. I only come for him—because he loves it & said he expected to be here with me. I am angry not only at him but at myself for hoping that he would at least stay here." Argonauta did not even have a telephone, and the nearest people were ten minutes away through the mud. Propane gas motors generated electricity—one for lights, the other for appliances; but, she wrote Lucia Valentine, she would gladly trade her few modern conveniences for a little company. What she found most discouraging was "the pattern of being left" and—after all her years of weeping to her therapist and wailing in her diary—her own inability to walk away from such unacceptable behavior.

She lay awake at night in silent fury, trying to plot the remainder of her marriage. "First," she realized, "I must harden my heart—not because I *don't* love him but because I *do*. I must harden my heart against him, against being vulnerable to him & his leaving, against being dependent on him. I must plan out my life alone. I must learn to cope with things alone here not only physically but emotionally." She spent the next few weeks readying the house for his return—mopping up, sweeping out dead animals, burning garbage, washing all their clothes. Through it all, it never dawned on Anne to pack her bags and go to a hotel . . . or to one of her other houses.

By the following year, Anne had made her peace with Argonauta. She routinely wrote up her shopping lists to Hasegawa's General Store, an impossibly cluttered emporium back in town—including such items as rat poison, animal traps, and a machete to hack at the wild bamboo that was overtaking many of the fruit trees they had planted—without batting an eye. "I have convinced your father that we will have to spray the walls with something strong (Ecology or no ecology) to get [the ants] out," she wrote Ansy. "It's either them or me!" But she could not convince Charles to fire up their second generator, the one that ran the lights—"because your father *likes* to use kerosene lamps." Yet again, Anne was "very disappointed" when her husband had to leave on business and cancel his return to Hawaii; but she was hardly surprised.

The night after she drove him to the airport she turned on the second generator and the lights. "It's OK to cook supper & eat by kerosene light if your husband is with you," she wrote Ansy, "but alone in the dark—NO!" The next morning she completely sprayed the outside of the house with more insecticide than Charles would ever have permitted. Anne's life in Hawaii would always be a struggle against the temperamental water and electrical systems and the vermin; but over the next few weeks, she surrendered to the intoxicating charms of Hana, enjoying its beauty and taking advantage of her isolation by reading through her diaries.

Lindbergh made a point of visiting Hawaii with increasing frequency, ultimately spending as much as two months a year there. He lobbied its senators to designate its Leeward chain as Wilderness Areas and Diamond Head as a national monument. In his efforts to preserve as much of the Hana coast as possible, he became active with The Nature Conservancy, an organization that obtained lands of exceptional natural beauty and conveyed their ownership to the United States Park Service. Both Anne and Charles contributed thousands of dollars toward the purchase of land in the Valley of the Seven Sacred Pools in the Kipahulu Valley, which would allow the existing Haleakala National Park to extend more than four thousand acres from the inland crater to the sea. As he had with the World Wildlife Fund, Lindbergh solicited money by writing letters and addressing small groups. (Anne endorsed the organization as well, deeding them Big Garden Island, off the coast of Maine, which her parents had given her as a wedding present in 1929.) The Nature Conservancy would not hesitate to call upon Lindbergh whenever they needed help raising money for difficult acquisitions—from the Lubrecht Forest in Montana to the Four Hole Swamp in South Carolina. This new cause gave him still more excuses to travel.

Richard M. Nixon also called upon his services, as his new administration proved eager to include him in their environmental policy-making. With Secretary of the Interior Walter Hickel informing Lindbergh that he was placing the eight species of great whales on America's Endangered Species List, and Secretary of State William P. Rogers encouraging him to "outline ways in which the field of conservation might be used to the advantage of diplomatic relationships," Lindbergh accepted the President's invitation to serve on The Citizen's Advisory Committee on Environmental Quality, chaired by Laurence S. Rockefeller. Through this committee, Lindbergh often provided language for an administration eager to show how "Green" it was. Nixon used Lindbergh as much as possible in "photo-opportunities," attaching his face to the Republicans' environmental protection activities.

Similarly, Lindbergh allowed himself to be publicly associated with the space program. In December 1968, the Lindberghs had accepted the invitation of the Lyndon Johnsons to one of their last official dinners, this one honoring the Apollo astronauts and James Webb, head of the National Aeronautics and Space Administration. Two weeks later they went to Cape Kennedy to watch the launch of Apollo VIII. At the request of astronauts Frank Borman, James Lovell, and William Anders, the Lindberghs joined them for lunch the day before their flight, their last meal on earth before blasting off on man's first voyage to the moon. Lindbergh inspired his hosts with tales of early aviation and of Robert Goddard, who had spoken to him forty years earlier of a multi-stage rocket that could one day reach the moon.

The next morning, the Lindberghs observed the launching from a special area reserved for astronauts and their families. "I have never experienced such a sense of power," he wrote one of the NASA directors afterward, having calculated that in its first second lifting off, the "thirty-six-story" rocket burned more than ten times the fuel Lindbergh had used flying from New York to Paris. After following the mission on television that Christmas at their son Land's ranch in Montana, Lindbergh called it "the greatest feat of teamwork in the history of the world." He and Anne sent the astronauts a congratulatory telegram, noting, "YOU HAVE TURNED INTO REALITY THE DREAM OF ROBERT GODDARD."

Only six months later, Lindbergh accepted an invitation from Neil A. Armstrong to attend the launch of Apollo XI, the mission that hoped to put the first man on the moon. The major television networks asked Lindbergh to appear on their news programs to provide commentary on the journey, particularly as it might compare to his own epochal flight. He refused all such offers, quietly attending the event with his son Jon. After what Lindbergh himself called a "fascinating, extraordinary, and beautifully executed mission," many drew parallels between the two shy, young Galahads of the sky. Television journalist David Brinkley, for one, could not help observing how the astronauts themselves "stood in the utmost respect, and even awe, of a man who had flown to Paris." Armstrong would later remind others that Lindbergh had flown solo with only a small team of technical backers, while he had been part of a three-man crew backed by a team of hundreds of thousands. And, Armstrong added, "Slim flew through miserable weather and stretched the science and art of navigation to find Le Bourget. We could see our destination throughout our entire voyage." Lindbergh heartily congratulated Armstrong afterward, adding in a postscript to his letter, "I wonder if you felt on the moon's surface as I did after landing at Paris in 1927—that I would like to have had more chance to look around."

In truth, the Apollo XI crewman with whom Lindbergh most empathized was Michael Collins, who circled alone in space while Armstrong and

"Buzz" Aldrin walked on the moon's surface. "Of course I feel sure that your sense of aloneness was regularly broken into by Mission Control at Houston," Lindbergh wrote him, "but there must have been intervals in between—I hope enough of them. In my flying, years ago, I didn't have the problem of coping with radio communication."

President Nixon invited Lindbergh to accompany him by helicopter to the U.S.S. *Hornet* to receive the returning astronauts. He refused. "My declining was based on the fact that I spent close to a quarter century, after my flight from New York to Paris, in 1927, reachieving a position in which I could live, work, and travel under normal circumstances," Lindbergh explained. He felt that the splashdown of the astronauts would, quite properly, "attract the greatest concentration of publicity in the history of the world, and that I could not avoid involvement because of my 1927 flight." This, Lindbergh added, "would, of course, tend to take me back into a press relationship and way of life I am most anxious not to re-enter."

Lindbergh would disappoint Nixon again just a few months later, when he went public with his opposition to the administration's billion-dollar support of the supersonic transport. Having long considered the SST a costly, noisy, impractical polluter, he concluded in a 1972 Op-Ed piece in *The New York Times:* "the regular operation of SST's in their present state of development will be disadvantageous both to aviation and to the peoples of the world. I believe we should prohibit their scheduled operation on or above United States territory as long as their effect on our over-all environment remains unsatisfactory."

During the span of the Apollo XI mission, Lindbergh hopscotched from Tellina to Argonauta, with stops in San Francisco and Seattle. It was a typical week of travel for him. As Anne had feared, the building of a third house encouraged her husband's travels rather than curtailed them. Whatever time they scheduled to be together invariably got cut in half by some environmental emergency. In 1969, he circled the globe five times, stopping wherever he felt he could do good.

That October, he went to Minnesota, where he helped establish the Voyageurs National Park on the Kabetogama peninsula at the Canadian border. For two days he explored the rugged region by air, boat, and on foot with Elmer L. Andersen, the former governor, and Russell W. Fridley, director of the Minnesota Historical Society, publicly pronouncing it "an extraordinary place" and telling the press it would be "tragic" not to make it a national park. Before leaving the state, Lindbergh visited his childhood home in Little Falls, then being restored as a museum. He enjoyed a reunion there with his seventy-seven-year-old half-sister, Eva Christie, whom he had hardly seen since their father's death forty-five years earlier. After little more than an hour together, he was gone.

Obsessive about remaining active, affixing purpose to every action, Lindbergh became the conservation movement's most tireless freelance. No person or place on earth was off-limits to him; no time was wasted. When a canceled flight to New York in the winter of 1969 left him stranded in Los Angeles for a few hours, he rented a Volkswagen and drove to Santa Barbara, to inspect the site of a recent oil spill. He followed up a five-day survey trip through Baja California in 1968 with a mission to Mexico City in 1972, voicing his concerns about the gray whale and the need to protect a dozen areas in Baja because of its extraordinary flora and fauna. Upon learning in 1970 that Akihoto wanted to see the *Tingmissartoq*, which was on display in Osaka for the World's Fair, he squeezed in a trip to Japan because he thought he could promote conservation firsthand with the Crown Prince. At several meetings in 1972 he successfully encouraged His Majesty King Taufa-ahau Tupou IV of Tonga to establish parks on his exotic islands. And in a handwritten note to Prince Philip of Great Britain, he suggested that a word from him to the Chief Minister of the Fiji Islands would go a long way in the marine conservation efforts there. In his efforts to see Brazil make the Reserve Forestal do Tumucumaque a national park, Lindbergh flew to Rio de Janeiro and met with a cadre of ambassadors, government ministers, and newspaper owners; he also flew to Brasilia, where he delivered a written appeal from the WWF to President Costa e Silva and appeared before the Senate.

In late 1968, Lindbergh traveled to the northern frontier of Brazil, near the Surinam border, where he lived for several days among the Indians in the Tumucumaque region. Members of the tribe subsisted primarily on the meat of wild pigs, birds, and monkeys killed by bows and arrows. Not completely unaccustomed to visitors, the tribesmen amused themselves by serving the flesh of wild animals to their civilized guests, delighting in watching their reactions. Most visitors, Lindbergh was told, passed up the bowl of stewed monkey; but he treated himself to three helpings. "Do you really like it?" one of the natives asked through a Catholic monk who translated. "Yes," Lindbergh replied with a straight face, "it's almost as good as *human* flesh."

As the fine line separating primitive man from the rest of the animal kingdom increasingly fascinated him, Lindbergh's conservation work kept drawing him to the Philippines. His love affair with this island nation began with the tamaraw, a wild buffalo just forty inches tall, which was indigenous to Mindoro, the fifth-largest island in the Philippines. By 1966, when Lindbergh first learned of the animal at IUCN headquarters in Switzerland, an estimated one hundred remained on earth, all prey to hunters, disease, and other elements of civilization.

In January 1969, Lindbergh arrived in the Philippines, without advance notice and with only the names of a few contacts. One was Thomas Harrisson, an English anthropologist whose work was partially funded by the IUCN. Upon their meeting, Harrisson observed how Lindbergh "lent his whole influence and energy" to conservation efforts for ten days. Harrisson arranged for Lindbergh to meet Dr. Sixto Roxas, one of the country's leading bankers and an economic adviser to President Ferdinand Marcos, who in turn scheduled a meeting between Lindbergh and Marcos himself. Lindbergh—staying at the Embassy as a guest of Ambassador G. Mennen Williams—expected ten minutes of pleasantries with the President and his wife. But he found them both "sincerely interested in conservation," and they kept him at Malacañang Palace for two hours. Lindbergh returned to the palace later in the week for a luncheon with Marcos's cabinet. He also visited the national legislature and met with the press.

Lindbergh made friends everywhere, especially on the wild, mountainous Mindoro, which he surveyed on foot and by helicopter. There, Professor Harrisson observed, "Lindbergh very effectively spoke to the crowds assembled to see him and enormously impressed them with the visible fact that a man of such world status *could* be interested enough to visit them for this conservation purpose." When Lindbergh returned to the Philippines in June, he learned that Marcos had ordered a seventy-five-thousand-hectare preserve around the principal tamaraw area and assigned thirty guards to protect it. Within two years, the tamaraw's numbers were increasing.

During these visits, Lindbergh also learned of the plight of the monkey-eating eagle, the largest eagle in the world, indigenous to Mindanao. In August 1969, Lindbergh rallied local support there by addressing a radio audience for the first time in twenty years. He even allowed a newspaper reporter—Alden Whitman of *The New York Times*—to accompany him on his travels, sending dispatches of his missionary work around the world. When Lindbergh returned to the Philippines that October, Marcos presented him with a Presidential Plaque of Appreciation "for inspiring and spurring action to save the country's prized fauna . . . from extinction; and for his pace-setting advancement of the cause of wildlife conservation throughout the world."

While in the Philippines, Lindbergh learned of sixty tribal groups that still inhabited its islands, many subsisting at prehistoric cultural levels. President Marcos expressed interest in protecting his country's heritage by appointing an adviser on national minorities, a controversial young man named Manuel Elizalde, Jr. "Manda," as he was known to his friends, was an heir to one of the largest conglomerates in the country—interests that extended from sugar to steel. A Harvard-educated, hard-drinking playboy, he turned his life around once exposed to the losing struggle the tribal peoples were waging against land developers. He established an organization called Panamin—an acronym for Private Association for National Minorities—the goal of which was to ensure the welfare of these people forgotten by time.

Finding a kindred spirit in Lindbergh, Elizalde gave him a brief tour of some settlements of the uncivilized tribes, generally spending a few hours, on one occasion the entire night. "As you know," Lindbergh wrote Elizalde after his second visit to the Philippines, "I am deeply interested in primitive peoples and the impact our civilization is having on them. . . . and the ways you are bringing assistance to them. I am thoroughly in accord with your philosophy of making assistance available to these minority peoples, but of not attempting to push them too far beyond their needs and desires." With every intention of returning soon, Lindbergh asked if it would be possible to arrange for him to "live quietly" among them. Because he slept well on split-bamboo floors and would carry his own blanket, he said he needed only a corner in one of the native huts.

When Lindbergh returned to Manila in October 1969, he rented a Consolidated-Vultee L-5 from the Philippine Air Transport Service and flew anthropologist Dr. Robert Fox of Panamin to an abandoned logging strip on the northeast coast of Luzon. There, beyond roads and radio contact, he lived among the semi-naked, black-skinned Agta tribe, sleeping on the beach beneath a leaf-sheaved lean-to. During his stay he learned that businessmen from the cities were threatening the lives of the Agta by deceitfully acquiring their territory. "If they keep on taking our land away," an Agta hunter told Lindbergh through an interpreter, "we will put poison back on our arrows."

Lindbergh lived among other tribes the following June, this time bringing Alden Whitman and a photographer. He hoped Whitman would report the crises the aborigines were facing, not only the shady real estate deals in Mindanao, Mindoro, Palawan, and northern Luzon but also the cultural war the "Christian-Filipino world" was waging against them. Lindbergh recognized it as a "war of shame," one in which the minorities were told they were ignorant, their dress was silly, and their names ugly. Elizalde's policy was to encourage the tribes to respect their own cultures and to partake in legal services if they wished to remain separate from the rest of the country or in social services if they wished to assimilate. Lindbergh became a director of Panamin.

On July 18, 1970, he rode with a busload of Panamin officials through South Cotabato on Mindanao. Passing through Surallah, where opposition to Panamin was known to be high, a truck sat before them blocking the road to the next town. The Panamin bus driver blasted his horn and slowed down, but the truck did not move. Instead fifteen men suddenly appeared, armed with automatic rifles. A member of the Philippine Constabulary who worked with Panamin emerged from their bus wielding his automatic weapon, and rifle barrels poked out of every one of its windows. Lindbergh was armed with a 9mm. Swiss HK submachine gun. Gunbolts clicked all round, but the ambush ended there.

Realizing the tension between Panamin and many Christian settlers, however, Lindbergh suggested to Elizalde that they call on the Mayor of Surallah—who had stood behind the truck that night with a hundred armed men. "No shooting was intended," he explained to Lindbergh when he and Elizalde returned to the region, "but if anyone had shot, it could have been very serious." After two or three days together, Lindbergh was made an Adopted Son of Surallah and Honorary Chief of Police, and the Mayor had become an adviser to Panamin. "I remain highly apprehensive," Lindbergh wrote Alden Whitman; "but as of the time we left South Cotabato, there was a reasonably friendly working relationship between Panamin and the Christians of Surallah."

Through his repeated visits to the Philippines, Lindbergh cultivated a cordial relationship with President Marcos, who remained sympathetic to his causes despite growing opposition from businessmen eager to exploit the land. Within a few years, Panamin was able to help the Agta in northern Luzon by establishing a school to teach the children how to maintain their property rights. Panamin also helped the more culturally advanced Taboli in southern Mindanao by sending troupes of their native-costumed dancers to Manila and other countries to display the beauty of their culture.

During their now occasional visits together, Anne came to understand the hold the Philippines had on her husband. "It is not simply wild-life & wilderness and its preservation," she wrote in her diary, ". . . nor is it entirely his study of & fascination with the impact of civilization on primitive life (which one can see there as in few places in the world) but it is also his extreme interest & admiration for what some Filipinos . . . are attempting to preserve & to build in their country—a multi-racial nation, living harmoniously together & preserving their divergences and dissimilarities." The country was one great laboratory for Lindbergh, where the laws of human nature could be tested. For all her festering resentment because of her husband's chronic absence, Charles's ever-expanding mind never ceased to amaze his wife.

"I must say Father has really done it this time!" Anne wrote daughter Ansy in April 1972, from Argonauta, where she had just heard on the radio that "Lindbergh & the anthropologists have been living in isolation with . . . the world's only surviving cavemen . . . on the side of a steep mountain deep in this southern Philippine rain forest." For one of the few times, media reports about Lindbergh did not exaggerate. A cave-dwelling, primitive tribe called the Tasaday had been discovered in the mountainous rain forests of southern Mindanao, a people with but the slightest knowledge of the world beyond their secluded foraging grounds; and Lindbergh helped organize the first expedition into their colony.

Jumping from a helicopter onto a treetop platform, which Panamin had previously erected in the rain forest, seventy-year-old Lindbergh felt he had leapt through time. "In seconds," he later wrote, "my environment had transformed from that of civilization to that of a stone-age-cave-dwelling culture. I felt that I might have been on a visit to my ancestors a hundred thousand years ago." Across a sharp-toothed mountain ridge and a "deep, thorny, rainsoaked valley" loomed the Tasaday caves. The expedition pitched camp in the forest.

The next morning, Lindbergh and his Panamin colleagues climbed the slippery mud trail until they reached the high caves at the jungled cliff edge. A few small, brown men with black, bushy hair, wearing loincloths, stood at the openings of the caves above. Grabbing at vines, Lindbergh hoisted himself up and into the thirty-foot-deep dwelling, where eighteen people sat around a pair of fires. "No sign of any attempt to improve or modify cave in any way although generation after generation apparently has lived in it— probably for centuries," Lindbergh noted.

Observing the Tasaday over the next week, Lindbergh had never seen "a happier people." The jungle supplied them with all their needs, and they knew of no threats to take anything away. Elizalde managed to ask the tribesmen what they wanted most from the outside; and one of them said, "We do not know what to ask for because we do not know what we want." When asked how long they had lived in that cave, one replied, "Since time began." Outside, over the sound of the rain pattering on his tent at night, Lindbergh heard human howls.

With the discovery of the Tasaday came practical and ethical questions as to how the Philippine government should treat them. Exploitation—from the media and foresters—was sure to follow. Lindbergh recognized that this Panamin expedition helped paved their way; but he also felt that they were in a position to protect the tribe preemptively, for logging roads would otherwise approach their caves within a few years. Lindbergh and Panamin returned to the caves the following month, bringing cloth for blankets and a doctor with medicines. By then, in response to a Panamin request, President Marcos had proclaimed a reserve around the Tasaday. Panamin offered them their choice of futures, isolation or integration. The natives said they would like to remain in their cave culture, as they had since the dawn of man. But within a few months the outsiders proved to have infected the tribe with curiosity, which gradually drew them beyond the forest.

Lindbergh's intense interest in the Philippines was as visceral as it was intellectual. While living among the primitives, he found himself stripping his life of "civilized accoutrements" and going native himself. On one of his Panamin expeditions, he was especially attracted to a young woman. Anne would later discover a photograph of the nubile Filipina, one provocative enough for her to assume that Charles had slept with her. She and her husband never discussed the liaison, just as they had never discussed Anne's earlier affair with Dana Atchley; but there was no doubt in her mind that it had occurred. Lindbergh had skinny-dipped all his life; but now, back at Tellina, he took to wading nude in the Long Island Sound at low tide, wallowing in the ooze and covering himself in mud, like some primitive man. Then he would splash himself clean and sunbathe in the hollow of the big rock on the edge of the cove, naked.

His boundless awe of nature drew Lindbergh into searching for its creator. Always a loner rather than part of any flock, Lindbergh had long eschewed formal religion. But in 1971, he retreated one day to the Regina Laudis Priory in Bethlehem, Connecticut, at the suggestion of Anne, who periodically found solace there. Communing with the Benedictine nuns on their pastoral grounds, Lindbergh was surprised, as he wrote one of the sisters afterward, by "the welcome, the singing, the sense of earth, the spiritual atmosphere, and with these qualities, a broadness of viewpoint and sense of humor that result in a character I have never encountered before in a religious organization." He would return several more times over the next few years, when he felt the need to center himself, a chance to search his soul.

Lindbergh showed signs of mellowing, appearing more frequently in public, even dressing in black tie without complaint. His non-conservation activities of late were a chary selection from the hundreds of invitations that continued to arrive every year. He accepted the National Institute of Social Sciences Gold Medal Award in 1968 and was made an honorary fellow of The Society of Experimental Test Pilots in 1969. At both ceremonies, his message was not much different from the one he delivered in 1973 at the dedication of the Interpretive Center at the one-hundred-and-ten-acre Lindbergh State Park in Little Falls, Minnesota. From the front porch of his boyhood home, he told two thousand well-wishers, "I believe our civilization's latest advance is symbolized by the park rather than by satellites and space travel."

Although he still had no interest in celebrating the past, Lindbergh took part in commemorative events if he thought the attendant publicity might honor unsung friends. And so in 1968 he accepted, in a private ceremony, an Honorary Doctorate of Science from Georgetown University, largely because of the care with which they curated the Alexis Carrel collection. And after spending several afternoons in Sands Point, Long Island, when his friend Harry Guggenheim was dying, Lindbergh appeared at the 1973 posthumous dedication of Falaise as a county museum. There he spoke to interviewers and strolled freely among the guests through the twenty-six-room Norman mansion where he had written *"We,"* courted his wife, and found sanctuary from the press with his new bride. Upon reaching his former bedroom, one woman noticed the four-foot-by-seven-foot bed and could not help asking, "General, how did you ever sleep in this bed?" Anne could not resist interjecting, "Oh, he likes to curl up." That made Charles laugh, all the way down the grand staircase.

He also made exceptions for the military. In 1969, he attended a reunion in Colorado Springs of the 475th Fighter Group, his war buddies from the South Pacific. And in 1973, he accepted the National Veterans Award, presented on behalf of twenty-eight million American veterans. Both events were happy occasions for him, public reminders that the man many accused of having been a traitor was, in fact, a patriot.

More than thirty years after his explosive Isolationist statements, Lindbergh still refused to recant anything. And though he said he never cared what the public thought of him, private actions occasionally revealed otherwise. He sometimes blurted out nonsequiturs, which revealed that his fall from grace stuck in his craw. One weekend, while David Read, a young psychiatrist friend of the Lindberghs, was visiting, Charles said suddenly, "Dave, they didn't pay attention to the rest of the speech." Noticing that Lindbergh suddenly looked hurt and puzzled, Read asked what he meant. Lindbergh told him about that night in Des Moines in September 1941. "I did explain," Lindbergh said with great sincerity, "why the Jews would be concerned."

Ever since he had become famous, Lindbergh had been aware of false statements about his life and beliefs; and a generation later, many of those mistakes were reappearing in new books and articles. After discussing this problem with his closest new friend, William Jovanovich—a dynamic young publisher who had become president of Harcourt, Brace & World—Lindbergh reread the journals he had kept between 1938 and 1945 and decided to publish them. He believed those two thousand entries were, "to the best of my ability, an accurate record."

He cut his six hundred thousand words by a third. While he prided himself on doing no rewriting—not even to correct the occasional bad grammar—several excisions were of an editorial nature. Without fully realizing that some of his comments were anti-Semitic, he intuitively deleted many of them. His admiration for Germany's accomplishments got soft-pedaled. The result of his labors, which he squeezed in between his travels, was a thousand-page tome.

The Wartime Journals of Charles A. Lindbergh was published in September 1970 to great fanfare. It received attention not only in book reviews but also on editorial pages and the front sections of news magazines, reigniting the old America First debate. Reaction to the book fell almost en-

tirely along political lines, echoing prewar attitudes. Lindbergh's own introduction to the book revealed a stubborn adherence to the beliefs he had
voiced decades earlier, a failure to admit any mistakes.

> In order to defeat Germany and Japan we supported the still greater
> menaces of Russia and China [he wrote]—which now confront us in
> a nuclear-weapon era. Poland was not saved. The British Empire has
> broken down with great suffering, bloodshed, and confusion. England
> is an economy-constricted secondary power. France had to give up her
> major colonies and turn to a mild dictatorship itself. Much of our
> Western culture was destroyed. We lost the genetic heredity formed
> through aeons in many million lives. Meanwhile, the Soviets have
> dropped their iron curtain to screen off Eastern Europe, and an an-
> tagonistic Chinese government threatens us in Asia.

In reviewing *The Wartime Journals* for the *New York Times Book Review,* Professor Eric Goldman wrote perhaps the most objective appraisal
that appeared anywhere, evaluating Lindbergh's style as well as his sub-
stance. Commenting on Lindbergh's visit to Camp Dora, Goldman wrote:
"In a five-page entry so moving that it may well find a place in American literature, he cries out against 'the shame and degradation' of which nations are
capable. He did not add what he might have been witnessing if the United
States had followed the leadership of men like himself, who let the finest in
themselves be overwhelmed by addiction to the apparent present and fear of
the onrushing future." The book became a solid bestseller and was a semifi-
nalist for a National Book Award. Lindbergh's fan mail included letters from
Nixon as well as Kennedys ("That family—and me—admire you more than
anyone," wrote Jacqueline Onassis). But *Wartime Journals* did not foster
new opinions of Lindbergh so much as reinforce old ones. It did, however,
temper some of the long-standing hatred toward him, as it revealed at least
a man who had been loyal to his country.

By the 1970s, Lindbergh was devoting as much time to other people's
writings as he was to his own. While writing "sketches" and chapters of what
he was calling an "autobiography of values," Lindbergh also wrote intro-
ductions to books on Maui, the Vanguard rocket, and the Tasaday tribe, as
well as Michael Collins's autobiography, *Carrying the Fire: An Astronaut's
Journeys.* He provided detailed answers—both by mail and in person—to authors researching the lives of many of his friends, from Henry Ford to John
P. Marquand; and he was especially generous with anyone writing about Dr.
Carrel. Lindbergh championed the work of several authors enough to recommend them to William Jovanovich—including Bruce Larson, who wrote

a biography of Lindbergh's father, and Wayne Cole, who wrote an account of Lindbergh's battle against intervention.

Lindbergh also began to read a new generation of biographies about himself, all of which he found so riddled with errors that he typed up detailed memorandums of the mistakes and filed them with the Library of Congress.

No writer received more of Lindbergh's encouragement than his wife. Several ecological pieces she wrote for *Life* were but a suggestion of the extent to which he impacted upon her work. She credited him further with goading her into a major project, a "companion piece" to his war journals. The process of sifting through more than a quarter century of diaries and letters and editing them into publishable form would occupy Anne for the next decade. She was ambivalent about the process, approving of it in principle but dreading "the reaction, the invasion of my privacy, the publicity, the insultable letters." The more he pushed her, the more she realized her diaries would be "a counter & filler-in for the misapprehensions & false pictures given by some of the reaction to his." The first volume, *Bring Me a Unicorn: Diaries and Letters, 1922–1928,* was published in 1972 to critical and popular acclaim, enough to get her through the next few years of entries, which climaxed with the kidnapping and killing of her child.

"Even though I have read the last part (1932) six or seven times—perhaps more," Anne wrote in her diary in April 1972, "I still go blind with tears at places. It is so far in the past and that girl who suffered is not me. She died & was reborn again—slowly. It is because I'm reading about a stranger that I cry." When the book, *Hour of Gold, Hour of Lead,* was published the following year, hundreds of thousands of readers felt they were reading about a friend. Another three bestselling volumes would be published over the next seven years, making Anne Morrow Lindbergh one of the century's most popular diarists.

The hardest volume for Anne to assemble proved to be the years between 1939 and 1945, which she entitled *War Within and Without.* Her purpose in publishing it, she wrote in a long introductory essay, was "to show the unwritten side of [my husband's] *Wartime Journals,* to say the things he could never say. By looking at the inner side of a tapestry, one can often uncover patterns and colors that reveal a complexity and meaning invisible on the surface." To her friend Lucia Valentine, Anne wrote, "I must not struggle so hard to defend him, but there are sides that must be shown— the record should be there. Only then can I be free to let him go—to let the public figure go." She would publish no new books after that.

After a half-century of the practice, Anne became dilatory in her diary-keeping. Preparing the earlier works for publication was only part of the reason. The Lindbergh marriage had become a one-sided affair, at Charles's disposal whenever he chose to partake; and that proved too dispiriting to record. When they were together, he expected her attention to be focused on him, his self-absorption reaching comical proportions. He sometimes forbade her to pick up the telephone when it rang; and if he found her spending too much time gabbing to friends, he sometimes grabbed his gun from the closet and threatened to shoot the phone. When Anne replaced some seventy-five-year-old mattresses in the guestroom with a new set—bought on sale at Bloomingdales—it sparked a sermon on her contributing to the fall of civilization. He became obsessed with the general breakdown of law and order and the upsurge in anarchy, and he often groused about "what's happening to the country." In some cases, he had just cause—especially in discussing airplanes, which had become crime zones, as terrorist hijackings were becoming epidemic. He would say "It's no time to be living around a big city." And she would reply, "It's no time to be flying between homes."

Their conversations became more contentious, with Anne constantly wondering when her husband would reappear next. The children provided all the emotional support they could. "I don't think [Father's] fair to do this to you *again*, even without torrential rainstorms," Reeve wrote her mother in the spring of 1972, when Lindbergh was returning from yet another trip to the Philippines. "What does the monkey-eating eagle got that you don't got, I'd like to know." But with Jon pursuing oceanographic interests and raising salmon in Washington, Land ranching in Montana, Ansy writing children's books in France, and Reeve teaching in Vermont—all raising children of their own—there was little any of them could do for their mother.

Ironically, Scott was the one who brought his parents together, but only for a moment. After sharing their shock over the news of his marriage, Anne's feelings turned to remorse while Charles's turned to rage. She visited Scott on her visits to Europe and wrote sympathetic letters to him. He stopped seeing his son and fired off curt, and occasionally cruel, letters. "I am disgusted with you and ashamed of you," he wrote one year after Scott's marriage; "but I still care for you, deeply. What relationship this will bring between us in the future, I do not know." A few more rounds of letters in 1969 brought them to an impasse. "When you awake to what you have been and are doing to yourself," he wrote on June second, "if I can be of help please let me know." Closing the letter, "My love to you always," he stopped writing him.

Through Anne's visits and reports from his other children, Lindbergh remained apprised of Scott's progress, of his graduate work in animal psychology at Strasbourg University and his creating an eighty-acre research preserve in the Dordogne, where he and his wife studied South American howler monkeys. But Lindbergh maintained his silence for almost three years. In April 1972, shortly after his seventieth birthday, he tried to break the deadlock, writing, "I do not know whether I will see you, hear from you, or write to you again. If not, then I would like to leave this with you as my last message. . . . You have the ability to succeed in about anything you seriously apply yourself to. But I want to again emphasize to you that professional and material success, no matter how great, is trivial in comparison to what you make of yourself as a man."

Scott invited his father to visit him and his wife in their animal habitat. But Lindbergh refused, still disapproving of "the standards and the way of life you have apparently laid out for yourself." While he said he would always welcome Scott's letters, another year of silence lapsed between them. In April 1973, Scott sent his father a compelling description of his work, which involved studying monkey societies and relating their feelings to human emotions. Lindbergh replied, recalling the days when he and Dr. Carrel had talked of raising apes on a small island. Then he chilled his response by adding that he hoped the second half of Scott's life "is not going to be expended largely in raising and experimenting with monkeys." He asked, "Are you going to be content as an American living on an inherited income in a chateau in southern France while the world about you is aflame in many areas and in a state of flux unparalleled in history?" The former silence returned.

There was, in fact, an unspoken explanation for Lindbergh's sudden reaching out and his irrational withdrawals. This decade-long struggle over control had become part of a larger battle of body and emotions in which Lindbergh found himself engaged. During a routine physical examination in October 1972, Dr. George Hyman had discovered an abnormal node that proved to be a lymphoma; another irregular node further suggested cancer. At the end of the month Lindbergh checked into a small room in the Harkness Pavilion at the Columbia-Presbyterian Medical Center in New York as Mr. August to have the growths removed and biopsied. The diagnosis had been correct, and on January 31, 1973, he began three days of radiation therapy.

Lindbergh had a severe anemic reaction to his treatment and had never felt so terrible in his life. For the next few months he was weak and tired. He shed thirty pounds from his already lean frame, and he looked drawn. He and Anne told everyone, including their children, that he had contracted a virus during his travels. He chose to recuperate in Maui, where the Hawaiian sun brought some color to his face. He was soon eating again and sleeping well.

One morning, he walked to the Pryors and asked his friend a question with enough nonchalance not to arouse any suspicion. "Sam," he queried, "where are you going be buried?" Pryor was startled but answered without hesitation. "Right behind the little church I've restored about twenty minutes walk from here." Lindbergh said he would like to see it; and they hiked down a dirt road to the Ho'omau Congregational Church, built by missionaries from Connecticut more than one hundred years earlier. Far enough off the main road to go unnoticed, and sheltered by a banyan tree, pines, and coconut palms stood a small, white house of worship, made of lava rock and stucco. From its wooden tower, the original missionary bell tolled every Sunday. Inside, light flooded through six large windows onto the white walls, unadorned except for one simple wooden cross and a few pewter sconces. Two chandeliers hung over the ten pews. Outside lay an old Hawaiian burial ground, with some new graves set among the palm trees. Beyond this shaded area, where the Pryors had already interred some of their apes, a pasture stretched to a high cliff that looked onto the Kipahulu Bay, white water crashing over a jagged mound of lava rock near the shore.

Walking cliffward, at the center of that great sward, Lindbergh asked, "Who is over there?" Upon learning that the land was available, Lindbergh arranged with the state and church authorities to secure a thirty-foot-wide burial plot on that very spot. Lindbergh helped Pryor restore the church, and some days he could be seen clearing foliage from the neglected graveyard.

Later that spring, Lindbergh suffered from an excruciating case of shingles, which limited his travels and cost him another ten pounds. His blood count low, flu and other minor maladies plagued him for months. He discouraged visitors, though he and Anne did entertain Imelda Marcos and Manda Elizalde at lunch one day in Darien. While he never completely recovered that year, he put up a good front, carrying on his essential business, sandwiching trips to his three houses.

Anne finally got to spend more time with her husband. "This, of course, has a reaction on my life," she wrote her sister, "because it virtually isolates me from the people I used to see when he went off. . . . What I have to face is a new and different un-balance in our relationship and in our life. And I must somehow learn how to right it . . . so that I am not either exhausted, or so frustrated that I lose my temper over minor and unrelated details, or so depressed because of the apparent monotony or sense of imprisonment, that I draw in to my shell & give up." Months passed between diary entries. When she finally found a moment to catch up in her little "Cuckoo Clock chalet" above the main house in Switzerland, she wrote, "It has been a year of pressures & anxieties. 'Alarms and excursions.' " Regular blood tests and additional biopsies suggested that the radiation had Lindbergh's cancer in remission.

His vitality never completely bounced back, but his appetite, weight, and spirit did. Into 1974, Lindbergh made one nonessential trip to Europe that year. In February, he met with J. Paul Getty at Sutton Place, the billionaire's Tudor castle outside London, to garner extra publicity for the $50,000 Getty was donating to the World Wildlife Fund. That month, Lindbergh turned seventy-two, the mandatory retirement age from the Pan American Board of Directors. Although he was made an honorary member of the board, he was no longer obliged to make any trips anywhere.

At the start of the year, the Lindberghs changed their legal residence from Connecticut to Hawaii. He planned future journeys—including the Midwestern Governors' Conference in Minnesota and a tour of Brazil in July—but he traveled only to Maui, resting there four times by May. During that fourth visit, he and Sam Pryor and a Hawaiian named Joseph "Tevi" Kahaleuahi, a local bulldozer operator and builder, walked around the graveyard of the Ho'omau Congregational Church and marked a burial site with thick stakes and twine. Back in Darien, Lindbergh spoke of summering in Switzerland.

On June second, however, he came down with a fever, which spiked to 104 degrees. Lindbergh checked into Harkness Pavilion and found himself bedridden for several days. After two weeks, he seemed strong enough to return home, but the doctors worried about their inability to correct his bloodcount. He still did not want anybody to know how ill he was; and he forbade Anne from informing the children. By chance—"miracle from heaven," wrote Anne—Jon showed up in New York on business mid-June. He insisted on seeing his father, whose condition could no longer be completely concealed.

The "virus" that kept Lindbergh's fever from breaking was, in fact, cancer that had invaded his lymphatic system, affecting the bone marrow, which produced "bad blood." He began to respond well, however, to a new drug. After more than a month in the hospital, he was told he could go home and, with continued progress, on to Switzerland for the summer. On the third of July, he decided to take a "trial run," by attending a Pan Am meeting midtown Manhattan. Starting out, he felt so good he thought of taking the subway—to save the cabfare. After the effort of walking from his hospital room down to Broadway, however, he hailed a taxi. The outing was enervating but successful. He began a course of chemotherapy and blood transfusions.

Lindbergh returned to Tellina on Saturday, July seventh. It was brutally hot, and the trip home exhausted him. He slept most of the day, with a fever and chills. But he began improving every day after that, walking around the house, sitting on the terrace, eating and sleeping well. Jim Newton called from New York, and Charles invited him to supper, regaling his friend with tales of the Philippines until midnight.

While the results of Lindbergh's chemotherapy would not be immediate, those of the blood transfusions were. They stimulated him, and he was told he could have them as often as necessary. As he seemed to be on the rebound, the Lindbergh children were given the complete story of their father's health, though Anne never spoke the name of his disease, euphemizing it as "the basic problem."

Despite the regular freshening of his blood supply, Lindbergh's strength ebbed. After a few weeks of test results, it became obvious that "the basic problem" was worsening. He canceled his trip to Minnesota, and the possibility of going to Switzerland became more remote every day. On Wednesday, July twenty-fourth, he returned to the hospital, where the doctors told Anne they could no longer offer any hope of recovery. They would step up his chemotherapy, but they believed he could survive but a few weeks at most. Still fighting off the possibility of death, Lindbergh asked all sorts of medical questions. "It is as if the fire of the disease were raging in him, devouring him," Anne confessed to the Reverend Mother at Regina Laudis. "Since his nature has always had so much of fire in it, this seems rather fitting."

Lindbergh's children gathered around him, Ansy coming in from Paris, Reeve from Vermont. Land telephoned his younger brother in France; and though Scott was then suffering from hepatitis, he was prepared to visit if his father so wished. Thinking it would take a miracle for the two most stubborn members of the family ever to speak to each other again, Anne did everything in her powers to enable it. She prayed; and she suggested that Scott write a letter to his father first—"to make some kind of a bridge." It did not have to be a long letter, she told him—any subject that might open a dialogue. Scott wrote at once, mostly about his work; but there was no mistaking the underlying purpose of his missive. "I am getting increasingly uncomfortable about the number of years that are collecting into the time that has passed since I last saw you," he wrote. ". . . I've been all wrong in waiting for the problems to dissipate into a more or less distant past, in anticipating that my work would eventually create new levels on which we could get together. If lack of consideration and negligence are at the base of our differences, then what I've done, relegate our relationship to temporary oblivion, could only increase those differences." Anne read the letter to Charles in the hospital, and he was visibly pleased.

Scott immediately flew to New York and made his way to the Harkness Pavilion. Alone in Room 1148, he and his father talked for hours. "Charles has seemed so much happier . . . with this painful knot loosed," Anne wrote from the hospital waiting room to a friend. "And it may save Scott's life in the future. It would have been a hard burden to live with." Anne shared the news of the reunion, and her husband's condition, with his half-sister, Eva Lindbergh Christie Spaeth—from whom Charles had been estranged most of a lifetime. "Now they find they are alike much more deeply in thought and philosophy and work," Anne wrote Eva on August tenth. "He feels his own thoughts and beliefs being continued in Scott's work and writings. It makes him very happy and I am so grateful we have had this time for both of them."

Word leaked that Lindbergh was lying in the Intensive Care Unit at Columbia-Presbyterian, and well-wishing messages streamed in. Anne read him those she thought would please him most—from President Nixon, the DeWitt Wallaces, and Eva, who said she was "proud to know you are my brother." Jim Newton flew to New York for a bedside visit. Lindbergh's dear friend and publisher Bill Jovanovich closed a long letter by noting, "I am, as always, at your service and in your debt as your happy companion and unwavering friend. You have my good wishes, Charles, and my hope and my love, and that is the whole of it."

Over the next few days, Lindbergh accepted his fatal condition. On August fourteenth, he telephoned Jovanovich and said, "It is time we talked. Can you come to Columbia-Presbyterian?" When the publisher arrived, Lindbergh spoke to him about the book of memoirs he had been assembling over the years. He asked Jovanovich to read four hundred pages of manuscript to determine "whether it is any good and if it should be published." Jovanovich read all night and returned to say that it was and it should be. Lindbergh then directed him to the brown leather bag in the hospital room, which contained half the pieces that would make up the final manuscript. Another thousand pages, he explained, were at Tellina or in his locked files at Yale. As instructed, Jovanovich drew up a contract and a letter to the Trustees of Yale in which Lindbergh's wishes were spelled out, that Jovanovich should serve as editor as well as publisher, that he should "establish a sequence" out of the sometimes unconnected pieces of manuscript, and that he should inform the reader that while the writing was all Lindbergh's, "parts of the text were subject to editing consistent with his purpose."

Over the next two days, Lindbergh weakened visibly, though his voice grew stronger. On Friday, August sixteenth, he asked for a copy of his will, which he had amended the preceding year by removing Scott's name as either a trustee or a beneficiary. He went through the fourteen-page document, and, in a discernibly feeble hand, printed Scott's name five times, careting him back among his siblings. Later that day, he shook up everybody in the room with an extraordinary request. "I want to go home," he said, turning to Anne, "—to Maui."

Most of the doctors would not hear of it. An argument could be made to let him return to Tellina, but Argonauta was out of the question. Dana Atchley understood the patient better than any of the others, however, and knew nobody would be able to change his thinking. He said he would sign him out of the hospital. They reached Dr. Milton Howell in Hawaii, who had discreetly assisted in treating Lindbergh's condition over the past two years, and Lindbergh said to him, "Milton, I have eleven physicians here. . . . and they advise me that they aren't going to be able to help me any more. I have eight to ten days to live, and I want to come back home to die. I'd rather spend two days alive on Maui than two months alive in this hospital here in New York City."

Howell tried to dissuade him, arguing that his doctors there knew his condition best and that he thought nobody would sign a certificate of fitness to travel. But Lindbergh's mind was made up. He asked Howell to locate a house where he might spend his last days, one closer to the medical clinic in Hana than Argonauta. Howell arranged for Lindbergh to move into the guest cottage belonging to Jeannie and Edwin Pechin, friends who had just left on a cruise to Alaska.

Jon Lindbergh took charge of transporting his father from Harkness Pavilion to Hana. Dr. Atchley recommended an Air Force ambulance plane, but Sam Pryor, then in New York, said that would be politically difficult. He offered a special plane from his fleet, but Jon said his father's principles would not rest well with that or with a private charter. A regularly scheduled United Airlines flight seemed the only alternative, despite the high risk of publicity. Pryor said Lindbergh's stretcher could be placed over the first-class seats, and privacy curtains could enclose the entire compartment of the plane. Lindbergh was thinking of making the flight sometime the following week; but Atchley said he did not think they should wait that long. They targeted Sunday morning.

On Saturday, Lindbergh received two blood transfusions. Revitalized, he spent much of the day reminiscing with Jon about growing up in Minnesota. He called Sam Pryor, who said United Airlines was prepared for the special situation and that the airline doctor would sign the consent form necessary for so unfit a passenger. Then one of Lindbergh's attending physicians announced that he and all the doctors involved in his case had unanimously agreed that the plan was "medically unsound" and "incompletely thought out." He said he wanted at least thirty-six hours in which he would put together a small medical team to accompany the patient. Lindbergh asked the doctor to elucidate, in strictly medical terms. The physician described the worsening pneumonia, the spreading cancer, and the recurring infections; he mentioned the possibilities of hemorrhage, discomfort, lack of privacy in the plane, and an emergency landing should he become worse en route.

Lindbergh praised the doctors for having done "a magnificent job," but he realized they were fighting a losing battle. He did not want to chance "another 36 hours," which might bring enough deterioration to prevent his going at all. The doctor accused the patient of turning his back on medical science. Lindbergh replied that science had done all it could, that the problem was no longer medical but philosophical.

William Jovanovich appeared twice that day, to discuss the final manuscript and contract. Before leaving, Lindbergh gazed at his friend and asked, "Do you think I am dying well?" Jovanovich said yes.

Later that day, Lindbergh discussed his burial plans with Jon. He described the plot he had arranged at the Kipahulu church and the kind of grave he wanted, right down to its drainage system. Scott was not sure whether their father meant for him to come to Hawaii, where he had never been. But there was no question in anybody else's mind about his making the trip. That evening, Lindbergh spoke by telephone to his daughters, who had gone with their children to North Haven. Anne, Scott, and Jon packed up Lindbergh's belongings and returned to Darien. For the sake of logistics, Lindbergh insisted they meet him the next morning at Kennedy airport, without stopping off in the city.

Bill Jovanovich arrived at the hospital at 6:30 that morning and met one of the attending doctors, who said there was a good chance Lindbergh would die in the air. The publisher rode with Lindbergh in the ambulance to the airport, where Sam Pryor awaited, having arranged the getaway without any publicity. A little after eight, the family and Pryor stood in the first-class section of the United jet, leaving room for a pair of stretcher-bearers to carry Lindbergh aboard. As they were about to transfer him onto the bed that had been made over two knocked-down seats, Lindbergh, referring to Jovanovich, said, "I know you are strong fellows but let my friend here hold my middle: I am pretty tall." After doing his part, Jovanovich leaned over and kissed him twice.

By the time Sam Pryor said good-bye, Lindbergh's eyes began to well up with tears. The curtain was drawn around the bed, which was six inches too short for its patient and was lengthened with a stack of pillows. The family took their seats on the opposite side of the cabin; and then the other passengers, unaware of the proceedings up-front, boarded.

United Airlines flight 987, a DC-8, departed at 10:30 that morning. Lindbergh nodded off through much of the trip and drank some water and milk along the way. Scott administered his father's medicine during the journey. For the most part, Anne sat by his side, watching the country pass below, commenting to her sons that this trip was analogous to the historic flight in 1927, as "No one believed he could do either and survive."

As the Hawaiian Islands came into view, Lindbergh perked up and looked out the window with obvious pleasure. Approaching Honolulu, the captain wanted first to circle Maui, providing his special passenger with a panorama of the island. Lindbergh rejected the idea, noting that all the others on board had schedules to keep.

Land Lindbergh had traveled from Montana to Honolulu, arriving two hours before his father. He used the time to ensure Lindbergh's smooth transfer to an ambulance plane, a twin-engine Beechcraft, which Sam Pryor had arranged to be drawn up to the side of the jet. As he entered the first-class cabin of the United jet, Land was shocked to see how much weight his father had lost; but he took heart in the brightness in his eyes and the firmness of his handshake. A young medical attendant cursorily checked Lindbergh over and cheerily said he would be up in no time. Despite the young man's kind intentions, the fatuousness of the remark made Lindbergh angry, and he told him off. As the patient was moved from one plane to the other, three pilots stood off in the distance, holding their caps in their hands. Land accompanied his parents in the Beechcraft, his brothers following a little later.

Lindbergh had asked Milton Howell not to bother meeting him at the Hana airstrip, but the doctor disobeyed. Before deplaning, Lindbergh motioned him to his side. "Now, it is understood why I have come here, isn't it?" Lindbergh asked. "I know I am going to die. . . . I know that I have only a short time to live. I don't want anything unnecessary. I don't want any heroics." He asked Howell to assist in making his demise "a constructive act."

The Pechins' small guest cottage sat atop a hill, its living room opening onto a large lanai with a beautiful view of the coast. Oxygen and intravenous equipment were set up in the bedroom, which looked directly out onto tropical foliage and the Pacific. Lindbergh appeared extremely pleased to be there; and to the sound of the surf below, he fell asleep.

The new day began with Dr. Howell outlining his basic program, which was to keep Lindbergh as alert as possible, though never at the expense of comfort. He explained that the malignancy had already blocked one lung and there were indications that it had spread to the other. Once it attacked the pleura or heart covering, there could be severe pain, which Howell said he would control with sedatives.

Lindbergh began this journey as he had all his others, with checklists. Usually in the mornings, when he was feeling strongest, he funneled all his energies into final preparations, particularizing how he wished each step of his departure carried out. "Details," Jon noted in a log he kept, "to a minute degree that appalls the rest of us. How do you talk about such things with someone that close to you who is dying. It may be rational enough, but it takes some getting used to. . . . He is looking at death as one last adventure and throwing himself into the preparation to the fullest."

Lindbergh started with the grave, which he wanted Tevi Kahaleuahi to prepare in the traditional Hawaiian style. Island superstition generally restricted the digging of a man's final resting place until he had died; but, having already been condemned to death, Lindbergh urged Tevi to start digging right away. A local Kahuna, a holy man, blessed the site before Tevi put more than a dozen workers on the job. The fourteen-by-fourteen-by-twelve-foot pit was partitioned, leaving room for Anne, and lined with lava rock, two feet thick along the sides. Tevi inspected every rock for size, shape, and smoothness. "Father was obsessed about drainage," Jon observed; and that led to a lengthy argument about the removal of a wild plum tree in one corner of the burial plot. When Tevi said he would be sad to see the plum tree go, Lindbergh agreed to let it stay.

The Lindbergh sons worked on the grave as well. "It might seem that helping build your father's grave even before he died would be very strange," Jon Lindbergh wrote that week. "But in actuality it felt an intimate, very loving family project. To do something physical in this respect was very strong therapy for me." More vigorous since arriving in Hana, Lindbergh thought for a moment that the move there might just have bought him a few extra days, possibly weeks. But on August twenty-third, he felt "rather punk" and suggested adding men to the digging crew.

Lindbergh asked his friend John Hanchett, vice president of the Hana Ranch, to oversee the building of his coffin. He wanted it made by hand of native wood—rough-sawn, flat-sided and -topped, with no curves. Two ranch hands built the box as specified, using one-inch-thick planks of eucalyptus robusta, known locally as "swamp mahogany."

Another discussion dealt with the lining of the coffin. Lindbergh wanted several layers of different biodegradable materials, starting with a tarpaulin on the bottom. On top of that he wanted cowhide, until Hanchett said the only hides readily available were greasy and smelly. Anne suggested an old Hudson Bay blanket that Charles had once given his mother. Calls were made to the family members stateside to locate it, and it was express-mailed that day. Lindbergh wished to be covered with tapa cloth and cotton sheets from Argonauta. Nobody could find pure cotton sheets there, so he settled on fifty-percent cotton, fifty-percent polyester.

Lindbergh also asked Hanchett to order his headstone, a slab of granite two-feet-by-three-and-a-half feet and almost a foot-and-a-half thick—so heavy that it would not be disturbed. It would come from the Rock of Ages quarry in Barre, Vermont. He wanted the sides rough-hewn, polished on top only where it would be inscribed. From a sample book Lindbergh selected a simple typeface to be cut one-quarter of an inch into the stone, just deep enough so that the elements would keep it clean. Below his name, he wanted to note the dates and places of his birth and death, Michigan and Maui; and beneath that, he and his wife and their three sons agreed on a two-line passage from the 139th Psalm, which suggested a supreme belief in the Lord: "If I take the wings of the morning, / And dwell in the uttermost parts of the sea." The remainder of the passage, which would not be inscribed, went on to say: "Even there would Thy hand lead me. / And Thy right hand would hold me."

They turned their attention next to the funeral services. Lindbergh wanted one short service before the burial, a prayer and hymn at the gravesite, and a slightly longer memorial service a day or two later. He insisted on no eulogy. Instead, he wanted passages read from a broad range of thought, evidencing his belief that "no one culture or religion had a monopoly on truth." Anne presented a potpourri from which he selected readings from Isaiah, St. Bernard of Clairvaux, Gandhi, St. Augustine, the Hindu Mundaka Upanishad, and a Navajo prayer. Anne also offered her husband a sampling of hymns. While singing one she thought suitable, Charles shook his head and said it was no good. "But," Anne replied, "the music is by Bach, and you can't do better than that." Charles said, "The music is all right, but the words are corny." Anne wondered what to do, until he resolved the situation: "Let's just have Hawaiian hymns," he said, "then nobody will know what they mean."

Lindbergh also requested that at least part of the service be conducted by a Hawaiian deacon, Henry Kahula, who was the proprietor of the local Chevron station. Anne paid a call on him, and he suggested a number of Hawaiian poems, prayers, and hymns, which he would sprinkle through the service. Lindbergh wanted the funeral kept private, noting that anyone from Kipahulu was welcome. He asked Dr. Howell to see that his pallbearers, local men who were working on the coffin and grave, attended in work clothes. Howell protested, explaining that they would want to show their respect by wearing their finest clothes. Besides, he told Lindbergh, "You can't tell people what to wear."

Lindbergh then asked Milton Howell if he would perform perhaps the most difficult task, that of representing the family to the press. Lindbergh felt that the articulate physician, who had once served as Mayor of Glencoe, Minnesota, could best protect Anne. When it came time to face the inevitable barrage of journalists, Lindbergh said, "I would like for you to answer the questions just as they are. I would hope that it would be kept dignified—which you do very well." To Howell's surprise, Lindbergh said that he wanted the editor of the *Maui News*—and nobody else—to be informed of the impending death right away, so that when the moment came, the obituary would be practically written. By establishing this exclusive arrangement, Lindbergh believed he could buy his family a few extra hours. Indeed, the island was already talking.

A minister from California named John Tincher had been assigned to the Congregational Church in Hana for the month of August. The young reverend was just a few days from leaving the island when he learned that Charles Lindbergh had recently been flown in to die and that he was staying in a secret location. One day, while shopping in the little Hana Ranch Grocery, Tincher could not help noticing the small woman in front of him at the cash register who seemed to be buying out the store. Tincher watched as Anne Lindbergh signed for her provisions. After making his purchase, he followed her to her car and introduced himself, indicating that he was "available if she wanted to talk to somebody at this time." On Friday, the twenty-third, she drove to his beach house and left a note with her telephone number. He called, and they met the next day for an hour. Neither committed to his conducting a service, because Tincher had to leave the island the following Tuesday.

When they needed a break from the emotionally difficult tasks at hand, Anne and her three sons went to Argonauta, where they hacked away with machetes at the mimosa brush, cane grass, and banana patches that had grown around the house. Exerting themselves in the hot sun made them feel they were sweating out their "troubles and tensions."

For hours at a time, between Lindbergh's naps or in the evenings, at least one family member would sit with him as he reminisced—about his mother and "Brother," about the early days of aviation, about the war. America First was on his mind as well; and he told Land one day, "Don't let your mother spend a lot of time defending me." Each night he wanted an update on the progress of his grave.

Surrounded by their sons one evening, Anne asked Charles if he would describe what he was feeling, because, she said, "you're going through an experience we all have to go through." He said he had never before realized that "death is so close all the time—it's right there next to you," and that he felt totally "relaxed" about it. "It's harder on you watching than it is on me," he added. One day, they tried to get him out on the lanai to behold the beautiful view, but the effort proved too great. "I can't do this," he said; "I have to go back in." He lost a little ground every day and said he had already come close to crossing over two or three times.

Each of the sons had enough private moments with his father to prevent later regrets about things left unsaid. In surviving the last two weeks, Lindbergh had made up for the lost time with Scott. Their mutual love and respect became obvious to them and everybody around them. "Great relief to M[other]," Jon observed in his diary. "A ray of light in a rather dark scene." Having left his wife alone to care for their troops of primates, Scott had to return to France. The whole family, however, rejoiced in the reconciliation, including Ansy and Reeve, who remained in North Haven, receiving regular reports.

On August twenty-fifth, the grave and casket were completed; and Jon returned to Seattle. He expected to see his father again but realized there was a good chance he would be too late in returning.

Lindbergh's breathing became labored that afternoon, and he felt chest pains. Dr. Howell, who had been visiting twice a day, gave him aspirin with codeine, half-grain tablets which Lindbergh broke up, swallowing quarter-grain bits only when necessary. Because he steadily drank enough fluids,

Howell never had to hook him up to an intravenous drip. He did keep an oxygen mask at Lindbergh's side, however, which he replaced that afternoon with a larger breathing apparatus. "Now, Doctor," Lindbergh asked that Sunday night, "is the calibre of the oxygen tube really large enough to supply me with the amount of oxygen I need?" In fact, it was not, as the lymphosarcoma was filling his lungs. Later that night, reaching over to adjust a valve so that he might get more air, his arm dropped and he drifted into a coma. Dr. Howell sedated him and planned to move him to the clinic the next day at nine. Anne, Land, and a nurse remained by his side through the night, his wife holding his hand.

In the morning—Monday, August twenty-sixth—Lindbergh seemed at peace. After an early breakfast, Anne and Land went into the bedroom and found him barely breathing. The Howells arrived a few minutes after seven; and after examining him, the doctor said, "He's going now." Anne took his hand and could hardly believe how lifeless it had become since the night before. Land instinctively wanted to hold his father, but he knew how much he disliked being touched. And so, with his mother at one end of the bed, he sat at the other, putting his hand on his father's foot. For more than ten minutes they sat there as the room became increasingly still. "And then," recalled Land, "he just went."

Silently, everybody left the room, leaving Anne alone with Charles. She gave him a last kiss. She wanted to have a longer moment alone with him, but there was no time. He had prepared everybody to move him from his bed to his grave as swiftly as possible, not only to beat the invasion of the press but also for legal reasons.

Lindbergh had insisted that he not be embalmed. A "natural" burial was legal in Hawaii so long as it occurred within eight hours of death. But the law also prohibited interment until a death certificate had been signed by the coroner, and he was on "the other side" of the island. At Lindbergh's urging, Dr. Howell had already made preparations. He had filled out the certificate with everything except the date of death; he had apprised the coroner of the situation; and he had his son standing by to drive the document to him in Wailuku, two hours away. Howell followed all of Lindbergh's instructions to the letter. He dispatched his son; he summoned Tevi, on a construction job on the other side of the island; he notified the police, asking them to provide security around the cottage and the church; and he called the newspaper editor, telling him that Lindbergh had died and asking him to hold the news at least until noon.

Minutes later, the local radio station got word. Not three hours after Land had called Jon in Seattle to tell him their father had died, he heard it on the radio. A few women rushed to the church to sweep it clean and to strew ginger stalks and hibiscus onto the deep window ledges. John Hanchett and a dozen ranch hands pulled up to the Pechin guest cottage and unloaded the heavy eucalyptus casket. The Hudson Bay blanket arrived that morning.

Tevi, flown into Hana by private plane, arrived at the house to perform the most personal duties of the day. Lindbergh had asked the sixty-three-year-old laborer to dress him. Anne handed him the outfit Charles had selected—a pair of old, gray cotton pants and a khaki shirt; he would wear neither a belt, because of the metal buckle, nor shoes. Tevi, John Hanchett, and two ranch hands then carried the dressed corpse to the blanket-lined coffin and set him down, tucking in the sheets exactly as prescribed. Just as one of the men prepared to hammer down the lid, Anne called out, "No, wait." She approached for a final look and lost her composure. With tears in her eyes, she placed four white flowers inside the casket, which was finally nailed shut. Eight men carried the heavy box out to Hanchett's blue pickup. Tevi hopped in back so that he could ride alongside the coffin, which was covered with canvas.

It was early afternoon when the local police sergeant began his drive from the Pechin cottage down to the Kipahulu church, followed by Hanchett's truck, and a small convoy of other vehicles. As they passed the Ohe'o Stream, none of the sightseers at the Seven Sacred Pools had any idea that the funeral cortege of Charles Lindbergh was passing by.

The service was scheduled for three o'clock, and Milton Howell had said he would talk to the press at four. But by two o'clock, the coffin had been carried inside to the front of the church, and all the intended guests were present—no more than fifteen people, most of the men in their work clothes. Candles flickered in the sconces and the smell of ginger filled the small church. Knowing that the serenity of the moment could not last much longer, Anne and Land asked for the service to begin.

In a moment of absolute tranquility just before the Reverend John Tincher spoke, a barefooted Hawaiian woman, who occasionally helped with the housekeeping at Argonauta, walked to the front of the church, her apron full of flowers. She knelt by the coffin; and, placing one blossom at a time, she covered it with a blanket of plumeria. Exactly as scripted, the service of silent prayer and Tincher's reading of five selections took less than twenty minutes.

Because the casket was so heavy, six or seven men carried it back to the truck, and John Hanchett drove it to the gravesite. It was difficult lowering the coffin into the deep stone-lined hole; and, as it was done, Tincher spoke the words of committal. People tossed flowers into the tomb, and Land actually climbed in to place one white plumeria blossom on the coffin for his mother. Henry Kahula led the singing of a Hawaiian hymn with three other voices; and the music, Land recalled, "just soared out and away with the wind and the crashing of the waves below us."

Only one local reporter was present for the service, respectfully in the background. By three o'clock, when the mourners were driving off, the first television crew was on its way to the church, not a half-mile away. The dozen members of the press who followed felt they had been tricked. But Milton Howell explained the situation and invited them to his house, where he answered all their questions.

For the last time, Charles Lindbergh captured the attention of the world media. News of his death commanded the entire upper-left corner of the front page of *The New York Times*. The paper paid further homage with a two-page obituary by Alden Whitman, a column of tributes, including one from the President of three weeks, Gerald Ford. The *Times* editorial, titled "Passing of a Hero," spoke of Lindbergh as "both the beneficiary and the victim of a celebrity experienced by no other American in this century." It was fitting, it noted, that he chose to die and be buried "in the utmost simplicity, far from the crowds that had hailed and repelled him in his lifetime." Beginning that afternoon, close to one thousand messages of condolence began to pour in, from around the world.

At two o'clock the following afternoon, two dozen people arrived at the Ho'omau Church for Lindbergh's memorial service. Another dozen reporters had arrived early to cover the event; and Anne Lindbergh invited them to take seats in the rear pews. Jon and Sam Pryor sat up front with Anne and Land. John Tincher, in his final hours on Maui, conducted the multifaith service, again with Henry Kahula. Anne was especially moved by the singing of the last hymn, a sublime rendition of "Hawaii Aloha." The entire program lasted less than thirty minutes, without any suggestion of Lindbergh's accomplishments. When it was over, Anne thanked each person who attended, even the reporters. She would return to the mainland later that week, and settle into a progressively reclusive widowhood in Connecticut, reducing her life to visits with her children and seventeen grandchildren. In time, she stopped going to Switzerland and Hawaii at all.

Lindbergh's *Autobiography of Values* would be published in 1978, exposing a more philosophical, even poetic, man than most readers expected. It concludes on a transcendental note. "After my death," he wrote, "the molecules of my being will return to the earth and the sky. They came from the stars. I am of the stars."

And on certain days at that quiet graveyard overlooking Kipahulu Bay, the molecules collide in such a way that the water and sky blend into one seamless spectrum of blue—a deep sapphire far out to sea that brightens almost to the color of glacial ice as it ascends, that very same pale but radiant blue that the sky over Sweden sometimes casts in the last summer.

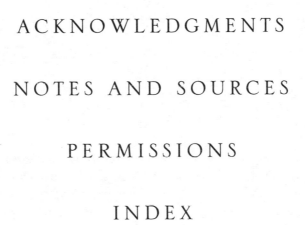

ACKNOWLEDGMENTS

NOTES AND SOURCES

PERMISSIONS

INDEX

ACKNOWLEDGMENTS

In 1989, Phyllis E. Grann, Chairman and CEO of Putnam Berkley, asked if I would be interested in writing a book she had been wanting to read for fifteen years—a biography of Charles Lindbergh. "Yes and no," I told her. Lindbergh had long been on my short list of potential subjects, I explained; but, alas, I had already ascertained that his papers were under lock and key and that his family had no interest in opening them to researchers. Mrs. Grann did not care; she simply wanted to read about Lindbergh. I explained that the only circumstances under which I would attempt such a book would be with the complete cooperation of the Lindbergh family, which would allow me to see and quote from what was rumored to be hundreds of boxes of material.

After almost a year of correspondence, Charles Lindbergh's widow, Anne Morrow Lindbergh, asked if we could meet. And after a week of meals and conversations together—usually in the company of her youngest daughter, her sister, and two of her closest friends—she handed me a light-blue envelope containing the legal permissions—handwritten in ballpoint pen—to undertake this biography. She offered complete access, imposed no restrictions, and made no demands, expressing only her hope that I would not rush through the material. A few weeks later, I received another letter from Mrs. Lindbergh—what I feared, at first, was a withdrawal of the permission. "You can't write about Charles without writing about me," she explained, as she granted access to all *her* papers as well, including some sixty years of diaries.

I am profoundly grateful to Anne Morrow Lindbergh not only for the access to what proved to be some two thousand boxes—counting the personal papers of her parents and siblings as well as her in-laws—but also for the time she contributed to this project and for her trust. I am equally beholden to the five remarkable Lindbergh children, all of whom made themselves (and their papers and diaries) available to me. Jon, Land, Anne, Scott, and Reeve Lindbergh also provided hours of unusually thoughtful, articulate, and candid reflections of their father. I have seldom encountered such generosity of spirit. I hope this book offers some compensation for their investment. I am especially indebted to Reeve Lindbergh, the family shepherd, who never failed to put her own work aside in order to answer just one more question or to help me locate just one more source. Quite simply, this book would not exist were it not for her.

Other Lindbergh relatives also contributed lavishly to this book. Anne Lindbergh's sister Constance, the late Mrs. Aubrey Morgan, was a great fount of inspiration and information. I also had the pleasure of spending time with Dwight Morrow, Jr.'s former wife, Margot—Mrs. John Wilkie—who mixed her sharp insights with invigorating humor. Charles Lindbergh's niece, Lillian Johnson, provided a most memorable day of memories. While not related to the Lindberghs by either blood or marriage, James and Eleanor Forde Newton have been part of their family for sixty years. I learned as much about friendship from Jim and Ellie as I did about the Lindberghs.

Because the majority of this book is based on the Lindbergh archives, I am grateful to the institutions that preserve them. More important, I would like to thank the individuals at those libraries that helped make my years of research so pleasurable. The team in Manuscripts and Archives at Yale University's Sterling Memorial Library became friends as well as colleagues, always two steps ahead of me. I am most grateful to Judith A. Schiff, who helped chart my two-year course through the massive collection there; she also offered her own memories of Lindbergh. William R. Massa, Jr., performed countless deeds above and beyond the call of duty; Christine Connolly and Sandra Staton combined extraordinary efficiency with uncommon cheerfulness.

Many thanks as well to Jean Streeter, Martha Clevenger, John Furlong, and Sharon Smith at the Missouri Historical Society, who were exceptionally helpful. I am equally obliged to: Margery Sly, the former archivist at Smith College, and curator Amy Hague; Emily Silverman in Archives at the Robert Frost Library at Amherst College; John Decker at the Stearns County Historical Society; Rebecca DuBey at the Southern Museum of Flight in Birmingham, Alabama; Adele Wall at Falaise at the Sands Point Preserve, Long Island; Lieutenant C. Thomas DeFeo, archivist Mark Falzini, and Dolores Raisch at the New Jersey State Police Museum in West Trenton; Michael Hoarn at High Fields; Dr. William Joyce, Jane Snedeker, and my longtime friend Mary Ann Jensen at the Princeton University Library. The Minnesota Historical Society is fortunate to have so knowledgeable and accommodating a site manager as Donald Westfall at the Charles A. Lindbergh House in Little Falls, where I spent several days. Gene Bratsch, Executive Director of the Charles A. and Anne Morrow Lindbergh Foundation in Minneapolis, came to my rescue so many times during the writing of this book that I have lost count; thanks also to Dacia Durham and Marlene K. White at the Foundation.

Researching this work demanded considerable travel beyond the continental United States; and many people helped to make those voyages especially fulfilling. In Sweden, I am most grateful to Richard Lucas for a full day of history and hospitality. Thanks also to Kerstin Lappea, Professor Karl-Gustaf Hildebrand (who interrupted his moose-hunting to talk to me), and the Svensson family—Helga, Sven, and Sune—who gave up an afternoon so that we might tour Ola Månsson's former farm. In Great Britain, my thanks go to Ludovic Kennedy, Betty Gow, Anthea Secker, and

Evelyn C. Molesworth; Nigel Nicolson provided a wonderful lunch, a tour of the gardens at Sissinghurst, and a study in which I could read his father's personal papers and make notes. In France, I received especially gracious assistance from Ambassador Pamela Harriman, Denise Cardinet, and Louis Le Jouan, who took me to the top of Coz Costel at Buguélès and pointed the way to Illiec. In Hawaii, Jeannie Pechin showed me all the Lindbergh sites and the local points of interest in between.

For interviews, informative correspondence, legal permissions, supplying letters and other information pertaining to the life of Charles Lindbergh, I am indebted to: Governor Elmer L. Andersen, Dr. Richard Bing, Richard W. Brown, Robert R. Bryan, Esq., Ev Cassagneres, Colonel Raymond H. Fredette, Russell Fridley, Paul E. Garber, Susanna Beck Hatt, Anna Hauptmann, Charles G. Houghton III, Peter Kahn, Esq., John Konchellah, Lyle Leverich, Mary Jo Lewis, James W. Lloyd, Esq., James Lord, Benjamin Lupica, Dr. Theodore I. Malinin, Glenn Messer, Susan Miller, Richard Moore, Karen Pryor, Dr. David Read, Oren Root, General H. Norman Schwarzkopf, Jr., General Robert Lee Scott, Robert J. Serling, Mrs. Truman Smith, James Stewart, R. Douglas Stuart, Jr., the Reverend John Tincher, Russell Train, Billy Wilder, the Honorable David Wilentz, and Helen Wolff. Years ago, T. Willard Hunter interviewed several of the supporting players in Charles Lindbergh's life. The transcripts of those conversations have proved invaluable to me, as has Willard's friendship.

When I began work on this book, I received a call from actor-director-pilot-producer-restaurateur-writer Tony Bill. He said it was urgent that I meet him at his house. There he revealed one of the most remarkable private collection of books I have ever seen, with its emphasis on aviation, Lindbergh a specialty. "Consider this your library," he said with characteristic magnanimity. And I did. He has been this biography's greatest booster, infusing my past eight years with the spirit of Lindbergh.

The friendship and innumerable kindness of many others sustained me through the last decade. When my fifteen-year-old Altos 8500 broke down, threatening to take much of this book with it, my brilliant friend John Riley saved the day. Were it not for him, I believe my protagonist would be forever lost in the fog of cyberspace. Heartfelt thanks as well to Helen Bartlett, Leonora Hornblow, Fiona Lewis, Alan and Nancy Olson Livingston, Lucille LoRicco, Professor Theodore and Jan Marmor, Irene Mayer Selznick, Professor Kim and Marty Gwinn Townsend, and Nathaniel Tripp. Katharine Hepburn has been my Lady Bountiful for two decades, but never more so than during my years of research in New Haven, during which time she provided a weekend-home away from home. Margaret "Peg" Perry provided a very hot lunch and even hotter conversation every Saturday that I was in Connecticut. My parents, Barbara and Richard Berg, have ceaselessly provided encouragement and loving support, as have my brothers—Jeffrey, Tony, and Rick.

At a time when publishing has been engulfed by conglomerates, this volume has been fortunate enough to be nurtured and protected by many individuals who simply love books. Lynn Nesbit has proved to be a caring friend as well as a dazzling agent, sorting out every matter with exceptional intelligence and grace. Her associate Bennett Ashley solved many of our legal riddles. I am grateful as well for the business wizardry and friendship of Robert Bookman. At Putnam, this book has received nothing but total support from many people in every department—notably the book's designers, Claire Vaccaro and Jennifer Daddio, the copy editor, Claire Winecoff, and the eagle-eyed attorney, Alex Gigante. I am especially grateful to the late George Coleman, whose passion for this project fueled me in the early days, and to Neil S.

Nyren, whose editorial advice greatly enhanced this manuscript as he guided it toward completion.

Nobody has done more to help bring this work to fruition than those named on the dedication page. After seeing that it got started, Phyllis Grann provided eight years of unflagging support, which culminated in a superb display of line editing. She has made every detail of the book a top priority in her life. As has Kevin McCormick, who has shared in every aspect of its development. He remains my lodestar; and his wise counsel, astute criticism, and constant sacrifice of his own time for the sake of my work benefited this book beyond measure. My love and gratitude to them both. The last decade certainly would not have been as much fun without them.

—A.S.B.
Los Angeles
May 1998

NOTES AND SOURCES

Most of the documents cited below are part of the Charles A. Lindbergh Collection (#325) or the Anne Morrow Lindbergh Collection (#829), which are housed in Manuscripts and Archives in Sterling Memorial Library at Yale University in New Haven, Connecticut. A number of papers, particularly those pertaining to the building of the *Spirit of St. Louis* and the preparation of its flight to Paris (including the letters from Lindbergh's mother) are part of the Charles A. Lindbergh Collection at the Missouri Historical Society in St. Louis, Missouri. The letters and diaries of Anne Lindbergh's mother and sister, Elizabeth C. Morrow and Elisabeth R. M. Morgan, respectively, are part of the Sophia Smith Collection at Smith College, Northampton, Massachusetts; those of Anne Lindbergh's father come from the Dwight W. Morrow Papers in the Amherst College Library, Amherst, Massachusetts. Much of the material pertaining to Charles Lindbergh's ancestors is part of the Lindbergh Collection at the Minnesota Historical Society in St. Paul, Minnesota; miscellaneous documents pertaining to his early years and the transcripts of interviews T. Willard Hunter conducted with people who were part of Lindbergh's final days can be found at the Charles A. Lindbergh House, within Charles A. Lindbergh State Park, in Little Falls, Minnesota. Documents relating to the reaction of the Franklin D. Roosevelt administration to Lindbergh's involvement with the America First movement are located at the FDR Library in Hyde Park, New York. Most of the aforementioned archives include numerous newspaper and magazine clippings—many without sources, headlines, dates, or page numbers; this explains the occasional omission of such data. Information obtained through interviews is designated with an (I).

Other abbreviations are:

AC   Dr. Alexis Carrel
ACL   Amherst College Library

AML	Anne Morrow Lindbergh (wife of CAL)
ASB	A. Scott Berg
ASL	Anne Spencer Lindbergh (daughter of CAL)
AOV	CAL, *Autobiography of Values* (New York: Harcourt Brace Jovanovich, 1978)
AW	Autobiographical writings (includes unpublished drafts of books, articles, sketches)
BMAU	AML, *Bring Me a Unicorn* (New York: Harcourt Brace Jovanovich, 1972)
BUM	CAL, *Boyhood on the Upper Mississippi* (St. Paul: Minnesota Historical Society, 1972)
CA	Charles August Lindbergh (father of CAL)
CAL	Charles Augustus Lindbergh
CMM	Constance Morrow Morgan (sister of AML)
DWM	Dwight Whitney Morrow (father of AML)
(D)	Diary
DAVIS	CAL (U-M) on Kenneth Davis's *The Last Hero: Charles A. Lindbergh and the American Dream* (Garden City, NY: Doubleday, 1959)
E	Epigraph
ECM	Elizabeth Cutter Morrow (mother of AML)
ELCS	Eva Lindbergh Christie Spaeth (half-sister of CAL)
ELL	Evangeline Lodge Land (grandmother of CAL)
ELLL	Evangeline Lodge Land Lindbergh (mother of CAL)
ERMM	Elisabeth Reeve Morrow Morgan (sister of AML)
FN	AML, *The Flower and the Nettle* (New York: Harcourt Brace Jovanovich, 1976)
FRDT	CAL, biographical notes to Colonel Raymond Fredette, 1972
GS	AML, *Gift from the Sea* (New York: Pantheon Books, 1955)
HB	Henry Breckinridge
HG	Harry Guggenheim
HGHL	AML, *Hour of Gold, Hour of Lead* (New York: Harcourt Brace Jovanovich, 1973)
JML	Jon Morrow Lindbergh (son of CAL)
L	Lindbergh (CAL)
LML	Land Morrow Lindbergh (son of CAL)
LROD	AML, *Locked Rooms and Open Doors* (New York: Harcourt Brace Jovanovich, 1974)
LTW	AML, *Listen! The Wind* (New York: Harcourt, Brace , 1938
(M)	Memorandum
MHS	Missouri Historical Society
MNHS	Minnesota Historical Society
(N)	Notes
NTO	AML, *North to the Orient* (New York: Harcourt, Brace, 1935)
NYT	*The New York Times*
OFAL	CAL, *Of Flight and Life* (New York: Charles Scribner's Sons, 1948)
RHG	Robert H. Goddard
RML	Reeve Morrow Lindbergh (daughter of CAL)

ROSS   CAL (U-M) on Walter S. Ross's *The Last Hero* (New York: Harper
          & Row, 1968)
SML   Scott Morrow Lindbergh (son of CAL)
SSL   CAL, *The Spitit of St. Louis* (New York: Charles Scribner's Sons,
          1953)
(T)   Telegram
(U)   Unpublished
WE   CAL, *"We"* (New York: G. P. Putnam's Sons, 1927)
WF   AML, *The Wave of the Future* (New York: Harcourt Brace & Co.,
          1938)
WJ   CAL, *Wartime Journals* (New York: Harcourt Brace Jovanovich,
          1970)
WWW   AML, *War Within and Without* (New York: Harcourt Brace
          Jovanovich, 1980)
Y   Lindbergh archives at Yale University

1   KARMA

E: CAL, "Preface" to Milton Lehman, *This High Man: The Life of Robert H. Goddard* (New York: Farrar, Straus and Company, 1963), p. xv.

ANTICIPATING CAL'S ARRIVAL: T. Bentley Mott, *Myron T. Herrick: Friend of France* (Garden City, NY: Doubleday, Doran, 1930), pp. 340–1; John Zuckerman (of Stockton, CA) to "Dear Abby" (Abigail Van Buren), "Who Saw Lindy Land in Paris?" *Los Angeles Times,* c. 1990; "Tilden and Hunter Lose in Fast Match," *NYT,* May 22, 1927, p. X:1; Edwin L. James, "L Does It," *NYT,* May 22, 1927, p. 2; George H. Muller (Manager, Concepts and Features Department, Car Engineering, Ford Motor Company), text of speech, "I Was There," July 9, 1977; n.a. "Lindbergh" (U article), Jan. 3, 1938 [MHS, B31/F8]; Harry Crosby (ed. by Edward Germain), *Shadows of the Sun: The Diaries of Harry Crosby* (Santa Barbara: Black Sparrow Press, 1977), p. 146. [N.B. Crosby spelled "Lindbergh" without an "h"; I have made similar corrections in spelling whenever I felt the error interrupted the flow of the quotation.]

LE BOURGET AND AFTERMATH: *SSL,* p. 492; *AML, (U-D),* Jan. 25, 1953; CAL (U-AW), IV-2 (218/626), 1947; Harry Crosby, *Shadows of the Sun,* p. 146; *AOV,* pp. 79, 402.

2   NORTHERN LIGHTS

E: CAL quoted in AML to ELLL, Sept. 15, 1933 [*LROD,* p. 110].

OLA MÅNSSON IN SWEDEN: CAL to ELCS, Jan. 6, 1960; Grace Nute to CAL, Oct. 30, 1936 and Sept. 12, 1938; Grace Nute to ELCS, Dec. 15, 1939; Richard B. Lucas, *Charles August Lindbergh, Sr.: A Case Study of Congressional Insurgency, 1906–12* (Uppsala, Sweden: Acta Universitatis Upsaliensis, 1974), pp. 18–20; Marianne Bergstedt, "Ola Månsson in Parliament and His Fast Disappearance to the United States" (graduate paper at University of Uppsala), April, 1972; Gunnar Westin to CAL, Oct. 30, 1936; Gunnar Westin, "Appendices," Sept. 28, 1935; Grace Lee Nute to CAL, c. late June, 1938, Sept. 12, 1938, Nov. 20, 1940, and Jan. 28, 1941; Gunnar Westin to Grace Lee Nute, Apr. 14, 1937; Sten Carlsson to Debbie Stultz, Jan. 7, 1977; Gunnar Westin to Debbie Stultz, Dec. 8, 1977; Linda Lindbergh Seal to CAL, Mar. 30, 1953; Grace Nute (N) on (I) with P. P. Ornberg, Dec. 10 and 15, 1936; Sven Svensson to ASB (I), Sept. 18, 1993.

The name Lindbergh was fashioned from the Swedish words for linden tree and mountain. Had Ola Månsson (August Lindbergh) adhered to the traditional system of patronyms, his son Karl (Charles) would have used the surname Olsson (the son of Ola).

EMIGRATION TO AMERICA; SETTLING IN MINNESOTA: Grace Lee Nute, ed., "The Lindbergh Colony," *Minnesota History, 20,* Sept., 1939, pp. 243–58; Norman Thompson and Major J. H. Edgar, *Canadian Railway Development from the Earliest Times* (Toronto: The Macmillan Co., 1933), pp. 68, 76–7; Grace Nute (N) of (I) with Frank Lindbergh, June 9, 1936; George W. Prescott, clerk, "Declaration of Intention" of August Lindbergh, Aug. 4, 1859; *CAL* to Grace Nute, Dec. 30. 1936; C. S. Harrison, *Adorning the Beulah Land of the Hither Shore and How to Become an Extinguished Minister* (York: Nebraska), pp. 42–3; Mrs. L. E. Tubbs, "Letter Written . . . From Los Angeles," *Sauk Center Herald,* June, 1927; "Melrose First Home of Ls in America," *Melrose Beacon,* July 21, 1927, pp. 1, 4; "Pioneer Settler Called Beyond," Apr. 21, 1921, p. 1; Linda Seal to CAL, Dec. 25, 1939 and Apr. 9, 1960; AML (N) of (I) with Juno Lindbergh, July 29, 1935, accompanying CAL to Grace Nute, Apr. 10, 1936; Perry Lindbergh to ELLL, May 25, 1930, Sept. 6 and 20, 1932; Frank Lindbergh to CAL, Feb. 6, 1940; Linda Lindbergh Seal to ELLL, n.d. [Y: 245/437]; ELLL to Grace Nute, Dec. 16, 1939; CAL (U) draft of family history [MHS], n.d.; August Lindbergh, Homestead application #797, Oct. 31, 1867, and purchase certificate #3919, Mar. 11, 1868; Grace Nute (N) of (I) with Myrom D. Taylor, Oct. 7, 1936; Grace Nute (N) of (I) with Juno Lindbergh Butler, June 4, 1936; Grace Nute (N) of (I) with Perry Lindbergh, June 16–19, 1936; ELCS (N) of family history, c. Nov., 1958; CAL (N) of family history, Jan. 20, 1922 [prob. 1923]; *AOV,* pp. 44–7.

Most prior accounts of August Lindbergh's immigration asserts that he entered the United States in New York. This error emanates from Lynn and Dora B. Haines, *The Lindberghs* (New York: The Vanguard Press, 1931), p. 8. August Lindbergh's sworn "Declaration of Intention to Become a Citizen of the United States" clearly names Detroit as his point of entry.

C.A.: Grace Nute to CAL, Dec. 18, 1936; Bruce L. Larson, *Lindbergh of Minnesota: A Political Biography* (New York: Harcourt Brace Jovanovich, 1973), pp. 11–23; CA campaign pamphlet, n.d. [MNHS: P1675, Box 13]; Grace Nute (N) of (I) with Perry Lindbergh, June 16–19, 1936; Frank A. Lindbergh (N) on family, n.d. (MNHS: "Corr. And Misc." undated 1908–60); CAL to Grace Nute, Sept. 20, 1936; Grace Nute (N) of (I) with Frank Lindbergh, June 9, 1936; Grace Nute (N) of (I) with Perry Lindbergh, June 16–19, 1936; Thomas Pederson, "CAL, Sr. (As I Knew Him)," n.d.

The marriage between August Lindbergh and Louisa Carlin [*sic*] was recorded in the records of the Stearns County Court House: *Marriage Record Book I,* p. 363.

MARY LA FOND: Grace Nute (N) of (I) with Mrs. Robert Herron, Sept. 9, 1937 and with Mr. and Mrs. A. M. Opsahl, May 11, 1937; Dr. A. W. Abbott to Dr. Trace, 1898.

THE LODGES OF DETROIT: Silas Farmer, *The History of Detroit and Michigan* (Detroit: Silas Farmer, 1889), pp. 3, 6, 704; Edwin A. Lodge to Edwin Lodge (son) Oct. 31, 1868 (MHS); Edwin A. Lodge to Harriett (Clubb) Lodge Lindsay, Feb. 21, 1852, Oct. 5, 1852, Nov. 5, 1852, Nov. 14, 1861, Aug. 7, 1864, Aug., 1865, Nov.

11, 1866; C. Burton, M. D., *Beginnings of Homeopathy* (n.d.), pp. 13, 20, 24, 31 [Y: 274/731]; Edwin A. Lodge, "Private Lecture to Young Men," 1860; Daniel Gano to Edwin A. Lodge, Nov. 5, 1858; "Funeral of Late Reuben H. Lloyd," *San Francisco Chronicle,* Mar. 12, 1909; Edwin A. Lodge to Edwin Lodge (son), Feb. 18, 1875; Don Lochbiler, *Detroit's Coming of Age: 1873 to 1973* (Detroit: Wayne State University Press, 1973), p. 310; ELLL, "Unvarnished Memories of the Lodge Family," (U), c. 1940.

THE LANDS: Ray E. Garrison to Francis De Tarr, Sept. 22, 1955; John Scott Land to Charles Henry Land, Sr., July 4, 1861; CAL to Mr. Meyers, Apr. 3, 1964; Alfred R. Henderson to CAL, Apr. 7, 1969; CAL to North Callahan, May 6, 1966; "Some Conflicts and Unresolved Problems in the Historical Account of Robert Land," attached to Alfred Henderson to CAL, ca. Mar. 23, 1971; "Contributions of Charles H. Land to Dentistry," attached to Alfred Henderson to CAL, Mar. 10, 1969; CAL, "(Previous Lodge & Land records)," n.d.; "A Lot of Mad Doctors," (Detroit) *Evening News,* Mar. 21, 1888, p. 1.

Some of Dr. Charles Henry Land's patents were for artificial teeth, artificial dentures, improvements on the filling of decayed teeth, methods of operative dentistry, and a baby jumper. He also invented a gold inlay system and a porcelain inlay system, as well as numerous gas and oil burners and furnaces for use in the manufacture of pottery and artificial teeth. According to Curt Proskauer, Curator of the Museum at the Dental School of Columbia University, Dr. Land "introduced the all-porcelain jacket crown which was patented in 1889 and is now in common use." (Curt Proskauer to CAL, Nov. 5, 1952.)

ELLL: CAL to Bruce Larson, July 24, 1968; Everett M. Lodge to Dr. L. Laszlo Schwartz, Nov. 29, 1957; *BUM,* pp. 1–3; Capt. Willard Glazier, *Down the Great River* (Philadelphia: Hubbard Brothers, Publishers, 1892), p. 154; ELLL, "Little Falls, Minnesota," (U), n.d.; ELLL to Evangeline Land, Tuesday [ca. 1900], Nov. 21, 1900, ca. Nov., 1900, Nov. 8, 1900; Susan Hayden Land (grandmother) to ELLL, Mar. 20, 1901; ELLL, "Facto," n.d. [Y:259/591].

ELLL MARRIES CA: Olive Adele Evers (principal of Stanley Hall) to CA, Nov. 29, 1900 and Oct 22, 1901; ELCS, (N), 1959; ELLL, "For CAL, Jr.," (N), n.d. [Y:259/595]; ELLL, two different pieces titled "The Home at Little Falls," n.d.

BIRTH OF CAL: ELLL, "All that I can tell—from the time you were born," n.d.; ELLL, untitled notes about CAL birth, n.d.; *AOV,* p. 3.

3   NO PLACE LIKE HOME

E: *AOV,* p. 43.

CAL EARLY CHILDHOOD, 1902–6: ELCS to AML, Feb. 4, 1975, ELLL (handwritten N), c. 1930; CA to ELLL, Feb. 8, 1902; Haines, *Lindberghs,* pp. 71, 81–2; CAL (N), n.d. (MHS); CAL to Bruce Larson, Apr. 7, 1967; CAL, "Chronology" [Y: 276/738]; CAL (N), n.d. [Y:182/123]; Grace Nute (N) of (I) with Mr. and Mrs. Robert Herron, Sept. 9, 1937; Grace Nute (N) of (I) with Mr. and Mrs. A. M. Opsahl, May 11, 1937; "Fine Residence Burned," Little Falls *Daily Transcript,* Aug. 7, 1905; CAL (N), Apr. 16, 1966; CAL to Bruce Larson, Oct. 23, 1972; *BUM,* pp. 5–6, 9–10; CAL (N) on Larson's *L of Minnesota,* Oct. 17, 1971; *SSL,* pp. 372–3; CA to ELLL, ca. Dec. 15, 1905; CAL to Bruce Larson, Jan. 24, 1971.

CA GOES TO WASHINGTON: Lucas, *CAL, SR.,* pp. 29–49, 78; Haines, *Lindberghs,* pp. 98, 102–3 (citations from CA's speeches), 115 (first votes in Congress), 116–7, 129, 134–5; Larson, *L of Minnesota,* pp. 38–68, 73; ELCS to Grace Nute,

Apr. 8, 1936; H. P. Bell to CA, Apr. 16 and 24, 1906; CA to Carl Bolander, Oct. 15, 1906; Thomas Pederson, "CAL, Sr. (As I Knew Him)," (U), n.d. [Y:277/763]; Grace Nute (N) of (I) with Mr. and Mrs. A. M. Opsahl, May 11, 1937; misc. CA letters, n.d. [MNHS, P1675, Folder 1]; *SSL,* pp. 308–11; the Panic of 1907 is discussed in Ron Chernow, *The House of Morgan* (New York: Atlantic Monthly Press: 1990), pp. 121–9; Ida Tarbell, "The Hunt for a Money Trust," *American Magazine,* May, 1913, p. 11; CA, speech, cited in *Congressional Record, Appendix,* pp. 12072–12077, July 22, 1935.

The common background of the "insurgent" legislators was observed by James Holt in *Congressional Insurgents and the Party System, 1909–1916* (Cambridge: Harvard University Press, 1967), p. 3, and cited in Lucas's study of CA, p. 13. The other outstanding insurgents in the House of Representatives included George W. Norris of Nebraska, Edmond H. Madison of Kansas, Victor Murdock of Kansas (an urban journalist), John M. Nelson of Wisconsin, and Miles Poindexter of Washington.

FAMILY DISCORD AND DISCONTENT: *SSL,* pp. 373–5; ELLL to CAL, Jan 5, 1938; Lillian Roberts to ELLL, Jan. 14, 29, and Feb. 20, 1908; ELCS to CAL, May 24, 1974; ELCS to CAL, Apr. 15, 1966; ELLL to ELL, Feb. 10, 1909 and Feb. 8, 1910; Lillian Johnson to ASB (I), July 18, 1993; ELCS to AML, Mar. 11, 1977; ELLL to ELL, two letters, n.d. (each dated "Sunday"), June 30, 1909, July 8, 1909, June 22 and 30, 1909, Dec. 10, 1909; ELLL (N), n.d.; ELLL, "Notes, 1909"; ROSS, Aug. 3, 1968; CA to CAL, Sept. 18, 1914 and Nov. 5, 1915; *AOV,* p. 60; FRDT, pp. 2–3; *SSL,* p. 376–7; *BUM,* p. 8; CAL to Bruce Larson, Feb. 19, 1966; DAVIS, Aug. 4, 1969; ELLL to ELL, June 6 and July 31, 1915; ELL to ELLL, n.d. [Y:224/62]; CA's affair is discussed in M. N. Koll to CA, Feb. 13, 1910, CA to Koll, Feb. 16, 1910, ELLL to ELL, Apr. 8, 1918, and is further documented in Grace Nute to CAL (recording memories of Mrs. Charles Weyerhauser), Apr. 16, 1941; RML (quoting ELCS) to ASB (I), Aug. 1, 1993; ELL TO ELLL, n.d. (c. Aug., 1918); CAL to Grace Nute, Aug. 10, 1937.

CAL BOYHOOD; DETROIT AND D.C.: CAL, (U) "English" draft of *SSL,* c. 1937; CAL (N) on life of Charles Henry Land, Nov. 29, 1952; CAL to Alfred Henderson, Jan. 12, 1974, May 8 and 31, 1971, June 20, 1966, Mar. 2, 1974; CAL (D), "Paris," Dec., 1938; *SSL,* pp. 316–21; ELLL, (N), n.d.; CAL, copybooks [Y:198/1]; CAL, "Paris" draft of *SSL,* Mar., 1939; Grace Nute (N) of (I) with Mr. and Mrs. A. M. Opsahl, May 11, 1937; CA to ELLL, n.d. (ca. 1910); William R. and Mary Anne MacKaye, *Mr. Sidwell's School* (Washington, D.C.: Acropolis Books, 1983), pp. 100–1; "L a Member of 'Roosevelt Gang,' " *Detroit Free Press,* June 3, 1927; ELLL to ELL, Jan. 8, 1910; *AOV,* p. 55; CAL, "Foreword" to Larson's *L of Minnesota,* p. xiv; *SSL,* pp. 311, 313, 314; ELLL to ELL, Feb. 21, 1916; CAL, notebook, 1912.

CAL EARLY ADOLESCENCE: *AOV,* pp. 57, 59–60; CA quoted in *Congressional Record,* 63rd Congress, 2nd session, p. 15708, cited in Larson, *L of Minnesota,* p. 179; *BUM,* pp. 25, 29–30; CAL to Kevin Hammerbeck, Feb. 22, 1970; CAL, notebook, "Auto Trip," Spring, 1916; *Northern Lights* (official publication of Antique Automobile Club of America), July, 1969, p. 4.

CALIFORNIA: ELCS to AML, Apr. 13, 1979; ROSS, Aug. 3, 1968; CAL, timeline, Aug., 1957; *BUM,* p. 31; *AOV,* p. 7; CAL to CA, n.d. (c. 1916); ELCS to AML, Apr. 13, 1979; CA to ELCS, n.d. (c. 1916) and Oct. 15, 1916; CA, "Some Recollections of My Daughter Lillian, 1916," Little Falls *Daily Transcript,* Nov. 6, 1916;

ELCS to AML, Dec. 9, 1976; ELLL (N), n.d.; ELL to ELLL, Feb. 28 and Apr. 11, 1917.

CA LEAVES D.C.: Haines, *Lindberghs*, pp. 221–3, 262; Larson, *L of Minnesota*, pp. 207, 209, 250–52, 329; *Congressional Record*, 64th Congress, 2nd session, Feb. 12, 1917, pp. 1–4, 81147–16998; CA to ELCS, Feb. 17, 1917; CA to CAL, Apr. 5, 1917; CA's quote, "The trouble with war . . ." is cited in CAL introduction to Larson, *L of Minnesota*, p. xiv; CA, *Why Is Your Country at War?* (Washington, D. C.: National Capital Press, Inc., 1917), p. 8; CA to CAL, June 12, 1918; Harrison Salisbury, *A Journey for Our Times* (New York: Harper & Row, 1983), p. 16; Walter Quigley, introduction of reprint of CA's *Your Country at War* (Philadelphia: Dorrance & Co., Inc., 1934), pp. 7–13; CA to ELCS, Sept, 13, 1918.

CAL ON THE FARM: CA to ELLL, ca. Apr., 1917; CAL to ELCS, Jan. 28, 1956; CA to CAL, ca. Apr., 1917; *BUM*, pp. 32–3, 39–40, 43–5; DAVIS, Aug. 5, 1969; ROSS, Aug. 3, 1969; "What L's Town Thinks of Him," *PIC*, Sept. 30, 1941; *AOV*, pp. 61–3; ELLL, (N); *SSL*, pp. 380–2, 384–5; CAL to Grace Nute, Jan. 12, 1938; CA to CAL, Feb. 1, 1919 (MHS); Alex Johnson to T. Willard Hunter (I), June 14, 1981 [CAL House, Little Falls]; CAL, timeline, Aug., 1957.

4   UNDER A WING

E: *SSL*, p. 261.

CAL AT WISCONSIN AND ROTC: ELLL, "Madison," (U-N), n.d.; Daniel H. Borus (ed.), *These United States* (Ithaca, NY: Cornell University Press, 1992), p. 398; ELLL to "64" (family at 64 W. Elizabeth St., Detroit), Oct. 22, 1920; George Buchanan Fife, *Lindbergh: The Lone Eagle* (Cleveland: The World Syndicate Publishing Co., 1927), pp. 134–40; CAL, timeline, n.d.; *SSL*, pp. 247, 357–8, 403–4; ELLL (N), 1920; FRDT; *WE*, p. 24; F. Scott Fitzgerald, "Echoes of the Jazz Age," *The Crack-up* (New York: New Directions, 1945) p. 15; DAVIS, Aug. 6, 1969; CA to ELCS, Feb. 29, 1920, and Apr. 23, 1921; CAL (D), Aug., 1921; CA to CAL, July 11, July 23, another on July 23, Sept. 9 and 19, 1921; ELLL to CA, ca. 1921; CA to ELLL, Feb. 10, 1922; Univ. of Wisconsin, College of Mechanics and Engineering, grades, June 24, 1921; *BUM*, pp. 45–6; CAL, journal, July 20–Aug. 21, 1921; R. D. Herzog (Nebraska Aircraft Corp) to CAL, Dec. 28, 1921; Ralph C. Diggins School to CAL, Feb. 28, 1922; P. H. Hyland to ELLL, Feb. 7, 1922.

Camp Knox, Kentucky, would later become Fort Knox.

HISTORY OF FLIGHT: Prof. Peter Wegner, "What Makes Airplanes Fly" (lectures) at Yale University, 1990–1; Francis Trevelyan Miller, *The World in the Air* (New York: G. P. Putnam's Sons, 1930), vols. I and II; Walter J. Boyne, *The Smithsonian Book of Flight* (Washington, D. C.: Smithsonian Books, 1987), pp. 33–114; C. H. Gibbs-Smith, AVIATION: AN HISTORICAL SURVEY (London: H. M. Stationery Office, 1970), pp. xi–xiv, 1–179; Tom D. Crouch, *The Bishop's Boys: A Life of Wilbur and Orville Wright* (New York: W. W. Norton and Co., 1989), pp. 242–99.

LEARNING TO FLY: R. D. Herzog to CAL, Jan. 31, 1922; ROSS, Aug. 4, 1968; *AOV*, p. 9; Secretary of Admissions, Teachers College, Columbia University to ELLL, Aug. 14, 1922; ELLL to CAL, Apr. 8, 14, 28, and 30, 1922, Aug. 14, 1922; *WE*, p. 25; CAL to Richard Plummer, Apr. 22, 1922; CAL to ELLL, Apr. 5, 8, 10, and 22, 1922; *SSL*, pp. 247–9, "Personnel of Page's Aerial Pageant," flyer, n.d.

BARNSTORMING: *SSL*, pp. 253–68, 430; *WE*, pp. 28–31, 34–9; CAL to ELLL, June 22, 1922, Aug. 11, 1922; Billings (Montana) *Gazette Sun*, Aug. 27, 1922, n.p.;

ELLL to CAL, May 26, 1922, Aug. 14, 1922, Sept. 5, 1922; CAL, timeline; CAL to Richard Glendenning, Sept. 17, 1969; Edward W. Kraske to CAL, Mar. 3, 1953; CA's condition is discussed in CAL to Bruce Larson, July 7, 1967 and CA to ELLL, Sept. 17, 1921, n.d. (c. 1922), and Mar. 18, 1924; ELCS to CA, Mar. 30, 1922; CA to CAL, Jan. 23, 1922 and Feb. 7, 1923.

CAL AND HIS OWN PLANE: CAL to CA, Mar. 21, 23, and 31, 1923, Apr. 4, 20, and 29, 1923; CA to CAL, Apr. 11, 12, and 14, 1923, May 17, 1923; CAL to Secretary of Committee on Attractions, ca. 1923; "John Wyche Rites Today," n.s., c. July 1, 1962; *SSL*, pp. 436–50; *WE*, pp. 39–50, 52–67, 70–77; CAL to Mr. Sloan, July 11, 1957; CAL to ELLL, Apr. 9, 1923, May 23, 1923; Rudy Hayes, "L Visisted Here," *Americus Times Recorder*, Aug. 28, 1979, p. 1; Glenn Messer to ASB (I), Mar. 5, 1993; Phyllis Cheryl Love, "Charles L's Visit in Maben" (essay at Mississippi State University), Jan. 7, 1969; "L's Son Detained in Flight to Join Father," n.s., n.d.; CAL to Bruce Larson, Apr. 7, 1967; "Plane Damaged Near Glencoe," *Glencoe Enterprise*, June 14, 1923; CA to ELCS, July 3, 1923; CA to ELLL, Dec. 25, 1923; CAL to Stan Bleazard, Jan. 8, 1965; *BUM*, p. 46.

CAL CONSIDERS AND JOINS ARMY: *WE*, pp. 78–104, 109; FRDT; Lieutenant Harold McGinnis to CAL, Nov. 14, 1923; L. H. Drennan to C. H. Land (meaning CAL), Dec. 6, 1923; Reed Inert, *American Racing Planes and Historic Air Races* (Chicago: Willcox and Follett, 1952), pp. 49–51; editorial referred to in Harold Bixby to CAL, prob. Jan. 14, 1961; CAL to ELLL, Oct. 17, 1923 and Jan. 16, 1924; *SSL*, pp. 279–80, 408, 417–8; CAL to CA, Feb. 29, 1924, Mar. 21, 1924; ELLL to CAL, Nov. 29, 1923 and Mar. 21, 1924; CA to ELCS, Feb. 11, 1924; CA to CAL, Jan. 16, 1924.

CA'S DEMISE: ELC to CAL (T), Apr. 16, 1924, and Apr. 18, 1924 (T), Apr. 23, 1924, May 12, 22, and 24 (T), 1924, June 2, 1924; ELC, "Memoir of Last Illness of C. A.," (U), n.d.; ELC to George Christie, Apr. 23, 25, and 27, 1924, May 5, 1924; Dr. A. W. Adson to CAL (T), Apr. 23, 1924; CAL to Leon Klink, Apr. 24, 1924; CAL to ELLL, Apr. 28, 1924, May 25 and 28, 1924, June 2, 1924, July 8, 1924; ELLL to CAL, "Monday," Apr., 1924, April, 23, 1924, May 22, 24, 26, 27, 28, 29, and 30, 1924, June 5, 1924; ELC to AML, Nov. 28, 1976; ELLL to "Brother" (Charles H. Land, Jr.), May 2, 3, and 4, 1924; "C. A. Lindbergh Dies Saturday," *Red Lake Falls Courier*, May 29, 1924, pp. 1, 5; "Funeral Honors Paid to L in Minneapolis," Minneapolis *Daily Star*, May 28, 1924; "Statement of Facts," State of Minnesota Appellant's Brief #24994, 1925; *AOV*, pp. 396–7.

CAL IN ARMY: Elmer Beckstrand to CAL, Feb. 12, 1925; *WE*, pp. 121–51; CAL to CA, Apr. 4, 1924; DAVIS, Aug. 12, 1969; Ross Jordan to CAL, Jan. 10, 1968; *SSL*, pp. 214–7, 278–281, 420–2; ELLL to CAL, June 10, Aug. 9 and 13, Sept. 12, 1924, Mar. 9, 1925; CAL to ELLL, Sept. 17 and 19, Nov. 19, 1924, Jan. 10, Mar. 21, 1925; *Air Service News Letter*, Apr. 2, 1925; C. D. McAllister, quoted in Orange County *Register*, Feb. 22, 1995, n.p.; Harold Fisher to CAL, Feb. 11, 1925; CAL (U-N) on Dale Van Every and Morris DeHaven Tracy, *Charles Lindbergh: His Life* (New York: D. Appleton, 1927), Dec. 5, 1968; FRDT; Earl Potts to CAL, Feb. 15, 1953; CAL to "Gang" (Army friends), Jan. 26, 1926.

5   SPIRIT

E: *OFAL*, p. 49.

CAL ARRIVING IN ST. LOUIS: Manley O. Hudson, "Missouri: Doesn't Want to Be Shown," in Borus, *These United States*, p. 206; A. B. Lambert to CAL, June 5,

1925; A. B. Lambert, "A Brief Summary of the Lambert-St. Louis Municipal Airport," Oct., 1941 [MHS]; *SSL*, pp. 20, 122, 281; *35th Division Air Service News*, May, 1926; George Oonk to CAL, Feb. 17, 1925; "Harold Bixby, a Chief Supporter of L," *NYT*, Nov. 20, 1965; *AOV*, p. 66; Harlan "Bud" Gurney to CAL, Feb. 10, ca. Feb. 16, May 11, 1925; the man who wished to urinate on his hometown is mentioned in CAL, timeline; "Vera May Dunlop's Flying Circus," handbill, n.d. [MHS]; "Who Wants to Ride Airplane," n.s., June 26, 1925; CAL to ELLL, May 20, July 7 and 10, Aug. 10, 1925; clipping from St. Louis *Globe-Democrat*, May 22, 1927; "O. E. Scott, Airport Manager in '20s, Dies," St. Louis *Globe-Democrat*, July 8, 1948, p. 7A; "Fliers Arrive for Big Four Flying Circus," St. Charles *Daily Banner*, June 25, 1925, p. 1; FRDT; Col. Tenney Ross, Special Orders #154, Headquarters 7th Corps Area, July 3, 1925; CAL to Raymond Fredette, July 15, 1971.

COLORADO; PREPARING FOR AIR MAIL: *WE*, pp. 156–69; J. Wray Vaughan to CAL, Aug. 7 (T) and 9 (T), 1925; CAL to ELLL, Aug. 10, 19, 29, Sept. 1, and Oct. 5, 1925; *SSL*, p. 281; Mil-Hi Airways business card, 1925; William B. Robertson to CAL, Aug. 24, 1925; CAL to ELLL, Nov. 6 and 22, 1925, Jan. 6, 12, Feb. 5 and 26, Mar. 14, 1926; Miller, *World in the Air*, pp. 275–95; CAL to "Sir," (Detroit Aviation Society), Jan. 2, 1926; C. B. Fritsch (Detroit Aviation Society) to CAL, Jan. 7, 1926; *SSL*, pp. 287, 325; FRDT; *WE*, p. 170; CAL, Last Will and Testament, Dec. 11, 1925; DAVIS, Aug. 9, 1969; *AOV*, pp. 66–7; Philip Love to CAL, Aug. 14, Nov. 13, Dec. 17, 1925; "Steve" to CAL, Sept. 19, 1925; Joseph Wecker, "News of St. Louis Aviation 'Old-Timers,' " Dec. 1967; Mrs. Eva Martin (Reliance Correspondence Club) to "Sir" (CAL), n.d.

AIR MAIL COMMENCES: CAL to ELLL, Apr. 10, 1926; CAL to Josephine Austin, Aug. 2, 1972; "St. Louis Mail By Air to New York in 15 Hours," n.s., Apr. 16, 1926; "Air Mail Day," advertisement, ca. May 19, 1926; *WE*, pp. 172–93; "Airmail Payments Put on Pound Basis," n.s., June 18, 1926; CAL to William Conkling, June 14, 1938; CAL to Billy Wilder, May 20, 1954; CAL to William P. MacCracken, Jr., July 21, 1968; *AOV*, p. 68; *SSL*, pp. 5–9, 11–4, 324–6; *Rip Cord* (publication of Caterpillar Club), n.d., pp. 48–51; Constance Fetzer to CAL, Nov. 10, 1969; W. H. Conkling to CAL, Sept. 17, 1926; Sgt. A. W. Thiemann to CAL, Sept. 18 and Nov. 27, 1926; CAL's reports of his parachute drops reprinted in *Aeronautic Review*, Nov., 1926, pp. 174–5; Wecker, "St. Louis Old-Timers," Dec., 1967; CAL to E. E. Larabee, July 18, 1967; CAL to ELLL, June 8 and Aug. 29, 1926; O. P. Austin (of National Geographic Society) to CAL, Oct. 18, 1926; "CAL," *National Guardsman*, May, 1957, pp. 11–13, 39; "Physical Examination for Flying" for CAL, Dec. 13, 1926 [MHS].

ORTEIG PRIZE; CAL SEEKS PLANE: Graham Wallace, *The Flight of Alcock and Brown* (London: Putnam, 1955), pp. 287–300; Edward Jablonski, *Atlantic Fever* (New York: Macmillan, 1972), pp. 27, 53–4; Richard K. Smith, "Fifty Years of Transatlantic Flight," AIAA 6th Annual Meeting, paper #69–1044, pp. 1–2; "History of the Prize," menu from presentation of Orteig Prize, June, 1927; CAL to Ed Pendray, July 22, 1963; *WE*, pp. 198–9; *SSL*, pp. 17–20, 25–7, 30–4, 41, 45–6, 51–75; FRDT; CAL, prospectus, n.d. [MHS]; CAL to ELLL, Oct. 30, Dec. 26 and 28, 1926, Jan. 15, 1927. Feb. 11, 15, and 18, 1927; A. B. Lambert to Nettie Beauregard, Dec. 10, 1937; Giuseppe Bellanca to CAL, Dec. 4, 1926; "L, Mail Pilot, May Fly For . . . Award," prob. *NYT*, ca. Feb. 9, 1927; A. B. Lambert, "Suggested procedure," (U-N), ca. Jan. 1927 [MHS: 291/85]; CAL, (D), Feb. 18–27, 1927.

One of Sikorsky's financial backers was fellow expatriate Sergei Rachmaninoff.

SAN DIEGO: *WPA Guide to California* (New York: Pantheon, 1984), pp. 258–64; *SSL*, pp. 79–86, 90–98, 101, 104, 112, 116, 118–22, 132–4, 503–4; Ryan Airlines, Inc., "Order," Feb. 25, 1927; CAL to ELLL, Feb. 25, Mar. 3, 8, 12, 27, Apr. 24, May 7, 1927; H. H. Knight to CAL (T), Feb. 25, 1927; CAL to H. H. Knight (T), Feb. 26, 1928 (actually 1927); Walter Balderston, "Lindbergh" (U memoir), Apr., 1928; U. S. Grant Hotel bills, Mar. 3, 10, 17, 1927; *WE*, pp. 198–212; Donald Hall, "Technical Notes," NACA #257, July, 1927; CAL to Ev Cassagneres, Jan. 29, 1974; C. W. Ambrust to CAL, Mar. 15 and 28, 1927; A. G. Spalding to Ryan Air Lines (T), Mar. 24, 1927; ELLL to CAL, Mar. 3, 4, 7, 9, 21, Apr. 8 and 27, 1927; Douglas Corrigan, *That's My Story* (New York: E. P. Dutton, 1938), pp. 91, 93–4; Ev Cassagneres, *The Spirit of Ryan* (Blue Ridge Summit, PA: TAB Books, 1982), pp. 56, 60; Gus the Sign Painter, bill, n.d.; CAL to Harry Knight (T), Apr. 25, 1927; for specifications of plane, see *SSL*, pp. 531–40; Harry Knight to CAL, Mar. 21, 1927.

The plastic used in the windows and skylight of the *Spirit of St. Louis* was Pyralin, a nitro-cellulose.

In 1938 Douglas Corrigan would capture the imagination of the press and the public after taking off in his $900 "crate" of a plane, "intending" to fly from Bennett Airport, Long Island, to California. Twenty-eight hours later he landed in Dublin, a stunt to which he never owned up, reveling instead in the publicity and celebrity that crowned him "Wrong-Way Corrigan."

ON TO ST. LOUIS AND NEW YORK: *SSL*, pp. 134–45, 150–73; Rev. R. B. Schuler, "Statement in Regard to the L Medal," n.d. [Y]; E. J. Mulligan and Ken Boedecker, "Mulligan, Boedecker and Lane Recall Days," *Trade Winds* (published by Wright Aeronautical Corporation), May, 1937, p. 6; CAL to S. Dillon Ripley, Mar. 12, 1971; CAL, notebook, 1927; "Mrs. L Bids Calm Good-by to Son," *NYT*, May 15, 1927; Cassagneres, *Spirit*, p. 72; Lauren D. Lyman, "When L Went to Paris," *Bee-Hive* (United Aircraft Corp.), Spring, 1967, pp. 18–9; HG to Milton Lehman, Oct. 15, 1962; CAL to Milton Lehman, Sept. 30, 1962; Harry Bruno, *Wings over America* (New York: Robert M. McBride, 1942) pp. 173–4; William Morris to CAL (T), May 13, 1927; R. M. Allen (president of Vitamin Food Co.) to CAL, May 13, 1927; ELLL to CAL, May 18, 1927; CAL, (U-N), regarding Bruno's *Wings*, July, 1971.

L's other pre-flight visitors, who would rise to great prominence in aviation, included Grover Loening, who had his own plant, Roy Grumman, a young engineer who worked at Loening, and Chance Vought.

6   PERCHANCE TO DREAM

E: *AOV*, p. 397.

PRE-TAKEOFF: *AOV*, p. 71; Russell Owen, "L Is Set to Fly," *NYT*, May 20, 1927, pp. 1–2, and "L Leaves New York at 7:52 A.M.," May 21, 1927, pp. 1–2; *SSL*, pp. 173–5, 178, 182–185, 225, 538; K. J. Boedecker, "Mulligan, Boedecker and Lane Recall Days," *Trade Winds*, p. 8; DAVIS, Aug. 11, 1969; CAL (U-N) on Bruno's *Wings*, p. 3; CAL to Leland Hayward (T) Oct. 20, 1955; Charles E. Blake to CAL (T), ca. Dec. 1938; "Nungesser Quest Fails," *NYT*, May 20, 1927, p. 2; Richard Lockridge (of New York *Sun*) quoted in clipping "L Off Ten Years Ago in Sea Flight," n.s., n.d. n.p.; Walter E. Dauch to CAL, May 20, 1946; Harris, Winthrop & Co., to CAL, May 13, 1927; Esther Mueller to Percy Ebbott of Chase National Bank, Oct. 15, 1952; "L's Speed Surprises Aviators," *NYT*, May 21, 1927, p. 4; CAL, (U-AW), p. IV-2 [Y:218/626]; Madeline McNamara to CAL and AML, Dec. 6, 1955; R. F. McNamara, "An Anonymous Gift For Lucky Lindy," *The Catholic Transcript*,

June 11, 1976; CAL flying log; Linda Bruder, "Lucky Lindy's Lift-Off Relived," *Pennysaver,* June 18, 1988, n.p.

The woman who gave CAL her compact mirror has never been satisfactorily identified. The likeliest claimant is one Ada Bielenberg, then Mrs. Amos Ferguson, who was living nearby.

TAKEOFF AND FIRST STAGE OF FLIGHT: Boedecker, *Trade Winds,* p. 8; *SSL,* pp. 185–92, 197–210, 233, 239, 293–5, 298–9; Owen, "L Leaves New York," May 2l, 1927; "Other Fliers Wish L All Luck," p. 4, "Lloyd's Refuses Risk on L's Chances," p. 4, "Home Town Eager for News," p. 3, "Lone Flight Grips French Imagination," p. 3, "Two English Airmen on Non-Stop Hop to India," p. 6, "Vessels in Track Taken By L," p. 6, "Ship Alter Course to Seek L," p. 3, "L Speeds Across North Atlantic, p. 1, *NYT,* May 21, 1927; Lyman, "When L Went," p. 21; R. R. Blythe to ELLL (T), May 20, 1927, 8:48 A.M.; "Mother of Flier Sure He Will Win," *NYT,* May 21, 1927, p. 2; Van Every and Tracy, *L: His Life,* p. 181; Cassagneres, *Spirit of Ryan,* p. 78; HG, *The Seven Skies* (New York: G. P. Putnam's Sons, 1930), pp. 67–91; Umlauf quoted in Neville Small, "Pegasus and the Gargoyle," *The Compass* (Mobil International, 1988), no. 2; Juan Trippe, "CAL and World Travel," The Wings Club "Sight" lecture, 1977; CAL to Francis Drake, Feb. 9, 1948; CAL, (U-AW), [Y:218/626], p. IV-1; *WE,* p. 220; CAL to Billy Wilder, July 26, 1955.

CAL OVER THE OCEAN; REACTION ON EARTH: *AOV,* p. 78; "L's Venture Grips City's Interest," p. 6, "40,000 Join in Prayer that L Wins," p. 13, "Coolidge Is Praised in Gary's Forecast," p. 29, *NYT,* May 21, 1927, p. 6; Ruth Oliff to AML, Jan. 29, 1968; Paul Garber to ASB (I), June 6, 1990; James Stewart (with Joseph Laitin), "Lucky to Be Lindy," *Colliers,* March, 30, 1956; James Stewart to ASB (I), May 21, 1990; Will Rogers (ed. by Donald Day), *The Autobiography of Will Rogers* (Boston: Houghton Mifflin Co., 1949), pp. 149–50; Harold M. Anderson, "L Flies Alone," *The New York Sun,* May 21, 1927; *SSL,* pp. 303, 305, 323–6, 331–2, 340–1, 351–4, 362, 366, 379, 387–90, 399–403, 425–9, 433, 451–2, 457–66; *WE,* p. 218–20; CAL to Billy Wilder, July 26, 1955.

FINAL HOURS OF FLIGHT: *SSL,* pp. 465–6, 468–72, 478–92; "Bulletins Record Progress of Flier," p. 2, "Lloyd's Gave 10-3 Odds," p. 4, "Paris Spent Day Wishing Success," p. 2, "10,000 Telephone Inquiries on L," p. 3, "Mother Glad First for Flier's Safety," p. 4; *NYT,* May 22, 1927; Stewart, "Lucky to Be Lindy"; Alistair Cooke, *Alistair Cooke's America* (New York: Alfred A. Knopf, 1973), p. 322; Juno Lindbergh Butler to CAL, May 21, 1927; *AOV,* p. 79; Denise Cardinet (quoting Mme. J. Citroën) to ASB (I), Sept. 14, 1993.

LE BOURGET AND PARIS: *SSL,* pp. 492–500; Mott, *Herrick,* p. 341–2, 345; George Delage to CAL, May 4, 1929; Jack Glenn to CAL, Oct. 11, 1936; Carlyle Mac Donald, "L Does It," *NYT,* May 22, 1927, pp. I: 1–2; Myron T. Herrick to ELLL (T), May 21, 1927, 10:10 P.M.

7   ONLY A MAN

E: *AOV,* p. 310.

INITIAL REACTIONS; FRANCE PAYS TRIBUTE: Mott, *Herrick,* pp. 345–6, 348–50; *AOV,* pp. 311–2, 314, "New York Stages Big Celebration," pp. 1–2, "Crowd Cheers News," p. 3, "St. Louis Rejoices," p. 4, "Mother Glad First For Flier's Safety," p. 4, "Town Wild Over L," p. 2, "Italians Emphasize Flier's Bold Daring," p. 4, "L's Victory Thrills England, p. 2, "Brown, One of First Two Ocean Fliers, Elated," p. 5, *NYT,* May 22, 1927; "L's Daring Praised in Pulpits," p. 3, "Baby

Named for Air Hero," p. 3, "Orville Wright Lauds," p. 2, "L's Success is Hailed in Germany," p. 4, "Intrigued by L's Cat," p. 5, "Flier Has a Busy Day," p. 2, "L Talks to Mother By Phone," p. 3, "L's First Call Is On Mme. Nungesser," p. 1, "Italians Acclaim L's Flight," p. 2, *NYT,* May 23, 1927; "L Talk Relayed," p. 3, "France Pins on L the Cross of Legion of Honor," pp. 1–2, "Explains Compass," p. 3, *NYT,* May 24, 1927; "Tact of Flier Wins the French," p. 2, "Jam to See L Bursts Window," pp. 1–2, "American in Paris Greet L," p. 2, "L Feted by French Fliers," p. 2, "Tribute From Argentine President," "Would Pay L's Tax," p. 2, May 25, 1927; "L Donates His 150,000–Franc Gift," p. 1, "L Greets Bleriot as Master," p. 1, "French Deputies Acclaim L," pp. 1–2, "Dole Gives $35,000," p. 3, May 26, 1927; "L Drinks First Champagne," prob. *Washington Post,* May 24, 1927, p. 8; Corrigan, *My Story,* p. 95; Fitzgerald, "Echoes," *Crack-up,* p. 20; "An Appreciation of L from India," *Air Corps News Letter,* Oct. 15, 1927, p. 293; *SSL,* p. 501; Francis Kellogg to CAL (T), May 21, 1927; Calvin Coolidge to CAL (T), May 21, 1927; Theodore Roosevelt, Jr. to CAL (T), May 22, 1927; HG to CAL (T), May 22, 1927; Adolph Ochs to CAL (T), prob. May 22, 1927; Fitzhugh Green, "A Little of What the World Thought of L," epilogue of *WE,* pp. 238–40; "Tears Dim L's Eyes" and "L Choked with Emotion," prob. *Boston Herald,* prob. May 23, 1927; reference to Herrick's dog Max appears in "L Sees Flying Boats Next," *NYT,* June 9, 1927, p. 4; the calling card ["You're a God"] was from Gerard Fourment [MHS B81/F28]; CAL to Hobart Lewis, July 3, 1967, CAL to Raymond Fredette, May 21, 1973; Will Rogers quoted in "How to Reward L," *NYT,* June 22, 1927, p. 25; Carlyle MacDonald, "500,000 Parisians Cheer L," pp. 1–2, "Brussels Prepares to Greet L," p. 2, *NYT,* May 27, 1927; Edwin L. James, "L Thrills Paris In Air Stunts," pp. 1–2, *NYT,* May 28, 1927; Francis S. Altendorf to "Mother and Dad," May 28, 1927; Raymond Orteig, "Account of L's Farewell Note to Paris," in privately printed booklet, June, 1927, pp. 6–7; "L Drops Farewell to Paris," CAL, "King Albert Decorates L . . . L Defends His 'Stunts' in the Air," *NYT,* May 29, 1927, pp. 1–2.

BELGIUM; ENGLAND: CAL, "King Albert Decorates," pp. 1–2, *NYT,* May 29, 1927; Green, epilogue, *WE,* pp. 248–64; CAL, "Belgian Rulers Knows a Lot About Flying," pp. 1–2, "Brussels Burghers Honor L," p. 3, "London Wildly Welcomes L," pp. 1–2, *NYT,* May 30, 1927; CAL, "L Explains Early Return," pp. 1–2, *NYT,* May 31, 1927; "Program for Reception of Capt. L in London," May 29–June 1, 1927 [MHS]; "L Decorated by King George," "Coolidge Offers Him a Cruiser," CAL, "L Finds King Democratic," pp. 1, 2, *NYT,* June 1, 1927; "L Sees English Derby Run," "Meets President's Wish," pp. 1–2, *NYT,* June 2, 1927; CAL, "L Calls London 'Bully,' " "L Starts Flight to Paris," pp. 1–2, "Cruiser Memphis One of the Fastest," p. 2, *NYT,* June 3, 1927; King George's inquiring about L's "peeing" comes from unpublished diaries of Harold Nicolson, quoted in Leonard Mosley, *Lindbergh: A Biography* (Garden City, NY: Doubleday, 1976), pp. 116, 406, "L in Paris," pp. 1, 3, "Cruiser Reaches Cherbourg," p. 3, *NYT,* June 4, 1927; CAL, "L Sails; Royal French Send-Off," "Good-bye Tributes Bid to L," and CAL, "God Bless You All; L Farewell," pp. 1, 28, "Honored Like a Sovereign," pp. 7, 8, "Levine, Owner Steps Aboard Plane," pp. 1–2, *NYT,* June 5, 1927; CAL, "L on the Memphis Hears," pp. 1, 5, *NYT,* June 6, 1927.

AMERICA PREPARES AS CAL RETURNS: L. Gilman, "L's Flight Set to Music," New York HERALD-TRIBUNE, Mar. 29, 1931; "The Lindy Hop," *Life,* Aug. 23, 1943, n.p.; Chip Deffaa (quoting Norma Miller) to ASB, July 10, 1990; n.a., "Poems on L," *Bulletin of the Carnegie Institute,* vol. I, no. 8, pp. 19–20, June, 1928; William

Rose Benet, *With Wings as Eagles* (New York: Dodd, Mead, 1940), pp. 45–6; Sacha Guitry to CAL (T), Nov. 22, 1928; James E. West, *The Lone Scout of the Sky* (Philadelphia: Boy Scouts of America, 1928), p. 13; CAL, "L Calls London 'Bully,' " *NYT*, June 3, 1927; "The Man of Vision," cartoon, *The Christian Science Monitor*, May 28, 1927, n. p.; *AOV*, p. 316; CAL, "L on Memphis Hears of Sighting of Columbia Fliers," *NYT*, June 6, 1927, pp. 1, 5; CAL, "L in Peril," *NYT*, June 7, 1927, pp. 1, 8; CAL, "L Sees Flying Boats Next," *NYT*, June 9, 1927, p. 4; CAL, "Memphis Makes Record," pp. 1–2, "Air and Sea Escort Ready for Memphis," p. 3, *NYT*, June 11, 1927; "L Lands at Capital Today for Nation's Welcome," pp. 1–2, "L Wonders 'If I Deserve All This,' " and "L's Mother Guest of Coolidges," p. 2, *NYT*, June 11, 1927; ECM (D), June 11 and 12, 1927.

WASHINGTON, D.C., RECEPTION: Green, *WE*, pp. 265–96; "500,000 Air Letters Expected for L," June 10, 1927, *NYT*, p. 3; "Nation Pays Its Homage to L," "L Crowd Shatters Record," pp. 1–2, CAL, "Washington Reception Best of All," pp. 1, 3, "Path One of Memories," pp. 1, 2, "Memphis Moves Up to Din of Welcome," p. 3, "L Parade is Triumph Anew," p. 3, "Aerial Cavalcade Greets L," p. 4, "Guns and Cheers Thunder at Docks," p. 4, "Millions Visualize the Scene by Radio," p. 14; "Hail L at Press Welcome," p. 7, "300,000 Take Part in Capital Tribute," p. 8; *NYT*, June 12, 1927; Madge Graves Ballard, "Historic Celebrations of Past Dimmed," *The Saturday Spectator*, June 25, 1927, n.p.; Lamar Trotti, "Sending L to the World Through the Motion Picture," *The Southern Club Woman*, n.d., pp. 18–9; A. W. Hall, director of Bureau of Engraving and Printing to Postmaster General, June 11, 1927; "His Final Day in Capital One of Continuous Ovation" and "L Moved by War Wounded," pp. 1–2, "L's Ride One Rolling Cheer," pp. 1, 3, "L to Fly Spirit of St. Louis," pp. 1, 4, " 'We' Meet Again, Ready for the Air," p. 3, "Flag Honor Cross Given to L," p. 4, *NYT*, June 13, 1927.

NEW YORK: *WE*, pp. 297–314; "Millions Roar Welcome to L," pp. 1–2, "Air Hero Lionized at Social Function," pp. 1, 13, "L Says His Mind Is Ablaze," pp. 1, 3, "Son's Glory Brings Homage to Mother," pp. 1, 12, "Capital Bids Flier a Warm Farewell," p. 4, "A Mighty Paean in Harbor," pp. 1, 10, "Flier Sports in Air on Quick Dash Here," pp. 1, 4, "A Boy's Day in a Big City," pp. 1–3, "Radio Keeps Pace With L," p. 16, "Palisades Crowd Cheers," p. 4, "Mayor Welcomes Flier at City Hall" and "Cardinal Blesses L," p. 2, "Flier Lays Wreath at Eternal Light" and "Vast Throng Roars Greeting in Park," p. 3, "10,000 Pupils Watch," p. 8, "City Vast Gallery of 'Lindy' Pictures," p. 9, "L Parade Has 10,000 Troops," p. 6, "5000 Cubic Yards of Paper," p. 13, "Films on L Set Speed Record," p. 14, *NYT*, June 14, 1927; T. M. Hesburgh to AML, Aug. 27, 1974; Trotti, "Sending L," *Southern Club Woman*, p. 32; Paul Garber to ASB (I), June 6, 1990; "Cheers of 3700 Acclaim L," pp. 1–2, "Visits Long Island Twice," pp. 2–3, *NYT*, June 15, 1927; "L Flies Off at 3 This Morning," pp. 1–2, "Brooklyn Parade Today," pp. 1, 3, "Business Leaders Lionize L," p. 2, *NYT*, June 16, 1927; "L Flies to St. Louis Today," pp. 1–2, "$25,000 Orteig Prize Presented to Flier," pp. 1, 3, "Hero Back at Field Where Fame Began," pp. 1, 2, "200,000 Hail Pilot in Prospect Park," pp. 1–2, "Brooklyn Parade Cheered by 700,000," p. 2, *NYT*, June 17, 1927.

ST. LOUIS WELCOME: *WE*, pp. 315–8; "L Flies to St. Louis Welcome," pp. 1–2, "L Gives Treat to Columbus on Way," p. 2, "L Beams as He Takes Air" and "L Evokes Flood of Letters," p. 2, *NYT*, June 18, 1927; "St. Louis Roars Welcome," *NYT*, June 19, 1927, pp. 1–2; "L Frolics on an Air Holiday," *NYT*, June 20, 1927, pp. 1–2; "Ignores L For His New Car," *NYT*, June 21, 1927, p. 7.

OFFERS AND REQUESTS: Esther B. Mueller, "Decorations, Awards, Trophies, and Gifts Presented to Capt. L," Appendix to *SSL*, pp. 517–30; Nettie H. Beauregard, *L's Decorations and Trophies* (St. Louis: MHS, 1935); T. L. Murphy to CAL, contract, Sept. 8, 1927; Harold van Doren to CAL, Apr. 26, 1929; HB to Secretary of Commerce of Turkey, Sept. 28, 1932; advertisement in *Aviation Magazine*, c. Jan. 26, 1928, n.d., n.p.; A. B. Reed of Hookless Fastener Co. to Bruno & Blythe, May 16, 1928; Lynwood Thompson of Thompson Mfg. Co. to Guggenheim Foundation, May 25, 1929; advertising suggestions from W. S. Gallatin, York, PA; E. G. Milne (representing Pantages) to R. Blythe, May 23, 1927; E. Castel to CAL, May 24, 1927; W. H. Miller (of Thomas Edison, Inc.) to CAL, June 15, 1927; C. Laemmle to James Bryson (T), May 23, 1927; James Bryson to CAL, May 28, 1927; W. R. Hearst to CAL (T), June 17, 1927; HB to CAL, Oct. 5, 1927; CAL to Milton Lomask, Aug. 15, 1963; W. R. Hearst, "Stuff and Nonsense at Washington," n.s., Feb. 20, 1934; *AOV*, pp. 317–8; "Government Seeks L's Ideas," *NYT*, June 22, 1927, p. 5; "Dayton Is Disappointed," *NYT*, June 24, 1927, p. 3.

HG; PLANNING TOUR; WE: "L Gets Advice at Capital," *NYT*, June 24, 1927, n.p.; Daniel Guggenheim to Board members, Jan. 24, 1926; CAL (U) preface to book on Guggenheims, c. 1930 [Y:376/1051], *Report of Daniel Guggenheim Fund for Promotion of Aeronautics*, 1926 and 1927, pp. ii, 15, 20–1; Seward Prosser to Hereford of Bankers Trust (T), June 3, 1927; Daniel Guggenheim Fund, press release, June 28, 1927; Harry Knight to DWM, June 29 and July 7, 1927 [ACL]; DWM to Harry Knight, June 29 and 30, 1927 [ACL], HG to DWM, July 5, 1927 [ACL], DWM to HG, July 9, 1927 [ACL]; George P. Putnam, *Wide Margins* (New York: Harcourt, Brace & Co., 1942), pp. 232–6; CAL to E. B. Mueller, Mar. 22, 1942; Fitzhugh Green to CAL, June 28, 1927, and Nov. 1, 1928; CAL, "Recollections of HG and Falaise" (U), Apr. 30, 1973; CAL, (U) comments on reading *WE*, Oct. 24, 1971; CAL (U) comments on notes by Raymond Fredette, May 21, 1973; DAVIS, Aug. 12, 1969; G. P. Putnam to CAL, Mar. 1, 1928; CAL, (U) "Misc. Notes and Information," July 1955; HB to G. P. Putnam, Mar. 12, 1928; CAL, log of 48–state tour, appears in *SSL*, pp. 506–11; tales of tour appear in Donald F. Keyhoe, *Flying With L* (New York: Grosset & Dunlap, 1928), pp. 17, 76, 95; CAL to Bruce Larson, June 24, 1967; "When 'Lindy' Flew Over Fond du Lac," (Fond du Lac) *Commonwealth Reporter*, Apr. 22, 1966, pp. II, 5; Michael Parfit, "Flying Where Lindy Flew," *Smithsonian*, Oct., 1987, pp. 201–2; *AOV*, pp. 81, 83; Bruce Larson, "L's Return to Minnesota, 1927," *Minnesota History*, Winter, 1970, pp. 141–152; *L the Flier of Little Falls* (Little Falls: Little Falls High School, 1928) [MNHS: P1675, Box 14]; "L Given Title By Oklahoma Indians," n.s., c. July 31, 1927; Otto Robert Landelius, *Swedish Place-Names in North America* (Carbondale: South Illinois University Press, 1985), pp. 3, 29, 80, 110, 156, 158, 162, 183, 187, 201, 256, 262, 273–4; "Town Names for L," *NYT*, June 14, 1928, p. 2; polls of heroes cited in Dixon Wecter, *The Hero in America* (New York: Charles Scribner's Sons, 1941), p. 432–4; Thomas Moore to CAL, May 9, 1952; Vacuum Oil Co. to HB, Nov. 21, 1928; "L Crate . . . in Canaan," (Waterville, Maine) *Morning Sentinel*, Mar. 31, 1990, pp. 1, 8; Edward Kraske to CAL, Mar. 3, 1953; L. M. Campbell to Mayor Victor Miller (of St. Louis), ca. Jan. 31, 1928; Paul Garber to ASB (I), June 6, 1990; CAL to George Plagenz (of *The Cleveland Press*), Apr. 23, 1973.

IMPACT OF U.S. TOUR: HG to CAL, Oct. 26, 1927; "Ryan Gets 29 Orders," *NYT*, June 18, 1927, p. 3; Corrigan, *My Story*, p. 97; *Shell Aviation News* #185, 1953; Davis, *Hero*, p. 236; Ross, *Last Hero*, p. 160; CAL, "St. Louis Has Opportunity to Become Leading Aviation Center," *Greater St. Louis,* Aug., 1927, p. 11 (MHS: B74/F47); Lambert, "Brief Summary"; A. B. Lambert to CAL, May 21, 1928; Lordsburg (N. M.) Chamber of Commerce to CAL, July 13, 1927; Chattanooga Chamber of Commerce to Adolph Ochs, Oct. 4, 1978; "Flashbacks—Sixty Years Ago in *Forbes,*" *Forbes,* June 15, 1987, p. 279; HG, *Seven Skies,* p. 76; J. D. Rockefeller to CAL, Dec. 7, 1927; Gershwin anecdote related in Dwight Taylor, *Joy Ride* (London: Victor Gollancz Ltd., 1959), pp. 134–143.

LATIN AMERICAN TOUR AND AFTERMATH: CAL to DWM, Sept. 29, 1927; Harold Nicolson, *Dwight Morrow* (New York: Harcourt, Brace, 1935) pp. 309–14; Stanley R. Ross, "DWM, Ambassador to Mexico," *The Americas,* vol. XIV, no. 3, Jan., 1958, pp. 273–89; DWM to HG, Nov. 18, 1927 (ACL); *AOV,* pp. 83–96, 318–24; ECM (D), Dec. 14 and 28, 1927; ECM to Amey Aldrich, Dec. 18, 1927; CMM to "Rhea and Anne," n.d. (ca. Dec. 15, 1927); BMUA, pp. 81, 99; ECM to Maude Hulst, Jan. 5, 1928; CAL to Paul S. Johnston, Nov. 30, 1958; CAL to Prof. Wesley Newton, Mar. 1, 1971; "60,000 Children Acclaim Lindy," St. Louis *Globe-Democrat,* Feb. 15, 1928, pp. 1–2; *Time*'s "Man of the Year" as a "marketing gimmick" is cited in Walter Isaacson, *Kissinger* (New York: Simon & Schuster, 1992), p. 479; *SSL,* p. 530.

8   UNICORNS

E: *AOV,* p. 118.

DWM AND ECM: Walter Lippmann, "DWM: A Tribute," *New York Herald-Tribune,* Oct. 7, 1931; Nicolson, *Morrow,* pp. 3–20, 22–41, 51–2, 69–78, 80, 103, 110, 113 124, 129–31, 164, 206, 211, 259; DWM to President Benjamin Harrison, Jan 3, 1891 [ACL]; Charles Burnett to DWM, Apr. 16, 1914 [ACL]; Margot Wilkie to ASB (I), Apr. 26, 1993; ECM, notebook, n.d. [Smith College]; DWM to ECM, June 12, 1895, July 10, 1899; ECM to "Mother," July 26, 1901; *BMAU,* p. xiii; n.a. *The History of Englewood* [MHS: Box 114]; ERMM, "The Little Brown House" and "Move to Palisade Avenue (U), n.d. [Smith College]; Chernow, *House of Morgan,* p. 150; ECM (D), Jan. 30, Feb. 25, Mar. 31, and Apr. 8, 1914; CMM to ASB (I), Mar. 3, 1993.

DWM's brother Jay Johnson Morrow distinguished himself in the Engineer Corps of the United States Army, rising to the rank of General and serving as Governor of the Canal Zone. [N.B. DWM actually joined the law firm of Reed, Simpson, Thacher & Barnum, which became Simpson, Thacher & Bartlett in 1904.]

AML, BACKGROUND AND MEETING CAL: Corliss Lamont to ASB (I), June 4, 1993; RML to ASB (I), May 8, 1993; Susanna Beck Hatt to ASB (I), May 6, 1993; Dorothea Bolton to AML, Dec. 15, 1974; *BMAU,* pp. v (E), xvi, xx, 5–6, 15, 19–21; AML to ERMM, June 7, 1922 and late-Sept. 1922; ERMM to AML, July 4, 1923; AML, "Ships," *The Wheel* (Chapin School), Dec., 1923 (also: "Distance Lends Enchantment," Mar., 1924 and "Disillusions of Childhood," n.d.); Mary Walker Delafield to AML, Mar. 22, 1966; ERMM (D), Apr. 22, 1924 [MHS]; CMM to ASB (I), Mar. 3, 1993; AML to ECM, Sept. 28, 1924, Apr. 22 and May 23, 1925, Jan. 31, July 23, 1927; AML to John Krout, Jan. 22, 1965; "Obituaries," *Smith Alumnae Quarterly,* Winter, 1986, pp. 68–9; Elizabeth Bacon Rodewald to AML, Feb. 9, 1972, Aug. 28, 1974, Feb. 9, 1977; Margot Wilkie to ASB (I), Apr. 26, 1993; AML, *Dearly Beloved* (New York: Harcourt, Brace & World, Inc., 1962), p. 79; Corliss Lamont to AML, Feb. 8, 1928; ECM (D), July 19, 1927; Nicolson, *Morrow,* p. 292; Stanley Ross, "DWM," p. 288.

CAL IN MEXICO; AML FALLS IN LOVE: *BMAU*, pp. 80–89, 91–2, 94–7, 99–100, 104, 106–8; 118, 135, 139, 147; AML (D), Dec. 20, 21, 28, 1927, Feb., Apr. 5, May 3, 1928; ECM (D), Dec. 14–20, 27, 1927, Jan. 26, 1928; AML to ECM, Jan. 15, Feb., Mar. 18, "after [Easter] vacation," May 3, 1928; AML to ERMM, Apr. 23, 1928; Fanny Heaslip Lea, "Galahad Himself," *Saturday Evening Post*, Mar. 31, 1928.

CAL AND AVIATION INDUSTRY: CAL, "Air Transport," Feb. 1, 1930; CAL, "Articles No. 1, 3, and 4," *NYT*, 1928; *AOV*, pp. 96–105, 107–8, 112; Gore Vidal, *United States* (New York: Random House: 1993), pp. 1061–2, 1067; "History of Transcontinental & Western Air, Inc." (remarks of Hon. Simeon D. Fess), *Congressional Record*, Apr. 20, 1934; CAL (N), Jan. 26, 1958; C. M. Keys to Stockholders of TAT, Inc., Feb. 20, 1928; CAL, "Report," to D. M. Sheaffer, c. 1930; CAL, "TAT Report," Winter, 1928–9; Paul Henderson, "Report" to CAL, Feb. 1, 1928; C. M. Keys to CAL, May 23, 1928; Cheever Cowdin to CAL, June 19, 1929 [MHS]; CAL to Cheever Cowdin, June 19, 1929 [MHS]; correspondence between CAL and Acme Milling and Refining Co., Sept., 1930–Apr., 1931, W. D. Coolidge (of General Electric) and CAL, Jan. 30, 1929; Ford Motor Company, Oct. 15, 1932; Goodyear, 1928–1931, and A. Wittnauer Co., to CAL, June 5, 1930 [MHS]; DAVIS, Aug. 13, 1969; CAL to D. A. Colussy, Feb. 11, 1971; CAL to Prof. Newton, June 6, 1970; CAL, "Lindy Earns Vacation," St. Louis *Globe-Democrat*, Feb. 12, 1928; Juan Trippe to CAL, May 15, 1928, Jan. 7, 1929; CAL to Juan Trippe, Nov. 12, 1929; CAL, "Form 1040," Individual Income Tax Return, 1928 and 1929; HB to CAL, July 9, 1928 (two letters); CAL to ELLL, ca. July 10, 1928; "Mrs. L and Miss Morrow Join Faculty," *Near East Colleges News Letter*, Oct., 1928, p. 1.

CAL-AML COURTSHIP: *AOV*, pp. 117, 119, 121–4; RML to ASB (I), May 8, 1993; Susanna Beck Hatt to ASB (I), May 6, 1993; ERMM to AML, Mar. 10 and Nov. 6, 1928; AML (D), March 1 and 26, May 3, June 22, July 13, 1928; *BMAU*, pp. 116, 127, 153, 157, 160, 168, 172, 175–7, 180–205, 208–11, 219–20, 227–8; ECM (D), Aug. 9, Nov. 13, 18, 22, 1928; "Mother Declares Lindy Marriage Rumors 'Silly,' " n.s., n.d.; AML to CMM, Oct. 4, 12, 19, 22, 26, and 29, Nov. 5 and 19, 1928: ERMM (D), Nov. 11, 1928; AML to ECM, June 28, 1929; AML to Stephen D. Bodayla, Oct. 21, 1980; CMM to ASB (I), Mar. 3, 1993; AML to ERMM, late-Nov., 1928; CAL to ELLL, Nov. 12, 1928, Feb. 20, 1929; ELLL to CAL, Dec. 20, 1928; ELLL to AML, Dec. 6, 1928; AML to ELLL, Jan. 4, 1929; CAL to AML, Apr. 16, 1929; *HGHL*, p. 1; AML to Corliss Lamont, n.d.; AML to Mrs. Norton, ca. Feb. 11, 1929.

Besides the Jordan Prize, AML won the Elizabeth Montagu Prize for a paper on Mme. D'Houdetot; her poem "Height" was published in the March, 1928 issue of *Scribner's Magazine*.

ENGAGEMENT: Ruth Dean, "Mrs. DWM's Garden," *Charm*, Aug. 1930; ECM (D), Jan. 27, Feb. 12, 13, 16, 27, and 28, 1929; "L to Wed Anne S. Morrow . . ." (Philadelphia?) *Inquirer*, Feb. 13, 1929; ERMM to "D. C.," Mar. 12, 1929; ECM to Alice Morrow, Feb. 24, 1929; DAVIS, Aug. 13, 1969; AML to ASL, Mar. 5, 1972; *HGHL*, pp. 1–2, 4, 16–8; ERMM to ECM, Feb. 2, 1929; CMM to ERMM, Feb. 13, 1929; AML, "Misc Note," (D), June 5, 1929; AML to CMM, Mar. 8, 1929; ECM to Katherine Norton[?], Mar. 21, 1929; *AOV*, pp. 125–7; CAL, timeline, 1929.

CAL-AML WEDDING: AML (D), May 27, 1929 (written on D pp. July 11–18, 1929); CAL, holograph will, May 27, 1929; Madame Blanche to CAL, June 16, 1939; ECM (D), May 28, 1929, and May 7, 1939; ELLL (N), May, 1929; *AOV*,

p. 127; AML to ECM, May 27, 1929; "L and Miss Morrow Wed . . . ," (St. Louis) *Globe Democrat,* May 28, 1929.

9   "WE"

E: *AOV,* p. 128.

HONEYMOON: AML to ECM, June, 18, 1929; *HGHL,* pp. 40–6; CAL to Edw. T. Richardson, Jr., Sept. 8, 1969, CAL to Senator Spong, Sept. 4, 1972; AML to DWM, Jr., June 23, 1929; *AOV,* p. 128; ECM (D), June 20, 1929; AML to Sue Beck, June 26, 1929.

"Mouette" (the name of the Ls' honeymoon boat) is French for "sea gull."

NEWLYWEDS AND AVIATION: Simeon D. Fess, "History of Transcontinental & Western Air, Inc.," *Congressional Record,* Apr. 20, 1934; CAL, "Report" to Col. Paul Henderson, May 26, 1929; n.a., "Transcontinental & Western Air," *Aero Digest,* Feb., 1934, n.p.; ECM (D), June 20, 1929; AML to ECM, June 18 and 28, July 6 and 13, Sept. 5, 1929, Jan. 18, Apr. 4, 1930; *HGHL,* pp. 9, 45, 47–62, 72–3, 97–9, 120–1, 157–8; AML to CMM, June 27, July 4, 8, and 9, Aug. 6, 1929; AML to ERMM, July 2, 1929; CAL, "Statement," ca. 1929 [Y:124/508]; *AOV,* p. 106, 107–9, 203–5, Gene Coughlin, "When L Saved the Day for Me," *Reader's Digest,* Feb., 1958, pp. 81–4; Kevin Starr, *Material Dreams* (New York: Oxford University Press, 1990), pp. 115–7; CAL, "Travelling By Air in 1929" (Daniel Guggenheim Fund), 1929; Pan American Airways System (M), 1931; Vidal, *United States,* pp. 1067–9; Capt. Benjamin B. Lipsner (as told to Leonard Finley Hilts), *The Airmail: Jennies to Jets* (New York: Wilcox & Follett, 1951), pp. 220, 224–37; AML to ELLL, Jan. 24, Apr. 9, and n.d., 1930; Bob Meakin, "Spirit of Lebec," *Westways,* Mar., 1974, pp. 19–23, 75; William L. Van Dusen, "Charlie L—Glider Pilot," *Western Flying,* May, 1930, pp. 50–3, 143; Marlen Pew, "Shop Talk at Thirty," *Editor & Publisher: The Fourth Estate,* July 26, 1930, draft of article with CAL revisions, n.d. [MHS: B59/F5]; Paul Garber to ASB (I), June 6, 1990; A. V. Kidder, "Col. And Mrs. L Aid Archaeologists," *News Service Bulletin* (Carnegie Institution of Washington), Part I, Dec. 1, 1929, pp. 109–13, and Part II, pp. 115–21; CAL to Harry Davison, Nov. 26, 1967; FRDT; Trippe, "CAL and World Travel," pp. 6–9; Dr. Walter M. Simpson to CAL, May 16, 1935; CAL to Miss Cunningham, July 13, 1970; AML to Sue Beck, Oct. 5, 1929.

ROCKETS AND RHG: *AOV,* pp. 15, 335–43, 381; CAL to Frederick Duvant III, Jan. 30, 1970; CAL (N) for Lehman's *This High Man,* June 27, 1956; Lehman, *High Man,* pp. 54, 159, 176–83, 208–21; Henry Du Pont to CAL, Oct. 23, 1929; Charles Stine to CAL, Nov. 6, 1929; "Finds New Explosive For Rocket Planes," *NYT,* Nov. 6, 1929; CAL to Milton Lehman, May 11, 1963; John Merriam, (M) re Goddard Rocket Project, Dec. 10, 1929; John Merriam to CAL, Jan. 25, 1930; CAL to HG, May 19, 1930; HG to CAL, May 28, 1930; "Goddard Backs Rocket Sky-Study,"*NYT,* July 10, 1930; *HGHL,* pp. 6, 64–6, 68–9; RHG to HG, Feb. 18, July 15, and Oct. 29, 1935; HG to RHG, Mar. 4, 1935; RHG to CAL, June 10 and Oct. 29, 1935; HG to CAL, Aug. 8, 1935.

SETTLING DOWN: AML to ERMM, Aug. 17, 1929, Apr. 3 and 8, 1930; FRDT; AML to CMM, Aug. 4 and 6, 1929; Vidal, *United States,* p. 1069; Sue Beck Hatt to ASB (I), May 6, 1993; *HGHL,* pp. 7–8, 102–7, 126–9, 131–2, 134–6; AML to ECM, Oct. 13 and 30, 1929, Mar. 4, Apr. 10, 1930; AML to ELLL, n.d. [1929]; Nicolson, *Morrow,* pp. 350–3, 377–89; AML, "Dedication of Chilton House" (U speech), Oct. 17, 1972; CAL to Mrs. Carl Squier, Nov. 7, 1969; FRDT; R. S. Allen,

"The Lockheed Sirius," *MHS Journal,* Winter, 1965, pp. 266–70; R. S. Allen, *Revolution in the Sky* (Brattleboro, VT: The Stephen Greene Press, 1964), pp. 36–9; CAL to Paul Johnston, Feb. 27, 1966.

BIRTH OF CAL, JR.: AML to CMM, May 12 and Nov. 10, 1930; *HGHL,* pp. 132, 134–6, 138–40, 142, 144–5, 151–4, 160; AML to ELLL, June 10 and 23–4, Sept. 29, and Nov., 1930, prob. Mar., Mar. 5 and 31, May 10, 1931; CAL (N) on Pew, "Shop Talk" draft; ECM (D), June 22, 1930; ECM to ELLL, June 23, 1930; CAL, "To the Wire Services," June 22, 1930; Mollie Wells, "Stars Propitious For the Lindys' Boy," *Daily Mirror,* June 24, 1930, p. 3; FDR to CAL, June 29, 1929; "A L Memorial," St. Louis *Post Dispatch,* c. Jan. 14, 1930; A. A. Graham, "The Next President of the U. S.," n.s., c. Oct. 30, 1930; Ralph Sordillo to CAL, Aug. 1, 1931; Rev. Paul Hamborszky to CAL, Oct. 7, 1930; J. V. McAree, "Col. L Disliked By Quite a Few People," n.s., Oct. 7, 1930; H. W. Ross to HB, Sept. 29, 1930; Russell Owen to CAL, Sept. 18, 1930; "Not Touched By Baby," "War and Lindy," "Looks and Lindy," clippings, n.s., n.d.; AML to ERMM, July 30–Aug. 3, 1930; Laura Lou Brookman, "How Ls Live in Rented Home," n.s., ca. Dec. 10, 1930; J. R. Donovan, "Lone Eagle Plans His Nest in the Sky," (Philadelphia) *Evening Bulletin,* Apr. 7, 1931; AML to Lucia Norton Valentine, Dec. 1930; Betty Gow to ASB (I), Sept. 25, 1993; Post Office Inspector D. P. Looney to CAL, Nov. 25, 1930, P. O. Inspector W. K. Halliday to CAL, Sept 29, 1930; AML (U-N) re Betty Gow, Mar., 1932.

BIOLOGY AND DR. CARREL: *AOV,* pp. 129–35; CAL to Father Joseph Durkin, May 20, 1966; CAL, (U-AW), [Y:218/626]; Dr. Paluel Flagg to CAL, Dec. 1, 1930, June 22, 1935; Dr. Paluel Flagg, "L's Introduction to Medicine" (U memoir), June 22, 1930; James Thomas Flexner, *An American Saga* (Boston: Little, Brown and Co., 1984), p. 351; W. Sterling Edwards and Peter Edwards, *AC: Visionary Surgeon* (Springfield, IL: Charles C. Thomas, 1974), pp. 8, 15; Simon Flexner, "AC: 1873–1944," n.s., n.d.; AC, *Man, the Unknown* (New York: Halcyon House, 1935), pp. 60, 214, 296, 321; Albert H. Ebeling, "Carrel's Immortal Tissue," *American Druggist,* Jan., 1942, n.p.; Dr. Richard Bing, (U) memoir, "Carrel, L, Rockefeller Institute, and NYC," n.d., pp. 32–49; CAL, "Preface" to AC, *The Voyage to Lourdes* (New York: Harper & Brothers, 1950), pp. v–viii; CAL to Dr. William Glenn, Apr. 9, 1965; CAL to Dr. Houston, Jan. 3, 1960; "Col. L Gets Degree at Princeton," *NYT,* June 17, 1931; Dr. Richard Bing to ASB (I), Feb. 17, 1994; AML to Jack Moseley, Oct. 20, 1980; CAL, quoted in "Paying Tribute to Dr. Carrel," *American Medical News,* Aug. 20, 1973, pp. 16–7; CAL, "AC Centenary," draft, June 28, 1973; CAL, "AC," draft, Dec. 29, 1973; CAL, "Speech" at Huntington Memorial Hospital, Dec. 2, 1970.

TRIP NORTH TO ORIENT: CAL, (U-AW) [Y:218/626]; CAL, "Autobiographical" (U-AW), 1947; *NTO,* pp. 11–2, 15, 23–5, 27–9, 37–40, 65–8, 162–200, 210–221, 226–34; CAL to William Leary, Jr., July 21, 1968; Nelson A. Rockefeller to CAL, July 17, 1931; Leonard Baldwin (of Lomen Reindeer Corp.) to CAL, July 23, 1931; Vilhjalmur Stefansson to CAL, June 19, 1931; CAL to Vilhjalmur Stefansson, July 13, 1931; *HGHL,* pp. 8, 160–2, 188–94; Betty Gow to ASB (I), Sept. 25, 1993; AML to ELLL, May 10, 1931; AML to ECM, July 17 and 22, Aug. 6, 8, 10, 17–8, 29, Sept. 17, 26, 28, and 30, early Oct., 1931; ECM (U) account of CAL, Jr., c. Spring, 1932; ELLL to CAL, July 8, 1931; CAL to John Grierson, Mar. 17, 1964; "Ls in Tokyo Cheered by 100,000," *NYT,* Aug. 27, 1931; CAL (U-M) re his revolver, June 27, 1933; *AOV,* pp. 250–5; CAL, "Report" to China's National Flood

Relief Commission, Sept. 26, 1931; J. Heng Liu, "An Experience with L," n.s., n.d.; AML to ERMM, Oct., 1931.

DEATH OF DWM AND RETURN TO U.S.: ERMM to AML (T), Oct. 6, 1931; Ekins of United Press to CAL (T), Oct. 6, 1931; DWM, "You Dare Not Fail," speech, printed in *The Survey,* Nov. 15, 1931, pp. 193–4; Nicolson, *Morrow,* pp. 399–400; "Morrow is Buried," *NYT,* Oct. 6, 1931; Walter Lippmann, "Dwight Morrow," *New York Herald Tribune,* Oct. 7, 1931; ECM (D), Oct. 5–8, 1931; ECM to AML, Oct. 15, 1931; B. T. Chiu to CAL and AML, Oct. 30, 1934; Gilbert Grovenor to B. T. Chiu, Jan. 25, 1934; Amb. Cameron Forbes to CAL, Feb. 13, 1932; "Ls in China," *NYT,* Sept. 29, 1931.

HOUSE IN HOPEWELL: AML to ELLL, Nov. 12, 1931; *HGHL,* pp. 202–5; AML to CMM, Nov. 16, 1931; ECM (U-N) re CAL, Jr., Spring, 1932; AML (U-N) re Betty Gow, Mar., 1932; AML (U), "The Tulips," Winter, 1940; Betty Gow to ASB (I), Sept. 25, 1993; "L To Celebrate 30th Birthday," n.s., Jan. 28, 1932; "CAL on 30th Birthday," n.s., ca. Feb. 4, 1932; James C. Young, "L Adding to His Trophies," *NYT Magazine,* Nov. 1, 1931; CAL, "A Method for Washing Corpuscles in Suspension," *Science,* Apr. 15, 1932, pp. 415–6; CAL to Dr. Michael Weiner, July 16, 1965; CAL and AML, income tax returns, 1930, 1931; Dr. David Read to ASB (I), May 2, 1993; AML to ELLL, Dec., 1931.

10 SOURLAND

E: *AOV,* p. 139.

AT HOME WITH "THE BABY": "Heroes—'Cunning Little Rascal,' " *Time,* Nov. 30, 1931, p. 11; Will Rogers, "Will Rogers Recalls. . . ," *NYT,* Mar. 3, 1932, p. 8; AML to Sue Beck Vaillant, ca. Jan. 13, 1932; AML to ELLL, Feb. 7 and 10, 1932; "Mrs. L Aids China Flood Appeal," *NYT,* Feb. 22, 1932, p. 18; Frank Doubleday to AML, Oct. 9, 1930; *HGHL,* pp. 222–4; CAL (D), Nov. 11, 1931 and Feb. 24, 1932.

NIGHT OF KIDNAPPING: AML, "Statement" to Lt. J. J. Sweeney and Det. Hugh Strong, Newark Police Dept., Mar. 13, 1932; Betty Gow, "Statement" to J. J. Lamb, May 12, 1932; Elsie Mary Whateley, "Statement" to J. J. Sweeney and Hugh Strong, Mar. 10, 1932; Olly Whateley, "Statement" to P. J. Brady, L. J. Bornmann, and J. J. Sweeney, Mar. 3, 1932; CAL, "Statement" to J. J. Sweeney, Mar. 11, 1932; "Kidnapping and Murder of CAL, Jr.," FBI Summary Report, New York File 62–3057, p. 49; Hugh Larimer, "Unknown Subjects," FBI Report, Mar. 4, 1933; Lt. Dunn quoted by Det. L. J. Bornmann to C. D. Plebani in Jim Fisher, *The Lindbergh Case* (New Brunswick, NJ: Rutgers University Press, 1987), pp. 7–8; "Police Information," teletype, Mar. 1, 1932 (New Jersey State Police Museum); Corp. Jos. A. Wolfe, "Major Initial Report," Mar. 1, 1932; AML to ELLL, Mar. 2 and 3, 1932; *HGHL,* pp. 224, 226–7; "Kidnapping Holds First Place on Radio," *NYT,* Mar. 4, 1932, p. 8; Oren Root to ASB (I), Apr. 10, 1994; ransom note #1 as well as those that followed are housed at the New Jersey State Police Museum, West Trenton, New Jersey; the Schwarzkopf detractors are quoted in Ludovic Kennedy, *The Airman and the Carpenter* (New York: Viking, 1985), p. 86; "Father Searches Grounds for Child," *NYT,* Mar. 2, 1932, pp.1, 3.

DAYS FOLLOWING KIDNAPPING: "L Baby Kidnapped," *NYT,* Mar. 2, 1932, pp. 1, 3; Sidney B. Whipple, *The Lindbergh Crime* (New York: Blue Ribbon Books, 1935), pp. 14–18, 28–9; "Home Now Police Centre," *NYT,* Mar. 4, 1932, pp. 1, 8; AML to ELLL, Mar. 3 and Apr. 8, 1932; *HGHL,* pp. 226–7, 237; Fisher, *L Case,* pp. 17, 20–8; "Federal Aid in Hunt Order By Hoover," p. 8, "Roosevelt Orders State Police Hunt," p. 8, "L Hopeful, Is Ready to Ransom Son," pp. 1, 9, "100,000 in The Manhunt," pp. 1, 8, "Kidnapping Arouses Sympathy of Nation," pp. 1, 10, "Diet Needed by L Baby," p. 1, " 'Baby Is Safe,' Says Card from Newark," p. 10, "Kidnapping Wave Sweeps Nation," p. 9, *NYT*, Mar. 3, 1932; F. Trubee Davison to CAL (T), Mar. 2, 1932; "Kidnapping of Baby Speeds Federal Law," *NYT*, Mar. 2, 1932, pp. 1, 3; press release re Boy Scouts of America, c. Mar. 7, 1932 [MHS]; "AF of L in 7 States Asked to Aid in Hunt," *NYT*, Mar. 6, 1932; D. M. Sheaffer to CAL (T), Mar. 2, 1932; "Westchester Women Aid L Search," p. 8, "World Waits Hopefully," pp. 1, 8, "Television Used in Search," p. 9, *NYT*, Mar. 4, 1932; Betty and Will Rogers to CAL and AML (T), Mar. 2, 1932; Herbert Hoover to CAL and AML, Mar. 2, 1932; Benjamin Lupica to ASB (I), Apr. 7, 1994; FBI "Summary Report," p. 255; T. P. Crockett to CAL (T), Mar. 11, 1932; Carl Egge to CAL (T), Apr. 15, 1932; Janie Dietz to CAL (T), Mar. 3, 1932; Anon. to Hopewell Chief of Police, Mar. 5, 1932; "Kidnapping Notes Swamp Police," Mar. 5, 1932, *NYT*, p. 6; Irene Mayer Selznick to ASB (I), Apr. 4, 1987; Chernow, *House of Morgan*, p. 301.

THEORIES AND INVESTIGATION: "CHJF" to AML, May 4, 1932; ECM (D), Mar. 8, 1932; Anon. to AML (from England), Oct. 13, 1933; Maurice Sendak comment expressed in Joyce Milton, *Loss of Eden: A Biography of C and AML* (New York: HarperCollins, 1993), p. 300; Dr. J. W. Hall to CAL, Mar. 14, 1932 [MHS]; Whipple, *L Crime*, pp. 27–8, 47 (Capone quoted on p. 55); Whited quoted in Kennedy, *Airman*, pp. 215–6; "No Trace of L Kidnappers," pp. 1, 9, Mar. 4, 1932, "Flier's Mother Composed," p. 7, "Col and Mrs. L's Offer," p. 1, "Friend of L Nurse is Seized," pp. 1, 7, Mar. 5, 1932, *NYT*; AML to ELLL, Mar. 3, 5, 1932; *HGHL*, pp. 227–9; Fisher, *L Case*, p. 14; Betty Gow to ASB (I), Sept. 25, 1993; ransom note #2; "Ls in Message to Abductors," pp. 1, 23, "Text of Announcement," p. 1, Mar. 6, 1932, *NYT*; "L Ignored Police in New Move," p. 12, Mar. 7, 1932, *NYT*; ECM to ELLL, Mar. 4, 1932; D. P. Weimer (of Weimer & Bennett) to HB, Mar. 7, 1932; Barrett Wendell, Jr. to Jerome D. Green, Mar. 2, 1932 [MHS].

In *Murder on the Orient Express*, Agatha Christie wrote of the fictitious "Armstrong Kidnapping Case," in which a Colonel Armstrong's only child was abducted during his wife's second pregnancy. Shortly after Armstrong paid an enormous ransom, the child's dead body was discovered; and in the surrounding hysteria, a nursemaid who could not bear the police interrogation committed suicide.

MEANS, CURTIS, AND "JAFSIE": George Waller, *Kidnap* (New York: Dial Press, 1961), pp. 35–48, 50; Condon letter appeared in Bronx *Home News*, Mar. 8, 1932, cited in Fisher, *L Case*, pp. 40, 42, 45, 47–9, 56–61; FBI "Summary Report," pp. 80–1, 157–76, 178–9, 305; Kennedy, *Airman*, pp. 98–103; Larimer, FBI report, Mar. 4, 1933; ECM(D), Mar. 10, 11, 12, 16, 1932; AML to ELLL, Mar. 10 and 12, Apr. 29, 1932; *HGHL*, pp. 232–3, 243; W. Merrick (M), FBI Files #62–3057, Mar. 18, 1932; J. E. Seykora, FBI report re Condon, Mar. 8, 1934; John F. Condon, grand jury testimony, May 20, 1932; Edward F. Bergman, *Woodlawn Remembers* (New York: North Country Books, 1988), pp. 3–11; J. F. Condon, "Meeting the Kidnapper, Mar. and Apr., 1932 at Woodlawn Cemetery," n.d. [NJ State Police Museum]; J. F. Condon "Statement" to District Attorney, May 14, 1932; "11 Days of Failure in L Case" and "Spitale Acquitted on Liquor Charge," Mar. 13, 1932, *NYT*, p. 3; "L Case Commercialized," *NYT*, Mar. 7, 1932, p. 11.

Condon used a pseudonym with all except the innermost circle at the Lindberghs'. Even Mrs. Morrow called him "Mr. Stice" for weeks, thinking his name was J. U. Stice.

WAITING; PAYING RANSOM: CAL, "Statement," *The Detriot News,* Mar. 20, 1932, n.p.; AML to ELLL, Mar. 8, 12, 16, 21, and 23, Apr. 1, 6, 8, 13, 18, 29, 1932; ECM (D), Mar. 20, 22, 26, 29, and 31, Apr. 2–5, 7–9, 11, 1932; J. M. Keith (FBI) report to J. E. Hoover, Apr. 9, 1932; FBI "Summary Report," pp. 183–8, 208–10; Fisher, *L Case,* pp. 72, 76–7, 79; Kennedy, *Airman,* p. 104; *HGHL,* pp. 231–3, 235–7, 242–3; AML, (U) fragment, "The Tulips," late winter, 1940; AML to ERMM, Mar. 18, 1932; John F. Condon, *Jafsie Tells All!* (New York: Jonathan Lee, 1936), p. 148; CAL, "Statement" to Harry W. Walsh, May 20, 1932; J. E. Seykora, "Report" re Condon, Mar. 3, 1934; J. F. Condon, "From Memory: Meeting Kidnapper at St. Raymond's," Mar. 23, 1934; Larimer, FBI Report, n.d.; John F. Condon, grand jury testimony, May 20, 1932; CAL, grand jury testimony, Sept. 26, 1934; J. E. Seykora, "Title: Unknown Subjects," re Condon, Mar. 8, 1934; CAL (N) on back of Secretary of Treasury to CAL, May 7, 1932; Waller, *Kidnap,* p. 79; ELLL to AML, Apr. 13, 1932.

WAITING; PURSUING ALTERNATIVE LEADS: Fisher, *L Case,* pp. 94–5, FBI Summary Report, pp. 384, 390–8; ECM (D), Apr. 14, 19, 20, 24, and 29, May 8–11, 1932; C. Lloyd Fisher, "The Case New Jersey Would Like to Forget," *Liberty,* Aug. 1–Sept. 12, 1936 (seven weekly installments), esp. Aug. 8, pp. 31, 33, and Aug. 15, p. 15; CAL, "Statement" to Harry Walsh, May 20, 1932; CAL, "Outline of Information" re Curtis, Apr. 20, 1932; AML (D), May 11, 1932; *HGHL,* p. 245.

DISCOVERY OF CORPSE: "Two Distinct Fractures," pp. 1,2, and "Trenton Negro Tells of Finding Body," n.p., *Trenton State Gazette;* FBI Summary Report, pp. 58, 108–11; Larimer report, "Alpine 1230," Condon Ex. #29; Fitzgerald and Zapolsky report, and Corp. Frank Kelley report, May 12, 1932 [NJ State Police Hq., L case archives]; Betty Gow to ASB (I), Sept. 25, 1993; ECM (D), May 12, 1932; AML (D), May 12, 1932; *HGHL,* pp. 246–8, 252; AML to ELLL, May 12, and 17, 1932; Whipple, *L Crime,* pp. 98–9; Waller, *Kidnap,* p. 104; Ross, *Last Hero,* pp. 211–28; Fisher, *L Case,* pp. 112–4; Betty Gow, "Statement" to Robert Coar and Samuel Leon (NJ State Police), May 13, 1932; Walter Swayze, "Report on Unknown Baby," May 12, 1932.

L subscribed to the theory that the baby fell to his death when the ladder broke. (Larimer report, Mar. 4, 1933, p. 11.)

11   APPREHENSION

E: *AOV,* p. 390.

CONDOLENCES AND AFTERMATH: HB comment comes from Oren Root to ASB (I), Apr. 19, 1994; CAL papers include lists of "Ts Received from Organizations," "Letters of Condolence Received from Organizations," May–June, 1932, "Letters Received from Personal Friends," May–June, 1932; "Ts Received from Officials," "Flowers and Gifts," c. week of May 13, 1932, "Ts—Personal," May, 1932; Ortíz Rubio to CAL, May 18, 1932; Mayor Frank Kiewele to CAL and AML, May 13, 1932; ELCS to CAL, May 14, 1932; Elsie Allen to AML, May 16, 1932; James F. Spink, "The Little Eaglet" (Buffalo: Sword & Shield Bookstore, 1932), pamphlet; n.a. "Oshamnu," *The Hungarian Jew,* May 24, 1932, p. 4; Kathleen Norris, "Save All 'Lost Children,'" n.s., c. May 15, 1932; Charles Elliott, NJ Commissioner of Education to CAL (re Puerto Rican schoolchildren), July 7, 1932; Joseph Stehlin (of

Jacksonville Beach Chamber of Commerce) to CAL, Oct. 4, 1932; Z. Szabodosz (of *Amerikai Magyar Nepszava*) to AML (re Hungarian woman offering her son for adoption), June 15, 1932; AML to ELLL, May 18 and 22, June 10, 1932; ECM (D), Mar. 15 and May 23, 1932; AML (D), May 20-23, 31, June 4, 1932, *HGHL,* pp. 254-8, 262, 265, 269; *AOV,* p. 140.

Ls REASSEMBLE THEIR LIVES; CASE WINDS DOWN: Amelia Earhart quip related by CMM to ASB (I), Mar. 3, 1993 and Dr. David Read to ASB (I), May 2, 1993; AML to ERMM, June 10, 1932; *HGHL,* pp. 269-272, 282-7, 292, 296-7; FBI, "Summary Report," NY-62-3057, pp. 80-93; AML to ELLL, June 13, July 2 and 5, 1932; ECM (D), June 10 and 11, 1932; AML (D), June 11 and 12, July 9 and 24, 1932, Aug. 14, 1932; H. Norman Schwarzkopf to "All Law Enforcement Officials," flier, May 21, 1932; AML to ERMM, Aug. 8, 1932; Mina Curtis, "CL: A Personal Portrait," c. 1941, p. 6 [Sophia Smith Library]; DAVIS, Aug. 19, 1969.

BIRTH OF JML; MARRIAGE OF ERMM: AML (D), Aug. 16-7, 20, 24, 28, Sept. 3, 8, 14, 17, Dec. 28, 1932; *HGHL,* pp. 297-301, 303, 305-7, 309-11, 313, 315, 318-23; AML to ELLL, Aug. 16 and 18, Sept. 15, ca. Oct. 15, Dec. 15, 1932; ECM (D), Aug. 16 and 17, 1932; Dr. Hawks is quoted by Lynn Frost in a letter from Thomas B. Congdon, Jr., to ASB, Apr. 22, 1991; CAL to United Press (T), Aug. 16, 1932; Fred Ferguson of NEA Service Inc., to HG, Aug. 17, 1932; ERMM to ELLL, Oct. 29, 1932; "Another Morrow Bride," (NY) *Daily News,* Dec. 29, 1932.

In 1933, the Lindberghs gave away their property outside Hopewell, New Jersey. It was named High Fields and has since been used as a home for children in need.

RENEWED SOCIAL LIFE; NEW TRAVELS: AML (D), Jan. 13, 18, 21, 24, 30, Feb. 6, Apr. 26-30, May 6-71933; *LROD,* pp. 5, 8-13, 18-20, 26-37; AML to ECM, Mar. 2, 1933, AML to ELLL, Mar. 2 and May 11, 1933; AML pouring water on CAL related by CMM to ASB (I), Mar. 3, 1993; CAL to ELLL, June 5, Sept. 3, 1932; CAL, log of flights, Mar. 30-Apr. 25, 1932; CAL to Nettie Beauregard, May 17, 1933; "L Visits Friends," St. Louis *Post Dispatch,* Apr. 22, 1933, n.p.; "L Flies Again," Detroit *Times,* Apr. 20, 1933, p. 1; "Ls Reach Ohio," *NYT,* Apr. 21, 1933, n.p.; "Ls Here," Kansas City *Times,* Apr. 25, 1933, p. 1; AML to ERMM, May 1933; "Ls Held By a Sandstorm," *NYT,* May 8, 1933, p.1.

PLANNING ATLANTIC SURVEY TRIP: CAL, "Foreword," *LTW,* pp. v-viii; *AOV,* pp. 108-9; CAL, "North Atlantic Survey—1933," July 28, 1934; Richard Sanders Allen, "The Lockheed Sirius," *A. A. H. S, Journal,* Winter, 1965, pp. 269-70; DAVIS, Aug. 19. 1969; F. C. Meier to CAL, Dec. 20, 1933; Fred C. Meier, "Collecting Micro-Organisms From the Arctic Atmosphere," *The Scientific Monthly,* Jan., 1935, pp. 5-20; Vilhjalmur Stefansson to CAL, June 8 and July 8, 1933; F. Gledhill (of Pan American) to V. Stefansson (M), July 7, 1933; CAL to Milton Lehman, Apr. 6, 1963; AML to ELLL, June 12 and 20, 1933; *LROD,* pp. 40-4; ERMM to AML, May 28, 1933; AML (D), June 25, 1933; AML to ERMM, June 24, 1933.

GREENLAND AND EUROPE: CAL, "Lockheed Sirius," log, July 1-Sept. 17, 1933; "Ls Start Flight to Arctic," *NYT,* July 10, 1933, n.p.; AML (D), July 9, 21, and 22, 1933; AML to ELLL, June 20, Sept. 15, Oct. 10, 22, 25, 1933, *LROD,* pp. xviii-xix, 42-3, 46-58, 60-94, 110, 112-4, 132-8, 153-4; AML to ECM, Aug. 11 and 20, 1933; AML quoted in "Ls," *Smithsonian World,* Mar. 1984, p. 27; "L Rumor Creates Worry Throughout the World" and "The Rumors About L," (Copenhagen) *Politiken,* Aug. 11 and 12, 1933; John Grierson quoted in (Tom Crouch, ed.) *CAL: An American Life* (Washington, D. C.: National Air and Space Museum, 1977), p. 13; AML (U) draft of "Introduction" to John Grierson, *I Re-*

member L (New York: Harcourt Brace Jovanovich, 1977); AML (D), Aug. 17–20, Sept. 17, Nov. 22–3, 1933; John Grierson to Editor, "Letters," *Flight International,* Sept. 19, 1974, n.p.; AML to ERMM, Nov. 6, 1933; "L Pays Homage . . . Shows Wife Bourget," Chicago *Daily Tribune* (European edition), Oct. 31, 1933, n.p.; AML quoted in Winifred Rogers, "Does Baby Jon Need His Mother?," *The Cleveland Press,* Dec. 1, 1933, n.p.

AFRICA; SOUTH AMERICA: AML (D), Nov. 27, Dec. 5, 9, 11, and 12, 1933; *LROD,* pp. 157–8, 168–75, 178–9; *AOV,* pp. 113–5; *LTW,* pp. 203–17, La Varre to William A. Orr, Jan. 5, 1934; William Orr to CAL, Mar. 8, 1934.

RETURN TO AMERICA: FDR to CAL and AML (T), Dec. 16, 1933; AML and CAL to FDR, Dec. 17, 1933; CAL, "Foreword," *LTW,* p. ix; FRDT; CAL to Dr. H. E. Anthony (American Museum of Natural History), May 1, 1934; CAL to Clarence Hay, Feb. 20, 1934; Clarence Hay to AML and CAL, Nov. 11, 1934; "Ls Sign Off After Flight," *Newsweek,* Dec. 30, 1933, p. 19; CAL to Orville Wright, Jan. 5, 1933; Orville Wright to Dr. Charles G. Abbot, Dec. 23, 2933, Orville Wright to CAL, Jan. 11, 1934; AML to ERMM, Feb. 19 and June 7, 1934; AML to ELLL, Mar. 2, 1933, Jan. 24, c. Feb. 25, Apr. 26, 1934; *LROD,* pp. 19, 190, 192–3; FDR to CAL and AML, c. Jan., 1934; CAL and AML to FDR and Eleanor Roosevelt, c., Jan., 1934.

AIR-MAIL CONTROVERSY: FDR, Executive Order #6591, Feb. 9, 1934; Lipsner, *Airmail,* pp. 238–43, 245–50, 252–3; Arthur M. Schlesinger, Jr., *The Coming of the New Deal* (Boston: Houghton Mifflin, 1958), pp. 448–54; A. G. Patterson to CAL, Dec. 8, 1933; CAL to Hugo Black, Jan. 11, 1934; Grace Robinson, "The Rentschlers Fly the Dollar," p. 33, "Are the Rentschler Boys Good?" p. 31, "Capitalism at its Damndest," n.p., *New York Daily News,* Jan. 19, 1934; Richard Robbins to Postmaster General Farley; *AOV,* pp. 140–2; AML, fragment, n.d. with CAL emendations; CAL to FDR (T), Feb. 11, 1934; "Cracking Down on the Colonel," *Washington Star,* Feb. 13, 1934; "Roosevelt Rebukes Lindy," *Herald and Examiner,* Feb. 13, 1934, n.p.; CAL to W. R. Hearst, Feb. 21, 1934; the "plain citizen" who wired in CAL's behalf was Maurice Goodman to Stephen Early (T), Feb. 13, 1934; Will Rogers, "Will Is Stumped by Air Mail Cleanup Order," Kansas City *Star,* Feb. 12, 1934, n.p., which is also referred to in Owen Lovejoy to CAL, Feb. 26, 1934; James A. Farley to CAL (T), Feb. 13, 1934; AML to ERMM, Feb. 11, 1934, *LROD,* pp. 188–90; R. W. Robbins to "All T & WA Personnel," (M), Feb. 18, 1934; Secretary George Dern to CAL (T), Mar. 13 and 15, 1934; CAL to George Dern (T), Mar. 14 and 15, 1934; George Durno, "Lindy," (Philadelphia) *Evening Public Ledger,* Oct. 2, 1934, n.p.; "L Testifies," *New York American,* Mar. 19, 1934, n.p., "L Testifies," *Washington Star,* Mar. 18, 1934, n.p.; CAL (U-N), Mar. 1934; Carl L. Ristine to CAL, Mar. 16, 1934; HB (M), c. Mar. 16, 1934; CAL, "Statement," to Carl Ristine, Mar. 16, 1934; CAL to Carl Ristine (T), Apr. 7, 1934; Montague (of Paramount News) to CAL (T), Feb. 13, 1934; Ralph Renaud (of *Washington Post*) to CAL (T), Feb. 12, 1934; Charles Ford (of Universal Newsreel) to CAL (T), Feb. 12, 1934; John Royal (of NBC) to CAL, Feb. 12, 1934; Paul White (of CBS) to CAL (T), Mar. 15, 1934; "The Weight of Evidence," *NYT,* Mar. 19, 1934, n.p.; Hamilton Fish, remarks, *Congressional Record,* Feb. 21, 1934, pp. 3108–10; Walter Lippmann, "The Air-Mail Fiasco," *New York Herald Tribune,* Mar. 20, 1934; "Mr. Farley Hoists the White Flag," *Philadelphia Inquirer,* Apr. 17, 1934, n.p.; "The Sore Spot," *U. S. Air Services,* Apr., 1934, n.p.; Henry Suydam, "Critics Show Roosevelt Is Only Human," n.s., Feb. 26, 1934, n.p.

SUMMER, 1934; CLOSING IN ON HAUPTMANN: AML to ELLL, Apr. 26,

July 11, 1934; *LROD,* pp. 192–202; AML to ERMM, June 7, July 11 and 29, Aug. 23 and 28, Sept. 1, 1934; FRDT; ERMM to AML, Sept. 4, 1934; AML to ECM, Sept. 19, 1934; AML to CAL, quoted in Kennedy, *Airman,* p. 13, and verified by AML to ASB (I), Feb. 28, 1990; L Case Archives and "L Kidnapping—A State Police Review With Annexes," NJ State Police Headquarters, Mar. 15, 1980; Arthur Koehler, "Technique Used in Tracing the L. Kidnaping Ladder," *American Journal of Police Science,* incorporated in *Journal of Criminal Law and Criminology,* vol. 27, no. 5, 1937, pp. 712–24; W. O. Woods, Treasurer of the U. S. to "President of the Banking Institution Addressed," Apr. 14, 1933; Treasury Dept. (M) re L bills, ca. Aug. 16, 1932 [MHS: B24/F1]; FBI File, NY 62–3057, "Chronology," pp. 26–43; L. C. Haag, "L Case Revisited," *Journal of Forensic Sciences,* vol. 28, no. 4, Oct., 1983, pp. 1044–8.

HAUPTMANN'S ARREST: H. C. Leslie, Special Agent, (M) for File, Oct. 6, 1934; W. F. Seery, "Bruno Richard Hauptmann," report for U. S. Bureau of Investigation, Sept. 26, 1934; Special Agent Thomas H. Sisk, trial testimony, Jan. 17, 1935; Fisher, *L Case,* p. 195, 212, 249; Sgt. A. H. Albrecht, "Investigation of Bruno Richard Hauptmann's employment record at the Majestic Hotel," Sept. 20, 1934; B. R. Hauptmann interrogation, transcript, L Case Archives, NJ State Police; Anna S. Hauptmann, "Statement," Apr. 20, 1935; L. G. Turrou (M) re "Unknown Suspects," Sept. 21, 1934; Kennedy, *Airman,* p. 195, 240; Lewis J. Bornmann, "Searching Apartment and garage of . . . Hauptmann," Sept. 26, 1934; Anna S. Hauptmann to ASB (I), June 11, 1990; n.t., *NYT,* Oct. 9 and 10, 1934, n.p.; Tamm of FBI to J. Edgar Hoover, Jan. 22, 1936.

LIFE AT NEXT DAY HILL; PREPARING FOR TRIAL: Harold Nicolson to Vita Sackville-West, Sept. 30, Oct. 2, 4, 6, 13, 14, 15, Nov. 7, 8, 14, 1934; Nigel Nicolson, ed., *Vita and Harold* (New York: G. P. Putnam's Sons, 1992), pp. 255, 259; Mina Curtiss comment related by CMM to ASB (I), Mar. 3, 1993; AML (D), Oct. 13, Nov. 15, Dec. 3–5,. 11, 29 1934; *LROD,* pp. 209, 216, 223–4, 226, 232; ECM (D), Dec. 3, 1934; Margot Wilkie to ASB (I), Apr. 26, 1993; "L Asks Permission," *New York Evening Journal,* Dec. 31, 1934, p. 4; "Life in Flemington Is Transformed," p. 12, "Hauptmann Trial Will Start Today," pp. 1, 12, "Hauptman Spends Day on Cot," p. 12, *NYT,* Jan. 2, 1935; Lt. Allen L. Smith (of NJ State Police), report, Jan. 1, 1935.

Mina Curtiss came to admire CAL. In "Charles L: A Personal Portrait," (U), c. 1941 [Sophia Smith Collection], she wrote of the penetrating quality of his mind. "He's like a radium beam," Mrs. Curtiss told AML. Years later she concluded that he was "a man of honor and integrity, a scientist of great distinction . . . [a man who] has by an accident of fate been placed in a position where it is impossible for more than a few people ever to know him as a simple human being."

12   CIRCUS MAXIMUS

E: DAVIS, Aug. 13, 1969.

TRIAL COMMENCES; L TESTIFIES: "State [of New Jersey] vs. Hauptmann," transcript, Jan. 2–Feb. 13, 1935 [a satisfactory redaction of which exists in *The Trial of Bruno Richard Hauptmann* (Birmingham, AL: The Notable Trials Library, Division of Gryphon Editions, Inc., 1989)]; Russell B. Porter, "Hauptmann Trial Will Start Today," pp. 1, 12, "Life in Flemington Is Transformed," "Highlights of Trial Will Be Broadcast," "Huge Wire Service Set Up For Trial," Porter, "55 Witnesses Go To Jersey Today," p. 12, *NYT,* Jan. 2, 1935; "10 Hauptmann Case Jurors Quickly

Chosen," pp. 1, 3, "Foreman of Jury 25 Years in Same Job," pp. 1, 4, "Stopping of Clock Prolongs First Session," p. 4, Kathleen Norris, "Novelist Sketches the Trial Scene," p. 4, "First Day's Speed Pleases Defense," p. 5, *NYT*, Jan. 3; "Extra Jobs at Trial End Flemington Depression," p. 4, "Bookkeeper 55, Carpenter 60, Fill Jury," p. 5, Porter, "Col. and Mrs. L on Stand," pp. 1, 3, "Inside Job Says Reilly," pp. 1, 6, "Court Room Walls Lined By Standees," p. 7, *NYT*, Jan. 4, 1935; "Photographing of Ls Stirs Court," "Church Lunch Served to Many at the Trial," p. 8, "Youthful Crowd Waits at Court," p. 8, "L Stops Carrying Revolver," p. 8, Porter, "Col. L Names Hauptmann," pp. 1, 8, "Condon Defense Target," pp. 1, 8, *NYT*, Jan. 5; "Reilly Declares He Will Name Four," Jan. 6, p. 26, *NYT*, L. D. Lyman, "Col. L Wants Trial to be Scrupulously Fair," pp. 1, 7, *NYT*, Jan. 7, 1935; Neil Gabler, *Winchell* (New York: Alfred A. Knopf, 1994), pp. 208–13; Lee Israel, *Kilgallen* (New York: Dell, 1979), p. 51; Milton, *Loss of Eden*, p. 301; Whipple, *L Crime*, p. 317; Robert Wilentz to ASB (I), Oct. 20, 1993; David Davidson, "The Story of the Century," *American Heritage*, Feb., 1976, pp. 23–4; CAL (U-M), Dec. 28, 1934; Charles Katz, "Only Confession Can Convict Hauptmann?" (Bridgeport) *Herald*, Jan. 20, 1935, n.p.; ECM (D), Jan. 3, 1935; HB is quoted by Oren Root to ASB (I), Apr. 10, 1994; AML to ELLL, Jan. 9–10, 1935; *LROD*, p. 235.

PROSECUTION CONTINUES: "State vs. Hauptmann," transcript; Betty Gow to CAL (T), Dec. 13 and 16, 1934; Betty Gow to ASB (I), Sept. 25, 1993; AML to ELLL, Jan. 9–10, 1935; *LROD*, pp. xxii–xxv, 226, 237–8, 240–2; L. D. Lyman, "Col. L Wants Trial to Be Scrupulously Fair," pp. 1, 4, Russell B. Porter, "Miss Gow on Stand for State Today," pp. 1, 4, "60,000 See Scenes of L Case," p. 4, "Hauptmann Uneasy, Jail Guards Report," p. 4, *NYT*, Jan. 7, 1935; Kathleen Norris, "Betty Gow's Poise Praised By Writer," pp. 1, 8, "Miss Gow Firm in Her Story," pp. 1, 11, "Miss Gow Is Overcome After Leaving the Stand," pp. 11, *NYT*, Jan. 8, 1935; "Hauptmann Is Treated for a Cold in Chest," p. 1, Porter, "Hauptmann Near the Scene With Ladder, Says Witness," pp. 1, 10, "Hochmuth Story Surprises Family," p. 11, *NYT*, Jan. 9, 1935; Porter, "Condon Names Hauptmann," pp. 1, 11, "Prosecution Pleased By Condon Testimony," p. 1, *NYT*, Jan. 10, 1935; "Condon Gave Ransom to Fisch, Reilly Says," p. 1, Porter, "Breckinridge Backs Condon," pp. 1, 10, *NYT*, Jan. 11, 1935; Porter, "Hauptmann Asks to Go On the Stand," pp. 1, 30, "Jurors Get Bus Ride," p. 30, *NYT*, Jan. 13, 1935; "Jurors Play Cards and Chat in Rooms," p. 6, Porter, "Week's Fight Due Over Handwriting in Hauptmann Case," *NYT*, Jan. 14, 1935; Porter, "Woman Swears She Saw Hauptmann Watch Condon," pp. 1, 15, "Two Handwriting Experts Quit the Defense," p. 1, *NYT*, Jan. 15, 1935; Porter, "Two More Experts Name Hauptmann," pp. 1, 10, *NYT*, Jan. 16, 1935; "Defense in a Rift in Reilly Methods," p. 15, "'You Stop Lying,' Hauptmann Rages," pp. 1, 12, *NYT*, Jan. 18, 1935; Porter, "Woman Says Hauptmann Limped," pp. 1, 7, "Everybody Against Us," p. 7, *NYT*, Jan. 19, 1935; Lyman, "L Ready To Testify Again," pp. 1, 4, Jan. 20, 1935; "87 Have Testified," p. 12, *NYT*, Jan. 24, 1935; Lyman, "Koehler Tells of 18-Month Hunt," pp. 1, 13, Porter, "Expert Traces Tool Marks," pp. 1, 13, "Trial 'Booked Up' Weeks in Advance," p. 13, *NYT*, Jan. 24, 1935; "Judge and L Made Late By Storm," p. 16, Ford Madox Ford, "Tribute to Judge Paid By Novelist," p. 18, *NYT*, Jan. 25, 1935; J. Vreeland Haring, *The Hand of Hauptmann* (Plainfield, NJ: Hamer Publishing Co., 1936), pp. 197–310; AML (D), Jan. 12, 20, and 23, 1935; Lt. Allen Smith, "Guard Detail M," Jan. 16, 1935 [cited in Fisher, *L Case*, p. 313].

DEFENSE; HAUPTMANN TESTIFIES: "State vs. Hauptmann," transcript;

Porter, "Hauptmann Takes Stand," pp. 1, 17, "A Thrilling Trial," p. 20, "L Is Wilentz Guest at Trenton," p. 18, *NYT,* Jan. 25, 1935; Porter, "Admissions By Hauptmann Open Cross-Examination," pp. 1, 9, "Mention of Word 'Baby' Mars Hauptmann's Calm," p. 9, Kathleen Norris, "Mrs. Norris Finds Prisoner 'Pitiful,' " p. 9, Alexander Woollcott, "Hauptmann Story Shed No Light," p. 9, *NYT,* Jan. 26, 1935; Edna Ferber, "Miss Ferber Views Vultures At Trial," p. 4, Lyman, "L Is Sure of Voice He Heard," p. 4, Craig Thompson, "Air-Hero Complex Laid to Hauptmann," p. 4, *NYT,* Jan. 28, 1935; "Hauptmann Admits Lying And Says Wilentz Lies Too," pp. 1, 4, "Defense to Cite Laughter in Courtroom," p. 1, *NYT,* Jan. 29, 1935; Porter, "Hauptmann's Own Letters Discredit Story of Fisch," pp. 1, 12, Craig Thompson, "Hauptmann Is Calm After Ordeal," pp. 1, 12, " 'Good Witness,' Counsel for Both Sides Agree," p. 12, Norris, "Marvels At Faith of Mrs. Hauptmann," p. 12, *NYT,* Jan. 30, 1935; "On Stand For 17 1/2 Hours," p. 13, Thompson, "Harried Housewife Tired, Puzzled," pp. 1, 13, Fannie Hurst, "Loyalty of Wife Impresses Writer," p. 13, *NYT,* Jan. 31, 1935; Porter, "Witness Says He Saw Fisch With Sharpe Girl and Baby," pp. 1, 7, "Trial Again Takes a Recess for Week-End," p. 7, "Wilentz Demands Suppression of Newsreels," pp. 1, 7, *NYT,* Feb. 2, 1935; Porter, "L To Take Stand in Rebuttal," pp. 1, 26, *NYT,* Feb. 3, 1935; Porter, "5 Alibi Witnesses Fail to Appear for Defense," pp. 1, 15, *NYT,* Feb. 5, 1935; Porter, "Café Man Swears Fisch Was at Bronx Cemetery," pp. 1, 12, *NYT,* Feb. 6, 1935; Porter, "Mrs. Morrow Last Witness," pp. 1, 29, *NYT,* Feb. 10, 1935; Jack Benny quoted in Fisher, *L Case,* p. 327; Whipple, *L Crime,* pp. 306–7, 317–8, 320–1; an additional verse of the "schnitzelbank song" appears in Kennedy, *Airman,* p. 258; the State's psychiatrist wrote a book, Dr. Dudley D. Shoenfeld, *The Crime and the Criminal—a Psychiatric Study of the L Case* (New York: Covici-Freide, 1936); Hauptmann to Fisher, quoted in Waller, *Kidnap,* p. 449; AML (D), Feb. 9, 1935; *LROD,* pp. 246–8.

Ludovic Kennedy, for one, subscribed to the rumor that Jafsie's address and telephone number written inside his closet was the handiwork of *Daily News* reporter Tom Cassidy (Kennedy, *Airman,* pp. 204–7).

TRIAL CONCLUDES, TAKING ITS TOLL: ECM (D), Feb. 11, 1935; AML (D), Feb. 11 and 13, 1935; *LROD,* p. 249; Porter, "Reilly Accuses Servants, Charges Police Frame-Up In Hauptmann's Final Plea to Jury," pp. 1, 17, Thompson, "Reilly Bangs Fist, Shakes Finger At Jury," pp. 1, 16, *NYT,* Feb. 12, 1935; Porter, " 'No Mercy,' Wilentz Plea," pp. 1, 15, *NYT,* Feb. 13, 1935; Ford, "Trial Is Likened to a Bullfight," p. 11, Porter, "Hauptmann Guilty, Sentenced to Death," pp. 1, 12, "Jury Courageous, Wilentz Declares," pp. 1, 11, Thompson, "Hauptmann in Cell, Falls in Collapse," pp. 1, 12, "Jury in Thaw Case Was Out 25 Hours," p. 11, "L Not At Home," p. 11, "6000 Jam Street to Cheer Verdict," p. 11, "Bell at Court House Announces Verdict," p. 11, *NYT,* Feb. 14, 1935; "After the Verdict," p. 18, "CCC Juryman Last to Vote for Death, p. 6, *NYT,* Feb. 15, 1935; Whipple, *L Crime,* pp. 329–32; Harold Nicolson to Vita Sackville-West, Feb. 13 and 14, 1935; Nicolson, *Vita and Harold,* pp. 270–2; juror Ethel Stockton quoted on dustjacket of Fisher, *L Case; AOV,* p. 142; Anna Hauptmann to ASB (I), June 11, 1990; Alan Dershowitz, "Introduction," *The Trial* (Notable Trials Edition), p. v.

CAL, AML RESUME LIVES: AML (D), Feb. 14, Apr. 30, July 16, 22, 26, 29, and 30, Aug. 25, 29, and 30, Sept. 2, 3, 4, 5, and 17, 1935; AML to ECM, Feb. 21–3, 1935; *LROD,* pp. 249, 252–4, 268–71, 285–8, 290–5, 299, 301–6, 309–13; Alfred Harcourt to AML, May 15, 1935; Mina Curtiss to AML, Sept. 2, 1935; Virginia Woolf to AML, Oct. 6, 1935; Alfred Harcourt to CAL, Aug. 19, 1935; Harcourt,

Brace and Co., press release, Dec. 12, 1935; AC and CAL, *The Culture of Organs* (New York: Paul B. Hoeber, Inc., 1938), pp. 6–15, 212, 220–21; AC and CAL, "The Culture of Whole Organs," *Science*, June 21, 1935, pp. 621–3; Peyton Rous to CAL, July 22, 1935; "Carrel's Man," *Time*, Sept. 16, 1935, pp. 40–3; Ernest Lundeen, "L the Scientist," *Congressional Record*, Aug. 2, 1935, pp. 12851–2 [quoting William Laurence in *Today*, Aug. 3, 1935, pp. 5, 20]; Alice Payne Hackett, *Fifty Years of Best-Sellers: 1895–1945* (New York: R. R. Bowker Co., 1945), pp. 71–4; *AOV*, p. 142; ECM (D), July 4, 1935.

DEATH OF WILL ROGERS: notification came via Phelan to S. Banks [c/o ECM] (T), ca. Aug. 16, 1935; AML (D), Aug. 16, 1935; *LROD*, p. 297; CAL to Mr. Croy, Oct. 11, 1952; CAL to Henry Greist (draft of T), Aug. 16, 1935; Bill Rogers to CAL (T), Aug. 19, 1935.

REPERCUSSIONS OF TRIAL; CAL PREPARES TO LEAVE U.S.: Eleanor Roosevelt quoted Fisher, *L Case*, p. 380 [quoting *NYT*, Feb. 23, 1935, p. 1]; William M. Marston, "A Famous Psychologist Analyzes the Twisted Brains," *The Denver Post*, Mar. 3, 1935, n.p.; Anon. [from Port Chester, NY] to CAL, Feb. 18, 1935 [MHS]; Anon. to CAL, Feb. 14, 1935 [MHS]; Anon. to "Lindy," Feb. 15, 1935 [MHS]; *AOV*, pp. 142–4; CAL to ELLL, Dec. 18, 1935; AML (D), Dec. 7, 21, and 22, 1935; *LROD*, pp. 331–3; Lyman, "L Family Sails For England To Seek a Safe, Secluded Residence," *NYT*, Dec. 23, 1935, pp. 1, 3; AC to Dr. Moynihan, Dec. 16, 1935; ECM (D), Dec. 15, 20, 21, 1935; Meyer Berger, *The Story of the New York Times* (New York: Simon & Schuster, 1951), pp. 414–9; Monte Millar to AML, Dec. 25, 1935; "L," *U.S. Air Service*, May, 1953, p. 22.

13   RISING TIDES

E: *AOV*, pp. 151–2.

CROSSING; SETTLING IN ENGLAND: AML (D), Jan. 28, 29, and 31, Feb. 20, 1936; *LROD*, pp. 335–6; CAL to HB, Apr. 2, May 14, 1936; HG to CAL, Feb. 11, Apr. 17, and May 18, 1936; Clara H. Clark to CAL and AML, Jan. 28, 1936; HB to CAL, Jan. 3, 1936; ELLL to CAL and AML, Jan. 1, 1936; L. D. Lyman to CAL, Jan. 2, 1936; CAL to Harry Davison, Jan. 2, 1936; AML to ECM, Dec. 5, 1935–Jan., 1936, Mar. 17, 1936; AML to ELLL, Jan. 10 and Feb. 23, 1936; *FN*, pp. 3–4, 12–5, 20–3, 29–31, 335; Archduke Joseph Francis to CAL, Jan. 6, 1936; R. Brutnell (on behalf of Lord Sempill) to CAL, Jan. 8, 1936; Mrs. John Downie to CAL, Mar. 1, 1936; Nicolson, *Vita and Harold*, p. 50; CAL to Dr. J. C. Merriam, Jan. 22 and Apr. 15, 1936; CAL to H. N. Schwarzkopf, Jan. 27, 1937; Harold Nicolson to AML, Mar. 8, 1936; Vita Sackville-West to AML, Feb. 24 and Mar. 4, 1936; CAL secretary to Nicolsons' solicitor, "Dear Sir," Apr. 7, 1936; AML to CMM, Mar. 23, 1936; CAL to ELLL, June 11, 1936; *AOV*, pp. 18, 145; CAL to HG, May 1, 1936; Lehman, *High Man*, pp. 231, 234–5; CAL, "The Rocket Offers Freedom From the Air," *Astronautics Journal*, July, 1937, p. 8; RHG to CAL, Sept. 11 and Oct. 8, 1937; Dr. Richard Bing, "Autobiography," (U), pp. 37–43; Carrel, *Man, Unknown*, pp. 220, 291, 299; James Newton, *Uncommon Friends* (New York: Harcourt Brace Jovanovich, 1987), pp. 132, 136–7; Carrel, (U-M), ca. 1936 [Y:7/178]; CAL to AC, Jan. 1, 6, and 9, Mar. 7, June 3, 14, and 23, July 21, 23, 24, 1937; C. M. Wenyon to CAL, Mar. 25, 1936; John Merriam to CAL, Apr. 3, 1936; CAL to Dr. Theodore Malinin, Jan. 24, 1971.

HAUPTMANN EXECUTION: Gov. H. Hoffman to H. Norman Schwarzkopf, Jan. 26, 1936; Kennedy, *Airman*, p. 378, 400; "Hauptmann Gets a Stay," *NYT*, Apr. 1, 1936, pp. 1, 2; "The Shame of N. J.," *The Boston Herald*, Apr. 2, 1936, p. 16;

Hauptmann 'Torture" Assailed By Maurois," *NYT,* Apr. 2, 1936, p. 2; Russell B. Porter, "Hauptmann Put to Death," *NYT,* Apr. 4, 1936, pp. 1, 2; Harry Flory (United Press) to CAL (T), Mar. 31, 1936; CAL to HB, Apr. 16, 1936; "Hoffman to Oust Col. Schwartzkopf," *NYT,* June 2, 1936, n.p.; CAL to Dr. A. Flexner, Nov. 16, 1936.

CAL AND AML'S LIFE IN ENGLAND: Wogan Philipps (writing of Churchill) to CAL, Dec. 22, [prob.] 1936; H. Nicolson to CAL, Apr. 4, 1936; CAL to H. Nicolson, Apr. 9, 1936; AML (D), Jan. 10, Apr. 23–6, May 12, 15, and 27, 1936; *FN,* pp. 4, 35, 38–40, 42–6, 48–9, 51–5; "King's Derby Night Party," (London) *Times,* n.d., p. 16; CAL to ELLL, May 29, June 11 and 15, 1936; AML to CMM, Mar. 23, 1936; CAL to Guy Vaughan, June 29, 1936; CAL to Juan Trippe, Aug. 20 and Oct. 28, 1936, Jan. 12, 1937; CAL to André Priester, Apr. 15 and Dec. 3, 1936; Guy Vaughan to CAL (T), June 26, 1936; "Airline Seeks 100–Passenger Ocean Planes," *Washington Post,* Dec. 11, 1937, n.p.; CAL, "Intelligence Report" (fragment), n.d.; CAL to Clare Bunch, Aug. 20, 1936; F. G. Miles to CAL, July 8, 1936; CAL to HG, June 18, 1936; CAL to AC, June 12, 1936; CAL (M), May 2, 1936; CAL to HB, June 30, 1936; CAL to Dr. Raymond C. Parker, July 4, 1936.

FIRST VISIT TO GERMANY: Truman Smith (ed. by Robert Hessen), *Berlin Alert* (Stanford, CA: Hoover Institution Press, 1984), pp. 80, 82, 86–8, 92–105; Alfred Price, *Pictorial History of the Luftwaffe: 1933–1945* (New York: Arco Publishing Co., 1969), p. 11, Katharine (Mrs. Truman) Smith to ASB (I), May 18, 1990; Truman Smith to CAL, May 25 and July 2, 1936; CAL to ELLL, June 15, 1936; CAL to Truman Smith, June 5 and Sept. 16, 1936, May 31, 1955; CAL to HB, May 15 and Sept. 23, 1936; AML (D), July 22, 23, and 28, 1936; *FN,* pp. 70–7, 85–6; CAL to Harry Davison, Jan. 23, 1937; DAVIS, Aug. 20, 1969; CAL, "Revolutionary Changes Wrought By Aviation" (speech), July 23, 1936; CAL to Jim Smith, Sept. 13, 1953; "New Colonel," *The Literary Digest,* Aug. 1, 1936, p. 16; "Airman to Earthman," *Time,* Aug. 3, 1936, pp. 15–6; Dorothy Thompson, "As the Twig Is Bent," *Herald Tribune,* July 28, 1936, n.p.; (Roger Straus via) HB to CAL (T), July 20, 1936; William Shirer, *The Rise and Fall of the Third Reich* (New York: Simon & Schuster, 1960), p. 233; HG to CAL, Aug. 1, 1936; *AOV,* p. 146.

COPENHAGEN; REACTIONS TO GERMAN TRIP: "L Adds to Fame as Scientist," *The Literary Digest,* Aug. 22, 1936, pp. 16–7; CAL, (U-M), Aug. 8, 1936; CAL to AC, July 27, 1936; CAL to Truman Smith, Aug. 6, 1936; CAL to ELLL, Oct. 16, 1936; Bing, "Autobiography," (U), pp. 40–3; Dr. Richard Bing to ASB (I), Feb. 17, 1994 and Apr. 22, 1998; CAL to HG, Sept. 15, 1936; CAL to Harry Davison, Jan. 27, 1937; CAL to Hermann Goering, Aug. 20, 1936; Helen Wolff to AML, Feb. 8, 1974; AML to ECM, Aug. 5, 1936; *FN,* pp. 87–9; Toynbee quoted in *FN,* p. xv; Thomas Jones, *A Diary with Letters: 1931–50* (London: Oxford University Press, 1954), p. 181; Shirer, *Rise and Fall,* p. 232; CAL to HB, Sept. 23, 1936; CAL to Maj. Theodore Koenig, Sept. 25, 1936; Truman Smith to CAL, Aug. 12 and Sept. 5, 1936; Smith, *Berlin Alert,* pp. 104–5.

WANDERLUST; IRELAND TO INDIA: CAL to ELLL, Dec. 1 and 17, 1936, Jan. 15, 1937; Karl Bickel (United Press) to CAL (T), Nov. 25, 1936; AML (D), Christmas, 1936; *FN,* pp. 100–1, 126–32; *AOV,* pp. 148–51; AML to ECM, Feb. 21 and Mar. 8, 1937; CAL, (U-AW) [Y: 218/626]; "Still Modest," *NYT,* n.d., n.p.

RETURN TO ENGLAND; BIRTH OF LML: CAL to ELLL, Nov. 15, 1936, Mar. 12, May 12 and 13, 1937; CAL to H. Norman Schwarzkopf, Jan. 27, 1937; *AOV,* p. 155; CAL to Harry Knight, Mar. 10, 1937; CAL to Truman Smith, Nov. 17, 1936; AML (D), May 20 and 22, 1937; *FN,* pp. 138–44, 146; AML to Mme. Carrel, May

16, 1937; AML to ELLL, May 14, 1937; CAL to ECM, May 27, 1937; ECM (D), May 13, 1937; A. J. Read (registrar of births and deaths) to CAL, June 22, 1937; AML to ECM, June 17, 1937; CAL to Thomas Lamont, May 12, 1937; "The Age of Air Transport," *NYT,* May 20, 1937, n.p.; Ferdinand Kuhn, "L Ignores Today's Tributes," *NYT,* May 20, 1937, n.p.; "L Flight Celebrated By All Save 'Lone Eagle,' " *Christian Science Monitor,* May 20, 1937, p. 1; CAL to Tiffany & Co., Ltd., May 25 and June 8, 1937.

RETURN TO GERMANY; VISIT TO AMERICA: William E. Dodd to CAL, Jan. 18, 1957; CAL to William E. Dodd, Mar. 11, 1937; CAL to ELLL, Dec. 20, 1936 and Sept. 20, 1937; Smith, *Berlin Alert,* pp. 109–20; CAL to Adolf Baeumker, Nov. 11, 1937; CAL to AC, Nov. 7 and 9, 1937; CAL to Amey Aldrich, Nov. 28, 1937; CAL to Adm. E. S. Land, Nov. 5, 1937; CAL to Earl N. Findley, Nov. 9, 1937; CAL to Jack Allard, Nov. 11, 1937; Julian E. Gillespie (Commercial Attaché, U. S. Dept. of Commerce) to CAL, Jan. 30, 1937; CAL to William Jovanovich, Dec. 18, 1969 [quoted in *WJ,* p. xiii]; CAL to Truman Smith, Dec. 2, 1937; CAL (D), Nov. 25, Dec. 5 and 10, 1937, Jan. 15 and 25, 1938; "Leave L Alone," Rochester *Times,* Dec. 7, 1937, n.p.; Paul White (CBS) to CAL (T), Dec. 6, 1937; CAL to A. A. Schechter, Dec. 13, 1937; CAL to A. F. DuPont, Dec. 15, 1937; *NYT* to CAL (T), Dec. 5, 1937; CAL to Maj. Gen. F. R. McCoy, Jan. 31, 1938; CAL to Harry Davison, Oct. 28, 1937; Joseph P. Kennedy to FDR (M), n.d., attached to Gen. Malin Craig to Col. Watson, Feb. 11, 1938 [FDR papers]; Newton, *Uncommon Friends,* pp. 3, 84, 123, 151–7; Amey Aldrich to CAL, Sept. 25, 1937; CAL to Amey Aldrich, Sept. 16 and Oct. 1, 1937; Conger Goodyear to CAL, Jan. 30, 1938; AML (D), Feb. 20, 1938; *FN,* p. 186.

FAREWELL TO ENGLAND; ILLIEC: CAL, (D), Feb. 25, Mar. 11, 16, and 31, Apr. 2 and 5, May 23, June 1, July 3, 6, and 28, 1938; *WJ,* pp. 11–3, 39, 42; CAL to ELLL, July 4, Sept. 1, and Nov. 3, 1937; *Côtes D'Armor* (Paris: Editions Nouveaux-Loisirs, 1992), pp. 18–9, 367; AML to ELLL, July 8–9, 1937; CAL to AC, July 29, 1937, Apr. 9, 1938; "L Visits Carrel," n.s., c. July 5, 1937; *AOV,* pp. 161–2, 364–7; CAL to Mme. Carrel, Mar. 31, 1938; AML (D), Apr. 8 and 30, May 1, 5, and 23, June 1, July 7 and 29, 1938; *FN,* pp. 206–9, 220–1, 224–8, 237–41, 247–53, 279, 289; Harold Nicolson, *Diaries and Letters: 1930–1939* (New York: Atheneum, 1961), p. 343; Raymond Lee to Truman Smith, Oct. 10, 1938; Carrel, *Man, Unknown,* pp. 299–300; AC to CAL, Mar. 15, 1939; *AOV,* pp. 152, 373.

SHUTTLE DIPLOMACY: CAL (D), Aug. 2, Sept. 8, 9, 21, 26, 27, and 29, Oct. 3, 10, and 11, 1938; *WJ,* pp. 39, 44, 72, 75–88, 93–5; *AOV,* pp. 163–8, 172–8; Raymond Lee to CAL, June 9, 1938 attached to Philip Faymonville to Raymond Lee, May 27, 1938; CAL to ELLL, Sept. 4, 1938; CAL to J. P. Kennedy, Sept. 22, 1938; J. P. Kennedy to Secretary of State, Sept 22, 1938; CAL to Jean Monnet, Oct. 7, 1938; Felmy report to Goering quoted in David Irving, *Göring* (London: Macmillan, 1989), p. 228; AML (D), Sept. 26, 1938; *FN,* pp. 359–62, 379; DAVIS, Aug. 21, 1969; *The Week,* No. 284, Oct. 5, 1938, p. 4; P. Faymonville to R. Lee (T), Oct. 10, 1938.

BERLIN; NAZI MEDAL: CAL (D), Oct. 12, 18, Nov. 13, 1938; *WJ,* pp. 96–103, 115–6; AML (D), Oct. 18, 21, 22, 27, 29–30, Dec. 19, 1938, *FN,* p. 379–81, 411; Smith, *Berlin Alert,* pp. 127–35; DAVIS, Aug. 20, 1969; *AOV,* pp. 180–82; CAL to Truman Smith, May 9, 1938, and May 31, 1955; ; CAL to John T. Flynn, May 2, 1941; Hugh R. Wilson to CAL, Aug. 4, 1941; CAL to AC, Oct. 28 and Dec. 10, 1938; CAL to Jim Smith, Sept. 13, 1953; Cajus Bekker, *The Luftwaffe Diaries* (Garden City: Doubleday & Co., 1968), p. 376; CAL to H. Goering, Oct. 25, 1938; CAL to Gen. H. H. Arnold, Nov. 2, 1938; Gen. H. H. Arnold to CAL, Nov. 17, 1938; CAL to J. P. Kennedy, Nov. 9, 1938; AML to Kay (Mrs. Truman) Smith, Nov. 16, 1938; Shirer, *Rise and Fall,* pp. 430–2; Frederick L. Collins, "Why Did Hitler Give L a Medal," *Liberty,* Dec. 17, 1938, pp. 6–8; *NYT* report of L wearing medal reported Oct. 20, 1938, and quoted by Congressman R. O. Woodruff in *Congressional Record—House,* May 31, 1940, p. 11117; "Talk of the Town: Notes and Comment," *The New Yorker,* Nov. 26, 1938, n.p.; Aubrey Morgan to CAL, Christmas, 1938; AC to CAL, Nov. 18, 1938; Mary Scandrett to AML, Dec. 5, 1938.

L subsequently contributed the Service Cross of the German Eagle to the Missouri Historical Society, where it has occasionally been displayed as part of the collection of his awards.

MOVE TO PARIS; HEADING HOME: *AOV,* pp. 156, 182–7; CAL, (D), Nov. 22, Dec. 18 and 22, 1938, Jan. 16 and 17, Mar. 30, Apr. 1 and 2, 1939; WJ, pp. 118, 127, 131, 139–41, 169–70, 173; AML (D), Nov. 22, 1938; *FN,* pp. 396–7, 408–9; " 'L Line' Slogan Is Dropped by T. W. A.," *NYT,* Dec. 5, 1938, n.p.; AML to ECM, Dec. 11, 1938.

14   THE GREAT DEBATE

E: *AOV,* p. 61.

CAL RETURNS; BEGINS GOVT. WORK: Walter Winchell, "Reveal 'Inside' of Lindy's Role in Munich Pact," *Daily Mirror,* Jan. 2, 1939; R. Fredette to Philip Geyelin, Apr. 18, 1976; David E. Koskoff, *Joseph P. Kennedy* (Englewood Cliffs, NJ: Prentice-Hall, 1974), p. 524; R. Fredette, "L and Munich: A Myth Revived," *The Bulletin* [MHS], Apr., 1977, pp. 197–202; Arthur Krock, "In the Nation: The Invaluable Contribution of Col. L," *NYT,* Feb. 1, 1939; CAL (D), Apr. 8–15, 17, 20, 21, June 10 and 12, 1939; WJ, pp. 175–89, 210, 212; William Jovanovich, "Introduction," WJ, p. xviii; *AOV,* pp. 158–9, 190; Sol Bloom to CAL (radiogram), Apr. 9, 1939; Robert E. Gross to CAL (radiogram), Apr. 11, 1939; John Victory to CAL (radiogram), Apr. 13, 1939; Gen. H. H. Arnold (radiogram), Apr. 13, 1939; Newton, *Uncommon Friends,* pp. 175–6; ECM (D), Apr. 14, 1939; "Heroes," *Time,* June 19, 1939, p. 21; Henry H. Arnold, *Global Mission* (New York: Harper, 1949), pp. 187–9; E. C. Desobry to CAL (M), Apr. 18, 1939; H. H. Arnold to CAL (M), Apr. 18, 1939; CAL to AC, Apr. 18, 1939; E. M. Watson to FDR (M), Apr. 17, 1939; FDR, *The President's Press Conferences,* vol. XIII, pp. 313–9, Apr. 20, 1939; First Staff Squadron, Air Corps, "List of CAL Flights," May 15, 1939; CAL to HG, May 27, 1939; Lehman, *High Man,* pp. 271–2; "Extract from Report of Subcommittee on Independent Offices," House Appropriations Committee, Report #1515, 76th Congress, 3rd Session, Jan. 16, 1940.

AML RETURNS TO U.S.; CAL SPEAKS OUT: CAL to AML, Apr. 21, 1939; AML (D), Apr. 28, May 2, 28, and 30, Aug. 4–7 [Saint-Exupéry passages], Sept. 11, 12, 15, Oct. 28, 1939; *WWW,* pp. 3–5, 9–10, 20–35 [Saint-Exupéry passages], 52–3, 56–8, 63–6; ECM (D), May 27, 1939; CAL (D), May 30, June 1, Aug. 5–7, 23, Sept. 2, 7, 10, 14, 15, 26, and 27, Oct. 7, 11, 13, 16, 22, and 24, 1939; WJ, pp.205–6, 238–9, 245, 250, 252–8, 263–5, 271–6, 278–82; CAL to Anne Carrel, July 17 and Nov. 14, 1939; "Heroes: Press v. L," *Time,* June 19, 1939, p. 20; Sue Beck Hatt to ASB (I), May 6, 1993; Margot L. (Morrow) Wilkie to ASB (I), Apr. 26, 1993; William Castle to CAL, Jan. 19, Apr. 12, and c. July, 1939; CAL, "Aviation, Geography, and Race," *Reader's Digest,* Nov. 1939, pp. 64–7; Carrel, *Man, Unknown,* pp. 212, 214; DeWitt Wallace to CAL, Sept. 27, 1939; CAL, "What Substitute for War?," *Atlantic Monthly,* Mar., 1940, pp. 304–5; CAL, "America and European Wars," speech, Sept.

15, 1939; AML to ELLL, Sept. 12 and 30, 1939; Kay Smith to ASB (I), May 18, 1990; Newton, *Uncommon Friends,* pp. 195, 212; James Newton to ASB (I), Feb. 28, 1990; Ward W. Keesecker to CAL, Sept. 16, 1939; H. H. Arnold to CAL, Sept. 18, 1939; Peter Kurth, *American Cassandra: The Life of Dorothy Thompson* (Boston: Little, Brown, 1990), pp. 312–3; Dorothy Thompson, "On the Record," Sept. 20, 1939; CAL, *Herald Tribune,* "Neutrality and War," speech, Oct. 13, 1939; CAL to AC, May 8, 1940; AML to Anne Carrel, Dec. 19, 1939; CAL to ELLL, Nov. 14, 1939.

Regarding the position as Secretary of Air: CAL later stated that General Arnold said that if he did not accept the offer, there would be no record of the conversation. (CAL to Murray Green, Feb. 15, 1971.)

"PHONY WAR"; FLORIDA TRIP; AML YEARNINGS: CAL (D), Oct. 21, 1939, May 15–23, 1940; *WJ,* pp. 278, 307–16, 348–50; James Newton to CAL, Jan. 9, 1940; CAL to ELLL, Feb. 6 and 22, Mar. 6, May 19, 1940; CAL (D) Jan. 21, 1940–Feb. 7, 1940; *WWW,* pp. 77–81, 89–94, 102–4, 129–31, 161–2; Newton, *Uncommon Friends,* pp. 196, 200–1, 219–26; AML to Mary Scandrett, Jan. 13, 1937; *FN,* pp. 107–8; AML to Mina Curtiss, May 27, 1939; AML to Ruth Oliff, Aug. 23, 1940; AML (D), Apr. 3 and 29, May 27, June 7 and 21, July 23, 1940, Jan. 1941; CAL, "The Air Defense of America," speech, May 19, 1940; "The Small Minority Threatens U. S. Peace," *Social Justice,* June 3, 1940; AML to ECM, June 5–7, 1940; AC to CAL, Sept. 12, 1939; AC to Dr. Scovel, Feb. 24, 1940; Stacy Schiff, *Saint-Exupéry: A Biography* (New York: Alfred A. Knopf, 1994), pp. 150–2.

WAVE OF THE FUTURE; BIRTH OF ASL: AML (D), Aug. 16 and 26, Oct. 27, 1940; *WWW,* pp. 137, 141–5, 147–8; AML to ECM, Sept. 4, 1940; ECM (D), Sept. 6, 1940; ECM to AML, Sept. 6 and Dec. 3, 1940; CAL (D), June 21, Sept. 17 and 25, Oct. 2, Nov. 5, Dec. 10, 1940; *WJ,* pp. 360, 390, 392, 394–5, 414, 425; *WF,* pp. 18–9, 23–7, 33–4, 37; CMM to ASB (I), Mar. 3, 1993; AML to ASB (I), Feb. 27, 1990; Alfred Harcourt to CAL, Nov. 22, 1940; DeWitt Wallace to CAL, Sept. 27, 1940; W. H. Auden to AML, Oct. 21, 1940; E. B. White writes of *WF* in *One Man's Meat* (New York: Harper Brothers, 1944), pp. 203–10; Dorothy Thompson, "An Open Letter to AML," *Look,* Mar., 1941, n.p.; Ickes quoted in Wayne Cole, *CAL and the Battle Against American Intervention in World War II* (New York: Harcourt Braace Jovanovich, 1974), p. 130; CL to AML, ca. 1941 [Y:10/216]; ECM to William A. White, Dec. 2, 1940; AML, "Reaffirmation," *The Atlantic Monthly,* June, 1941, pp. 681–6.

CAL'S PUBLIC ADDRESSES; AMERICA FIRST: CAL (D), June 5–15, 22, and 26, Aug. 3–4, Oct. 22, 24, and 30, 1940; *WJ,* pp. 353–8, 360, 362, 374–5, 409–11; CAL, "Our Relationship With Europe," speech, Aug. 4, 1940; R. D. Stuart, Jr. to CAL, Aug. 5, 1940; Cole, *CAL and Battle,* pp. 106, 123–4, 128–9; "The Attack on L," *The Christian Century,* Aug. 21, 1940, pp. 1022–3; H. Morgenthau, "Presidential Diaries," May 20, 1940, p. 563 [FDR Library]; FDR to H. L. Stimson, May 21, 1940 [Y: Stimson Papers]; Ralph Ingersoll, "Denouncing CAL," *PM,* Aug. 6, 1940, p. 1; Lippmann quoted in Ronald Steel, *Walter Lippmann and the American Century* (Boston: Little, Brown & Co., 1980), p. 375, calling CAL a "Nazi lover"; C. B. Allen, "L Today," *Scribner's Commentator,* Aug., 1940, pp. 11–2, 21–6; "L vs. Byrnes," *Chicago Daily Tribune,* May 25, 1940, p. 10; Herman Klurfeld, *Winchell: His Life and Times* (New York: Praeger Publishers, 1976), p. 89; John S. Bugas to Director (J. Edgar Hoover), FBI file #65–11449–7, June 14, 1940; AML (D), Aug. 26, 1940; *WWW,* pp. 141; Robert E. Sherwood, *Roosevelt & Hopkins* (New York:

Harper & Brothers, 1948), pp. 152–3; Anon. to CAL, c. Aug., 1940; Anon. to Col. Charles Lindburger Cheese, May 22, 1940; J. J. Breslin (Post Office Dept Inspector) to CAL, June 14, 1940; Paul Palmer, "America Speaks to CAL" (ms), Aug. 31, 1940; Norman Thomas to CAL, May 24, 1940; John Foster Dulles to CAL, May 20, 1940; Chester Bowles to CAL, May 24, 1940; F. L. Wright quoted in Palmer, "America Speaks"; Frank Lloyd Wright in his *Autobiography* (New York: Duell, Sloan and Pearce, 1943), p. 500, wrote that he wired L: ". . . now when everywhere is equivocation and cowardice, you not only think straight but you dare speak straight"; Daniel V. McNamee, Jr., Potter Stewart, R. Douglas Stuart, Jr., Wyndham Gary, Willard Brown, Sargent Shriver to CAL, Nov. 1, 1939; Eugene Locke, R. D. Stuart, Jr., Gerald Ford, Potter Stewart, "Dear ___" (mimeographed form letter), n.d.; America First's principles appear in Richard Moore, *The Great Debate and Me: A Memoir for my Grandchildren* (U), n.d.; Richard A. Moore to ASB (I), May 30, 1994; R. Douglas Stuart, Jr. to ASB (I), Mar. 26, 1994; CAL, "Impregnable America" (Yale speech), Oct. 30, 1940; K. R. McIntyre to Mr. Kramer, (M), FBI Serial #100–4712–140X.

The name "Committee to Defend America First" was meant to mimic William Allen White's organization, "Committee to Defend America by Aiding the Allies." Another early recruit to the organization was Peter Dominick, who would become a United States Senator from Colorado.

LEND-LEASE TESTIMONY; RETURN TO FLORIDA: Hamilton Fish to CAL (T), Jan. 14, 1941; CAL (D), Jan. 23, Feb. 5, 6, and 13, Mar. 5–27, 1941; *WJ*, pp. 442–3, 446–8, 450, 455–71; CAL, "Statement: Lend-Lease Bill," H.R. 1776 (Washington, D. C.: U. S. Govt. Printing Office, 1941), p. 3; "Lend-Lease Bill," *Congressional Record*, Jan. 23, 1941, pp. 373, 379, 412, 420, 435; "Promote Defense of the U. S.," hearings on S275, *Congressional Record*, Feb. 6, 1941, pp. 490, 512, 522, 525; Jacob J. Leibson to CAL, Feb. 10, 1941; Cornelius Vanderbilt, Jr. to CAL (T), n.d.; "L and the Like," *The Richmond News Leader*, Jan. 28, 1941, p. 10; James Newton to CAL, Feb. 14, 1941; CAL to ELLL, Feb. 19 and Mar. 6, 1941; *WWW*, pp. 167–9; Newton, *Uncommon Friends*, p. 238.

AMERICA FIRST SPEECHES: CAL, "Chicago Speech," April 17, 1941; CAL (D), Apr. 17–8, 23, 25–7, May 3, 10, 23, 28, and 29, June 18 and 20, July 27, Aug. 9, 26–9, 1941; *WJ*, pp. 474–82, 484–6, 492–4, 496–8, 503–5, 522, 524–5, 529–32; Cole, *CAL and Battle*, pp. 123, 130, 147–9; CAL, "Manhattan Center Speech," Apr. 23, 1941; AML (D), May 9 and 23, June 18 and 20, 1941; *WWW*, pp. 177–8, 186–92, 196–9; L. M. Birkhead to CAL, Mar. 11, 1941; n.t., *PM*, Apr. 24, 1941, n.p.; "Ickes Charges Hitler's Helpers Undermine U. S.," *Chicago Tribune*, Apr. 14, 1941, p. 11; FDR Presidential Press Conference #738, Apr. 25, 1941 [FDR Library: vol. :17:2925]; CAL to Secy. H. L. Stimson, Apr. 28, 1941; CAL to FDR, original and final draft, Apr. 28, 1941; ECM (D), Apr. 29, 1941; R. D. Stuart, Jr. to CAL (T), ca. Apr. 28, June 30, July 14, 1941; John and Adelaide Marquand to CAL (T), Apr. 29, 1941; Robert McCormick to CAL, Apr. 28, 1941; CAL, final drafts of speeches, Mar. 3, 10, 23, and May 29, June 20, July 1, Aug. 9, 1941; Friends of Democracy flyer, n.d.; McIntyre, FBI (M), Sept. 12, 1941; Norman Thomas (with Bertram Wolfe), *Keep America Out of War* (New York: Frederick A. Stokes, 1939), p. 19; n.t., *Time*, June 2, 1941, p. 15; n.t., *Life*, June 9, 1941, p. 56; CAL to Truman Smith, Mar. 6, 1941; James E. West to CAL, June 20, 1941; Maj. A. C. Wedemeyer to CAL, May 2, 1941; Franklin Alter, Jr. to Editor (Dayton) *Journal-Herald*, May 18, 1941; "In the News," *Washington News Letter*, May 21, 1941, p. 3; Clare Swisher, "It's A Great

Life," press release re Buffalo, Aug. 19, 1940; "Lindy Ousted as Honorary Member of Memorial Unit," n.s., n.d.; "The Dissenters," *Life,* May 5, 1941, p. 28; CAL to R. D. Stuart, Jr., June 21, 1941; CAL to W. R. Hearst, Feb. 27 and July 2, 1941.

An oratorical note: CAL pronounced the word "Nazi" as though it rhymed with "jazzy."

CAL VS. FDR AND ICKES; ANTI-CAL SENTIMENT BUILDS: Harold Ickes, "France Forever," speech, July 14, 1941; CAL (D), July 16, 1941; *WJ,* pp. 518; CAL to FDR, July 16, 1941; Stephen Early to CAL, July 19, 1941; Harold Ickes, "Ickes Asserts L Errs In Story of Nazi Decoration," *Washington Star,* July 25, 1941, p. A-2 and "Ickes Rejects Apology Demanded by L," n.s., July 24, 1941, sent by John Wheeler (North American Newspaper Alliance) to CAL, July 25, 1941; "A Reprimand for Mr. Ickes," *Liberty,* Aug. 2, 1941, p. 9; R. E. Wood to CAL, Aug. 12, 1941; Billy Rose to CAL (T), July 18, 1941; Richard A. Moore to ASB (I), May 30, 1994; Harold Ickes, *The Secret Diary of Harold L. Ickes: 1939–1941,* vol. III (New York: Simon & Schuster, 1954), p. 501.

MARTHA'S VINEYARD; DES MOINES SPEECH: AML to Kay Smith, July 16, 1941; CAL to Truman Smith, Aug. 1, 1941; CAL (D), Aug. 15, Sept. 11–3, 17, 18, Oct. 3, 6, 10, and 14, Nov. 1 and 30, Dec. 1, 1941; *WJ,* pp. 522, 527, 536–42, 544, 546–9, 552, 558–60; AML (D), July, Sept. 11, 13, 14, 1941; *WWW,* pp. 211–2, 220–5, 231; CAL to Wayne Cole, Feb. 17, 1972 and Mar. 19, 1973; CAL, drafts of Des Moines speech, Aug. 18 and Sept. 11, 1941; AML, "Suggestions—1st typed draft," n.d.; AML to Sue Vaillant, Sept. 8, 1941; Newton, *Uncommon Friends,* p. 250; D. Meyer, "Today's Guest Editorial," *Phoenix Gazette,* Sept. 5, 1941, n.p.; AML to ECM, Sept. 27, 1941; Cole, *CAL and Battle,* pp. 174–5; Reinhold Niebuhr to John T. Flynn, Sept. 13, 1941 [University of Oregon, Eugene, OR: Flynn Papers]; "Assail L For Iowa Speech," *NYT,* Sept. 13, 1941, p. 1; "L—The Most Dangerous Man in America," *Liberty,* Oct. 18, 1941, n.p.; Rabbi Reichart quoted in Erich J. P. Sturm to CAL, Sept. 14, 1941; Sol Schwartz to CAL, Sept. 29, 1941; Norman Thomas to R. E. Wood, Sept. 17, 1941; Norman Thomas to CAL, Sept. 24, 1941; Francis E. McMahon, "L and the Jews," *Liberty,* Jan. 3, 1942, n.p.; HG to Milton Lehman, Apr. 16, 1963; Winchell quoted in Klurfeld, *Winchell,* p. 90; CAL to Mayor H. W. Baals, Oct. 16, 1941; CAL to Katrina McCormick, Oct. 16, 1941; CAL to R. E. Wood (draft), c. Sept. [Y:39/1175] and Oct. 27, 1941; R. D. Stuart, Jr. to "All Chapter Chairmen," Sept. 23, 1941; R. E. Wood to CAL, Sept. 22, 1941; CAL, final draft of speech, Oct. 3, 1941; Moore, "Autobiography," pp. 39–40, 43–4; Richard Moore to ASB (I), May 30, 1994; Lyle Leverich to ASB, Nov. 3, 1990; CAL to Rev. John A. O'Brien, Dec. 1, 1941.

PEARL HARBOR: CAL, "What Do We Mean by Democracy and Freedom," preliminary draft of speech, meant to be delivered Dec. 12, 1941; Thomas (and Wolfe), *Keep America Out,* pp. 156–7; CAL (D), Dec. 7 and 8, 1941; *WJ,* pp. 560–1; AML (D), Dec. 8, 1941; *WWW,* p. 239–42; CAL to R. D. Stuart, Jr., (T), Dec. 8, 1941.

15   CLIPPED WINGS

E: *AOV,* p. 195.

CAL ATTEMPTS TO JOIN WAR EFFORT: CMM to ASB (I), Mar. 3, 1993; CAL (D), June 22, Dec. 12, 16, 18, 20, and 30, 1941, Jan. 3, 8, 10, 12, 13, 15, 19, Feb. 1, 2, 10, 13, and 25, Mar. 12, 1942; *WJ,* pp. 506–7, 567–69, 576–7, 570, 572–4, 578–84, 587, 589–90, 593–5, 597, 602; R. D. Stuart, Jr., to "All Chapter

Chairmen," Dec. 8, 1941; CAL to Gen. H. H. Arnold, Dec. 20, 1941; Gen. H. H. Arnold to CAL, Dec. 23, 1941; "Mr. L volunteers," *NYT*, Dec. 31, 1941, n.p.; Victor Reisel, "L Regrets White Race 'Is Divided In This War,' " *New York Post*, Jan. 9, 1942; "L Deplored Split of White Race," *New York World-Telegram*, Jan. 9, 1942; "Do You Want the Man Who Said These Things," *PM*, Jan. 9, 1942; Harold Ickes to FDR, Dec. 30, 1941; Frank Knox to FDR (M), Jan. 1, 1942; FDR to Harold Ickes, Dec. 30, 1941; Henry L. Stimson to FDR, Jan. 13, 1942; "Lindy to Technical Army Job," (Chicago?) *American*, Jan. 15, 1942; CAL to R. E. Wood, Dec. 26, 1941; FDR's line about clipping wings cited in CAL, "Timeline," Aug., 1957; CAL to Phil Love, Jan. 30, 1942 and Mar. 7, 1942; CAL to Jerry Land, Dec. 22, 1941; Phil Love to CAL, Jan. 28 and Feb. 22, 1942; CAL to Maj. Reuben Fleet, Mar. 14, 1942; R. Fleet to CAL, Mar. 21, 1942, Dec. 21, 1951, Aug. 24, 1957.

FORD MOTOR CO.: CAL (D), Mar. 16, 21, 23, 24, Apr. 1–3, 9, 10, 15, 1942; *WJ*, pp. 603, 607–8, 612–4, 621–3, 625; Allan Nevins and Frank Ernest Hill, *Ford: Decline and Rebirth, 1933–1962* (New York: Charles Scribner's Sons, 1963), pp. 186–9, 198–9; AML (D), Mar. 12, Apr. 8, 1942; *WWW*, pp. 251–7; AML to CMM, Apr. 2, 1942; CAL to Father O'Brien, Oct. 29, 1942; I. A. Capizzi to Managing Editor of *Michigan Daily*, May, 19, 1942; CAL to I. A. Capizzi, May 27, 1942; "Have You Changed Your Mind?," *Liberty*, July 25, 1942, pp. 20–1; Ernest V. Heyn (of *Liberty*) to *CAL*, attached to "Suggested Outline For Reply," July 6, 1942; CAL to "Sirs" (*Liberty*), unsent letter, ca. July, 1942; Clinton Green (of International News Service) to CAL, Apr. 4, 1942; CAL to Clinton Green, June 15, 1942; John Walters (of *Sunday Pictorial* in London) to CAL (T), Jan. 28, 1942; Non-Sectarian Anti-Nazi League to CAL (T), Dec. 30, 1941; CAL to Marjory Douglas of MHS, Jan. 2, 1942; Marjory Douglas to CAL, June 6, 1942.

Henry Ford employed two other "former heroes" during the war, both at the Ford Rouge plant: Jesse Owens worked at a desk in the Employment division; and Jim Thorpe worked in the Plant Protection department (*Ford Times*, Apr. 2, 1943, pp. 1, 7).

LIFE IN DETROIT; BIRTH OF SML: CAL to James Newton, May 21, 1942; AML to CAL, June 13, 1942; *WWW*, pp. 269–70, 273–5, 277, 279–80, 282–5, 287–94, 306; CAL to AML, Apr. 14, June 4, 1942; CAL (D), May 22, 29, and 31, June 5, July 9, 21, 28, and 30, Aug. 1, 4, 11, Sept. 17–8, 1942; *WJ*, pp. 653, 658–9, 663, 674, 679, 683–5, 688–9, 694; AML (D), July 18, 21, and 28, Aug. 2, 4, 12, Nov. 28, 1942; CAL to Frank Ernest Hill, Nov. 13, Dec. 6, 1959; AML to ECM, Dec. 2, 1942; AML to CMM, Aug. 24, 1942; CAL to Donald Shelley (Director, Henry Ford Museum), Oct. 31, 1957; CAL (N) re trailer, Sept. 13, 1957; "Meet L's Travel Trailer," *Trailering Guide*, Jan., 1965, pp. 20–1; CAL to C. E. Sorenson, June 3, 1942, Jan. 2, 1943; CAL, "The Future of the Large Bomber" (submitted to C. E. Sorenson), Apr. 18, 1942; CAL to Dr. J. C. Hunsaker, Aug. 19, 1942; *AOV*, pp. 23–5; CAL to Henry Ford, July 30, 1942; CAL to Paul Palmer, July 6, 1942; CAL to Harry Bennett, Dec. 22, 1942; "L In the News," *The Roanoke* (Va.) *Times*, Aug. 14, 1942, p. 6; Theodore Dreiser to Mrs. Hortense N. Dillon, Oct. 20, 1942; the story of Beatrice Kaufman and Adelaide Marquand is related in Stephen Birmingham, *The Late John Marquand* (Philadelphia: J. B. Lippincott, 1972), pp. 159–60.

MAYO CLINIC; HIGH-ALTITUDE TESTS: CAL (D), Sept. 22–Oct. 3, 19, 21, 23, Nov. 2, 14, 1942; *WJ*, pp. 718–731, 734–5, 741, 746–7; D. B. Dill, "Walter M. Boothby, Pioneer in Aviation Medicine," *Science*, Oct. 29, 1954, p. 688; *AOV*, pp. 24–5; CAL, "Training For the Recognition of Oxygen Emergencies in High-Altitude

Flying," *Handbook of Respiratory Physiology,* Sept., 1954, pp. v–vii; Walter M. Boothby, Kenneth G. Wilson, CAL, and Charles J. Clark, "M —Report to Army Air Forces Material Center," Series A, No. 1, Oct. 3, 1942; Walter Boothby to CAL, May 20, 1952; CAL to Dr. Charles Mayo, Oct. 16, 1942; CAL to Dr. W. M. Boothby, Oct. 16, 1942; *OFAL,* pp. 3–10; CAL to E. E. Wilson, Nov. 25 and Dec. 4, 1942; E. E. Wilson to CAL, Nov. 27, 1942; "Army & Navy Report," *Time,* Oct. 1, 1943, pp. 69–71; CAL, "Trips to Bridgeport & Hartford," (M), n.d.; L. D. Lyman, "L: 'Tech Rep,' " *The Bee-Hive,* Jan. 1950, p. 14; L. D. Lyman to E. E. Wilson, "Confidential—M," ca. Oct. 15, 1943.

CAL IN COMBAT: CAL (D), Jan. 5, 6, 19–23, Apr. 2, 3, May 22, 29, and 30, June 21, 26, July 10, 12, 16, 19, 24, 26, 28, Aug. 1, 15, 21, 22, Sept. 1–4, 6, 8, 12, 13, 16, 17, 1944; *WJ,* pp. 755–6, 759–60, 774–5, 814–9, 835–7, 853–4, 856, 870–4, 876–8, 881–5, 887–93, 906, 910–2, 915–8, 920–2, 924; ROSS, Aug. 8, 1968; Boyne, *Smithsonian Book,* p. 190; Charles H. Gibbs-Smith, *Aviation,* p. 209; CAL to AML, Apr. 23, May 12, 1944; Col. Charles MacDonald, "Long-legged Fighters," typescript, later published as "L In Battle," *Colliers,* Feb. 16, 1946, pp. 11–2, 75–6; CAL to R. Fredette, May 15, 1971; Edwards Park, "The Jug in New Guinea," appears in Boyne, *Smithsonian Book,* p. 178; Carroll R. "Bob" Anderson to Bob Considine, July 18, 1957; *AOV,* pp. 195–202; CAL, "Individual Combat Report," Mission No. 3–407, July 29, 1944; Col. C. H. MacDonald, "Individual Combat Report," Mission No. 30407, July 29, 1944; CAL to Col. Danforth Miller, Sept. 29, 1956; *OFAL,* pp. 10–14; CAL, "Individual Combat Report," Mission No. 3–413, Aug. 2, 1944; CAL to Paul Baker, Apr. 26, 1953.

CAL's means of achieving "maximum range cruise" involved flying slowly, setting throttles and propeller controls so that "the engines turn slowly but labor hard," and running on a lean mixture, such that the "engines suck in more air and less gasoline." (W. Langewiesche, "How They Fly the Atlantic," *Harper's,* May, 1948, p. 449.)

AML ON THE HOME FRONT: AML (D), Apr. 17, June 13, 1943, Feb. 4, Mar. 4–18, July 3, Oct. 8 and 27, 1944; *WWW,* pp. 338–40, 360, 381–2, 407–8, 417–9, 432, 438–9, 446–52; AML to Alfred Harcourt, Aug., 1943; CAL to AML, Aug. 7, 1944; AML to Margot L. Morrow, Sept. 7, 1944; CAL (D), Sept. 18, 20, and 22, 1944; *WJ,* pp. 925–8.

16   PHOENIX

E: *OFAL,* p. 50.

READJUSTING TO "CIVILIAN" LIFE: CAL (D), Sept. 21–2, 1944; *WJ,* pp. 927–8; CAL to Charles MacDonald, Mar. 22, 1947; Harry Johansen to CAL (T), June 3, 1943; CAL to R. E. Wood, July 9, 1943; CAL to O. K. Armstrong, Mar. 28, 1944; CAL to Mrs. Thomas McGuire, Apr. 28, 1945; ROSS, Aug. 21, 1969; John LaFarge, "Alexis Carrel," *America,* Nov. 18, 1944, p. 129; Anne and AC to Frederic Coudert, c. Oct., 1944; T. Bentley Mott to Frederic Coudert, Dec. 10, 1944; CAL to Roy McClure, Nov. 10, 1944; Corliss Lamont, "Argument from Ignorance," *The Modern Monthly,* July, 1936, pp. 28–9; CAL to Dr. Irene McFaul, May 11, 1945; CAL to Edward Moore, Feb. 24, 1946; "By-laws of AC Foundation," n.d.; CAL to Rev. Father E. Rooney, S. J., Aug. 14, 1953; Cass Canfield to CAL, Oct. 26, 1949; AML to CAL, June 6, 1945.

CAL'S EUROPEAN MISSION: CAL to John F. Sinclair, Apr. 27, 1945; CAL to Gen. R. E. Wood, Nov. 16, 1949; CAL to ELLL, May 10, 1945; CAL (D), May 11–5, 17–9, 21, 23, June 4, 10, 11, and 13–5, 1945; *WJ,* pp. 933–40, 942–57, 960–1,

972, 990–1000; *AOV,* pp. 344–351; Gibbs-Smith, *Aviation,* pp. 213–4; CAL, "Supersonic Transport," July 14, 1972; Lehman, *High Man,* pp. 402–3; CAL to Rt. Rev. Walter H. Gray, Apr. 10, 1972; CAL to Wayne Cole, Dec. 23, 1973; AML to William Jovanovich, Sept. 5, 1976.

NEW ATTITUDES; GODDARD; ATOMIC BOMB: J. L. Bourbon to CAL, May 13, 1945; John Armstrong to "The Editor," n.s., c. May 14, 1945; Bernard De Voto, "The Easy Chair," *Harper's,* Jan. 1944, p. 143; CAL to Wayne Cole, Mar. 11, 1974; CAL "final draft of comments to *Chicago Tribune,*" July 25, 1945; CAL to ELLL, July 30, 1945; CAL to H. B. Sallada, July 24, 1945; RHG to CAL, June 19, 1940; CAL to Milton Lehman, Nov. 12, 1961; Lehman, *High Man,* pp. 389–91; AML to André de Lattre, Aug. 7, 1945; FRDT; *AOV,* pp. 214–7, 226; CAL to AML, Sept. 19, 1945; CAL to Robert M. Hutchins, Nov. 25, 1946; "L Said to Advise Secrecy on Atomic Bomb," *NYT,* Nov. 14, 1945, n.p.; CAL, "Phoned to A. P.," Nov. 18, 1945; "L Wants Bomb Controlled by World Group," *Washington Post,* Nov. 18, 1945, n.p.; CAL, "Aero Club Address," Dec. 17, 1945.

AIR FORCE AND POSTWAR GOVT. WORK: Townsend Hoopes and Douglas Brinkley, *Driven Patriot: The Life and Times of James Forrestal* (New York: Alfred A. Knopf, 1992), pp. 341–5; W. Stuart Symington to CAL, Nov. 24, 1947; CAL to Gen. Hoyt Vandenberg, reports, Sept. 14, 1948 and Feb. 18, 1949; *AOV,* pp. 29–30, 36, 219–2, 231, 237, 356; Col. J. J. Judge to Commanding Generals (M), Aug. 4, 1948; FRDT; CAL to AML, Aug. 8, 1947, Jan. 6 and Aug. 29, 1948; CAL to Stuart Symington, Nov. 15, 1949; CAL, "Statement," Apr. 7, 1947; "L Urges U. S. World Role," n.s., Apr. 14, 1947, n.p.

BIRTH OF RML; DOMESTIC LIFE IN DARIEN: ECM (D), Oct. 2 and Nov. 29, 1945, Dec. 29, 1949, Apr. 26, 1950; CAL to ELLL, May 10, 1945; CAL to James Newton, Apr. 29, 1945; CAL to Dr. Alfred R. Henderson, Mar. 3, 1974; CMM to ASB (I), Mar. 3, 1993; Dr. David Read to ASB (I), May 2, 1993; AML (D), Feb. 4, 1944; *WWW,* p. 407; ASL to ASB (I), May 9, 1993; AML to JML, July 27, 1947; AML to ELLL, Nov. 24, 1944; CAL to Harold Bixby, Mar. 28, 1946; CAL, accounts, specifically Dec. 3, 1947 [Y:373/998]; Wendell Wilson (Teton Valley Ranch) to CAL, Sept. 3, 1943; LML to ASB (I), Aug. 18, 1993; Ruth Thomas to AML, July 23, 1945; Brookside School (Bloomfield Hills, MI) to CAL and AML, comments, June 1943; CAL, "Policy" (for secretary Barbara Mansfield), ca. 1947–8.

MEETING DR. ATCHLEY; AML-CAL MARRIAGE: AML to CMM, Dec. 15 and 22, 1946, Feb. 21, Mar. 20, 1947; AML to Adelaide Marquand, Mar. 1, 1947; AML to Dr. E. M. Hawks, n.d.; AML (D), Feb. 13, 1947; AML to ECM. Apr. 12, 1947; AML to ELLL, Apr. 24 and July 27, 1947; F. L. Wright, *Autobiography,* p. 500; CAL to AML, Dec. 13 and 21, 1947; AML to Janet de Coux, July 23, 1947; AML, "The Flame of Europe," *Reader's Digest,* Jan., 1948, pp. 141–6; AML to CAL, Sept. 28 and 30, Dec. 18, 1947; Edna St. Vincent Millay to AML, Aug., 1948; Edward Sheldon to AML, Apr. 25, 1945; ECM (D), Aug. 31 and Nov. 16, 1948, May 16 and Dec. 29, 1949.

AML'S other pieces about postwar Europe included: "One Starts at Zero," *Reader's Digest,* Feb., 1948; "Anywhere in Europe," *Harper's,* Apr., 1948; "Airliner to Europe," *Harper's,* Sept., 1948; "Our Lady of Risk," *Life,* July 29, 1950.

OFAL; REASCENDANCE OF CAL: OFAL, pp. v–vii, 10, 14, 21, 26, 40, 50; John P. Marquand to CAL, May 26, 1948; Charles Scribner to CAL, Apr. 5, May 11 (T), May 31, 1948; John W. Chase, "L Apologia and Attack," *NYT Book Review,* n.d., n.p.; Edward Witsell to CAL, Dec. 26, 1947; Omar N. Bradley to CAL, Oct. 22,

1948; George C. Kenney to CAL, Mar. 14, 1955; James D. McIntyre to Truman Smith, Sept. 19, 1954; Stuart Symington to CAL (T), Jan. 17, 1950; Crouch, *Bishop's Boys*, pp. 520, 527–8; A. Wetmore to CAL, May 7, 1948; CAL to A. Wetmore, May 17, 1948; Luther Evans to CAL, Jan. 18, 1949; CAL to Mrs. Henry Keil, Jan. 10, 1947; Martha Knowlton to CAL, Feb. 7, 1947; Supt. Paul J. Janson, Aug. 15, 1951; Theodore M. Hesburgh to CAL (T), Apr. 7, 1956; John S. Dickey to CAL, Feb. 8, 1954; CAL to Charles Honce, Feb. 15, 1952; CAL to Alan J. Gould, Mar. 20, 1952; CAL to J. F. Sinclair, Jan. 29, 1946; CAL to Amyas Ames, Mar. 2, 1949; AML to ASB (I), Feb. 27, 1990; CAL to Dr. Magdalene Wenzel, Dec. 18, 1952; Effie and Bruce Hopper to CAL, Nov. 9, 1949; Richard Davis, "L Still Solos in Anonymity," *Newsweek,* Dec. 5, 1949; CAL to Wayne S. Cole, May 29, 1949; CAL, "Wright Dinner Speech," Dec. 17, 1949, reprinted in *U.S. Air Services,* Jan., 1950, pp. 11, 13; CAL and HG's speeches of Jan. 25, 1954 (awarding of Guggenheim Medal) reprinted in supplement *Pioneering in Aeronautics* (Daniel Guggenheim Medal Board of Award, 1954); Gen. R. L. Scott to ASB (I), Apr. 23, 1998.

  SSL: CAL (N), Feb. 5, 1939; CAL to Hobart Lewis, Sept. 28, 1966; *SSL,* pp. ix, 3, 492; DAVIS, Aug. 22, 1969; ROSS, Aug. 10, 1968; R. D. Lyman, "How L Wrote a Book," *Bee-Hive,* Summer, 1954, pp. 18–20; ECM (D), Oct. 24, 1951; Charles Scribner to CAL, Dec. 6, 1951, July 2, 1952; John Hall Wheelock to CAL, Mar. 26 and 31, Apr. 1, July 2, 1952, Sept. 11, 1953; CAL to Charles Scribner, July 28, 1952; CAL to John Hall Wheelock, Mar. 10, Apr. 16, 27, 28, 1952; Ben Hibbs (of *Saturday Evening Post*) to George T. Bye, Dec. 8, 1952; Wesley Price to CAL, Jan. 17, 1953; "Biggest Sales in *Post* History," advertisement in *New York World Telegram,* Apr. 15, 1953, p. 18; George T. Bye to CAL, Apr. 27, 1953; Charles Scribner, *In the Company of Writers* (New York: Charles Scribner's Sons, 1990), p. 100; AML (D), Jan. 25, Sept. 23, 1953; Whitney Darrow to CAL, Feb. 10, 1954; AML to Lucia Norton, Jan. 8, 1954; Carl W. Ackerman to CAL, May 3, 1954.

  CAL donated his Pulitzer prize-money, five hundred dollars, to Columbia's School of Dental and Oral Surgery, to be used in connection with its program of historical research, in honor of his grandfather, the pioneering dentist Dr. Charles H. Land. (Grayson Kirk to CAL, June 30, 1954.)

17   DOUBLE SUNRISE

  E: CAL to Robert Wenkam, July 22, 1953.

  EMERGENCE OF AML: AML (D), Mar. 1–9, 1948, Mar. 4, 28, 1951, July 22 and Nov. 5, 1953, Jan. 19, May 27, 1954, May 31, 1957; GS, pp. 9–11, 63, 69, 76, 96; John Marquand to CAL, Feb. 8, 1951; AML to ECM, Easter, 1951; J. P. Marquand to Alfred McIntyre, Apr. 6, 1946; AML to Ruth Oliff, c. 1950; Margot Wilkie to ASB (I), Apr. 26, 1993 and May 23, 1994; ECM (D), Feb. 24, 1949, Apr. 26, Dec. 7, 1950; RML to ASB (I), Jan. 25, 1953; CAL, "Books read and studied," n.d. [Y:360/975]; CAL, "Travelling Case," 1956; CAL to L. D. Lyman, July 5, 1957; CAL to Walter Boothby, Dec. 19, 1942; CAL to J. H. Wheelock, June 1, 1953; CAL to Anne Carrel, Dec. 27, 1950; CAL to AML, July 9, Sept. 12, Oct. 14, 1950.

  CAL'S NEW ACTIVITIES: J. R. Killian, Jr. (of MIT) to CAL, Oct. 15, 1954; CAL (N), re Secretary of Air, Aug. 19, 1955; tearsheets, *The American Mercury,* Jan., 1956, p. 12; CAL to Harold E. Talbott, June, 1954; n.a., "Sites Inspected," Apr. 9–15, 1954, July 1, 1954; *AOV,* p. 31; CAL to George [prob. Troutman], Nov. 3, 1959; "Agenda of 20th Meeting of Scientific Advisory Committee," Jan. 28–9, 1960, "Agenda," Apr. 7, and "Agenda," Mar. 17, 1960; CAL, "Foreword" to C.M. Green and Milton Lomask, *Vanguard: A History* (Washington, D.C.: NASA, 1970), pp. v–vi; André Priester to CAL, Dec. 16, 1953; Pan American map with CAL (N), Jan. 1, 1954; CAL to Alfonso Cadena, Aug. 26, 1955; Juan Trippe to CAL, Mar. 11, Apr. 9, Nov. 2, 1953; CAL to Harold Gray, Sept. 11, 1956; CAL to Juan Trippe, Jan. 29, 1958.

Other members of the Air Force site committee included Virgil Hancher, H. B. Harmon, Merrill Meigs, and Carl Spaatz.

GS: AML (D), July 22, 1953, Sept. 18, 1954, July 18, 1955; James Lord, *Six Exceptional Women* (New York: Farrar Straus Giroux, 1994), p. 347; Dana Atchley to AML, Feb. 1, and Dec. 22, 1952; GS, p. 56; CAL to AML, July 5, 1953; Kurt Wolff to AML, Mar. 29 and Apr. 21, 1954; Michael Ermarth [ed.], "Foreword," *Kurt Wolff: A Portrait in Essays and Letters* (Chicago: University of Chicago Press, 1991), pp. vii–xiv, and Helen Wolff, "Kurt Wolff: A Biographical Sketch," p. xxvii; CAL to Milton Lehman, Apr. 19, 1960; AML, "*GS* Re-opened" (Twentieth Anniversary Edition of) *GS* (New York: Vintage Books, 1978), pp. 131, 136–7; AML to CAL, Sept. 9, 1954, RML to ASB (I), May 8, 1993; ELLL's demise in CAL to James Newton, Dec. 3, 1954, ECM's demise discussed in AML to Monte Millar, Dec. 23, 1954 and to Ruth Oliff, n.d.; CAL to DeWitt Wallace, Jan. 2, 1956.

THE UNICORN: AML, *The Unicorn and Other Poems: 1935–1955* (New York: Pantheon Books, 1956), pp. 11, 55–6, 86; John Ciardi, "A Close Look at *Unicorn*," *Saturday Review,* Jan. 12, 1957, pp. 54–5; "Letters to the Editor," *Saturday Review,* Feb. 9, 1957, pp. 23–4; Norman Cousins, *Present Tense: An American Editor's Odyssey* (New York: McGraw-Hill, 1967), p. 55, and "John Ciardi and the Readers," *Saturday Review,* Feb. 16, 1957, pp. 22–3; John Ciardi, "The Reviewer's Duty to Damn," *Saturday Review,* Feb. 16, 1957, pp. 24–5, 54–5; AML to Ruth Thomas, n.d. [Y:829–114/139]; AML (D), Jan. 25, 1957.

SSL, THE MOVIE: Leland Hayward to George Bye, Dec. 18, 1953; "L's Idealism," *The Philadelphia Inquirer,* Jan. 27, 1943; Billy Wilder to CAL, July 22, 1955; CAL to Billy Wilder, June 6, 1954; James Stewart (with Joseph Laitin), "Lucky to Be Lindy," *Colliers,* Mar. 30, 1956, pp. 30–1; Slim Keith with Annette Tapert, *Slim* (New York: Simon & Schuster, 1990), pp. 176–8; CAL to Paul Palmer, Apr. 24, 1955; Maurice Zolotow, *Billy Wilder in Hollywood* (New York: G. P. Putnam's Sons, 1977), pp. 192–5, 314; Billy Wilder to ASB (I), Apr. 1, 1990; James Stewart to ASB (I), May 21, 1990; Bud Gurney to CAL, Apr. 4 and Aug. 21, 1954, ca. May, 1955, May 4, 1956; Leland Hayward to CAL, Apr. 6, 1955, and May 4 and July 28, 1955, Feb. 6, 1957; David Krauss, "Aviation on Film," *USAir Magazine,* Oct. 1990, p. 62; R. J. Obringer (Warner Brothers legal dept.) to Leland Hayward, July 28, 1955; J. L. Warner to CAL (T), Apr. 8, 1957; CAL to Bud Gurney, July 7, 1963; CAL to Leland Hayward, Mar. 29, 1957.

CAL'S FAMILY: ASL to ASB (I), May 9, 1993; CAL to JML and LML, Apr. 5, 1949, and June 16, 1959; CAL to JML, Dec. 27, 1950, Sept. 3, 1952, and May 17, 1953, Dec. 28, 1954, Feb. 24, 1955; CAL to AML, Jan. 12, 1951, June 15, 1957; JML to ASB (I), Aug. 17, 1993; Explosive Engineering Corp. announcement, c. 1961; CAL to Anne Carrel, Apr. 9, 1955; CAL to J. E. Wallace Sterling, Jan. 3, 1955; Robert Wells, "Lindy's Son Shuns Spotlight," n.s., n.d. [Y:271/693]; CAL to Kenneth Ross, June 2, 1950; CAL to Ben Jaffe, Mar. 29, 1955; Ben Jaffe to CAL, Aug. 23, 1955; AML to LML, Feb. 23, 1956; AML to Kathleen O. Elliott, Sept. 12, 1958; ASL to AML, Mar. 1, 1972; AML (D), Aug. 31, 1958; AML to CAL, June 21, 1949; RML to ASB (I), Mar. 1, 1990.

AML'S SOCIAL AWAKENING: Alan Valentine to AML, Mar. 11, Apr. 29, and Dec. 17, 1958; Corliss Lamont to AML, June 26, 1954; AML (D), Nov. 1, 1954, July 8, c. Aug. 10, 1956, Jan. 25, Aug. 1, Oct. 14, 1957; Katharine Hepburn to ASB (I), Apr. 2, 1991; James Lord to ASB (I) May 20, 1994; Dana Atchley to AML, Mar. 6, Aug. 10, and Dec. 18, 1956, July 8, 1958; ASL to ASB (I), May 9, 1993; CMM to ASB (I), Mar. 3, 1993; AML to CAL, Aug. 11, 1956; AML to CMM, Aug. 12, 1956, Aug. 18, 1957; AML to Lucia Valentine, Mar. 11, 1957; Helen Wolff to AML, July 7, 1956; Helen Wolff to ASB (I), May 9, 1993; RML to ASB (I), Oct. 10 and May 5, 1994.

18   ALONE TOGETHER

E: *AOV,* p. 39.

SWITZERLAND; NEW HOUSE IN CONNECTICUT: AML (D), Feb. 12, 1959, May 7, June 7, Oct. 7–8, 1960, Feb. 1–2, Apr. 6–7, 1962; ASL to ASB (I), May 9, 1993; Helen Wolff to AML, Mar. 13, 1959; AML to Lucia and Alan Valentine, July, 1959, Dec. 16, 1963; AML to Dana Atchley, July 9–13, 1959, Feb. 9, 1961, Apr. 11, 1963; Helen and Kurt Wolff to AML, July 15, 1959; CAL to Helen Wolff, Dec. 11, 1968 and Jan. 11, 1969; Helen Wolff to CAL, Dec. 20, 1968; *AOV,* pp. 281–2; AML, "Prologue," (U), c. Aug., 1961 [Y:157/398]; CAL to Dr. Clark B. Millikan, May 16, 1960; AML to CMM, Dec. 12, 1960; AML to CAL, Mar. 18, June 18, 1960, Sept. 23 and 28, 1961, Jan. 19 and Nov. 11, 1962; CAL to ASL, June 21, Aug. 23, 1962; AML to LML, Apr. 12, Sept. 29, 1960; CAL to Paul Johnston, July 17, 1962; CAL (N), "Planorbe," Sept. 21 and 22, 1973; CAL to Geoffrey Platt, May 16, 1962 and Apr. 5, 1964; Crosson Kearny (Hudson Institute) to CAL, May 16, 1962; LML to ASB (I), Aug. 18, 1993; AML to Mina Curtiss, Apr. 16, 1961; "Daughter of the Ls Wed to Student in France," *NYT,* Dec. 27, 1963, n.p., CAL to M. and Mme. Feydy, Jan. 1, 1964; AML to ASL, Nov. 7, 1964.

One night shortly before Land married, his fiancée, Susan Miller, and CAL happened to be in Paris at the same time. One evening, strolling along the Seine together, CAL pointed out some gaslights and casually remarked, "These lights are so much more beautiful from the air than electric lights." Utterly lost in the beauty of the evening, Susie innocently asked, "Have you ever flown over Paris?" Without giving it a thought, Lindbergh quietly replied, "I did once . . . years ago." (Susan Miller to ASB (I), Aug. 27, 1994.)

STATESIDE INVITATIONS: CAL to Raymond Bisplinghoff, Aug. 18, 1966; Arthur H. Sulzberger to CAL, Aug. 18, 1961; CAL to Arthur H. Sulzberger, Nov. 4, 1961; CAL to Henry Luce, Feb. 21, 1963; CAL to Grayson Kirk, Apr. 10, 1966; Barry Goldwater to CAL (T), Nov. 10, 1961; Adlai E. Stevenson to CAL, Dec. 22, 1964; CAL to Adlai E. Stevenson, Jan. 3, 1965; CAL to AML, Nov. 7, 1960; CAL to JFK, Mar. 2 and May 23, 1962; CAL to Evelyn Lincoln, Apr. 9 and 15, 1962; Jacqueline Kennedy Onassis, "America's First Ladies Honor CAL," *Good House-keeping,* June, 1977, p. 72; AML to Dana Atchley, May 13, 1962; AML (D), Apr. 18 and May 13, 1962; Jacqueline Kennedy to CAL and AML, May 22, 1962; CAL to William M. Allen, Apr. 7, 1966; CAL to Joe Wecker, Mar. 19, 1963; CAL to John L. Crone, Apr. 26, 1965; CAL to James W. Jacobs, Feb. 10, 1968; S. Paul Johnston to CAL, May 31, 1967; CAL to Bruce Larson, July 18, 1966; CAL to J. H. Wheelock, Feb. 28, 1953; CAL to Min Miller, Nov. 7, 1963; Lady Bird Johnson to AML, Jan. 29, 1963; Lady Bird Johnson, "Guest list," Mar. 22, 1966; CAL to ELCS, Oct. 27, 1964; AML to Pres. and Mrs. Lyndon B. Johnson, June 1, 1967; FRDT; *AOV,* p. 31;

CAL to Gen. Frederick Osborn, Nov. 1, 1959; Najeeb E. Halaby to CAL, Apr. 13, 1962; CAL to N. E. Halaby, Apr. 26, 1962; CAL to Secy. Robert S. McNamara, July 11, 1966; CAL to William M. Allen, Feb. 2, 1966; TWA press release, May 20, 1962; Boyne, *Smithsonian Book,* p. 260; Robert J. Serling, *Legend & Legacy: The Story of Boeing and Its People* (New York: St. Martin's Press, 1992), p. 284; CAL to Father J. T. Durkin, June 14, 1965.

WISDOM OF WILDNESS: *AOV,* pp. 33–4, 307; CAL to Stewart Udall, June 12, 1966; the Henry David Thoreau quotation is from his essay "Walking"; CAL, "Wisdom of Wildness," *Life,* Dec. 12, 1967, p. 9; James Newton to ASB (I), Mar. 3, 1993; Newton, *Uncommon Friends,* pp. 317–8; CAL to JML and LML, June 11, 1961; CAL to James Newton, Apr. 14 and July 24, 1961; CAL (N), "Meeting with Jilin Konchellah," June 16, 1961; Paul Pry View, "John Konchellah," (Nairobi?) *Sunday Nation,* Nov. 25, 1962, n.p.; John Konchellah to ASB (I), Aug. 15, 1992.

AFRICA: CAL to John Konchellah, Dec. 21, 1961 and Apr. 11, 1963; Noel Simon to Ian Grimwood, Sept. 22, 1962; CAL to Denis Zaphiro, Dec. 17, 1962, Oct. 12, 1965; CAL to Ronald Ngala, Dec. 13, 1962; Newton, *Uncommon Friends,* p. 318; *AOV,* pp. 269–71, 278–81, 283–5, 380, 386; CAL to Ian Grimwood, Jan. 31, Mar. 11, and Apr. 24, 1964, Feb. 4, 1966; CAL (N), "Dr. L. S. B. Leakey," Feb. 23, 1964; L. S. B. Leakey to CAL, n.d.; Richard Logan, "L Refined Philosophy of Life," (CAL Fund, Inc.) *Newsletter,* Spring, 1994, pp. 3, 6; CAL To L.S.B. Leakey, May 18 and July 8, 1964; L.S.B. Leakey to CAL, June 2, 1964; CAL to Anne Carrel, Apr. 12, 1965; AML (D), May 26, 1965; CAL to Amb. William Atwood, Nov. 16, 1965; CAL to Jon, Barbara, Land, Susan, Julien, Anne, Scott, and Reeve, Oct. 11, 1965; LML to ASB (I), Aug. 18, 1993; AML to Lucia Valentine, Jan. 22, 1966; CAL to SML, Nov. 24, 1965.

WILDLIFE: Kermit Roosevelt to CAL, Sept. 17, 1962; "What Is IUCN," brochure, Aug., 1962; CAL to Noel Simon, Sept. 25, 1963, Oct. 2 and Nov. 15, 1964, May 5, 1967; Noel Simon to CAL, Nov. 8, 1963; CAL to Harold J. Coolidge, Dec. 27, 1963; CAL, "Is Civilization Progress?," *Reader's Digest,* July, 1964, pp. 67–74; *AOV,* pp. 272, 274, 285; CAL to Hobart Lewis, Apr. 24, 1968; CAL to DeWitt Wallace, Apr. 23 and Nov. 16, 1964, June 3 and Aug. 30, 1966; CAL to Ira Gabrielson, Apr. 27 and July 27, 1965; Ira Gabrielson to CAL, Aug. 17, 1965; CAL, draft of form letter, c. Aug. 1965; CAL (N), re World Wildlife Fund; Max Lerner to ASB (I), Nov. 3, 1993; n.a., "Extermination of the Great Whale" (suggested press release from unknown conservation org.), n.d.; IUCN statement as read by CAL, International Whaling Comission, June 30, 1967; CAL to Prime Minister Eisaku Sato, Jan. 14, 1965; CAL to Pres. F. B. Terry, Feb. 7, 1968; CAL to Amb. Ralph Dungan, Apr. 9, 1967; Ralph Dungan to CAL, Apr. 18 and May 31, 1967; Ralph Graves to CAL, Jan. 6, 1967; CAL to David Mannes, Apr. 6, 1967; Stan Wayman to CAL, May 15, 1967; "L and the Blue Whale," *The Washington Post,* Nov. 5, 1966, n.p.; CAL to Erwin A. Olson, Oct. 9, 1966; "The Uniqueness of Aldabra" [prob. IUCN newsletter], ca. Aug. 21, 1967; CAL to Secy. Robert S. McNamara, Sept. 28, 1967; Tufele-Faia'oga to CAL, June 17, 1964.

SCIENTIFIC VOYAGES: CAL, "Notes concerning the Udjung Kulon," June 4, 1967 and Aug. 3, 1970; "Change of Schedule of H. E. Adam Malik's Trip," May 14, 1967; CAL to Sultan Hamengku Buwono IX, May 31, 1967; CAL, "Wisdom of Wildness," pp. 8–10; CAL, "Conservation notes . . . Indonesia," c. Nov., 1967; *AOV,* pp. 282–3, 399–400; Dr. Theodore I. Malinin and Vernon P. Perry, "Observations on Contracting Monkey Hearts . . . ," *Johns Hopkins Medical Journal* (vol. 122, no. 6),

June, 1968, pp. 380–6; Dr. Theodore I. Malinin to ASB (I), May 30, 1993; Dr. Frank Glenn to CAL, Feb. 3, Apr. 27, and Sept. 19, 1969; CAL to Dr. Denton Cooley, Nov. 16, 1967; Dr. Denton Cooley to CAL, Oct. 26, 1967; Nate Haseltine, "Scientists Aided by L," *World Journal Tribune,* Mar. 15, 1967; CAL to Anne Carrel, Apr. 22, 1964; G. Edward Pendray, "Summary of Progress: Man's Relation to Man Project," Aug. 1, 1965; CAL to HG, May 10, 1963.

CAL ADVISES HIS CHILDREN; DRIFTS FROM AML: CAL to RML, July 8, 1966 and June 14, 1967, Jan. 31, 1968; LML to ASB (I), Aug. 18, 1993; ASL to ASB (I), May 9, 1993; CAL to ASL, Nov. 23, 1963; CAL to JML, Nov. 20, 1960, Dec. 7, 1967; CAL to Barbara Robbins Lindbergh, Jan. 8, 1960; Vietnam discussed in Edgar Needham, "Travels With Charlie," *Esquire,* Mar. 1971, pp. 90–1; CAL to SML, Jan. 30, 1966, Nov. 16, 1967, Jan. 15, Mar. 28, 1968; SML to CAL, May 26, 1963, Apr. 1, 1968; SML to CAL and AML, also Apr. 1, 1968; CAL to Jon, Land, Anne, and Reeve, Dec. 10, 1967; ASL to CAL, Dec. 13, 1967; AML (D), Mar. 27, Aug. 20, and Nov. 19, 1967, Feb. 7, 1968; AML to CAL, May 26, 1963; RML to CAL, Dec. 13, 1967 and Jan. 14, 1968; AML to CMM, Jan. 31, 1968.

ALASKA: CAL to Mr. Bechtel, Mar. 23, 1968; Stanton Patty, "The Lone Eagle And The Alaska Legislature," *Seattle Times,* Jan. 5, 1969, pp. 12–3; CAL to Gov. Walter Hickel, Apr. 14, 1968; CAL to Lowell Thomas, Mar. 30, 1968; CAL to Fritz Vollmar, June 3, 1968; Lowell Thomas to CAL, Apr. 3, 1968; Lowell Thomas, Jr. to CAL, Apr. 30, 1968; "L Speaks on Conservation," *Alaska Conservation Review,* Summer, 1968, p. 2; "Lindy Urges Protection of Natural Resources," *The Oregonian,* Mar. 22, 1968.

19   ALOHA

E: *AOV,* p. 309.

HANA: Steven L. Walker and Matti P. Majorin, *Hawaiian Islands* (Scottsdale, AZ: Camelback Design Group and Elan Publishing, 1992), pp. 9–11, 41–2; Ron Youngblood, *On the Hana Coast* (Hong Kong: Emphasis International, Ltd. and Carl Lindquist, 1987), pp. 16–23, 81, 90–99; AML to ASL, Mar. 20, 1969, Jan. 13, Feb. 8, 1971, Feb. 25 and Mar. 5, 1972; Beverly Creamer, "Sam Pryor: The L Connection," reprinted in Youngblood, *Hana Coast,* p. 74; CAL, "Maui," introduction to *Maui: The Last Hawaiian Place* (San Francisco and New York: Friends of the Earth, 1970); Jeannie Pechin to ASB (I), Aug. 27, 1994; CAL to Sam Pryor, Apr. 12, 1968, Feb. 25, 1971; Sam Pryor to CAL, c. Apr. 1968; AML to James Lloyd, Feb. 5, 1975; CAL to Jack O. Tobin, Apr. 16, 1969; CAL to Edward M. Brownless, Sept. 19, 1969; CAL to Taylor A. Pryor, Jan. 29, 1970; AML (D), May 6, 1969, July 2, 1970, Jan. 22, 1971; AML to Dana Atchley, Jan. 21, 1971; AML to Lucia and Alan Valentine, Jan. 29 and Feb. 9, 1971, Apr. 2, 1972, Feb. 12, 1974; AML to CAL, Jan. 19, 1970, Jan. 31, 1971, Mar. 10, 1972; AML to RML, Feb. 8, 1971; AML to Mina Curtiss, Mar. 8, 1973.

CONSERVATION: CAL to Sen. Daniel Inouye, May 12, 1968; CAL to Sen. Hiram Fong, June 6, 1968; The Nature Conservancy, press release, Jan. 10, 1969; CAL to Thomas W. Richards, Oct. 12, 1968 and Mar. 15, 1969; Mary Alice Rogers to CAL, Sept. 24, 1968; CAL to Austin Lamont, Dec. 16, 1968; Huey D. Johnson to CAL, June 31, 1972; CAL to Edward Kingman, Feb. 12, 1969; CAL form letter, Apr. 9, 1970; Walter J. Hickel to CAL, Nov. 25, 1970; CAL to William P. Rogers, July 26, 1969; Laurence S. Rockefeller to Richard M. Nixon, "Draft Language for Possible Inclusion in the State of the Union Message," n.d.; John C. Whitaker to CAL, Apr.

23, 1970; "L Visits Replica of 'Spirit,' " *San Diego Union,* Dec. 16, 1972; "Nixon Visits S. F., Pushes Bay Park," *San Francisco Chronicle,* Sept. 6, 1972.

ASTRONAUTICS AND AVIATION: Lady Bird Johnson, *A White House Diary* (New York: Holt, Rinehart & Winston, 1970), p. 749; Social Secretary of The White House to CAL and AML (T), Nov. 29, 1968; CAL to The Apollo VIII Crew, Dec. 9, 1968; AML, *Earth Shine* (New York: Harcourt, Brace, 1969), pp. 9–14, 19–23; CAL to Frank Borman, July 20, 1969; CAL to Jerome Lederer, Dec. 29, 1968; CAL to Scott McLeod, Feb. 21, 1969; CAL and AML to Col. Frank Borman (T), Dec. 28, 1968; CAL to Neil Armstrong, June 15, 1969, July 27, 1969; David Brinkley, *NBC Nightly News,* transcript, Aug. 26, 1974; Neil Armstrong, "Remarks," accepting 1997 Lindbergh Award, May 10, 1997; CAL to Michael Collins, July 27, 1969; CAL to Richard Nixon, July 26, 1969; CAL, "For Me, Aviation Has Value Only to the Extent that It Contributes to the Quality of the Human Life It Serves," *NYT,* July 27, 1972, p. 31; CAL to Ralph Graves, Oct. 16, 1969.

ENVIRONMENTAL PROTECTION TRIPS: " 'Lindy' Sees Kabetogama," Minneapolis *Star,* Oct. 6, 1969; "L Visits Park Site," (International Falls) *Daily Journal,* Oct. 6, 1969; CAL to Elmer Andersen, Oct. 22, 1969; CAL to AML, Aug. 7, 1970; CAL to Samuel F. Pryor, Jr., Feb. 22 and Aug. 7, 1969; George Lindsay, "Some Natural Values of Baja California," *Pacific Discovery,* Mar.–Apr., 1970, pp. 1–10; "Schedule of C. A. L.," Mar. 10, 1972; "Programme for Visit of Laurence Rockefeller party," Dec. 15, 1972; CAL to King Taufa-ahau Tupou IV, May 31, 1972; CAL, "W. W. F. Mission to Brazil," (M), Sept. 4, 1968; CAL to Peter Scott, Sept. 3, 1968.

PHILIPPINES: CAL to Alden Whitman, July 12, 1971; CAL to Ken Bechtel, Oct. 30, 1971; Tom Harrisson, "The Tamaraw and its Survival," *IUCN Bulletin,* Apr./June, 1969, pp. 85–6; Eduardo Lachica, "Save the Tamaraw—L," *Philippines Herald,* Feb. 1, 1969; CAL (N), "Comments" (on *NYT* article by Alden Whitman of June 23, 1969), Aug. 3, 1969; CAL, transcript of radio address, Digos Broadcasting System, Aug. 23, 1969; CAL to Lt. Gov. Thomas Gill, June 23, 1969; Ferdinand E. Marcos, "Copy of Plaque," Oct. 31, 1969; Alden Whitman, "Philippine Tribes Struggle to Survive" and "Tribesmen's Mentor: Manuel Elizalde, Jr.," *NYT,* Aug. 13, 1970; CAL to Manuel Elizalde, Jr., May 30 and Sept. 21, 1969, June 26, 1970, (T) Apr. 5, 1972; CAL to Sixto Roxas, May 30, 1969; CAL to Dr. Robert Fox, July 13, 1969; *AOV,* pp. 34–6, CAL, "Introduction" to book about Panamin, May 10, 1971; CAL to Ralph Graves, Nov. 13, 1969 and Jan. 19, 1970; unauthorized "L Statement," July 23, 1970 (re ambush in Surallah); CAL to Alden Whitman, Aug. 29, 1970; CAL to Ferdinand Marcos, May 25, 1970, May 31, 1971, Apr. 8, 1972; CAL to Mary Tay Pryor, Apr. 26, 1971; AML (D), Aug. 28, 1970; AML to CAL, Apr. 27, 1971; AML to ASL, May 3, 1971, Apr. 3, 1972; CAL, "Foreword" to John Nance, *The Gentle Tasaday: A Stone-Age People in the Philippine Rain Forest* (New York: Harcourt Brace Jovanovich, 1975); CAL, "Comments on ms. for *The Tasaday* by John Nance," Mar. 12, 1974; CAL (N), Mar. 28, Apr. 21, May 19, 1972; CAL to Filipina [who shall remain unnamed], Apr. 19, 1972; AML's discovery of photograph related by an intimate of AML who asked to be unidentified; CAL to William Jovanovich, Aug. 12, 1971; CAL to AML, July 5, 1971.

PRIVATE COMMUNION; PUBLIC APPEARANCES: CAL to Sister Hildegard, June 24, 1971; CAL, speech, National Institute of Social Sciences, Nov. 21, 1968; CAL, speech, Society of Experimental Test Pilots, Sept. 27, 1969; CAL, as quoted in Peter Weller, "Interpretive Center is Dedicated in Little Falls," *Minnesota Progressive,* Nov., 1973, p. 5; "CAL Given Hero's Welcome," (Little Falls) *Daily Transcript,* Oct.

1, 1973; George Vecsey, "L Revisits Scene of Old Friendship on L. I.," *NYT,* May 17, 1973; Adele Wall to ASB (I), May 20, 1994; Harold W. Gray, Jr. to CAL, July 31, 1969; Raymond Weeks to CAL, Sept. 12, 1973; CAL, speech, "National Veterans Day Address, Oct. 21, 1973; Dr. David Read to ASB (I), May 2, 1993.

CAL and AML donated several hundred books to Falaise to help fill the library shelves. (CAL to George Fontaine, Nov. 18, 1973.)

WJ: CAL to William Jovanovich, Dec. 18, 1969 [reprinted in *WJ,* pp. xii–xv], Jan. 27 and Nov. 13, 1970; Alden Whitman, "L Journal on War Era Is Due," *NYT,* Mar. 11, 1970; William Jovanovich to Alden Whitman, Jan. 22, 1970, attached to Ethel Cunningham to William Jovanovich (M), Jan. 20, 1970; CAL to Leland Hayward, Apr. 11, 1970; Harcourt Brace World (M), "Cutting," enclosed with William Jovanovich to CAL, Aug. 24, 1969; "American Notes—According to Lindy," *Time,* Sept. 14, 1970, p. 12; "L Wrong Again," *Long Island Press,* Sept. 3, 1970; The American Jewish Committee, press release, Sept. 8, 1970; S. L. A. Marshall, "Lindy Book: 1000 pages, mostly dull," *Chicago Sun-Times,* Sept. 1, 1970, p. 28; Eric Goldman, "WJ of CAL," *NYT,* Sept. 20, 1970; Henry Raymont, "Judges of Book Awards Revolt," *NYT,* Jan. 26, 1971; CAL to Julie N. Eisenhower, Nov. 7, 1970; Jacqueline Onassis to CAL, Aug. 23, 1971; CAL to Burton Wheeler, Jan. 19, 1971; William Jovanovich, "Foreword" to *WJ,* p. xiv.

PUBLISHING AML'S DIARIES; IMPASSE WITH SML: AML (D), Sept. 10, 1970, Apr. 19, 1971, Apr. 29. 1972; *WWW,* p. xxviii; AML to Lucia Valentine, July 31, 1977; AML to Dana Atchley, Dec. 26, 1969; AML to ASL, Apr. 17, 1969, Nov. 17, 1971; "Analysis of Hijacking Mail and Wires," Pan American Corp. office, Sept. 15, 1970; RML to AML, Mar. 26, 1972; AML to SML, Apr. 5, 1968; CAL to SML, Mar. 24, Apr. 20, and June 2, 1969, Apr. 19, May 14, 1972, May 1, 1973; SML to CAL, Apr. 8, 1969; CAL to ASL, Mar. 2 and Apr. 24, 1972, Apr. 8, 1973.

CAL'S ILLNESS: Dr. Milton Howell to T. Willard Hunter (I), Dec. 4, 1984; CAL (N), "Dana Atchley," Oct. 6, 1972; CAL to Ian Grimwood, May 11, 1974; Dana Atchley to AML, Mar. 5, 1973; Samuel F. Pryor to T. Willard Hunter (I), Dec. 31, 1980; Samuel F. Pryor and CAL to Hawaii Conference Foundation Trustees, Mar. 23, 1973; Milton M. Howell, "The Lone Eagle's Last Flight," *Journal of the American Medical Association,* May 19, 1975, p. 715; CAL to Manuel Elizalde, June 12, 1973; CAL to Imelda Marcos, June 14, 1973; Imelda Marcos to CAL, Aug. 2, 1973; AML to CMM, July 22, 1973; AML to Margot L. (Morrow) Wilkie, July 27, 1973; AML (D), July 16, 1973; "Getty Prize," *World Wildlife News,* Apr., 1974, p. 7; "A Pragmatist and a Pioneer," *Time,* Feb. 18, 1974, p. 25; CAL to Francis I. Kellogg, Mar. 17, 1974; Peter Gove to CAL, May 17, 1974; Jeannie Pechin to ASB (I), Aug. 27, 1994; AML to ASL, May 22, June 11, June 19, 23, and 29, July 5, 9, and 14, 1974; CAL to William Jovanovich, June 14, 1974; AML to CMM, June 4, 1974; AML to SML, June 17, 1974; CAL to Raymond Fredette, June 30, 1974; AML to LML, July 19, 1974.

CAL HOSPITALIZED: AML to Marthe Sturm, Aug. 9, 1974; CAL to Gov. Wendell Anderson, July 21, 1974; CAL to Russell Fridley, July 21, 1974; AML to Reverend Mother (Regina Laudis Priory, Bethlehem, CT), July 25, 1974; AML to ASL, July 20, 1974; AML to SML, July 23, 1974; SML to CAL, July 23, 1974; Judge E. Donald Steinbrugge to CAL, Aug. 18, 1974; AML to Yvonne (deLattre?), Aug. 2, 1974; AML to ELCS, Aug. 10, 1974; Richard M. Nixon to CAL, July 31, 1974; DeWitt and Lila Wallace to CAL (T), Aug. 2, 1974; ELCS to CAL, Aug. 1, 1974; Newton, *Uncommon Friends,* p. 340; William Jovanovich to CAL, July 28, 1974;

Jovanovich quoted in *AOV*, pp. xiii–xv; JML (D), Aug. 15–28, 1974; CAL, "Will of Apr. 11, 1973 amended"; AML "Affidavit," Feb. 18, 1975; Dr. Milton Howell to T. Willard Hunter (I), Dec. 4, 1984; Roselle Howell to T. Willard Hunter (I), Jan. 2, 1981; AML to Margot L. (Morrow) Wilkie," Aug. 18, 1974; AML to Juan Trippe, Sept. 4, 1974.

FINAL PREPARATIONS IN HAWAII: Milton Howell quoted in Tom Stevens, *The Maui News,* Sept. 19, 1974, p. B7; JML (D), Aug. 15–28, 1974; AML 9 (and others), "Lists," Aug. 20–2, 1974, re burial, service, etc. [Y:220/85]; Mary Anne Cravens, "Tevi and L: An Old Maui Native Buries His Friend," *People,* Sept. 16, 1974, pp. 12–3; Edward Oxford, "Final Flight," *American History Illustrated,* pp. 25–35, 72; Joseph "Tevi" Kahaleuahi to T. Willard Hunter (I), Dec. 19, 1980; LML to ASB (I), Aug. 18, 1993; JML to ASB (I), Aug. 17, 1993; John Hanchett to T. Willard Hunter (I), Dec. 31, 1980; AML to John Grierson, c. May, 1975; Henry Kahula to T. Willard Hunter (I), Jan. 3, 1981; Rev. John Tincher to ASB (I), Aug. 26, 1994; AML to Susan Miller Lindbergh, Oct. 20, 1978; SML to ASB (I), Jan. 9, 1994; RML to ASB (I), June 19, 1997; AML to Mrs. Saunders, Aug. 20, 1974.

CAL DEATH AND POST-MORTEM: AML to CMM, Sept. 26, 1985; AML to ELCS, Oct. 9, 1974; "Tevi" quoted in Leigh Fenly, "L's final home," (Port Washington-Manhasset) *Pennysaver*, Oct. 5, 1981; Roselle Howell to "Dear Friends," Apr. 6, 1974; Beverly Creamer, "The Death of a Hero—August, 1974," quoted in Youngblood, *Hana Coast,* p. 78; LML to ASB, May 18, 1998; "L Dies of Cancer in Hawaii at the Age of 72," *NYT,* Aug. 27, 1974, pp. 1, 17; "President Leads the Nation in Tribute to L," *NYT,* Aug. 27, 1974, p. 17; Alden Whitman, "Daring L Attained the Unattainable with Historic Flight Across Atlantic," *NYT,* Aug. 27, 1974, pp. 18–9; "Passing of a Hero," *NYT,* Aug. 28, 1974, p. 30; "Burial Service for CAL" (U program), Aug. 26, 1974; "Graveside Prayers" (U program), Aug. 26, 1974; "Memorial Service for CAL" (U program), Aug. 27, 1974; Dan Carmichael, "L's last flight," (Honolulu) *The Sunday Star-Bulletin & Advertiser,* Sept. 1, 1974; AML to Dr. Milton Howell, Aug. 30, 1974; *AOV,* p. 402.

PERMISSIONS

Grateful acknowledgment is made to Anne Morrow Lindbergh, as well as the Charles A. Lindbergh Papers and the Anne Morrow Lindbergh Papers, Manuscripts and Archives, Yale University Library, for permission to quote extensively from the unpublished papers of Charles and Anne Morrow Lindbergh.

Very special thanks to everyone who granted permission to quote from the following heretofore unpublished material: Excerpts of letters dated March 6 and December 18, 1956, and July 8, 1958, from Dr. Dana W. Atchley to Anne Morrow Lindbergh appear by permission of Dr. John Atchley; excerpt of "Lindbergh" by Walter P. Balderston by permission of the W. P. Balderston Estate; excerpt of "Charles Lindbergh: A Personal Portrait" by Mina Kirstein Curtiss by permission of the Mina Kirstein Curtiss Papers, Sophia Smith Collection, Smith College, Northampton, Massachusetts; excerpt of an October 20, 1942, letter from Theodore Dreiser to Mrs. Hortense N. Dillon by permission of the Trustees of the University of Pennsylvania; excerpts of an October 26, 1927, letter from Harry Guggenheim to Charles A. Lindbergh and an October 15, 1962, letter from Harry Guggenheim to Milton Lehman by permission of Peter Lawson-Johnston; excerpt of a July 28, 1974, letter from William Jovanovich to Charles A. Lindbergh by permission of William Jovanovich; excerpt of a November 3, 1990, letter from Lyle Leverich to A. Scott Berg by permission of Lyle Leverich; excerpts of August 1974 diary entries of Jon M. Lindbergh by permission of Jon M. Lindbergh; excerpt of May 18, 1998 letter from Land M. Lindbergh to A. Scott Berg by permission of Land M. Lindbergh; excerpt of a March 26, 1972, letter from Reeve Lindbergh to Anne Morrow Lindbergh by permission of Reeve Lindbergh; excerpts of letters dated May 26, 1963, and July 23, 1974, from Scott M. Lindbergh to Charles A. Lindbergh by permission of Scott M. Lindbergh; excerpt of a February 8, 1951, letter from John P. Marquand to Charles A. Lindbergh by permission of the Estate of

INDEX